SO-CCG-645

BUSINESS PLUG-INS

TECHNOLOGY PLUG-INS

Business
Driven
Technology

Business Driven Technology

Stephen Haag

Daniels College of Business

University of Denver

Paige Baltzan

Daniels College of Business

University of Denver

Amy Phillips

Daniels College of Business

University of Denver

McGraw-Hill
Irwin

Boston   Burr Ridge, IL   Dubuque, IA   Madison, WI   New York
San Francisco   St. Louis   Bangkok   Bogotá   Caracas   Kuala Lumpur
Lisbon   London   Madrid   Mexico City   Milan   Montreal   New Delhi
Santiago   Seoul   Singapore   Sydney   Taipei   Toronto

 **McGraw-Hill**
Irwin

BUSINESS DRIVEN TECHNOLOGY

Published by McGraw-Hill/Irwin, a business unit of The McGraw-Hill Companies, Inc., 1221
Avenue of the Americas, New York, NY, 10020. Copyright © 2006 by The McGraw-Hill
Companies, Inc. All rights reserved. No part of this publication may be reproduced or distributed
in any form or by any means, or stored in a database or retrieval system, without the prior written
consent of The McGraw-Hill Companies, Inc., including, but not limited to, in any network or
other electronic storage or transmission, or broadcast for distance learning.

Some ancillaries, including electronic and print components, may not be available to customers
outside the United States.

This book is printed on acid-free paper.

1 2 3 4 5 6 7 8 9 0 VNH/VNH 0 9 8 7 6 5 4

ISBN: 0-07-298301-9

Editorial director: *Brent Gordon*
Publisher: *Stewart Mattson*
Senior sponsoring editor: *Paul Ducham*
Developmental editor: *Jennifer Wisnowski*
Senior marketing manager: *Douglas Reiner*
Media producer: *Greg Bates*
Lead project manager: *Mary Conzachi*
Production supervisor: *Gina Hangos*
Senior designer: *Mary E. Kazak*
Senior photo research coordinator: *Jeremy Cheshareck*
Photo researcher: *Jennifer Blankenship*
Senior supplement producer: *Rose M. Range*
Senior digital content specialist: *Brian Nacik*
Cover design: *Lodge Design*
Cover image: © *Haslin/Corbis Sygma*
Interior design: *Amanda Kavanagh*
Typeface: *10/12 Utopia*
Compositor: *ElectraGraphics, Inc.*
Printer: *Von Hoffmann Corporation*

Library of Congress Cataloging-in-Publication Data

Haag, Stephen.
    Business driven technology / Stephen Haag, Paige Baltzan, Amy Phillips.—1st ed.
        p. cm.
    Includes bibliographical references and index.
    ISBN 0-07-298301-9 (alk. paper)
    1. Information technology—Management. 2. Management information systems. 3.
Information resources management. 4. Industrial management—Technological innovations.
I. Baltzan, Paige. II. Phillips, Amy. III. Title.
HD30.2.H32 2006
658.4'038—dc22
                                                                                2004057923

www.mhhe.com

DEDICATION

In memory of Allan R. Biggs, my father, my
mentor, and my inspiration.
Paige

To my mother, Jane E. Phillips, with much
love and affection. Without you, I would
not be here.
Amy

For Al and Fern, my wife's parents, and just
as important, my best friends.
Stephen

TABLE OF CONTENTS

FEATURES

Unlike any other MIS text, *Business Driven Technology* discusses various business initiatives first and how technology supports those initiatives second. The premise for this unique approach is that business initiatives should drive technology choices. Every discussion first addresses the business needs and then addresses the technology that supports those needs. *Business Driven Technology* offers the flexibility to customize courses according to your needs and the needs of your students by covering only essential concepts and topics in the five core units, while providing additional in-depth coverage in the business and technology plug-ins.

Business Driven Technology contains 20 chapters (organized into 5 units), 10 business plug-ins, and 7 technology plug-ins offering you the ultimate flexibility in tailoring content to the exact needs of your MIS or IT course. The unique construction of this text allows you to cover essential concepts and topics in the five core units while providing you with the ability to customize a course and explore certain topics in greater detail with the business and technology plug-ins.

Plug-ins are fully developed modules of text that include student learning outcomes, case studies, business vignettes, and end-of-chapter material such as key terms, individual and group questions and projects, and case study exercises.

We realize that instructors today require the ability to cover a blended mix of topics in their courses. While some instructors like to focus on networks and infrastructure throughout their course, others choose to focus on ethics and security. *Business Driven Technology* was developed to easily adapt to your needs. Each chapter and plug-in is independent so you can:

- Cover any or all of the *chapters* as they suit your purpose
- Cover any or all of the *business plug-ins* as they suit your purpose
- Cover any or all of the *technology plug-ins* as they suit your purpose
- Cover the plug-ins in any order you wish

This text is organized around the traditional sequence of topics and concepts in information technology; however, the presentation of this material is nontraditional. That is to say, the text is divided into four major sections: (1) Units, (2) Chapters, (3) Business plug-ins, and (4) Technology plug-ins. This represents a substantial departure from existing traditional texts; the goal of which is to provide both students and faculty with only the most essential concepts and topical coverage in the text, while allowing faculty to customize a course by choosing from among a set of plug-ins that explore topics in more detail. All of the topics that form the core of the discipline are covered, including CRM, SCM, Porter's Five-Forces model, value-chain analysis, competitive advantage, information security, and ethics.

Business-Driven Technology
includes four major components:
- 5 Core Units
- 20 Chapters
- 10 Business Plug-ins
- 7 Technology Plug-ins.

UNITS

1. **Achieving Business Success through Information Technology**
   Chapter 1: Business Driven Technology Overview
   Chapter 2: Identifying Competitive Advantages
   Chapter 3: Strategic Initiatives for Implementing Competitive Advantages
   Chapter 4: Measuring the Success of Strategic Initiatives
   Chapter 5: Organizational Structures That Support Strategic Initiatives

2. **Managing Information for Business Initiatives**
   Chapter 6: Valuing Organizational Information
   Chapter 7: Storing Organizational Information—Databases
   Chapter 8: Viewing and Protecting Organizational Information

3. **Enhancing Business Decisions**
   Chapter 9: Enabling the Organization—Decision Making
   Chapter 10: Extending the Organization—Supply Chain Management
   Chapter 11: Building a Customer-centric Organization—Customer Relationship Management
   Chapter 12: Integrating the Organization from End to End—Enterprise Resource Planning

4. **Creating Collaborative Partnerships in Business**
   Chapter 13: Creating Collaborative Partnerships through E-Business
   Chapter 14: Enhancing Collaborative Partnerships
   Chapter 15: Outsourcing Collaborative Partnerships
   Chapter 16: Integrating Collaborative Partnerships

5. **Transforming Organizations**
   Chapter 17: Fostering an Innovative Organization
   Chapter 18: Creating a Wireless Organization
   Chapter 19: Building Software to Support an Agile Organization
   Chapter 20: Developing a 21st Century Organization

BUSINESS PLUG-INS

B1	Information Security	B6	Strategic Outsourcing
B2	Ethics	B7	E-Business Models
B3	Supply Chain Management	B8	Emerging Trends and Technologies
B4	Customer Relationship Management	B9	Systems Development
B5	Enterprise Resource Planning	B10	Project Management

TECHNOLOGY PLUG-INS

T1	Hardware and Software	T5	Touring Access
T2	Networks and Telecommunications	T6	Object-Oriented Technologies
T3	Decision-Analysis Tools in Excel	T7	Valuing Technology
T4	Designing Database Applications		

Format, Features, and Highlights

Business Driven Technology is state-of-the-art in its discussions, presents concepts in an easy-to-understand format, and allows students to be active participants in learning. The dynamic nature of information technology requires all students, more specifically business students, to be aware of both current and emerging technologies. Students are facing complex subjects and need a clear, concise explanation to be able to understand and use the concepts throughout their careers. By engaging students with numerous case studies, exercises, projects, and questions that enforce concepts, *Business Driven Technology* creates a unique learning experience for both faculty and students.

- **Logical Layout.** Students and faculty will find the text well organized with the topics flowing logically from one unit to the next and from one chapter to the next. The definition of each term is provided before it is covered in the chapter and an extensive glossary is included at the back of the text. Each core unit offers a comprehensive opening case study, introduction, learning outcomes, unit summary, closing case studies, key terms, making business decision questions, and making collaborative business decision questions. The plug-ins follow the same pedagogical elements with the exception of the exclusion of opening case and closing case studies in the technology plug-ins. Plug-in pointers at the end of the chapters indicate that the discussion at that point may be usefully augmented by specific plug-ins.

- **Thorough Explanations.** Complete coverage is provided for each topic that is introduced. Explanations are written so that students can understand the ideas presented and relate them to other concepts presented in the core units and plug-ins.

- **Solid Theoretical Base.** The text relies on current theory and practice of information systems as they relate to the business environment. Current academic and professional journals cited throughout the text are found in the Notes at the end of the book—a roadmap for additional, pertinent readings that can be the basis for learning beyond the scope of the unit, chapter, or plug-in.

- **Material to Encourage Discussion.** All units contain a diverse selection of case studies and individual and group problem-solving activities as they relate to the use of information technology in business. Two comprehensive cases at the end of each unit reflect the concepts from the chapters. These cases encourage students to consider what concepts have been presented and then apply those concepts to a situation they might find in an organization. Different people in an organization can view the same facts from different points of view and the cases will force students to consider some of those views.

- **Flexibility in Teaching and Learning.** While most textbooks that are "text only" leave faculty on their own when it comes to choosing cases, *Business Driven Technology* goes much further. Several options are provided to faculty with case selections from a variety of sources including *CIO, Harvard Business Journal, Wired, Forbes, Business 2.0,* and *Time,* to name just a few. Therefore, faculty can use the text alone, the text and a complete selection of cases, or anything in between.

- **Integrative Themes.** Several integrative themes recur throughout the text which adds integration to the material. Among these themes are value added techniques and methodologies, ethics and social responsibility, globalization, and gaining a competitive advantage. Such topics are essential to gaining a full understanding of the strategies that a business must recognize, formulate, and in turn implement. In addition to addressing these in the chapter material, many illustrations are provided for their relevance to business practice. These include brief examples in the text as well as more detail presented in the corresponding plug-in(s) (business or technical).

Visual Content Map

Visual Content Map. Located at the beginning of each unit and serving as a logical outline, the visual content map illustrates the relationship between each unit and its associated plug-ins.

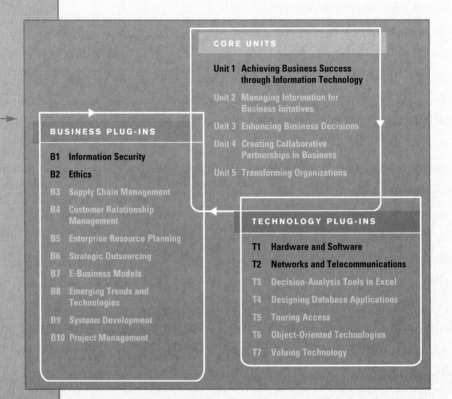

CORE UNITS

Unit 1 Achieving Business Success through Information Technology

Unit 2 Managing Information for Business Initatives

Unit 3 Enhancing Business Decisions

Unit 4 Creating Collaborative Partnerships in Business

Unit 5 Transforming Organizations

BUSINESS PLUG-INS

B1 Information Security

B2 Ethics

B3 Supply Chain Management

B4 Customer Relationship Management

B5 Enterprise Resource Planning

B6 Strategic Outsourcing

B7 E-Business Models

B8 Emerging Trends and Technologies

B9 Systems Development

B10 Project Management

TECHNOLOGY PLUG-INS

T1 Hardware and Software

T2 Networks and Telecommunications

T3 Decision-Analysis Tools in Excel

T4 Designing Database Applications

T5 Touring Access

T6 Object-Oriented Technologies

T7 Valuing Technology

Plug-In Pointers

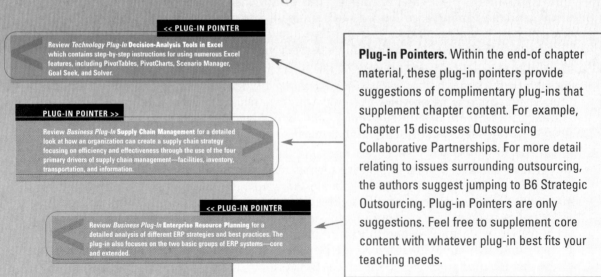

<< PLUG-IN POINTER

Review *Technology Plug-In* **Decision-Analysis Tools in Excel** which contains step-by-step instructions for using numerous Excel features, including PivotTables, PivotCharts, Scenario Manager, Goal Seek, and Solver.

PLUG-IN POINTER >>

Review *Business Plug-In* **Supply Chain Management** for a detailed look at how an organization can create a supply chain strategy focusing on efficiency and effectiveness through the use of the four primary drivers of supply chain management—facilities, inventory, transportation, and information.

<< PLUG-IN POINTER

Review *Business Plug-In* **Enterprise Resource Planning** for a detailed analysis of different ERP strategies and best practices. The plug-in also focuses on the two basic groups of ERP systems—core and extended.

Plug-in Pointers. Within the end-of chapter material, these plug-in pointers provide suggestions of complimentary plug-ins that supplement chapter content. For example, Chapter 15 discusses Outsourcing Collaborative Partnerships. For more detail relating to issues surrounding outsourcing, the authors suggest jumping to B6 Strategic Outsourcing. Plug-in Pointers are only suggestions. Feel free to supplement core content with whatever plug-in best fits your teaching needs.

Learning Outcomes and Introduction

> **Introduction.** Located after the Unit Opening Case, the introduction familiarizes students with the overall tone of the chapters. Thematic concepts are also broadly defined.

> **Learning Outcomes.** These outcomes focus on what students should learn and be able to answer upon completion of the chapter or plug-in.

INTRODUCTION

Decision making and problem solving in today's electronic world encompass large-scale, opportunity-oriented, strategically focused solutions. The traditional "cookbook" approach to decisions simply will not work in the e-business world. Decision-making and problem-solving abilities are now the most sought-after traits in up-and-coming executives, according to a recent survey of 1,000 executives by Caliper Associates, as reported in *The Wall Street Journal*. To put it mildly, decision makers and problem solvers have limitless career potential.[8]

E-business is the conducting of business on the Internet, not only buying and selling, but also serving customers and collaborating with business partners. (Unit 4 discusses e-business in detail.) With the fast growth of information technology and the accelerated use of the Internet, e-business is quickly becoming standard. This unit focuses on technology to help make decisions, solve problems, and find new innovative opportunities. The unit highlights how to bring people together with the best IT processes and tools in complete, flexible solutions that can seize business opportunities (see Figure 3.1). The chapters in Unit 3 are:

- **Chapter Nine**—Enabling the Organization—Decision Making
- **Chapter Ten**—Extending the Organization—Supply Chain Management
- **Chapter Eleven**—Building a Customer-centric Organization—Customer Relationship Management
- **Chapter Twelve**—Integrating the Organization from End to End—Enterprise Resource Planning

LEARNING OUTCOMES

14.1. Identify the different ways in which companies collaborate using technology.

14.2. Define the different categories of collaboration technologies.

14.3. List, describe, and provide an example of a content management system.

14.4. Evaluate the advantages of using a workflow system.

14.5. Differentiate between a groupware system and a peer-to-peer system.

14.6. Define the fundamental concepts of a knowledge management system.

14.7. Explain the current tools and trends used in a collaborative working environment.

Unit Opening Case and Opening Case Study Questions

Unit Opening Case. To enhance student interest, each unit begins with an opening case study that highlights an organization that has been time-tested and value proven in the business world. This feature serves to fortify concepts with relevant examples of outstanding companies. Discussion of the case is threaded throughout the chapters in each unit.

Opening Case Study Questions. Located at the end of each chapter, poignant questions connect the Unit Opening Case Study with important chapter concepts.

Projects and Case Studies

Case Studies. This text is packed with 55 case studies illustrating how a variety of prominent organizations and business have successfully implemented many of this text's concepts. All cases are timely and promote critical thinking. Company profiles are especially appealing and relevant to your students, helping to stir classroom discussion and interest. For a full list of cases explored in *Business Driven Technology,* turn to the inside back cover.

Project 1:
The Importance of Information Technology

Managers need to be involved in information technology—any computer-based tool that people use to work with information and support the information and information-processing needs of an organization—for the following (primary) reasons:

- The sheer magnitude of the dollars spent on IT must be managed to ensure business value.
- Research has consistently shown that when managers are involved in IT, IT enables a number of business initiatives, such as gaining a competitive advantage, streamlining business processes, and even transforming entire organizations.
- Research has consistently shown that when managers are not involved in IT, systems fail, revenue is lost, and even entire companies can fail all as a result of poorly managed IT.[1]

Project Focus:

One of the biggest challenges your organization will face is, "How do we get general business managers involved in IT?" Research has shown that involvement is highly correlated with personal experience with IT and IT education, including university classes and IT executive seminars. Once general business managers understand IT through experience and education, they are more likely to be involved in IT, and more likely to lead their organizations in achieving business success through IT.

Chapter Three Case: Consolidating Touchpoints for Saab

Saab Cars USA imports more than 37,000 Saab sedans, convertibles, and wagons annually and distributes the cars to 220 U.S. dealerships. Saab competes in the premium automotive market and its primary challenge is to compete with rivals who attract customers through aggressive marketing campaigns, reduced prices, and inexpensive financing. Saab decided that the answer to beating its competition was not to spend capital on additional advertising, but to invest in Siebel Automotive, a customer relationship management system.

Until recently, the company communicated with its customers through three primary channels: (1) dealer network, (2) customer assistance center, (3) lead management center. Traditionally, each channel maintained its own customer database and this splintered approach to managing customer information caused numerous problems for the company. For example, a prospective customer might receive a direct mail piece from Saab one week, then an e-mail with an unrelated offer from a third-party marketing vendor the next week. The local dealer might not know of either activity, and therefore might deliver an ineffective pitch when the customer visited the showroom that weekend. Al Fontova, direct marketing manager with Saab Cars USA, stated that he had over 3 million customer records and 55 files at three different vendors. Analyzing this information in aggregate was complicated, inefficient, and costly.

Saab required a solution that would provide a consolidated customer view from all three touchpoints. In 2002, Saab implemented the Siebel CRM solution, which provides Saab's call center employees with a 360-degree view of each customer, including prior service-related questions and all the marketing communications they have received. Known internally as "TouchPoint," the Siebel application provides Saab's dealers with a powerful Web-based solution for coordinating sales and marketing activities. These tracking capabilities enable Saab to measure the sales results of specific leads, recommend more efficient selling techniques, and target its leads more precisely in the future. Using Siebel Automotive, Saab received the following benefits:

- Direct marketing costs decreased by 5 percent.
- Lead follow-up increased from 38 percent to 50 percent.
- Customer satisfaction increased from 69 percent to 75 percent.
- Saab gained a single view of its customers across multiple channels.[12]

Questions

1. Explain how implementing a CRM system enabled Saab to gain a competitive advantage.
2. Estimate the potential impact to Saab's business if it had not implemented a CRM system.
3. What additional benefits could Saab receive from implementing a supply chain management system?

Applying Your Knowledge. At the end of this text, there is a set of 20 projects aimed at reinforcing the business initiatives explored in this text. These projects help to develop the application and problem-solving skills of your students through challenging and creative business-driven scenarios.

Project 1: The Importance of Information Technology
Project 2: Strategic and Competitive Advantage
Project 3: Assessing the Value of Information
Project 4: Network Security
Project 5: Qualitative Analysis
Project 6: Small Business Analysis
Project 7: Mining Information
Project 8: Data Warehouse and CRM Challenge
Project 9: Analyzing a Supply Chain
Project 10: Outsourcing Information Technology
Project 11: E-Business
Project 12: Emerging Trends and Technology
Project 13: Open Source on a Large Scale
Project 14: Aligning IT with Business Goals
Project 15: Transforming Campaign Finance
Project 16: Relational Data Structure
Project 17: Building a Relational Database
Project 18: Buy or Lease
Project 19: Gathering Business Requirements
Project 20: Project Management

Making Decisions

Making Business Decisions. Small scenario-driven projects that help students focus *individually* on decision making as they relate to the topical elements in the chapters and plug-ins.

1. Improving Information Quality

HangUps Corporation designs and distributes closet organization structures. The company operates five different systems including order entry, sales, inventory management, shipping, and billing. The company has severe information quality issues including missing, inaccurate, redundant, and incomplete information. The company wants to implement a data warehouse containing information from the five different systems to help maintain a single customer view, drive business decisions, and perform multidimensional analysis. Identify how the organization can improve its information quality when it begins designing and building its data warehouse.

2. Mining the Data Warehouse

Janet Smith is a senior buyer for a large wholesaler that sells different types of arts and crafts to greeting card stores such as Hallmark. Janet's latest marketing strategy is to send all of her customers a new line of hand-made picture frames from Russia. All of Janet's information supports her decision for the new line. Her analysis predicts that the frames should sell an average of 10 to 15 per store, per day. Janet is excited about the new line and is positive it will be a success.

One month later Janet learns that the frames are selling 50 percent below expectations and averaging between 5 to 8 frames sold daily in each store. Janet decides to access the company's data warehouse information to determine why sales are below expectations. Identify several different dimensions of information that Janet will want to analyze to help her decide what is causing the problems with the picture frame sales.

3. Determining Information Quality Issues

Real People is a magazine geared toward working individuals that provides articles and advice on everything from car maintenance to family planning. *Real People* is currently expe-

1. Finding Innovation

Along with disruptive technologies there are also disruptive strategies. The following are a few examples of companies that use disruptive strategies to gain competitive advantages:

- **Circuit City, Best Buy**—Disrupted the consumer electronics departments of full-service and discount department stores, which has sent them up-market into higher-margin goods.
- **Ford**—Henry Ford's Model T was so inexpensive that he enabled a much larger population of people, who historically could not afford cars, to own one.
- **JetBlue**—Whereas Southwest Airlines initially followed a strategy of new-market disruption, JetBlue's approach is low-end disruption. Its long-range viability depends on the major airlines' motivation to run away from the attack, as integrated steel mills and full-service department stores did.
- **McDonald's**—The fast food industry has been a hybrid disruptor, making it so inexpensive and convenient to eat out that they created a massive wave of growth in the "eating out" industry. Their earliest victims were mom-and-pop diners.
- **Plastic manufacturers**—Plastics as a category have disrupted wood and steel, in that the "quality" of plastic parts often was inferior to those of wood and steel. However, plastics' low cost and ease of shaping have replaced wood and steel in many areas. For example, look at how little plastics were used in automobiles 30 years ago versus extensive use today.[54]

There are numerous other examples of corporations that have used disruptive strategies to create competitive advantages. In a team, prepare a presentation highlighting three additional companies that used disruptive strategies to gain a competitive advantage.

2. Approving a Project

You are working in the IT development team for Gear International, a privately held sports and recreational equipment manufacturer. To date, you have spent the majority of your

Making Collaborative Decisions. Similar to "Making Business Decisions," but students are encouraged to *work in groups* to solve the problems presented (units only).

End-of-Unit Elements

eBay's Cosmos Business Intelligence System

"In Cosmos, we have built a platform with the flexibility and scalability to grow and meet our needs for the foreseeable future. The global scale of our trading community and the competitive pressures we face have made this new analytic system a necessity. Cosmos has opened our eyes and allowed through our site. The a vided us with a compe manager, eBay.

eBay Overview

eBay, founded in 1995, i vices. eBay's business i

- 22 million registe
- 500 million items
- Over $6 billion in
- 2 million unique

1. Information Timeliness

Information timeliness is a major consideration for all organizations. Organizations need to decide the frequency of backups and the frequency of updates to a data warehouse. In a team, describe the timeliness requirements for backups and updates to a data warehouse for

- Weather tracking systems
- Car dealership inventories
- Vehicle tire sales
- Interest rates
- Restaurant invent
- Grocery store inv

2. Entities and Attr

Martex Inc. is a mar clude running, tenni rently supplies four and Maximum Work In a group, identify th

Agile methodology, 200
Analysis phase, 197
Business requirement, 197
Design phase, 197
Development phase, 197
Disruptive technology, 185
Electronic tagging, 209
Extreme programming (XP) methodology, 199
Feature creep, 201
Implementation phase, 197

IT infrastructure, 206
Maintenance phase, 197
Mobile commerce, 209
Planning phase, 196
Project management, 202
Project management software, 202
Prototype, 199
Radio frequency identifica (RFID), 209

Each unit contains complete pedagogical support in the form of:

- **Unit Summary.** Revisiting the unit highlights in summary format.
- **Key Terms.** With page numbers referencing where they are discussed in the text.
- **Two Closing Case Studies.** Reinforcing importance concepts with prominent examples from businesses and organizations. Discussion Questions follow each case study.
- **Making Business Decisions.** Small scenario-driven projects that help students focus individually on decision making as they relate to the topical elements in the chapters.
- **Making Collaborative Decisions.** Similar to "Making Business Decisions," but students are encouraged to work in groups to solve the problems presented.

About the Plug-Ins

The plug-ins are designed to allow faculty to customize their course and cover selected topics in more detail. Students will read core material related to all of the plug-ins in the 5 units.

As an example, students will learn about various facets of customer relationship management (CRM) most notably in Chapters 1, 2, and 3. However, customer relationship management has its own business plug-in. The CRM business plug-in gives both faculty and students the ability to cover CRM in more detail if desired. Likewise, students will receive an introduction to O-O technologies in Unit 5. The O-O technology plug-in allows coverage of O-O topics such as polymorphism, inheritance, and encapsulation in more detail.

PLUG-IN

B5 Enterprise Resource Planning

LEARNING OUTCOMES

1. Compare core enterprise resource planning components and extended enterprise resource planning components.
2. Describe the three primary components found in core enterprise resource planning systems.
3. Describe the four primary components found in extended enterprise resource planning systems.
4. Explain the benefits and risks associated with enterprise resource planning systems.
5. Assess the future of enterprise resource planning systems.

Introduction

The core units discussed *enterprise resource planning (ERP)*, which integrates all departments and functions throughout an organization into a single IT system (or integrated set of IT systems) so that employees can make enterprisewide decisions by viewing enterprisewide information on all business operations. This plug-in focuses on the two basic groups of ERP systems—core and extended.

Management Focus. By focusing on the Business Plug-ins, your course will take on a managerial approach to MIS.

Business Plug-ins include:

B1	Information Security
B2	Ethics
B3	Supply Chain Management
B4	Customer Relationship Management
B5	Enterprise Resource Planning
B6	Strategic Outsourcing
B7	E-Business Models
B8	Emerging Trends and Technologies
B9	Systems Development
B10	Project Management

PLUG-IN

T7 Valuing Technology

LEARNING OUTCOMES

1. Summarize the three areas an organization can use to assess the financial health of an information technology project.
2. Describe the different financial metrics an organization can use to determine the value of an information technology project.
3. Explain customer metrics and their importance to an organization.
4. Describe the different types of comparative metrics an organization can use to determine the efficiency and effectiveness of its information technology resources.

Introduction

The core units introduced efficiency and effectiveness metrics, which are the two primary types of IT metrics. *Efficiency IT metrics* measure the performance of the IT system including throughput, speed, availability, etc. *Effectiveness IT metrics* measure the impact IT has on business processes and activities including customer satisfaction, conversion rates, sell-through increases, etc.

An organization's *strategic resources* include those assets available after an organization has cautiously spent what it must to keep its existing business operating at its current level. Strategic resources are typically used to fund more promising strategic ventures. Decisions regarding strategic resource allocation for IT projects are among the most difficult of all tactical resource decisions. Many organizations routinely analyze efficiency and effectiveness metrics to measure the performance of IT projects. This plug-in takes a step beyond simple efficiency and effectiveness metrics by covering a number of tools commonly used in IT investment decisions including financial, customer, and comparative metrics.

Metrics—Measuring IT Value

In today's highly automated business world, the strategies and directions of the IT department increasingly form the basis for the overall corporate strategy. Once regarded as merely a service department, decisions made regarding IT can influence a company's competitive position and often dictate its ability to exploit market

---

Technical Focus. If hands-on, Technical skills are more important, include Technical Plug-ins in your MIS course.

Technology Plug-ins include:

T1	Hardware and Software
T2	Networks and Telecommunications
T3	Decision-Analysis Tools in Excel
T4	Designing Database Applications
T5	Touring Access
T6	Object Oriented Technologies
T7	Valuing Technology

End-of-Plug-in Elements

Each plug-in contains complete pedagogical support in the form of:

- **Plug-in Summary.** Revisiting the plug-in highlights in summary format.
- **Key Terms.** With page numbers referencing where they are discussed in the text.
- **Two Closing Case Studies.** Reinforcing important concepts with prominent examples from businesses and organizations. Discussion Questions follow each case study. (Business Plug-ins only.)
- **Making Business Decisions.** Small scenario-driven projects that help students focus individually on decision making as they relate to the topical elements in the chapters.

PLUG-IN SUMMARY

Advances in technology have made ethics a concern for many organizations. Consider how easy it is for an employee to e-mail large amounts of confidential information, change electronic communications, or destroy massive amounts of important company information all within seconds. Electronic information about customers, partners, and employees has become one of corporate America's most valuable assets. However, the line between the proper and improper use of this asset is at best blurry. Should an employer be able to search employee files without employee consent? Should a company be able to sell customer information without informing the customer of its intent? What is a responsible approach to document deletion?

The law provides guidelines in many of these areas, but how a company chooses to act within the confines of the law is up to the judgment of its officers. Since CIOs are responsible for the technology that collects, maintains, and destroys corporate information, they sit smack in the middle of this potential ethical quagmire.

One way an organization can begin dealing with ethical issues is to create a corporate culture that encourages ethical c...
Not only is an ethical culture a...
ing prevent customer problem...
ment of and adherence to we...
ethical corporate culture. Thes...

- ePolicies
- Ethical Computer Use P...
- Information Privacy Pol...
- Acceptable Use Policy
- E-Mail Privacy Policy
- Internet Use Policy

KEY TERMS

Analytical CRM, 262
Automatic call distribution, 269
Call scripting system, 269
Campaign management
    system, 265
Click-to-talk, 269
Contact center, 268
Contact management
    system, 267
Cross-selling, 265
Customer relationship
    management (CRM), 262

Employee relationship
    management (ERM), 272
Interactive voice response
    (IVR), 269
List generator, 265
Operational CRM, 262

Sales force automation
    (SFA), 266
Sales management system, 266
Supplier relationship
    management (SRM), 271
Up-selling, 265

CLOSING CASE ONE

Sarbanes-Oxley: Where Information Technology, Finance, and Ethics Meet

The Sarbanes-Oxley Act (SOX) of 2002 is legislation enacted in response to the high-profile Enron and WorldCom financial scandals to protect shareholders and the general public from accounting errors and fraudulent practices by organizations. One of the primary components of the Sarbanes-Oxley Act is the definition of which records are to be stored and for how long. For this reason, the legislation not only affects financial departments, but also IT departments whose job it is to store electronic records. The Sarbanes-Oxley Act states that all business records, including electronic records and electronic messages, must be saved for "not less than five years." The consequences for noncompliance are fines, imprisonment, or both. The following are the three rules of Sarbanes-Oxley that affect the management of electronic records.

1. The first rule deals with destruction, alteration, or falsification of records and states that persons who knowingly alter, destroy, mutilate, conceal, or falsify documents shall be fined or imprisoned for not more than 20 years, or both.

2. The second rule defines the retention period for records storage. Best practices indicate that corporations securely store all business records using the same guidelines set for public accountants which state that organizations shall maintain all audit or review workpapers for a period of five years from the end of the fiscal period in which the audit or review was concluded.

3. The third rule specifies all business records and communications that need to be stored, including electronic communications. IT departments are facing the challenge of creating and maintaining a corporate records archive in a cost-effective fashion that satisfies the requirements put forth by the legislation.

Support and Supplemental Material

A complete set of materials are available that will assist students and faculty in accomplishing course objectives.

INSTRUCTOR'S RESOURCE CD-ROM. Available to adopting faculty, the Instructor's Resource CD contains all of the supplements in one convenient place: Instructor's Manual, Test Bank, PPTs, Sample Syllabi, Classroom Exercises, and Image Library.

- **Instructor's Manual (IM).** The IM, written by the authors, includes suggestions for designing the course and presenting the material. Each chapter is supported by answers to end-of-chapter questions and problems, and suggestions concerning the discussion topics and cases.

- **Test Bank.** This computerized package allows instructors to custom design, save, and generate tests. The test program permits instructors to edit, add, or delete questions from the test banks; analyze test results; and organize a database of tests and student results.

- **PowerPoint Presentations.** A set of PowerPoint slides, created by the authors, accompanies each chapter that features bulleted items that provide a lecture outline, plus key figures and tables from the text, and detailed teaching notes on each slide.

- **Sample Syllabi.** Several syllabi have been developed according to different course lengths—quarters and semesters, as well as different course concentrations such as a business emphasis or a technology focus.

- **Classroom Exercises.** Choose from over 30 different detailed classroom exercises that engage and challenge students. For example, if you are teaching systems development start off the class with the "Skyscraper Activity" where the students build a prototype that takes them through each phase of the systems development life cycle.

- **Image Library.** Text figures and tables, as permission allows, are provided in a format by which they can be imported into PowerPoint for class lectures.

ONLINE LEARNING CENTER (www.mhhe.com/bdt)
The McGraw Hill Higher Education Web site for *Business Driven Technology* includes support for students and faculty. These support materials enhance the learning experience. A few of the features found on the Web site include:

- **Project Files.** The authors have provided files for all projects that need further support, such as data files.

- **Internet Links.** Throughout the text are Web site addresses where related material can be obtained from the World Wide Web. These Web locations provide valuable information that, when used with the text material, provides a complete, up-to-date coverage of information technology and business.

Supplements:

- Online Learning Center
- Instructor's Manual
- Test Bank
- PowerPoint Presentations
- Sample Syllabi
- Classroom Exercises
- Image Library
- MISource CD
- Classroom Performance System
- Problem Solving Video Vignettes
- MBA MIS Cases
- Application Cases for MIS

Empowered Instruction

Classroom Performance System

Engage students and assess real-time lecture retention with this simple yet powerful wireless application.You can even deliver tests that instantly grade themselves.

MIS Case Videos

Choose from our library of original video cases to illustrate important concepts or generate class discussion.

PowerPoint Presentations

Robust, detailed, and designed to keep students engaged. Detailed teaching notes are also included on every slide.

Introduction

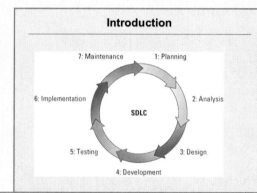

- Walk the students through the systems development life cycle:
  - *Planning phase*—involves establishing a high-level plan of the intended project and determining project goals
  - *Analysis phase*—involves analyzing end-user business requirements and refining project goals into defined functions and operations of the intended system
  - *Design phase*—involves describing the desired features and operations of the system including screen layouts, business rules, process diagrams, pseudo code, and other documentation
  - *Development phase*—involves taking all of the detailed design documents form the design phase and transforming them into the actual system
  - *Testing phase*—involves bringing all the project pieces together into a special testing environment to test for errors, bugs, and interoperability, in order to verify that the system meets all the business requirements defined in the analysis phase
  - *Implementation phase*—involves placing the system into production so users can begin to perform actual business operations with the system
  - *Maintenance phase*—involves performing changes, corrections, additions, and upgrades to ensure the system continues to meet the business goals

MISOURCE

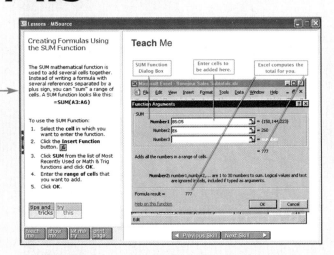

Software Skills & Computer Concepts

MISource provides animated tutorials and simulated practice of the core skills in Microsoft Excel, Access, and PowerPoint. MISource also animates 47 important computer concepts.

Spend less time reviewing software skills and computer literacy.

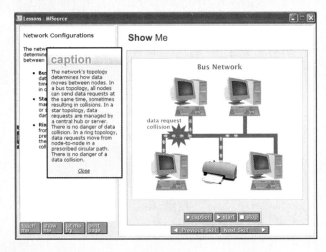

MIS Practice and Principles

MISource includes three video vignettes about the problems and opportunities facing a growing beverage company. Use the questions that follow each vignette as homework assignments or for discussion. Animated presentations of data mining, online transaction processing, and the systems development life cycle give students more perspective.

PROBLEM SOLVING VIDEO VIGNETTES

Three separate segments show how a growing beverage company comes to terms with problems and opportunities that can be addressed with database systems, telecommunications technology, and system development. Use the questions that follow each segment to inspire discussion or test students' critical thinking skills.

MBA MIS CASES

Developed by Richard Perle of Loyola Marymount University, these 14 comprehensive cases allow you to add MBA-level analysis to your course. Visit our Web site to review a sample case.

APPLICATION CASES FOR MIS

Looking for a more substantial hands-on component? The Fifth Edition of Application Cases in MIS (ISBN 0072933631) by James Morgan is the proven answer.

ONLINE LEARNING CENTER

Visit www.mhhe.com/BDT for additional instructor and student resources.

ONLINE COURSES

Content for *Business Driven Technology* is available in WebCT, Blackboard, and PageOut formats to accommodate virtually any online delivery platform.

Compiling the first edition of *Business Driven Technology* has been a tremendous undertaking and there are numerous people whom we want to heartily thank for their hard work, enthusiasm, and dedication.

This text draws from the efforts of a number of people at McGraw-Hill/Irwin. Paul Ducham, our Senior Sponsoring Editor, thank you for your insight, your intellect, and your continuous support and belief in our abilities—we simply could not have succeeded without you! Jennifer Wisnowski, our Development Editor, thank you for always taking the extra time to ask those all-important questions that everyone else seemed to miss. Mary Conzachi, our Lead Project Manager, thank you for making the difficult production process smooth and effortless.

In addition we would like to thank Brent Gordon (Editorial Director), Stewart Mattson (Publisher), Douglas Reiner (Marketing Manager), Mary Kazak (Designer), Gregory Bates (Media Producer), Rose Range (Supplements Producer), Gina Hangos (Production Supervisor), Jen Blankenship (Photo Researcher), and Jeremy Cheshareck (Photo Coordinator), for your support and dedication to the success of this text.

Last, but certainly not least, we offer our sincerest gratitude and deepest appreciation to our valuable reviewers whose feedback was instrumental in successfully compiling the first edition of this text.

Dennis Adams
University of Houston

Syed Imtiaz Ahmad
Eastern Michigan University

Lawrence Andrew
Western Illinois University

Jean-Pierre Auffret
George Mason University

Kristi-Ann L. Berg
Minot State University

Nora M. Braun
Augsburg College

Judith P. Carlisle
Dowling College

Gerald J. Carvalho
University of Utah

Edward J. Cherian
George Washington University

Joobin Choobineh
Texas A&M University

Samuel Coppage
Old Dominion University

Joanna DeFranco-Tommarello
New Jersey Institute of Technology

Roy Dejoie
Purdue University

Robert Denker
Baruch College–CUNY

Uldarico Rex Dumdum
Marywood University

Roland Eichelberger
Baylor University

Juan Esteva
Eastern Michigan University

Roger Flynn
University of Pittsburgh

Janos T. Fustos
Metropolitan State College of Denver

Sharyn Hardy Gallagher
University of Massachusetts Lowell

Edward J. Glantz
Pennsylvania State University

Marvin L. Golland
Polytechnic University, Brooklyn

Robert Gordon
Hofstra University

Diane Graf
Northern Illinois University

Dale D. Gust
Central Michigan University

Jun He
University of Pittsburgh

Gerald L. Hershey
University of North Carolina, Greensboro

Fred H. Hughes
Faulkner University

Surinder Kahai
SUNY, Binghamton

Rex Karsten
University of Northern Iowa

Joseph Kasten
Dowling College

Tracie Kinsley
George Mason University

Fred L. Kitchens
Ball State University

Brian J. Klas
Montclair State University

Barbara D. Klein
University of Michigan–
Dearborn

Richard Klein
Clemson University

Chang E. Koh
University of North Texas

Gerald Kohers
Sam Houston State University

Rebecca Berens Koop
University of Dayton

Brett J. L. Landry
University of New Orleans

William Lankford
University of West Georgia

Robert Lawton
Western Illinois University

Al Lederer
University of Kentucky

John D. (Skip) Lees
California State University,
Chico

Bingguang Li
Albany State University

Shin-Jeng Lin
Le Moyne College

Dana McCann
Central Michigan University

Charlotte McConn
Pennsylvania State University

Matthew McGowan
Bradley University

John Melrose
University of Wisconsin–
Eau Claire

Jim Mensching
California State University,
Chico

Pam Milstead
Louisiana Tech University

Ellen F. Monk
University of Delaware

Philip F. Musa
The University of Alabama
at Birmingham

George Nezlek
Grand Valley State University

Jennifer Nightingale
Duquesne University

Floyd D. Ploeger
Texas State University–
San Marcos

Mahesh S. Raisinghani
University of Dallas

Paula Ruby
Arkansas State University

Werner Schenk
University of Rochester

Roy Schmidt
Bradley University

David Schroeder
Valparaiso University

Sherri Shade
Kennesaw State University

Nancy C. Shaw
George Mason University

Betsy Page Sigman
Georgetown University

Marcos P. Sivitanides
Texas State University

Marion S. Smith
Texas Southern University

Ute H. St. Clair
Binghamton University

Suzanne Testerman
University of Akron

Amrit Tiwana
Emory University

Yung-Chin Alex Tung
University of Connecticut

Douglas E. Turner
State University of West Georgia

David A. Vance
Mississippi State University

Linda Wallace
Virginia Tech

Barbara Warner
University of South Florida

John Wee
University of Mississippi

Dennis Williams
California Polytechnic
State University

Karen Williams
University of Texas
at San Antonio

G. W. K. Willis
Baylor University

Kathleen Wright
Salisbury University

Judy Wynekoop
Florida Gulf Coast University

Ruben Xing
Montclair State University

James E. Yao
Montclair State University

Robert Zwick
Baruch College–CUNY

Paige Baltzan

Paige Baltzan teaches in the Department of Information Technology and Electronic Commerce at the Daniels College of Business at the University of Denver. She holds a B.S.B.A specializing in Accounting/MIS and an M.B.A. specializing in MIS from the University of Denver. She is a coauthor of several books in the *I-Series* and a contributor to *Management Information Systems for the Information Age.*

Prior to joining the Daniels College faculty in 1999, Paige spent several years working for a large telecommunications company and an international consulting firm where she participated in client engagements in the United States as well as South America and Europe. Paige lives in Lakewood, Colorado, with her husband, Tony, and daughters Hannah and Sophie.

Amy Phillips

Amy Phillips teaches in the Department of Information Technology and Electronic Commerce at the Daniels College of Business at the University of Denver. Amy has 20 years of teaching experience and has coauthored several textbooks in the *I-Series* and is a contributor to *Management Information Systems for the Information Age.* Recently Amy earned her M.C.A.D., M.C.S.D., and M.C.T. certification, which has allowed her to facilitate numerous workshops and seminars on behalf of Microsoft.

Stephen Haag

Stephen Haag is Chair of the Department of Information Technology and Electronic Commerce in the Daniels College of Business at the University of Denver. Stephen is also the Director of the Masters of Science in Information Technology program and the Director of the Advanced Technology Center. Stephen holds a B.B.A. and M.B.A. from West Texas State University and a Ph.D. from the University of Texas at Arlington.

Stephen is the coauthor of numerous books including *Interactions: Teaching English as a Second Language* (with his mother and father), *Information Technology: Tomorrow's Advantage Today* (with Peter Keen), *Excelling in Finance,* and more than 40 books within the *I-Series.* He has also written numerous articles appearing in such journals as *Communications of the ACM, Socio-Economic Planning Sciences,* the *International Journal of Systems Science, Managerial and Decision Economics, Applied Economics,* and the *Australian Journal of Management.* Stephen lives with his wife, Pam, and their four sons—Indiana, Darian, Trevor, and Zippy—in Highlands Ranch, Colorado.

Business
Driven
Technology

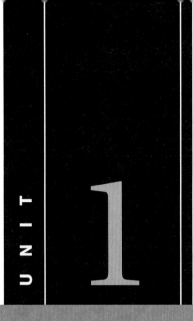

UNIT 1

Achieving Business Success through Information Technology

How Levi's Got Its Jeans into Wal-Mart

People around the world recognize Levi's as an American icon, the cool jeans worn by movie stars James Dean and Marilyn Monroe. For one reason or another, however, the company failed to keep up with the fast-changing tastes of American teenagers. In particular, it missed the trend to baggy jeans that caught hold in the mid-1990s. Sales plummeted from $7.1 billion in 1996 to $4.1 billion in 2003 and Levi's U.S. market share dropped from 18.7 percent in 1997 to 12 percent in 2003, a huge decline of almost one-third in both dollars and market share.

Analyzing and Responding to What Happened

Competition hit Levi's on both the high and low ends. Fashion-conscious buyers were drawn to high-priced brands like Blue Cult, Juicy, and Seven, which had more fashion cachet than Levi's. On the low end, parents were buying Wrangler and Lee jeans for their kids because on average they cost about $10 less than Levi's Red Tab brand. Wrangler and Lee were also the brands they found at discount retailers such as Wal-Mart, Target, and T. J. Maxx. David Bergen, Levi's chief information officer (CIO), described the company as "getting squeezed," and "caught in the jaws of death."

Levi's new CEO, Philip A. Marineau, came to Levi's from PepsiCo in 1999, a year after he helped PepsiCo surpass Coke in sales for the first time. Marineau recruited Bergen in 2000 from Carstation.com. Marineau quickly realized that turning Levi's around would entail manufacturing, marketing, and distributing jeans that customers demanded, particularly customers at the low end where the mass market was located.

Bergen was anxious to join Marineau's team because of his background in clothing, retailing, and manufacturing with companies such as The Gap and Esprit de Corps in the 1980s. He knew that Marineau's plan to anticipate customer wants would require up-to-date IT applications such as data warehousing, data mining, and customer relationship management (CRM) systems. He also knew that selling to mass market retailers would require upgrades to Levi's supply chain management (SCM) systems, and he understood that globalization would necessitate standardized enterprise resource planning (ERP) systems. Overall, it was a challenge any ambitious CIO would covet. After all, designing and installing IT systems that drive and achieve key business initiatives is what it is all about.

Joining Wal-Mart

Wal-Mart was a pioneer in supply chain management systems, having learned early on that driving costs out of the supply chain would let it offer products to customers at the lowest possible prices, while at the same time assuring that products the customers demanded were always on the stores' shelves. Becoming one of Wal-Mart's 30,000 suppliers is not easy. Wal-Mart insists that its suppliers do business using up-to-date IT systems to manage the supply chain—not just the supply chain between Wal-Mart and its suppliers, but the supply chains between the suppliers and their suppliers as well. Wal-Mart has strict supply chain management system requirements that its business partners must meet.

Wal-Mart's requirements presented Levi's with a serious hurdle to overcome because its supply chain management systems were in bad shape. Levi's executives did not even have access to key information required to track where its products were moving in the supply chain. For example, they did not know how many pairs of jeans were in the factory awaiting shipment, how many were somewhere en route, or how many had just been unloaded at a customer's warehouse. According to Greg Hammann, Levi's U.S. chief customer officer, "Our supply chain could not deliver the services Wal-Mart expected."

Bergen created a cross-functional team of key managers from IT, finance, and sales to transform Levi's systems to meet Wal-Mart's requirements. Their recommendations included network upgrades, modifications to ordering and logistics applications, and data warehouse improvements, among others. Although Bergen realized that about half the changes required to Levi's current IT systems to accommodate the state-of-the-art demands of Wal-Mart would be a waste of resources since these systems were being replaced by a new SAP enterprise software system over the next five years, nevertheless, Levi's could not wait for the SAP installation if it wanted Wal-Mart's business now, so it decided to move forward with the changes to the current systems.

Levi's successful transformation of its supply chain management system allowed the company to partner with Wal-Mart. The company introduced its new signature line at Wal-Mart, which sells for around $23 and has fewer details in the finish than Levi's other lines, no trademark pocket stitching or red tab, for example. Wal-Mart wants big-name brands to lure more affluent customers into its stores, while still maintaining the low price points all Wal-Mart customers have come to expect. Wal-Mart Senior Vice President Lois Mikita notes that Wal-Mart "continues to tailor its selection to meet the needs of customers from a cross section of income levels and lifestyles." She also states she is impressed with the level of detail Levi's has put into its systems transformation efforts to "make the execution of this new launch 100 percent."

Achieving Business Success through IT

Bergen's changes were a success and the percentage of products delivered on time quickly rose from 65 percent to 95 percent primarily because of the updated supply chain management system. Levi's total sales were also up in the third and fourth quarters of 2003, for the first time since 1996. NPD Group's Fashionworld is a research group that tracks apparel and footwear market trends. In 2003, Levi's appeared on NPD Fashionworld's top 10 list of brands preferred by young women, ending an absence of several years. Marshall Cohen, a senior industry analyst at NPD Fashionworld, noted that Levi's "hadn't been close to that for a while. Teens hadn't gravitated toward Levi's in years. That was incredible. A lot of that has to do with having the right style in the right place at the right time." The improved systems, Cohen noted, also helped the company get the right sizes to the right stores.

Another highly successful IT system implemented by Levi's is a digital dashboard that executives can display on their PC screens. The dashboard lets an executive see the status of a product as it moves from the factory floor to distribution centers to retail stores. For example, the dashboard can display how Levi's 501 jeans are selling at an individual Kohl's store compared to forecasted sales. "When I first got here I didn't see anything," Hammann says. "Now I can drill down to the product level."

The digital dashboard alerts executives to trends that under the previous systems would have taken weeks to detect. For example, in 2002 Levi's started to ship Dockers Stain Defender pants. Expected sales for the pants were around 2 million pairs. The digital dashboard quickly notified key executives that the trousers were selling around 2.5 million pairs. This information enabled them to adjust production upward in time to ship more pants, meet the increased demand, and avoid lost sales. Levi's also uses the systems to control supply during key seasonal sales periods such as back-to-school and Christmas.

"If I look overconfident, I'm not," says Bergen. "I'm very nervous about this change. When we trip, we have to stand up real quick and get back on the horse, as they say." As if to reinforce Bergen's point, Gib Carey, a supply chain analyst at Bain, notes, "The place where companies do fail is when they aren't bringing anything new to Wal-Mart. Wal-Mart is constantly looking at 'How can I get the same product I am selling today at a lower price somewhere else?' "[1]

INTRODUCTION

Information is everywhere. Most organizations value information as a strategic asset that can directly affect their bottom line. Consider General Motors (GM)—its GMAC operation, which handles financing for car sales and leases, is now actually more profitable than its manufacturing and sales operations.

GM's success depends heavily on information about its customers, suppliers, markets, and operations. For example, GM must be able to predict the number of people who will graduate from college this year and the percentage of those graduates who will buy cars (and which models) within the next two years. Estimating too many buyers will lead GM to produce an excess of inventory; estimating too few buyers will potentially mean lost sales (and worse yet, lost revenues from financing or leasing).

GM must also gain business intelligence about its suppliers, such as Gates (rubber components) and Fisher (auto body components), including their production schedules, projected drop-shipment dates, volume discounts, and levels of quality. Supplier quality levels are crucial in the automobile industry, because any car that is a "lemon" means bad word-of-mouth advertising. Having to recall an entire automobile line because of defects can be devastating. Therefore, supplier information is just as important to GM's business as customer information.

Understanding the direct impact information has on an organization's bottom line is crucial to running a successful business. This text focuses on information, business, technology, and the integrated set of activities used to run most organizations. Many of these activities are the hallmarks of business today—supply chain management, customer relationship management, enterprise resource planning, outsourcing, integration, e-business, and others. The five core units of this text cover these important activities in detail. Each unit is divided into chapters that provide individual learning outcomes and case studies. In addition to the five core units, there are technology and business "plug-ins" (see Figure 1.1) that further explore topics presented in the five core units. "Plug-in pointers" provided at the end of each chapter identify the relevant plug-ins.

The chapters in Unit 1 are:

- **Chapter One**—Business Driven Technology Overview
- **Chapter Two**—Identifying Competitive Advantages
- **Chapter Three**—Strategic Initiatives for Implementing Competitive Advantages
- **Chapter Four**—Measuring the Success of Strategic Initiatives
- **Chapter Five**—Organizational Structures That Support Strategic Initiatives

FIGURE 1.1

The Format and Approach of This Text

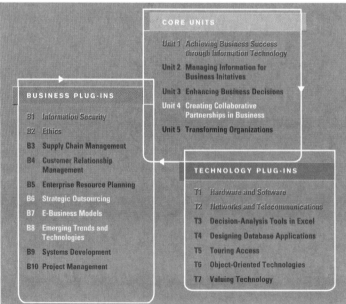

Chapter One: Business Driven Technology Overview

1.1. Compare management information systems (MIS) and information technology (IT).

1.2. Describe the relationships among people, information technology, and information.

1.3. Describe why people at different levels of an organization have different information needs.

This chapter provides an overview of the units in this text and introduces a few of the important business and technology concepts covered in each unit.

UNIT 1—ACHIEVING BUSINESS SUCCESS THROUGH INFORMATION TECHNOLOGY

Information technology (IT) is any computer-based tool that people use to work with information and support the information and information-processing needs of an organization. Information technology can be an important enabler of business success and innovation. This is not to say that IT *equals* business success and innovation or that IT *represents* business success and innovation. Information technology is most useful when it leverages the talents of people. Information technology in and of itself is not useful unless the right people know how to use and manage it effectively.

Management information systems is a business function just as marketing, finance, operations, and human resource management are business functions. Formally defined, *management information systems (MIS)* is the function that plans for, develops, implements, and maintains IT hardware, software, and the portfolio of applications that people use to support the goals of an organization. To perform the MIS function effectively, almost all organizations today, particularly large and medium-sized ones, have an internal IT Department, often called Information Technology (IT), Information Systems (IS), or Management Information Systems (MIS).

The plans and goals of the IT Department must align with the plans and goals of the organization. For example, if a primary goal of the organization is to increase sales, as at Levi's, information technology can facilitate Levi's relationship with Wal-Mart. Information technology can enable an organization to increase efficiency in manufacturing, retain key customers, seek out new sources of supply, and introduce effective financial management.

It is not always easy for managers to make the right choices when using IT to support (and often drive) business initiatives. Most managers understand their business initiatives well, but are often at a loss when it comes to knowing how to use and manage IT effectively in support of those initiatives. Managers who understand what IT is, and what IT can and cannot do, are in the best position to help their organization succeed.

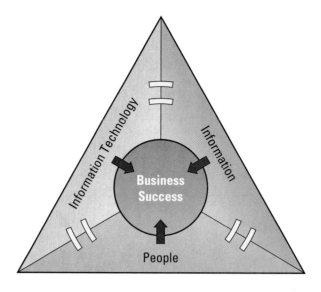

In essence,

- *people* use
- *information technology* to work with
- *information* (see Figure 1.2)

Those three key resources—people, information, and information technology (in that order of priority)—are inextricably linked. If one fails, they all fail. Most important, if one fails, then chances are the business will fail.

Unit 1 introduces several business strategies, such as Porter's Five Forces, value chain, supply chain management, and customer relationship management, that organizations can use to achieve success. The unit then focuses on how to measure the success of these strategies and finishes with a discussion on implementing the correct organizational structure to support these strategies.

UNIT 2—MANAGING INFORMATION FOR BUSINESS INITIATIVES

Like any resource, an organization must manage information properly. That is, an organization must:

1. Determine what information it requires.
2. Acquire that information.
3. Organize the information in a meaningful fashion.
4. Assure the information's quality.
5. Provide software tools so that employees throughout the organization can access the information they require.

At the very heart of most—if not all—management information systems is a database and a database management system (see Figure 1.3). A ***database*** maintains information about various types of objects (inventory), events (transactions), people (employees), and places (warehouses). A ***database management system (DBMS)*** is software through which users and application programs interact with a database. Think of it this way: A DBMS is to a database as word processing software is to a document or as spreadsheet software is to a spreadsheet. One is the information and the other is the software people use to manipulate the information.

The primary task of a database is to store and organize every piece of information related to transactions (for instance, the sale of a product) and business events (such as the hiring of a new employee). As such, databases store a tremendous amount of detailed information. The primary task of a DBMS then is to allow users to create, access, and use information stored in a database.

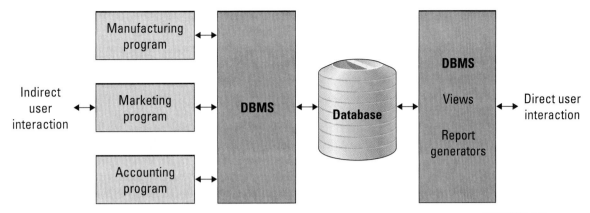

FIGURE 1.3

Managing Information
with a Database and
Database Management
System (DBMS)

As displayed in Figure 1.3, a user can directly interact with a database of information using different types of information technology tools such as views and report generators. Users can also interact with a database of information by using application programs such as accounting, marketing, and manufacturing applications.

Unit 2 covers databases and database management systems in detail and highlights why and how information adds value.

UNIT 3—ENHANCING BUSINESS DECISIONS

The structure of a typical organization is similar to a pyramid. The array of organizational activities occur at different levels of the pyramid. People in the organization have unique information needs and thus require various sets of information technology tools (see Figure 1.4). At the lower levels of the pyramid, people perform daily tasks such as processing transactions. This is ***online transaction processing (OLTP)***—the capturing of transaction and event information using technology to (1) process the information according to defined business rules, (2) store the information, and (3) update existing information to reflect the new information. At this level during OLTP, the organization must capture every detail of transactions and events. The activities of processing, storing, and updating information occur within the context of databases and DBMSs.

FIGURE 1.4

Activities, Information,
and Information
Technology within
an Organization

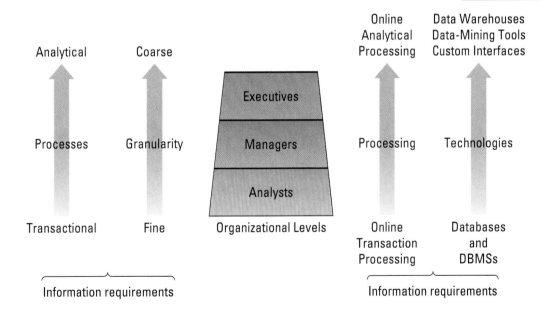

Moving up through the organizational pyramid, people (typically managers) deal less with the details ("finer" information) and more with meaningful aggregations of information ("coarser" information) that help them make broader decisions on behalf of the organization. This is **online analytical processing (OLAP)**—the manipulation of information to create *business intelligence* in support of strategic decision making. **Business intelligence** is a broad, general term describing information that people use to support their decision-making efforts.

While DBMS tools help managers obtain various aggregations of information in a database, many organizations today employ data warehouses and data-mining tools to support their strategic decision making. A **data warehouse** is a logical collection of information—gathered from many different operational databases—that supports business analysis activities and decision-making tasks. The tools that people use to work with information in a data warehouse are called data-mining tools. **Data-mining tools** use a variety of techniques to find patterns and relationships in large volumes of information and infer rules from them that predict future behavior and guide decision making.

Unit 3 introduces the role of information technology in strategic decision making and covers in detail topics such as data marts, data-mining tools, digital dashboards, supply chain management, and customer relationship management.

UNIT 4—CREATING COLLABORATIVE PARTNERSHIPS IN BUSINESS

To be successful—and avoid being eliminated by the competition—an organization will constantly undertake new initiatives, address both minor and major problems, and capitalize on significant opportunities. In support of these activities, an organization will create and utilize teams, partnerships, and alliances because all the requisite expertise needed is beyond the scope of a single individual or even the organization. An organization can form teams, partnerships, and alliances internally among its employees or externally with other organizations (see Figure 1.5).

The increasingly complicated nature of business often requires the expertise from many functional areas. IT-based collaboration tools can help organizations make efficient and effective use of their resources, namely their people and infor-

FIGURE 1.5

Teams, Partnerships, and Alliances within and External to an Organization

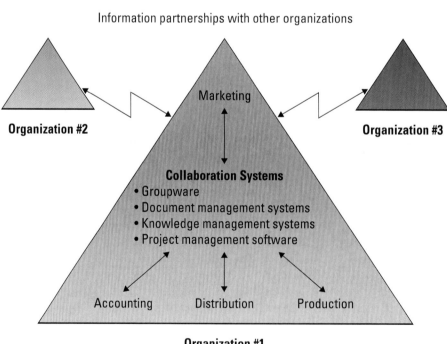

Information partnerships with other organizations

Organization #2

Organization #3

Marketing

Collaboration Systems
- Groupware
- Document management systems
- Knowledge management systems
- Project management software

Accounting   Distribution   Production

Organization #1

mation, when they use teams. A **collaboration system** is an IT-based set of tools that supports the work of teams by facilitating the sharing and flow of information. Many successful organizations today have utilized some or all of the following collaboration systems in support of teams:

- **Groupware**—software tools that support team interaction and dynamics including calendaring, scheduling, and videoconferencing.
- **Document management systems (DMS)**—support the electronic capturing, storage, distribution, archival, and accessing of documents. Document management systems are ideal for moving standard business documents, such as purchase orders, among various functions including order processing, inventory management, billing, warehousing, and shipping.
- **Knowledge management systems (KMS)**—systems that support the capturing and use of an organization's "know how."
- **Project management software**—specifically supports the long-term and day-to-day management and execution of the steps in a project (such as building a new warehouse or designing and implementing a new IT system).

For example, Project Management Advisors, Inc. (PMA), provides its clients with expertise in project management for real estate design, construction, and occupancy processes. PMA required a system for sharing project information such as project plans, budgets, and progress reports with its project team members who were typically located in cities across the United States. PMA implemented Synergy, a Web-based collaboration tool that provides the various team members access to project information. The tool even offers the functionality to control which team members can update documents and which team members can only view documents. The system replaced e-mail discussions with Web-based discussion forums, which in turn provide an organized record of project-related discussions among team members. The use of Synergy has permitted PMA to undertake larger, more complex projects and reduce its administrative costs at the same time.[2]

In the same way that organizations use internal teams, they are increasingly forming alliances and partnerships with other organizations. The **core competency** of an organization is its key strength, a business function that it does better than any of its competitors. For example, Apple Computer is highly regarded for its strength in product design, while Accenture's core competency is the design and installation of information systems. A **core competency strategy** is one in which an organization chooses to focus specifically on what it does best (its core competency) and forms partnerships and alliances with other specialist organizations to handle nonstrategic business processes.

Information technology systems make such business partnerships and alliances easier to establish and manage. An **information partnership** occurs when two or more organizations cooperate by integrating their IT systems, thereby providing customers with the best of what each can offer. The advent of the Internet has greatly increased the opportunity for IT-enabled business partnerships and alliances. For example, Amazon.com developed a profitable business segment by providing e-business outsourcing services to other retailers who use Amazon's Web site software. Some well-known retailers partnering with Amazon.com include Marshall Fields, Office Depot, and Target.[3]

Information partnerships are an integral foundation for many business initiatives, including supply chain management, as with Wal-Mart and Levi's in the opening case study. Levi's core competency is brand-name differentiation and recognition, while Wal-Mart's core competency is retail cost leadership. The information partnership between those two organizations enables cost-leadership selling of a widely recognized brand name. It is a win-win situation for both organizations.

Unit 4 specifically focuses on IT support for collaborative partnerships, both internally to an organization and externally with its business partners.

Traditional Businesses	Internet Competitors
Automobile dealers	Autobyte, AutoTrader
Bookstores	Amazon, BarnesandNoble
Mortgage bankers	DiTech, HomeLoanAdvisor
Music retailers	Apple i-Tunes, Pressplay
Stockbrokers	E-Trade, Ameritrade
Travel agents	Expedia, Travelocity
U.S. Postal Service	AOL, MSN, Hotmail
Auctions	eBay, ubid

FIGURE 1.6

Traditional Business Changed by Internet-Enabled Competition

UNIT 5—TRANSFORMING ORGANIZATIONS

Some observers of our business environment have an ominous vision of the future—*digital Darwinism*. **Digital Darwinism** implies that organizations which cannot adapt to the new demands placed on them for surviving in the information age are doomed to extinction.[4]

Rapid changes in technology coupled with recent trends toward the globalization of business have raised the intensity of the competitive environment in just about every industry. In the words of one long-time business consultant, "Nothing's easy any more." What this means is that managers will need all of the tools at their disposal to ensure that their business thrives in the information age by continuously transforming itself. Figure 1.6 shows several business segments that have changed dramatically because of Internet-based competition.

There are numerous examples of organizations losing revenue because of advances in technology. For example, the airline industry lost revenue from business travelers after the invention of videoconferencing technologies because managers no longer have to travel to distant places to meet with their co-workers. The airline industry also lost revenue with the invention of networking technologies that give individuals the ability to access systems remotely to make updates, changes, and fixes. Technical specialists do not have to physically travel to the location of the system; they can simply log in from wherever they are located. Thus, managers must continually watch for Internet competition and technology advances that have the potential to corrode market share.

Unit 5 explores the power of IT to transform an organization. Information technology is a powerful tool that can transform an organization from doing "business as usual" to becoming what some observers call an *agile organization,* capable of anticipating and/or reacting to business opportunities and threats. Unit 5 focuses on how to manage the development of IT systems to support agile organizations in keeping with the requirements of a 21st century organization.

OPENING CASE STUDY QUESTIONS

1. Explain how Levi's achieved business success through the use of information, information technology, and people.

2. Describe the types of Levi's jeans information staff employees at a Wal-Mart store require and compare it to the types of Levi's jeans information the executives at Wal-Mart's corporate headquarters require.

3. Arrange the five units covered in this text and rank them in order of greatest impact to least impact on Levi's competitive strategy.

Technology, specifically the Internet, is changing the way businesses operate. Internet-based business such as online retail sales and online advertising generates over $100 billion in revenue per year. Organizations must understand the potential value that can be unleashed from embracing technology and Internet-based business. The following are a few statistics about the Internet that organizations can use to estimate future revenue potential:

■ Forester Research predicted online retail sales would hit $101.1 billion in the United States by 2002. This prediction came true a year later in 2003 (see Figure 1.7).

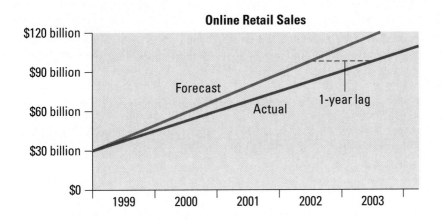

FIGURE 1.7

Online Retail Sales

■ eMarketer estimated that 22.3 million households would have broadband connections in the United States by 2000. The actual figure for 2002 was 17.2 million and reached 24 million by the end of 2003 (see Figure 1.8).

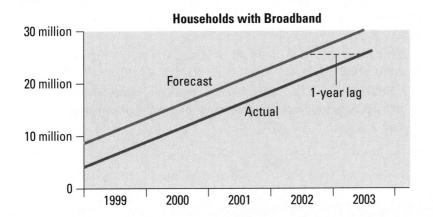

FIGURE 1.8

Households with Broadband

■ Online advertising revenue was expected to hit $3 billion in 2001 and actually did in 2003 (see Figure 1.9).

FIGURE 1.9

Online Advertising
Revenue

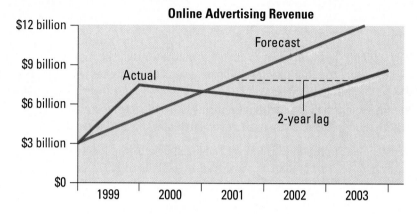

Online Advertising Revenue

■ Jupiter Research estimated the world's online population would hit 498.1 million by 2003. According to eMarketer, the global Internet population was over 633 million in 2003 (see Figure 1.10).[5]

FIGURE 1.10

Internet Users
Worldwide

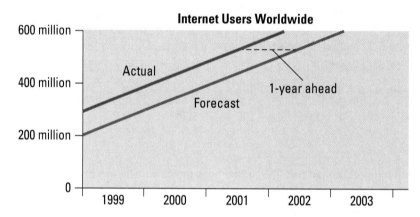

Internet Users Worldwide

Questions

1. Review the graphs in Figures 1.7 through 1.10 and explain why it is critical that businesses understand and embrace the Internet.
2. Explain the correlation between the online retail sales graph (Figure 1.7) and the online advertising revenue graph (Figure 1.9).
3. The number of Internet users worldwide is two years ahead of its forecast. What are the potential impacts that underestimating the number of global Internet users might have on a business?

PLUG-IN POINTERS >>

Review the *Technology Plug-In* **Hardware and Software** for an overview of hardware devices, application software, system software, storage devices, and connecting devices.

Review the *Technology Plug-In* **Networks and Telecommunications** for a comprehensive overview of networks including LAN, WAN, MAN, VPN, TCP/IP, network topologies, network operating systems, and guided and unguided media.

Chapter Two: Identifying Competitive Advantages

2.1. Explain why competitive advantages are typically temporary.

2.2. List and describe each of the five forces in Porter's Five Forces Model.

2.3. Compare Porter's three generic strategies.

2.4. Describe the relationship between business processes and value chains.

To survive and thrive, an organization must create a competitive advantage. A *competitive advantage* is a product or service that an organization's customers value more highly than similar offerings from a competitor. Unfortunately, competitive advantages are typically temporary because competitors often seek ways to duplicate the competitive advantage. In turn, organizations must develop a strategy based on a new competitive advantage.

When an organization is the first to market with a competitive advantage, it gains a first-mover advantage. The *first-mover advantage* occurs when an organization can significantly impact its market share by being first to market with a competitive advantage. FedEx created a first-mover advantage several years ago when it developed its customer self-service software allowing people and organizations to request a package pick-up, print mailing slips, and track packages online. Other parcel delivery services quickly followed with their own versions of the software. Today, customer self-service on the Internet is a standard for doing business in the parcel delivery industry.

As organizations develop their competitive advantages, they must pay close attention to their competition through environmental scanning. *Environmental scanning* is the acquisition and analysis of events and trends in the environment external to an organization. Information technology has the opportunity to play an important role in environmental scanning. For example, Frito Lay, a premier provider of snack foods such as Cracker Jacks and Cheetos, does not just send its representatives into grocery stores to stock shelves—they carry hand-held computers and record the product offerings, inventory, and even product locations of competitors. Frito Lay uses this information to gain business intelligence on everything from how well competing products are selling to the strategic placement of its own products.

There are three common tools used in industry to analyze and develop competitive advantages: (1) the Five Forces Model, (2) the three generic strategies, and (3) value chains.

THE FIVE FORCES MODEL—EVALUATING BUSINESS SEGMENTS

Organizations frequently face a decision as to whether to enter a new industry or industry segment. Michael Porter's Five Forces Model is a useful tool to aid in this challenging decision. The *Five Forces Model* helps determine the relative attractiveness of an industry and includes the following five forces (see Figure 1.11):

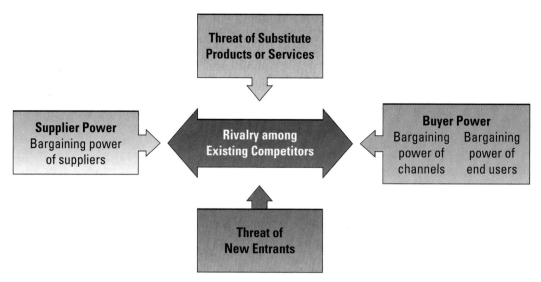

FIGURE 1.11

Porter's Five Forces
Model in the Internet
Economy

1. Buyer power
2. Supplier power
3. Threat of substitute products or services
4. Threat of new entrants
5. Rivalry among existing competitors

The following introduction to each force provides detailed examples of how information technology can develop a competitive advantage.

Buyer Power

Buyer power in the Five Forces Model is high when buyers have many choices of whom to buy from and low when their choices are few. To reduce buyer power (and create a competitive advantage), an organization must make it more attractive for customers to buy from them than from their competition. One of the best IT-based examples is the loyalty programs that many organizations offer. ***Loyalty programs*** reward customers based on the amount of business they do with a particular organization. The travel industry is famous for its loyalty programs such as frequent-flyer programs for airlines and frequent-stayer programs for hotels.

Keeping track of the activities and accounts of many thousands or millions of customers covered by loyalty programs is not practical without large-scale IT systems. Loyalty programs are a good example of using IT to reduce buyer power. Because of the rewards (e.g., free airline tickets, upgrades, or hotel stays) travelers receive, they are more likely to be loyal to or give most of their business to a single organization.

Supplier Power

Supplier power in the Five Forces Model is high when buyers have few choices of whom to buy from and low when their choices are many. Supplier power is the converse of buyer power: A supplier organization in a market will want buyer power to be low. A ***supply chain*** consists of all parties involved, directly or indirectly, in the procurement of a product or raw material. In a typical supply chain, an organization will probably be both a supplier (to customers) and a customer (of other supplier organizations) (see Figure 1.12).

As a buyer, the organization can create a competitive advantage by locating alternative supply sources. IT-enabled business-to-business (B2B) marketplaces can help. A ***business-to-business (B2B) marketplace*** is an Internet-based service which brings together many buyers and sellers. One important variation of the B2B mar-

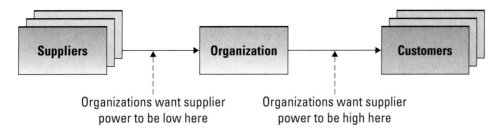

FIGURE 1.12

An Organization within the Supply Chain

Suppliers → Organization → Customers

Organizations want supplier power to be low here

Organizations want supplier power to be high here

ketplace is a private exchange. A *private exchange* is a B2B marketplace in which a single buyer posts its needs and then opens the bidding to any supplier who would care to bid. Bidding is typically carried out through a reverse auction. A *reverse auction* is an auction format in which increasingly lower bids are solicited from organizations willing to supply the desired product or service at an increasingly lower price. As the bids get lower and lower, more and more suppliers drop out of the auction. Ultimately, the organization with the lowest bid wins. Internet-based reverse auctions are an excellent example of the way that information technology can reduce supplier power for an organization and create a competitive advantage.

Threat of Substitute Products or Services

The *threat of substitute products or services* in the Five Forces Model is high when there are many alternatives to a product or service and low when there are few alternatives from which to choose. Ideally, an organization would like to be in a market in which there are few substitutes for the products or services it offers. Of course, that is seldom possible in any market today, but an organization can still create a competitive advantage by using switching costs. *Switching costs* are costs that can make customers reluctant to switch to another product or service.

A switching cost need not have an associated *monetary* cost. Amazon.com offers an example. As customers purchase products at Amazon.com over time, it begins to develop a unique profile of their shopping and purchasing habits. When a customer visits Amazon.com repeatedly, it can begin to offer products tailored to that particular customer based on their profile. If the customer decides to shop elsewhere, there is an associated switching cost because the new site will not have the profile of the customer's past purchases. In this way Amazon.com has reduced the threat of substitute products or services in a market in which there are many by tailoring customer offerings and creating a "cost" to the consumer to switch to another online retailer.

Threat of New Entrants

The *threat of new entrants* in the Five Forces Model is high when it is easy for new competitors to enter a market and low when there are significant entry barriers to entering a market. An *entry barrier* is a product or service feature that customers have come to expect from organizations in a particular industry and must be offered by an entering organization to compete and survive. For example, a new bank must offer its customers an array of IT-enabled services, including ATM use, online bill paying, and account monitoring. These are significant barriers to entering the banking market. At one time, the first bank to offer such services gained a valuable first-mover advantage, but only temporarily, as other banking competitors developed their own IT systems.

Rivalry among Existing Competitors

Rivalry among existing competitors in the Five Forces Model is high when competition is fierce in a market and low when competition is more complacent. Although competition is always more intense in some industries than in others, the overall trend is toward increased competition in just about every industry.

The retail grocery industry is intensively competitive. While Kroger, Safeway, and Albertson's in the United States compete in many different ways, essentially they try to beat or match the competition on price. Most of them have loyalty programs that give shoppers special discounts. Customers get lower prices while the store gathers valuable information on buying habits to craft pricing strategies. In the future, expect to see grocery stores using wireless technologies to track customer movement throughout the store and match it to products purchased to determine purchasing sequences. Such a system will be IT-based and a huge competitive advantage to the first store to implement it.

Since margins are quite low in the grocery retail market, grocers build efficiencies into their supply chains, connecting with their suppliers in IT-enabled information partnerships such as the one between Wal-Mart and its suppliers. Communicating with suppliers over telecommunications networks rather than using paper-based systems makes the procurement process faster, cheaper, and more accurate. That equates to lower prices for customers and increased rivalry among existing competitors.

THE THREE GENERIC STRATEGIES—CREATING A BUSINESS FOCUS

Once the relative attractiveness of an industry is determined and an organization decides to enter that market, it must formulate a strategy for entering the new market. An organization can follow Porter's three generic strategies when entering a new market: (1) broad cost leadership, (2) broad differentiation, or (3) a focused strategy. Broad strategies reach a large market segment, while focused strategies target a niche market. A focused strategy concentrates on either cost leadership or differentiation. Trying to be all things to all people, however, is a recipe for disaster, since it is difficult to project a consistent image to the entire marketplace. Porter suggests that an organization is wise to adopt only one of the three generic strategies.

To illustrate the use of the three generic strategies, consider Figure 1.13. The matrix shown demonstrates the relationships among strategies (cost leadership versus differentiation) and market segmentation (broad versus focused).

FIGURE 1.13

Three Generic Strategies in the Auto Industry

- **Hyundai** is following a broad cost leadership strategy. Hyundai offers low-cost vehicles, in each particular model stratification, that appeal to a large audience.

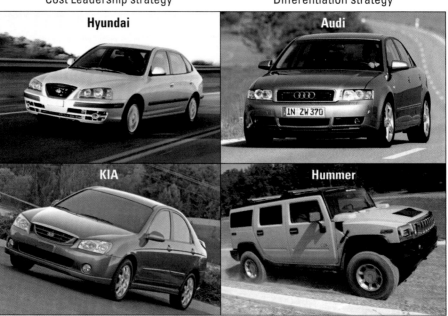

Cost Leadership strategy   Differentiation strategy

Hyundai   Audi

Broad markets

KIA   Hummer

Focused markets

- **Audi** is pursuing a broad differentiation strategy with its Quattro models available at several price points. Audi's differentiation is safety and it prices its various Quattro models (higher than Hyundai) to reach a large, stratified audience.

- **KIA** has a more focused cost leadership strategy. KIA mainly offers low-cost vehicles in the lower levels of model stratification.

- **Hummer** offers the most focused differentiation strategy of any in the industry (including Mercedes-Benz).

VALUE CHAINS—TARGETING BUSINESS PROCESSES

An organization must understand, accept, and successfully execute its business strategy. Every aspect of the organization contributes to the success (or failure) of the chosen strategy. The business processes of the organization and the value chain they create play an integral role in strategy execution.

A **business process** is a standardized set of activities that accomplish a specific task, such as processing a customer's order. To evaluate the effectiveness of its business processes, an organization can use Michael Porter's value chain approach. The **value chain** approach views an organization as a chain, or series, of processes, each of which adds value to the product or service for each customer. To create a competitive advantage, the value chain must enable the organization to provide *unique* value to its customers.

Organizations can achieve this by offering lower prices or by competing in a distinctive way. Examining the organization as a value chain (actually numerous distinct but inseparable value chains) leads to the identification of the important activities that add value for customers and then identifying IT systems that support those activities. Figure 1.14a provides a graphical depiction of a value chain. *Primary value activities,* shown at the bottom of the graph, acquire raw materials and manufactures, delivers, markets, sells, and provides after-sales services. *Support value activities,* along the top of the graph, such as firm infrastructure, human resource management, technology development, and procurement, support the primary value activities.

The goal here is to survey the customers and ask them the extent to which they believe each activity adds value to the product or service. This generates a quantifiable metric, displayed in percentages in Figure 1.14, for how each activity adds value (or reduces value). The competitive advantage decision then is to (1) target high value-adding activities to further enhance their value, (2) target low value-adding activities to increase their value, or (3) perform some combination of the two.

FIGURE 1.14a

A Graphical Depiction of a Value Chain

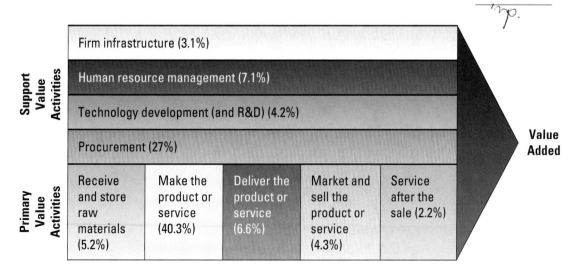

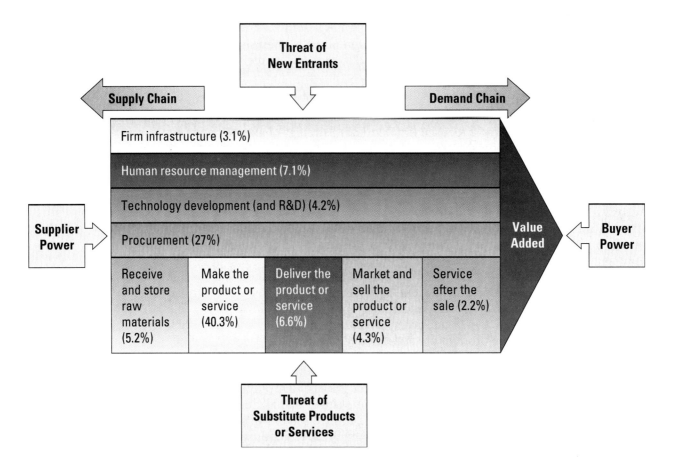

FIGURE 1.14b

The Value Chain and
Porter's Five Forces

Value chain analysis is a highly useful tool in that it provides hard and fast numbers for evaluating the activities that add value to products and services. An organization can find additional value by analyzing and constructing its value chain in terms of Porter's Five Forces (see Figure 1.14b). For example, if an organization wants to decrease its buyer's or customer's power it can construct its value chain activity of "service after the sale" by offering high levels of quality customer service. This will increase the switching costs for its customers, thereby decreasing their power. Analyzing and constructing its support value activities can help an organization decrease the threat of new entrants. Analyzing and constructing its primary value activities can help an organization decrease the threat of substitute products or services.

OPENING CASE STUDY QUESTIONS

1. How can Levi's use environmental scanning to gain business intelligence?

2. Using Porter's Five Forces Model, analyze Levi's buyer power and supplier power.

3. Which of the three generic strategies is Levi's following?

Chapter Two Case: Say "Charge It" with Your Cell Phone

Wireless operators, credit card companies, and retailers are working on a technology that allows customers to purchase items by using their cell phones. For example, a customer could purchase a can of soda by dialing a telephone number on the dispensing machine and have the charge for the soda show up on their cell phone bill. Working prototypes are currently in use in South Korea, Japan, and Europe.

The ability to charge items to a cell phone has significant business potential because, unlike in the United States, credit cards are not nearly as popular in other countries. In Japan and China, for example, people are much more likely to have a cell phone than a credit card. Japanese consumers use credit cards for only 5.6 percent of their personal spending compared with 33 percent of U.S. consumer spending.

The payoff for credit card companies and cell phone operators from this technology could be enormous. By associating a credit card with a cell phone, banks and credit card companies hope to convince consumers to buy products, such as soda, with their cell phones instead of pocket change. Of course, they will reap transaction fees for each transaction. Mobile phone operators see the technology as a way to increase traffic on their networks as well as to position cell phones as an even more useful and, thus, essential device for consumers. Retailers envision easier transactions also leading to more sales.

MasterCard International and Nokia are currently testing a cell phone credit card for the U.S. market. The phones have a special chip programmed with the user's credit card information and a radio frequency transmitting circuit. Consumers can simply tap their phone on a special device at a checkout counter equipped with a receiving device that costs the retailer about $80. Betsy Foran-Owens, vice president for Product Services at MasterCard International commented that with this technology, "You don't even have to get off your phone to pay. You can just tap this thing down at the register." She also noted, "If you're not going to carry cash around, what are you going to carry? Your mobile phone."

The only players who might not look favorably on the technology are the traditional telephone companies, who must certainly view the technology as just one more threat to their traditional telephone business.[6]

Questions

1. Do you view this technology as a potential threat to traditional telephone companies? If so, what counterstrategies could traditional telephone companies adopt to prepare for this technology?
2. Using Porter's Five Forces describe the barriers to entry for this new technology.
3. Which of Porter's three generic strategies is this new technology following?

Chapter Three: Strategic Initiatives for Implementing Competitive Advantages

3.1. List and describe the four basic components of supply chain management.

3.2. Explain customer relationship management systems and how they can help organizations understand their customers.

3.3. Summarize the importance of enterprise resource planning systems.

Trek, a leader in bicycle products and accessories, gained more than 30 percent of the worldwide market by streamlining operations through the implementation of several IT systems. According to Jeff Stang, director of IT and Operational Accounting, the most significant improvement realized from the new systems was the ability to obtain key management information to drive business decisions in line with the company's strategic goals. Other system results included a highly successful Web site developed for the 1,400 Trek dealers where they could enter orders directly, check stock availability, and view accounts receivable and credit summaries. Tonja Green, Trek channel manager for North America, stated, "We wanted to give our dealers an easier and quicker way to enter their orders and get information. Every week the number of Web orders increases by 25–30 percent due to the new system."[7]

This chapter introduces three high-profile strategic initiatives that an organization can undertake to help it gain competitive advantages and business efficiencies—supply chain management, customer relationship management, and enterprise resource planning.

SUPPLY CHAIN MANAGEMENT

To understand a supply chain, consider a customer purchasing a Trek bike from a dealer. On one end, the supply chain has the customer placing an order for the bike with the dealer. The dealer purchases the bike from the manufacturer, Trek. Trek purchases raw materials such as packaging material, metal, and accessories from many different suppliers to make the bike. The supply chain for Trek encompasses every activity and party involved in the process of fulfilling the order from the customer for the new bike.

Supply chain management (SCM) involves the management of information flows between and among stages in a supply chain to maximize total supply chain effectiveness and profitability. The four basic components of supply chain management are:

1. **Supply chain strategy**—the strategy for managing all the resources required to meet customer demand for all products and services.

2. **Supply chain partners**—the partners chosen to deliver finished products, raw materials, and services including pricing, delivery, and payment processes along with partner relationship monitoring metrics.

3. **Supply chain operation**—the schedule for production activities including testing, packaging, and preparation for delivery. Measurements for this component include productivity and quality.

4. **Supply chain logistics**—the product delivery processes and elements including orders, warehouses, carriers, defective product returns, and invoicing.

Dozens of steps are required to achieve and carry out each of the above components. SCM software can enable an organization to generate efficiencies within these steps by automating and improving the information flows throughout and among the different supply chain components.

Wal-Mart and Procter & Gamble (P&G) implemented a tremendously successful SCM system. The system linked Wal-Mart's distribution centers directly to P&G's manufacturing centers. Every time a Wal-Mart customer purchases a P&G product, the system sends a message directly to the factory alerting P&G to restock the product. The system also sends an automatic alert to P&G whenever a product is running low at one of Wal-Mart's distribution centers. This real-time information allows P&G to efficiently make and deliver products to Wal-Mart without having to maintain large inventories in its warehouses. The system also generates invoices and receives payments automatically. The SCM system saves time, reduces inventory, and decreases order-processing costs for P&G. P&G passes on these savings to Wal-Mart in the form of discounted prices.[8]

Figure 1.15 diagrams the stages of the SCM system for a customer purchasing a product from Wal-Mart. The diagram demonstrates how the supply chain is dynamic and involves the constant flow of information between the different parties. For example, the customer generates order information by purchasing a product from Wal-Mart. Wal-Mart supplies the order information to its warehouse or distributor. The warehouse or distributor transfers the order information to the manufacturer, who provides pricing and availability information to the store and replenishes the product to the store. Payment funds among the various partners are transferred electronically.

Effective and efficient supply chain management systems can enable an organization to:

■ Decrease the power of its buyers.

■ Increase its own supplier power.

■ Increase switching costs to reduce the threat of substitute products or services.

FIGURE 1.15

Supply Chain for a Product Purchased from Wal-Mart

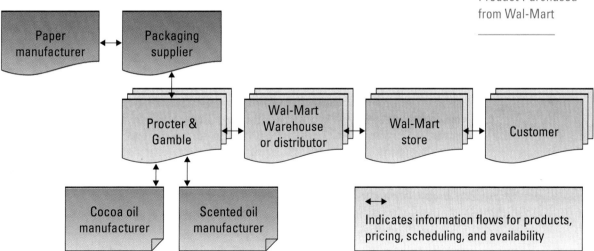

Paper manufacturer ↔ Packaging supplier

Procter & Gamble ↔ Wal-Mart Warehouse or distributor ↔ Wal-Mart store ↔ Customer

Cocoa oil manufacturer   Scented oil manufacturer

↔ Indicates information flows for products, pricing, scheduling, and availability

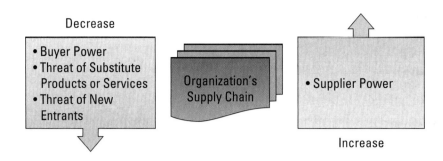

- Create entry barriers thereby reducing the threat of new entrants.
- Increase efficiencies while seeking a competitive advantage through cost leadership (see Figure 1.16).

CUSTOMER RELATIONSHIP MANAGEMENT

Today, most competitors are simply a mouse-click away. This intense marketplace has forced organizations to switch from being sales focused to being customer focused.

Charles Schwab recouped the cost of a multimillion-dollar customer relationship management system in less than two years. The system, developed by Siebel, allows the brokerage firm to trace each interaction with a customer or prospective customer and then provide services (retirement planning, for instance) to each customer's needs and interests. The system gives Schwab a better and more complete view of its customers, which it can use to determine which customers are serious investors and which ones are not. Automated deposits from paychecks, for example, are a sign of a serious investor, while stagnant balances signal a nonserious investor. Once Schwab is able to make this determination, the firm allocates its resources accordingly, saving money by not investing time or resources in subsidizing nonserious investors.[9]

Customer relationship management (CRM) involves managing all aspects of a customer's relationship with an organization to increase customer loyalty and retention and an organization's profitability. CRM allows an organization to gain insights into customers' shopping and buying behaviors in order to develop and implement enterprisewide strategies. Kaiser Permanente, for example, undertook a CRM strategy to improve and prolong the lives of diabetics. After compiling CRM information on 84,000 of its diabetic patients among its 2.4 million northern California members, Kaiser determined that only 15 to 20 percent of its diabetic patients were getting their eyes checked routinely. (Diabetes is the leading cause of blindness.) As a result, Kaiser is now enforcing more rigorous eye-screening programs for diabetics and creating support groups for obesity and stress (two more factors that make diabetes even worse). This CRM-based "preventive medicine" approach is saving Kaiser considerable sums of money and saving the eyesight of diabetic patients.[10]

It is important to realize that CRM is not just technology, but a strategy that an organization must embrace on an enterprise level. Although there are many technical components of CRM, it is actually a process and business goal simply enhanced by technology. Implementing a CRM system can help an organization quickly identify types of customers, design specific marketing campaigns tailored to each customer type, and thereby increase customer spending. A CRM system also allows an organization to treat customers as individuals, gaining important insights into their buying preferences and behaviors leading to increased sales, greater profitability, and higher rates of customer loyalty.

Figure 1.17 provides an overview of a typical CRM system. Customers contact an organization through various means including call centers, Web access, e-mail, faxes, and direct sales. A single customer may access an organization multiple

FIGURE 1.17

CRM Overview

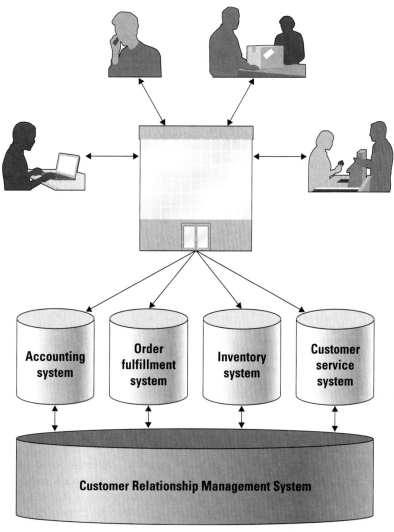

Accounting system

Order fulfillment system

Inventory system

Customer service system

Customer Relationship Management System

←→ Customer information flows are represented by arrows.

times through many different channels. The CRM system tracks every communication between the customer and the organization and provides access to CRM information within different systems from accounting to order fulfillment. Understanding all customer communications allows the organization to communicate effectively with each customer. It gives the organization a detailed understanding of each customer's products and services record regardless of the customer's preferred communication channel. For example, a customer service representative can easily view detailed account information and history through a CRM system when providing information to a customer such as expected delivery dates, complementary product information, and customer payment and billing information.

Eddie Bauer ships 110 million catalogs a year, maintains two Web sites, and has over 600 retail stores. The company collects information through customer transactions and analyzes the information to determine the best way to market to each individual customer. One thing Eddie Bauer discovered was that customers who shop across all three of its distribution channels—catalogs, Web sites, and stores—spend up to five times more than customers who shop through only one channel.

Michael Boyd, director of CRM at Eddie Bauer, stated that "our experience tells us that CRM is in no way, shape, or form a software application. Fundamentally, it is a business strategy to try to optimize profitability, revenue, and satisfaction at an individual customer level. Everything in an organization, every single process, every single application, is a tool that can be used to serve the CRM goal."[11]

ENTERPRISE RESOURCE PLANNING

Enterprise resource planning (ERP) integrates all departments and functions throughout an organization into a single IT system (or integrated set of IT systems) so that employees can make enterprisewide decisions by viewing enterprisewide information on all business operations. The key word in ERP is "enterprise" and not necessarily resource or planning.

Understanding that typical organizations operate by functional areas, which are often called functional silos if they are not integrated, is the best way to see the value of ERP. Figure 1.18 provides a graphical depiction of an organization with functional silos. Each functional area undertakes a specific core business function:

- **Sales and Marketing:** demand forecasting, sales forecasting, market segmentation, advertising, campaigns and promotions, bids and quotes, order processing, order management, customer relationship management, and customer support.
- **Operations and Logistics:** purchasing, supplying, receiving, transportation, production, shipping, manufacturing and maintenance, production planning, materials management, order entry and order processing, warehouse management, transportation management, and customer service management.
- **Accounting and Finance:** financial and cost accounting, planning, budgeting, cash flow, tax compliance, general ledger, accounts payable, treasury management, and cost control.
- **Human Resources:** hiring, training, benefits, and payroll.

Functional areas are anything but independent in an organization. In fact, functional areas are *interdependent*. For example, sales must rely on information from operations to understand inventory and be able to place orders, calculate transportation costs, and gain insight into product availability based on production schedules. It is critical to an organization's success that every department or functional area work together sharing common information and not be a "silo." This requires that all IT systems—including hardware, software, information, and people—be integrated with one another. This is the goal of ERP, but it is no small task.

FIGURE 1.18

Functional Organization
Overview

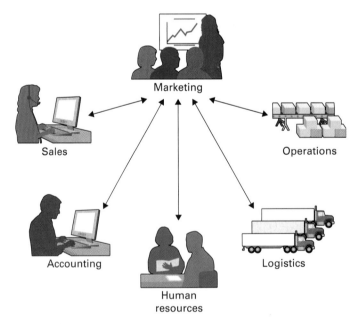

Functional organization—Each functional area has its own systems and communicates with every other functional area (diagram displays Marketing communicating with all other functional areas in the organization).

An **IT infrastructure** includes the hardware, software, and telecommunications equipment that, when combined, provide the underlying foundation to support the organization's goals. The problem with maintaining a consistent IT infrastructure occurs when a single department decides to implement a new system without taking into consideration the other departments or overall organizational IT infrastructure. This makes it difficult to integrate IT systems throughout the organization. Organizations must ensure that the integration of their separate systems occurs; otherwise, ERP is not possible.

To integrate the IT infrastructures of separate and distinct systems, organizations need the help of integration tools including:

- **Intranets**—an internalized portion of the Internet, protected from outside access, that allows an organization to provide access to information and application software to only its employees. Intranets support information and application software sharing across different IT infrastructures.

- **Enterprise information portals (EIP)**—an Internet site owned and operated by an organization to support its operations. EIPs often operate within an intranet and work in a fashion similar to popular Internet search tools such as Google.

mySAP ERP Web site

ERP solutions can provide tremendous value to an organization by offering the flexibility that gives employees their own unique interface to the system. ERP solutions meet the individual needs of each employee in the organization while supporting the enterprise-level needs of the overall organization.

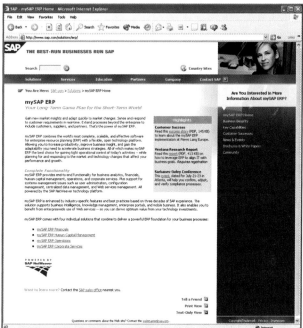

As an alternative to integrating existing systems, many organizations are turning to the acquisition of enterprisewide ERP solutions, offered by such vendors as SAP, PeopleSoft, and Oracle. SAP was one of the first vendors to develop a comprehensive ERP system, and today is one of the dominant market leaders. SAP's mySAP Business Suite offers a variety of business solutions in areas such as business intelligence, customer relationship management, enterprise information portals, financials, human resources, product lifecycle management, supplier relationship management, and supply chain management. As an organization acquires these various tools, it can integrate them to develop a complete ERP solution.

To summarize—initiatives in customer relationship management, supply chain management, and enterprise resource planning are integral parts of a strategic business tool set that enable organizations to create competitive advantages.

OPENING CASE STUDY QUESTIONS

1. Which of Porter's Five Forces did Levi's address through the implementation of its updated supply chain management system?

2. Evaluate how Levi's can gain business intelligence through the implementation of a customer relationship management system.

3. Create an argument against the following statement: "Levi's should not invest any resources to upgrade its current supply chain management system."

Chapter Three Case: Consolidating Touchpoints for Saab

Saab Cars USA imports more than 37,000 Saab sedans, convertibles, and wagons annually and distributes the cars to 220 U.S. dealerships. Saab competes in the premium automotive market and its primary challenge is to compete with rivals who attract customers through aggressive marketing campaigns, reduced prices, and inexpensive financing. Saab decided that the answer to beating its competition was not to spend capital on additional advertising, but to invest in Siebel Automotive, a customer relationship management system.

Until recently, the company communicated with its customers through three primary channels: (1) dealer network, (2) customer assistance center, (3) lead management center. Traditionally, each channel maintained its own customer database and this splintered approach to managing customer information caused numerous problems for the company. For example, a prospective customer might receive a direct mail piece from Saab one week, then an e-mail with an unrelated offer from a third-party marketing vendor the next week. The local dealer might not know of either activity, and therefore might deliver an ineffective pitch when the customer visited the showroom that weekend. Al Fontova, direct marketing manager with Saab Cars USA, stated that he had over 3 million customer records and 55 files at three different vendors. Analyzing this information in aggregate was complicated, inefficient, and costly.

Saab required a solution that would provide a consolidated customer view from all three touchpoints. In 2002, Saab implemented the Siebel CRM solution, which provides Saab's call center employees with a 360-degree view of each customer, including prior service-related questions and all the marketing communications they have received. Known internally as "TouchPoint," the Siebel application provides Saab's dealers with a powerful Web-based solution for coordinating sales and marketing activities. These tracking capabilities enable Saab to measure the sales results of specific leads, recommend more efficient selling techniques, and target its leads more precisely in the future. Using Siebel Automotive, Saab received the following benefits:

- Direct marketing costs decreased by 5 percent.
- Lead follow-up increased from 38 percent to 50 percent.
- Customer satisfaction increased from 69 percent to 75 percent.
- Saab gained a single view of its customers across multiple channels.[12]

Questions

1. Explain how implementing a CRM system enabled Saab to gain a competitive advantage.
2. Estimate the potential impact to Saab's business if it had not implemented a CRM system.
3. What additional benefits could Saab receive from implementing a supply chain management system?

Chapter Four: Measuring the Success of Strategic Initiatives

4.1. Compare efficiency IT metrics and effectiveness IT metrics.

4.2. List and describe five common types of efficiency IT metrics.

4.3. List and describe four types of effectiveness IT metrics.

4.4. Explain customer metrics and their importance to an organization.

In an effort to offer detailed information to all layers of management, General Electric Co. (GE) invested $1.5 billion in employee time, hardware, software, and other technologies to implement a real-time operations monitoring system. GE's executives use the new system to monitor sales, inventory, and savings across its 13 different global business operations every 15 minutes. This allows GE to respond to changes, reduce cycle times, and improve risk management on an hourly basis instead of waiting for month-end or quarter-end reports. GE estimates that the $1.5 billion investment will provide a 33 percent return on investment over the five years of the project.[13]

Organizations spend enormous sums of money on IT to compete in today's fast-paced business environment. Some organizations spend up to 50 percent of their total capital expenditures on IT. To justify expenditures on IT, an organization must measure the payoff of these investments, their impact on business performance, and the overall business value gained.

Efficiency and effectiveness metrics are two primary types of IT metrics. *Efficiency IT metrics* measure the performance of the IT system itself including throughput, speed, availability, etc. *Effectiveness IT metrics* measure the impact IT has on business processes and activities including customer satisfaction, conversion rates, sell-through increases, etc. Peter Drucker offers a helpful distinction between efficiency and effectiveness. Drucker states that managers "Do things right" and/or "Do the right things." Doing things right addresses efficiency—getting the most from each resource. Doing the right things addresses effectiveness—setting the right goals and objectives and ensuring they are accomplished.[14]

Effectiveness focuses on how well an organization is achieving its goals and objectives, while efficiency focuses on the extent to which an organization is using its resources in an optimal way. The two—efficiency and effectiveness—are definitely interrelated. However, success in one area does not necessarily imply success in the other.

BENCHMARKING—BASELINING METRICS

Regardless of what is measured, how it is measured, and whether it is for the sake of efficiency or effectiveness, there must be *benchmarks,* or baseline values the system seeks to attain. *Benchmarking* is a process of continuously measuring system results, comparing those results to optimal system performance (benchmark values), and identifying steps and procedures to improve system performance.

Efficiency	Effectiveness
1. United States (3.11)	1. Canada
2. Australia (2.60)	2. Singapore
3. New Zealand (2.59)	3. United States
4. Singapore (2.58)	4. Denmark
5. Norway (2.55)	5. Australia
6. Canada (2.52)	6. Finland
7. United Kingdom (2.52)	7. Hong Kong
8. Netherlands (2.51)	8. United Kingdom
9. Denmark (2.47)	9. Germany
10. Germany (2.46)	10. Ireland

FIGURE 1.19

Comparing IT Efficiency and Effectiveness Metrics for E-Government Initiatives

Consider e-government worldwide as an illustration of benchmarking efficiency IT metrics and effectiveness IT metrics (see survey results in Figure 1.19). From an effectiveness point of view, Canada ranks number one in terms of e-government satisfaction of its citizens. (The United States ranks third.) The survey, sponsored by Accenture, also included such attributes as CRM practices, customer-service vision, approaches to offering e-government services through multiple-service delivery channels, and initiatives for identifying services for individual citizen segments. These are all benchmarks at which Canada's government excels.[15]

In contrast, the *United Nations Division for Public Economics and Public Administration* ranks Canada sixth in terms of efficiency IT metrics. (It ranked the United States first.) This particular ranking based purely on efficiency IT metrics includes benchmarks such as the number of computers per 100 citizens, the number of Internet hosts per 10,000 citizens, the percentage of the citizen population online, and several other factors. Therefore, while Canada lags behind in IT efficiency, it is the premier e-government provider in terms of effectiveness.[16]

Governments hoping to increase their e-government presence would benchmark themselves against these sorts of efficiency and effectiveness metrics. There is a high degree of correlation between e-government efficiency and effectiveness, although it is not absolute.

THE INTERRELATIONSHIPS OF EFFICIENCY AND EFFECTIVENESS IT METRICS

Efficiency IT metrics focus on the technology itself. The most common types of efficiency IT metrics include:

- *Throughput*—the amount of information that can travel through a system at any point in time.
- **Speed**—the amount of time a system takes to perform a transaction.
- **Availability**—the number of hours a system is available for use by customers and employees.
- **Accuracy**—the extent to which a system generates the correct results when executing the same transaction numerous times.
- *Web traffic*—including a host of benchmarks such as the number of pageviews, the number of unique visitors, and the average time spent viewing a Web page.
- *Response time*—the time it takes to respond to user interactions such as a mouse click.

While these efficiency metrics are important to monitor, they do not always guarantee effectiveness. Effectiveness IT metrics are determined according to an organization's goals, strategies, and objectives. Here, it becomes important to consider the strategy an organization is using, such as a broad cost leadership strategy (Wal-Mart for example), as well as specific goals and objectives such as increasing new customers by 10 percent or reducing new product development cycle times to six months. Broad, general effectiveness metrics include:

- **Usability**—the ease with which people perform transactions and/or find information. A popular usability metric on the Internet is degrees of freedom, which measures the number of clicks to get to desired information or processing capabilities.

- **Customer satisfaction**—as measured by such benchmarks as satisfaction surveys, percentage of existing customers retained, and increases in revenue dollars per customer.
- **Conversion rates**—the number of customers an organization "touches" for the first time and convinces to purchase its products or services. This is a popular metric for evaluating the effectiveness of banner, pop-up, and pop-under ads on the Internet.
- **Financial**—such as return on investment (the earning power of an organization's assets), cost-benefit analysis (the comparison of projected revenues and costs including development, maintenance, fixed, and variable), and break-even analysis (the point at which constant revenues equal ongoing costs).

In the private sector, eBay is an organization that constantly benchmarks its information technology efficiency and effectiveness. In 2003, eBay posted impressive year-end results with revenues increasing 74 percent while earnings grew 135 percent. Maintaining constant Web site availability and optimal throughput performance is critical to eBay's success.[17]

eBay's Web site

Jupiter Media Metrix ranked eBay as the Web site with the highest visitor volume (efficiency) in 2003 for the second year in a row, with an 80 percent growth from the previous year. eBay averaged 4.5 million unique visitors during each week of the holiday season that year with daily peaks exceeding 5 million visitors. To ensure constant availability and reliability of its systems, eBay implemented ProactiveNet, a performance measurement and management-tracking tool. The tool allows eBay to monitor its environment against baseline benchmarks, which helps the eBay team keep tight control of its systems. The new system has resulted in improved system availability with a 150 percent increase in productivity as measured by system uptime.[18]

Do not forget to consider the issue of security while determining efficiency and effectiveness IT metrics. When an organization offers its customers the ability to purchase products over the Internet it must implement the appropriate security—such as encryption and Secure Sockets Layers (SSLs; denoted by the lock symbol in the lower right corner of a browser window and/or the "s" in https). It is actually inefficient for an organization to implement security measures for Internet-based transactions as compared to processing non-secure transactions. However, an organization will probably have a difficult time attracting new customers and increasing Web-based revenue if it does not implement the necessary security measures. Purely from an efficiency IT metric point of view, security generates some inefficiency. From an organization's business strategy point of view, however, security should lead to increases in effectiveness metrics.

Figure 1.20 provides a graph depicting the interrelationships between efficiency and effectiveness. Ideally, an organization should operate in the upper right-hand corner of the graph, realizing both significant increases in efficiency and effectiveness. However, operating in the upper left-hand corner (minimal efficiency with increased effectiveness) or the lower right-hand corner (significant efficiency with minimal effectiveness) may be in line with an organization's particular strategies. In general, operating in the lower left-hand corner (minimal efficiency and minimal effectiveness) is not ideal for the operation of any organization.

FIGURE 1.20

The Interrelationships
between Efficiency and
Effectiveness

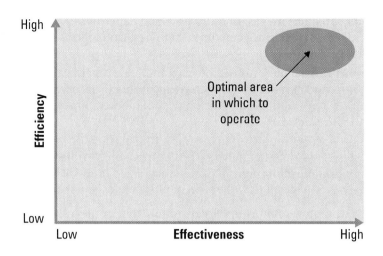

DETERMINING IT EFFICIENCY AND EFFECTIVENESS

Stock market analysts tend to have a bias toward financial metrics. Clearly this emphasis is important—however, focusing only on financial measurements is limiting since financial metrics are only one factor that an organization can use to determine IT effectiveness. ***Customer metrics*** assess the management of customer relationships by the organization. These effectiveness metrics typically focus on a set of core measurements including market share, customer acquisition, customer satisfaction, and customer profitability.

Traffic on the Internet retail site for Wal-Mart has grown 66 percent in the last year. The site has over 500,000 visitors daily, 2 million Web pages downloaded daily, 6.5 million visitors per week, and over 60,000 users logged on simultaneously. Wal-Mart's primary concern is maintaining optimal performance for online transactions. A disruption to the Web site directly affects the company's bottom line and customer loyalty. The company monitors and tracks the hardware, software, and network running the company's Web site to ensure high quality of service, which saved the company $1.1 million dollars in 2003.[19]

Customers are primarily concerned with the quality of service they receive from an organization. Anyone using the Internet knows that it is far from perfect and often slow. One of the biggest problems facing Internet users is congestion caused by capacity too small to handle large amounts of traffic. Corporations are continually benchmarking and monitoring their systems in order to ensure high quality of service. The most common quality of service metrics that are benchmarked and monitored include throughput, speed, and availability.

A company must continually monitor these behaviors to determine if the system is operating above or below expectations. If the system begins to operate below expectations, system administrators must take immediate action to bring the system back up to acceptable operating levels. For example, if a company suddenly began taking two minutes to deliver a Web page to a customer, the company would need to fix this problem as soon as possible to keep from losing customers and ultimately revenue.

Web Traffic Analysis

Most companies measure the traffic on a Web site as the primary determinant of the Web site's success. However, a lot of Web site traffic does not necessarily indicate large sales. Many organizations with lots of Web site traffic have minimal sales. A company can go further and use Web traffic analysis to determine the revenue generated by Web traffic, the number of new customers acquired by Web traffic, any reductions in customer service calls resulting from Web traffic, and so on. The Yankee Group reports that 66 percent of companies determine Web site success solely by measuring the amount of traffic. New customer acquisition ranked second on the list at 34 percent, and revenue generation ranked third at 23 percent.[20]

Analyzing Web site traffic is one way organizations can understand the effectiveness of Web advertising. A *cookie* is a small file deposited on a hard drive by a Web site containing information about customers and their Web activities. Cookies allow Web sites to record the comings and goings of customers, usually without their knowledge or consent. A *click-through* is a count of the number of people who visit one site and click on an advertisement that takes them to the site of the advertiser. A *banner ad* is a small ad on one Web site that advertises the products and services of another business, usually another dot-com business. Advertisers can track how often customers click on banner ads resulting in a click-through to their Web site. Often the cost of the banner ad depends on the number of customers who click on the banner ad. Tracking the number of banner ad clicks is a great way to begin to understand the effectiveness of the ad on its target audience.

Tracking effectiveness based on click-throughs guarantees exposure to target ads; however, it does not guarantee that the visitor liked the ad, spent any substantial time viewing the ad, or was satisfied with the information contained in the ad. In order to help understand advertising effectiveness, interactivity measures are tracked and monitored. *Interactivity* measures the visitor interactions with the target ad. Such interaction measures include the duration of time the visitor spends viewing the ad, the number of pages viewed, and even the number of repeat visits to the target ad. Interactivity measures are a giant step forward for advertisers, since traditional methods of advertising through newspapers, magazines, outdoor such as billboards and buses, and radio and television provide no way to track effectiveness metrics. Interactivity metrics measure actual consumer activities, something that was impossible to do in the past and provides advertisers with tremendous amounts of useful information.

The ultimate outcome of any advertisement is a purchase. Knowing how many visitors make purchases on a Web site and the dollar amount of the purchases creates critical business information. It is easy to communicate the business value of a Web site or Web application when an organization can tie revenue amounts and new customer creation numbers directly back to the Web site, banner ad, or Web application.

Behavioral Metrics

Firms can observe through click-stream data the exact pattern of a consumer's navigation through a site. Click-stream data can reveal a number of basic data points on how consumers interact with Web sites. Metrics based on click-stream data include:

- The number of page views (i.e., the number of times a particular page has been presented to a visitor)
- The pattern of Web sites visited, including most frequent exit page and most frequent prior Web sites
- Length of stay on the Web site
- Dates and times of visits
- Number of registrations filled out per 100 visitors
- Number of abandoned registrations
- Demographics of registered visitors
- Number of customers with shopping carts
- Number of abandoned shopping carts

Figure 1.21 provides definitions of common metrics based on click-stream data. To interpret such data properly, managers try to benchmark against other companies. For instance, consumers seem to visit their preferred Web sites regularly, even checking back to the Web site multiple times during a given session. Consumers tend to become loyal to a small number of Web sites, and they tend to revisit those Web sites a number of times during a particular session.

FIGURE 1.21

Web Site Metrics

Visitor	Visitor Metrics
Unidentified visitor	A visitor is an individual who visits a Web site. An "unidentified visitor" means that no information about that visitor is available.
Unique visitor	A unique visitor is one who can be recognized and counted only once within a given period of time. An accurate count of unique visitors is not possible without some form of identification, registration, or authentication.
Session visitor	A session ID is available (e.g., cookie) or inferred by incoming address plus browser type, which allows a visitor's responses to be tracked within a given visit to a Web site.
Tracked visitor	An ID (e.g., cookie) is available which allows a user to be tracked across multiple visits to a Web site. No information, other than a unique identifier, is available for a tracked visitor.
Identified visitor	An ID is available (e.g., cookie or voluntary registration), which allows a user to be tracked across multiple visits to a Web site. Other information (name, demographics, possibly supplied voluntarily by the visitor) can be linked to this ID.
Exposure	**Exposure Metrics**
Page exposures (page-views)	The number of times a particular Web page has been viewed by visitors in a given time period, without regard to duplication.
Site exposures	The number of visitor sessions at a Web site in a given time period, without regard to visitor duplication.
Visit	**Visit Metrics**
Stickiness (visit duration time)	The length of time a visitor spends on a Web site. Can be reported as an average in a given time period, without regard to visitor duplication.
Raw visit depth (total Web pages exposure per session)	The total number of pages a visitor is exposed to during a single visit to a Web site. Can be reported as an average or distribution in a given time period, without regard to visitor duplication.
Visit depth (total unique Web pages exposure per session)	The total number of unique pages a visitor is exposed to during a single visit to a Web site. Can be reported as an average or distribution in a given time period, without regard to visitor duplication.
Hit	**Hit Metrics**
Hits	When visitors reach a Web site, their computer sends a request to the site's computer server to begin displaying pages. Each element of a requested page (including graphics, text, interactive items) is recorded by the Web site's server log file as a "hit."
Qualified hits	Exclude less important information recorded in a log file (such as error messages, etc.).

Evolving technologies are continually changing the speed and form of business in almost every industry. Organizations spend an enormous amount of money on IT in order to remain competitive. Some organizations spend up to 50 percent of their total capital expenditures on IT investments. More than ever, there is a need to understand the payoff of these large IT investments, the impact on business performance, and the overall business value gained with the use of technology. One of the best ways to demonstrate business value is by analyzing an IT project's efficiency and effectiveness metrics.

OPENING CASE STUDY QUESTIONS

1. Formulate a strategy for how Levi's can use efficiency IT metrics to improve its business.

2. Formulate a strategy for how Levi's can use effectiveness IT metrics to improve its business.

Chapter Four Case: How Do You Value Friendster?

Jonathan Abrams is keeping quiet about how he is going to generate revenue from his Web site, Friendster, which specializes in social networking. Abrams is a 33-year-old Canadian software developer whose experiences include being laid off by Netscape and then moving from one start-up to another. In 2002, Abrams was unemployed, not doing well financially, and certainly not looking to start another business when he developed the idea for Friendster. He quickly coded a working prototype and watched in amazement as his Web site took off.

The buzz around social networking start-ups has recently been on the rise. A number of high-end venture capital (VC) firms, including Sequoia and Mayfield, have invested more than $40 million into social networking start-ups such as LinkedIn, Spoke, and Tribe Networks. Friendster received over $13 million in VC capital from Kleiner, Perkins, Caufield, Byers, and Benchmark Capital, which reportedly valued the company at $53 million—a startling figure for a company that had yet to generate even a single dime in revenue.

A year after making its public debut, Friendster is one of the largest social networking Web sites, attracting over 5 million users and receiving over 50,000 page-views per day. The question is how do efficiency metrics, such as Web traffic and page-views, turn into cash flow? Everyone is wondering how Friendster is going to begin generating revenue.

The majority of Abrams's competitors make their money by extracting fees from their subscribers. Friendster is going to continue to let its subscribers meet for free but plans to charge them for premium services such as the ability to customize their profile page. The company also has plans to extend beyond social networking to an array of value-added services such as friend-based job referrals and classmate searches. Abrams is also looking into using his high-traffic Web site to tap into the growing Internet advertising market.

Abrams does not appear concerned about generating revenue or about potential competition. He states, "Match.com has been around eight years, has 12 million users, and has spent many millions of dollars on advertising to get them. We're a year old, we've spent zero dollars on advertising, and in a year or less, we'll be bigger than them—it's a given."

The future of Friendster is uncertain. Google recently offered to buy Friendster for $30 million even though there are signs, both statistical and anecdotal, that Friendster's popularity may have peaked.[21]

Questions

1. How could you use efficiency IT metrics to help place a value on Friendster?
2. How could you use effectiveness IT metrics to help place a value on Friendster?
3. Explain how a venture capital company can value Friendster at $53 million when the company has yet to generate any revenue.
4. Explain why Google would be interested in buying Friendster for $30 million when the company has yet to generate any revenue.

Chapter Five: Organizational Structures That Support Strategic Initiatives

5.1. Compare the responsibilities of a chief information officer (CIO), chief technology officer (CTO), chief privacy officer (CPO), and chief security officer (CSO).

5.2. Explain the gap between IT people and business people and the primary reason this gap exists.

5.3. Define the relationship between security and ethics.

Employees across the organization must work closely together to develop strategic initiatives that create competitive advantages. Understanding the basic structure of a typical IT department including titles, roles, and responsibilities will help an organization build a cohesive enterprisewide team.

IT ROLES AND RESPONSIBILITIES

Information technology is a relatively new functional area, having only been around formally in most organizations for about 40 years or so. Therefore, job titles, roles, and responsibilities often differ dramatically from organization to organization. Nonetheless, there are some clear trends developing toward elevating some IT positions within an organization to the strategic level.

Most organizations maintain positions such as chief executive officer (CEO), chief financial officer (CFO), and chief operations officer (COO) at the strategic level. Recently there are more IT-related strategic positions such as chief information officer (CIO), chief technology officer (CTO), chief security officer (CSO), and chief privacy officer (CPO).

The ***chief information officer (CIO)*** is a senior executive who (1) oversees all uses of information technology and (2) ensures the strategic alignment of IT with business goals and objectives. The CIO often reports directly to the CEO. CIOs must possess a solid and detailed understanding of every aspect of an organization coupled with tremendous insight into the capability of IT. Broad functions of a CIO include:

1. *Manager*—ensuring the delivery of all IT projects, on time and within budget.
2. *Leader*—ensuring that the strategic vision of IT is in line with the strategic vision of the organization.
3. *Communicator*—building and maintaining strong executive relationships.

Although CIO is considered a position within IT, CIOs must be concerned with more than just IT. According to a recent survey (see Figure 1.22), most CIOs ranked "enhancing customer satisfaction" ahead of their concerns

FIGURE 1.22

What Concerns CIOs the Most?

Percentage	CIO's Concerns
94%	Enhancing customer satisfaction
92	Security
89	Technology evaluation
87	Budgeting
83	Staffing
66	ROI analysis
64	Building new applications
45	Outsourcing hosting

for any specific aspect of IT. CIOs with the broad business view that customer satisfaction is more crucial and critical than specific aspects of IT should be applauded.[22]

The **chief technology officer (CTO)** is a senior executive responsible for ensuring the throughput, speed, accuracy, availability, and reliability of an organization's information technology. CTOs are similar to CIOs, except that CIOs take on the additional responsibility for effectiveness of ensuring that IT is aligned with the organization's strategic initiatives. CTOs have direct responsibility for ensuring the *efficiency* of IT systems throughout the organization. Most CTOs possess well-rounded knowledge of all aspects of IT, including hardware, software, and telecommunications.

The **chief security officer (CSO)** is a senior executive responsible specifically for ensuring the security of IT systems and developing strategies and IT safeguards against attacks from hackers and viruses. The role of a CSO has been elevated in recent years because of the number of attacks from hackers and viruses. Most CSOs possess detailed knowledge of networks and telecommunications as hackers and viruses usually find their way into IT systems through networked computers.

The **chief privacy officer (CPO)** is a senior executive responsible for ensuring the ethical and legal use of information within an organization. CPOs are the newest senior executive position in IT. In 2001, 150 of the Fortune 500 companies added the CPO position to their list of senior executives. Not surprising, many CPOs are lawyers by training, enabling them to understand the often complex legal issues surrounding the use of information.

All the above IT positions and responsibilities are critical to an organization's success. While many organizations may not have a different individual for each of these positions, they must still have leadership in place taking responsibility for all these areas of concern. Employees must seek the guidance and support of the individuals in these roles who are responsible for enterprisewide IT and IT-related issues.

THE GAP BETWEEN BUSINESS PERSONNEL AND IT PERSONNEL

One of the greatest challenges today is effective communication between business personnel and IT personnel. Business personnel possess expertise in functional areas such as marketing, accounting, sales, and so forth. IT personnel have the technological expertise. Unfortunately, there often exists something of a communications gap between the two. IT personnel have their own vocabularies consisting of acronyms and technical terms. Business personnel have their own vocabularies based on their experience and expertise. Effective communication between business and IT personnel should be a two-way street with each side making the effort to better understand the other (including written and oral communication).

Business personnel must seek to achieve an increased level of understanding of IT. Although they do not need to know every technical detail, it will be beneficial to business personnel's careers to understand what they can and cannot accomplish using IT. There are numerous business-oriented IT magazines including *InformationWeek* and *CIO* that business managers and leaders can read to increase their IT knowledge.

At the same time, an organization must develop strategies for integrating its IT personnel into the various business functions. All too often, IT personnel are left out of strategy meetings because "they do not understand the business so they will not add any value." That is a dangerous position to take. If IT personnel are not going to understand the business, how is the organization going to determine which technologies can benefit (or hurt) the business? On the other hand, with a little effort to communicate, by providing information on the functionality available in CRM systems, IT personnel might greatly enhance a meeting about how to improve customer service. Working together, business and IT personnel have the potential to create customer-service competitive advantages.

It is the responsibility of the CIO to ensure effective communications between business and IT personnel. While the CIO assumes the responsibility on an enterprisewide level, it is each employee's responsibility to see to it that the business and IT sides of an organization are communicating effectively.

FUNDAMENTAL SUPPORT STRUCTURES—ETHICS AND SECURITY

Ethics and security are two fundamental building blocks that organizations must base their businesses on. In recent years, such events as the Enron and Martha Stewart fiascos along with 9/11 have shed new light on the meaning of ethics and security. When the behavior of a few individuals can literally destroy billion dollar organizations because of a lapse in ethics or security, the value of highly ethical and highly secure organizations should be evident. It is recommended to review the Ethics and Security plug-ins to gain a detailed understanding of these topics. Due to the importance of these topics, they will be readdressed throughout this text.

Ethics

Ian Clarke, the inventor of a file-swapping service called Freenet, decided to leave the United States for the United Kingdom, where copyright laws are more lenient. Wayne Rosso, the inventor of a file-sharing service called Grokster, decided to leave the United States for Spain, again saying goodbye to tough United States copyright protections. File sharing encourages a legal network of shared thinking that can improve drug research, software development, and the flow of information. The United States copyright laws, designed decades before the Internet was ever invented, make file sharing and many other Internet technologies illegal.[23]

The ethical issues surrounding copyright infringement and intellectual property rights are consuming the e-business world. Advances in technology are making it easier and easier for people to copy everything from music to pictures. Technology poses new challenges for our *ethics*—the principles and standards that guide our behavior toward other people. Review Figure 1.23 for an overview of concepts, terms, and ethical issues stemming from advances in technology.

In today's electronic world, privacy has become a major ethical issue. *Privacy* is the right to be left alone when you want to be, to have control over your own personal possessions, and not to be observed without your consent. Some of the most problematic decisions organizations face lie in the murky and turbulent waters of privacy. The burden comes from the knowledge that each time employees make a decision regarding issues of privacy, the outcome could sink the company some day.

The SEC began inquiries into Enron's accounting practices on October 22, 2001. David Duncan, the Arthur Andersen partner in charge of Enron, instructed his team to begin destroying paper and electronic Enron-related records on October 23, 2001. Kimberly Latham, a subordinate to Duncan, sent instructions on October 24, 2001, to her entire team to follow Duncan's orders and even compiled a list of computer files to delete. Arthur Andersen blames Duncan for destroying thousands of Enron-related documents. Duncan blames the Arthur Andersen attorney, Nancy Temple, for sending him a memo instructing him to destroy files. Temple blames Arthur Andersen's document deletion policies.[24]

Regardless of who is to blame, the bigger issue is that the destruction of files after a federal investigation has begun is both unethical and illegal. A direct corporate order to destroy information currently under federal investigation can pose a real dilemma for any professional. Comply, and you participate in potentially criminal activities; refuse, and you might find yourself looking for a new job.

Privacy is one of the biggest ethical issues facing organizations today. Trust between companies, customers, partners, and suppliers is the support structure of

FIGURE 1.23

Ethical Issues Stemming from Technology Advances

Intellectual property	Intangible creative work that is embodied in physical form.
Copyright	The legal protection afforded an expression of an idea, such as a song, video game, and some types of proprietary documents.
Fair use doctrine	In certain situations, it is legal to use copyrighted material.
Pirated software	The unauthorized use, duplication, distribution, or sale of copyrighted software.
Counterfeit software	Software that is manufactured to look like the real thing and sold as such.

the e-business world. One of the main ingredients in trust is privacy. Widespread fear about privacy continues to be one of the biggest barriers to the growth of e-business. One way or another, people are concerned their privacy will be violated as a consequence of interactions on the Web. Unless an organization can effectively address this issue of privacy, its customers, partners, and suppliers may lose trust in the organization, which in effect hurts its business. Figure 1.24 displays the results from a recent CIO survey as to how privacy issues lose trust for e-business.[25]

Primary Reasons Privacy Issues Lose Trust for E-Business
1. Loss of personal privacy is a top concern for Americans in the 21st century.
2. Among Internet users, 37 percent would be "a lot" more inclined to purchase a product on a Web site that had a privacy policy.
3. Privacy/security is the #1 factor that would convert Internet researchers into Internet buyers.

FIGURE 1.24

Primary Reasons Privacy Issues Lose Trust for E-Business

Security

Organizational information is intellectual capital. Just as organizations protect their assets—keeping their money in an insured bank or providing a safe working environment for employees—they must also protect their intellectual capital. An organization's intellectual capital includes everything from its patents to its transactional and analytical information. With security breaches on the rise and hackers everywhere, an organization must put in place strong security measures to survive.

The Health Insurance Portability and Accountability Act (HIPAA) protects the privacy and security of personal health records and has the potential to impact every business in the United States. HIPAA affects all companies that use electronic data interchange (EDI) to communicate personal health records. HIPAA requires health care organizations to develop, implement, and maintain appropriate security measures when sending electronic health information. Most important, these organizations must document and keep current records detailing how they are performing security measures for all transmissions of health information. On April 21, 2005, security rules for HIPAA will become enforceable by law.

According to recent Gartner polls, less than 10 percent of all health care organizations have begun to implement the security policies and procedures required by HIPAA. The Health Information Management Society estimates that 70 percent of all health care providers failed to meet the April 2003 deadline for privacy rule compliance. Health care organizations need to start taking HIPAA regulations seriously since noncompliance can result in substantial fines and even imprisonment.[26]

Beyond the health care industry, all businesses must understand the importance of information security, even if it is not enforceable by law. *Information security* is a broad term encompassing the protection of information from accidental or intentional misuse by persons inside or outside an organization. With current advances in technologies and business strategies such as CRM, organizations are able to determine valuable information—such as who are the top 20 percent of their customers who produce 80 percent of their revenues. Most organizations view this type of information as valuable intellectual capital and they are implementing security measures to prevent the information from walking out the door or falling into the wrong hands.

Adding to the complexity of information security is the fact that organizations must enable employees, customers, and partners to access all sorts of information electronically to be successful. Doing business electronically automatically creates tremendous information security risks for organizations. There are many technical aspects of security, but the biggest information security issue is not technical, but a people issue. Most information security breaches result from people misusing an organization's information either intentionally or inadvertently. For example, many individuals freely give up their passwords or leave them on sticky notes next to their computers, leaving the door wide open to intruders.

FIGURE 1.25

Organizational
Spending on
Information Security

Source: Computer Security
Institute

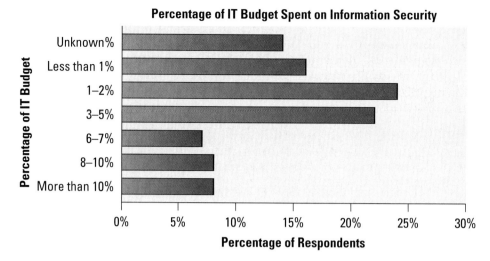

Figure 1.25 displays the typical size of an organization's information security budget relative to the organization's overall IT budget from the CSI/FBI 2004 Computer Crime and Security Survey. Forty-six percent of respondents indicated that their organization spent between 1 and 5 percent of the total IT budget on security. Only 16 percent indicated that their organization spent less than 1 percent of the IT budget on security.

Figure 1.26 displays the spending per employee on computer security broken down by both public and private industries. The highest average computer security spending per employee ($608) was found in the transportation industry. The highest average computer security operating expenditures per employee was found in the federal government ($261).[27]

Security is perhaps the most fundamental and critical of all the technologies/disciplines an organization must have squarely in place in order to execute its business strategy. Without solid security processes and procedures, none of the other technologies can develop business advantages.

FIGURE 1.26

Computer Security
Expenditures/
Investments

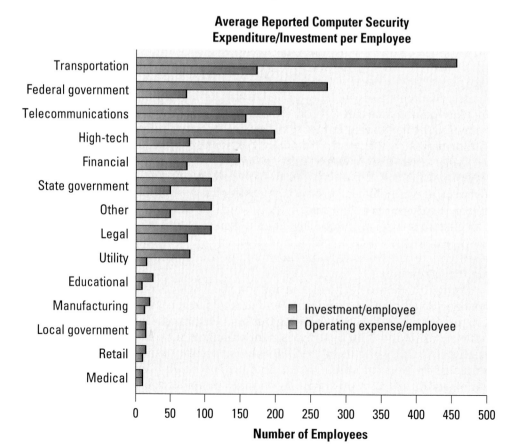

1. Predict what might have happened to Levi's if its top executives had not supported investments in IT.

2. David Bergen, Levi's CIO, put together a cross-functional team of key managers from IT, finance, and sales to transform Levi's systems to meet Wal-Mart's requirements. Analyze the relationships between these three business areas and determine why Bergen chose them to be a part of his cross-functional team.

3. Explain why it would be unethical for Wal-Mart to sell Levi's jeans sales information to another jeans manufacturer.

4. Evaluate the ramifications for Wal-Mart's business if it failed to secure its partner's information and all sales information for all products were accidentally posted to an anonymous Web site.

Chapter Five Case: CCRM—Customer's Customer Relationship Management

Perceptive CIOs recognize that rewards come from implementing effective solutions for not only their own organizations but also their customers' organizations. This concept is known as CCRM—customer's customer relationship management. It is a balancing act.

Ticketmaster, one of the world's largest ticket vendors, has two sets of customers: (1) the people who actually buy the tickets, and (2) the stadiums, venues, teams, leagues, bands and acts that sell the tickets. Ticketmaster's CIO Sean Moriarty often finds himself dealing with the challenge of meeting the needs of both sets of customers.

Moriarty's challenge is to convince his customers to give him access to their customers so Ticketmaster can serve both. For example, when Ticketmaster sells tickets to a Knicks game at Madison Square Garden, it would also like to book dinner for that customer at a restaurant close to the venue. This might be nice for the ticket buyer. The dilemma is that the primary customer in this example, Madison Square Garden, might not benefit from adding additional value for its customers since dinner could cut into lucrative concession sales at the sporting event. On the other hand, the Garden and the Knicks will be better off if the fans have an excellent experience and come to more games.

Almost all organizations in every industry face this type of channel conflict. With the advancements in technology it is now even easier for channel conflicts (and opportunities) to arise. For example, many brokers will think twice before giving detailed information about their customers to a mutual fund. The mutual fund would benefit greatly from marketing directly to the customers; however, the brokers would not want the competition. In the information age advantages and opportunities abound—but so do threats—posing challenges and calling for strategic management.

Today, CIOs must become advocates of collaborative initiatives to be successful. CIOs must convince their customers to co-invest with them. Ironically, a successful collaborative initiative may take some revenue away from a customer in the short run. If customers do not see any larger benefits, the collaboration may collapse. If Ticketmaster began selling Big Head Todd albums online as well as concert tickets, chances are the promoter and the record company would be furious with the intermediary for stepping on what they consider their territory.

The key to successfully implementing strategic initiatives (managing customers' customer relationships) is to ensure that the benefits for *all* parties significantly outweighs the costs.[28]

Questions

1. Describe the dilemma an organization faces when attempting to access its customer's customers.

2. Compare customer relationship management and customer's customer relationship management.

3. Explain why directly accessing a customer's customer is considered unethical.

4. Assess the adverse impact to Ticketmaster if it failed to ensure the security of its customer information such as credit card numbers.

PLUG-IN POINTERS >>

Review the *Business Plug-In* **Information Security** for an overview of security issues and features including information security policies and plans, hackers, viruses, public key encryption, digital certificates, digital signatures, firewalls, and authentication, authorization, and detection and response technologies.

Review the *Business Plug-In* **Ethics** for an overview of privacy laws, ethical computer use policy, Internet use policy, information privacy policy, acceptable use policy, e-mail privacy policy, anti-spam policy, monitoring technologies, and monitoring polices.

Understanding and working with technology have become an integral part of life in the 21st century. Most students take courses in various disciplines in their educational careers, such as in marketing, operations management, management, finance, accounting, and information technology, each of which is designed to provide insight into the tasks of each functional area. In the business world, these are all intertwined and inextricably linked.

Information technology can be an important enabler of business success and innovation and is most useful when it leverages the talents of people. Technology in and of itself is not useful unless the right people know how to use and manage it effectively.

Organizations use information technology to capture, process, organize, distribute, and massage information. Information technology enables an organization to:

- Integrate all functional areas and the tasks they perform.
- Gain an enterprisewide view of its operations.
- Efficiently and effectively utilize resources.
- Realize tremendous market and industry growth by gaining insight into the market at large (through environmental scanning) and insight into internal operations.

Banner ad, 33
Benchmark, 29
Benchmarking, 29
Business intelligence, 10
Business process, 19
Business-to-business (B2B) marketplace, 16
Buyer power, 16
Chief information officer (CIO), 36
Chief privacy officer (CPO), 37
Chief security officer (CSO), 37
Chief technology officer (CTO), 37
Click-through, 33
Collaboration system, 11
Competitive advantage, 15
Cookie, 33
Copyright, 38
Core competency, 11
Core competency strategy, 11
Counterfeit software, 38
Customer metric, 32
Customer relationship management (CRM), 24
Database, 8
Database management system (DBMS), 8

Data-mining tool, 10
Data warehouse, 10
Digital Darwinism, 12
Document management system (DMS), 11
Effectiveness IT metrics, 29
Efficiency IT metrics, 29
Enterprise information portal (EIP), 27
Enterprise resource planning (ERP), 26
Entry barrier, 17
Environmental scanning, 15
Ethics, 38
Fair use doctrine, 38
First-mover advantage, 15
Five Forces Model, 15
Groupware, 11
Information partnership, 11
Information security, 39
Information technology (IT), 7
Intellectual property, 38
Interactivity, 33
Intranet, 27
IT infrastructure, 27
Knowledge management system (KMS), 11
Loyalty program, 16

Management information system (MIS), 7
Online analytical processing (OLAP), 10
Online transaction processing (OLTP), 9
Pirated software, 38
Privacy, 38
Private exchange, 17
Project management software, 11
Response time, 30
Reverse auction, 17
Rivalry among existing competitors, 17
Supplier power, 16
Supply chain, 16
Supply chain management (SCM), 22
Switching cost, 17
Threat of new entrants, 17
Threat of substitute products or services, 17
Throughput, 30
Value chain, 19
Web traffic, 30

Motivating and Rewarding an Organization's Most Valuable Asset— Its Employees

As companies focus on achieving gains in productivity and profitability, more are rethinking how to automate their incentive and compensation processes. Starbucks Coffee Co., which describes its two-year-old Starbucks Card program as "a flexible marketing tool that businesses can use as a thank you, an incentive, or a reward for customers and employees," has a long list of satisfied customers. Starbucks Cards come in $3 to $500 denominations and can be personalized by adding a message or a business logo.

One client, a national newspaper with a circulation of 1.3 million, offered a $10 Starbucks Card to subscribers who agreed to convert from paper billing to automated credit card billing. The newspaper got an amazing 36 percent response to its offer with over 4,100 conversions, 1,500 more than anticipated. Another client, a large national bank, used a $10 Starbucks Card to motivate existing customers to add a check card to their accounts. The bank got over 68,000 responses, exceeding expectations by more than 1,200 percent.

Enterprise incentive management (EIM) programs such as the Starbucks Card is just one of many new techniques helping organizations boost profits and raise revenues. According to the Aberdeen Group, a Boston-based IT market-research firm, sales of EIM software, service, and support are estimated to increase from $200 million in 2003 to $2.5 billion in 2006. HR.com, an online resource center for industry professionals, defines enterprise incentive management as a solution that automates the process of designing, developing, and administering incentive-based compensation plans. Essentially, any business issue involving a measurable objective can be helped by an incentive program.

Tom Wilson, president of a Concord, Massachusetts, consulting firm that specializes in designing corporate compensation plans and author of *Innovative Reward Systems for the Changing Workplace* (McGraw-Hill, 2003), states, "Most companies have a plan that says if a person sells 'x' he gets paid 'y.' That sounds simple enough, but research suggests that there is a 1 percent to 3 percent error rate in how people are actually paid, and some studies say it can even be as high as 8 percent to 10 percent. Some people get paid more than they should, which you never know about, but you always hear about it when a salesperson isn't paid enough. One problem is the cost of these errors. Another is the impact on morale that can affect employee turnover. How much confidence do your sales people have in the firm's management team? And are they spending the bulk of their time doing backup accounting for themselves, or are they out visiting and selling to clients?"

EIM systems provide organizations with a way to track and analyze incentive plans and eliminate costly errors associated with the majority of incentive plans. They also give managers a tool to run "what if" calculations through profit and loss statements, which gives organization a way to identify the impact a change in a compensation plan will have on the organization. One of the greatest benefits of EIM systems is that they are typically Web-enabled, allowing sales people to see how they are performing on a real-time basis. If managers have access to the same information, they can make immediate corrections to sales or product pricing strategies. The primary vendors of EIM systems today include Callidus Software, Synygy, and Centive.

EIM systems offer organizations a competitive advantage by allowing them to change compensation plans as their strategic initiatives change, which can directly affect an organization's bottom line.[29]

Questions

1. Using Porter's Five Forces determine if you would enter the EIM market. Provide support for your answer.

2. Explain why you think the EIM market is expected to grow so significantly over the next few years.

3. Describe how managers can change an organization's efficiency and effectiveness by being able to view incentive plans online.

4. Explain why EIM software can have a direct impact on an organization's bottom line.

5. Summarize how an EIM can impact a company's value chain.

6. Define ethics and explain why it is unethical for people to fail to report when they are overpaid for their sales efforts.

7. Explain why an organization would want to ensure that its incentive program information is highly secure.

UNIT CLOSING CASE TWO

Delta Airlines Plays Catch-Up

The airline industry has a well-deserved reputation for creative use of IT. American Airlines is known as a leader in using IT to drive its business and United Airlines is known as a fast follower. Delta Airlines, while highly regarded as a well-run airline, has been a slow follower in IT. Recently, however, this has changed. In the past few years, Delta has invested more than $1.5 billion in technology, automating everything from gate and boarding tasks to baggage-handling, inventory control, and revenue accounting.

SABRE and APOLLO were the earliest examples of significant forays into business driven IT in the airline industry. These were the airline reservation systems introduced by American Airlines and United Airlines, respectively. The SABRE and APOLLO programs are inventory control systems that sell and manage available seats on future flights. Travel agents received a special computer terminal from the airline when they signed up for the programs. Usually, a travel agent would sign up for one or the other system, but not both. Airline companies who did not have their own reservation systems (Frontier Airlines, for example) could become "co-hosts" on SABRE or APOLLO. A fee was charged to co-hosts for the privilege of listing their flights on the reservation systems.

American and United obtained significant competitive advantages as owners of the reservation systems for several reasons. First, they were very profitable. Second, they gave American's and United's IT and operations personnel early and valuable experience with online transaction processing (OLTP) systems. Finally, they gave American and United access to information on the sales volumes of their competitors, such as Frontier, because the information was available in the reservation system's database. For example, if American wanted to consider adding a flight from Denver to Chicago, it could simply examine the historical information in the SABRE system to see if there was enough demand for the new route. It could also see what sort of traffic a competitor like Frontier was generating on the same route in order to pick the best time to schedule a new flight along with the best price. American and United offered the same competitive intelligence information to their co-host airlines, but charged them for it, and often took weeks to provide it to them.

It was not long until American and United realized they had a gold mine of customer-related information available in their reservation systems. They conceived and rolled out hugely successful frequent flyer programs, which increased the likelihood that frequent business travelers, their most profitable customers, would fly with them instead of with a competitor. Frequent flyer programs require sophisticated computer systems to properly account for and manage the flight activity of millions of customers, together with their eligibility for awards—another noteworthy example of business driven IT. Ultimately, frequent flyer programs became an entry barrier for the industry because all airline companies felt they could not compete for the best customers without having their own frequent flyer systems.

Follow-on IT Innovations

Yield management systems are the IT systems that alter the price of available seats on a flight. The systems operate on a minute by minute basis as the date of the flight approaches, depending on the number of seats sold compared to the number expected. This is why an airfare quoted over the phone can be $100 higher if the airfare is quoted again an hour later. Most airlines use yield management systems to sell as many seats as possible at the best price. From the airlines' standpoint, it's better to sell a seat at a lower price than to have a plane take off with a vacant seat. At the same time, airlines want to avoid selling a seat for a price lower than what a passenger is willing to pay. Yield management systems are a great example of solving a business problem with IT because they help business managers maximize the revenue generated by each flight.

American Airlines went so far as to sell some of its systems, like yield management, to other airlines. When asked why, American's then CIO, Max Hopper, said American might as well recover some of its development costs by selling systems to competitors because eventually competitors would develop their own systems. Besides, Hopper believed that by the time lagging competitors like Delta figured out how to use the systems, American would have reached the next plateau of IT innovation.

Delta's IT Success

Delta always had a reputation in the industry as a slow follower, being reluctant to give up its paper-based systems for modern IT systems. The company did a turnaround, however, when former Frito-Lay CIO and "CIO for Hire" Charlie Feld joined Delta in 1997. Feld quickly addressed some of Delta's most pressing IT issues including projects and people in disarray, departments hiring their own IT consultants to develop systems with no attention given to coordination with other Delta systems, as well as the pending Y2K problem. He established a separate wholly owned subsidiary called Delta Technology, and set out to replace Delta's antiquated IT systems with new applications to run the airline.

Feld began by building the gate and boarding application along with the supporting technical hardware, software, and network infrastructure. The gate and boarding application was chosen because it was most visible to Delta's 104 million passengers. The new system provided gate agents' information on which passengers had checked in, seat assignments, and standby status, and saved an average of 8 to 10 minutes of gate activity per flight. As Chief Technical Officer (CTO) Dean Compton recalled, "I remember when we put in the systems in Jacksonville. I saw an overbooked widebody 767—where there is normally a lot of confusion around the gate—boarded by two agents on time and ahead of schedule. I'd seen a similar situation in Salt Lake City where we hadn't put in the technology yet, and they had to use nine agents to board the plane, and it still left late."

Delta Technology continued to roll out applications, but by early 2001, the airline industry began to feel the effects of the economic downturn. Delta's board of directors questioned the need to spend additional funds on IT when the airline was under great pressure to reduce its costs. After Delta Technology executives gave an overview of projects they were working on, Vickie Escarra, the chief marketing officer, spoke up in support of the IT initiatives like the gate and boarding application by saying, "Man, we couldn't have done what we're doing today if it wasn't for the technology." The overview from IT coupled with the endorsement from a satisfied business unit customer convinced the board that the IT projects should proceed. They insisted, however, that all projects be supported and justified by a solid business case analysis with emphasis placed on either lowered operating costs or increased revenues.

After September 11, when traffic fell off even more, Delta began to postpone projects showing a longer payoff (like new HR systems) and to speed up projects showing a faster payoff (like increasing the number of self-service check-in kiosks and replacing call center technology).

Currently, Delta processes almost 300 million transactions on its new IT infrastructure each month. The company installed SAP software for inventory management, but altered the "flight plan" for Delta's new technology platform. "Today, we're working only on projects that pay off in 12 months and have ongoing impact for at least three years—either building revenue or lowering operating costs," says current CIO Curtis Robb. He went on to say, "I see this work going on for another five years. We'll be done when we run out of ideas."[30,31,32]

Questions

1. What business risks would Delta be taking if it decided not to catch up with industry leaders in using IT to gain a competitive advantage?

2. What competitive advantages can a company reap if it is the first-mover in introducing an innovative IT system? What are the pros and cons of being a fast follower?

3. What other industries could potentially benefit from the use of yield management systems?

4. Explain how American and United used customer information to gain a competitive advantage and how the competitive advantage affected their value chains.

5. Select two efficiency and effectiveness metrics that Delta can implement to measure the success of its gate and boarding application.

6. Delta's board of directors questioned the need to spend additional funds on IT when the airline was under great pressure to reduce its costs. Determine a strategy for how the CEO, CIO, CTO, and CPO can work together to ensure IT projects are supported by both the business and IT departments.

7. Explain how an airline can use information technology to ensure the security of its airplanes.

MAKING BUSINESS DECISIONS

1. Opportunity Analysis

Cheryl O'Connell is the owner of a small, high-end retailer of women's clothing called Excelus. Excelus's business has been successful for many years, largely because of Cheryl's ability to anticipate the needs and wants of her loyal customer base and provide them with personalized service. Cheryl does not see any value in IT and does not want to invest any capital in something that will not directly affect her bottom line. Develop a proposal describing the potential IT-enabled competitive opportunities or threats Cheryl might be missing by not embracing IT. Be sure to include a Porter's Five Forces analysis and discuss which one of the three generic strategies Cheryl should pursue.

2. Using Efficiency and Effectiveness Metrics

You are the CEO of a 500-bed acute care general hospital. Your internal IT department is responsible for running applications that support both administrative functions (e.g., patient accounting) as well as medical applications (e.g., medical records). You need assurance that your IT department is a high quality operation in comparison to similar hospitals. What metrics should you ask your CIO to provide you to give the assurance you seek? Provide the reasoning behind each suggested metric. Also, determine how the interrelationship between efficiency metrics and effectiveness metrics can drive your business's success.

3. Building Business Relationships

Synergistics Inc. is a start-up company that specializes in helping businesses build successful internal relationships. You have recently been promoted to Senior Manager of the Business and IT Relationship area. Sales for your new department have dwindled over the last two years for a variety of reasons including the burst of the technological bubble, recent economic conditions, and a poorly communicated business strategy. Your first task on the job is to prepare a report detailing the following:

- Fundamental reasons for the gap between the IT and business sides
- Strategies you can take to convince your customers that this is an area that is critical to the success of their business
- Strategies your customers can follow to ensure that synergies exist between the two sides

4. Information Security over the Web

Jack Provenzo is the new chief security officer at Trends, a fast-growing information storage company. Soon after starting his new job, Jack realizes that Trends has many holes in its information security. Just from walking around the office, Jack spots employees leaving their computers unlocked when heading out to lunch, passwords stuck on bulletin boards and sticky notes, and personal employee software loaded on company machines. Jack is even able to convince several employees to reveal their user names and passwords to him. Jack is frightened by the blatant lack of security found throughout Trends and has requested your help to determine the best ways to safeguard the company from security breaches. Research the Web to find information on security strategies and techniques that Jack can use to protect Trends' intellectual capital.

5. Acting Ethically

Assume you are an IT manager and one of your projects is failing. You were against the project from the start; however, the project had powerful sponsorship from all of the top executives. You know that you are doomed and that the project is doomed. The reasons for the failure are numerous including the initial budget was drastically understated, the technology is evolving and not stable, the architecture was never scaled for growth, and your resources do not have the necessary development skills for the new technology. One of your team leads has come to you with a plan to sabotage the project that would put the project out of its misery without assigning any blame to the individuals on the project. Create a document detailing how you would handle this situation.

6. Determining IT Organizational Structures

You are the Chief Executive Officer for a start-up telecommunications company. The company currently has 50 employees and plans to ramp up to 3,000 by the end of the year. Your first task is to determine how you are going to model your organization. You decide to address the IT department's organizational structure first. You need to consider if you want to have a CIO, CPO, CSO, and CTO, and if so, what their reporting structure will look like and why. You also need to determine the different roles and responsibilities for each executive position. Once you have compiled this information, put together a presentation describing your IT department's organizational structure.

★ MAKING COLLABORATIVE DECISIONS

1. Comparing CRM Vendors

As a team, search the Internet for at least one recent and authoritative article that compares or ranks customer relationship management systems. Select two packages from the list and compare their functions and features as described in the article(s) you found as well as on each company's Web site. Find references in the literature where companies that are using each package have reported their experiences, both good and bad. Draw on any other comparisons you can find. Prepare a presentation for delivery in class on the strengths and weaknesses of each package, which one you favor, and why.

2. Performing a Competitive Analysis

Assume your team is made up of associates in a venture capital firm. You have been tasked with recommending whether or not to invest in Datria (www.datria.com), a young company in the voice-enabled field services space. The company has achieved some recent successes and is in need of additional funds to expand. Evaluate the company in comparison to its competition and prepare a report on how well it compares. Based on your research, come to a conclusion on the investment action your firm should take.

3. Creating a Digital Dashboard

Assume each member of your team is a member of the IT Department at Levi's. David Bergen, the CIO, wants you to design a digital dashboard for him. He wants to be sure the key performance indicators for the IT function are readily available for him to view and monitor on a continuing basis. He had suggested that you first prepare a list of key factors that other CIOs are using to monitor their departments so that you do not "reinvent the wheel." Once he reviews the list, he will select the ones that he feels apply to his needs and then he will give you additional direction to complete your task. Search the Internet to come up with an initial list of possibilities for his review. We suggest you start your research at the site www.cio.com/research/itvalue/. This is a section of the *CIO* magazine site, which discusses how CIOs can demonstrate the value of IT to themselves and their business manager colleagues.

4. Applying the Three Generic Strategies

The unit discussed examples of companies that pursue differentiated strategies so that they are not forced into positions where they must compete solely on the basis of price. Pick an industry and have your team members find and compare two companies, one which is competing on the basis of price, and another which has chosen to pursue a differentiated strategy enabled by the creative use of IT. Some industries you may want to consider are clothing retailers, grocery stores, airlines, and personal computers. Prepare a presentation for the class on the ways that IT is being used to help the differentiating company compete against the low cost provider. Before you begin, spend some class time to make sure each team selects a different industry if at all possible.

5. The Five Forces Model

Your team is working for a small investment company that specializes in technology investments. A new company, Geyser, has just released an operating system that plans to compete with Microsoft's operating systems. Your company has a significant amount of capital invested in Microsoft. Your boss, Jan Savage, has asked you to compile a Porter's Five Forces analysis for Microsoft to ensure that your company's Microsoft investment is not at risk.

6. Researching Competitive Intelligence

The Society for Competitive Intelligence Professionals Web site can be located at www.scip.org. Review the Web site and determine if this is an organization your team would consider joining. Be sure to justify your answer in terms of gaining insight into business advantages and competitive intelligence.

U N I T

2

Managing Information
for Business Initiatives

Searching for Revenue—Google

Google founders Sergey Brin and Larry Page recently made *Forbes* magazine's list of world billionaires. Google is a privately held company with revenues between $750 million and $1 billion. The company, famous for its highly successful search engine, experienced a 620 percent revenue growth in 2003.

How Google Works

Figure 2.1 displays the life of an average Google query. The Web server sends the query to the index servers. The content inside the index server is similar to the index at the back of a book—it tells which pages contain the words that match any particular query term. Then the query travels to the document servers, which actually retrieve the stored documents and generate snippets to describe each search result. Finally, the search engine returns the results to the user. All these activities occur within a fraction of a second.

Google consists of three distinct parts:

1. The Web crawler, known as Googlebot, finds and retrieves Web pages and passes them to the Google indexer. Googlebot functions much like a Web browser. It sends a request for a Web page to a Web server, downloads the entire page, and then hands it off to Google's indexer. Googlebot can request thousands of different Web pages simultaneously.

FIGURE 2.1

How Google Works

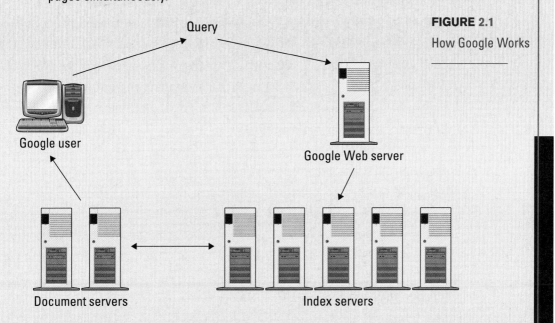

Query

Google user

Google Web server

Document servers

Index servers

2. The indexer indexes every word on each page and stores the resulting index of words in a huge database. This index is sorted alphabetically by search term, with each index entry storing a list of documents in which the term appears and the location within the text where it occurs. Indexing the full text of Web pages allows Google to go beyond simply matching single search terms. Google gives more priority to pages that have search terms near each other and in the same order as the query. Google can also match multi-word phrases and sentences.

3. The query processor compares the search query to the index and recommends the documents that it considers most relevant. Google considers over a hundred factors in determining which documents are most relevant to a query, including the popularity of the page, the position and size of the search terms within the page, and the proximity of the search terms to one another. The query processor has several parts, including the user interface (search box), the "engine" that evaluates queries and matches them to relevant documents, and the results formatter.

Selling Words

Google's primary line of business is its search engine; however, the company does not generate revenue from people using its site to search the Internet. It generates revenue from the marketers and advertisers that are paying to place their ads on the site.

Around 200 million times each day, people from all over the world access Google to perform searches. AdWords, a part of the Google site, allows advertisers to bid on common search terms. The advertisers simply enter in the keywords they want to bid on and the maximum amounts they want to pay per click, per day. Google then determines a price and a search ranking for those keywords based on how much other advertisers are willing to pay for the same terms. Pricing for keywords can range from 5 cents to $3 a click. A general search term like "tropical vacation" costs less than a more specific term like "Hawaiian vacation." Whoever bids the most for a term appears in a sponsored advertisement link either at the top or along the side of the search-results page.

Paid search is the ultimate in targeted advertising because consumers type in exactly what they want. One of the primary advantages of paid search Web programs such as AdWords is that customers do not find it annoying, as is the problem with some forms of Web advertising such as banner ads and pop-up ads. According to the Interactive Advertising Bureau, overall industry revenues from paid search surpassed banner ads in the third quarter of 2003.

"A big percentage of queries we get are commercial in nature," confirms Salar Kamangar, Google's director of product management. "It is a marketplace where the advertisers tell us about themselves by telling us how much each lead is worth. They have an incentive to bid how much they really want to pay, because if they underbid, their competitors will get more traffic." Kamangar came up with the AdWords concept and oversees that part of the business today. AdWords, which launched two years ago, accounts for the vast majority of Google's annual revenue and the company has over 150,000 advertisers in its paid-search program, up from zero in 2002.

Expanding Google

Google has a secret weapon working for its research and development department—hackers. Hackers actually develop many of the new and unique ways to expand Google. The company elicits Hacker ideas through its application program interface (API), a large piece of the Google code. The API enables developers to build applications around the Google search engine. By making the API freely available, Google has inspired a community of programmers that are extending Google's capabilities. "It's working," states Nelson Minar, who runs the API effort. "We get clever hacks, educational uses, and wacky stuff. We love to see people do creative things with our product." A few of the successful user developed applications include:

- **Banana Slug**—www.bananaslug.com. For customers who hit a dead end with Google search, the site adds a random word to search text that generates surprising results.
- **Cookin' with Google**—www.researchbuzz.org. Enter in the ingredients that are in the fridge and the site returns potential recipes for those ingredients.
- **Google Alert**—www.googlealert.com. Google Alert automatically searches the Web for information on a topic and returns the results by e-mail.
- **RateMyProfessors.com**—www.ratemyprofessors.com. The goal of this site was to create a place where students could rank their teachers. However, too many jokesters typing in false professor names such as "Professor Harry Leg" and "Professor Ima Dog" left the information on the site questionable. The developers turned to the Google API to create an automatic verification tool. If Google finds enough mentions in conjunction with a professor or university then it considers the information valid and posts it to the Web site.

Given all the exciting new technologies that Google has invented or exploited, it is easy to imagine that the future of Google might include Google e-mail, Google auctions, or even Google software.[1,2,3,4]

INTRODUCTION

Information is powerful. Information tells an organization everything from how its current operations are performing to estimating and strategizing how future operations might perform. New perspectives open up when people have the right information and know how to use it. The ability to understand, digest, analyze, and filter information is a key to success for any professional in any industry. Unit 2 demonstrates the value an organization can uncover and create by learning how to manage, access, analyze, and protect organizational information. The chapters in Unit 2 are:

- **Chapter Six**—Valuing Organizational Information
- **Chapter Seven**—Storing Organizational Information—Databases
- **Chapter Eight**—Viewing and Protecting Organizational Information

Chapter Six: Valuing Organizational Information

oogle recently reported a 200 percent increase in sales of its new Enterprise Search Appliance tool released in 2002. Companies use the tool within an enterprise information portal (EIP) to search corporate information for answers to customer questions and to fulfill sales orders. Hundreds of Google's customers are already using the tool—Xerox, Hitachi Data Systems, Nextel Communications, Procter & Gamble, Discovery Communications, Cisco Systems, Boeing. The ability to search, analyze, and comprehend information is vital for any organization's success. The incredible 200 percent growth in sales of Google's new Search Appliance tool is a strong indicator that organizations are coveting technologies that help organize and provide access to information.[5]

Information is everywhere in an organization. When addressing a significant business issue, employees must be able to obtain and analyze all the relevant information so they can make the best decision possible. Organizational information comes at different levels and in different formats and "granularities." (Granularity means fine and detailed or "coarse" and abstract information.) Employees must be able to correlate the different levels, formats, and granularities of information when making decisions. For example, if employees are using a supply chain management system to make decisions, they might find that their suppliers send information in different formats granularity at different levels. One supplier might send detailed information in a spreadsheet, another supplier might send summary information in a Word document, and still another might send aggregate information from a database. Employees will need to compare these different types of information for what they commonly reveal to make strategic SCM decisions. Figure 2.2 displays types of information found in organizations.

Successfully collecting, compiling, sorting, and finally analyzing information from multiple levels, in varied formats, exhibiting different granularity can provide tremendous insight into how an organization is performing. Taking a hard look at organizational information can yield exciting and unexpected results such as potential new markets, new ways of reaching customers, and even new ways of doing business.

Samsung Electronics took a detailed look at over 10,000 reports from its resellers to identify "lost deals" or orders lost to competitors. The analysis yielded the enlightening result that 80 percent of lost sales took place in a single business unit, the

Information Types	Range	Examples
Information Levels	Individual	Individual knowledge, goals, and strategies
	Department	Departmental goals, revenues, expenses, processes, and strategies
	Enterprise	Enterprisewide revenues, expenses, processes, and strategies
Information Formats	Document	Letters, memos, faxes, e-mails, reports, marketing materials, and training materials
	Presentation	Product, strategy, process, financial, customer, and competitor presentations
	Spreadsheet	Sales, marketing, industry, financial, competitor, customer, and order spreadsheets
	Database	Customer, employee, sales, order, supplier, and manufacturer databases
Information Granularities	Detail (Fine)	Reports for each sales person, product, and part
	Summary	Reports for all sales personnel, all products, and all parts
	Aggregate (Course)	Reports across departments, organizations, and companies

health care industry. Furthermore, Samsung was able to identify that 40 percent of its lost sales in the health care industry were going to one particular competitor. Prior to performing the analysis, Samsung was heading into its market blind. Armed with this valuable information, Samsung is changing its selling strategy in the health care industry to recoup its losses by implementing a new strategy to work more closely with hardware vendors to win back lost sales.[6]

Not all companies are successful when it comes to managing information. Staples, the office-supplies superstore, opened its first store in 1986 with state-of-the-art technology. The company experienced rapid growth and soon found itself overwhelmed with the resulting volumes of information. The state-of-the-art technology quickly became obsolete and the company was unable to obtain any insight into its massive volumes of information. A simple query such as identifying the customers who purchased a computer, but not software or peripherals, took hours. Some of the queries required several days to complete and by the time the managers received answers to their queries it was too late.[7]

After understanding the different levels, formats, and granularities of information, it is important to look at a few additional characteristics that help determine the value of information. These characteristics include transactional, analytical, timeliness, and quality.

THE VALUE OF TRANSACTIONAL AND ANALYTICAL INFORMATION

Transactional information encompasses all of the information contained within a single business process or unit of work and its primary purpose is to support the performing of daily operational tasks. Examples of using transactional information are withdrawing cash from an ATM, making an airline reservation, or purchasing stocks. Organizations capture and store transactional information in databases, and they use it when performing operational tasks and repetitive decisions such as analyzing daily sales reports and production schedules to determine how much inventory to carry.

Analytical information encompasses all organizational information and its primary purpose is to support the performing of managerial analysis tasks. Analytical information includes transactional information along with other information such as market and industry information. Examples of analytical information include trends, sales, product statistics, and future growth projections. Analytical information is used when making important ad hoc decisions such as whether the organization should build a new manufacturing plant or hire additional sales personnel.

THE VALUE OF TIMELY INFORMATION

The need for timely information can change for each business decision. Some decisions require weekly or monthly information while other decisions require daily information. Timeliness is an aspect of information that depends on the situation. In some industries, information that is a few days or weeks old can be relevant while in other industries information that is a few minutes old can be almost worthless. Some organizations, such as 911 centers, stock traders, and banks, require consolidated, up-to-the-second information, 24 hours a day, 7 days a week. Other organizations, such as insurance and construction companies, require only daily or even weekly information.

Real-time information means immediate, up-to-date information. *Real-time systems* provide real-time information in response to query requests. Many organizations use real-time systems to exploit key corporate transactional information. In a December 2003 survey of 700 IT executives by Evans Data Corp., 48 percent of respondents said they were already analyzing information in or near real-time, and another 25 percent reported plans to add real-time systems.[8]

Real-time systems provide valuable information for supporting corporate strategies such as customer relationship management. Bell Mobility Inc., Canada's largest wireless carrier, staffs over 550 customer service representatives and uses E.piphany Inc.'s Real-Time tool to make the right customer offers at the right time without having to rely on guesswork. Figure 2.3 display's Bell Mobility's results from the first month after implementation of the Real-Time tool.[9]

The growing demand for real-time information stems from organizations' need to make faster and more effective decisions, keep smaller inventories, operate more efficiently, and track performance more carefully. But timeliness is relative. Organizations need fresh, timely information to make good decisions. Information also needs to be timely in the sense that it meets employees' needs—but no more. If employees can absorb information only on an hourly or daily basis, there is no need to gather real-time information in smaller increments. For example, MBIA Insurance Corp. uses overnight updates to feed its real-time systems. Employees use this information to make daily risk decisions for mortgages, insurance policies, and other services. The company found that overnight updates were sufficient, as long as users could gain immediate access to the information they needed to make business decisions during the day.[10]

Most people request real-time information without understanding one of the biggest pitfalls associated with real-time information—continual change. Imagine the following scenario: Three managers meet at the end of the day to discuss a business problem. Each manager has gathered information at different times during the day to create a picture of the situation. Each manager's picture may be different because of this time discrepancy. Their views on the business problem may not

FIGURE 2.3

Results from Bell Mobility's Real-Time Tool

Bell Mobility's Real-Time Tool Results
■ 18 percent increase in sales per hour
■ 16 percent increase in total inbound marketing revenue
■ 75 percent decrease in total time to create and deploy a new marketing campaign

match since the information they are basing their analysis on is continually changing. This approach may not speed up decision making, and in fact it may slow it down.

The timeliness of the information required must be evaluated for each business decision. Organizations do not want to find themselves in the position of using real-time information to make a bad decision faster.

THE VALUE OF QUALITY INFORMATION

Westpac Financial Services (WFS), one of the four major banks in Australia, serves millions of customers from its many core systems, each with its own database. The databases maintain information and provide users with easy access to the stored information. Unfortunately, the company failed to develop information capturing standards, which led to inconsistent organizational information. For example, one system had a field to capture e-mail addresses while another system did not. Duplicate customer information among the different systems was another major issue and the company continually found itself sending conflicting or competing messages to customers from different operations of the bank. A customer could also have multiple accounts within the company, one representing a life insurance policy and one representing a credit card. WFS had no way to identify that the two different customer accounts were for the same customer.

WFS had to solve its information quality problems immediately if it was to remain competitive. The company purchased NADIS (Name & Address Data Integrity Software), a software solution that filters customer information, highlighting missing, inaccurate, and redundant information. Customer service ratings are on the rise for WFS now that the company can operate its business with a single and comprehensive view of each one of its customers.[11]

Business decisions are only as good as the quality of the information used to make the decisions. Review Figure 2.4 for an overview of five characteristics common to high-quality information: accuracy, completeness, consistency, uniqueness, and timeliness. Figure 2.5 highlights several issues with low-quality information including:

- The first issue is *missing* information. The customer's first name is missing. (See #1 in Figure 2.5.)
- The second issue is *incomplete* information since the street address contains only a number and not a street name.
- The third issue is a probable *duplication* of information since the only slight difference between the two customers is the spelling of the last name. Street addresses and phone numbers being the same make this likely.

Characteristics of High-Quality Information	
Accuracy	Are all the values correct? For example, is the name spelled correctly? Is the dollar amount recorded properly?
Completeness	Are any of the values missing? For example, is the address complete including street, city, state, and zip code?
Consistency	Is aggregate or summary information in agreement with detailed information? For example, do all total fields equal the true total of the individual fields?
Uniqueness	Is each transaction, entity, and event represented only once in the information? For example, are there any duplicate customers?
Timeliness	Is the information current with respect to the business requirements? For example, is information updated weekly, daily, or hourly?

FIGURE 2.4

The Five Common Characteristics of High-Quality Information

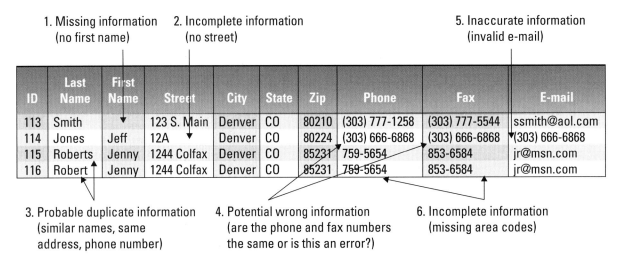

1. Missing information (no first name)
2. Incomplete information (no street)
5. Inaccurate information (invalid e-mail)

3. Probable duplicate information (similar names, same address, phone number)
4. Potential wrong information (are the phone and fax numbers the same or is this an error?)
6. Incomplete information (missing area codes)

FIGURE 2.5

Low-Quality
Information Example

- The fourth issue is potential *wrong* information because the customer's phone and fax numbers are the same. Some customers might have the same number for phone and fax line, but the fact that the customer also has this number in the e-mail address field is suspicious.

- The fifth issue is definitely an example of *inaccurate* information since a phone number is located in the e-mail address field.

- The sixth issue is *incomplete* information since there is not a valid area code for the phone and fax numbers.

Recognizing how low-quality information issues occur will allow organizations to begin to correct them. The four primary sources of low-quality information are:

1. Online customers intentionally enter inaccurate information to protect their privacy.

2. Information from different systems that have different information entry standards and formats.

3. Call center operators enter abbreviated or erroneous information by accident or to save time.

4. Third party and external information contains inconsistencies, inaccuracies, and errors.[12]

Addressing the above sources of information inaccuracies will significantly improve the quality of organizational information and the value that can be extracted from the information.

Understanding the Costs of Low-Quality Information

Using the wrong information can lead to making the wrong decision. Making the wrong decision can cost time, money, and even reputations. Every business decision is only as good as the information used to make the decision. Bad information can cause serious business ramifications such as:

- Inability to accurately track customers, which directly affects strategic initiatives such as CRM and SCM.

- Difficulty identifying the organization's most valuable customers.

- Inability to identify selling opportunities and wasted revenue from marketing to nonexistent customers and nondeliverable mail.

- Difficulty tracking revenue because of inaccurate invoices.

- Inability to build strong relationships with customers—which increases their buyer power.

Understanding the Benefits of High-Quality Information

High-quality information can significantly improve the chances of making a good decision and directly increase an organization's bottom line. Lillian Vernon Corp., a catalog company, used Web analytics to discover that men preferred to shop at Lillian Vernon's Web site instead of looking through its paper catalog. Based on this information, the company began placing male products more prominently on its Web site and soon realized a 15 percent growth in sales to men.[13]

Another company discovered that Phoenix, Arizona, is not a good place to sell golf clubs, even with its high number of golf courses. An analysis revealed that typical golfers in Phoenix are either tourists or conventioneers. These golfers usually bring their clubs with them while visiting Phoenix. The analysis further revealed that two of the best places to sell golf clubs in the United States are Rochester, New York, and Detroit, Michigan.[14]

There are numerous examples of companies that have used their high-quality information to make solid strategic business decisions. High-quality information of course does not automatically guarantee that every decision made is going to be a good one, since people ultimately make decisions. But high-quality information ensures that the basis of the decisions is accurate. The success of the organization depends on appreciating and leveraging the true value of timely and high-quality information.

OPENING CASE STUDY QUESTIONS

1. Determine if Google's search results are examples of transactional information or analytical information.

2. Describe the ramifications on Google's business if the search information it presented to its customers was of low quality.

3. Review the five common characteristics of high-quality information and rank them in order of importance to Google's business.

4. Explain how the Web site RateMyProfessors.com solved its problem of low-quality information.

Chapter Six Case: Fishing for Quality

The Alaska Department of Fish and Game requires high-quality information to manage the state's natural resources, specifically to increase fishing yields, while ensuring the future of many species. Using fish counts the department makes daily decisions as to which districts will be open or closed to commercial fishing. If the department receives low-quality information from fish counts then either too many fish escape or too many are caught. Allowing too many salmon to swim upstream could deprive fishermen their livelihoods. Allowing too many to be caught before they swim upstream to spawn could diminish fish populations—yielding devastating effects for years to come.

Because of the incredible size of Alaskan fisheries, the Commercial Fisheries Division's decisions have global impact. Its information is relied upon by individual fishermen who want to know the best places to fish, by corporations around the world that need information on which to base business strategies for seafood processing and marketing, by researchers, and by legislators. With so much at stake, the Division of Commercial Fisheries set out to improve the quality of its information by implementing a system that can gather the information from remote parts of the state and analyze it quickly to determine the daily outcomes.

Originally, the department captured information in spreadsheets that were e-mailed from station to station before being entered into the system. There was no central information set to work from, and more often than not, the information was low quality. Decisions were based on inaccurate and, because of delays in posting, untimely information.

With the implementation of an Oracle database, the department significantly improved the quality and timeliness of its information. Each time a commercial fishing boat within Alaska's jurisdiction unloads at a processing plant, the catch is weighed and details of the catch, such as species caught, weight, and quantity, are recorded on a fish ticket. This information is entered into the new system. To gather fish escapement information from remote areas, field workers positioned in towers scan rivers to visibly count fish. This information is radioed in the next morning.

Information from fish processed the previous day is keyed in by 10:00 A.M., and one hour later, the managers and fisheries across the state have all the information they require to make accurate decisions. They then announce on the radio and on their Web site, which receives more that 3,000 hits on an average day, whether or not fishermen can fish that day.

Fisheries are now managed with timely, centralized, and accurate information. Web pages summarize daily catches for certain areas, like Bristol Bay, whose annual Sockeye Salmon season, which lasts only a few weeks, is closely monitored by fish processors worldwide. With the enormous quantities of fish caught, salmon fisheries worldwide adjust their production levels based on the results of the annual Bristol Bay Sockeye Salmon season. This is just one reason why producing fast, high-quality information is critical to managing Alaska's natural resources.[15]

Questions

1. Describe the difference between transactional and analytical information and determine which type the Alaska Department of Fish and Game is using to make decisions.
2. Explain the importance of high-quality information for the Alaska Department of Fish and Game.
3. Review the five common characteristics of high-quality information and rank them in order of importance for the Alaska Department of Fish and Game.

Chapter Seven: Storing Organizational Information—Databases

LEARNING OUTCOMES

7.1. Define the fundamental concepts of the relational database model.

7.2. Evaluate the advantages of the relational database model.

7.3. Compare operational integrity constraints and business-critical integrity constraints.

7.4. Describe the role and purpose of a database management system.

7.5. List and describe the four components of a database management system.

7.6. Describe the two primary methods for integrating information across multiple databases.

Austrian Federal Railways maintains its entire railway system—which includes over 5,849 kilometers of track, 5,993 bridges and viaducts, 240 tunnels, and 6,768 crossings—with an Oracle database. Multiple applications run on the database including accounting, order processing, and geographic applications that pinpoint railway equipment locations. The database contains over 80 billion characters of information and supports more than 1,200 users. Many organizations use databases similar to Austrian Federal Railways' to manage large amounts of information.[16]

RELATIONAL DATABASE FUNDAMENTALS

There are many different models for organizing information in a database, including the hierarchical database, network database, and the most prevalent—the relational database model. Broadly defined, a **database** maintains information about various types of objects (inventory), events (transactions), people (employees), and places (warehouses). The **hierarchical database** stores related information in terms of predefined categorical relationships in a "tree-like" fashion. The **network database** is used by a network installation tool to allocate and track network resources. The **relational database model** is a type of database that stores its information in the form of logically related two-dimensional tables. This text focuses on the relational database model.

Consider how the Coca-Cola Bottling Company of Egypt (TCCBCE) implemented an inventory-tracking database to improve order accuracy by 27 percent, decrease order response time by 66 percent, and increase sales by 20 percent. With over 7,400 employees, TCCBCE owns and operates 11 bottling plants and 29 sales and distribution centers, making it one of the largest companies in Egypt.

Traditionally, the company sent distribution trucks to each customer's premises to take orders and deliver stock. There were many problems associated with this process including numerous information entry errors, which caused order-fulfillment time to take an average of three days. To remedy the situation, Coca-Cola decided to create presales teams equipped with hand-held devices to visit customers and take orders electronically. On returning to the office, the teams synchronized orders with the company's inventory-tracking database to ensure automated processing and rapid dispatch of accurate orders to customers.[17]

Entities, Entity Classes, and Attributes

Figure 2.6 illustrates the primary concepts of the relational database model—entities, entity classes, attributes, keys, and relationships. An *entity* in the relational database model is a person, place, thing, transaction, or event about which information is stored. An *entity class* (often called a table) in the relational database model is a collection of similar entities. The entity classes of interests in Figure 2.6 are *CUSTOMER, ORDER, ORDER LINE, PRODUCT,* and *DISTRIBUTOR.* Notice that each entity class (the collection of similar entities) is stored in a different two-dimensional table. *Attributes,* also called fields or columns, are characteristics or properties of an entity class. In Figure 2.6 the attributes for *CUSTOMER* include *Customer ID, Customer Name, Contact Name,* and *Phone.* Attributes for *PRODUCT* include *Product ID, Product Description,* and *Price.* Each specific entity in an entity class (e.g., Dave's Sub Shop in the *CUSTOMER* table) occupies one row in its respective table. The columns in the table contain the attributes.

Keys and Relationships

To manage and organize various entity classes within the relational database model, developers must identify primary keys and foreign keys and use them to create logical relationships. A *primary key* is a field (or group of fields) that uniquely identifies a given entity in a table. In *CUSTOMER,* the *Customer ID* uniquely identifies each entity (customer) in the table and is the primary key. Primary keys are important because they provide a way of distinguishing each entity in a table.

A *foreign key* in the relational database model is a primary key of one table that appears as an attribute in another table and acts to provide a logical relationship among the two tables. Consider Hawkins Shipping, one of the distributors appearing in the *DISTRIBUTOR* table. Its primary key, *Distributor ID,* is DEN8001. Notice that *Distributor ID* also appears as an attribute in the ORDER table. This establishes the fact that Hawkins Shipping (*Distributor ID* DEN8001) was responsible for delivering orders 34561 and 34562 to the appropriate customer(s). Therefore, *Distributor ID* in the ORDER table creates a logical relationship (who shipped what order) between *ORDER* and *DISTRIBUTOR.*

RELATIONAL DATABASE ADVANTAGES

From a business perspective, database information offers many advantages, including:

- Increased flexibility
- Increased scalability and performance
- Reduced information redundancy
- Increased information integrity (quality)
- Increased information security

Increased Flexibility

Databases tend to mirror business structures and a good database can handle changes quickly and easily, just as any good business needs to be able to handle changes quickly and easily. Equally important, databases provide flexibility in allowing each user to access the information in whatever way best suits his or her needs. The distinction between logical and physical views is important in understanding flexible database user views. The *physical view* of information deals with the physical storage of information on a storage device such as a hard disk. The *logical view* of information focuses on how users logically access information to meet

CUSTOMER

Customer ID	Customer Name	Contact Name	Phone
23	Dave's Sub Shop	David Logan	(555)333-4545
43	Pizza Palace	Debbie Fernandez	(555)345-5432
765	T's Fun Zone	Tom Repicci	(555)565-6655

ORDER

Order ID	Order Date	Customer ID	Distributor ID	Distributor Fee
34561	7/4/2004	23	DEN8001	$22.00
34562	8/6/2004	23	DEN8001	$12.95
34563	6/5/2004	765	NY9001	$29.50

ORDER LINE

Order ID	Line Item	Product ID	Quantity
34561	1	12345AA	75
34561	2	12346BB	50
34561	3	12347CC	100
34562	1	12349EE	300
34563	1	12345AA	100
34563	2	12346BB	100
34563	3	12347CC	50
34563	4	12348DD	50
34563	5	12349EE	100

DISTRIBUTOR

Distributor ID	Distributor Name
DEN8001	Hawkins Shipping
CHI3001	ABC Trucking
NY9001	Van Distributors

PRODUCT

Product ID	Product Description	Price
12345AA	Coca Cola	$0.55
12346BB	Diet Coke	$0.55
12347CC	Sprite	$0.55
12348DD	Diet Sprite	$0.55
12349EE	Vanilla Coke	$0.55

their particular business needs. This separation of logical and physical views is what allows each user to access database information differently. That is, while a database has only one physical view, it can easily support multiple logical views. In the previous database illustration, for example, users could perform a query to determine which distributors delivered shipments to Pizza Palace last week. At the same time, another person could perform some sort of statistical analysis to determine the frequency at which Sprite and Diet Coke appear on the same order. These represent two very different logical views, but both views use the same physical view.

Consider another example—a mail-order business. One user might want a CRM report presented in alphabetical format, in which case last name should appear before first name. Another user, working with a catalog mailing system, would want customer names appearing as first name and then last name. Both are easily achievable, but different logical views of the same physical information.

Increased Scalability and Performance

The official Web site of The American Family Immigration History Center, www.ellisisland.org, generated over 2.5 billion hits in its first year of operation (see page 65). The site offers easy access to immigration information about people who entered America through the Port of New York and Ellis Island between 1892 and 1924. The database contains over 25 million passenger names correlated to 3.5 million images of ships' manifests.[18]

Only a database could "scale" to handle the massive volumes of information and the large numbers of users required for the successful launch of the Ellis Island Web site. *Scalability* refers to how well a system can adapt to increased demands. *Performance* measures how quickly a system performs a certain process or transaction. Some organizations must be able to support hundreds or thousands of online users including employees, partners, customers, and suppliers, who all want to access and share information. Databases today scale to exceptional levels, allowing all types of users and programs to perform information-processing and information-searching tasks.

Reduced Information Redundancy

Redundancy is the duplication of information, or storing the same information in multiple places. Redundant information occurs because organizations frequently capture and store the same information in multiple locations. The primary problem with redundant information is that it is often inconsistent, which makes it difficult to determine which values are the most current or most accurate. Not having correct information is confusing and frustrating for employees and disruptive to an organization. One of the primary goals of a database is to eliminate information redundancy by recording each piece of information in only one place in the database. Eliminating information redundancy saves space, makes performing information updates easier, and improves information quality.

Increased Information Integrity (Quality)

Information integrity is a measure of the quality of information. Within a database environment, *integrity constraints* are rules that help ensure the quality of information. Integrity constraints can be defined and built into the database design. The database (more appropriately, the database management system, which is discussed below) ensures that users can never violate these constraints. There are two types of integrity constraints: (1) operational integrity constraints and (2) business-critical integrity constraints.

Operational integrity constraints are rules that enforce basic and fundamental information-based constraints. For example, an operational integrity constraint would not allow someone to create an order for a nonexistent customer, provide a markup percentage that was negative, or order zero pounds of raw materials from a supplier.

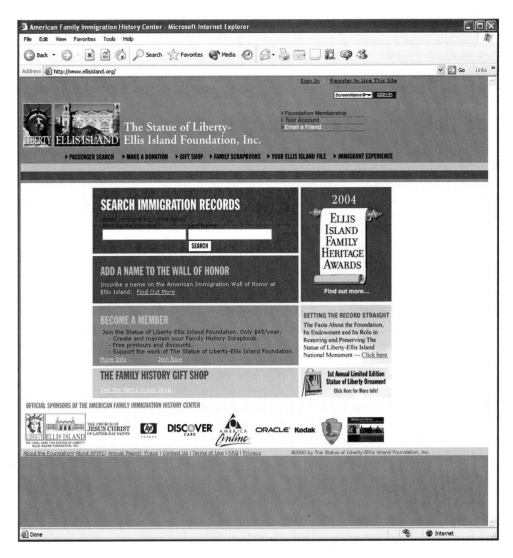

Business-critical integrity constraints are rules that enforce business rules vital to an organization's success and often require more insight and knowledge than operational integrity constraints. Consider a supplier of fresh produce to large grocery chains such as Kroger. The supplier might implement a business-critical integrity constraint stating that no product returns are accepted after 15 days past delivery. That would make sense because of the chance of spoilage of the produce. These types of integrity constraints tend to mirror the very rules by which an organization achieves success.

The specification and enforcement of integrity constraints produces higher quality information that will provide better support for business decisions. Organizations that establish specific procedures for developing integrity constraints typically see a decline in information error rates and an increase in the use of organizational information.

Increased Information Security

Information is an organizational asset. Like any asset, the organization must protect its information from unauthorized users or misuse. As systems become increasingly complex and more available over the Internet, security becomes an even bigger issue. Databases offer many security features including passwords, access levels, and access controls. Passwords provide authentication of the user who is gaining access to the system. Access levels determine who has access to the different types of information and access controls determine what type of access they have to the information. For example, customer service representatives might need read-only access to customer order information so they can answer customer order inquiries; they might not have or need the authority to change or delete order information. Managers might require access to employee files, but they should have access only to their own employees' files, not the employee files for the entire company. Various security features of databases can ensure that individuals have only certain types of access to certain types of information.

Databases can increase personal security as well as information security. Since 1995, the Chicago Police Department (CPD) has relied on a crime-fighting system called Citizen and Law Enforcement Analysis and Reporting (CLEAR). CLEAR electronically streamlines the way detectives enter and access critical information to help them solve crimes, analyze crime patterns, and ultimately promote security in a proactive manner. The CPD enters 650,000 new criminal cases and 500,000 new arrests into CLEAR each year.[19]

DATABASE MANAGEMENT SYSTEMS

Ford's European plant manufactures more than 5,000 vehicles a day and sells them in over 100 countries worldwide. Every component of every model must conform to complex European standards, including passenger safety standards and pedestrian and environmental protection standards. These standards govern each stage of Ford's manufacturing process from design to final production. The company needs to obtain many thousands of different approvals each year to comply with the standards. Overlooking just one means the company cannot sell the finished vehicle, which brings the production line to a standstill and could potentially cost Ford up to 1 million Euros per day. Ford built the Homologation Timing System (HTS), based on a relational database, to help it track and analyze these standards. The reliability and high performance of the HTS system have helped Ford substantially reduce its compliance risk.[20]

A database management system is used to access information from a database. A ***database management system (DBMS)*** is software through which users and application programs interact with a database. The user sends requests to the DBMS and the DBMS performs the actual manipulation of the information in the database. There are two primary ways that users can interact with a DBMS: (1) directly and (2) indirectly, as displayed in Figure 2.7. In either case, users access the DBMS and the DBMS accesses the database.

FIGURE 2.7

Interacting Directly and Indirectly with a Database through a DBMS

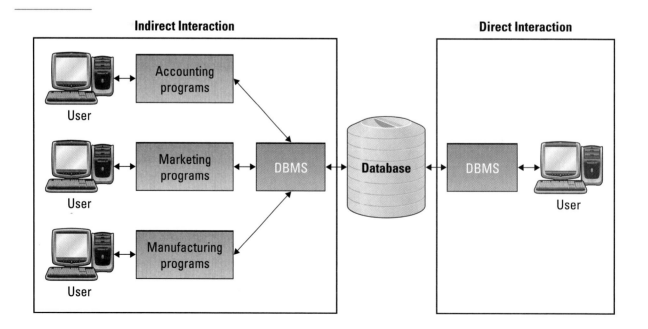

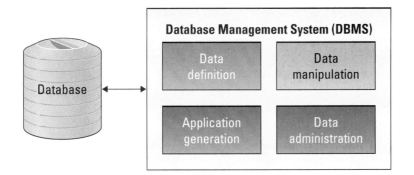

FIGURE 2.8

Four Components of a
Database Management
System

A DBMS is composed of four primary components including data definition, data manipulation, application generation, and data administration (see Figure 2.8).

Data Definition Component

The *data definition component* of a DBMS helps create and maintain the data dictionary and the structure of the database. The *data dictionary* of a database is a file that stores definitions of information types, identifies the primary and foreign keys, and maintains the relationships among the tables. The data dictionary essentially defines the logical properties of the information that the database contains. See Figure 2.9 for typical logical properties of information.

All the logical properties shown in Figure 2.9 are important and they vary depending on the type of information. For example, a typical address field might have a *Type* logical property of alphanumeric, meaning that the field can accept number, letters, and special characters. This would be an example of an operational integrity constraint. The validation rule requiring that a discount cannot exceed 100 percent is an example of a business-critical integrity constraint.

The data dictionary is an important part of the DBMS because users can consult the dictionary to determine the different types of database information. The data dictionary also supplies users with vital information when creating reports such as column names and information formats.

Data Manipulation Component

Of the four DBMS components, users probably spend the most time working with data manipulation. The *data manipulation component* of a DBMS allows users to create, read, update, and delete information in a database. A DBMS contains a variety of data manipulation tools including views, report generators, query-by-example tools, and structured query language.

A *view* allows users to see the contents of a database, make any required changes, perform simple sorting, and query the database to find the location of specific information. *Report generators* allow users to define formats for reports along with what information they want to see in the report (see Figure 2.10).

Logical Property	Example
Field name	Name of field such as *Customer ID* or *Product ID*
Type	Alphanumeric, numeric, date, time, currency, etc.
Form	Each phone number must have the area code (XXX) XXX-XXXX
Default value	The default value for area code is (303)
Validation rule	A discount cannot exceed 100 percent
Entry rule	The field must have a valid entry—no blanks are allowed
Duplicate rule	Duplicate information is not allowed

FIGURE 2.9

Logical Field Properties
in a Database

FIGURE 2.10

Sample Report Using
Microsoft Access

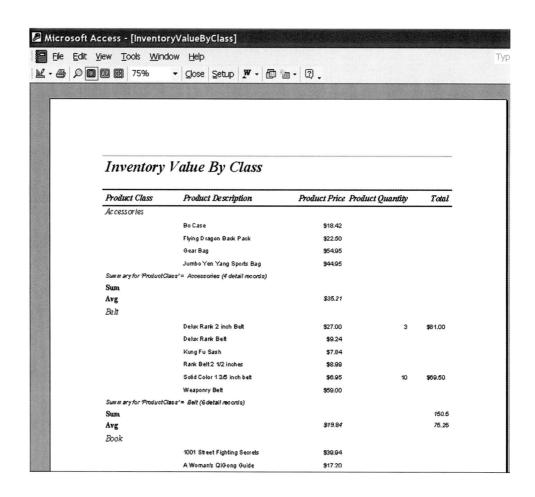

Most often, users will create queries to access information in a database. A query is simply a question, such as "How many customers live in California?" ***Query-by-example (QBE)*** tools allow users to graphically design the answers to specific questions. Figure 2.11 displays Microsoft's Access QBE tool with a query asking which customers have ordered which products. Using a QBE, a user can design this query by asking the DBMS to pull all of the product descriptions for each order for every customer. Figure 2.12 displays the results to this query.

Structured query language (SQL) is a standardized fourth-generation query language found in most DBMSs. SQL performs the same function as QBE, except that the user must type statements instead of pointing, clicking, and dragging in a graphical environment. The basic form of an SQL statement is SELECT...... FROM......WHERE. Figure 2.13 displays the corresponding SQL statement required to perform the query from Figure 2.11. To write queries in SQL, users typically need some formal training and a solid technical background. Fortunately, QBE tools and their drag-and-drop design features allow nonprogrammers to quickly and easily design complex queries without knowing SQL.

Application Generation and Data Administration Components

For the most part, users will be focusing on data manipulation tools to build views, reports, and queries. IT specialists primarily use the application generation and data administration components. Even though most users will probably not be using these components, it is still important that they understand what they are and the functions they support.

The ***application generation component*** includes tools for creating visually appealing and easy-to-use applications. IT specialists use application generation components to build programs for users to enter and manipulate information with

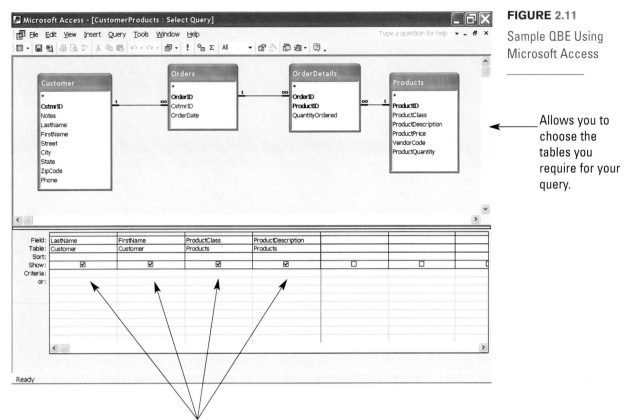

FIGURE 2.11

Sample QBE Using Microsoft Access

Allows you to choose the tables you require for your query.

This is where you define which fields you want to see for the results of your query. This query asks for the customer's last name and first name, along with the customer's corresponding product class and product description from the customer's orders.

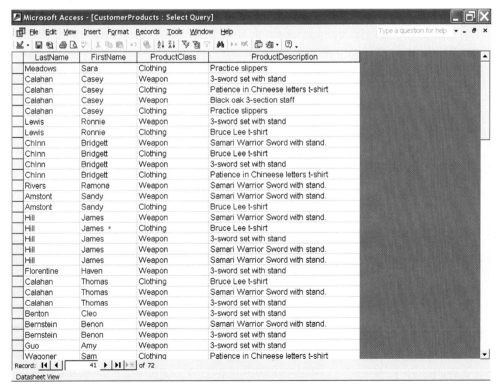

FIGURE 2.12

Results to the QBE Query in Figure 2.11

```
SELECT  Customer.LastName, Customer.FirstName,
        Products.ProductClass, Products.ProductDescription
FROM    Products
        INNER JOIN ((Customer INNER JOIN Orders ON
        (Customer.CstmrID = Orders.CstmrID) AND (Customer.CstmrID
        = Orders.CstmrID))
        INNER JOIN OrderDetails ON Orders.OrderID =
        OrderDetails.OrderID) ON Products.Product ID =
        OrderDetails.ProductID;
```

FIGURE 2.13

SQL Version of the QBE
Query in Figure 2.11

an interface specific to their application needs. Consider a manager involved in the management of an organization's supply chain. Using the application generation component, an IT specialist could build an SCM application software tool for the manager that would contain various menu options including add a supplier, order from a supplier, check the status of an order, and so on. This application would be easier and more intuitive for the manager to use on a consistent basis than requiring the manager to use views, report generators, and QBE tools.

The *data administration component* provides tools for managing the overall database environment by providing facilities for backup, recovery, security, and performance. Again, IT specialists directly interact with the data administration component. There are several strategic-level IT positions in most organizations—CIOs (chief information officers), CTOs (chief technology officers), CSOs (chief security officers), and CPOs (chief privacy officers). People in these positions oversee the use of the data administration component. For example, the chief privacy officer (CPO) is responsible for ensuring the ethical and legal use of information. Therefore, he or she would direct the use of the security features of the data administration component, implement policies and procedures concerning who has access to different types of information, and control what functions they can perform on that information (read-only, update, delete). The chief technology officer (CTO), responsible for ensuring the efficiency of IT systems, would direct the use of the backup, recovery, and performance features of the data administration component.

The focus this far has been on a single database. However, almost all organizations maintain multiple systems—for billing, order entry, order fulfillment, etc.—and hence have multiple databases, one to support each system. The number of databases in an organization can range from just a few to several hundred. Issues of redundancy and consistency become prevalent and problematic. Having multiple databases, some containing the same information, adds another layer of complexity to managing information and ensuring its quality in an organization.

INTEGRATING INFORMATION AMONG MULTIPLE DATABASES

Until the 1990s, each department in the UK's Ministry of Defense (MOD) and Army headquarters had its own systems, each system had its own database, and sharing information among the departments was difficult. Manually inputting the same information multiple times into the different systems was also time consuming and inefficient. In many cases, management could not even compile the information it required to answer questions and make decisions.

The Army solved the problem by integrating its systems, or building connections between its many databases. These integrations allow the Army's multiple systems to automatically communicate by passing information between the databases, eliminating the need for manual information entry into multiple systems because after entering the information once, the integrations sent the information immediately to all other databases. The integrations not only enable the different departments to share information, but have also dramatically increased the quality of the information. The Army can now generate reports detailing the Army's state of readiness and other vital issues, nearly impossible tasks prior to building the integrations among the separate systems.[21]

An ***integration*** allows separate systems to communicate directly with each other. Similar to the UK's Army, an organization will probably maintain multiple systems, with each system having its own database. Without integrations, an organization will (1) spend considerable time entering the same information in multiple systems and (2) suffer from the low quality and inconsistency typically embedded in redundant information. While most integrations do not completely eliminate redundant information, they can ensure the consistency of it across multiple systems.

There are two integration methods an organization can follow. The first is to create forward and backward integrations that link together processes (and their underlying databases) in the value chain. A ***forward integration*** takes information entered into a given system and sends it automatically to all downstream systems and processes. A ***backward integration*** takes information entered into a given system and sends it automatically to all upstream systems and processes.

Figure 2.14 demonstrates how this method works across the systems or processes of sales, order entry, order fulfillment, and billing. In the order entry system, for example, an employee can update the information for a customer. That information, via the integrations, would be sent upstream to the sales system and downstream to the order fulfillment and billing systems.

Ideally, an organization wants to build both forward and backward integrations, which provide the flexibility to create, update, and delete information in any of the systems. However, integrations are expensive and difficult to build and maintain and most organizations build only forward integrations (sales through billing in Figure 2.14). Building only forward integrations implies that a change in the initial system (sales) will result in changes occurring in all the other systems. Integration of information is not possible for any changes occurring outside the initial system, which again can result in inconsistent organizational information. To address this issue, organizations can enforce business rules that all systems, other than the initial system, have read-only access to the integrated information. This will require users to change information in the initial system only, which will always trigger the integration and ensure that organizational information does not get out of sync.

The second integration method builds a central repository for a particular type of information. Figure 2.15 provides an example of customer information integrated using this method across four different systems in an organization. Users can create, update, and delete customer information only in the central customer information database. As users perform these tasks on the central customer information database, integrations automatically send the new and/or updated customer information to the other systems. The other systems limit users to read-only access of the customer information stored in them. Again, this method does not eliminate redundancy—but it does ensure consistency of the information among multiple systems.

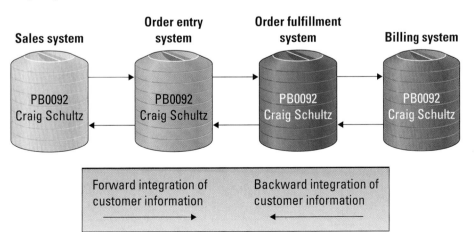

Sales system **Order entry system** **Order fulfillment system** **Billing system**

PB0092 Craig Schultz   PB0092 Craig Schultz   PB0092 Craig Schultz   PB0092 Craig Schultz

Forward integration of customer information

Backward integration of customer information

FIGURE 2.14

A Forward and Backward Customer Information Integration Example

FIGURE 2.15

Integrating Customer
Information among
Databases

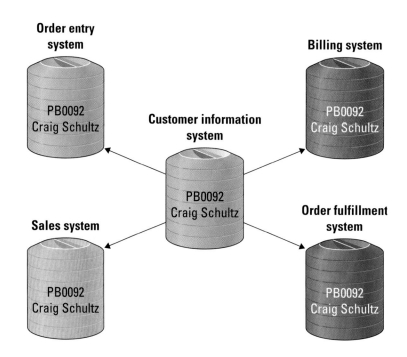

1. Identify the different types of entity classes that might be stored in Google's indexing database.

2. Explain why database technology is so important to Google's business model.

3. Explain the difference between logical and physical views and why logical views are important to Google's employees.

Chapter Seven Case: Hotcourses Increases Revenues by 60 Percent

Hotcourses, one of the hottest new e-businesses in London, offers a comprehensive online educational marketplace. One of the biggest online databases of professional, higher, and further education courses in the United Kingdom, Hotcourses receives more than 5,000 unique visits per day on its Web site. The site attracted 7,500 course providers during its first 12 months, including every university in the UK, and is growing at a rate of 600 percent or 2,000 new courses each week.

The company was launched by the UK's leading publisher of retail guides to courses and colleges in June 2000. Hotcourses enables people to find the right course, at the right price, in the location they choose to study and estimates annual revenues for 2003 between $101 million and $500 million.

The company's IT goals are to provide the scalability and performance required to deploy Web applications quickly, manage content dynamically, and support tens of thousands of users concurrently. These goals are being accomplished through Hotcourses' flexible IT infrastructure which is based upon Oracle databases. "Leveraging the internet to put our business online and extend the service on a national basis was always part of our growth strategy," said Jeremy Hunt, joint chief executive at Hotcourses. "Providing an online portal and Web-enabled fulfillment systems would extend our reach and drive demand, both from course providers and students."

Resources available through Hotcourses are free to users, who can select and book their chosen course online. The site allows colleges to upload and amend information themselves and list their courses free of charge, but a fee is payable for the facility to allow prospective students to e-mail them with further inquiries. Hotcourses also derives revenue from value-added services to course providers such as extended profiles, banners, hotlinks to Web sites, and priorities in search returns. The search engine is based on Oracle InterMedia, a core feature of Oracle database, which provides an integrated data management environment enabling users to search for, analyze, and profile information.

The business intelligence integrated with the database enables Hotcourses to assess key factors such as the number of hits and regularity of visits. "The internet and Oracle's e-business technology have transformed our business from a London-focused directory publisher to a countrywide service, advertising and selling thousands of courses from a huge range of providers," said Hunt.

The number of courses listed on Hotcourses rose from 35,000 to over 600,000 at the end of 2003. Since that time, Hotcourses has begun to extend the service by creating databases in Chinese, Japanese, and Portuguese to attract foreign students who wish to study in Britain. The company also plans to create an online, interactive directory for students and course providers, implement robust, scalable platforms to support rapid expansion, and capture key information and analyze it to provide real-time business intelligence.[22]

Questions

1. Identify the different types of entity classes and attributes potentially maintained in the Hotcourses database.
2. Describe the two different ways that employees at Hotcourses might access the information in their databases.
3. Create two questions that a manager at Hotcourses could turn into queries and run against its database to discover business intelligence.

<< PLUG-IN POINTERS

Review *Technology Plug-In* **Designing Database Applications** for a complete overview of the steps to follow while designing a small database application, including defining entity classes, identifying primary and foreign keys, and completing the first three steps of normalization (up through and including eliminating many-to-many relationships).

Review *Technology Plug-In* **Touring Access** for a comprehensive tour of Microsoft Access including how to build tables, define relationships, perform simple and advanced queries, and generate reports.

Chapter Eight: Viewing and Protecting Organizational Information

LEARNING OUTCOMES

8.1. Describe the roles and purposes of data warehouses and data marts in an organization.

8.2. Compare and contrast the multidimensional nature of data warehouses (and data marts) with the two-dimensional nature of databases.

8.3. Summarize the importance of ensuring the cleanliness of information throughout an organization.

8.4. Define the relationship between backup and recovery.

8.5. Illustrate the five characteristics of adaptable systems.

A pplebee's Neighborhood Grill & Bar posts annual sales in excess of $3.2 billion and is actively using information from its data warehouse to increase sales and cut costs. The company gathers daily information for the previous day's sales into its data warehouse from 1,500 restaurants located in 49 states and 7 countries. Understanding regional preferences, such as patrons in Texas preferring steaks more than patrons in New England, allows the company to meet its corporate strategy of being a neighborhood grill appealing to local tastes. The company has found tremendous value in its data warehouse by being able to make business decisions about customers' regional needs. The company also uses data warehouse information to perform the following:

- Base its labor budgets on actual number of guests served per hour.
- Develop promotional sale item analysis to help avoid losses from overstocking or understocking inventory.
- Determine theoretical and actual costs of food and the use of ingredients.[23]

DATA WAREHOUSE FUNDAMENTALS

A *data warehouse* is a logical collection of information—gathered from many different operational databases—that supports business analysis activities and decision-making tasks. The primary purpose of a data warehouse is to aggregate information throughout an organization into a single repository in such a way that employees can make decisions and undertake business analysis activities. Therefore, while databases store the details of all transactions (for instance, the sale of a product) and events (hiring a new employee), data warehouses store that same information but in an aggregated form more suited to supporting decision-making tasks. Aggregation, in this instance, can include totals, counts, averages, and the like. Because of this sort of aggregation, data warehouses support only analytical processing or OLAP.

The data warehouse modeled in Figure 2.16 compiles information from internal databases or transactional/operational databases and external databases through

Data Warehouse Model

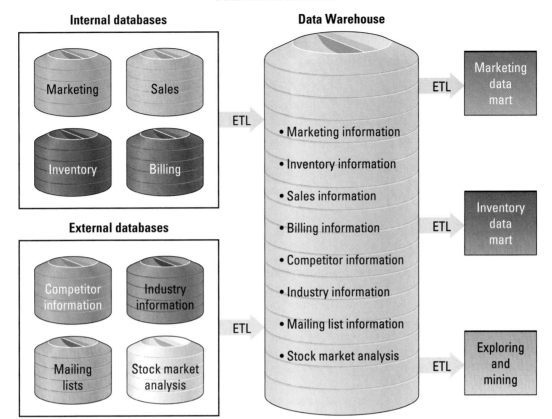

Internal databases

Marketing | Sales
Inventory | Billing

External databases

Competitor information | Industry information
Mailing lists | Stock market analysis

ETL

Data Warehouse

- Marketing information
- Inventory information
- Sales information
- Billing information
- Competitor information
- Industry information
- Mailing list information
- Stock market analysis

ETL → Marketing data mart

ETL → Inventory data mart

ETL → Exploring and mining

FIGURE 2.16

Model of a Typical Data Warehouse

extraction, transformation, and loading (ETL), which is a process that extracts information from internal and external databases, transforms the information using a common set of enterprise definitions, and loads the information into a data warehouse. The data warehouse then sends subsets of the information to data marts. A *data mart* contains a subset of data warehouse information. To distinguish between data warehouses and data marts, think of data warehouses as having a more organizational focus and data marts having focused information subsets particular to the needs of a given business unit such as finance or production and operations.

Lands' End created an organizationwide data warehouse so all its employees could access organizational information. Lands' End soon found out that there could be "too much of a good thing" because many of its employees would not use the data warehouse because it was simply too big, too complicated, and had too much irrelevant information. Lands' End knew there was valuable information in its data warehouse and it had to find a way for its employees to easily access the information. Data marts were the perfect solution to the company's information overload problem. Once the employees began using the data marts, they were ecstatic at the wealth of information. Data marts were a huge success for Lands' End.[24]

Multidimensional Analysis and Data Mining

A relational database contains information in a series of two-dimensional tables. In a data warehouse and data mart, information is multidimensional, meaning it contains layers of columns and rows. For this reason, most data warehouses and data marts are *multidimensional databases*. A *dimension* is a particular attribute of information. Each layer in a data warehouse or data mart represents information according to an additional dimension. A *cube* is the common term for the representation of multidimensional information. Figure 2.17 displays a cube (cube *a*) that represents store information (the layers), product information (the rows), and promotion information (the columns).

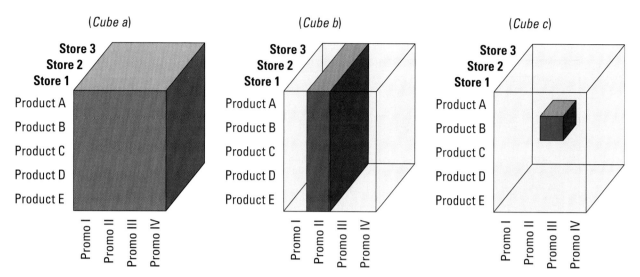

FIGURE 2.17

A Cube of Information
for Performing a
Multidimensional
Analysis on Three
Different Stores, for
Five Different Products,
and Four Different
Promotions

Once a cube of information is created, users can begin to slide-and-dice the cube to drill down into the information. The second cube (cube *b*) in Figure 2.17 displays a slice representing promotion II information for all products, at all stores. The third cube (cube *c*) in Figure 2.17 displays only information for promotion III, product B, at store 2. By using multidimensional analysis, users can analyze information in a number of different ways and with any number of different dimensions. For example, users might want to add dimensions of information to a current analysis including product category, region, and even forecasted versus actual weather. The true value of a data warehouse is its ability to provide multidimensional analysis that allows users to gain insights into their information.

Data warehouses and data marts are ideal for off-loading some of the querying against a database. For example, querying a database to obtain an average of sales for product B at store 2 while promotion III is under way might create a considerable processing burden for a database, essentially slowing down the time it takes another person to enter a new sale into the same database. If an organization performs numerous queries against a database (or multiple databases), aggregating that information into a data warehouse could be beneficial.

Data mining is the process of analyzing data to extract information not offered by the raw data alone. For example, Ruf Strategic Solutions helps organizations employ statistical approaches within a large data warehouse to identify customer segments that display common traits. Marketers can then target these segments with specially designed products and promotions.[25]

Data mining can also begin at a summary information level (coarse granularity) and progress through increasing levels of detail (drilling down), or the reverse (drilling up). To perform data mining, users need data-mining tools. ***Data-mining tools*** use a variety of techniques to find patterns and relationships in large volumes of information and infer rules from them that predict future behavior and guide decision making. Data-mining tools for data warehouses and data marts include query tools, reporting tools, multidimensional analysis tools, statistical tools, and intelligent agents.

Sega of America, one of the largest publishers of video games, uses a data warehouse and statistical tools to distribute its advertising budget of more than $50 million a year. With its data warehouse, product line specialists and marketing strategists "drill" into trends of each retail store chain. Their goal is to find buying trends that help them determine which advertising strategies are working best and how to reallocate advertising resources by media, territory, and time.[26]

Information Cleansing or Scrubbing

It should come as no surprise that maintaining high-quality information in a data warehouse or data mart is extremely important. The Data Warehousing Institute estimates that low-quality information costs U.S. businesses $600 billion annually. That number may seem high, but it is not. If an organization is using a data warehouse or data mart to allocate dollars across advertising strategies (such as in the case of Sega of America), low-quality information will definitely have a negative impact on its ability to make the right decision.[27]

To increase the quality of organizational information and thus the effectiveness of decision making, businesses must formulate a strategy to keep information clean. This is the concept of information cleansing or scrubbing. *Information cleansing or scrubbing* is a process that weeds out and fixes or discards inconsistent, incorrect, or incomplete information.

Specialized software tools exist that use sophisticated algorithms to parse, standardize, correct, match, and consolidate data warehouse information. This is vitally important because data warehouses often contain information from several different databases, some of which can be external to the organization. In a data warehouse, information cleansing occurs first during the ETL process and second on the information once it is in the data warehouse. Companies can choose information cleansing software from several different vendors including Oracle, PeopleSoft, SAS, Ascential Software, and Group 1 Software. Ideally, scrubbed information is error free and consistent.

Dr Pepper/Seven Up, Inc., was able to integrate its myriad databases in a data warehouse (and subsequently data marts) in less than two months, giving the company access to consolidated, clean information. Approximately 600 people in the company regularly use the data marts to analyze and track beverage sales across multiple dimensions, including various distribution routes such as bottle/can sales, fountain food-service sales, premier distributor sales, and chain and national accounts. The company is now performing in-depth analysis of up-to-date sales information that is clean and error free.[28]

KEEPING BUSINESS OPERATIONS RUNNING SMOOTHLY

A 66-hour failure of an FBI database that performed background checks on gun buyers was long enough to allow criminals to buy guns. The database failed at 1:00 P.M. on a Thursday and restoration did not take place until Sunday at 7:30 A.M. The FBI must complete a gun check within three days; if it fails to do so, a merchant is free to go ahead with the sale. During this outage, any gun checks that were already in progress were not finished, allowing merchants to complete those gun sales at their own discretion.[29]

Storage Devices

Organizations must protect themselves from system failures and crashes. There are three primary steps an organization can take to protect its systems so they operate as expected. First, develop an appropriate backup and recovery strategy that fits organizational needs. Second, create a disaster recovery plan to help the business stay on track if a disaster ever strikes. Third, build adaptable business systems that can grow and change as the business transforms.

BACKUP AND RECOVERY STRATEGY

Millions of dollars are lost every year because of system crashes and failures or nonexistent backup and recovery strategies. One way to minimize the damage of a system crash or failure is to have a backup and recovery strategy in place. A *backup* is an exact copy of a system's information. *Recovery* is the ability to get a system up and running in the event of a system crash or failure and includes restoring the information backup. There are many different types of backup and recovery media available including redundant storage servers, tapes, disks, and even CDs and DVDs. All the different types of backup and recovery media are reliable with the primary differences being the speed of the backup and recovery and the associated costs.

7Eleven Taiwan supports a chain of more than 4,000 franchise locations and it downloads and uploads backup and recovery information from its central location to all its chain locations daily. The company implemented a new technology solution by Digital Fountain that could quickly and reliably download and upload backup and recovery information to all its store locations. In addition, when a connection fails during the download or upload process, the technology automatically resumes the download without having to start over, saving valuable time.[30]

Organizations should choose a backup and recovery strategy that is in line with its corporate goals. For example, if the organization deals with large volumes of critical information, it will require daily backups, perhaps even hourly backups, to redundant storage servers. If the organization deals with small amounts of noncritical information, then it might require only weekly backups to tapes, CDs, or DVDs. Deciding how often to back up computer information and what media to use is a critical business decision. If an organization decides to back up on a weekly basis then it is taking the risk that, if a total system crash occurs, it could lose an entire week's worth of work. If this risk is acceptable, then a weekly backup strategy will work. If this risk is unacceptable, then the organization needs to move to a daily backup strategy. Some organizations find the risk of losing an entire day's worth of work too high and move to an hourly backup strategy.

DISASTER RECOVERY PLAN

Disasters such as power outages, floods, and even harmful hacking strike businesses every day. Organizations must develop a disaster recovery plan to prepare for such occurrences. A ***disaster recovery plan*** is a detailed process for recovering information or an IT system in the event of a catastrophic disaster such as a fire or flood.

A comprehensive disaster recovery plan takes into consideration the location of the backup information. Many organizations choose to store backup information in an off-site storage facility. StorageTek is a company that specializes in providing off-site information storage and disaster recovery solutions. A comprehensive disaster recovery plan also foresees the possibility that not only the computer equipment but also the building where employees work may be destroyed. A ***hot site*** is a separate and fully equipped facility where the company can move immediately after a disaster and resume business. A ***cold site*** is a separate facility that does not have any computer equipment, but is a place where employees can move after the disaster.

A ***disaster recovery cost curve*** charts (1) the cost to the organization of the unavailability of information and technology and (2) the cost to the organization of recovering from a disaster over time. Figure 2.18 displays a disaster recovery cost curve and shows that where the two lines intersect is the best recovery plan in terms of cost and time. Creating an organization's disaster recovery cost curve is no small task. It must take into account the cost of losing information and technology within each department or functional area, and it must consider the cost of losing information and technology across the whole enterprise. During the first few hours of a disaster, those costs will be low but become increasingly higher over time. With

FIGURE 2.18

Disaster Recovery Cost Curve

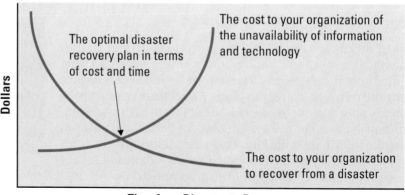

those costs in hand, an organization must then determine the costs of recovery. Recovery during the first few hours of a disaster is exceedingly high and then diminishes over time.

BUILDING ADAPTABLE SYSTEMS

As an organization changes, its systems must be able to change to support its operations. For example, if an organization grows by 50 percent in a single year, its systems must be able to handle a 50 percent growth rate. Systems that cannot adapt to organizational changes can severely hinder the organization's ability to operate. The future of an organization might depend on its ability to meet its partners and customers on their terms, at their pace, any time of the day, in any geographic location. When reviewing or developing systems, use the following five characteristics to ensure that the systems are adaptable: (1) flexibility, (2) scalability, (3) reliability, (4) availability, (5) performance.

Flexibility

Organizations must watch today's business, as well as tomorrow's, when designing and building systems. Systems must be *flexible* enough to meet all types of business changes. For example, when designing a system it might include the ability to handle multiple currencies and languages, even though the company is not currently performing business in other countries. When the company starts growing and performing business in multiple countries, the systems will already have the flexibility to handle multiple currencies and languages. If the company failed to recognize that its business would someday be global, it would need to redesign all its systems to handle multiple currencies and languages, not an easy task once the systems are up and running.

Scalability

Estimating organizational growth is a challenging task. Growth can occur in a number of different forms including more customers and product lines and expanding into new markets. **Scalability** refers to how well a system can adapt to increased demands. A number of factors can create organizational growth including market, industry, and economywide factors. If an organization grows faster than anticipated, it might experience all types of performance degradations, ranging from running out of disk space to a slowdown in transaction speeds. Anticipating expected—and unexpected—growth is key to building scalable systems that can support that growth.

MSNBC's Web site typically received moderate traffic. On September 11, 2001, the company's Web site was inundated with more than 91 million page views as its customers were trying to find out information about the terrorist attacks. Fortunately, MSNBC had anticipated this type of unexpected growth and built adaptable systems accordingly, allowing it to handle the increased page view requests.[31]

Reliability

Reliability ensures all systems are functioning correctly and providing accurate information. Reliability, in this instance, is another term for accuracy when discussing the correctness of systems within the context of efficiency IT metrics. Inaccurate information processing occurs for many reasons, from the incorrect entry of information to information corruption. Whatever the reason, if information is not reliable, the organization is at risk when making decisions based on the information.

Availability

Availability (another efficiency IT metric) addresses when systems can be accessed by employees, customers, and partners. Some companies have systems available $24 \times 7 \times 365$ to support business operations and global customer and employee needs. With the emergence of the Web, companies expect systems to operate $24 \times 7 \times 365$. A customer that finds that a Web site closes at 9:00 P.M. is not going to be a customer for long.

Systems, however, must come down for maintenance, upgrades, and fixes. One of the challenges facing organizations is determining when to schedule system downtime if the system is expected to operate continually. Exacerbating the negative impact of scheduled system downtime is the global nature of business. Scheduling maintenance during the evening might seem like a great idea—but the evening in one city is the morning somewhere else in the world, and global employees may not be able to perform their jobs if the system is down (see Figure 2.19). Many organizations overcome this problem by having redundant systems, allowing the organization to take one system down by switching over to a redundant, or duplicate, system.

Performance

Performance measures how quickly a system performs a certain process or transaction in terms of efficiency IT metrics of both speed and throughput. Not having enough performance capacity can have a devastating, negative impact on a business. A customer will wait only a few seconds for a Web site to return a request before giving up and moving on to another Web site. To ensure adaptable systems performance, capacity planning helps an organization determine future IT infrastructure requirements for new equipment and additional network capacity. It is cheaper for an organization to design and implement an IT infrastructure that envisions performance capacity growth than to update all the equipment after the system is already operational.

FIGURE 2.19

Time Zone Differences
Around the World

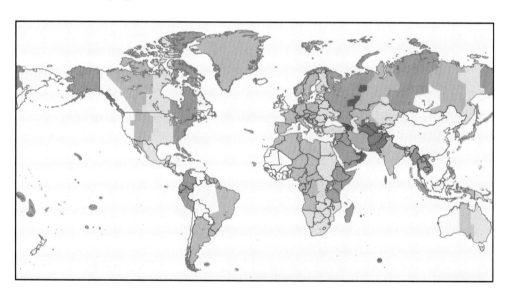

OPENING CASE STUDY QUESTIONS

1. Determine how Google could use a data warehouse to improve its business operations.

2. Explain why Google would need to scrub and cleanse the information in its data warehouse.

3. Identify a data mart that Google's marketing and sales department might use to track and analyze its AdWords revenue.

4. Describe the fundamentals of a disaster recovery plan along with a recommendation for a plan for Google.

5. Describe why availability and scalability are critical to Google's business operations.

Chapter Eight Case: Connecting Austria

For years, Austria has been the fastest growing mobile communications market in Europe. Now almost 6 million of the 8 million people in Austria have mobile phones, and T-Mobile Austria serves approximately 36 percent of these users. As Austria's mobile market boom ends, T-Mobile is starting to focus on building stronger relationships with its current customers instead of using low-priced introductory rate plans to attract new customers.

T-Mobile Austria depends on detailed customer information and current marketing and sales campaigns to stay ahead of its competitors. To help implement its new CRM strategies, the company built a multi-terabyte enterprise data warehouse, which quickly became one of the largest and most successful data warehouse implementations in Austria. The data warehouse integrates information from all the critical operational systems, including raw data from telecommunication switches, billing records, customer care applications, financial data, and several other applications. The company runs over 40 different applications off the data warehouse including subscriber and user reporting, CRM reporting, campaign management analysis, churn analysis, fraud analysis, and risk scoring analysis.

Today, approximately two terabytes of information are available to support analyses, reports, and data-mining applications, and T-Mobile adds more than 10 gigabytes of information on a daily basis to its data warehouse. The company also supports advanced analytical analysis using several different multidimensional analysis tools from Oracle, Cognos, MIS, SAS, Quadstone, and Prime. The data warehouse currently stores more than 90 OLAP cubes based on 600 database tables.

T-Mobile Austria attributes a large part of its business success to its data warehouse and the high-quality and real-time business information it provides, keeping it ahead of its competitors.[32,33]

Questions

1. Explain how T-Mobile Austria is using information from its data warehouse to remain successful and competitive in a saturated market.
2. Identify why information cleansing and scrubbing is critical to T-Mobile Austria's data warehouse success.
3. Assess the potential impacts on T-Mobile Austria's business if it failed to create a disaster recovery plan.
4. Review the five characteristics of adaptable systems and rank them in order of importance to T-Mobile Austria's business.

<< PLUG-IN POINTER

Review *Technology Plug-In* **Decision-Analysis Tools in Excel** which contains step-by-step instructions for using numerous Excel features, including PivotTables, PivotCharts, Scenario Manager, Goal Seek, and Solver.

The five common characteristics of high-quality information include accuracy, completeness, consistency, uniqueness, and timeliness. The costs to an organization of having low-quality information can be enormous and could result in revenue losses and ultimately business failure. Databases maintain information about various types of objects, events, people, and places and help to alleviate many of the problems associated with low-quality information such as redundancy, integrity, and security.

A data warehouse is a logical collection of information—gathered from many different operational databases—that supports business analysis activities and decision-making tasks. Data marts contain a subset of data warehouse information. Organizations gain tremendous insight into their business by mining the information contained in data warehouses and data marts.

Understanding the value of information is key to business success. Employees must be able to optimally access and analyze organizational information. The more knowledge employees have concerning how the organization stores, maintains, provides access to, and protects information the better prepared they will be when they need to use that information to make critical business decisions.

★ KEY TERMS

Analytical information, 56
Application generation
    component, 68
Attribute, 62
Backup, 77
Backward integration, 71
Business-critical integrity
    constraint, 65
Cold site, 78
Cube, 75
Data administration
    component, 70
Database, 61
Database management system
    (DBMS), 66
Data definition component, 67
Data dictionary, 67
Data manipulation
    component, 67
Data mart, 75

Data mining, 76
Data-mining tool, 76
Data warehouse, 74
Disaster recovery cost
    curve, 78
Disaster recovery plan, 78
Entity, 62
Entity class, 62
Extraction, transformation, and
    loading (ETL), 75
Foreign key, 62
Forward integration, 71
Hierarchical database, 61
Hot site, 78
Information cleansing or
    scrubbing, 77
Information integrity, 64
Integration, 71
Integrity constraint, 64
Logical view, 62

Network database, 61
Operational integrity
    constraint, 64
Performance, 64
Physical view, 62
Primary key, 62
Query-by-example (QBE)
    tool, 68
Real-time information, 56
Real-time system, 56
Recovery, 77
Redundancy, 64
Relational database model, 61
Report generator, 67
Scalability, 64
Structured query language
    (SQL), 68
Transactional information, 55
View, 67

★ UNIT CLOSING CASE ONE

HARRAH'S—GAMBLING BIG ON TECHNOLOGY

The large investment made by Harrah's Entertainment Inc. in its information technology strategy has been tremendously successful. The results of Harrah's investment include:

- 10 percent annual increase in customer visits.
- 33 percent increase in gross market revenue.

- Yearly profits of over $208 million.
- Highest three-year ROI (return on investment) in the industry.
- A network that links over 42,000 gaming machines in 26 casinos across 12 states.
- Rated #6 of the 100 best places to work in IT for 2003 by ComputerWorld magazine.
- Recipient of 2000 Leadership in Data Warehousing Award from the Data Warehousing Institute (TDWI), the premier association for data warehousing.

The casino industry is highly competitive (rivalry among existing competitors is fierce). Bill Harrah was a man ahead of his time when he opened his first bingo parlor in 1937 with the commitment of getting to know each one of his customers. In 1984, Phil Satre, president and CEO of Harrah's, continued the late Bill Harrah's commitment to customers. In search of its competitive advantage, Harrah's invested in an enterprisewide technology infrastructure to maintain Bill Harrah's original conviction: "Serve your customers well and they will be loyal."

Harrah's Commitment to Customers

Harrah's recently implemented its patented Total Rewards™ program to help build strong relationships with its customers. The program rewards customers for their loyalty by tracking their gaming habits across its 26 properties and currently maintains information on over 19 million customers, information which the company uses to analyze, predict, and maximize each customer's value.

One of the major reasons for the company's success is Harrah's implementation of a service-oriented strategy. Total Rewards™ allows Harrah's to give every single customer the appropriate amount of personal attention, whether it's leaving sweets in the hotel room or offering free meals. Total Rewards™ works by providing each customer with an account and a corresponding card that the player swipes each time he or she plays a casino game. The program collects information on the amount of time the customers gamble, their total winnings and losses, and their betting strategies. Customers earn points based on the amount of time they spend gambling, which they can then exchange for comps such as free dinners, hotel rooms, tickets to shows, and even cash.

Total Rewards™ helps employees determine which level of service to provide each customer. When a customer makes a reservation at Harrah's, the service representative taking the call can view the customer's detailed information including the customer's loyalty level, games typically played, past winnings and losses, and potential net worth. If the service representative notices that the customer has a Diamond loyalty level, for example, the service representative knows that customer should never have to wait in line and always receive free upgrades to the most expensive rooms.

"Almost everything we do in marketing and decision making is influenced by technology," says Gary Loveman, Harrah's chief operating officer. "The prevailing wisdom in this business is that the attractiveness of property drives customers. Our approach is different. We stimulate demand by knowing our customers. For example, if one of our customers always vacations at Harrah's in April, they will receive a promotion in February redeemable for a free weekend in April."

Gaining Business Intelligence with a Data Warehouse

Over 90 million customers visit Harrah's each year and tracking a customer base larger than the population of Australia is a challenging task. To tackle this challenge Harrah's began developing a system called WINet (Winner's Information Network). WINet links all Harrah's properties together allowing it to collect and share customer information on an enterprisewide basis. WINet collects customer information from all the company transactions, game machines, and hotel management and reservations systems and places the information in a central data warehouse. Information in the data warehouse includes both customer and gaming information recorded in hourly increments. The marketing department uses the data warehouse to analyze customer information for patterns and insights, which allows it to create individualized marketing programs for each customer based on spending habits. Most important, the data warehouse allows the company to make business decisions based on information, not intuition.

Casinos traditionally treat customers as though they belong to a single property, typically the place the customer most frequently visits. Harrah's was the first casino to realize the potential of rewarding customers for visiting more than one property. Today, Harrah's has found that customers who visit more than one of its properties represent the fastest growing revenue segment. In the first two years of the Total Rewards™ program, the company received a $100 million increase in revenue from customers who gambled at more than one casino.

Harrah's also uses business intelligence to determine gaming machine performance. Using the data warehouse, Harrah's examines the performance and cost structure of each individual gaming machine. The company can quickly identify games that do not deliver optimal operational performance and can make a decision to move or replace the games. The capability to assess the performance of each individual slot machine has provided Harrah's with savings in the tens of millions of dollars. CIO Tim Stanley stated, "As we leverage more data from our data warehouse and increase the use and sophistication of our decision science analytical tools, we expect to have many new ways to improve customer loyalty and satisfaction, drive greater revenues, and decrease our costs as part of our ongoing focus on achieving sustainable profitability and success."

Information Security and Privacy

Some customers have concerns about Harrah's information collection strategy since they want to keep their gambling information private. The good news for these customers is that casinos are actually required to be more mindful of privacy concerns than most companies. For example, casinos cannot send marketing material to any underage persons. To adhere to the strict government regulations, casinos must ensure that the correct information security and restrictions are in place. Many other companies actually make a great deal of money by selling customer information. Harrah's will not be joining in this trend since its customer information is one of its primary competitive advantages.

The Future of Harrah's

Harrah's current systems support approximately $140,000 in revenue per hour (that's almost $25 million weekly). In the future, Harrah's hopes to become device independent by allowing employees to access the company's data warehouse via PDAs, hand-held computers, and even cell phones. "Managing relationships with customers is incredibly important to the health of our business," says Stanley. "We will apply whatever technology we can to do that."[34,35,36,37,38,39,40]

Questions

1. Identify the effects low-quality information might have on Harrah's service-oriented business strategy.
2. Summarize how Harrah's uses database technologies to implement its service-oriented strategy.
3. Harrah's was one of the first casino companies to find value in offering rewards to customers who visit multiple Harrah's locations. Describe the effects on the company if it did not build any integrations among the databases located at each of its casinos.
4. Estimate the potential impact to Harrah's business if there is a security breach in its customer information.

5. Explain the business ramifications if Harrah's fails to implement a backup policy.
6. Identify three different types of data marts Harrah's might want to build to help it analyze its operational performance.
7. Predict what might occur if Harrah's fails to clean or scrub its information prior to loading it into its data warehouse.

EVALUATING SWISS ARMY'S SUCCESS

Swiss Army Brands, Inc., is recognized throughout the world as the importer, distributor, and manufacturer of premium consumer products, including the Swiss Army Brand watches and Victorinox Original Swiss Army knives. Along with these signature products, the 65-year-old company distributes many other premier consumer products under three brands: Swiss Army, Victorinox, and R. H. Forschner. Swiss Army Brands has operations in the United States, Canada, and Europe and customers, sales teams, and distributors around the world.

Originally, the company had five separate product departments, each with its own legacy system, and Swiss Army Brands was seeking an integrated software solution. The company implemented a PeopleSoft solution to enhance the efficiency of the inventory and shipping processes, while also allowing easy integration of new products in the future. The business drivers for the new system included:

- Unification of multiple divisions
- Flexibility to accommodate changing processes and products
- Streamlined order processing

The results of the new system include:

- Closing time cut by approximately 80 percent
- Order process expedited through real-time information
- Manual effort reduced by multicurrency capability

"We turned to PeopleSoft first and foremost to provide a system that could give us a single view into our inventory, and also one that could accommodate new products and interfaces to other systems. In short, we expected both reliability and flexibility. With the system in place, we know what we have, where it is, and how fast we can get it to customers. It just makes life a lot easier," says Doug Imri, director of Materials Management. "One of the biggest benefits of PeopleSoft for us has been the accuracy and reliability of the data—a single view into all our inventory. Sales orders are applied in real-time to available stock, which improves customer service as well as sales rep performance."[41]

Questions

1. Why is accurate and reliable data considered a system benefit for Swiss Army?
2. How would unintegrated information affect Swiss Army's ability to operate its business?
3. What types of data marts might Swiss Army choose to gain business intelligence?
4. Explain the disaster recovery cost curve and the optimal place for Swiss Army to operate on it.
5. Assess the importance of backup and recovery strategies for Swiss Army.

1. Improving Information Quality

HangUps Corporation designs and distributes closet organization structures. The company operates five different systems including order entry, sales, inventory management, shipping, and billing. The company has severe information quality issues including missing, inaccurate, redundant, and incomplete information. The company wants to implement a data warehouse containing information from the five different systems to help maintain a single customer view, drive business decisions, and perform multidimensional analysis. Identify how the organization can improve its information quality when it begins designing and building its data warehouse.

2. Mining the Data Warehouse

Janet Smith is a senior buyer for a large wholesaler that sells different types of arts and crafts to greeting card stores such as Hallmark. Janet's latest marketing strategy is to send all of her customers a new line of hand-made picture frames from Russia. All of Janet's information supports her decision for the new line. Her analysis predicts that the frames should sell an average of 10 to 15 per store, per day. Janet is excited about the new line and is positive it will be a success.

One month later Janet learns that the frames are selling 50 percent below expectations and averaging between 5 to 8 frames sold daily in each store. Janet decides to access the company's data warehouse information to determine why sales are below expectations. Identify several different dimensions of information that Janet will want to analyze to help her decide what is causing the problems with the picture frame sales.

3. Determining Information Quality Issues

Real People is a magazine geared toward working individuals that provides articles and advice on everything from car maintenance to family planning. *Real People* is currently experiencing problems with its magazine distribution list. Over 30 percent of the magazines mailed are returned because of incorrect address information and each month it receives numerous calls from angry customers complaining that they have not yet received their magazines. Below is a sample of *Real People*'s customer information. Create a report detailing all of the issues with the information, potential causes of the information issues, and solutions the company can follow to correct the situation.

ID	First Name	Middle Initial	Last Name	Street	City	State	Zip Code
433	M	J	Jones	13 Denver	Denver	CO	87654
434	Margaret	J	Jones	13 First Ave.	Denver	CO	87654
434	Brian	F	Hoover	Lake Ave.	Columbus	OH	87654
435	Nick	H	Schweitzer	65 Apple Lane	San Francisco	OH	65664
436	Richard	A		567 55th St.	New York	CA	98763
437	Alana	B	Smith	121 Tenny Dr.	Buffalo	NY	142234
438	Trevor	D	Darrian	90 Fresrdestil	Dallas	TX	74532

4. Disaster Recovery Planning

You are the new senior analyst in the IT department at Beltz, a large snack food manufacturing company. The company is located on the beautiful shoreline in Charleston, North Carolina. The company's location is one of its best and also worst features. The weather and surroundings are beautiful—but the threat of hurricanes, tornados, and other natural disasters is high. Compile a disaster recovery plan that will minimize any risks involved with a natural disaster.

5. **Comparing Backup and Recovery Systems**

Research the Internet to find three different vendors of backup and recovery systems. Compare and contrast the three different systems and determine which one you would recommend if you were installing a backup and recovery system for a medium-sized business with 3,500 employees that maintains information on the stock market. Compile your findings in a presentation that you can give to your class that details the three systems and their strengths and weaknesses, along with your recommendation.

MAKING COLLABORATIVE DECISIONS

1. **Information Timeliness**

Information timeliness is a major consideration for all organizations. Organizations need to decide the frequency of backups and the frequency of updates to a data warehouse. In a team, describe the timeliness requirements for backups and updates to a data warehouse for

- Weather tracking systems
- Car dealership inventories
- Vehicle tire sales forecasts
- Interest rates
- Restaurant inventories
- Grocery store inventories

2. **Entities and Attributes**

Martex Inc. is a manufacturer of athletic equipment and its primary lines of business include running, tennis, golf, swimming, basketball, and aerobics equipment. Martex currently supplies four primary vendors including Sam's Sports, Total Effort, The Underline, and Maximum Workout. Martex wants to build a database to help it organize its products. In a group, identify the different types of entity classes and the related attributes that Martex will want to consider when designing the database.

3. **Integrating Information**

You are currently working for the Public Transportation Department of Chatfield. The department controls all forms of public transportation including buses, subways, and trains. Each department has about 300 employees and maintains its own accounting, inventory, purchasing, and human resource systems. Generating reports across departments is a difficult task and usually involves gathering and correlating the information from the many different systems. It typically takes about two weeks to generate the quarterly balance sheets and profit and loss statements. Your team has been asked to compile a report recommending what the Public Transportation Department of Chatfield can do to alleviate its information and system issues. Be sure that your report addresses the various reasons departmental reports are presently difficult to obtain as well as how you plan to solve this problem.

4. Multidimensional Analysis

You are currently working on a marketing team for a large corporation that sells jewelry around the world. Your boss has asked you to look at the following dimensions of information to determine which ones you want in your data mart for performing sales and market analysis. As a team, categorize the different dimensions ranking them from 1 to 5. 1 indicates that the dimension offers the highest value and must be in your data mart and 5 indicates that the dimension offers the lowest value and does not need to be in your data mart.

Dimension	Value (1–5)	Dimension	Value (1–5)
Product number		Season	
Store location		Promotion	
Customer net worth		Payment method	
Number of sales personnel		Commission policy	
Customer eating habits		Manufacturer	
Store hours		Traffic report	
Sales person ID		Customer language	
Product style		Weather	
Order date		Customer gender	
Product quantity		Local tax information	
Ship date		Local cultural demographics	
Current interest rate		Stock market closing	
Product cost		Customer religious affiliation	
Customer's political affiliation		Reason for purchase	
Local market analysis		Employee dress code policy	
Order time		Customer age	
Customer spending habits		Employee vacation policy	
Product price		Employee benefits	
Exchange rates		Current tariff information	
Product gross margin			

UNIT 3

Enhancing Business Decisions

Harley-Davidson Motorcycles

Revving Up Sales at Harley-Davidson

Harley-Davidson produces 290,000 motorcycles and generates over $4 billion in net revenues yearly. There is a mystique associated with a Harley-Davidson motorcycle. No other motorcycle in the world has the look, feel, and sound of a Harley-Davidson and many people consider it a two-wheeled piece of art. The company actually finds itself in the position that demand for its motorcycles outweighs its supply. Some models have up to a two-year wait list. Harley-Davidson has won a number of awards including:

- Rated second in *ComputerWorld*'s Top 100 Best Places to Work in IT in 2003.
- Rated 51st in *Fortune*'s 100 Best Companies to Work For in 2003.
- Rated first in *Fortune*'s 5 Most Admired Companies in the motor vehicles industry.
- Rated first in the Top 10 Sincerest Corporations by the *Harris Interactive Report*.
- Rated second in the Top 10 Overall Corporations by the *Harris Interactive Report*.

Harley-Davidson's Focus on Technology

Harley-Davidson's commitment to technology is paying off and in 2003 it decreased production costs and inventories by $40 million as a direct result of using technology to increase production capacity. The company's technology budget of $50 million is more than 2 percent of its revenue, which is far above the manufacturing industry average. More than 50 percent of this budget is devoted to developing new technology strategies.

Harley-Davidson focuses on implementing e-business strategies to strengthen its market share and increase customer satisfaction. Over 80 projects were in development in 2003 and the majority of the new projects focused on sharing information, gaining business intelligence, and enhancing decision making.

Talon, Harley-Davidson's proprietary dealer management system, is one of its most successful technology initiatives. Talon handles inventory, vehicle registration, warranties, and point-of-sale transactions for all Harley-Davidson dealerships. The system performs numerous time-saving tasks such as checking dealer inventory, automatically generating parts orders, and allowing the company to review and analyze information across its global organization. Talon gives Harley-Davidson managers a 360-degree view into enterprisewide information that supports strategic goal setting and decision making throughout all levels of the organization.

Building Supplier Relationships

Harley-Davidson invests time, energy, and resources into continually improving its company-to-company strategic business initiatives such as supply chain management. The company understands and values the importance of building strong relationships with its suppliers. To develop these important relationships the company deployed Manugistics, a supply chain management (SCM) system that allows it to do business with suppliers in a collaborative, Web-based environment. The company plans to use the SCM software to better manage its flow of materials and improve collaboration activities with its key suppliers.

Building Customer Relationships

Each time a customer reaches out to the company, Harley-Davidson has an opportunity to build a trusting relationship with that particular customer. Harley-Davidson realizes that it takes more than just building and selling motorcycles to fulfill the dreams of its customers. For this reason, the company strives to deliver unforgettable experiences along with its top quality products.

Harley-Davidson sells over $500 million worth of parts and accessories to its loyal followers. Ken Ostermann, Harley-Davidson's manager of Electronic Commerce and Communications, decided that the company could increase these sales if it could offer the products online. The dilemma facing Ostermann's online strategy was that selling jackets, saddlebags, and T-shirts directly to consumers would bypass Harley-Davidson's 650 dealers, who depend on the high-margin accessories to fuel their businesses' profits. Ostermann's solution was to build an online store, Harley-Davidson.com, which prompts customers to select a participating Harley-Davidson dealership prior to placing any online orders. The selected dealership is then responsible for fulfilling the order. This strategy has helped ensure that the dealers remain the focal point of customers' buying experiences.

To guarantee that each and every customer has a highly satisfying online buying experience the company asks the dealers to agree to a number of standards including:

- Checking online orders twice daily
- Shipping online orders within 24 hours
- Responding to customer inquiries within 24 hours

The company still monitors online customer metrics such as time taken to process orders, number of returned orders, and number of incorrect orders, ensuring that Harley-Davidson delivers on its message of prompt, excellent service consistently to all its loyal customers. The company currently receives over 1 million visitors a month to its online store. Customer satisfaction scores for the Web site have moved from the extremely satisfied level to the exceptional level over the past year.

Another of Harley-Davidson's customer-centric strategies is its Harley's Owners Group (HOG), established in 1983. HOG is the largest factory-sponsored motorcycle club in the world with more than 600,000 members. HOG offers a wide array of events, rides, and benefits to its members. HOG is one of the key drivers helping to build a strong sense of community among Harley-Davidson owners. Harley-Davidson has achieved the task of building a customer following that is extremely loyal, a difficult task to accomplish in any industry.

Harley-Davidson's Corporate Culture

Harley-Davidson employees are the engine behind its outstanding performance and the foundation of the company's overall success. Harley-Davidson believes in a strong sense of corporate ethics and values and the company's top five core values serve as a framework for the entire corporation:

1. Tell the truth
2. Be fair
3. Keep your promises
4. Respect the individual
5. Encourage intellectual curiosity

The company credits its core values as the primary reason it won the two prestigious awards from the *Harris Interactive Report,* one of the most respected consumer reviews for corporate sincerity, ethics, and standards. Sticking to strong ethics and values is and will continue to be a top priority for the company and its employees.

To enhance its enterprise further Harley-Davidson plans to keep taking advantage of new technologies and strategies including a Web-based approach to accessing information and an enterprisewide system to consolidate procurement at its eight U.S. facilities.[1,2,3,4,5,6,7]

INTRODUCTION

Decision making and problem solving in today's electronic world encompass large-scale, opportunity-oriented, strategically focused solutions. The traditional "cookbook" approach to decisions simply will not work in the e-business world. Decision-making and problem-solving abilities are now the most sought-after traits in up-and-coming executives, according to a recent survey of 1,000 executives by Caliper Associates, as reported in *The Wall Street Journal.* To put it mildly, decision makers and problem solvers have limitless career potential.[8]

E-business is the conducting of business on the Internet, not only buying and selling, but also serving customers and collaborating with business partners. (Unit 4 discusses e-business in detail.) With the fast growth of information technology and the accelerated use of the Internet, e-business is quickly becoming standard. This unit focuses on technology to help make decisions, solve problems, and find new innovative opportunities. The unit highlights how to bring people together with the best IT processes and tools in complete, flexible solutions that can seize business opportunities (see Figure 3.1). The chapters in Unit 3 are:

- **Chapter Nine**—Enabling the Organization—Decision Making
- **Chapter Ten**—Extending the Organization—Supply Chain Management
- **Chapter Eleven**—Building a Customer-centric Organization—Customer Relationship Management
- **Chapter Twelve**—Integrating the Organization from End to End—Enterprise Resource Planning

FIGURE 3.1

Decision-Enabling, Problem-Solving, and Opportunity-Seizing Systems

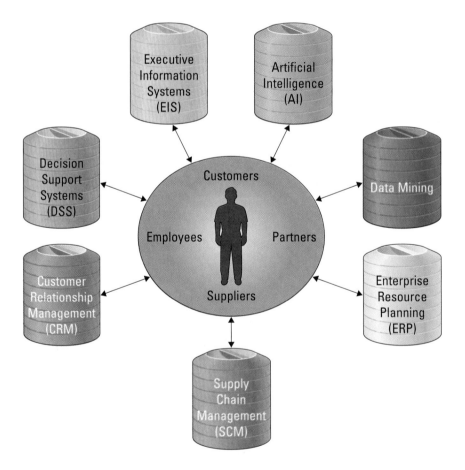

Chapter Nine: Enabling the Organization— Decision Making

9.1. Define the four systems organizations use to make decisions and gain competitive advantages.

9.2. Describe the three quantitative models typically used by decision support systems.

9.3. Describe the relationship between digital dashboards and executive information systems.

9.4. List and describe three types of artificial intelligence systems.

9.5. Describe three types of data-mining analysis capabilities.

W hat is the value of information? The answer to this important question varies. Karsten Solheim would say that the value of information is its ability to lower a company's handicap. Solheim, an avid golfer, invented a putter, one with a "ping," that led to a successful golf equipment company and the PING golf clubs. PING Inc., a privately held corporation, was the first to offer its customers customizable golf clubs. And PING thanks information technology for the explosion of its business over the past decade.

PING prides itself on being a just-in-time manufacturer that depends on a highly flexible information system to make informed production decisions. The system scans PING's vast amounts of order information and pulls orders that meet certain criteria such as order date, order priority, and customer type. PING then places the appropriate inventory orders allowing the company to maintain only 5 percent of its inventory in its warehouse. PING depends on its flexible information systems for both decision support and operational problem solving.[9]

In the electronic age, the amount of information people must understand to make good decisions is growing exponentially. In the past, people could rely on manual processes to make decisions because they had only limited amounts of information to deal with. Today, with massive volumes of available information it is almost impossible for people to make decisions without the aid of information systems. Figure 3.2 highlights the primary reasons dependence on information

FIGURE 3.2

Primary Reasons for Growth of Decision-Making Information Systems

---

Reasons for Growth of Decision-Making Information Systems

1. **People need to analyze large amounts of information**—Improvements in technology itself, innovations in communication, and globalization have resulted in a dramatic increase in the alternatives and dimensions people need to consider when making a decision or appraising an opportunity.

2. **People must make decisions quickly**—Time is of the essence and people simply do not have time to sift through all the information manually.

3. **People must apply sophisticated analysis techniques, such as modeling and forecasting, to make good decisions**—Information systems substantially reduce the time required to perform these sophisticated analysis techniques.

4. **People must protect the corporate asset of organizational information**—Information systems offer the security required to ensure organizational information remains safe.

systems to make decisions and solve problems is growing and will continue to grow in the future.

Decision-making information systems work by building models out of organizational information to lend insight into important business issues and opportunities. A ***model*** is a simplified representation or abstraction of reality. Models can calculate risks, understand uncertainty, change variables, and manipulate time. Each of the following systems uses different models to assist in decision making, problem solving, and opportunity capturing :

- Decision support systems (DSS)
- Executive information systems (EIS)
- Artificial intelligence (AI)
- Data mining

DECISION SUPPORT SYSTEMS

At limousine and transportation company BostonCoach, the most critical process for managers is dispatching a fleet of hundreds of vehicles as efficiently as possible. BostonCoach requires a real-time dispatching system that takes into account inventory, customer needs, and soft dimensions such as weather and traffic. Researchers at IBM's Thomas J. Watson Research Center built BostonCoach a mathematical algorithm for a custom dispatch system that combines information about weather, traffic conditions, driver locations, and customer pickup requests and tells BostonCoach dispatchers which cars to assign to which customers. The system is so efficient that, after launching it in Atlanta, BostonCoach experienced a 20 percent increase in revenues.

A ***decision support system (DSS),*** such as BostonCoach's, models information to support managers and business professionals during the decision-making process. Three quantitative models are typically used by DSSs: (1) sensitivity analysis, (2) what-if analysis, and (3) goal-seeking analysis.

- ***Sensitivity analysis*** is the study of the impact that changes in one (or more) parts of the model have on other parts of the model. Typically, users change the value of one variable repeatedly and observe the resulting changes in other variables.

- ***What-if analysis*** checks the impact of a change in an assumption on the proposed solution. For example, "What will happen to the supply chain if a hurricane in South Carolina reduces holding inventory from 30 percent to 10 percent?" Users repeat this analysis until they understand all the effects of various situations. Figure 3.3 displays an example of what-if analysis using Microsoft Excel. The tool is calculating the net effect of a 20 percent increase in sales on the company's bottom line.

- ***Goal-seeking analysis*** finds the inputs necessary to achieve a goal such as a desired level of output. Instead of observing how changes in a variable affect other variables as in what-if analysis, goal-seeking analysis sets a target value (a goal) for a variable and then repeatedly changes other variables until the target value is achieved. For example, "How many customers are required to purchase our new product line to increase gross profits to $5 million?" Figure 3.4 displays a goal-seeking scenario using Microsoft Excel. The model is seeking the monthly mortgage payment needed to pay off the remaining balance in 130 months.

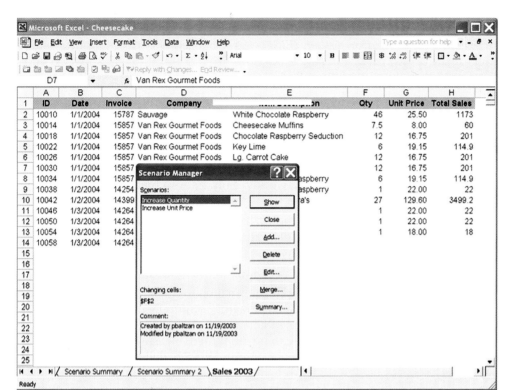

FIGURE 3.3

Example of What-If
Analysis in Microsoft
Excel

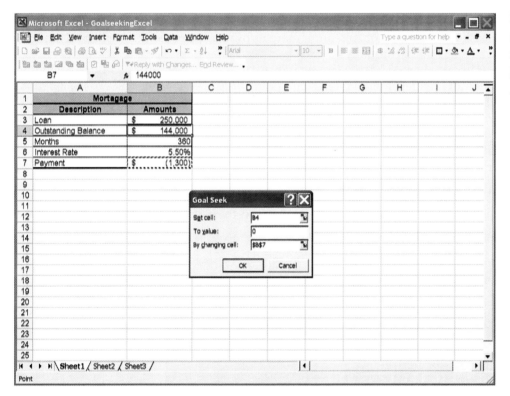

FIGURE 3.4

Examples of Goal-
Seeking Analysis in
Microsoft Excel

EXECUTIVE INFORMATION SYSTEMS

An *executive information system (EIS)* is a specialized DSS that supports senior level executives within the organization. Consolidation, drill-down, and slice-and-dice are a few of the capabilities offered in most EISs.

- **Consolidation** involves the aggregation of information and features simple roll-ups to complex groupings of interrelated information. Many organizations track financial information at a regional level and then consolidate the information at a single global level.

- **Drill-down** enables users to get details, and details of details, of information. For example, viewing monthly, weekly, daily, or even hourly information represents drill-down capability.

- **Slice-and-dice** is the ability to look at information from different perspectives. One slice of information could display all product sales during a given promotion. Another slice could display a single product's sales for all promotions.

An EIS that tailors these analysis capabilities to the preferences of the individuals using them, *digital dashboards* integrate information from multiple components and present it in a unified display. Digital dashboards commonly use indicators to help executives quickly identify the status of key information. Key information typically includes critical success factors that can be monitored, measured, and compared.

Digital dashboards, whether basic or comprehensive, deliver results quickly. As digital dashboards become easier to use, more executives can perform their own analyses without inundating IT personnel with queries and requests for reports. According to an independent study by Nucleus Research, there is a direct correlation between use of digital dashboards and companies' return on investment (ROI). Figure 3.5 displays two different digital dashboard formats.

TruServ, a member-owned hardware cooperative in Chicago, recently deployed digital dashboards that monitor metrics across its supply chain data mart. The system has reduced goods sold at a loss from $60 million to $10 million, and its forecasting ability has improved profit margins by nearly 1 percent, a significant amount for a $2.6 billion company.

The system works by collecting information from a variety of sources, including inventory management systems and point-of-sale systems at TruServ's 6,800 retail member stores. Employees then access the information through the digital dashboards. The goal of the system is to allow everyone in the supply chain—executives, warehouse managers, sales representatives, members, and suppliers—to measure and manage TruServ's distribution, pricing, and sales and marketing functions in real time. The digital dashboard allows TruServ to view real-time demand down to the product level by store and region so TruServ can immediately respond to inventory problems. The company can quickly transfer inventory from distribution centers supplying the stores with low demand to distribution centers supplying the stores with the greatest demand.[10]

FIGURE 3.5

InsightInformation's Sample Sales Digital Dashboard and InsightInformation's Sample Finance Digital Dashboard

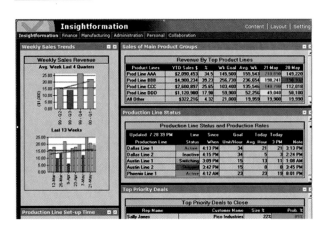

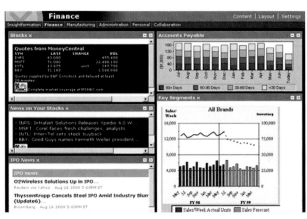

EIS systems, such as digital dashboards, allow companies to move beyond reporting to using information to directly impact business performance. Digital dashboards help executives react to information as it becomes available and make decisions, solve problems, and change strategies daily instead of monthly.

ARTIFICIAL INTELLIGENCE (AI)

RivalWatch, based in Santa Clara, California, offers a strategic business information service using artificial intelligence that enables organizations to track the product offerings, pricing policies, and promotions of online competitors. Clients can determine the competitors they want to watch and the specific information they wish to gather, ranging from products added, removed, or out of stock to price changes, coupons offered, and special shipping terms. Clients can check each competitor, category, and product either daily, weekly, monthly, or quarterly.

"Competing in the Internet arena is a whole different ballgame than doing business in the traditional brick-and-mortar world because you're competing with the whole world rather than the store down the block or a few miles away," says Phil Lumish, VP of Sales and Marketing at RivalWatch.com. "With new products and campaigns being introduced at a breakneck pace, e-businesses need new tools to monitor the competitive environment, and our service is designed specifically to meet that need."[11]

Intelligent systems are various commercial applications of artificial intelligence. *Artificial intelligence (AI)* simulates human intelligence such as the ability to reason and learn. AI systems can learn or understand from experience, make sense of ambiguous or contradictory information, and even use reasoning to solve problems and make decisions effectively. AI systems can perform such tasks as boosting productivity in factories by monitoring equipment and signaling when preventive maintenance is required. The ultimate goal of AI is the ability to build a system that can mimic human intelligence. AI systems are beginning to show up everywhere:

- At Manchester Airport in England, the Hefner AI Robot Cleaner alerts passengers to security and nonsmoking rules while it scrubs up to 65,600 square feet of floor per day. Laser scanners and ultrasonic detectors keep it from colliding with passengers.

- Shell Oil's SmartPump keeps drivers in their cars on cold, wet winter days. It can service any automobile built after 1987 that has been fitted with a special gas cap and a windshield-mounted transponder that tells the robot where to insert the pump.

- Matsushita's courier robot navigates hospital hallways, delivering patient files, X-ray films, and medical supplies.

- The FireFighter AI Robot can extinguish flames at chemical plants and nuclear reactors with water, foam, powder, or inert gas. The robot puts distance between the human operator and the fire.[12]

Examples of AI Systems

AI systems dramatically increase the speed and consistency of decision making, solve problems with incomplete information, and resolve complicated issues that cannot be solved by conventional computing. There are many categories of AI systems; three of the most familiar are: (1) expert systems, (2) neural networks, and (3) intelligent agents.

Expert Systems

Expert systems are computerized advisory programs that imitate the reasoning processes of experts in solving difficult problems. Human expertise is transferred to the expert system and users can access the expert system for specific advice. Most expert systems reflect expertise from many human experts and can therefore perform better analysis than any single expert. Typically, the system contains a knowledge base containing various accumulated experience and a set of rules for applying the knowledge base to each particular situation. The best-known expert systems play chess and assist in medical diagnosis. Expert systems are the most commonly used form of AI in the business arena because they fill the gap when human experts are difficult to find or retain or are too expensive.

Neural Networks

A *neural network,* also called an *artificial neural network,* is a category of AI that attempts to emulate the way the human brain works. The types of decisions for which neural networks are most useful are those that involve pattern or image recognition because a neural network can learn from the information it processes. Neural networks analyze large quantities of information to establish patterns and characteristics in situations where the logic or rules are unknown.

The finance industry is a veteran in neural network technology and has been relying on various forms of it for over two decades. The industry uses neural networks to review loan applications and create patterns or profiles of applications that fall into two categories: approved or denied. One neural network has become the standard for detecting credit card fraud. Since 1992, this technology has slashed fraud by 70 percent for U.S. Bancorp. Now, even small credit unions are required to use the software in order to qualify for debit-card insurance from Credit Union National Association.[13]

Shopping Bot Example
mySimon.com

Intelligent Agents

An **intelligent agent** is a special-purpose knowledge-based information system that accomplishes specific tasks on behalf of its users. Intelligent agents use their knowledge base to make decisions and accomplish tasks in a way that fulfills the intentions of a user. Intelligent agents usually have a graphical representation such as "Sherlock Holmes" for an information search agent.

One of the simplest examples of an intelligent agent is a shopping bot. A **shopping bot** is software that will search several retailer Web sites and provide a comparison of each retailer's offerings including price and availability. Increasingly, intelligent agents handle the majority of a company's Internet buying and selling and handle such processes as finding products, bargaining over prices, and executing transactions. Intelligent agents also have the capability to handle all supply-chain buying and selling.

Another application for intelligent agents is in environmental scanning and competitive intelligence. For instance, an intelligent agent can learn the types of competitor information users want to track, continuously scan the Web for it, and alert users when a significant event occurs.

By 2005, some 2 million AI robots will populate homes and businesses, performing everything from pumping gas to delivering mail. According to a new report by the United Nations and the International Federation of Robotics, more than half the AI robots will be toys and the other half will perform services. Bots will deactivate bombs, clean skyscraper windows, and vacuum homes.[14]

DATA MINING

Wal-Mart consolidates point-of-sale details from its 3,000 stores and uses AI to transform the information into business intelligence. Data-mining systems sift instantly through the information to uncover patterns and relationships that would elude an army of human researchers. The results enable Wal-Mart to predict sales of every product at each store with uncanny accuracy, translating into huge savings in inventories and maximum payoff from promotional spending. Figure 3.6 displays the average organizational spending on data-mining tools over the next few years.

Data-mining software typically includes many forms of AI such as neural networks and expert systems. Data-mining tools apply algorithms to information sets to uncover inherent trends and patterns in the information, which analysts use to develop new business strategies. Analysts use the output from data-mining tools to build models that, when exposed to new information sets, perform a variety of data analysis functions. The analysts provide business solutions by putting together the analytical techniques and the business problem at hand which often reveals important new correlations, patterns, and trends in information. A few of the more common forms of data-mining analysis capabilities include cluster analysis, association detection, and statistical analysis.

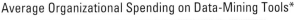

Average Organizational Spending on Data-Mining Tools*

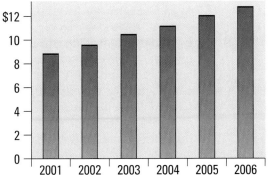

FIGURE 3.6

Data-Mining Tools
Investment Forecast

---

*In millions of dollars.
Source: Aberdeen Group.

Cluster Analysis

Cluster analysis is a technique used to divide an information set into mutually exclusive groups such that the members of each group are as close together as possible to one another and the different groups are as far apart as possible. Cluster analysis is frequently used to segment customer information for customer relationship management (CRM) systems to help organizations identify customers with similar behavioral traits such as clusters of best customers or one-time customers. Cluster analysis also uses neural networks because of their ability to uncover naturally occurring patterns in information.

Such data-mining tools that "understand" human language are finding unexpected applications in medicine. IBM and the Mayo Clinic unearthed hidden patterns in medical records, discovering that infant leukemia has three distinct clusters, each of which probably benefits from tailored treatments. Caroline A. Kovac, general manager of IBM Life Sciences, expects that mining the records of cancer patients for clustering patterns will turn up clues pointing the way to "tremendous strides in curing cancer."

Association Detection

Maytag Corporation, a $4.3 billion home and commercial appliance manufacturer, employs a team of hundreds of R&D engineers, data analysts, quality assurance specialists, and customer service personnel who all work together to ensure that each generation of appliances is better than the previous generation. Maytag is an example of an organization that is gaining business intelligence with *association detection* data-mining tools.

Association detection reveals the degree to which variables are related and the nature and frequency of these relationships in the information. Maytag's warranty analysis tool, for instance, uses statistical analysis to automatically detect potential issues, provide quick and easy access to reports, and perform multidimensional analysis on all warranty information. This association detection data-mining tool enables Maytag's managers to take proactive measures to control product defects even before most of its customers are aware of the defect. The tool also allows Maytag personnel to devote more time to value-added tasks such as ensuring high quality on all products rather than waiting for or manually analyzing monthly reports.[15]

Many people refer to association detection algorithms as *association rule generators* because they create rules to determine the likelihood of events occurring together at a particular time or following each other in a logical progression. Percentages usually reflect the patterns of these events, for example, "55 percent of the time, events A and B occurred together," or "80 percent of the time that items A and B occurred together, they were followed by item C within three days."

Market Basket Analysis

One of the most common forms of association detection analysis is market basket analysis. *Market basket analysis* analyzes such items as Web sites and checkout scanner information to detect customers' buying behavior and predict future behavior by identifying affinities among customers' choices of products and services. Market basket analysis is frequently used to develop marketing campaigns for cross-selling products and services (especially in banking, insurance, and finance) and for inventory control, shelf-product placement, and other retail and marketing applications.

Statistical Analysis

Statistical analysis performs such functions as information correlations, distributions, calculations, and variance analysis, just to name a few. Data-mining tools offer knowledge workers a wide range of powerful statistical capabilities so they can quickly build a variety of statistical models, examine the models' assumptions and validity, and compare and contrast the various models to determine the best one for a particular business issue.

Kraft is the producer of instantly recognizable food brands such as Oreo, Ritz, DiGiorno, and Kool-Aid. The company implemented two data-mining applications to assure consistent flavor, color, aroma, texture, and appearance for all of its lines of foods. One application analyzed product consistency and the other analyzed process variation reduction (PVR).

The product consistency tool SENECA (Sensory and Experimental Collection Application) gathers and analyzes information by assigning precise definitions and numerical scales to such qualities as chewy, sweet, crunchy, and creamy. SENECA then builds models, histories, forecasts, and trends based on consumer testing and evaluates potential product improvements and changes.

The PVR tool ensures consistent flavor, color, aroma, texture, and appearance for every Kraft product since even small changes in the baking process can result in huge disparities in taste. Evaluating every manufacturing procedure, from recipe instructions to cookie dough shapes and sizes, the PVR tool has the potential to generate significant cost savings for each product. Using these types of data-mining techniques for quality control and cluster analysis makes sure that the billions of Kraft products that reach consumers annually will continue to taste great with every bite.[16]

Forecasting is a common form of statistical analysis. Formally defined, **forecasts** are predictions made on the basis of time-series information. **Time-series information** is time-stamped information collected at a particular frequency. Examples of time-series information include Web visits per hour, sales per month, and calls per day. Forecasting data-mining tools allow users to manipulate the time-series for forecasting activities. When discovering trends and seasonal variations in transactional information, use a time-series forecast to change the transactional information by units of time, such as transforming weekly information into monthly or seasonal information or hourly information into daily information. Companies base production, investment, and staffing decisions on a host of economic and market indicators in this manner. Forecasting models allow organizations to take into account all sorts of variables when making decisions.

Nestlé Italiana is part of the multinational giant Nestlé Group and currently dominates Italy's food industry. The company improved sales forecasting by 25

Nestlé—Excelling at Forecasting

percent with its data-mining forecasting solution that enables the company's managers to make objective decisions based on facts instead of subjective decisions based on intuition.

Determining sales forecasts for seasonal confectionery products is a crucial and challenging task. During Easter, Nestlé Italiana has only four weeks to market, deliver, and sell its seasonal products. The Christmas time frame is a little longer, lasting from six to eight weeks, while other holidays such as Valentine's Day and Mother's Day have shorter time frames of about one week.

The company's data-mining solution gathers, organizes, and analyzes massive volumes of information to produce powerful models that identify trends and predict confectionery sales. The business intelligence created is based on five years of historical information and identifies what is important and what is not important. Nestlé Italiana's sophisticated data-mining tool predicted Mother's Day sales forecasts that were 90 percent accurate. The company has benefited from a 40 percent reduction in inventory and a 50 percent reduction in order changes, all due to its forecasting tool. Determining sales forecasts for seasonal confectionery products is now an area in which Nestlé Italiana excels.[17]

Today, vendors such as Business Objects, Cognos, and SAS offer complete data-mining decision-making solutions. Moving forward, these companies plan to add more predictive analytical capabilities to their products. Their goal is to give companies more "what-if" scenario capabilities based on internal and external information.

OPENING CASE STUDY QUESTIONS

1. Explain how Talon helps Harley-Davidson employees improve their decision-making capabilities and highlights potential business opportunities.

2. Assess the business impact Harley-Davidson could gain by using executive information systems.

3. Determine how Harley-Davidson can benefit from using artificial intelligence to support its business operations.

Chapter Nine Case: Finding the Best Buy

Best Buy, North America's number one specialty retailer of consumer electronics, personal computers, entertainment software, and appliances, has annual revenues of over $1 billion and employs over 10,000 people. The retailer offers customers an extensive selection of affordable, easy-to-use products in a fun, informative, and no-pressure shopping environment. Best Buy customers can purchase products whichever way is more convenient, at the brick-and-mortar retail stores or online.

In 1996, Best Buy decided to implement a data warehouse to enhance merchandising and supply chain management. The primary goal of Best Buy's data warehouse is to monitor margin analysis by product, product group, and region to determine what is moving and what factors contribute to sales. The information technology personnel explicitly sought a flexible IT infrastructure, anticipating that this would provide lots of long-term advantages. The key benefits the company has received from its data warehouse include:

- Simplified information
- Consolidated information
- Enhanced infrastructure for data warehousing operations
- Reduced complexity and administration costs
- Increased performance and scalability
- Streamlined business processes

Today, the data warehouse provides full details of every point-of-sale transaction from every Best Buy retail store over the last two years, as well as extensive detail on suppliers and products. Best Buy's employees have numerous tools that help them analyze the information in the data warehouse—decision support systems, executive information systems, digital dashboards, and data marts. Detailed information on every transaction in every store is loaded nightly into the data warehouse. As a result, retail managers are able to respond immediately to changes in customer behavior with respect to product purchase patterns, model preferences, returns, requests for service, and warranty claims. The implementation of the data warehouse has greatly improved Best Buy employees' ability to make decisions and solve problems.[18]

Questions

1. Summarize why decision making has improved at Best Buy with the implementation of a data warehouse.
2. Determine what types of information might be presented to a Best Buy marketing executive through a digital dashboard.
3. Evaluate how Best Buy could use the information in the data warehouse for sales forecasting.

Chapter Ten: Extending the Organization—Supply Chain Management

LEARNING OUTCOMES

10.1. List and describe the components of a typical supply chain.

10.2. Define the relationship between decision making and supply chain management.

10.3. Identify three of the factors driving supply chain management's explosive growth.

10.4. Summarize the best practices for implementing a successful supply chain management system.

The average company spends nearly half of every dollar that it earns on production needs—goods and services it needs from external suppliers in order to keep producing. Organizations must embrace technologies that can effectively manage and oversee their supply chains. Since its inception in the early 1990s, the field of supply chain management has become tremendously important to organizations in helping them create organizational efficiencies and competitive advantages. Best Buy checks inventory levels at each of its 750 stores in North America as often as every half-hour with its SCM system, thereby taking much of the guesswork out of inventory replenishment.[19]

In the past, companies focused primarily on manufacturing and quality improvements within their four walls; now their efforts extend beyond those walls to influence the entire supply chain including customers, customers' customers, suppliers, and suppliers' suppliers (refer to Figure 3.7).

Today's supply chain is a complex web of suppliers, assemblers, shipping/logistic firms, sales/marketing channels, third-party customer support firms, and other business partners linked primarily through information networks and contractual relationships. SCM systems enhance and manage the relationships. The supply chain has three main links:

1. Materials flow from suppliers and their "upstream" suppliers at all levels.
2. Transformation of materials into semifinished and finished products—the organization's own production processes.
3. Distribution of products to customers and their "downstream" customers at all levels. See Figure 3.7.

Collecting, analyzing, and distributing transactional information to all relevant parties, SCM systems help all the different entities in the supply chain work together more effectively. SCM systems provide dynamic holistic views of organizations. Users can "drill down" into detailed analyses of supply chain activities in a process analogous to what was described in the previous chapter on decision support systems.

Advances in SCM have significantly improved companies' forecasting in the last few years. Businesses today have access to modeling and simulation tools, algorithms, and applications that can combine information from multiple sources to build forecasts for days, weeks, and months in advance. Better forecasts for tomorrow result in better preparedness today.

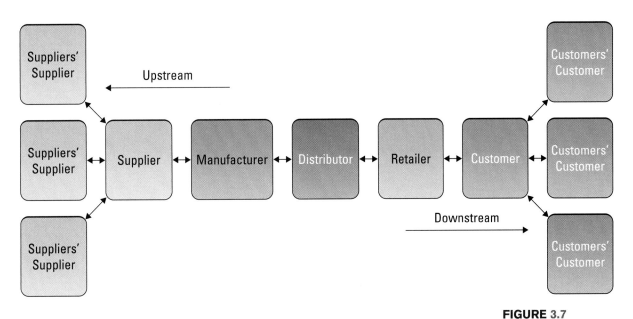

FIGURE 3.7

A Typical Supply Chain

Mattel Inc. has spent the last several years investing heavily in software and processes that simplify its supply chain, cut costs, and shorten cycle times. Using supply chain management strategies Mattel has cut weeks out of the time it takes to design, produce, and ship everything from Barbies to Hot Wheels. Mattel has installed optimization software that measure, tweak, and validate the operations of its seven distribution centers, seven manufacturing plants, and other facilities that make up its vast worldwide supply chain. Mattel has improved forecasting from monthly to weekly. The company no longer produces more inventory than stores actually require, and it delivers inventory when the stores request it. To keep up with more precise forecasting, Mattel's supply chain must move quickly to meet demand.[20]

SUPPLY CHAIN MANAGEMENT'S EXPLOSIVE GROWTH

As companies evolve into extended organizations, the roles of supply chain participants are changing. It is not uncommon for suppliers to be involved in product development and for distributors to act as consultants in brand marketing. Figure 3.8 depicts the top reasons more and more executives are turning to SCM to manage their extended enterprises.

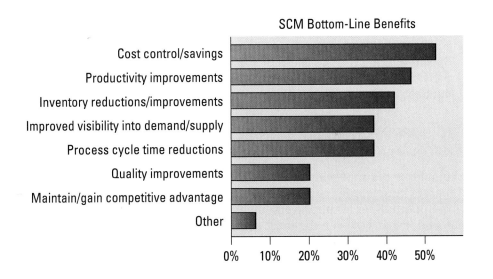

FIGURE 3.8

Top Reasons Executives Are Using SCM to Manage Extended Enterprises

Source: Aberdeen Group.

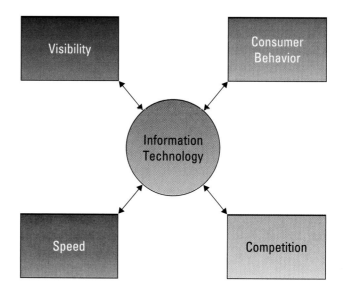

Changes in information technology, visibility, consumer behavior, competition, and speed are factors driving the increased attention being paid to supply chain management. See Figure 3.9 and the following short list to help envision how SCM technology is allowing organizations to focus on and integrate these important factors.

1. **Information technology**—Although people have been talking about the integrated supply chain for a long time, it has only been recently that advances in information technology have made it possible to bring the idea to life and truly integrate the supply chain.

2. **Visibility**—More visible models of different ways to do things in the supply chain have emerged. Managers can see more things more clearly. Some organizations have completely changed the dynamics of their industries because of competitive advantage gained from high visibility in the supply chain. Wal-Mart is the obvious example. The impact of the company's ability to get product to the customer and the impact of the economics have clearly changed the nature of competition. The sheer visibility of this has caused others to emulate this model.

3. **Consumer behavior**—Customers are more demanding than they have been in the past because they have information readily available, they know exactly what they want, and they know when and how they want it. Companies must respond with supply chain enhancements.

4. **Competition**—The behavior of customers has changed the way businesses compete. Customers will leave if a company does not continually meet their expectations.

5. **Speed**—During the past decade competition has focused on speed. A company must be able to satisfy changing customer requirements efficiently, accurately, and quickly.

USING SUPPLY CHAIN MANAGEMENT TO ENHANCE DECISION MAKING

The complexity of supply chains has led to the development of DSSs to assist decision makers in the design and operation of integrated supply chains. These DSSs identify opportunities for improvements across the supply chain far beyond the intuition and insights of even the most experienced manager. DSSs allow managers to examine performance and relationships over the supply chain, among suppliers, manufacturers, distributors, transportation options, product families, product demand, and a host of other factors to optimize supply chain performance. The DSSs use all supply chain information collected from the existing information systems and the supply chain data warehouse to help managers both solve broad problems and make daily decisions—such as a quick response to a scheduling problem, for instance.

Apple Computer, Inc., initially distributed its business operations over 16 legacy applications. Apple quickly realized that it needed a new business model centered around an integrated supply chain to drive performance efficiencies. Apple devised an implementation strategy that focused on specific SCM functions—finance, sales, distribution, and manufacturing—that would most significantly help its business. The company decided to deploy leading-edge functionality with a new business model that provided:

- Build-to-order and configure-to-order manufacturing capabilities.
- Web-enabled configure-to-order order entry and order status for customers buying directly from Apple at Apple.com.
- Real-time credit card authorization.
- Available-to-promise and rules-based allocations.
- Integration to advanced planning systems.

Since its SCM system went live, Apple Computer has experienced substantial benefits in many areas including measurable improvements in its manufacturing processes, a decrease by 60 percent in its build-to-order and configure-to-order cycle times, and the ability to process more than 6,000 orders daily.[21]

SUPPLY CHAIN MANAGEMENT SUCCESS FACTORS

To succeed in today's competitive markets companies must learn to align their supply chains with the demands of the markets they serve. Supply chain performance is now a distinct competitive advantage for companies proficient in the SCM area. Purdue Farms is an example of a company that excels at decision making based on its supply chain management system. Purdue Farms moves roughly 1 million turkeys, each within 24 hours of processing, to reach holiday tables across the nation yearly. The task is no longer as complicated as it was before Purdue Farms invested $20 million in SCM technology five years ago. SCM makes Purdue more adept at delivering the right number of turkeys, to the right customers, at the right time.[22]

To achieve success such as reducing operating costs, improving asset productivity, and compressing order cycle time, an organization should follow the seven principles of supply chain management outlined in Figure 3.10.

Seven Principles of Supply Chain Management

1. Segment customers by service needs, regardless of industry, and then tailor services to those particular segments.
2. Customize the logistics network and focus intensively on the service requirements and on the profitability of the preidentified customer segments.
3. Listen to signals of market demand and plan accordingly. Planning must span the entire chain to detect signals of changing demand.
4. Differentiate products closer to the customer, since companies can no longer afford to hold inventory to compensate for poor demand forecasting.
5. Strategically manage sources of supply, by working with key suppliers to reduce overall costs of owning materials and services.
6. Develop a supply chain information technology strategy that supports different levels of decision making and provides a clear view (visibility) of the flow of products, services, and information.
7. Adopt performance evaluation measures that apply to every link in the supply chain and measure true profitability at every stage.[23]

FIGURE 3.10

Seven Principles of Supply Chain Management

These seven principles run counter to previous built-in functional thinking of how companies organize, operate, and serve customers. Old concepts of supply chains are typified by discrete manufacturing, linear structure, and a focus on buy-sell transactions ("I buy from my suppliers, I sell to my customers"). Because the traditional supply chain is spread out linearly, some suppliers are removed from the end customer. The value proposition for collaboration to these companies is visibility. They benefit by knowing immediately what is being transacted at the customer end of the supply chain (the end customer's activities are visible to them). Instead of waiting days or weeks (or months) for the information to flow upstream through the supply chain, with all the potential pitfalls of erroneous or missing information, suppliers can react in near real-time to fluctuations in end customer demand.

Dell Computers offers one of the best examples of an extremely successful SCM system. Dell's highly efficient build-to-order business model enables it to deliver customized computer systems quickly. As part of the company's continual effort to improve its supply chain processes, Dell deploys supply chain tools to provide global views of forecasted product demand and materials requirements, as well as improved factory scheduling and inventory management.

Finally, organizations should study industry best practices to improve their chances of successful implementation of SCM systems. The SCM industry best practices are:

1. **Make the Sale to Suppliers**—The hardest part of any SCM system is its complexity because a large part of the system extends beyond the company's walls. Not only will the people in the organization need to change the way they work, but also the people from each supplier that is added to the network must change. Be sure suppliers are on board with the benefits that the SCM system will provide.

2. **Wean Employees Off Traditional Business Practices**—Operations people typically deal with phone calls, faxes, and orders scrawled on paper and will most likely want to keep it that way. Unfortunately, an organization cannot disconnect the telephones and fax machines just because they are implementing a supply chain management system. If the organization cannot convince people that using the software will be worth their time, they will easily find ways to work around it, which will quickly decrease the chances of success for the SCM system.

3. **Ensure the SCM System Supports the Organizational Goals**—It is important to select SCM software that gives organizations an advantage in the areas most crucial to their business success. If the organizational goals support highly efficient strategies be sure the supply chain design has the same goals.

4. **Deploy in Incremental Phases and Measure and Communicate Success**—Design the deployment of the SCM system in incremental phases. For instance, instead of installing a complete supply chain management system across the company and all suppliers at once, start by getting it working with a few key suppliers, and then move on to the other suppliers. Along the way, make sure each step is adding value through improvements in the supply chain's performance. The incremental approach does *not* mean to not take a big picture perspective (in fact, you *must* take a big picture perspective) but rather that the big picture should be implemented in digestible bites, and also measured for success one step at a time.

5. **Be Future Oriented**—The supply chain design must anticipate the future state of the business. Since chances are the SCM system will last for many more years than originally planned, managers need to explore how flexible the systems will be when (not if) changes are required in the future. The key is to be certain that the software will meet future needs, not only current needs.[24]

1. Describe how Harley-Davidson's SCM system, Manugistics, might improve its business operations.

2. Provide an illustration of Harley-Davidson's SCM system including all upstream and downstream participants.

Chapter Ten Case: BudNet

Every time a six-pack moves off the shelf, Anheuser-Busch's top-secret nationwide data network, BudNet, knows. BudNet is Anheuser-Busch's secret weapon and one of the reasons that Anheuser's share (by volume) of the $74.4 billion U.S. beer market inched up to 50.1 percent from 48.9 percent during 2003.

Dereck Gurden, a sales representative for Sierra Beverage, one of about 700 U.S. distributors that work for Anheuser-Busch, manages an 800-square-mile territory in California's Central Valley. His customers include 7-Eleven, Buy N Save, and dozens of liquor marts and restaurants. When Gurden enters one of his customers' stores he already knows what products are selling, which campaigns are successful, and what needs to be done to help the customer's business.

When entering a store, Gurden checks his hand-held PC, which displays vital store information. "First I'll scroll through and check the accounts receivable, make sure everything's current," he says. "Then it'll show me an inventory screen with a four-week history. I can get past sales, package placements—facts and numbers on how much of the sales they did when they had a display in a certain location." Gurden also walks around the store and inputs competitor information into his hand-held PC relating to product displays, pricing strategies, and promotions.

How BudNet Works

Information is entered into BudNet nightly from several thousand beer distributors and sales representatives. The information allows Anheuser-Busch managers to constantly adjust production and fine-tune marketing campaigns. The system works as follows:

1. Sales representatives collect new orders and track competitors' marketing efforts on PDAs and laptops.

2. Distributors compile the information and transmit it daily to Anheuser corporate headquarters.

3. Anheuser brand managers analyze the information and make decisions for distributors.

4. Distributors log on to BudNet to get the latest intelligence.

5. Sales representatives rearrange displays and rotate stock based on the recommendations.

Anheuser-Busch uses BudNet's information to constantly change marketing strategies, to design promotions to suit the ethnic makeup of its markets, and as early warning radar that detects where rivals might have an edge. "If Anheuser-Busch loses shelf space in a store in

Clarksville, Tennessee, they know it right away," says Joe Thompson, president of Independent Beverage Group, a research and consulting firm. "They're better at this game than anyone, even Coca-Cola."

According to dozens of analysts, beer-industry veterans, and distributor executives, Anheuser has made a deadly accurate science out of determining what beer lovers are buying, as well as when, where, and why. The last time you bought a six-pack of Bud Light at the corner store, Anheuser servers most likely recorded what you paid, when that beer was brewed, whether you purchased it warm or chilled, and whether you could have gotten a better deal down the street. BudNet has not just added efficiency into the beer supply chain; it is changing the dynamics of the industry.[25]

Questions

1. Describe how an SCM system can help a distributor such as Anheuser-Busch make its supply chain more effective and efficient.
2. SCM is experiencing explosive growth. Explain why this statement is true using BudNet as an example.
3. Evaluate BudNet's effect on each of the five factors that are driving SCM success.

PLUG-IN POINTER >>

Review *Business Plug-In* **Supply Chain Management** for a detailed look at how an organization can create a supply chain strategy focusing on efficiency and effectiveness through the use of the four primary drivers of supply chain management—facilities, inventory, transportation, and information.

Chapter Eleven: Building a Customer-centric Organization—Customer Relationship Management

11.1. Compare operational and analytical customer relationship management.

11.2. Identify the primary forces driving the explosive growth of customer relationship management.

11.3. Define the relationship between decision making and analytical customer relationship management.

11.4. Summarize the best practices for implementing a successful customer relationship management system.

1-800-Flowers.com achieved operational excellence in the late 1990s and turned to building customer intimacy to continue to improve profits and business growth. 1-800-Flowers.com turned brand loyalty into brand relationships by using the vast amounts of information it collected to better understand customers' needs and expectations. The company adopted SAS Enterprise Miner to analyze the information in its CRM systems. Enterprise Miner sifts through information to reveal trends, explain outcomes, and predict results so that businesses can increase response rates and quickly identify their profitable customers. With the help of Enterprise Miner, 1-800-Flowers.com is continuing to thrive and in the third quarter of 2003 revenues increased by 7.5 percent to $124 million.[26]

CRM is a business philosophy based on the premise that those organizations that understand the needs of individual customers are best positioned to achieve sustainable competitive advantage in the future. Many aspects of CRM are not new to organizations; CRM is simply performing current business better. Placing customers at the forefront of all thinking and decision making requires significant operational and technology changes, however.

A customer strategy starts with understanding who the company's customers are and how they help the company meet strategic goals. *The New York Times* understands this and has spent the past decade researching core customers to find similarities among groups of readers in cities outside the New York metropolitan area. Its goal is to understand how to appeal to those groups and make *The New York Times* a national newspaper, expanding its circulation and the "reach" it offers to advertisers. *The New York Times* is growing in a relatively flat publishing market and has achieved a customer retention rate of 94 percent in an industry that averages roughly 60 percent.[27]

As the business world increasingly shifts from product focus to customer focus, most organizations recognize that treating existing customers well is the best source of profitable and sustainable revenue growth. In the age of e-business, however, an organization is challenged more than ever before to truly satisfy its customers. More specifically, CRM will allow an organization to:

- Provide better customer service
- Make call centers more efficient
- Cross-sell products more effectively
- Help sales staff close deals faster
- Simplify marketing and sales processes
- Discover new customers
- Increase customer revenues

The National Basketball Association's New York Knicks are becoming better than ever at communicating with their fans. Thanks to a CRM solution, the New York Knicks' management now knows which season ticket holders like which players, what kind of merchandise they buy, and where they buy it. Management is finally able to send out fully integrated e-mail campaigns that do not overlap with other marketing efforts.[28]

CUSTOMER RELATIONSHIP MANAGEMENT'S EXPLOSIVE GROWTH

Brother International Corporation experienced skyrocketing growth in its sales of multifunction centers, fax machines, printers, and labeling systems in the late 1990s. Along with skyrocketing sales growth came a tremendous increase in customer service calls. When Brother failed to answer the phone fast enough product returns started to increase. The company responded by upping call center capacity, and the rate of returns began to drop. However, Dennis Upton, CIO of Brother International, observed that all the company was doing was answering the phone. He quickly realized that the company was losing a world of valuable market intelligence (business intelligence) about existing customers from all those telephone calls. The company decided to deploy SAP's CRM solution. The 1.8 million calls Brother handled in 2003 dropped to 1.57 million, which reduced call center staff from 180 agents to 160 agents. Since customer demographic information is now stored and displayed on the agent's screen based on the incoming telephone number, the company has reduced call duration by an average of one minute, saving the company $600,000 per year.[29]

In the context of increasing business competition and mature markets, it is easier than ever for informed and demanding customers to defect since they are just a click away from migrating to an alternative. When customers buy on the Internet, they see, and they steer, entire value chains. The Internet is a "looking glass," a two-way mirror, and its field of vision is the entire value chain. While the Internet cannot totally replace the phone and face-to-face communication with customers, it can strengthen these interactions and all customer touch points. Customer Web interactions become conversations, interactive dialogs with shared knowledge, not just business transactions. Web-based customer care can actually become the focal point of customer relationship management and provide breakthrough benefits for both the enterprise and its customers, substantially reducing costs while improving service.

According to a recent AMR Research survey of more than 500 businesses in 14 key vertical markets, half of all current CRM spending is by manufacturers. Current users are allocating 20 percent of their IT budgets to CRM solutions. Those who have not invested in CRM may soon come on board: Of the respondents in the study who are not currently using CRM at all, roughly one-third plan to implement

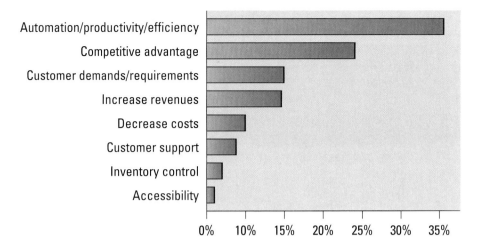

FIGURE 3.11

CRM Business Drivers

Source: AMR Research.

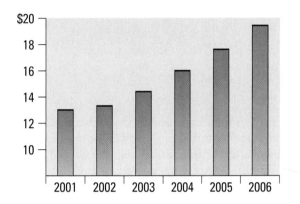

FIGURE 3.12

Forecasts for CRM
Spending ($ billions)

Source: Aberdeen Group.

these types of technology solutions within the next year. Figure 3.11 displays the top CRM business drivers and Figure 3.12 displays the forecasts for CRM spending over the next few years.[30]

USING ANALYTICAL CRM TO ENHANCE DECISIONS

Joe Guyaux knows the best way to win customers is to improve service. Under his leadership and with the help of Siebel CRM, the PNC retail banking team increased new consumer checking customers by 19 percent in 2003. Over the past two years, PNC has retained 21 percent more of its consumer checking households as well as improved customer satisfaction by 9 percent.[31]

The two primary components of a CRM strategy are operational CRM and analytical CRM. *Operational CRM* supports traditional transactional processing for day-to-day front-office operations or systems that deal directly with the customers. *Analytical CRM* supports back-office operations and strategic analysis and includes all systems that do not deal directly with the customers. The primary difference between operational CRM and analytical CRM is the direct interaction between the organization and its customers. See Figure 3.13 for an overview of operational CRM and analytical CRM.

Maturing analytical CRM and behavioral modeling technologies are helping numerous organizations move beyond "legacy benefits" like enhanced customer service and retention to systems that can truly improve business profitability. Unlike operational CRM that automates call centers and sales forces with the aim of enhancing customer transactions, analytical CRM solutions are designed to dig deep into a company's historical customer information and expose patterns of

FIGURE 3.13

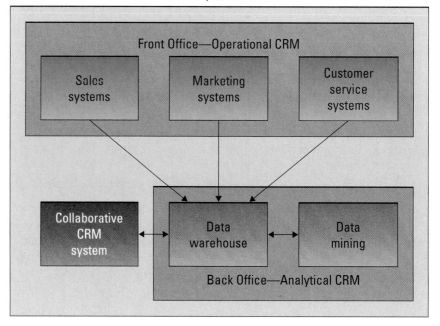

behavior on which a company can capitalize. Analytical CRM is primarily used to enhance and support decision making and works by identifying patterns in customer information collected from the various operational CRM systems.

For many organizations, the power of analytical CRM solutions provides tremendous managerial opportunities. Depending on the specific solution, analytical CRM tools can slice-and-dice customer information to create made-to-order views of customer value, spending, product affinities, percentile profiles, and segmentations. Modeling tools can identify opportunities for cross-selling, up-selling, and expanding customer relationships.

Personalization occurs when a Web site can know enough about a person's likes and dislikes that it can fashion offers that are more likely to appeal to that person. Many organizations are now utilizing CRM to create customer rules and templates that marketers can use to personalize customer messages.

The information produced by analytical CRM solutions can help companies make decisions about how to handle customers based on the value of each and every one. Analytical CRM can help make decisions as to which customers are worth investing in, which should be serviced at an average level, and which should not be invested in at all.

CUSTOMER RELATIONSHIP MANAGEMENT SUCCESS FACTORS

CRM solutions make organizational business processes more intelligent. This is achieved by understanding customer behavior and preferences, then realigning product and service offerings and related communications to make sure they are synchronized with customer needs and preferences. If an organization is implementing a CRM system, they should study the industry best practices to help ensure a successful implementation (see box on page 117).

1. **Clearly Communicate the CRM Strategy**—Boise Office Solutions recently spent $25 million implementing a successful CRM system. One of the primary reasons for the system's success was that Boise started with a clear business objective for the system: to provide customers with greater economic value. Only after establishing the business objective did Boise Office Solutions invest in CRM technology to help meet the goal. Ensuring that all departments and employees understand exactly what CRM means and how it will add value to the organization is critical. Research by Gartner Dataquest indicates that enterprises that attain success with CRM have interested and committed senior executives who set goals for what CRM should achieve, match CRM strategies with corporate objectives, and tie the measurement process to both goals and strategies.[32]

2. **Define Information Needs and Flows**—People who perform successful CRM implementations have a clear understanding of how information flows in and out of their organization. Chances are information comes into the organization in many different forms over many different touch points.

3. **Build an Integrated View of the Customer**—Essential to a CRM strategy is choosing the correct CRM system that can support organizational requirements. The system must have the corresponding functional breadth and depth to support strategic goals. Do not forget to take into account the system's infrastructure including ease of integration to current systems, discussed in greater detail later in this unit.

4. **Implement in Iterations**—Implement the CRM system in manageable pieces—in other words avoid the "big bang" implementation approach. It is easier to manage, measure, and track the design, building, and deployment of the CRM system when it is delivered in pieces. Most important, this allows the organization to find out early if the implementation is headed for failure and thus either kill the project and save wasted resources or change direction to a more successful path.

5. **Scalability for Organizational Growth**—Make certain that the CRM system meets the organization's future needs as well as its current needs. Estimating future needs is by far one of the hardest parts of any project. Understanding how the organization is going to grow, predicting how technology is going to change, and anticipating how customers are going to evolve are very difficult challenges. Taking the time to answer some tough questions up front will ensure the organization grows into, instead of out of, its CRM system.[33]

CRM is critical to business success. CRM is the key competitive strategy to stay focused on customer needs and to integrate a customer-centric approach throughout an organization. CRM can acquire enterprisewide knowledge about customers and improve the business processes that deliver value to an organization's customers, suppliers, and employees. Using the analytical capabilities of CRM can help a company anticipate customer needs and proactively serve customers in ways that build relationships, create loyalty, and enhance bottom lines.

OPENING CASE STUDY QUESTIONS

1 Assess the impact on Harley-Davidson's business if it decided to sell accessories directly to its online customers. Be sure to include a brief discussion of the ethics involved in this decision.

2. Evaluate the HOG CRM strategy and recommend an additional benefit Harley-Davidson could provide to its HOG members to increase customer satisfaction.

Chapter Eleven Case: Gearing Up at REI

Recreational Equipment Inc. (REI) boasts annual revenues between $500 million and $1 billion and an employee workforce of over 10,000. According to Forrester Research, Recreational Equipment Inc. (REI) deserves recognition as an industry leader for its "best practice" multi-channel CRM strategy, which allows customers to seamlessly purchase products at the company's 70 retail stores as well as by telephone, mail order, and on the Internet.

REI.com was one of the first stores to offer a broad selection of outdoor gear and expert advice and in-depth information about outdoor products and recreation online. The highly successful Web site currently receives over 2.5 million visitors per day and online sales represent 15 percent of its total sales revenue.

REI realized it could provide a consistent and seamless customer experience whether the customer is shopping via its Web site or at its in-store kiosks by consolidating its four disparate database systems into one customer relationship management system. The system integrates multiple sales channels to manage mail orders, in-store special orders, kiosk operations, and REI Adventures—the company's adventure travel service. This gives the company a complete view of all customers regardless of their shopping preference. In addition to finding items such as backpacks, bicycles, or tents through the system, customers can also research hiking trails, camping guides, and cycling techniques.

The system is providing REI with the confidence it needs to plan for expansions of customer service, such as the new REI Store Pickup and REI's soon-to-launch gift registries that function across all channels. Key benefits of the CRM system include:

- Minimizes maintenance costs
- Scales easily as company grows
- Provides sophisticated data warehouse for business intelligence
- Provides high availability[34]

Questions

1. Summarize why it is important for REI to use CRM strategies to consolidate its customer information.
2. Determine two pieces of customer information that REI could extrapolate from its CRM system that would help it manage its business more effectively.
3. Explain how REI could use personalization to give its customers a more satisfying shopping experience.

PLUG-IN POINTER >>

Review *Business Plug-In* **Customer Relationship Management** for a complete overview of CRM strategies along with a detailed look at the many different technologies that sales, marketing, and customer service departments can use to strengthen customer relationships.

Chapter Twelve: Integrating the Organization from End to End—Enterprise Resource Planning

LEARNING OUTCOMES

12.1. Describe the role information plays in enterprise resource planning systems.

12.2. Identify the primary forces driving the explosive growth of enterprise resource planning systems.

12.3. Explain the business value of integrating supply chain management, customer relationship management, and enterprise resource planning systems.

nterprise resource planning systems serve as the organization's backbone in providing fundamental decision-making support. In the past, departments made decisions independent of each other. ERP systems provide a foundation for collaboration between departments. ERP systems enable people in different business areas to communicate. ERP systems have been widely adopted in large organizations to store critical knowledge used to make the decisions that drive the organization's performance.

To be competitive, organizations always strive for excellence in every business process enterprisewide, a daunting challenge if the organization has multisite operations worldwide. To obtain operational efficiencies, lower costs, improved supplier and customer relations, and increased revenues and market share, all units of the organization must work together harmoniously toward congruent goals. An ERP system will help an organization achieve this.

One company that has blazed a trail with ERP is Atlanta-based United Parcel Service of America, Inc. (UPS). UPS has developed a number of Web-based applications that track information such as recipient signatures, addresses, time in transit, and other shipping information. These services run on an SAP foundation that UPS customers can connect to using real-time ERP information obtained from the UPS Web site. Currently, 6.2 million tracking requests pass through the company's Web site each day. By automating the information delivery process, UPS has dramatically reduced the demand on its customer service representatives. Just as important, UPS has improved relationships with its business partners—in effect integrating its business with theirs—by making it easier for consumers to find delivery information without leaving the Web site of the merchant.[35]

The heart of an ERP system is a central database that collects information from and feeds information into all the ERP system's individual application components (called modules), supporting diverse business functions such as accounting, manufacturing, marketing, and human resources. When a user enters or updates information in one module, it is immediately and automatically updated throughout the entire system, as illustrated in Figure 3.14.

ERP automates business processes such as order fulfillment—taking an order from a customer, shipping the purchase, and then billing for it. With an ERP system, when a customer service representative takes an order from a customer, he or she

FIGURE 3.14

ERP Integration Data
Flow

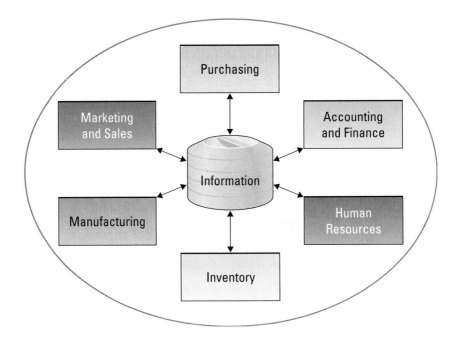

has all the information necessary to complete the order (the customer's credit rating and order history, the company's inventory levels, and the delivery schedule). Everyone else in the company sees the same information and has access to the database that holds the customer's new order. When one department finishes with the order, it is automatically routed via the ERP system to the next department. To find out where the order is at any point, a user need only log in to the ERP system and track it down, as illustrated in Figure 3.15. The order process moves like a bolt of lightning through the organization, and customers get their orders faster and with fewer errors than ever before. ERP can apply that same magic to the other major business processes, such as employee benefits or financial reporting.

To qualify as a true ERP solution, the system not only must integrate various organization processes, but also must be:

FIGURE 3.15

ERP Process Flow

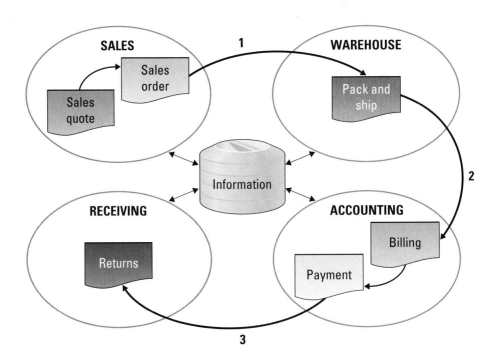

- **Flexible**—An ERP system should be flexible in order to respond to the changing needs of an enterprise.

- **Modular and open**—An ERP system has to have an open system architecture, meaning that any module can be interfaced with or detached whenever required without affecting the other modules. The system should support multiple hardware platforms for organizations that have a heterogeneous collection of systems. It must also support third-party add-on components.

- **Comprehensive**—An ERP system should be able to support a variety of organizational functions and must be suitable for a wide range of business organizations.

- **Beyond the company**—An ERP system must not be confined to organizational boundaries but rather support online connectivity to business partners or customers.

ENTERPRISE RESOURCE PLANNING'S EXPLOSIVE GROWTH

Cisco Systems Inc., a $22 billion producer of computer-network equipment, is using an ERP system to create a consolidated trial balance sheet and a consolidated income statement within a half day of a fiscal quarter's close, compared with two weeks five years ago when Cisco was a $4 billion company. What's more, during the past five years, the time devoted to transaction processing has fallen from 65 percent to 35 percent, and finance group expenses, as a percentage of the total company revenues, have fallen from 2 percent to 1.3 percent. All that has occurred even as Cisco added people to its finance department to keep pace with the company's growth. The ERP system gives Cisco executives a look at revenues, expenses, margins, and profits every day of every month.[36]

SAP, the leading ERP vendor, boasts 20,000 installations and 10 million users worldwide. These figures represent only 30 percent of the overall ERP market. Here are a few reasons why ERP solutions have proven to be such a powerful force:

- ERP is a logical solution to the mess of incompatible applications that had sprung up in most businesses.

- ERP addresses the need for global information sharing and reporting.

- ERP is used to avoid the pain and expense of fixing legacy systems.[37]

ERP as a business concept resounds as a powerful internal information management nirvana: Everyone involved in sourcing, producing, and delivering the company's product works with the same information, which eliminates redundancies, cuts down wasted time, and removes misinformation.

THE CONNECTED CORPORATION

Companies that are successful in the digital economy understand that current business designs and models are insufficient to meet the challenges of doing business in the e-business era. A close look at such leading companies as Amazon.com, Dell, and Cisco will provide insight into a new kind of business model that focuses on having a finely tuned integration of business, technology, and process. These companies frequently use technology to streamline supply chain operations, improve customer loyalty, gain visibility into enterprisewide information, and ultimately drive profit growth. To thrive in the e-business world, organizations must structurally transform their internal architectures. They must integrate their disparate systems into a potent e-business infrastructure.

FIGURE 3.16

Leading ERP Vendor
Overview

Component	Vendor		
	PeopleSoft	Oracle	SAP
Customer relationship management	X		X
Supply chain management	X	X	X
Financial management	X	X	X
Human resource management	X	X	X
Service automation	X		
Supplier relationship management	X		X
Enterprise performance management	X		
Business intelligence		X	
Learning management		X	
Order management		X	
Manufacturing		X	
Marketing		X	
Sales		X	

Applications such as SCM, CRM, and ERP are the backbone of e-business. Integration of these applications is the key to success for many companies. Integration allows the unlocking of information to make it available to any user, anywhere, anytime. Figure 3.16 displays the top three ERP vendors and their major components as defined by *CIO* magazine.

Each of the three ERP vendors highlighted in Figure 3.16 offers CRM and SCM modules. However, these modules are not as functional or flexible as the modules offered by industry leaders of SCM and CRM such as Siebel and i2 technologies, as depicted in Figure 3.17 and Figure 3.18. As a result, organizations face the challenge of integrating their new e-business systems with their preexisting applications and other vendor products.

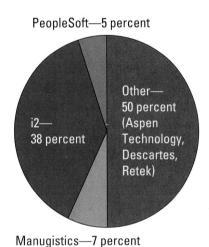

FIGURE 3.17

SCM Market Overview

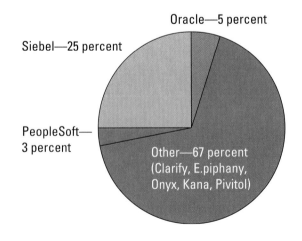

FIGURE 3.18

CRM Market Overview

INTEGRATING SCM, CRM, AND ERP

Most organizations today have no choice but to piecemeal their applications together since no one vendor can respond to every organization need; hence, customers purchase multiple applications from multiple vendors. As a result, large companies usually have multiple applications that are not designed to work together, and find themselves having to integrate business solutions. For example, a single organization might choose its CRM components from Siebel, SCM components from i2, financial components from Oracle, and HR management components from Peoplesoft. Figure 3.19 displays the general audience and purpose for each of these applications that have to be integrated.

Effectively managing the transformation to an integrated enterprise will be critical to the success of the 21st century organization. The key to an integrated enterprise is the integration of the disparate IT applications. An integrated enterprise infuses support areas, such as finance and human resources, with a strong customer orientation. Integrations are achieved using *middleware*—several different types of software which sit in the middle of and provide connectivity between two or more software applications. Middleware translates information between disparate systems. *Enterprise application integration (EAI) middleware* represents a new approach to middleware by packaging together commonly used functionality, such as providing prebuilt links to popular enterprise applications, which reduces the time necessary to develop solutions that integrate applications from multiple vendors. A few leading vendors of EAI middleware include Active Software, Vitria Technology, and Extricity.

Figure 3.20 displays the data points where these applications integrate and illustrates the underlying premise of e-business architecture infrastructure design: Companies run on interdependent applications. If one application of the company does not function well, the entire customer value delivery system is affected. The world-class enterprises of tomorrow must be built on the foundation of world-class applications implemented today.

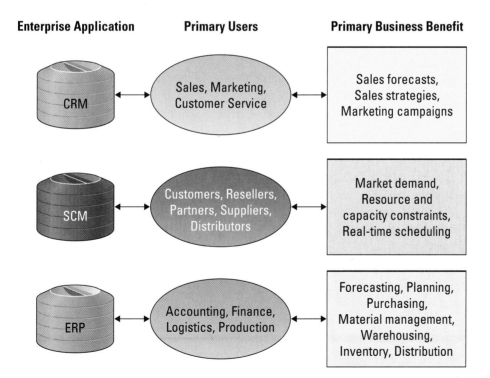

Enterprise Application	Primary Users	Primary Business Benefit
CRM	Sales, Marketing, Customer Service	Sales forecasts, Sales strategies, Marketing campaigns
SCM	Customers, Resellers, Partners, Suppliers, Distributors	Market demand, Resource and capacity constraints, Real-time scheduling
ERP	Accounting, Finance, Logistics, Production	Forecasting, Planning, Purchasing, Material management, Warehousing, Inventory, Distribution

FIGURE 3.19

Primary Users and Business Benefits of Strategic Initiatives

FIGURE 3.20

Integrations between
SCM, CRM, and ERP
Applications

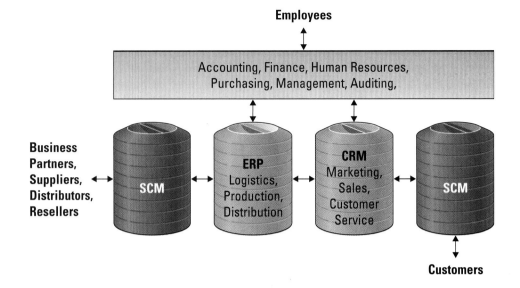

Companies are expecting e-business to increase profitability, create competitive differentiation, and support innovative business practices. To achieve these goals, companies must evolve through distinct stages, from integrated processes to truly synchronized inter-enterprise communities. Getting e-business applications based on different technologies and with differing business models and data models to work together is a key issue for 21st century organizations.

OPENING CASE STUDY QUESTIONS

1. Explain how an ERP system can help Harley-Davidson gain business intelligence in its operations.

2. Assess the business benefit for Harley-Davidson in integrating its CRM, SCM, and ERP systems.

Chapter Twelve Case: Hilton Purchases New Suite

The $4 billion Hilton Hotels Corporation based in Beverly Hills, California, is upgrading its enterprise systems. The company currently owns or manages 300 Hilton hotels and 1,600 properties in the DoubleTree, Embassy Suites, Hampton Inns, and Homewood Suites chains. The upgrade affects 1,500 people and the total cost, not counting internal labor, will come in at about $3.8 million. Hilton claims that the new system is increasing processing efficiency by a factor of six and expects to save $4.5 million to $5 million annually. Hilton also anticipates that the upgrade will greatly simplify maintenance and support and free up IT staff to concentrate on business process improvements.

The upgrade includes changing from PeopleSoft 7.5 client/server applications to PeopleSoft 8 on a three-tier, Web-based architecture. It also includes converting from Unix-based

Hewlett-Packard servers to Windows 2000 Server boxes from Dell and replacing its Sybase Inc. databases with SQL Server 2000 from Microsoft.

One of the primary reasons for the upgrade was the hodgepodge of information systems the company had as a result of its recent merger with Promus Hotel Corporation. "I was hired in April 2000 to pull the companies together," says Damien Bean, VP for Corporate Systems. "We had every platform and operating system under the sun. The two companies had too many servers, operating systems, and databases even before they merged. After the merger, the mix of technologies was untenable, a situation not improved by the instability of the production environment. The time had come to streamline, simplify, and standardize in order to cut costs."

Hilton decided to test its new system on a travel agent commission system that was developed using PeopleSoft's PeopleTools application development environment. Although it was big with over 60 tables and 100GB of information, it was relatively uncomplicated and noncritical and could be down for a day or two if there were problems. The new system proved up to the task and "ran like a scalded bat," performing six times faster than the previous system, Bean recalls. Gratified and emboldened, Hilton's IT shop moved on to migrate the PeopleSoft HR, payroll, and CRM systems for 71,000 employees. Hilton is now in the final phase of its IT architecture makeover and expects to have the remainder of the system upgrade in production by the end of the year.

Robert La Forgia, a senior vice president and Hilton's controller, states, "The upgrades will benefit Hilton customers by making it easier for the IT staffers to adapt systems that touch them, such as reservations and billing, to customers' changing needs."

As for internal customers, the new architecture has already so streamlined processing that La Forgia is now able to close the books in six days instead of 10. "We have decreased processing time considerably," he says. "We have a lot less blood, sweat and tears and a lot less overtime." All the migrations will save $4.5 million to $5 million out of Hilton's $150 million IT budget.[38]

Questions

1. Summarize why the merger of two separate corporations can cause significant issues for the integration of information.
2. Which component would you recommend if Hilton wanted to add an additional PeopleSoft component? Evaluate the business benefit of this additional component.
3. Analyze why it is critical for an organization like Hilton Hotels to have an enterprisewide system.
4. Assess the benefits Hilton Hotels Corporation could receive from implementing an integrated SCM, CRM, and ERP solution.

<< PLUG-IN POINTER

Review *Business Plug-In* Enterprise Resource Planning for a detailed analysis of different ERP strategies and best practices. The plug-in also focuses on the two basic groups of ERP systems—core and extended.

Today, organizations of various sizes are proving systems that support decision making and opportunity seizing are essential to thriving in the highly competitive electronic world. We are living in an era when information technology is a primary tool, knowledge is a strategic asset, and decision making and problem solving are paramount skills. The tougher, larger, and more demanding a problem or opportunity is, and the faster and more competitive the environment is, the more important decision-making and problem-solving skills become. This unit discussed numerous tools and strategic initiatives available that an organization can take advantage of to assist in decision making:

- Supply chain management (SCM)—managing information flows within the supply chain to maximize total supply chain effectiveness and profitability.
- Customer relationship management (CRM)—managing all aspects of customers' relationships with an organization to increase customer loyalty and retention and an organization's profitability.
- Enterprise resource planning (ERP)—integrating all departments and functions throughout an organization into a single IT system (or integrated set of IT systems) so that managers and leaders can make enterprisewide decisions by viewing enterprisewide information on all business operations.

Analytical CRM, 115
Artificial intelligence (AI), 99
Association detection, 102
Cluster analysis, 102
Consolidation, 98
Decision support system (DSS), 96
Digital dashboard, 98
Drill-down, 98
E-business, 94
Enterprise application integration (EAI) middleware, 123

Executive information system (EIS), 98
Expert system, 100
Forecast, 103
Goal-seeking analysis, 96
Intelligent agent, 101
Intelligent system, 99
Market basket analysis, 102
Middleware, 123
Model, 96
Neural network or artificial neural network, 100

Operational CRM, 115
Personalization, 115
Sensitivity analysis, 96
Shopping bot, 101
Slice-and-dice, 98
Time-series information, 103
What-if analysis, 96

Building LEGO's IT Systems One Block at a Time

They light up. They spin and hop. They talk and sing. The marketing of today's increasingly interactive, technologically advanced toys inundates children and their parents. As the latest toys hit the marketplace each year, more established, traditional toy companies work to keep their products fresh and innovative for a frequently fickle kids' toys audience. One toy classic, LEGO blocks, has not only endured for more than six decades but has grown continuously in popularity. While keeping its core product, the basic construction block toy, true to form, the LEGO Company has evolved to embrace new categories and audiences.

A family-owned enterprise since 1932, the LEGO Company employs 8,000 people around the world. Headquartered in Billund, Denmark, LEGO has annual global sales of more than $1.4 billion. As the company has expanded from a small corporation to a global business mainstay, its requirements for supply and demand planning have grown accordingly. The challenges facing the company are to:

- Increase forecast accuracy and velocity.
- Gain a clear view of demand by replacing disparate, localized legacy systems.
- Improve customer service on a global scale.
- Respond to opportunity for SCM with solutions for several large customers.
- Create eight global regions supported by i2 solutions to replace 25 LEGO sales companies.
- Establish common practices, processes, and tools.
- Employ an integrated approach to software products that support existing processes.
- Create an account planning system as a basis for SCM.

At the time of its search for a value chain solutions provider, a consulting firm employed by the LEGO Company highly recommended that the toy manufacturer look at i2 solutions. With its implementation of i2 solutions, the LEGO Company has experienced improved technical quality, increased forecasting accuracy, and enhanced customer satisfaction, and has bridged the process to support customer collaborative planning, forecasting, and replenishment (CPFR) opportunities.

"In the past, prior to utilizing i2 solutions, we would have taken as long as three to four weeks to consolidate a global forecast. Now, with i2, we're doing that within one day after the forecasts have been completed," states Bob Mincarelli, LEGO's director of Global Demand Management. The company experienced an immediate improvement in technical quality. When operating on a global level and continuously consolidating strategic plans that flow down to a supply chain, technical information quality is extremely important. The implementation of the i2 system has led to significant improvements for LEGO's forecasting accuracy. The results of the i2 system include:

- Reduced global forecast consolidation time from 3–4 weeks down to one day.
- Increased forecast accuracy and forecaster efficiency.
- Increased responsiveness to customer and marketplace requirements.
- Support for CPFR opportunity.[39]

Questions

1. Summarize why LEGO's managers and executives would want to use DSSs and EISs to gain business intelligence.
2. Prototype a potential digital dashboard for a sales executive at LEGO.
3. Describe a supply chain and explain why managing it is important to LEGO's business.
4. Summarize customer relationship management and explain how LEGO could use CRM to enhance its business.
5. Is it ethical for an employee at LEGO to sell the organizational information stored in its i2 system?
6. One of the challenges facing LEGO is its ability to forecast demand. Explain how implementing the ERP solution from i2 has helped the company improve its demand forecasting.

eBay's Cosmos Business Intelligence System

"In Cosmos, we have built a platform with the flexibility and scalability to grow and meet our needs for the foreseeable future. The global scale of our trading community and the competitive pressures we face have made this new analytic system a necessity. Cosmos has opened our eyes and allowed us to control the massive amounts of data and information flowing through our site. The analysis and action-enabling information this system provides has provided us with a competitive advantage that can't be matched."—Patrick Firouzian, senior manager, eBay.

eBay Overview

eBay, founded in 1995, is an online marketplace that specializes in the sale of goods and services. eBay's business is booming and the data about it are almost unbelievable:

- 22 million registered users
- 500 million items sold since inception
- Over $6 billion in goods sold in 2003
- 2 million unique visitors who add over 500,000 items to the site on a daily basis

eBay's senior managers found themselves excited about the organization's tremendous growth, but overwhelmed with how to maintain that growth especially with the incredible amounts of information the organization had to analyze to gain business intelligence and set strategic initiatives. In January 2002, the managers began focusing on how they could effectively capture, analyze, and process the enormous volumes of customer information and Web site statistics to gain business intelligence. Specifically, the managers were interested in having the ability to analyze and segment customer information at varying levels to measure the impact of partnerships and analyze new and existing site features on a timely basis.

The Solution—Cosmos

To tackle the problem the managers formed a Business Intelligence group with the goals of gaining a better understanding of market dynamics between buyers and sellers on eBay, improving customer relationships, and increasing revenues. The Business Intelligence group implemented a business intelligence system called "Cosmos" which is based on Informatica's PowerCenter enterprise information integration platform. Cosmos provides insight to users across the enterprise, improves the buying experience for customers, better targets customer markets, and manages enormous volumes of transactional and clickstream information. Some of the design features built into the Cosmos system include the ability to manage enormous amounts of information (80 to 100 million records daily), remain available $24 \times 7 \times 365$, and automatically reconcile the accuracy of the information reported externally.

Cosmos allows 1,000 users to quickly find answers to queries and share information with partner companies via an extranet. Cosmos also serves as the integration hub for customer and financial information from eBay sister companies to provide a consolidated enterprisewide view of customer and business performance. The Cosmos system integrates approximately 3 terabytes of information and the largest table contains over 500 million records. The different forms of integrated information include:

- Transaction and customer information from eBay's auction site, where millions of items and bids are handled daily.
- HTTP log files from over 200 Sun servers, which log more than 80 million transactions per day, including searches, listings, and page views.

Cosmos's Key Success Features

Cosmos has drastically improved eBay's financial visibility. eBay now has a better assessment of customer activity on its site, enabling increased average selling prices and sales conversion rates for bids. Moreover, by having better visibility into site activity, the company can better track revenue estimates and precisely allocate funds to advertisements, promotions, and other strategic projects.

Cosmos has also improved eBay's CRM because the company can now quantify the adoption or impact of a new feature or marketing campaign immediately after its launch. Examples of this are the new iPIX photo hosting services and the Buy-it-now auction format. Through the information contained in the Cosmos system, the ROI for planned features is estimated before development, helping to maximize resources and user community benefits. A better understanding of customer activity also allows eBay to improve customer experiences by making eBay a safer place to buy/sell practically anything.

Overall, Cosmos has improved eBay's managers' and executives' decision-making abilities. Business users can now access information without IT's assistance, reducing decision-making time from days to hours. Before implementing the Cosmos system, eBay managed a backlog queue of 25 to 30 report requests per month. Cosmos completely eliminated the backlog. The costs for maintenance and generation of the reports (seven developers, two managers) were also eliminated with the introduction of Cosmos. As a result, eBay's staff can now focus on more value-added tasks such as information quality, new releases, and helping users leverage information and tools.[40]

Questions

1. Explain why eBay's managers and executives decided to create the Business Intelligence team.
2. Define five types of information that eBay executives might want on their EISs.
3. Determine the strategy eBay is taking regarding its supply chain.
4. Assess the business benefits from implementing an analytical CRM solution at eBay.
5. Which component would you recommend eBay purchase if the company was interested in adding an additional ERP component.
6. One of the key success factors of Cosmos is its ability to provide a better understanding of customer activity, which allows eBay to improve customer experiences making eBay a safer place to buy/sell practically anything. Explain why eBay's unique business structure causes safety and security concerns for its customers.
7. What types of security issues should eBay be concerned with and what can it do to protect itself?

✳ MAKING BUSINESS DECISIONS

1. Making Decisions

You are the VP of Human Resources for a large consulting company. You are compiling a list of questions that you want each interviewee to answer. The first question on your list is, "How can information technology enhance your ability to make decisions at our organization?" On a single presentation slide, prepare a summary of what you consider to be the correct answer to this difficult question.

2. Implementing an ERP System

Blue Dog Inc. is a leading manufacturer in the high-end sunglasses industry. Blue Dog Inc. reached record revenue levels of over $250 million last year. The company is currently deciding on the possibility of implementing an ERP system to help decrease production costs and increase inventory control. Many of the executives are nervous about making such a large investment in an ERP system due to its low success rates. As a senior manager at Blue Dog Inc. you have been asked to compile a list of the potential benefits and risks associated with implementing an ERP system along with your recommendations for the steps the company can take to ensure a successful implementation.

3. DSS and EIS

Dr. Rosen runs a large dental conglomerate—Teeth Doctors—that staffs over 700 dentists in six states. Dr. Rosen is interested in purchasing a competitor called Dentix that has 150 dentists in three additional states. In order to make the decision to purchase Dentix, Dr. Rosen must consider several issues:

- The cost of purchasing Dentix
- The location of the Dentix offices
- The current number of customers per dentist, per office, and per state
- The merger between the two companies
- The professional reputation of Dentix
- Other competitors

Explain how Dr. Rosen and Teeth Doctors can benefit from the use of information systems to make an accurate business decision in regard to the potential purchase of Dentix.

4. SCM, CRM, and ERP

Jamie Ash is interested in applying for a job at a large software vendor. One of the criteria for the job is a detailed understanding of strategic initiatives such as SCM, CRM, and ERP. Jamie has no knowledge of any of these initiatives and cannot even explain what the acronyms mean. Jamie has come to you for help. She would like you to compile a summary of the three initiatives including an analysis of how the three are similar and how they are different. Jamie would also like to perform some self-training via the Web so be sure to provide her with several additional links to key Web sites that offer detailed overviews on SCM, CRM, and ERP.

✳ MAKING COLLABORATIVE DECISIONS

1. Customer Relationship Management Strategies

On average, it costs an organization six times more to sell to a new customer than to sell to an existing customer. As the co-owner of a medium-sized luggage distributor, you have recently been notified by your EIS systems that sales for the past three months have decreased by an average of 17 percent. The reasons for the decline in sales are numerous, including a poor economy, people's aversion to travel because of the terrorist attacks, and some negative publicity your company received regarding a defective product line. In a group, explain how implementing a CRM system can help you understand and combat the decline in sales. Be sure to justify why a CRM system is important to your business and its future growth.

2. **Finding Information on Decision Support Systems**

   You are working on the sales team for a small catering company that maintains 75 employees and generates $1 million in revenues per year. The owner, Pam Hetz, wants to understand how she can use decision support systems to help grow her business. Pam has an initial understanding of DSS systems and is interested in learning more about what types are available, how they can be used in a small business, and the cost associated with different DSS systems. In a group, research the Web site www.dssresources.com and compile a presentation that discusses DSS systems in detail. Be sure to answer all Pam's questions on DSS systems in the presentation.

3. **Analyzing Dell's Supply Chain Management System**

   Dell's supply chain strategy is legendary. Essentially, if you want to build a successful SCM system your best bet is to model your SCM system after Dell's. In a team, research Dell's supply chain management strategy on the Web and create a report discussing any new SCM updates and strategies the company is currently using that were not discussed in this text. Be sure to include a graphical presentation of Dell's current supply chain model.

4. **Assessing IT Capabilities**

   Hoover's Rentals is a small privately owned business that rents sports equipment in Denver, Colorado. The company specializes in winter rentals including ski equipment, snowboarding equipment, and snowmobile equipment. Hoover's has been in business for 20 years and, for the first time, it is starting to experience a decline in sales. Brian Hoover, the company's owner, is puzzled by the recent decreases in sales. The snowfall for the last two years has been outstanding and the ski resorts have opened earlier and closed later than most previous years. Reports say tourism in the Colorado area is up and the invention of loyalty programs has significantly increased the number of local skiers. Overall, business should be booming. The only reason for the decrease in sales might be the fact that big retailers such as Wal-Mart and Gart Sports are now renting winter sports equipment. Brian would like your team's help in determining how he can use the capabilities of IT described in this unit to help his company increase sales and compete with these big retailers.

5. **Gaining Business Intelligence from Strategic Initiatives**

   You are a new employee in the customer service department at Premier One, a large pet food distributor. The company, founded by several veterinarians, has been in business for three years and focuses on providing nutritious pet food at a low cost. The company currently has 90 employees and operates in seven states. Sales over the past three years have tripled and the manual systems currently in place are no longer sufficient to run the business. Your first task is to meet with your new team and create a presentation for the president and chief executive officer describing supply chain management, customer relationship management, and enterprise resource planning systems. The presentation should highlight the main benefits Premier One can receive from these strategic initiatives along with any additional added business value that can be gained from the systems.

UNIT 4

Creating Collaborative Partnerships in Business

Amazon.com—Just a Click Away

Mention the word "Amazon" and most people will not necessarily think of the largest river in the world. The common perception of Amazon.com is that it is a Web-based bookstore, but Amazon.com is much more than merely a place to buy books. Amazon.com and its sellers list millions of unique, new, and used items in categories ranging from baby products to tools and kitchen appliances.

When Amazon.com first opened its virtual doors on July 16, 1995, it was one of several online bookstores. As Amazon.com embraced the technology to categorize and display millions of books in one space, people welcomed the ability to search for and purchase books in a new way. The experience of building a successful business based on an open system like the Web has influenced Amazon.com throughout its history. Amazon.com has consistently pushed the technology envelope in its search to provide a satisfying, personalized experience for its customers. What started as a human-edited list of product suggestions has morphed into a sophisticated computer-generated recommendation engine that tailors product choices for millions of individuals by analyzing their purchase histories and the patterns of other Amazon.com customers. As the Web evolved into a two-way space for discussion and community, Amazon.com has developed features that allow anyone to post information and advice about products.

Amazon.com, perhaps best known for its highly effective and popular affiliate marketing program, has achieved much success during its short time in business (Figure 4.1). It has grown from a Web-based start-up in 1995 to become one of the most influential businesses in history with five international Web sites: (1) www.amazon.co.uk (Great Britain), (2) www.amazon.de (Germany), (3) www.amazon.fr (France), (4) www.amazon.co.jp (Japan), and (5) www.amazon.ca (Canada).

Amazon's e-Business Strategy

Under the direction of CEO Jeffrey Bezos, *Time*'s Man of the Year in 1999, Amazon.com has put into place sound principles for conducting e-business, such as having a strong business focus. Amazon.com pays close attention to its e-business strategy including:

- Promoting a sense of community
- Knowing its customers
- Building customer satisfaction

FIGURE 4.1

A View of
Amazon.com's Virtual
Storefront

- Providing safe and timely delivery of products
- Name branding
- Web development
- Reducing costs

Amazon.com does not work like a traditional retailer, since it does not run any physical storefronts. Its e-business strategy shifts much of Amazon.com's inventory burden to its suppliers and avoids the expensive real estate of retail stores. The company's central distribution system increases selections while decreasing inventory. Amazon.com gradually evolved from a "all-virtual-no-inventory" Web site to a well-established merchandising operation, with a few centralized warehouses covering the entire United States.

The company's perpetual pursuit for reinventing itself, mainly by adding more interesting features to its Web site, is an attempt to entertain its customers and create what is sometimes called "stickiness" (customer retention). Specific features include personalized recommendations, online customer reviews, and "1-click ordering"—the creation of a true one-stop shopping establishment where customers can find anything they want to buy online. Through the Amazon.com Auctions, zShops (independent third-party sellers), and more recently the Amazon.com Marketplace (where customers can sell pre-owned items), the company is able to offer its customers almost everything.

Amazon.com has become a true household brand, enjoying a high level of recognition among consumers; it has about 29 million customers, achieving profitability earlier than most analysts expected. The company is a massive online retailer, but it is capable of much more than just helping customers load up on new DVDs. In fact, learning to effectively use Amazon.com allows customers to harness an incredible array of information concerning an enormous variety of consumer products. Amazon.com is really a complex Web application, a tool that can be customized and adapted for personal uses. This includes participating in the Amazon.com community, earning money through Amazon.com's Marketplace, and improving the way users interact with its Web site.

Using Technology to Gain a Competitive Advantage

Over Amazon.com's lifetime, the company has invested $900 million in technology. Though Amazon.com's primary line of business is selling books, it is slowly transforming into a company that is creating its competitive advantage with its Web site and supply chain management system. More and more, Amazon.com is in the business of providing technology to other businesses, as well as its customers. For example, 30 percent of Amazon.com's business is from third-party sales. This means other businesses, and sometimes even competitors, are making money through Amazon.com.

Shaping Amazon.com's Future

It should not have been a surprise when Amazon.com released a free Web service that enables its business partners (whom Amazon.com calls "Associates") to interact with its Web site. More specifically, this Web service allows its partners access to catalog data, the ability to create and populate an Amazon.com shopping cart, and even initiate the checkout process. Over the past 16 months, the company has inspired 30,000 Associates to invent new ways to extend Amazon.com's visibility on the Internet.[1,2,3,4,5]

INTRODUCTION

Imagine being the CEO of Barnes and Noble, Leonard Riggio, and picking up *The Wall Street Journal* in July 1995. Grabbing the phone and calling his CIO, he demands to know, "Who is this Bezos?" Today most people know that it is Jeffrey Bezos, CEO and founder of Amazon.com, sometimes called "earth's biggest bookstore." The amazing story of Bezos's virtual bookstore can teach us many lessons about conducting business online. Out of nowhere, this digital bookstore turned an industry upside down. What happened here was more than creating a Web site. Bezos conceived and implemented an intelligent, global digital business. Its business is its technology; its technology is its business. Shocking traditional value chains in the book-selling industry, Amazon.com opened thousands of virtual bookstores in its first months of operation.

This unit focuses on the opportunities and advantages found with developing collaborative partnerships in e-business, outsourcing, and integration. Specific relationships between the use and deployment of technology and the creating of partnerships will be discussed. The chapters in Unit 4 are:

- **Chapter Thirteen**—Creating Collaborative Partnerships through E-Business
- **Chapter Fourteen**—Enhancing Collaborative Partnerships
- **Chapter Fifteen**—Outsourcing Collaborative Partnerships
- **Chapter Sixteen**—Integrating Collaborative Partnerships

Chapter Thirteen: Creating Collaborative Partnerships through E-Business

LEARNING OUTCOMES

13.1. Describe how IT accelerates and enhances e-business.

13.2. List and describe the importance of e-business models.

13.3. Explain why forming electronic partnerships and alliances is critical to an organization.

13.4. Differentiate between B2B and B2C e-business models.

13.5. Describe the major digital marketplace structures.

13.6. Describe the benefits of m-commerce.

The Internet is a powerful channel that presents new opportunities for an organization to touch customers, enrich products and services with information, and reduce costs. *E-commerce* is the buying and selling of goods and services over the Internet. *E-business,* derived from the term e-commerce, is the conducting of business on the Internet, not only buying and selling, but also serving customers and collaborating with business partners. E-business processes are now changing the nature of the buyer-seller relationship, the role of information technology (IT), and organizational structures and activities.

EVOLUTION OF E-BUSINESS

In everyday usage, the terms Internet commerce or I-commerce, Web-commerce, digital commerce, e-business, and e-commerce are interchangeable. Regardless of the e-label, the Internet extends a company's business processes to customers, trading partners, suppliers, and distributors. By eliminating time and distance the Internet makes it possible to do things in ways not previously imaginable. More important, and unlike the telephone and fax, the Internet connects people directly with the information source with which they work.

In the past few years, e-business seems to have permeated every aspect of daily life. In just a short time, both individuals and organizations have embraced Internet technologies to enhance productivity, maximize convenience, and improve communications globally. From banking to shopping to entertainment, the Internet has become integral to daily life. Twenty years ago, most people went into a financial institution and spoke with a teller or some other person to conduct regular banking transactions. Ten years ago, many people had embraced the ATM machine, which made banking activities more convenient. Today, millions of individuals rely on online banking services to complete a large percentage of their banking transactions.

The rapid growth and acceptance of Internet technologies have led some to wonder why the e-business phenomenon did not occur decades ago. The short answer is it was not possible. In the past, the necessary infrastructure did not exist to support e-business. Most businesses ran large mainframe computers with proprietary data formats. Even if the transfer of data from these large machines into homes had been achievable, the home computer was not yet a commodity, so there were few computers outside of businesses to receive information. As PCs became more popular, especially in the home, the ability to conduct e-business was still restricted because of the infrastructure required to support it, including customer and supplier interaction along with credit card processing systems. This has all changed. Refer to Figure 4.2 for an overview of several industries represented in e-business today.

To set up an e-business even a decade ago would have required an individual organization to assume the burden of developing the entire technology infrastructure, as well as its own business and marketing strategies. Today, the challenge of e-business is *integration*. Industry-leading companies have developed Internet-based products and services to handle many aspects of customer and supplier interactions. Integrating these technologies and services, however, around sound business and marketing strategies, on a real-time basis, can still be a monumental undertaking.

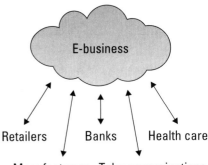

FIGURE 4.2

Overview of Several E-Business Industries

"In today's retail market, you cannot be a credible national retailer without having a robust Web site," says Dennis Bowman, senior vice president and CIO of Circuit City based in Richmond, Virginia, who adds that seamless retailing has become as much of a customer expectation as stores that are clean and well stocked. To that end, retailers are working furiously to integrate their e-business sites with their inventory and point-of-sale (POS) systems so that they can accept in-store returns of merchandise bought online and allow customers to buy on the Web and pick up in the store. Some companies, such as Best Buy, Circuit City, Office Depot, and Sears, already perform this. Their physical and online stores are completely integrated. These companies have been the fast movers because they already had an area in their stores for merchandise pick up (usually for big, bulky items like TVs and appliances), and because long before the Web they had systems and processes in place that facilitated the transfer of a sale from one store to another. Other retailers are partially integrated. Ann Taylor, Bed Bath & Beyond, Eddie Bauer, Linens 'n Things, Macy's, REI, Target, The Gap, and others let customers return but not pick up online-ordered merchandise in stores.[6,7]

E-Business Economy

As e-business continues to grow by both organizations and consumers who have access to the Internet from their homes and offices, the excitement spreads and potential for success increases. However, explosive growth of the Internet has also led to a growing number of integration challenges for e-businesses of all sizes and types.

E-business is not something a business can just go out and buy. A growing number of companies are already using the Internet to streamline their business processes, procure materials, sell products, automate customer service, and create new revenue streams. The Internet is forcing organizations to refocus their information systems from the inside out. Although the benefits of e-business systems are enticing—developing, deploying, and managing these systems is not always easy.

Competing for the future with e-business is not just about technology. Nor is it just about business. It is inseparably about both. According to an NUA Internet Survey, over 620 million people worldwide are linked to the Internet. Experts predict that global Internet usage will nearly triple between 2003 and 2006, making e-business an ever more significant factor in the global economy. Estimates suggest that by 2009 some 47 percent of all business will be conducted online.[8]

Just as BarnesandNoble.com created a digital mirror of its brick-and-mortar bookstore (see Figure 4.3), minus the coffee shop, the Internet will create a digital reflection of the economy.

FIGURE 4.3

A View of
BarnesandNoble.com's
Virtual Storefront

As one example, General Motors is bringing to the Web its response to AutobyTel
.com and Carpoint.com by allowing consumers to go online to configure and price
vehicles without bypassing dealers. Instead, the sites will direct customers to the
nearest dealer, allowing them to negotiate automobile purchases.

THE IMPORTANCE OF THE E-BUSINESS MODEL

An *e-business model* is an approach to conducting electronic business by which a
company can become a profitable business on the Internet. E-business models aim
to use and leverage the unique qualities of the Internet and the Web to conduct
business.

Simply "porting" a business to the Internet will most likely fail. The Internet can
change the customer experience, and that change is not always appropriate. For
example, there is a difference between convenience and specialty goods. Convenience goods are the basics of life, such as groceries, banking, and other commodities that people want to acquire while spending the least amount of time and effort.
Specialty goods, on the other hand, are highly valued and only complete information will satisfy the consumer in making these infrequent buying decisions. A Web
site must accommodate both of these.

The distinction between buying convenience and specialty is not removed with
the advent of the Internet. Buying aspirin and buying a car are different—the commodity versus the specialty good. On a Web site the nature of this difference must
be retained.

Exchanges take place between two major entities: (1) businesses and (2) consumers. All e-business activities happen within the framework of two types of business relationships: (1) the exchange of products and services with consumers

E-Business Term	Definition
Business-to-business (B2B)	Applies to businesses buying from and selling to each other over the Internet.
Business-to-consumer (B2C)	Applies to any business that sells its products or services to consumers over the Internet.
Consumer-to-business (C2B)	Applies to any consumer that sells a product or service to a business over the Internet.
Consumer-to-consumer (C2C)	Applies to sites primarily offering goods and services to assist consumers interacting with each other over the Internet.

	Business	Consumer
Business	B2B grainger.com	B2C carfax.com
Consumer	C2B ideas.com	C2C eBay.com

FIGURE 4.4

Basic Internet Business Models

(business-to-consumer) and (2) the exchange of products and services between businesses (business-to-business). ***Business-to-consumer (B2C)*** applies to any business that sells its products or services to consumers over the Internet. ***Business-to-business (B2B)*** applies to businesses buying from and selling to each other over the Internet. However, there is more to it than just purchasing. B2B has evolved to encompass supply chain management as more businesses outsource parts of their supply chain to their trading partners. It is worth mentioning that B2B e-business is the dominant e-business force by far representing 80 percent of present activities on the Internet. Figure 4.4 summarizes the basic business models developed for the Internet.

To be successful in e-business, an organization must master the art of electronic relationships. Building a Web site does not mean customers will come. Traditional means of customer acquisition such as advertising, promotions, and public relations are just as important with a Web site. Once customers are attracted, a Web site must create the "buzz," much like Amazon.com has done in the book-selling business. A company's Web site must be innovative, add value, and provide useful information. In short, the site must build a sense of community and become the "port of entry" for business.

Fruit of the Loom (FOL) understood this concept when it built its ActiveWear Web site and pioneered the notion of *coopetition* (cooperating with its competition) on the Web. It wanted to become the "port of entry" in its industry where everyone would come to transact business, tell stories, and display goods.

FOL positioned itself as the preeminent *cybermediary* (intermediator in e-business) by using its e-business systems to host its own site and also provide its expertise, software, and hosting to its distribution chain. Even the smallest "mom-n-pop" FOL distributor could have a sophisticated site, thanks to FOL, without having to acquire hardware or software. In addition, the distributors were not restricted to handling only FOL products. Customers could buy Hanes underwear from these distributors using the online facilities of FOL. Overall, a B2B or a B2C e-business Web site can:

- Reduce operational costs
- Increase efficiency from a rise in precision and speed
- Offer access to local, national, and international markets
- Offer personalized products and services
- Allow specialized marketing

Business-to-Business (B2B) Overview

Most of the early B2B procurements established tight links to a company's existing suppliers. They used their existing business practices and trading partners but lowered costs through automation. The savings resulted from dramatically reducing the costs. A few of the primary business advantages for B2B include:

- Managing inventory more efficiently
- Adjusting more quickly to customer demand
- Getting products to market faster
- Cutting the cost of paperwork
- Obtaining lower prices on supplies

Several examples of business-to-business are:

- United States carmakers Ford Motor, General Motors, and DaimlerChrysler (the Big Three) are cooperating on a B2B marketplace, called Covisint.
- US Steel Group, the United States' largest steel maker, has bought a stake in B2B steel exchange e-STEEL Corp.
- Oil giants including BP Amoco, Royal Dutch/Shell Group, and the Totalfina Elf Group formed a B2B site called Intercontinental Exchange.
- Buzzsaw.com, Bidcom, and Cephren have targeted areas of their industry by developing software and Web sites to connect real estate companies, architects, builders, engineers, and materials suppliers.[9]

Business-to-Consumer (B2C) Overview

A B2C Web site must attract customers and more importantly retain customers. This "stickiness" is the essence of e-business. Unlike the mass media of print and broadcasting, the Web is an interactive environment. A few advantages of the B2C market are:

- Access to a wider selection of products and services
- Access to products at lower costs
- Convenience for transactions or for obtaining information (saves time, etc.)

When most people think of B2C e-business, they think of Web sites such as Amazon.com and Dell.com. However, in addition to online retailers, B2C has grown to include services such as online banking, travel services, online auctions, health information, and real estate sites.

The Difference between B2B and B2C E-Business

The primary difference between B2B and B2C are the customers; B2B customers are other businesses while B2C customers are consumers. Overall, B2B relations are more complex and have higher security needs because of the volume of transactions that this market segment generates.

CHALLENGES OF THE E-BUSINESS MODELS

There are several challenges for the e-business models, such as the high cost of developing a dynamic Web site. The primary challenges include:

1. Security concerns
2. Taxation
3. Consumer protection

Security Concerns

A serious deficiency arises from the use of the Internet as a marketing means. Sixty percent of Internet users do not trust the Internet as a payment channel. Making purchases via the Internet is considered unsafe. This issue affects both the business and the consumer, as suggested in Figure 4.5. However, with encryption and the development of secure Web sites, security is becoming less of a constraint for e-businesses.

FIGURE 4.5

Security Concerns

Security Concerns	
Hackers	Although they receive the most attention and carry a rebel mystique, hackers are the least of a company's worries when it comes to securing its network. Basic security measures such as vulnerability assessment software, scanning tools, and updated password programs will keep hackers out and information safely in.
Insiders	A much more tangible threat comes from company insiders. Disgruntled current employees and former workers are often the most dangerous security threats and account for up to 75 percent of all security breaches, according to FBI statistics. In order to diminish the threat of insiders, organizations should establish strict security policies and develop internal processes to enforce those policies.
Passwords	In many cases, passwords are the first and last line of defense. Often, passwords are not changed frequently, are shared between users on a common desktop computer or are displayed in easy-to-see places such as on the computer itself.
Known software flaws	Perhaps the most preventable, and often overlooked, security risks are known software flaws. Each year security teams, security institutes, and software companies issue hundreds of alerts and patches for these known flaws.
General inattention to security	While it is hard to imagine that any organization or IT administrator could ignore security, it is not hard to understand why security may not be the most pressing issue. In e-business when continual uptime is essential and downtime can mean losses of millions of dollars, IT administrators are often focused on keeping systems running.

Taxation

While taxation should not discourage consumers from using electronic purchasing channels, it should not favor Internet purchases over store purchases either. Instead, a tax policy should provide a level playing field for traditional retail businesses, mail order companies, and Internet-based merchants. The Internet marketplace is rapidly expanding, yet it remains mostly free from traditional forms of taxation. In one recent study, uncollected state and local sales taxes from e-business exceeded $13 billion in 2001 and are projected to exceed $45 billion in 2006.[10]

Consumer Protection

In today's electronic marketplace, consumer protection must recognize that many consumers are unfamiliar with their digital choices and some e-businesses are well aware of these vulnerabilities. Therefore, consumers must be protected against:

- Unsolicited goods and communication
- Illegal or harmful goods, services, and content
- Insufficient information about goods or their suppliers
- Invasion of privacy
- Cyberfraud

Suppliers are in danger too, being exposed to unknown liabilities especially because Internet commerce law is vaguely defined and differs from country to country. The Internet and its use in e-business have raised many ethical, social, and political issues, such as identity theft and information manipulation.

THE EVOLUTION OF THE E-MARKETPLACE

Electronic marketplaces represent a new wave in e-business. ***Electronic marketplaces,*** or ***e-marketplaces,*** are interactive business communities providing a central market space where multiple buyers and sellers can engage in e business activities. They present structures for commercial exchange, consolidating supply chains, and creating new sales channels. Their primary goal is to increase market efficiency by tightening and automating the relationship between buyers and sellers. Existing e-marketplaces allow access to various mechanisms in which to buy and sell almost anything, from services to direct materials.

As e-business becomes more central to the operations of core companies, diverse marketplaces are arising in every industry. Most of the early movers have been small, aggressive dot.coms seeking first-mover advantages that they hope result in market dominance. For example, Microsoft's Small Business Center (formerly called bCentral) positions itself as the online partner for the more than seven million small businesses across the United States.

E-marketplaces have been largely composed of B2B electronic exchanges and auctions that have brought buyers and sellers together in a digital environment. This environment favors buyers more than sellers because buyers have been able to drive down prices based on their combined purchasing power and increased competition.

THE NEXT GENERATION: M-COMMERCE

In a few years, Internet-enabled mobile devices will outnumber PCs. ***Mobile commerce,*** or ***m-commerce,*** is the ability to purchase goods and services through a wireless Internet-enabled device. The emerging technology behind m-commerce is mobile devices equipped with Web-ready micro-browsers. In order to take advantage of the m-commerce market potential, handset manufacturers Nokia, Ericsson, Motorola, and Qualcomm are working with telecommunication carriers AT&T Wireless and Sprint to develop *smartphones*. Using new forms of technology, smartphones offer fax, e-mail, and phone capabilities all in one, paving the way for m-commerce to be accepted by an increasingly mobile workforce. Figure 4.6 gives a visual overview of m-commerce.

FIGURE 4.6

M-Commerce
Technology Overview

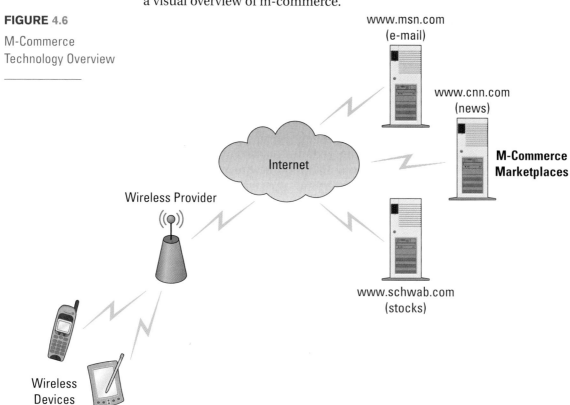

www.msn.com
(e-mail)

www.cnn.com
(news)

Internet

**M-Commerce
Marketplaces**

Wireless Provider

www.schwab.com
(stocks)

Wireless
Devices

Amazon.com has collaborated with Nokia to pioneer a new territory. With the launch of its Amazon.com Anywhere service, it has become one of the first major online retailers to recognize and do something about the potential of Internet-enabled wireless devices. As content delivery over wireless devices becomes faster, more secure, and scalable, m-commerce will surpass landline e-business (traditional telephony) as the method of choice for digital commerce transactions. According to the research firm Strategy Analytics, the global m-commerce market will be worth over $200 billion by 2005, and some 350 million customers will be generating almost 14 billion transactions annually. Additionally, information activities like e-mail, news, and stock quotes will progress to personalized transactions, "1-click" travel reservations, online auctions, and videoconferencing.[11]

OPENING CASE STUDY QUESTIONS

1. Explain whether Amazon.com is a B2B or B2C.

2. Identify how Amazon.com is already integrating its business in the e-marketplace.

3. Explain how m-commerce will influence the way Amazon.com conducts business.

Chapter Thirteen Case: 7-Eleven's Dream Team

In Japan, e-business is still in its infancy. The click-and-mortar retailers, those who sell both online and in stores, exceed those companies selling exclusively online. Surprisingly, convenience stores, which are geographically the closest stores for Japanese consumers, are establishing a new click-and-mortar standard for e-business, the Japanese way.

7-Eleven Japan has integrated its online site 7dream.com with its physical stores. Through the 7dream.com Web site, 7-Eleven Japan enables consumers to choose from an online assortment of 100,000 products, and then pay for and pick them up at one of the 8,400 7-Eleven stores nationwide, which are open 24 hours a day! 7-Eleven Japan believes that e-business does not necessarily run counter to conventional retailing. The key for them is to combine the features of the Internet into the existing retailing process.

The Japanese market has some unique characteristics. First, there are many non-PC Internet-accessible terminals. Mobile phones are in widespread use in Japan. Not only do one out of two people use them, but also more than 14 million cellular phone subscribers have Internet access. Furthermore, video game terminals with Internet access are also quite popular. Therefore, the number of consumers who can partake in e-business without the use of a PC is surprisingly large.

Second, convenience stores have blanket coverage across Japan's islands to an astounding degree. In total, there are approximately 40,000 convenience stores in Japan and approximately 8,400, or 20 percent, are 7-Eleven stores. In comparison, there are only 600 7-Eleven stores in California, which has a land mass approximately the same as Japan's.[12,13]

Questions

1. What 7dream.com sells is "convenience." Explain how integrating the Internet into its existing business is the key to its success.

2. Identify new electronic relationships 7-Eleven Japan can create to increase customer acquisitions.

3. Explain how 7-Eleven Japan can leverage the advantages of an e-marketplace to increase customer retention.

PLUG-IN POINTER >>

Review *Business Plug-In* **e-Business Models** for an overview of the complex network of suppliers, distributors, and customers who deal with each other via the Internet, and the e-business models they use.

Chapter Fourteen: Enhancing Collaborative Partnerships

14.1. Identify the different ways in which companies collaborate using technology.

14.2. Compare the different categories of collaboration technologies.

14.3. List, describe, and provide an example of a content management system.

14.4. Evaluate the advantages of using a workflow system.

14.5. Differentiate between a groupware system and a peer-to-peer system.

14.6. Define the fundamental concepts of a knowledge management system.

14.7. Explain the current tools and trends used in a collaborative working environment.

Heineken USA has shortened its inventory cycle time for beer production and distribution from three months to four weeks. By using its collaborative system to forecast demand and expedite shipping, the company has dramatically cut inventory levels and shipping costs while increasing sales.

Over the last few years most business processes have changed on various dimensions (e.g., flexibility, interconnectivity, coordination style, autonomy) because of market conditions and organizational models. Frequently, information is located within physically separated systems as more and more organizations spread their reach globally. This creates a need for a software infrastructure that enables collaboration systems.

A ***collaboration system*** is an IT-based set of tools that supports the work of teams by facilitating the sharing and flow of information. Collaboration solves specific business tasks such as telecommuting, online meetings, deploying applications, and remote project and sales management (see Figure 4.7). Collaboration allows people, teams, and organizations to leverage and build upon the ideas and talents of staff, suppliers, customers, and business partners. It involves a unique set of business challenges that:

- Include complex interactions between people who may be in different locations and desire to work across function and discipline areas.

- Require flexibility in work process and the ability to involve others quickly and easily.

- Create and share information rapidly and effortlessly within a team.

FIGURE 4.7

Collaborative Business Areas

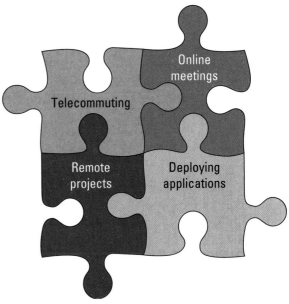

Most organizations collaborate with other organizations in some capacity. Consider the supplier-customer relationship, which can be thought of in terms of a continuous life cycle of engagement, transaction, fulfillment, and service activities. Rarely do companies excel in all four life cycle areas, either from a business process or from a technology-enabled aspect. Successful organizations identify and invest in their core competencies, and outsource or collaborate for those competencies that are not core to them.

THE NEED FOR COLLABORATION

Collaboration technologies fall into one of two categories:

1. *Unstructured collaboration* (sometimes referred to as *information collaboration*)—includes document exchange, shared whiteboards, discussion forums, and e-mail. These functions can improve personal productivity, reducing the time spent searching for information or chasing answers.

2. *Structured collaboration* (or *process collaboration*)—involves shared participation in business processes such as workflow in which knowledge is hardcoded as rules. This is beneficial in terms of improving automation and the routing of information.

Regardless of location or format—be it unstructured or structured—relevant accurate information must be readily and consistently available to those who need it—anytime, anywhere, and on any device. The integration of IT systems enables an organization to provide employees, partners, customers, and suppliers with the ability to access, find, analyze, manage, and collaborate on content. The collaboration can be done across a wide variety of formats, languages, and platforms. Figure 4.8 illustrates many of the typical collaborative functions within most organizations.

Lockheed Martin Aeronautics Company's ability to share complex project information across an extended supply chain in real-time was key in its win of a $19 billion Department of Defense (DoD) contract to build 21 supersonic stealth fighters. New government procurement rules require defense contractors to communicate effectively to ensure that deadlines are met, costs are controlled, and projects are managed throughout the life cycle of the contract.[14]

FIGURE 4.8

Typical Collaborative
Business Functions

Function	Collaborator(s)	Business Function(s)
Planning and forecasting	Supplier, Customer	Real-time information sharing (forecast information and sales information)
Product design	Supplier, Customer	Document exchange, computer-aided design (CAD)
Strategic sourcing	Supplier	Negotiation, supplier performance management
Component compatibility testing	Supplier	Component compatibility
Pricing	Supplier, Customer	Pricing in supply chain
Marketing	Supplier, Customer	Joint/coop marketing campaigns, branding
Sales	Customer	Shared leads, presentations, configuration and quotes
Make-to-order	Customer	Requirements, capabilities, contract terms
Order processing	Supplier, Customer	Order solution
Fulfillment: Logistics and service	Supplier, Customer	Coordination of distribution
International trade logistics	Customer	Document exchange, import/export documents
Payment	Customer	Order receipt, invoicing
Customer service/support	Supplier, Customer	Shared/split customer support

The Fort Worth, Texas, unit of Lockheed Martin Corporation developed a real-time collaboration system in anticipation of the contract that can tie together its partners, suppliers, and DoD customers via the Internet. The platform lets participants collectively work on product design and engineering tasks as well as supply chain and life cycle management issues. Lockheed will host all transactions and own the project information. The platform will let DoD and Lockheed project managers track the daily progress of the project in real-time. This is the first major DoD project with such a requirement. The contract, awarded to the Lockheed unit and partners Northrop Grumman Corp. and BAE Systems, is the first installment in what could amount to a $200 billion program for 3,000 jet fighters over a 40-year period.[15]

Strengths the collaboration process offers lie with the integration of many systems, namely:

- Content management systems
- Workflow management systems
- Groupware systems
- Peer-to-peer systems
- Knowledge management systems

Content Management Systems

At its foundation, a **content management system (CMS)** provides tools to manage the creation, storage, editing, and publication of information in a collaborative environment. As a Web site grows in size and complexity, the business must establish procedures to ensure that things run smoothly. At a certain point, it makes sense to automate this process and use a content management system to manage this effectively. Refer to Figure 4.9 for a listing of the major CMS vendors.

The CMS marketplace is complex, incorporating document management, digital asset management, and Web content management. Each one of these areas is distinct from the others:

- **Document management system (DMS)**—Supports the electronic capturing, storage, distribution, archival, and accessing of documents. A DMS optimizes the use of documents within an organization independent of any publishing medium (for example, the Web). A DMS provides a document repository with information about other information. The system tracks the editorial history of each document and its relationships with other documents. A variety of search and navigation methods are available to make document retrieval easy. A DMS manages highly structured and regulated content, such as pharmaceutical documentation.

- **Digital asset management system (DAM)**—Though similar to document management in some ways, DAM generally works with binary rather than text files, such as multimedia file types. DAM places emphasis on allowing file manipulation and conversion, for example, converting GIF files to JPEG.

- **Web content management system (WCM)**—Adds an additional layer to document and digital asset management that enables publishing content both to intranets and to public Web sites. In addition to maintaining the content itself, WCM systems often integrate content with online processes like e-business systems.

Content management software is helping BMW Group Switzerland accelerate personalized, real-time information about products, services, prices, and events to its dealers countrywide. BMW uses a process that allows dealers to specify what information is seen by which employee, as well as delivering marketing materials solely to members of the sales department, and technical specifications and support documents only to mechanics. That enhanced personalization eliminates the

Vendors	Strengths	Weaknesses	Costs
Documentum www.documentum.com	Document and digital asset management	Personalization features not as strong as competitors	Major components start at less than $100,000
FatWire www.fatwire.com	Web content management	May not scale to support thousands of users	SPARK, $25,000; Update Engine, $70,000 and up
InterWoven www.interwoven.com	Collaboration, enterprise content management	Requires significant customization	InterWoven 5 Platform, $50,000; average cost for a new customer, $250,000
Percussion www.percussion.com	Web content management	May not scale to support thousands of users	Rhythmyx Content Manager, about $150,000
Stellent www.stellent.com	Document conversion to Web-ready formats	Engineering for very large implementations with thousands of users	Content and Collaboration Servers, $50,000 to $250,000 each
Vignette www.vignette.com	Personalization	Document management and library services are not as robust as others	V6 Multisite Content Manager, $200,000 and up; V6 Content Suite, $450,000 and up

FIGURE 4.9

Content Management System Vendor Overview

chance that information is sent to the wrong dealership or to the wrong individual, which provides higher quality customer service. The content management software also enables nontechnical employees to create pages using predefined layout templates, simplifying the Web publishing process. More than 500 people use the solution daily, and all employees are able to publish information without calling on IT specialists, while maintaining the look and feel of the BMW brand.[16]

Workflow Management Systems

Workflow management systems control the movement of work through a business process. Work activities can be performed in series or in parallel and involve people and automated computer systems. In addition, many workflow management systems allow the opportunity to measure and analyze the execution of the process. Workflow management systems integrate with other organizational systems, such as document management systems, database systems, e-mail systems, and inventory management systems. This integration links otherwise independent systems and provides a method (such as a project folder) for organizing documents from diverse sources. Figure 4.10 lists some typical features associated with workflow management systems.

New York City was experiencing a record number of claims, ranging from injuries resulting from slips on sidewalks to medical malpractice at city hospitals. Claims are generally filed with the Comptroller's Office, which investigates them and offers to settle meritorious claims. The New York City Comptroller's Office, with the assistance of its consultants Xerox and Universal Systems Inc., utilized a workflow management system to enhance revenues and decrease operating costs.

NYC processes over 30,000 claims and incurs a quarter of a billion dollars in claim costs annually. With the implementation of the Omnibus Automated Image Storage Information System (OAISIS), processing contracts and claims, NYC will be saving over $20 million dollars using this workflow management system. Numerous organizations from NYC were involved, including:

- Bureau of Law and Adjustment
- Office of Contracts/Administration
- Management and Accounting Systems

Workflow Feature	Description
Process definition tool	A graphical or textual tool for defining a business process. Each activity within the process is associated with a person or a computer application. Rules are created to determine how the activities progress across the workflow and which controls are in place to govern each activity.
Simulation, prototyping, and piloting	Some systems allow workflow simulation or create prototype and/or pilot versions of a particular workflow to test systems on a limited basis before going into production.
Task initiation and control	The business process defined above is initiated and the appropriate resources (either human and/or IT related) are scheduled and/or engaged to complete each activity as the process progresses.
Rules-based decision making	Rules are created for each step to determine how workflow-related information is to be processed, routed, tracked, and controlled. As an example, one rule might generate e-mail notifications when a condition has been met. Another rule might implement conditional routing of documents and tasks based on the content of fields.
Document routing	In simple systems, this is accomplished by passing a file or folder from one recipient to another (e.g., an e-mail attachment). In sophisticated systems, document routing is completed by checking the documents in and out of a central repository. Both systems might allow for "redlining" of the documents so that each person in the process can add their own comments without affecting the original document.
Applications to view and manipulate information	Word-processors, spreadsheets, and production systems are used to allow workers to create, update, and view information.
Work list	Current tasks are quickly identified along with such things as a due date, goal date, and priority by using work lists. In some systems, an anticipated workload is displayed as well. These systems analyze where jobs are in the workflow and how long each step should take, and then estimate when various tasks will reach a worker's desk.
Task automation	Computerized tasks are automatically invoked. These might include such things as letter writing, e-mail notices, or execution of production systems. Task automation often requires customization of the basic workflow product.
Event notification	Employees can be notified when certain milestones occur or when workload increases.
Process monitoring	The workflow system can provide an organization with valuable information on current workload, future workload, bottlenecks (current or potential), turn-around time, or missed deadlines.
Tracking and logging of activities	Information about each step can be logged. This might include such things as start and completion times, worker(s) assigned to the task, and key status fields. Later, this information can be used to analyze the process or to provide evidence that certain tasks were in fact completed.

FIGURE 4.10

Workflow Management System Features

- Financial Information Systems Agency
- Office of Management and Budget
- Bureau of Accounting
- Bureau of Labor Law
- Bureau of Information Systems

The workflow management system has to support all these NYC organizations. The system performs many functions that were previously labor intensive and subtracted from the quality and efficiency of investigations. The workflow management system screens claims to determine accordance with statutory requirements. Acknowledgment letters are generated automatically, with little or no resource allocation involved in assignment of claims or routing of claims to specific work locations. Status letters are automatically generated by the system for certain claim types, thus allowing the Comptroller's office to keep the claimants informed of their claims two months, five months, and one year from the date of their filing. All this is done automatically by the workflow management system.

FIGURE 4.11

Workflow Process
Diagram

Workflow management systems allow management the ability to schedule individual systematic claim review without a disruption to the investigation. Management can also see the entire claim process graphically and determine bottlenecks. Deployment of additional resources to needed areas occurs without a management analysis of a particular process problem. Review Figure 4.11 for a workflow diagram of the process flow across processes.[17]

Business Processes

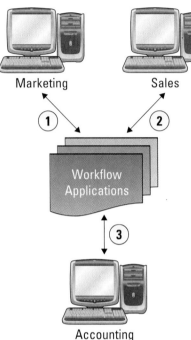

Groupware Systems

Groupware is software that supports team interaction and dynamics including calendaring, scheduling, and videoconferencing. Organizations can use this technology to communicate, cooperate, coordinate, solve problems, compete, or negotiate. While traditional technologies like the telephone qualify as groupware, the term refers to a specific class of technologies relying on modern computer networks, such as e-mail, newsgroups, videophones, and chat rooms. Groupware technologies fall along two primary categories (see Figure 4.12):

1. Users of the groupware are working together at the same time (real-time or synchronous groupware) or different times (asynchronous groupware).

2. Users are working together in the same place (colocated or face-to-face) or in different places (noncolocated or distance).

The groupware concept integrates various systems and functionalities into a common set of services or a single (client) application. In addition, groupware can represent a wide range of systems and methods of integration. Groupware offers an organization significant advantage over single-user systems, such as:

- Facilitating communication (make it faster, clearer, more persuasive)
- Enabling communication where it would not otherwise be possible
- Enabling telecommuting
- Reducing travel costs
- Collaborating expertise
- Forming groups with common interests where it would not be possible to gather a sufficient number of people face-to-face
- Saving time and cost in coordinating group work
- Facilitating group problem solving

FIGURE 4.12

Groupware
Technologies

	Same time "Synchronous"	Different time "Asynchronous"
Same place "Colocated"	Presentation support	Shared computers
Different place "Distance"	Videophones, Chat	E-mail, Workflow

Lotus Notes (or just Notes) is one of the world's leading software solutions for collaboration that combines messaging, groupware, and the Internet. The structure of Notes allows it to track, route, and manage documents. Systems that lend themselves to Notes involve tracking, routing, approval, document management, and organization.

Toyota developed an intranet system to promote information sharing within the company and to raise productivity. Unfortunately, the company's conventional e-mail system became overloaded, generating problems. Users did not receive incoming messages and were not able to send messages. Individual departments had introduced their own e-mail systems. Messages to other mail systems, including those outside the company, experienced delays, and the different mail systems were incompatible. As Internet use became more widespread, many companies associated with Toyota began to install e-mail systems. To deal with these difficulties, Toyota's information systems department reviewed the e-mail system and restructured it so that e-mail, now recognized as an important communication tool, is utilized more effectively in business transactions.[18]

Peer-to-Peer Systems

Peer-to-peer (P2P) systems allow collaboration in a shared information space to utilize, add to, or comment on any piece of information. Peer-to-peer systems is a concept known to many people only in its most recent and highly publicized incarnation: Napster. Yet P2P computing has been around for at least 30 years in one form or another. Not only does the technology remove the need for centralized servers, it avoids delays and security issues inherent in e-mail and messaging systems, such as chat rooms.

In P2P architecture, computers used traditionally as clients in a client/server network can instead communicate directly among themselves and, for maximum efficiency, can act as both client and server. Consequently, peer-to-peer computing can reduce the load on traditional servers and enable them to perform specialized services more effectively. Figure 4.13 displays a view of the client/server and peer-to-peer models.

Peer-to-peer networks, which interacted with 61,140 organization users in 2001, will grow to a staggering 6.2 million by 2007. Revenues for this market will grow to $4.35 billion by 2007 as estimated by the Gardner Group.[19]

While Napster may be the most widely known example of a P2P implementation, it may also be one of the most narrowly focused. That is because the Napster model takes advantage of only one of the many capabilities of P2P computing: file sharing. In fact, the technology has far broader capabilities, including the sharing of processing, memory, and storage, and support for collaboration among vast numbers of distributed computers. Peer-to-peer computing enables immediate interaction among people and computer systems and business processes, such as:

FIGURE 4.13

Client/Server and Peer-to-Peer Models

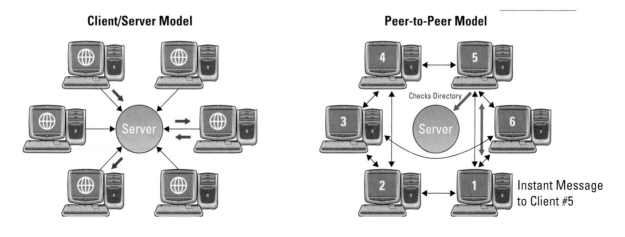

Client/Server Model   **Peer-to-Peer Model**

Server

Checks Directory

Server

Instant Message to Client #5

- Trading
- Conversing
- Chatting
- Designing
- Conducting research
- Planning
- Negotiating
- Clarifying
- Reporting

- Messaging
- Correcting errors
- Handling exceptions
- Sharing knowledge
- Mining shared marketplace information
- Auctioning
- Distributing and maintaining content
- Integrating ERP systems
- Managing projects

The Naval Postgraduate School is an academic institution whose emphasis is on study and research programs relevant to the Navy's interests, as well as on the interests of other branches of the Department of Defense. Nearly 1,500 students attend the school located in Monterey, California, 120 miles south of San Francisco. The student body consists of officers from the five United States uniformed services and from approximately 30 other countries, as well as a small number of civilians.

The Naval Postgraduate School uses a peer-to-peer technology called Groove Workspace to address its two primary challenges. The first was military-related and remains a prominent subject of study at NPS: how to establish distributed, collaborative, command and control centers in decentralized military environments. The second affected NPS directly: how to deliver coursework and learning to the school's primarily remote student population. Both challenges required a technology solution that would enable dispersed groups of individuals to interact and collaborate in a virtual environment. In one case, the environment was a virtual classroom; in the other, it was a virtual command center.

Groove Workspace uses in-class lecture interaction and Q&A, as well as project work and after-hours sessions. Students attend classes at designated times by logging into Groove and entering a shared space created specifically for that course. Students watch as others come online, or "enter" the classroom, and chat as they would in a normal class setting. The lecture is delivered from inside the Groove Web browser tool, allowing instructors to ensure each student is viewing the lecture in sync. Students submit questions to instructors using Groove's synchronous instant messaging capability, and instructors deliver answers to students using voice messaging.[20]

Knowledge Management Systems

Knowledge management involves capturing, classifying, evaluating, retrieving, and sharing information assets in a way that provides context for effective decisions and actions. These are daunting tasks within a single organization, but become even more challenging when all the participants in a value chain (e.g., supply chain) are included.

Knowledge is one of the real competitive advantages. In the same way that the computer itself announced the start of the information age, developments in network-centric computing facilitated a new age of knowledge rather than of information. Not only can future technology distribute information, but it can also distribute an organization's knowledge base by interconnecting people and digitally gathering their expertise.

Such knowledge management requires that organizations go well beyond providing information contained in spreadsheets, databases, and documents. It must include the information and digitally capture experts' expertise. A ***knowledge management system (KMS)*** is a system that supports the capturing and use of an organization's "know-how."

It is up to the organization to determine what information qualifies as intellectual and knowledge-based assets. In general, intellectual and knowledge-based assets fall into one of two categories: (1) explicit or (2) tacit. As a general rule, ***explicit*** *knowledge* consists of anything that can be documented, archived, and codified, often with the help of IT. Examples of explicit knowledge are assets such as patents, trademarks, business plans, marketing research, and customer lists. ***Tacit knowledge*** is the knowledge contained in people's heads. The challenge inherent in tacit knowledge is figuring out how to recognize, generate, share, and manage it. While information technology in the form of e-mail, groupware, instant messaging, and related technologies can help facilitate the dissemination of tacit knowledge, identifying it in the first place is a major hurdle.

The information gathered must reflect reality as perceived and understood by humans, not the artificial constructs of computer files characteristic of many systems. What happens when an organization translates its rules, policies, techniques, workflows, business processes, and decision making to its entire workforce as well as its customers and suppliers in digital form? By making customers, suppliers, and trading partners as smart as the organization itself, a completely new workforce will evolve. People inside and outside the organization become not just connected together, but work with the same knowledge base.

Mountains of information are of little use unless they are extracted and made available to the people or systems that need meaningful information at the right place and at the right time. To get the most value from intellectual assets, knowledge must be shared and serve as the foundation for collaboration. Consequently, an effective KMS program should help do one or more of the following:

- Foster innovation by encouraging the free flow of ideas.
- Improve customer service by streamlining response time.
- Boost revenues by getting products and services to market faster.
- Enhance employee retention rates by recognizing the value of employees' knowledge.
- Streamline operations and reduce costs by eliminating redundant or unnecessary processes.

These are the most prevalent examples. A creative approach to knowledge management can result in improved efficiency, higher productivity, and increased revenues in practically any business function. Figure 4.14 indicates the reasons why organizations launch KMS.

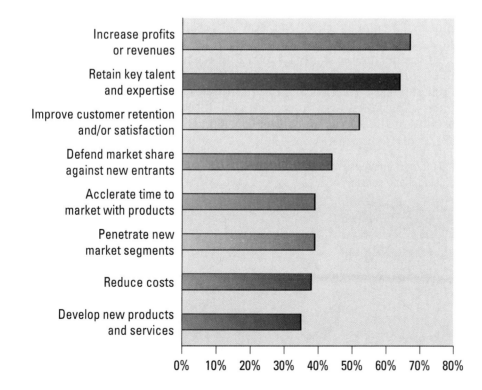

FIGURE 4.14

Why Organizations Launch Knowledge Management Programs

Source: IDC 2002 Knowledge Management Survey.

At ChevronTexaco Corporation, software is helping the company improve how its teams of employees manage the assets in oil fields by enabling employees in multiple disciplines to easily access and share the information they need to make decisions. ChevronTexaco employs teams composed of 10 to 30 people who are responsible for managing the assets, such as the drilling equipment, pipelines, and facilities for a particular oil field. Within each team, earth scientists and various engineers with expertise in production, reservoir, and facilities work together to keep the oil field up and running. Each member of the asset team needs to communicate with other members to make decisions based on the collection and analysis of huge amounts of information from various departments.

Individual team members can look at information from the perspective of their own department. This has helped ChevronTexaco achieve a 30 percent productivity gain, a 50 percent improvement in safety performance, and more than $2 billion in operating cost reductions. KMS techniques have also helped ChevronTexaco restructure its gasoline retailing business to drill oil and gas wells faster and cheaper.[21]

COLLABORATION TRENDS

E-mail is by far the dominant collaboration application, but real-time collaboration tools like instant messaging are creating a new communication dynamic within organizations. *Instant messaging* (sometimes called *IM* or *IMing*) is a type of communications service that enables someone to create a kind of private chat room with another individual in order to communicate in real-time over the Internet. In 1992, AOL deployed IM to the consumer market allowing users to communicate with other "IMers" through a "buddy list." Most of the popular instant messaging programs provide a variety of features, such as:

- Web links—Share links to favorite Web sites
- Images—Look at an image stored on someone else's computer
- Sounds—Play sounds
- Files—Share files by sending them directly to another IMer
- Talk—Use the Internet instead of a phone to talk
- Streaming content—Real-time or near-real-time stock quotes and news
- Instant messages—Receive immediate text messages

Commercial vendors such as AOL and Microsoft offer free instant messaging tools. Real-time collaboration, such as instant messaging, live Web conferencing, and screen or document sharing, creates an environment for decision making through the process of collaboration. AOL, Microsoft's MSN, and Yahoo! have begun to sell enterprise versions of their instant messaging services that match the capabilities of business-oriented products like IBM's Lotus Sametime. Figure 4.15 demonstrates the IM application presence within IT systems.

FIGURE 4.15

Instant Messaging Application Diagram

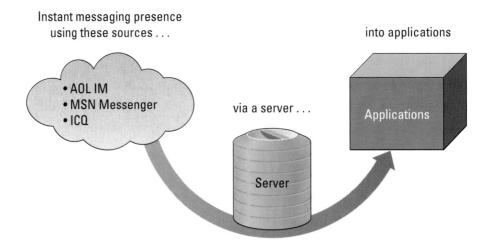

IBM Lotus software released new versions of its real-time collaboration platform, IBM Lotus Instant Messaging and IBM Lotus Web Conferencing, plus its mobile counterpart, IBM Lotus Instant Messaging Everyplace. These built-for-business products let an organization offer presence awareness, secure instant messaging, and Web conferencing in the organization. The products give employees instant access to colleagues and company information regardless of time, place, or device.

The bigger issue in collaboration for organizations is cultural. Collaboration brings teams of people together from different regions, departments, and even companies—people who bring different skills, perceptions, and capabilities. A formal collaboration strategy helps create the right environment, as well as the right systems for team members.

OPENING CASE STUDY QUESTIONS

1. Identify which systems Amazon.com could use to collaborate internally.

2. Explain which Internet technologies have facilitated the way in which Amazon.com collaborates with both its customers and business partners.

3. Describe how Amazon.com could leverage the power of a knowledge management system within its organization.

Chapter Fourteen Case: The Skinny on Knowledge Management at Frito-Lay

Frito-Lay, an $8.5 billion division of PepsiCo in Plano, Texas, had knowledge trapped in files everywhere. Corporate executives knew that capturing best practices and corporate information would increase productivity, thus increasing sales and profitability. However, information was scattered around the company in disparate systems, with no easy way for the geographically strewn sales force to get at it. The sales force also lacked a place for brainstorming and collaboration online. If somebody had a piece of valuable research information and wanted to get additional input from account executives in Baltimore and Los Angeles, online collaboration was impossible. Frito-Lay knew if the 15 member sales team could only access the same information, it would solve its ongoing problems with information sharing and communication.

Frito-Lay built a knowledge management system on its corporate intranet. A knowledge management portal would allow the employees a single point of access to the multiple sources of information as well as providing personalized access. A knowledge management portal would also give the sales department a central location for all sales-related customer and corporate information to cut down on the time it took to find and share research.

The executives from Frito-Lay chose a sales team as the portal pilot and dispersed them across the country, making it ideal for determining whether the portal would succeed in bridging geographic boundaries when it came to sharing internal information. Based on input from the pilot team, Frito-Lay established three goals for its portal: (1) to streamline knowledge, (2) to exploit customer-specific information, and (3) to foster team collaboration.

The portal has proven so successful that its use has now become a PepsiCo initiative. That means it will soon offer added functionality for all employees across the three divisions—Pepsi, Frito-Lay, and Tropicana.[22]

Questions

1. Identify new types of collaboration that Frito-Lay could use to increase its business communication.

2. Explain how Frito-Lay can use the portal technology to gain an advantage in its industry.

3. Describe how knowledge management and the portal application changed the jobs of salespeople at Frito-Lay?

Chapter Fifteen: Outsourcing Collaborative Partnerships

15.1. Describe the advantages and disadvantages of insourcing, outsourcing, and offshore outsourcing.

15.2. Describe why outsourcing is a critical business decision.

15.3. Assess the reasons for developing strategic outsourcing partnerships.

More than 400 people from Merrill Lynch, Thomson Financial (a large market data vendor), and a number of other vendors have been working feverishly on Merrill Lynch's biggest outsourcing initiative ever. This highly complex $1 billion makeover of its wealth management system is designed to improve the efficiency of Merrill's financial advisers. With the new system, Merrill Lynch's financial advisors can obtain more of the assets of their high-net-worth customers.

The new system also represents a major shift in the way Merrill approaches IT initiatives. In the 1990s, Merrill developed its previous system, Trusted Global Advisor (TGA), as it did any other major system—it developed it in-house. The thought of outsourcing a critical business system to a vendor was viewed as highly unfavorable by most financial services organizations. Last year, Merrill Lynch signed a contract that outsourced much of the responsibility for its new platform to Thomson Financial.[23]

In the high-speed global business environment, an organization needs to maximize its profits, enlarge its market share, and restrain its ever-increasing costs. Businesses need to make every effort to rethink and readopt new processes, especially the prospective resources regarding insourcing, outsourcing, and offshore outsourcing.

INSOURCING

Insourcing is a common approach using the professional expertise within an organization to develop and maintain the organization's information technology systems. Insourcing has been instrumental in creating a viable supply of IT professionals and in fact in creating a better quality workforce combining both technical and business skills.

Michael Palmer, the COO (and former CIO) of Allied Office Products, decided to bring in-house nearly all of the IT functions that had been outsourced. Palmer calculated that he could cut the $24,000-a-month hardware monitoring and maintenance costs by two-thirds and save several hundred thousand dollars on development by insourcing. Since Palmer turned to insourcing 85 percent of the IT work, he is now saving nearly $500,000 a year.[24]

OUTSOURCING

Outsourcing is an arrangement by which one organization provides a service or services for another organization that chooses not to perform them in-house. In some cases, the entire information technology department is outsourced, including planning and business analysis as well as the installation, management, and servicing of the network and workstations. Outsourcing can range from a large contract under which an organization like IBM manages IT services for a company such as Xerox, to the practice of hiring contractors and temporary office workers on an individual basis. Refer to Figure 4.16 for a comparison of the functions companies have outsourced.

Ever since Eastman Kodak announced that it was outsourcing its information systems function in 1988 to IBM, DEC, and Businessland, large organizations have found it acceptable to transfer their IT assets, leases, and staff to outsourcers. In view of the changes in sourcing, the key question now is not "should we outsource IT?" but rather "where and how can we take advantage of the rapidly developing market of IT services providers?" Organizations should consider outsourcing in order to achieve the following benefits:

- Financial savings
- Increase technical abilities
- Market agility

Financial Savings

Cost competitiveness has driven the Big Three—Ford, DaimlerChrysler, and General Motors—to collaborate in a unique way by building an IT service. Automotive Network eXchange (ANX) is a network that joins suppliers and buyers across the automotive supply chain and allows the sharing of CAD/CAM drawings, as well as exchanging trade e-mail messages and shipping communications. Ironing out such inefficiencies across the supply chain alone could decrease the cost of producing a car as much as $1,200.[25]

Increase Technical Abilities

Rapid technological change has become an issue for many businesses throughout all industries, resulting in more expense to upgrade systems, more time to install, and increased complexity to master. For a business whose IT department is a non-core function, maintaining a "best-of-breed" status under these conditions is next to impossible, especially for small and medium-sized enterprises where cost is a critical factor.

Nike's footwear business generates $6 billion in revenues per year. It requires an achievement in global communication to keep its global Web of Nike designers,

FIGURE 4.16

Common Departments Outsourced by Organizations

Source: 2003 Hewitt Survey Findings.

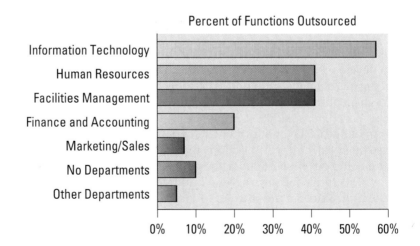

Percent of Functions Outsourced

product developers, marketing teams, sales staff, distributors, and dealers in line with product developments and marketing plans. Nike uses a system called GPIN (Global Product Information Network), an innovative IT service that allows Nike's employees to collaborate throughout their processes and keeps every partner up-to-date with developments.[26]

Market Agility

Market agility includes the ability to expand core businesses more rapidly depending on the outsourcer's capabilities to provide efficient transitions to new systems, better information management for decision making, and expansion to new geographical markets.

Kodak is over 100 years old. So is chemical-based photography. Therefore, Kodak moved its focus from being in the film business to being in the picture-processing business, and from this developed Kodak's exciting e-service, Photonet, a password-protected application that allows users to post photographs on the Internet, order copies, send picture postcards, and customize postcard greetings. [27]

IT outsourcing is a fast-growing industry since it provides access to state-of-the-art technologies with expert guidance, thus curtailing the need to open up expensive in-house departments. According to a report by IDC, global spending on IT services will rise to $700 billion by 2005, an increase from $440 billion in 2002. Many factors have converged to prompt firms to outsource. Figure 4.17 displays the reason why many organizations outsource key departments.[28]

Focusing a company's resources on core business functions allows outsourcing noncore functions. Outsourcing can give the right combination of people, processes, and technology to operate efficiently and effectively in the global marketplace without burdening time and budget. Some of the influential drivers affecting the growth of the outsourcing market include:

- **Core competencies**—Many companies have recently begun to consider outsourcing as a means to fuel revenue growth rather than just a cost-cutting measure. Outsourcing enables an organization to maintain an up-to-date technology infrastructure while freeing it to focus on revenue growth goals by reinvesting cash and human capital in areas offering the greatest return on investment.

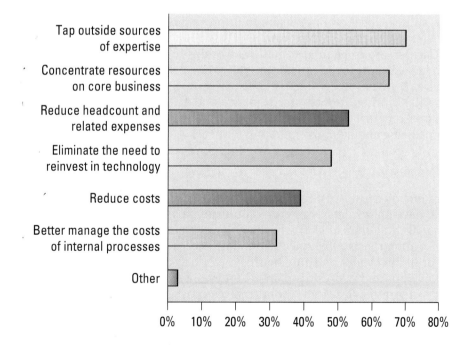

FIGURE 4.17

Reasons Why Companies Have Outsourced

Source: 2003 Hewitt Survey Findings.

- **Rapid growth**—A company's sustainability depends on both speed to market and ability to react quickly to changes in market conditions. By taking advantage of outsourcing, an organization is able to acquire best practices process expertise. This facilitates the design, building, training, and deployment of business processes or functions.

- **Industry changes**—High levels of reorganization across industries have increased demand for outsourcing to better focus on core competencies. The significant increase in merger and acquisition activity created a sudden need to integrate multiple core and noncore business functions into one business, while the deregulation of the utilities and telecom industries created a need to ensure compliance with government rules and regulations. Companies in either situation turned to outsourcing so they could better focus on industry changes at hand.

- **The Internet**—The pervasive nature of the Internet as an effective sales channel has allowed clients to become more comfortable with the outsourcing process.

DEVELOPING STRATEGIC OUTSOURCING PARTNERSHIPS

Business process outsourcing (BPO) is the contracting of a specific business task, such as payroll, to a third-party service provider. Business process outsourcing is increasingly becoming the strategic choice of companies looking to achieve cost reductions while improving their service quality, increasing shareholder value, and focusing on their core business capabilities. Many organizations are looking beyond traditional IT outsourcing to business process outsourcing as the next logical step.

Implementing BPO can assist with a cost-saving measure for tasks that an organization requires but does not depend upon to maintain its position in the marketplace. BPO is divided into two categories: (1) back-office outsourcing that includes internal business functions such as billing or purchasing, and (2) front-office outsourcing which includes customer-related services such as marketing or technical support.

Business process outsourcing is not a new field. Paychex, based in Rochester, New York, for example, has been outsourcing payroll processing for small businesses since 1971. However, the market is heating up these days, as companies' need for strategic cost cutting, desire to improve business methods, and comfort with outsourcing arrangements grow.

The Gartner Group estimates that the worldwide market for business process outsourcing will grow to $178 billion in 2005. Management consulting and technology services company Accenture is a BPO player. Accenture's first BPO deal came in the early 1990s, when it outsourced finance and accounting functions for British Petroleum. Accenture now handles a variety of outsourcing tasks, such as airline ticket processing and call center staffing for AT&T.[29]

SOURCING'S NEW SURGE—OFFSHORING

Offshore outsourcing is using organizations from developing countries to write code and develop systems. Numerous countries have substantially well-trained IT professionals and clerical staff who have lower salary expectations compared to their U.S. counterparts. Offshore outsourcing has become a small but rapidly growing sector in the overall outsourcing market. Nearly half of all businesses use offshore providers, and two-thirds plan to send work overseas in the near future, according to Forrester Research. India receives most of the outsourcing functions from all over the world. However, as more American companies seek to source globally, more countries are emerging to benefit from that demand—from Canada to Malaysia—each with its own particular strengths and weaknesses. Organizations have much to gain from offshore outsourcing.[30]

1. Explain the driving forces behind Amazon.com's need to keep all IT development and systems in-house.

2. Identify which business processes Amazon.com could or perhaps should outsource.

3. Discuss the pitfalls Amazon.com would encounter if it decided to outsource its IT department.

Chapter Fifteen Case: Outsourcing Can Change Everything

Outsourcing can change everything. Not only does it affect a company's relationships, its processes, and its technology environment, it also affects a business's culture.

With nearly $7 billion in sales, media giant Pearson is a leading provider of financial and business news, including the *Financial Times.* Pearson's education unit has imprints such as Addison-Wesley, Longman, Allyn & Bacon, and Prentice Hall. Pearson also publishes trade books through the Penguin Group, including Penguin, Putnam, Dorling Kindersley, and Viking. Its professional and technology group publishes leading computer, information technology, and business titles, such as Addison-Wesley Professional, New Riders, Peachpit Press, Prentice Hall PTR, Que, Sams, and Cisco Press.

IBM signed an outsourcing arrangement with Pearson to provide the company with managed operations services for its mainframe and server environment. Before the contract was signed, Pearson engaged the IBM relationship alignment team to create a "relationship launch." According to Frank McDonnell, vice president of Information Management for Pearson Technology, "The relationship alignment team was and continues to be an exceptional help in assisting us to initiate and sustain the actions necessary to build and maintain the relationship between Pearson and IBM." The team presented four separate launch events, planned so that expectations could be aligned across several layers of management, including members of the IT organization. The sessions enabled participants to understand the amount and nature of work needed to make the relationship a success. According to McDonnell, "Over the past year, I have learned that building the relationship between Pearson and IBM is a continuous process . . . it is a testament to the past and to the continued involvement of the relationship alignment team that we continue to work closely and successfully with our IBM outsourcing team."[31]

Working with IBM, Pearson plans to improve the efficiency and performance of its computer systems and reduce technology spending in The Penguin Group and Pearson Education. The companies will consolidate the operations of many of Pearson's less powerful servers into a smaller number of high-capacity systems and deploy a high-end server to support Pearson's critical business applications such as billing, inventory control, order entry, product distribution, inventory, payroll, human resources, and sales reporting. Pearson is also teaming with IBM's business recovery and continuity experts to ensure that its computer systems can continue to perform critical business functions in the event of a natural disaster.

As a result of the relationship with IBM, more than 70 Pearson employees will join IBM to support Pearson's data center operations, which will be managed from Pearson's facilities in New York City and New Jersey.

Questions

1. Summarize a few reasons why Pearson did not use an insourcing approach for its IT needs.

2. What are some of the advantages that IBM can offer Pearson as a result of outsourcing many of its critical business functions?

3. Explain the advantages of forming an outsourcing relationship with an international company, such as IBM has with Pearson.

PLUG-IN POINTER >>

Review *Business Plug-In* **Strategic Outsourcing** for an in-depth review of the reasons why American companies seek to source globally—from Canada to Malaysia—each with its own particular strengths and weaknesses.

Chapter Sixteen: Integrating Collaborative Partnerships

LEARNING OUTCOMES

16.1. Describe the benefits of deploying a virtual private network.

16.2. List, describe, and provide an example of an electronic trading network.

16.3. Differentiate between an Internet service provider, online service provider, and application service provider.

16.4. Assess the impact of portal technologies within e-business.

16.5. Describe the advantages of embracing open source technology.

There is no longer any doubt that the Internet is reshaping the business landscape. Over 92 percent of CEOs and members of top management agree that the Internet is profoundly transforming the global workplace. They also agree that tremendous competitive advantages belong to those companies that are quick to harness the power of the Internet to facilitate business processes. This includes businesses exchanging mission-critical information in real-time with trading partners around the world over every conceivable network, including:[32]

- **Value-added network (VAN)**—a private network, provided by a third party, for exchanging information through a high capacity connection.
- **Wide area network (WAN)**—a geographically dispersed telecommunication network.
- **Virtual private network (VPN)**—a way to use the public telecommunication infrastructure (e.g., Internet) to provide secure access to an organization's network (see Figure 4.18 for a brief overview of a VPN network diagram).

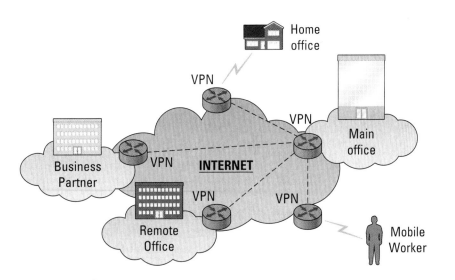

FIGURE 4.18

Virtual Private Network

Information integration within organizations and across trading communities will reduce costs and radically boost productivity. Real-time information flow will also allow quick response to the movements of a highly demanding global marketplace. With the Internet incorporated into a network strategy, an organization will be able to expand its network rapidly to encompass new partners, new customers, and new markets.

Volkswagen, A.G. (VWAG), a global industrial powerhouse based in Wolfsburg, Germany, is the third largest automaker in the world. To stay in the business forefront, to get the right products to market, and to maintain a highly successful global organization, VWAG has created a company to meet its information technology needs: gedas Inc. Owned and grown out of the VW family, gedas Inc. is the center for VW's large-scale information needs.

Due to VW's global extended nature, one of the first challenges that gedas Inc. needed to solve for Volkswagen of America (VWoA) was to secure remote business access. One of VWoA's most important business resources is its extranet that communicates with its growing pool of vendors and suppliers. An *extranet* is a private network that uses the Internet and the public telecommunication system to securely share part of a business's information or operations with suppliers, vendors, partners, customers, or other businesses. However, VWoA found that building extranet connections required a separate infrastructure.

VWoA found many issues to resolve when connecting separate, outside businesses. Along with the long lead times to set up each new partner, at the end of the vendor relationship each custom connection needed to be disconnected since they were using a modem pool for their communication. A virtual private network (VPN) was able to solve all the problems at the same time. The VPN solution provided many benefits, including:

1. No more connecting via modems greatly reduced the complexity of remote access.

2. Migrating to an extranet solution drove down the costs of both 800 number access and the creation of additional private infrastructures.

3. VWoA could provide vendor connectivity anytime, anywhere, connecting and disconnecting external vendors fast and easily.

PROVIDING WEB-BASED USER ACCESS

To take on the challenge of integration, an organization needs a secure and reliable infrastructure for mission-critical systems. The infrastructure must:

- Provide for the transparent exchange of information with suppliers, trading partners, and customers.

- Reliably and securely exchange information internally and externally via the Internet or other networks.

- Allow end-to-end integration and provide message delivery across multiple systems, in particular, databases, clients, and servers.

- Respond to high demands with scalable processing power and networking capacity.

- Serve as the integrator and transaction framework for both digital businesses and traditional brick-and-mortar businesses that want to leverage the Internet for any type of business.

To date, organizations engaging in B2B commerce have relied largely on a value-added network or other dedicated links handling electronic data interchange transactions. *Electronic data interchange (EDI)* is a standard format for exchanging business data. The traditional solutions, namely EDI, are still deployed in the market and for many companies will likely hold a strategic role for years to come. However, conventional technologies present significant challenges:

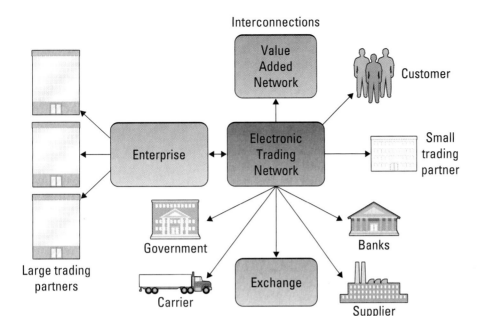

FIGURE 4.19

Diagram of an
Electronic Trading
Network

- By handling only limited kinds of business information, EDI contributes little to a reporting structure intended to provide a comprehensive view of business operations.
- EDI offers little support for the real-time business process integration that will be essential in the digital marketplace.
- EDI is relatively expensive and complex to implement, making it difficult to expand or change networks in response to market shifts.

Many organizations are now turning to providers of electronic trading networks for enhanced Internet-based network and messaging services. ***Electronic trading networks*** are service providers that manage network services. They support B2B integration information exchanges, improved security, guaranteed service levels, command center support, reporting, and auditability (see Figure 4.19). As online trading networks expand their reach and the number of Internet businesses continues to grow, so will the need for managed trading services. Using these services allows organizations to reduce time to market and the overall development, deployment, and maintenance costs associated with their integration infrastructures.

Traders at Vanguard Petroleum Corporation spent most days on the phone talking to prospective counterparties to patrol the market for pricing and volume information in order to strike the best possible deal. The process was slow and tied up traders on one negotiation at a time, making it inherently difficult to stay on top of quickly changing prices. One winter, for example, the weather got cold and stayed cold, causing propane prices to increase dramatically. The price was moving so fast that Vanguard was missing opportunities to buy, sell, and execute deals since it was able to complete only one deal at a time.

To bridge these shortcomings and speed the process, Vanguard became one of the first users of Chalkboard, a commodity markets electronic trading network that is now part of ChemConnect, a B2B e-marketplace. Vanguard now completes deals in real-time and is able to access a broader audience of buyers and sellers. Vanguard uses Chalkboard to put bids and offers in front of hundreds of traders and complete various trades at multiple delivery points simultaneously. In support of the communication infrastructure are service providers such as:[33]

- Internet service provider (ISP)
- Online service provider (OSP)
- Application service provider (ASP)

Internet Service Provider

An *Internet service provider (ISP)* is a company that provides individuals and other companies access to the Internet and other related services, such as Web site building. An ISP has the equipment and the telecommunication line access required to have a "point-of-presence" on the Internet for the geographic area served. Larger ISPs have their own high-speed leased lines so that they are less dependent on the telecommunication providers and can deliver better service to their customers. Among the largest national and regional ISPs are AT&T WorldNet, IBM Global Network, MCI, Netcom, UUNet, and PSINet.

Navigating the different options for an ISP can be daunting and confusing. There are over 7,000 ISPs in the United States; some are very large with household names, and others are literally one-person operations. Although Internet access is viewed as a commodity service, in reality there can be a tremendous difference in service features and performance from these ISPs including:[34]

1. *Web hosting*—Housing, serving, and maintaining files for one or more Web sites. Some Web hosts provide shared or dedicated servers.

2. Hard-disk storage space—Smaller sites may need only 300–500 MB (megabytes) of Web site storage space, whereas busier e-business sites may need at least 9 GB (gigabytes) of space or their own dedicated Web server.

3. Availability—To run an e-business, a site must be accessible to customers $24 \times 7 \times 365$. ISPs maximize the availability of the sites they host using techniques such as load balancing and clustering many servers together in order to reach 100 percent availability.

4. Support—A big part of turning to an ISP is that there is limited worry about keeping the Web server running. Most ISPs offer $24 \times 7 \times 365$ customer service.

Another member of the ISP family is the **wireless Internet service provider (WISP),** an ISP that allows subscribers to connect to a server at designated "hot spots" or "access points" using a wireless connection. This type of ISP offers access to the Internet and the Web from anywhere within the zone of coverage provided by an antenna. This is usually a region with a radius of one mile. Figure 4.20 displays a brief overview of how this technology works.

One example of a WISP is T-Mobile International, a company that provides access to wireless laptop users in 2,000 plus locations including airports, airline clubs, Starbucks coffeehouses, and Borders Books and Music stores. A wireless service called T-Mobile HotSpot allows customers to access the Internet and their corporate intranet via a wireless network from convenient locations away from their home or office. T-Mobile International is the first mobile communications company to extend service on both sides of the Atlantic, offering customers the advantage of using their wireless services when traveling worldwide.[35]

Online Service Provider

An *online service provider (OSP)* offers an extensive online array of services of their own apart from the rest of the Internet and sometimes their own version of a Web browser. The term online service provider has several different meanings. The name has had some popularity in distinguishing ISPs that have their own online independent content, such as America Online (AOL), from ISPs that simply connect users directly with the Internet, such as EarthLink or MSN. In general, the companies sometimes identified as OSPs (in this usage) offer an extensive online array of services of their own apart from the rest of the Internet and occasionally include their own version of a Web browser. Connecting to the Internet through an OSP is an alternative to connecting through one of the national ISPs, such as AT&T or MCI, or a regional or local ISP.

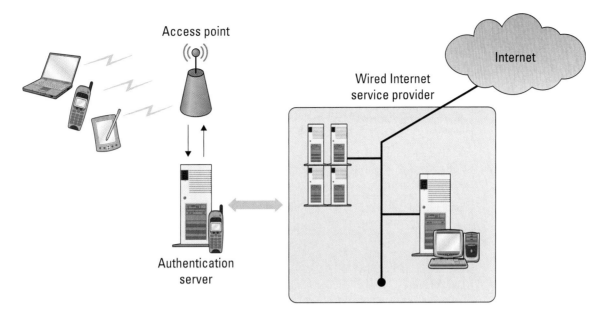

FIGURE 4.20

Wireless Access Diagram

Application Service Provider

An *application service provider (ASP)* is a company that offers an organization access over the Internet to systems and related services that would otherwise have to be located in personal or organizational computers. Sometimes referred to as "apps-on-tap," ASP services are an important alternative, not only for smaller companies with low IT budgets, but also for larger companies as a form of outsourcing. ASP services include:

- Remote access serving for the users of an organization.
- An off-premises local area network to which mobile users can be connected.
- Specialized systems that would be expensive to install and maintain within an organization or on a personal computer.

Hewlett-Packard, SAP, and Qwest have formed one of the first major alliances for providing ASP services. They plan to make SAP's popular R/3 systems available at "cybercenters" that will serve the systems to other companies. Microsoft is allowing some companies to offer its BackOffice products, including SQL Server, Exchange Server, and Windows NT Server on a rental, pay-as-you-use basis. Figure 4.21 displays a list of the top ASPs available.

British Airways, the $11.9 billion airline, had signed a contract with RightNow Technologies to automate the creation and management of different FAQ (frequently asked questions) pages on its Web site, www.BA.com. The focus for Right-Now was to customize and integrate an ASP solution. British Airways knew it would have to change the ASP's standard product to suit its specific needs. For instance, the airline needed to automatically develop, manage, and post different sets of FAQs for different customers, depending on whether they were members of British Air's loyalty program. If the customer enrolled in the program, the technology had to identify the tier that they belonged to (low, middle, or high end). That way, if British Air offered a special promotion exclusively to high-end tier members, it could post information about that promotion in a "Q&A" format on a page that was accessible only to high-end tier members and not to lower-tier participants or other customers.

PORTALS: A WINDOW INTO THE FUTURE

A *portal* is a Web site that offers a broad array of resources and services, such as e-mail, online discussion groups, search engines, and online shopping malls. There are *general portals* and specialized or *niche portals*. Some major general portals

FIGURE 4.21

Directory of Application
Service Providers

Company	Description	Specialty
Appshop www.appshop.com	Enterprise ASP	Oracle 11i e-business suite applications
BlueStar Solutions www.bluestarsolutions.com	Enterprise ASP	Managing ERP solutions with a focus on SAP
Concur www.concur.com	Enterprise ISP	Integrates B2B procurement
Corio www.corio.com	Enterprise ASP	Specializes in PeopleSoft applications
Employease www.employease.com	Online service provider	Human resource application services
Intacct www.intacct.com	Online service provider	Online general ledger service
LivePerson www.liveperson.com	Online service provider	Real-time chat provider
NetLedger www.netledger.com	Online service provider	Web based accounting platform
Outtask www.outtask.com	Enterprise ASP	Integration of budgeting, customer service, sales management, and human resources applications
RightNow www.rightnow.com	Online service provider, enterprise ISP	Suite of customer service applications
Salesforce.com www.salesforce.com	Online service provider	Suite of customer service applications
Salesnet www.salesnet.com	Online service provider	Suite of sales force automation products and services
Surebridge www.surebridge.com	Enterprise ASP	High-tech manufacturing, distribution, health care applications
UpShot www.upshot.com	Online service provider	Sales force automation products and services
USi www.usinternetworking.com	Enterprise ASP	Ariba, Siebel, Microsoft, Peoplesoft, and Oracle customer base

include Yahoo!, Excite, Netscape, Lycos, CNET, Microsoft Network, and America Online's AOL.com. Examples of niche portals include Garden.com (for gardeners), Fool.com (for investors), and SearchNetworking.com (for network administrators).

A number of large ISPs offer portals to the Web for their own users. Most portals have adopted the Yahoo! style of content categories with text-intensive, faster loading pages that are easy to use. Companies with portal sites have attracted much stock market investor interest because portals are able to command large audiences and numbers of advertising viewers.

Companies are implementing portals to support strategic business initiatives and using them as a tactical tool for managing organizational systems. By deploying a portal, Pratt & Whitney (one of the largest aircraft-engine manufacturers in the world) has saved millions of dollars through its portal initiatives. For example, Pratt & Whitney's sales and service field offices scattered throughout the world were formerly connected to headquarters through expensive dedicated lines. The company replaced the dedicated lines with high-speed Internet access to the portal, saving $2.6 million annually. The company estimates that this change will save another $8 million per year in "process and opportunity" savings. This is because the old dedicated lines were slow, whereas the new Internet connections are much faster. Field staff can find information they need in a fraction of the time it took before. Portal access speeds customer service helping field representatives resolve critical issues faster.

An *enterprise information portal (EIP)* is an Internet site owned and operated by an organization to support its operations. The EIP is a single point of contact between an organization, stakeholders, and prospects. Like the popular consumer portals, an enterprise portal organizes various information using indexes and visual presentation.

A company's Web presence is as important to brand identity, customer perception, and overall performance as storefronts, selling process, and business channels. Most organizational Web sites now contain huge amounts of information, managed by dozens of servers. Enterprise portals will help better organize all this information, partly by letting stakeholders create custom views of it.

Access, delivery, and personalization are the architectural bedrock to EIPs. However, EIPs also need to link and integrate information and processes, both online and offline, and provide new services and products. *Linkage* is the interconnection of different systems, information, and transactions to support a user action. For example, linking ordering, inventory status, and credit checking into a single user action requires coordinating three different systems. The enterprise resource planning system is linked with the customer relationship management and supply chain management systems for real-time information flow through the use of an EIP.

Properly designed enterprise information portals create enormous opportunities for organizational effectiveness and agility. Porter's "three generic strategies" suggest an organization is wise to adopt only one of three strategies: broad cost leadership, broad differentiation, or a focused strategy. This makes it possible to explore new business models, products, and ways of connecting with important entities. However, poor design, disjointed processes, system outages, and botched interactions can compromise these benefits. Success will require careful design, a robust infrastructure, and an architecture that can sustain value through rapid changes to portal content and organization. Figure 4.22 displays one example of an Enterprise Information Portal.

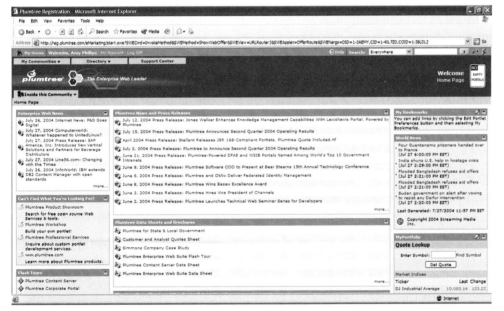

FIGURE 4.22

Example of an Enterprise Information Portal

THE FUTURE OF INTEGRATION IS OPEN

An **open architecture** (or **open system**) is a broad, general term that describes nonproprietary IT hardware and software made available by the standards and procedures by which their products work, making it easier to integrate them.

Amazon.com embraced open source technology in 2002, converting from Sun's proprietary operating system to Linux. *Linux* is an open source operating system created in 1991 as a hobby by a student, Linus Torvalds, at the University of Helsinki in Finland. The switch to an open source operating system, such as Linux, is simplifying the process by which Amazon.com associates can build links to Amazon.com applications into their Web sites, using Amazon.com's payment, fulfillment, and customer service without actually installing the software.

The designs of "open" systems allow for information sharing. In the past, different systems were very independent of each other and operated as individual islands of control. The sharing of information was accomplished through software drivers and devices that routed data allowing information to be translated and shared between systems. Although this method is still widely used, its limited capability and added cost are not an effective solution for most organizations. Another drawback to the stand-alone system is it can communicate only with components developed by a single manufacturer. The proprietary nature of these systems usually results in costly repair, maintenance, and expansion because of a lack of competitive forces. On the other hand, open system integration is designed to:

- **Allow systems to seamlessly share information.** The sharing of information reduces the total number of devices, resulting in an overall decrease in cost.

- **Capitalize on system infrastructure.** This avoids installing several independent systems, which creates duplication of devices as well as infrastructure.

- **Eliminate proprietary systems and promote competitive pricing.** Often a sole source vendor can demand its price and may even provide the customer with less than satisfactory service. Utilization of open systems allows users to purchase systems competitively.

In addition to the next generation of existing Internet standards, open architectures will play a dominant role for operating systems, such as Linux, as well as application-to-application interaction. Industry and vendor consortia such as the Web services-Interoperability Organization (WS-I), supported by BEA Systems, IBM, Microsoft and others, as well as the Universal Business Language promoted by Commerce One, SAP, and Sun are vying to create the combination of standards and applications. Each group has a slightly different definition of openness, but all the participants understand that they can sell new products and services to users only when collaboration across the value chain becomes economical and standardized.

Over the years, Caterpillar, Inc., the world's largest earth-moving equipment manufacturer, has accumulated an array of processing platforms to support its commercial, engineering, and manufacturing applications. These platforms include offerings from Microsoft, Digital Equipment Corporation, Hewlett-Packard, and IBM. As information technology has moved from a computer-centric to a network-centric environment, Caterpillar had to find ways to take advantage of its information technology investments.

Three years ago, Caterpillar organized a team to determine what an open systems architecture would look like. The team assembled a recommended architecture guide for Caterpillar, which defines the technology and industry standards that will enable Caterpillar to leverage the benefits of open systems.

By applying open systems architecture, Caterpillar has reduced development costs significantly and now uses its information resources far more effectively. Caterpillar also gained flexibility to deploy applications across a diverse set of operating platforms and responds more quickly to its users' needs.

Chapter Sixteen Case: JetBlue: Green with Envy

A start-up airline just a few years ago, JetBlue Airways has proved it has what it takes to succeed as a low-cost air carrier. That does not mean "no frills." In fact, leather seats and 24 channels of free DIRECTV programming at every seat have transformed an ordinary flight into an "experience." The New York City–based airline employs approximately 5,000 crew members and serves 20 cities around the United States. With further growth projected, the company continues to address the issues that give it a competitive edge.

JetBlue uses technology to enhance customer satisfaction and to keep the company at the forefront of the airline industry. JetBlue is the only U.S. airline to handle all its reservations through a 100-percent e-ticketing system. As the size of the company's fleet grows, so do the related Web-based transactions from additional flight reservations and inquiries.

According to Jeff Cohen, vice president and CIO at JetBlue, when he first joined the company, the IT infrastructure was composed of 12 Compaq servers in a single room. Gradually it grew to nearly 250 Compaq servers, three data centers, and 58 IT employees. To keep information technology costs down, JetBlue made a decision early on to run the majority of its mission-critical systems in-house in a standard Microsoft Windows environment.

JetBlue is involved in a joint development program to leverage the benefits of .NET. .NET is both a business strategy from Microsoft and its collection of programming support for what are known as Web services. The goal of .NET is to provide individual and business users with a seamlessly interoperable and Web-enabled interface for applications and computing devices and to make computing activities increasingly Web browser-oriented. Thanks to .NET, JetBlue is gaining the reliability, scalability, availability, and manageability it needs to support mission critical applications and its rapidly growing customer base. This includes an added benefit in providing automated maintenance facilities, systems inventory, and around-the-clock system monitoring. .NET will provide greater manageability and streamlined support for critical flight operations, including Maintenance, Weather, In-Flight Communications, Flight Calculator, Trip Trade, and Payroll.

Because of systems integration and collaboration, JetBlue can now enjoy real-time access to data about activities such as scheduling, booking, and check-in, and provide faster, more personalized customer service as a result. At the same time, the company can increase revenues by dropping less popular flights and scheduling more flights in cities that reflect the greatest market demand.[36]

Questions

1. Does JetBlue have a true competitive advantage by using a 100-percent e-ticketing system?

2. Should JetBlue invest resources in creating a portal for wireless access? What are the reasons?

3. How could JetBlue utilize the advantages of open source technology?

PLUG-IN POINTER >>

Review *Technology Plug-In* **Emerging Trends and Technologies** for a closer look at many emerging trends and new technologies that can help an organization prepare for the future.

I n a remarkably short time, the Internet has grown from a virtual playground into a vital, sophisticated medium for business, more specifically, e-business. Online consumers are flooding to the Internet, and they come with very high expectations and a degree of control that they did not have with traditional brick-and-mortar companies. The enticement of doing business online must be strengthened by the understanding that to succeed online, businesses will have to be able to deliver a satisfying and consistent customer experience, building brand loyalty and guaranteeing high rates of customer retention.

Strategic alliances enable businesses to gain competitive advantage(s) through access to a partner's resources, including markets, technologies, and people. Teaming up with another business adds complementary resources and capabilities, enabling participants to grow and expand more quickly and efficiently, especially fast-growing companies who rely heavily on outsourcing many areas of their business to extend their technical and operational resources. In the outsourcing process, they save time and boost productivity by not having to develop their own systems from scratch. They are then free to concentrate on innovation and their core business.

In a competitive business climate, an organization's ability to efficiently align resources and business activities with strategic objectives can mean the difference between succeeding and just surviving. To achieve strategic alignment, organizations are increasingly managing their activities and processes to monitor performance more closely and make better business decisions about their overall business portfolio.

Application integration is the focus on the combination of various applications, such as enterprise information applications. In recent years, the view has expanded to interoperability across large numbers of applications and data sources, both internal and external to an organization.

Businesses of all sizes and in all markets have gotten a taste in recent years of the benefits of leveraging their IT assets for the purposes of creating competitive advantage. Whereas information technology efforts in the past were aimed at increasing operational efficiency, the advent and proliferation of network-based computing (the Internet being the most visible, but not only, example) has enabled organizations to build systems with which all sorts of communities can interact. The ultimate result will allow organizations to "do business" with customers, business partners, suppliers, governments and regulatory agencies, and any other community relevant to their particular operation or activity.

Application service provider
  (ASP), 167
Business process outsourcing
  (BPO), 160
Business-to-business
  (B2B), 139
Business-to-consumer
  (B2C), 139
Collaboration system, 145
Consumer-to-business (C2B), 139
Consumer-to-consumer (C2C), 139
Content management
  system (CMS), 147

Digital asset management
  system (DAM), 147
Document management system
  (DMS), 147
E-business, 136
E-business model, 138
E-commerce, 136
Electronic data interchange
  (EDI), 164
Electronic marketplace
  (e-marketplace), 142
Electronic trading
  network, 165

Enterprise information portal
  (EIP), 169
Explicit knowledge, 153
Extranet, 164
Groupware, 150
Insourcing, 157
Internet service provider (ISP), 166
Knowledge management, 152
Knowledge management system
  (KMS), 152
Linkage, 169
Mobile commerce (M-commerce), 142
Offshore outsourcing, 160

✳ CLOSING CASE ONE

GM Drives Web Services

Just a few years ago, executives of the Big Three carmakers, General Motors, Ford Motor, and DaimlerChrysler, were bragging about the Internet and all the ways it would revolutionize their business. If everything worked according to plan, customers would one day stop in at a dealership, sit at an Internet kiosk, and type in their specifications for their dream car. The online order would go straight to automobile factories as well as the suppliers that feed the factories. Very quickly, everything needed to make that custom car, the right seat fabric, the chosen stereo, the desired color of exterior paint, would travel to the auto plant. In a week or so, the vehicle would be built and delivered.

This grand concept has not come close to panning out. Yet pursuing it has prompted General Motors (GM) to find profitable uses for Web services technologies. Right now, GM's Web services initiative is mostly about cutting costs. GM is using Web services so it does not have to keep upgrading software among its 3,000 different systems, some of which are brand new, while others have been around for years. Rather than ditch the old ones, GM is using a Web services platform to act as a translator between the old and the new systems. If an old software package works, there is no real reason to replace it.

Building the Framework

Thanks in large part to Web services, GM says its new vehicle engineering times have dipped as low as 18 months from the previous average of 40 months, assembly line defects have dropped 25 percent, and inventory costs have dropped 20 percent.

Information technology executives at the world's biggest carmaker think Web services can play a number of roles for the company. One of the biggest objectives for GM is to get information more easily about factory performance. The company has 30 plants worldwide and retools them on an average of every seven or eight years. That means plant IT ranges from state-of-the-art to (almost) obsolete. If the company wants to compare defect ratios for cars made at various plants, it has to have specific systems written for each generation of a plant, and then pull them together, a costly process.

Automakers have been aggressive adopters of standards-based communications technology. Web services is no exception. A Web service gives the company the ability to put a "wrapper" around all of its manufacturing systems, providing a consistent way to view the systems' performance. That view will help GM manage its performance more consistently.

Web Services Gears Up

General Motors is able to bring new vehicles to market faster with the help from E-vis, a real-time visualization and collaboration tool based on Web services. An engineer at GM's Powertrain division changes the cylinder head of the company's Ecotec 2.2-liter engine to improve oil flow. The change is minor, but because the engine is GM's first genuinely global effort, valve-train suppliers in North and South America, Europe, and Asia need to communicate.

Previously, an event like this would have launched a series of e-mail messages, phone calls, and face-to-face meetings; chances are several suppliers would have sent representatives to Detroit. However, with E-vis, the Powertrain engineer can send the pertinent (CAD/CAM) information to all parties that need to see it through the use of its Web service.

Cutting product development time is crucial since automakers have a shrinking window in which to meet consumer demand for low-production and high-profit vehicles. The core of the product development process is the company's engineers and the tools they use; E-vis allows GM to extend that process out to partners more economically.

The automaker's Powertrain division has a supplier with facilities in both Chatham, Ontario, and Juarez, Mexico. Previously, Powertrain engineers would drive from Detroit to Canada every other week to go through specifications and check parts for interferences. At least a couple of team members would fly to Juarez once a month; however, now that the suppliers have E-vis at both facilities, travel has nearly vanished. GM Powertrain engineers and supplier representatives all can view GM's information in real-time without the need of travel.

GM has also put resources into upgrading its consumer Web site, GMBuyPower.com, with new technology that allows car buyers faster access to the site and on a variety of platforms, such as from cell phones or hand-held devices. In addition to making the Web site available on platforms beyond the PC, a "bandwidth calculator" has been added that will speed up access to the site based on a user's Internet connection. This will allow GM to expand the Web site and make quick changes to its marketing and pricing structure.

GMBuyPower.com has become a valuable sales and marketing tool for GM. In addition to making content and information about GM cars and dealers available, the site allows consumers to configure GM cars virtually and communicate with more than 6,300 dealers, or about 83 percent of GM's retail dealers, on the Internet. GM says it generates about 1,000 leads per day, forwarding consumers to its local dealers around the world. New additions to the site have turned GMBuyPower.com into a central destination for car owners to visit for personal information on warranties, special offers, and service reminders.

Web Services Pays Off

The deployment of Web services is paying off. GM used to spend $4 billion a year on new software and support, and this figure has now been cut by $1 billion a year. Web services contributed to those savings by keeping GM from having to replace some of its data-tracking systems. In addition, at its assembly plants, GM now uses Web services to monitor information on quality, productivity, and inventory of cars and parts. Even older plants with aging software can speak to the company headquarters systems without trouble. The biggest contribution from deploying Web services is the quality and reliability of the software.

GM has some other ideas for Web services, including building cars with more and more software on-board. Every time GM wants to change software for a new car model, a Web services system could download the new programming directly to the assembly plant. Once there, the cars on the assembly line could download the software. That would be a big improvement from the current method, in which changing software requires changing the hardware, too.

None of this matches the sweeping designs for Web services that GM and other carmakers had a few years ago. However, just getting GM's varied software and computer systems connected has been a huge accomplishment.[37,38]

Questions

1. Explain how collaboration and electronic relationships are critical to GM's competitive structure.
2. What other types of services should GM be developing via its Web services?
3. GM outsources its IT operations. Is the outsourcing philosophy conducive to the development and deployment of its Web services?

4. How can establishing communications standards help reduce complexity, lower operating costs, influence buying power, and improve the quality of systems development and deployment?

Outsourcing at DuPont

DuPont is an icon in the global chemical industry, with 92,000 employees serving customers in 65 countries. DuPont's IT organization had long been viewed as being highly capable, having successfully supported the company's business objectives while reducing IT costs by 45 percent in just four years. Yet, information technology is not a core business for DuPont, nor did the company want it to be.

Rather than turn IT into a core business, DuPont preferred to focus its attention on the business of science, delivering science-based solutions that make a difference in people's lives in food and nutrition; health care; home and construction; electronics; and transportation. DuPont's IT organization needs to be flexible enough to support a changing mix of businesses and sophisticated enough to keep delivering innovative solutions, yet without adding costs. DuPont began to see outsourcing as a way to strategically and effectively move the organization forward.

DuPont decided to take an innovative step and enter into a groundbreaking 10-year, $4 billion outsourcing relationship with Accenture. This combines the business process management expertise of Accenture with DuPont's chemical leadership to ensure overall IT and business performance success. As part of this growing relationship, about 400 DuPont employees have been transferred to Accenture.

Accenture is providing solutions, which are critical to the support of DuPont's global manufacturing, marketing, distribution, and customer-service functions for the chemical business, including management of applications such as:

- Materials and resource planning
- Order processing
- Manufacturing and engineering systems
- Safety, health, and environmental analysis and reporting

The Benefits of Outsourcing

The alliance partnership is proving to be a smart move for DuPont. The company is reaping increased variability in spending, greater flexibility in responding to business needs, and access to diversified state-of-the-art business solutions, methods, skills, and techniques. "On-demand" information technology support is available, allowing DuPont to undertake new businesses quickly, or to get out of a market without being left with the residual costs of an IT infrastructure that is no longer needed. Furthermore, the alliance partnership has improved DuPont's ability to stay on top of evolving technology and a changing business environment. Through the partnership, DuPont is confident that its own technology will not only keep pace with the company's growth and changes, but will also speed up the creation of new systems while reducing IT costs by 5 percent or more.

Continued Partnership

DuPont needed to come up with a companywide e-business solution to head off the huge costs and inefficiency of its business segments creating individual e-business solutions. Two areas within the company faced urgent needs: (1) Internet order submission as a high-priority opportunity, and (2) distributor relations. DuPont needed to eliminate manual processing and get experience using the Web to improve shared supply chain processes. In addition, DuPont South America needed to implement an aggressive plan to automate customer order entry and offer self-service order management. Most important, whatever solution the company chose had to be implemented quickly, not only to meet the business segments' needs but also to satisfy a key component of DuPont's growth strategy that called for fast deployment of e-business.

Together, Accenture and DuPont built a joint team to manage the project. A hands-on group not only developed and deployed an e-business infrastructure that runs on DuPont's network and can be shared across business segments, but also constructed powerful development tools to allow the segments to create company-compatible e-business solutions on their own.[39,40]

Questions

1. What are DuPont's reasons for developing a strategic outsourcing partnership with Accenture?
2. Describe why outsourcing was a critical business decision for DuPont.
3. Explain Dupont's e-business model.
4. Identify the different ways that DuPont and Accenture are collaborating using technology.

MAKING BUSINESS DECISIONS

1. Leveraging the Competitive Value of the Internet

Physical inventories have always been a major cost component of business. Linking to suppliers in real-time dramatically enhances the classic goal of inventory "turn." The Internet provides a multitude of opportunities for radically reducing the costs of designing, manufacturing, and selling goods and services. E-mango.com, a fruit e-marketplace, is a company that must take advantage of these opportunities or find itself at a significant competitive disadvantage. Identify the disadvantages that confront e-mango.com if they do not leverage the competitive value of the Internet.

2. Integrating Wireless Worlds

Tele-Messaging is a next generation integrated Internet and wireless messaging service that offers services to ISPs, telecommunications carriers, and portal companies. According to Tele-Messaging's research, the primary reason that 90 percent of the people go online is for e-mail. However, the challenge for Tele-Messaging is how to successfully attract and retain these customers. Customers want more than free calls to sign up and are looking for a host of additional services with "whiz-bang" technology to give them the information that they want, when they want it, anywhere, and in the method most convenient to them. List the infrastructures discussed in the unit needed to deliver the technology with the necessary reliability, availability, and scalability demanded by Tele-Messaging's customers.

3. The Profit of Peer-to-Peer Systems

Founded in 2002, behindthemusic.com is hardly a household name, even among serious digital music fans. However, anyone who has ripped a CD has probably used its core product, CDDB (short for "compact disc database"). CDDB compares the arrangement and length of tracks on a CD with an online database to automatically provide information about the titles of songs on the disc, the artist, the release date, and the like. Business is booming. Behindthemusic.com makes money through royalties paid by companies that have embedded its technology in their music devices (Pioneer, Samsung, and Sony), audio software programs (RealNetworks), or online music stores (Apple Computer). While behindthemusic .com declined to provide detailed figures, its CEO Hans Palmer expects the firm to be cash flow positive by the second half of the year, with revenue growth of 90 percent by year-end.

Create a report detailing the ways in which you believe behindthemusic.com is able to meet their financial projections. In your report include any potential challenges that behindthemusic.com will need to overcome in order to meet their year-end goal.

4. The Know-How of Knowledge Management

thinktank.com is developing leading edge practices on contemporary business, information, technology, and knowledge management issues to facilitate organizational and individual performance, success, and fulfillment. Founder Paul Bauer says his vision for this site is to fill the gaps between business and technology, and data and knowledge. With the site's "knowledge map," the Web site has created a virtual library for business researchers. How is thinktank.com able to foster the innovation of ideas in a global community? How can thinktank.com improve efficiency and productivity for e-business?

5. Communicating with Instant Messages

You are working for a new start-up magazine, Jabber Inc., developed for information professionals that provides articles, product reviews, case studies, evaluation, and informed opinions. You have a need to collaborate on news items and projects, and exchange data with a variety of your colleagues inside and outside the Jabber Inc. walls. You know that many companies are now embracing the instant messaging technology. Prepare a brief report for the Jabber Inc. CIO that will explain the reasons IM is not just a teenage fad, but a valuable communications tool that is central to everyday business.

6. Collaboration on Intranets

myIntranet.com is a worldwide leader providing online intranet solutions. The myIntranet .com online collaboration tool is a solution for small businesses and groups inside larger organizations that need to organize information, share files and documents, coordinate calendars, and enable efficient collaboration, all in a secure, browser-based environment. myIntranet.com has just added conferencing and group scheduling features to its suite of hosted collaboration software. Explain why infrastructure integration is critical to the suite of applications to function within this environment.

★ MAKING COLLABORATIVE DECISIONS

1. Realizing the Worth of Outsourcing

The lure of offshore outsourcing is particularly enticing because of growing cost savings. With the help of improved VPN technology, IT managers can often implement offshore operations relatively easily. However, CIOs are very reluctant to allow mission-critical information out of their "sight." Develop a cost-based analysis (Microsoft Excel is an excellent tool to use for this) comparing a traditional insourcing implementation and an outsourced ASP service to develop a Call Center. Some categories to think about are:

■ Hardware—break this down further specifying server(s), desktop/laptop computers, and communication devices.

■ Software—elaborate more on this indicating type and cost of operating system.

■ Maintenance—for both hardware and software.

■ Personnel—costs relating to support and training.

2. Everybody Needs an Internet Strategy

An Internet strategy addresses the reasons businesses want to "go online." "Going online" because it seems like the right thing to do now or because everyone else is doing it is not a good enough reason. A business must decide how it will best utilize the Internet for its particular needs. It must plan for where it wants to go and how best the Internet can help shape that vision. Before developing a strategy a business should spend time on the Internet, see what similar businesses have grown, and what is most feasible, given a particular set of resources. Think of a new online business opportunity and answer the following questions:

1. Why do you want to put your business online?
2. What benefits will going online bring?
3. What effects will being connected to the Internet have on your staff, suppliers, and customers?

3. A Portal into Saab

Saab Cars USA, a marketing and distribution arm for the Swedish automaker, knew it had to improve communication with dealerships. Specifically, Saab wanted to ensure that dealers could communicate more reliably and easily access all the business systems and tools they needed. That meant upgrading their current system so dealers could tap into several of the company's legacy systems without having to install any Saab-specific hardware or software onsite. In addition, the refined system had to be reliable and inexpensive to maintain, easily support future upgrades, work within existing network and hardware designs, and integrate with existing systems. The portal was designed to make it easy for dealers across the United States to instantly access remote inventory, order parts, conduct online training sessions or research, and submit warranty claims. Identify the specific technological services Saab is looking to integrate into their new portal.

4. Developing an ASP Workspace Service

Workspace.com is a leading Internet solutions company dedicated to transforming the business of human resources through the use of technology, boasting years of experience creating and deploying an ASP service for large employers. Workspace.com offers ready access to:

- A best of breed application tool available $24 \times 7 \times 365$.
- The ability to reduce manual processes.
- An application platform that links to a company's existing ERP and HR systems.
- The highest level of security, flexibility, scalability, and reliability.
- Secure access via multiple media including Web, phone, fax, or wireless devices.

Identify how Workspace is able to deliver their high availability, assured information integrity, scalability, high performance, security, and access control. How can Workspace's ASP solution streamline the compensation planning and administration processes?

5. Gaining Efficiency with Collaboration

During the past year, you have been working for a manufacturing firm to help improve their supply chain management by implementing enterprise resource planning and supply chain management systems. For efficiency gains, you are recommending to the manufacturing firm that it should be turning toward collaborative systems. The firm has a need to share intelligent plans and forecasts with supply chain partners, reduce inventory levels, improve working capital, and reduce manufacturing changeovers. Given the technologies presented to you in this unit, what type of system(s) would you be recommending to your firm in order to facilitate their future needs?

UNIT 5

Transforming Organizations

Masters of Innovation, Technology, and Strategic Vision

There are several companies emerging today as leaders on the intensely competitive playing field of e-business. *Wired* magazine highlights The Wired 40—companies driven by innovative thinking, not marketplace brawn, which demonstrate a mastery of tomorrow's business essentials including innovation, technology, strategic vision, global reach, and networked communication.

Business Week magazine highlights The Web Smart 50—companies that are using technology to develop new e-business opportunities in the areas of collaboration, customer service, customization, streamlining, management, and cutting-edge technology. Cross-referencing the two lists reveals seven outstanding companies that are included in both The Wired 40 and The Web Smart 50:

- Amazon.com
- Charles Schwab
- Cisco
- Dell
- IBM
- Sony
- Wal-Mart

Amazon.com—It's a Mall World after All

- Ranked 7th on The Wired 40
- Featured on The Web Smart 50 under "Cutting Edge"

"Amazon.com and you're done!" was the e-business pioneer's slogan in 2002. Critics of Amazon.com said that CEO Jeff Bezos should have stuck with books; his online store would soon crumple under the debt it had taken on to expand into other goods. Jeff Bezos proved the critics wrong by reducing Amazon.com's debt while doubling its revenue growth rate over 2002.

In 2003, Amazon.com opened its site to independent developers, allowing merchants to use its gold-standard e-business technology to build their own stores on top of Amazons. To date, over 35,000 software developers have created programs from building customized Web stores to checking prices from hand-held devices. Currently, other retailers now account for 22 percent of all items sold on Amazon.com. Amazon.com continues to prove critics wrong and is demonstrating that a Web site can be the best storefront location of all.

Charles Schwab—Trading Places

- Ranked 37th on The Wired 40
- Featured on The Web Smart 50 under "Customer Service"

Charles Schwab, the full-service investment firm, continues to shock the investment industry by using technology innovations to transform its business. The company invested $20 million on Web technology to build the Schwab Equity Rating System, a computer-generated online service, which offers recommendations for the buying and selling of over 3,000 stocks. The system allows Schwab to avoid the $20-million-a-year cost of hiring new analysts and avoid conflicts of interest between analysts and business, something to watch in the wake of the recent Wall Street scandals.

Charles Schwab also rolled out Web-based services for financial advisers. Collaboration between Schwab and independent financial advisers gives retail investors the best of both worlds.

Cisco—The Network Connection

- Ranked 11th on The Wired 40
- Featured on The Web Smart 50 under "Cutting Edge"

Cisco, with its flat revenue and steady profit, has become a cash machine in just less than two decades. The company is continuing to transform to ensure it is evolving as the Internet evolves. First, it is switching 35,000 employees and consultants to Voice-over-IP (VOIP) Internet enabled telephone systems. Cisco workers worldwide now use Internet phones, cutting down on telephony services by $300,000 monthly.

Second, the company is changing its lines of business. John Chambers, the CEO of Cisco, understands that the market for routers and switches, which account for 70 percent of Cisco's sales, is headed for stagnation. To combat this, the company is investing 40 percent of its research and development dollars into areas that constitute a mere 15 percent of sales: optical and storage networking, wireless communications, security software, and VOIP. Cisco promises to be ready for companies that want to start investing in next-generation networks.

Dell—Just-in-Time Hardware

- Ranked 15th on The Wired 40
- Featured on The Web Smart 50 under "Cutting Edge"

Dell's core PC business is still "disruptive" (cutting edge) as the company installs robots to automate its e-business network. By installing robots on the assembly lines that process orders from the Web, the company can build 900 computers an hour, increasing output by over 40 percent. At Dell's plant in Nashville, assembly line robots retrieve online orders and fetch all of the required components to build the custom PCs. This new setup requires half as many workers and operates at three times the speed. The plant churns out one computer every four seconds.

Dell has a reputation for shattering every industry it targets. When the personal computer went from branded gizmo to commodity, Dell polished its famous strategy—assemble on demand, deliver high value at low cost, sell directly to customers—and drove IBM out of the PC market and Compaq into HP's arms. Dell is now focusing on attacking the server sector (of which it claims nearly a quarter), the workstation niche (where it has Sun on the run), the networking arena (where Cisco is looking vulnerable), and the consulting business specializing in systems integration.

IBM—The Ultimate IT Outsource

- Ranked 4th on The Wired 40
- Featured on The Web Smart 50 under "Collaboration"

Perhaps IBM's acronym should stand for It's Been Morphing. The 92-year-old company proved as nimble as a start-up by supporting Linux and promoting it as an enterprise-friendly solution. IBM is now promoting "e-business on demand," which envisions computing as a utility: Switch it on when needed and pay only for what is used. The services will allow everything including offering organizations the ability to expand at will.

IBM is also creating an online collaboration system for employees that has cut training costs by $375 million annually and travel expenses by $20 million annually. IBM's intranet allows its 300,000 workers to brainstorm. Web jams, big sessions with over 1,000 employees, encourage the free flow of ideas. Many organizations are now looking to IBM for expertise in the area of intranet development. IBM hopes to become to computing what "Ma Bell" once was to telephones.

Sony—That's Home Entertainment!

- Ranked 16th on The Wired 40
- Featured on The Web Smart 50 under "Collaboration"

Sony's CEO Nobuyuki Idei sees Sony's future in home networks that beam files among PCs, TVs, and portables. That means melding the company's music and video department together, which currently delivers more than half the company's profit. Nobuyuki Idei is restructuring the organization by moving away from departmental silos into a more seamless organization.

Wal-Mart—Retail-o-rama

- Ranked 13th on The Wired 40
- Featured on The Web Smart 50 under "Collaboration"

Wal-Mart squeezes big brands for low prices and passes the savings on to consumers. Then it pumps suppliers for information that will help it give shoppers what they want, when they want it. The newest technology innovation the company is pursuing to help streamline its supply chain is "smart tags," which will be placed in every product case for its top 100 suppliers. The tags will track product in every phase of the supply chain, allowing the company to know exactly where every product is and increase its ability to keep its shelves stocked. Analysts expect Wal-Mart to reap pretax savings of as much as $8 billion by 2007.

CEO Lee Scott is focusing on several other new investments including branding products like dog food and shouldering into pharmaceuticals, financial services, and DVD rentals. Global expansion continues: Wal-Mart has more stores in Mexico (551) than in its two biggest states, Texas and Florida, combined, plus 486 others in the UK, Brazil, China, and South Korea. Wal-Mart promises to continue to redefine efficiency in retailing.[1,2]

INTRODUCTION

The Polaroid camera was one of the most exciting advances in technology the photography industry had ever seen. By using a Polaroid camera, customers no longer had to depend on other people or companies to develop their film and they had instant access to their pictures. The technology was innovative and the product was high-end. Polaroid, founded in 1937, produced the first instant film and camera in the late 1940s. The company eventually went public, becoming one of Wall Street's most prominent enterprises, with its stock trading above $60 in 1997. In 2002, the stock was down to 8 cents and the company declared bankruptcy.[3]

How could a company like Polaroid, which had innovative technology and a captive customer base, go bankrupt? Perhaps the company executives failed to use Porter's Five Forces to perform an analysis of its threat of substitute products or services. If they had, would they have noticed the two threats, one-hour film processing and digital cameras, which eventually stole Polaroid's market share? Would they have understood that their customers, people who want instant access to their pictures without having a third party involved, would be the first to use one-hour film processing and purchase the new and exciting technology of digital cameras? Could they have found a way to compete with one-hour film processing and the digital camera to save Polaroid?

The dilemma that faced Polaroid is a dilemma that most organizations face—the criteria an organization uses to make business decisions for its present business could possibly create issues for its future business. Essentially, what is best for the current business could ruin it in the long term.

This unit focuses on how to build an organization that can transform itself to meet changing business, organization, and industry needs to sustain long-term business success. The chapters in Unit 5 are:

- **Chapter Seventeen**—Fostering an Innovative Organization
- **Chapter Eighteen**—Creating a Wireless Organization
- **Chapter Nineteen**—Building Software to Support an Agile Organization
- **Chapter Twenty**—Developing a 21st Century Organization

Chapter Seventeen: Fostering an Innovative Organization

LEARNING OUTCOMES

17.1. Compare disruptive and sustaining technologies.

17.2. Explain the innovator's dilemma.

17.3. Identify the four laws of disruptive technologies and their effects on an organization's ability to remain competitive.

W hat do steamboats, transistor radios, and Intel's 8088 processor have in common? They are all examples of "disruptive" technologies that redefined the competitive playing fields of their respective markets. Each of these innovations is a ***disruptive technology,*** a new way of doing things that initially does not meet the needs of existing customers. Disruptive technologies tend to open new markets and destroy old ones. A ***sustaining technology***, on the other hand, produces an improved product customers are eager to buy, such as a faster car or larger hard drive. Sustaining technologies tend to provide us with better, faster, and cheaper products in established markets. Incumbent companies most often lead sustaining technology to market, but virtually never lead in markets opened by new and disruptive technologies. Figure 5.1 displays companies that are expecting future growth to occur from new investments (disruptive technology) and companies that are expecting future growth to occur from existing investments (sustaining technology).

Digital Equipment Corporation's (DEC) strategic business plan was to steal IBM's lucrative mainframe sales by beefing up its VAX minicomputers. The basis of DEC's plan was to give minicomputers to midsized companies that could not yet afford mainframes, thereby winning many potential new customers. DEC thought its plan was brilliant. Unfortunately, it underestimated the impact PCs would have on the small and midsized business arena. DEC did not even consider PCs to be a threat to its business because they offered a lot less bang for the buck than a minicomputer. What DEC failed to realize was that PCs were sufficient to calculate payroll and other tasks for a small business that could not afford a minicomputer. Eventually DEC found itself a victim of the fate it had planned for IBM.[4]

Disruptive and new technologies typically cut into the low end of the marketplace and eventually evolve to displace high-end competitors and their reigning technologies. Sony is a perfect example of a company that entered the low end of the marketplace and eventually evolved to displace its high-end competitors. Sony started as a tiny company that built portable, battery-powered transistor radios people could carry around with them. The sound quality of Sony's transistor radios was poor because the transistor amplifiers were of lower quality than traditional vacuum tubes, which produce a better sound. Fortunately, customers were more than willing to overlook sound quality for the convenience of portability. Then, with the experience and revenue stream from the portables, Sony improved its technology to produce cheap, low-end transistor amplifiers that were "good enough" for home use and used those revenues to improve the technology further, which produced better radios.[5]

FIGURE 5.1

Expected Returns on
New Investments and
Existing Investments

_____

Source: CSFB/HOLT; Deloitte
Consulting analysis.

Fortune 500 Rank	Company	Expected Returns on New Investment	Expected Returns on Existing Investments
53	Dell Computer	78%	22%
47	Johnson & Johnson	66	34
35	Procter & Gamble	62	38
6	General Electric	60	40
77	Lockheed Martin	59	41
1	Wal-Mart	50	50
65	Intel	49	51
49	Pfizer	48	52
9	IBM	46	54
24	Merck	44	56
92	Cisco Systems	42	58
18	Home Depot	37	63
16	Boeing	30	70
11	Verizon	21	79
22	Kroger	13	87
32	Sears Roebuck	8	92
37	AOL Time Warner	8	92
3	General Motors	5	95
81	Phillips Petroleum	3	97

The Innovator's Dilemma, a book by Clayton M. Christensen, discusses how established companies can take advantage of disruptive technologies without hindering existing relationships with customers, partners, and stakeholders. Companies like Xerox, IBM, Sears, and DEC all listened to existing customers, invested aggressively in technology, had their competitive antennae up, and still lost their market-dominant positions. Christensen states that these companies may have placed too great an emphasis on satisfying customers' current needs, while forgetting to adopt new disruptive technology that will meet customers' future needs, thus causing the companies to eventually fall behind.[6]

FOCUSING ON THE UNEXPECTED

One of the biggest forces changing business is the Internet. Organizations must be able to transform as markets, economic environments, and technologies change. Most organizations today realize that it is not enough to put up "simple" Web sites for customers, employees, and partners. To take full advantage of new technologies such as the Internet and Web services, these companies must continually reinvent the way they do business, including changing how they distribute goods, manage their supply chains, and collaborate with partners and customers.

Technology companies like Intel and Cisco Systems were among the first to seize the Internet to overhaul their operations. Intel Corporation used Web-based automation to liberate its 200 sales clerks from tedious order-entry positions. Instead, sales clerks concentrate on CRM functions such as analyzing sales trends and pampering customers.

Cisco Systems Inc. handles 75 percent of its sales online, and 45 percent of its online orders for networking equipment never even touch employees' hands. This type of Internet-based ordering has helped Cisco systems hike productivity by 20 percent over the past two years.[7]

Focusing on the unexpected allows an organization to capitalize on the opportunity for new business growth from a disruptive technology. Figure 5.2 highlights

FIGURE 5.2

Companies That
Capitalized on
Disruptive
Technologies

_____

Source: CSFB/HOLT; Deloitte
Consulting analysis.

Company	Disruptive Technology
Charles Schwab	Online brokerage
Hewlett-Packard	Microprocessor-based computers; ink-jet printers
IBM	Minicomputers; personal computers
Intel	Low-end microprocessors
Intuit	QuickBooks software; TurboTax software; Quicken software
Microsoft	Internet-based computing; operating system software; SQL and Access database software
Oracle	Database software
Quantum	3.5-inch disks
Sony	Transistor-based consumer electronics

several companies that launched new businesses by capitalizing on disruptive technologies.

An organization must focus on the unexpected to ensure it is not only meeting its customers' current needs, but also their unspoken or future needs. This is particularly challenging since most customers will not even know or understand their future needs. The following four laws of disruptive technologies, identified by *The Innovator's Dilemma,* reveal how organizations can capitalize on innovation:

1. **Organizations Depend on Customers and Investors for Resources:** Successful organizations find it difficult to allocate resources for products that are not in line with mainstream demands. Perceptive managers need to find support for allocating resources toward disruptive technologies. One way to accomplish this is to align the unorthodox product with special customers who can put it to immediate use. As customer demand increases, more resources will flow toward the development of the disruptive technology.

    Quantum Corporation once led the minicomputer industry in making 8-inch disk drives. However, the company noticed an emerging market for PC 3.5-inch drives and decided to build a separate company to commercialize the smaller drives. In a little under 10 years, the market for 8-inch drives literally disappeared, and Quantum remained as the market leader for 3.5-inch drives.[8]

2. **Small Markets Do Not Meet the Growth Needs of Large Organizations:** Large organizations focus on maintaining stock prices and typically wait until new markets are "large enough to be interesting," which leaves the door to these new markets wide open to quick-acting start-ups. Organizations can have the best of both worlds by placing responsibility in small operating centers that can get excited about small opportunities and small wins.

    Johnson & Johnson found tremendous success by using this strategy. The organization maintains 180 autonomously operating companies and has launched products based on disruptive technologies through several small enterprises acquired specifically for that purpose.[9]

3. **It Is Difficult to Analyze a Market That Does Not Exist:** How do you ask for directions when you are going somewhere no one has ever been before? *The Innovator's Dilemma* points out that it is difficult to gain the essential first-mover advantage when nothing is known about the potential market. The key is continuously looking for and anticipating new markets.

    Honda's invasion of the North American motorcycle industry reflects this process of trial and error perfectly. Honda planned to introduce a fast, high-powered motorcycle in the United States in 1959. While in the quest for this market, Honda discovered an untapped market for small, inexpensive motorized bikes very different from the established market in which Harley-Davidson, BMW, and other traditional motorcycle manufacturers competed.

The 50cc motorbike, a disruptive technology in the American market, fueled Honda's growth and, by 1975, the company had captured a substantial share of the market with annual sales of 5 million units, largely from a disruptive technology in an unexpected market.[10]

4. **Technology Supply May Not Equal Market Demand:** The attributes that make disruptive technologies unattractive in the mainstream market are often the very ones that constitute their great value in emerging markets. Instead of racing toward higher performance and higher margins, companies who want to stay on top need to be aware of what their mainstream customers value at each stage of a product's life cycle, and be prepared to introduce more convenient, lower-priced products into established markets when the competitive environment demands them. Perhaps Polaroid could have avoided bankruptcy if it had attempted to move into the digital camera market.

OPENING CASE STUDY QUESTIONS

1. Determine which one of the seven companies profiled in the opening case has the most disruptive technology that is capable of making the greatest impact on e-business.

2. Describe how Amazon.com has used technology to disrupt the bookselling industry.

3. Do you think that Charles Schwab is a good example of disruptive technology? Why or why not?

4. Choose one of the seven companies and create a Porter's Five Forces analysis to highlight potential issues that company should acknowledge in terms of its disruptive technology.

Chapter Seventeen Case: Maintaining TiVo's Popularity

In 1997, Mike Ramsay and Jim Barton co-founded TiVo, the producer of the digital video recorder (DVR) that gives customers a huge array of recording and viewing options, including the ability to pause live programs. TiVo added 209,000 subscribers in the last quarter of 2003, up from 100,000 in the previous quarter. Sales for the first nine months of 2003 totaled nearly $100 million, a 35 percent increase from the previous year.

Unfortunately, TiVo is now facing the depressing reality that most disruptive technologies face—its competitors are stealing its revenues. According to Forrester Research, TiVo's overall DVR share is about one-third and shrinking. The market is flooded with cheaper, more efficiently distributed products, including a cable box made by Scientific-Atlanta that doubles as a DVR (over 500,000 units shipped in its first year). Cable companies like Time Warner Cable are distributing the boxes to customers free in return for a monthly service charge that ranges from $5 to $9. TiVo sells its DVRs at a minimum of $199, plus $13 a month for service.

TiVo is attempting to combat its competition by introducing new product improvements, including its own recordable DVDs, services that allow users to program TiVos from a remote PC, and a hard-drive "key" that allows users to transfer programs from their TiVo to their PC for later viewing. The company is also attempting to generate revenues from selling advertising on its programming guides, which allows viewers to see ads for soon-to-be-released movies and new cars. "We've taken some pretty strong steps to go beyond the DVR," says TiVo's Ramsay. "Besides we're in such an early phase of this technology, where there is so much upside, that to think DVR technology doesn't go forward from here is wrong."

TiVo is also attempting to stop others from infringing on its intellectual property. In January the company sued EchoStar, which has deployed a million DVRs to its satellite customers, for patent infringement. Should TiVo prevail, that will help its licensing business. Currently, Sony, Toshiba, and others are paying TiVo for its technology; manufacturers like Scientific-Atlanta and LG are not.[11]

Questions

1. Do you consider TiVo a disruptive technology? Why or why not?

2. Review the four laws of disruptive technologies on page 187 and formulate a strategy for TiVo to follow to remain competitive.

3. Do you consider it unethical for companies to copy TiVo's technology? Justify your answer.

4. Research the Internet and discover any new information relating to TiVo's lawsuit against EchoStar.

Chapter Eighteen: Creating a Wireless Organization

18.1. Explain how a wireless device helps an organization conduct business anytime, anywhere, anyplace.

18.2. Discuss three limitations to wireless devices and the effects they can have on an employee's job performance.

18.3. List and discuss the key factors inspiring the growth of wireless technologies.

18.4. Describe the impact a mobile organization has on an employee.

Wireless technologies are transforming how we live, work, and play. Hand-held devices are continuing to offer additional functionality and cellular networks are advancing rapidly in their increased speed and throughput abilities. These enabling technologies are fueling widespread adoption and creation of new and innovative ways to perform business. Common examples of wireless devices include:

- **Cellular phones and pagers**—provide connectivity for portable and mobile applications, both personal and business.
- **Global positioning system (GPS)**—allows drivers of cars and trucks, captains of boats and ships, backpackers, hikers, skiers, and pilots of aircraft to ascertain their location anywhere on earth.
- **Cordless computer peripherals**—the cordless mouse is a common example; keyboards and printers can also be wirelessly connected to a computer.
- **Home-entertainment-system control boxes**—the VCR control and the TV channel control are the most common examples; some hi-fi sound systems and FM broadcast receivers also use this technology.
- **Two-way radios**—this includes Amateur and Citizens Radio Service, as well as business, marine, and military communications.
- **Satellite television**—allows viewers in almost any location to select from hundreds of channels.

The next generations of disruptive technologies are already here, they work, and they are poised to change the way we live in the future. Here are a few examples of disruptive wireless technologies that promise to change our world:

- **WiMax wireless broadband**—enables wireless networks to extend as far as 30 miles and transfer information, voice, and video at faster speeds than cable. It is perfect for ISPs that want to expand into sparsely populated areas, where the cost of bringing in cable wiring or DSL is too high.
- **Radio frequency identification tags (RFID)**—have the potential to reinvent the supply chain. Wal-Mart is already making this happen and all of its suppliers must use the tags for pallets and cases of merchandise by 2005.

- **Micro hard drives**—offer gigabyte-level storage capacity and rapid data-transfer rates into tiny, matchbook-size casings.

- **Apple's G5 and AMD's Athlon 64 processors**—handle as much as 16 billion gigabytes of information at a time. That means dramatically lower IT costs for companies. Upstart airline JetBlue houses its frequent-flier and reservation information on two 64-bit servers, down from eight 32-bit servers.[12,13]

Soon, it will be difficult to remember how businesses operated prior to the invention of wireless technologies. The average employee uses three or more wireless devices (laptops, personal digital assistants, cell phones, etc.) in accomplishing daily activities. Gartner research estimates that in just a few years most enterprises will support as many as 50 different wireless devices. The wireless devices offered today have a few limitations, which is why people often use several of them to accomplish a single task. These limitations include:

- Cell phones increasingly include Web browsers, but lack the functionality and memory to run customized applications.

- Personal digital assistants (PDAs) originally lacking any communications capability are getting connectivity, but generally not to corporate networks.

- E-mail devices have surfaced in response to demand, but typically do not include such functions as voice.[14,15]

MOBILE AND WIRELESS TECHNOLOGIES

The terms "mobile" and "wireless" are often used synonymously, but actually denote two different technologies. *Mobile* means the technology can travel with the user, but it is not necessarily in real-time; users can download software, e-mail messages, and Web pages onto their PDA, laptop, or other mobile device for portable reading or reference. Information collected while on the road can be synchronized with a PC or corporate server.

Masters of Innovation

Wireless, on the other hand, gives users a live (Internet) connection via satellite or radio transmitters. International Data Corporation forecasts that by 2005 nearly one-third of hand-held devices will include integrated wireless networking. For instance, newly announced PDAs integrate phones, text messaging, Web browsers, and organizers.[16]

United Parcel Service and FedEx have been using wireless technologies for years to disrupt their industry, making it possible for information about dispatching and deliveries to travel between couriers and central stations. FedEx's famous tracking system that can find a package's location from its tracking number uses a wireless courier-management system.

BUSINESS DRIVERS FOR WIRELESS TECHNOLOGY

The big changes that will re-create workplaces, industries, and organizations are coming from these wireless technologies. The following factors are inspiring the growth of wireless technologies:

- **Universal access to information and applications**—People are mobile and have more access to information than ever before, but they still need to get to the point where they can access all information anytime, anywhere, anyplace.

- **The automation of business processes**—Wireless technologies have the ability to centralize critical information and eliminate redundant processes.

- **User convenience, timeliness, and ability to conduct business 24 × 7 × 365**—People delayed in airports no longer have to feel cut off from the world or their office. Through wireless tools and wireless solutions such as a BlackBerry RIM device, they can access their information anytime, anywhere, anyplace.

Number of U.S. Users	Wireless Device Technology
Less than 15,000	Smart phones
4,000,000	Web-enabled (WAP) phones
65,000,000	Digital cell phones

State government agencies, such as Departments of Transportation, use wireless devices for field information collection, which tracks inventory, reports time, monitors logistics, and completes forms—all from a mobile environment. The transportation industry is using wireless devices to offer location-based services that help determine current locations and alternate driving routes.

Wireless technology is rapidly evolving and is playing an increasing role in the lives of people throughout the world. The final key factor driving the increased use of wireless devices is the sheer number of U.S. wireless device users (see Figure 5.3). With such a large market, businesses simply must embrace wireless technologies.

WIRELESS INDUSTRY OUTLOOK

Analysts predict that more than 96 million U.S. consumers will use wireless devices for Internet access by 2005. Overall, there will be more than 1.4 billion wireless subscribers by the end of 2006, with about 500 million of those using wireless Internet access (see Figure 5.4). The growth of the wireless market will drive the development of new wireless technology, which in turn will create a larger market for *Bluetooth* connectivity, which allows wireless hand-held devices, personal computers, and laptops to work together. Analysts expect Bluetooth shipments to rise from fewer than 1 million in 2001 to 1.6 billion in 2006.[17]

Gartner predicts that the future will belong to "The Real-Time Enterprise," the organization that thrives in uncertain times because it can "detect sooner and respond faster." Wireless technologies clearly play a major role in increasing an organization's agility. Ovum predicts that by 2006, spending on global wireless enterprises will be over $28 billion, connecting 39 million workers wirelessly. IDC reports that annual spending on wireless and mobile network infrastructure will grow to $49 billion in 2007.[18]

Wireless access to corporate e-mail systems, often the primary catalyst to an organization's first significant venture into wireless technology, has become the focus of much attention. E-mail is the foremost communication system in most organizations, surpassing voicemail in importance and interest (refer to Figure 5.5).[19]

Organizations are fast approaching the point where they will have the technical wireless infrastructure to support an always-on connection that will let users roam seamlessly from Starbucks, to a customer site, to conference rooms, and even to a comfortable chair in front of the TV at home.

THE WIRELESS CULTURE

One of the trickiest issues in building a wireless organization is the simplest one in conventional organizations: dividing work from nonwork. Traditionally, when office workers are at the office, they are at work, accessible to managers, co-workers, and clients; when they are not, they are not. It is no longer that simple. In the last 10 to

Subscribers	2001	2004	2007
Internet users (millions)	533	945	1,460
Wireless Internet users as percent of all Internet users	16%	41.5%	56.8%

Application	Western Europe	Eastern Europe	United States
On 6-point interest scale, 6 = high interest, and 1 = low interest:			
E-mail	4.5	4.7	4.3
Payment authorization/enablement	3.4	3.8	3.0
Banking/trading online	3.5	3.4	3.2
Shopping/reservations	3.0	3.1	2.9
Interactive games	2.0	2.2	2.4

FIGURE 5.5

Current Mobile Phone Users' Applications Interest

Source: eMarketer.com.

15 years, employees, particularly in the United States, have seen a steady erosion of their personal time as their work day lengthens.[20]

Some of the same technological changes that now promote mobility have supported this change in business culture. Organizations must address these cultural issues if they are to redress the imbalance.

Kelley Drye & Warren's 350-plus attorneys were spending significant amounts of time searching out phone lines in order to plug in and check e-mail or link to contact and calendar information whenever they worked outside of the office. That changed when the firm implemented Cingular's Corporate Email PLUS service. These days the attorneys use a Research in Motion BlackBerry wireless hand-held that integrates wireless enterprise e-mail and organizer software, enabling them to send and receive e-mail and access contacts, calendars, and task functions.[21]

Wireless technology is here, and the business demand for it is growing. To get business value out of wireless, organizations will have to go beyond handing out laptops and cell phones to creating wireless organizations that truly support mobile workforces.

OPENING CASE STUDY QUESTIONS

1. Why would Dell want to explore the wireless market for new opportunities?

2. With the emergence of mobile technologies, why should leading edge companies be concerned with the lack of compatibility between wireless applications?

3. How could Charles Schwab use wireless technology to increase its market share?

4. Do you think organizations that do not embrace wireless technologies are at a disadvantage? Explain your answer.

Chapter Eighteen Case: Watching the Weather

Since its inception 20 years ago, The Weather Channel has spawned worldwide interest in forecasts and weather patterns. Consistently rated in the Top Five for News, Entertainment, and Information Web sites by Media Metrix, The Weather Channel's Web site, www.weather.com, features current conditions and forecasts for over 77,000 locations worldwide, along with local and regional radars.

The Weather Channel saw a unique opportunity to use wireless messaging to deliver "severe weather alerts" to subscribers' cell phones and pagers alerting them to dangerous weather conditions such as tornadoes and floods. The alerts include information regarding the duration of the storm warning as well as the affected location(s). "This wireless application is especially beneficial to those people who are frequently on the go and don't have continuous access to their local weather conditions," according to Tom Flournoy, vice president of product management for www.weather.com.

Weather.com subscribers set up profiles indicating weather notification preferences and the type of mobile device(s) they carry. After the brief provisioning process is complete, users are free to update and modify profiles when necessary. When weather conditions are bad, the database triggers weather alerts to subscriber profiles to warn potentially affected subscribers. Severe weather alerts are delivered across every major U.S. wireless network to virtually any wireless-enabled device including PDAs, WAP phones, and interactive pagers.[22]

Questions

1. Do you consider The Weather Channel's use of wireless technology disruptive? Why or why not?

2. Review the key factors inspiring the growth of wireless technology and brainstorm a new service The Weather Channel could provide to its customers based on these factors.

3. Determine who The Weather Channel's competitors are and evaluate what it can do to protect its business.

Chapter Nineteen: Building Software to Support an Agile Organization

19.1. Identify the business benefits associated with successful software development.

19.2. Describe the seven phases of the systems development life cycle.

19.3. Summarize the different software development methodologies.

19.4. Define the relationship between the systems development life cycle and software development methodologies.

19.5. Compare the waterfall methodology and the agile methodology.

Nike's SCM system failure, which spun out of control to the tune of $400 million, is legendary. Nike blamed the system failure on its SCM vendor i2 Technologies. Nike states that i2 Technologies' demand and supply planning module created serious inventory problems. The i2 deployment, part of a multimillion-dollar e-business upgrade, caused Nike CEO Philip Knight to famously say, "This is what we get for our $400 million?" i2 saw its stock plummet with the Nike disaster, along with its reputation. i2's chief marketing officer Katrina Roche asserted that Nike failed to use the vendor's implementation methodology and templates, which contributed to the problem.[23]

Organizations must learn how to build and implement disruptive technologies, such as software for wireless devices, to remain competitive. Software that is built correctly can support agile organizations and can transform as the organization and its business transforms. Software that effectively meets employee needs will help an organization become more productive and enhance decision making. Software that does not meet employee needs may have a damaging effect on productivity and can even cause a business to fail. Employee involvement along with using the right implementation methodology when developing software is critical to the success of an organization.

Software development problems often lead to high-profile disasters. Hershey Food's glitch in its ERP implementation made the front page of *The Wall Street Journal* and cost the company millions. Hershey said computer problems with its SAP software system created a backlog of orders, causing slower deliveries, and resulting in lower earnings. Statistics released in 2003 by the National Research Council show that U.S. companies spent $175 billion in 2002 to repair damage caused by software defects.[24]

If software does not work, the organization will not work. Traditional business risk models typically ignored software development, largely because most organizations considered the impact from software and software development on the business to be minor. In the digital age, however, software success, or failure, can lead directly to business success, or failure. Almost every large organization in the world relies on software, either to drive its business operations or to make its products work. As organizations' reliance on software grows, so do the business-related consequences of software successes and failures including:

- **Increase or decrease revenues**—Organizations have the ability to directly increase profits by implementing successful IT systems. Organizations can also lose millions when software fails or key information is stolen or compromised.

  Nike's poorly designed supply chain management software delayed orders, increased excess inventories, and caused third quarter earnings to fall 24 percent below expectations.

- **Repair or damage to brand reputation**—Technologies such as CRM can directly enhance a company's brand reputation. Software can also severely damage a company's reputation if it fails to work as advertised or has security vulnerabilities that affect its customers' trust.

  H&R Block customers were furious when the company accidentally placed its customers' passwords and social security numbers on its Web site.

- **Prevent or incur liabilities**—Technology such as CAT scans, MRIs, and mammograms can save lives. Faulty technology used in airplanes, automobiles, pacemakers, or nuclear reactors can cause massive damage, injury, or death.

  The parent company of bankrupt pharmaceutical distributor FoxMeyer sued SAP for $500 million over ERP software failure that allegedly crippled its operations.

- **Increase or decrease productivity**—CRM and SCM software can directly increase a company's productivity. Large losses in productivity can also occur when software malfunctions or crashes.

  The Standish Group estimates that defective software code accounted for 45 percent of computer-system downtime and cost U.S. companies $100 billion in lost productivity in 2003 alone.[25]

The lucrative advantages of successful software implementations provide significant incentives to manage software development risks. But according to the Standish Group's Chaos report, more than half the software development projects undertaken in the United States come in late or over budget and the majority of successful projects maintain fewer features and functions than originally specified. Organizations also cancel around 33 percent of these projects during development. Understanding the basics of software development, or the systems development life cycle, will help organizations avoid potential software development pitfalls and ensure that software development efforts are successful.[26]

DEVELOPING SOFTWARE—THE SYSTEMS DEVELOPMENT LIFE CYCLE (SDLC)

Information systems are the support infrastructure that helps an organization change quickly when adapting to changing business environments and markets. Many factors must come together to develop successful software. This chapter focuses on the *systems development life cycle (SDLC),* also known as the "software life cycle" or the "application life cycle," which is the overall process for developing information systems from planning and analysis through implementation and maintenance (see Figure 5.6).

1. **Planning**—The *planning phase* involves establishing a high-level plan of the intended project and determining project goals. Planning is the first and most critical phase of any systems development effort an organization undertakes, regardless of whether the effort is to develop a system that allows customers to order products over the Internet, determine the best logistical structure for warehouses around the world, or develop a strategic information alliance with another organization. Organizations must carefully plan the activities (and determine why they are necessary) to be successful.

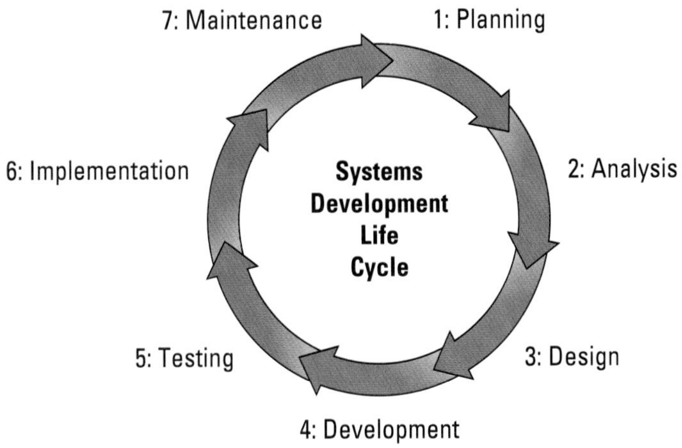

FIGURE 5.6

The Systems
Development Life Cycle

Figure shows a circular diagram labeled "Systems Development Life Cycle" with seven phases arranged around it: 7: Maintenance, 1: Planning, 6: Implementation, 2: Analysis, 5: Testing, 3: Design, 4: Development.

2. **Analysis**—The *analysis phase* involves analyzing end-user business requirements and refining project goals into defined functions and operations of the intended system. *Business requirements* are the detailed set of business requests that the system must meet in order to be successful. The analysis phase is obviously critical. A good start is essential and the organization must spend as much time, energy, and resources as necessary to perform a detailed, accurate analysis.

3. **Design**—The *design phase* involves describing the desired features and operations of the system including screen layouts, business rules, process diagrams, pseudo code, and other documentation.

4. **Development**—The *development phase* involves taking all of the detailed design documents from the design phase and transforming them into the actual system. In this phase the project transitions from preliminary designs to the actual physical implementation.

5. **Testing**—The *testing phase* involves bringing all the project pieces together into a special testing environment to test for errors, bugs, and interoperability and verify that the system meets all of the business requirements defined in the analysis phase.

    According to a report issued in June 2003 by the National Institute of Standards and Technology (NIST), defective software costs the U.S. economy an estimated $59.5 billion each year. Of that total, software users incur 64 percent of the costs and software developers 36 percent. NIST suggests that improvements in testing could reduce this cost significantly—by about a third, or $22.5 billion—but that unfortunately testing improvements would not eliminate most software errors.[27]

6. **Implementation**—The *implementation phase* involves placing the system into production so users can begin to perform actual business operations with the system.

7. **Maintenance**—Maintaining the system is the final sequential phase of any systems development effort. The *maintenance phase* involves performing changes, corrections, additions, and upgrades to ensure the system continues to meet the business goals. This phase continues for the life of the system because the system must change as the business evolves and its needs change, demanding constant monitoring, supporting the new system with frequent minor changes (for example, new reports or information capturing), and reviewing the system to be sure it is moving the organization toward its strategic goals.

SOFTWARE DEVELOPMENT METHODOLOGIES

Today, systems are so large and complex that teams of architects, analysts, developers, testers, and users must work together to create the millions of lines of custom-written code that drive enterprises. For this reason, developers have created a number of different system development life cycle methodologies including *waterfall; rapid application development (RAD); extreme programming;* and *agile.* The oldest of these, and the best known, is the waterfall methodology: a sequence of phases in which the output of each phase becomes the input for the next (see Figure 5.7).

Waterfall Methodology

The traditional ***waterfall methodology*** is a sequential, activity-based process in which each phase in the SDLC is performed sequentially from planning through implementation and maintenance. The waterfall methodology is one of the oldest software development methods and has been around for over 30 years. The success rate for software development projects that follow this approach is only about 1 in 10. One primary reason for such a low success rate is that the waterfall methodology does not sufficiently take into account the level of uncertainty in new projects and the creativity required to complete software development projects in several aspects:

- **The business problem:** Any flaws in accurately defining and articulating the business problem in terms of what the business users actually require flow onward to the next phase.

- **The plan:** Managing costs, resources, and time constraints is difficult in the waterfall sequence. What happens to the schedule if a programmer quits? How will a schedule delay in a specific phase impact the total cost of the project? Unexpected contingencies may sabotage the plan.

- **The solution:** The waterfall methodology is problematic in that it assumes users can specify all business requirements in advance. Defining the appropriate IT infrastructure that is flexible, scalable, and reliable is a challenge. The final IT infrastructure solution must meet not only current but also future needs in terms of time, cost, feasibility, and flexibility. Vision is inevitably limited at the head of the waterfall.

FIGURE 5.7

The Traditional
Waterfall Methodology

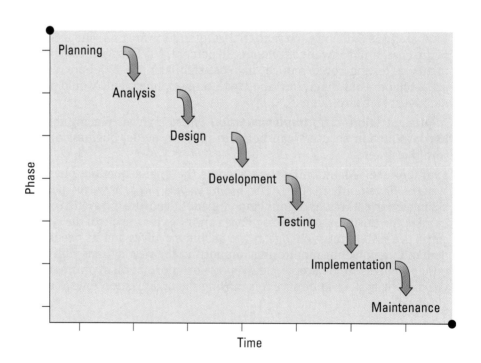

Unfortunately, business requirements change as the business changes, which calls for considerable feedback and iterative consultation for all business requirements. Essentially, software is "soft" and it must be easily changed and manipulated to meet the changing dynamics of an organization. As people's understanding of the business problems evolve over time, so must the software. For this reason, it is counterproductive to define all requirements precisely upfront since, by the time the software goes into production, which can be several months or even years after completing the initial analysis phase, chances are the business problems have changed as well as the business.

Rapid Application Development Methodology (RAD)

In response to the faster pace of business, rapid application development has become a popular route for accelerating systems development. *Rapid application development (RAD) (*also called *rapid prototyping) methodology* emphasizes extensive user involvement in the rapid and evolutionary construction of working prototypes of a system to accelerate the systems development process. The fundamentals of RAD include:

- Focus initially on creating a prototype that looks and acts like the desired system.
- Actively involve system users in the analysis, design, and development phases.
- Accelerate collecting the business requirements through an interactive and iterative construction approach.

A *prototype* is a smaller-scale representation or working model of the users' requirements or a proposed design for an information system. The prototype is an essential part of the analysis phase when using the RAD methodology.

PHH Vehicle Management Services, a Baltimore fleet-management company with over 750,000 vehicles, wanted to build an enterprise application that opened the entire vehicle information database to customers over the Internet. To build the application quickly, the company abandoned the traditional waterfall approach. Instead, a team of 30 developers began prototyping the Internet application and the company's customers evaluated each prototype for immediate feedback. The development team released new prototypes that incorporated the customers' feedback every six weeks. The PHH Interactive Vehicle application went into production seven months after the initial work began. Over 20,000 customers, using a common browser, can now access the PHH Interactive site at any time from anywhere in the world to review their accounts, analyze billing information, and order vehicles.[28]

Extreme Programming Methodology

Extreme programming (XP) methodology breaks a project into tiny phases, and developers cannot continue on to the next phase until the first phase is complete. The primary difference between the waterfall and XP methodologies is that XP divides its phases into iterations with user feedback. The waterfall approach develops the entire system, whereas XP develops the system in iterations (see Figure 5.8). XP is a lot like a jigsaw puzzle; there are many small pieces. Individually the pieces make no sense, but when they are combined together (again and again) an organization can gain visibility into the entire new system.

Microsoft Corporation developed Internet Explorer and Netscape Communications Corporation developed Communicator using extreme programming. Both companies did a nightly compilation (called a build) of the entire project, bringing together all the current components. They established release dates and expended considerable effort to involve customers in each release. The extreme programming approach allowed both Microsoft and Netscape to manage millions of lines of code as specifications changed and evolved over time. Most important, both companies frequently held user design reviews and strategy sessions to solicit and incorporate user feedback.[29]

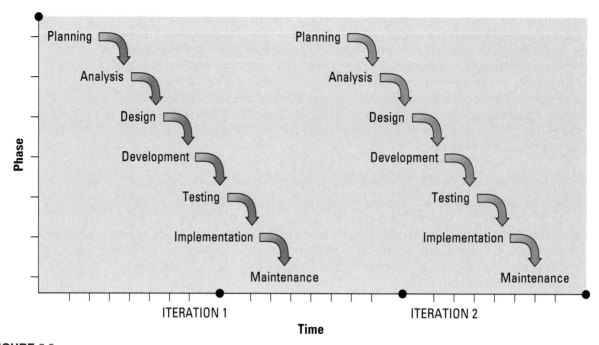

ITERATION 1   ITERATION 2

Time

FIGURE 5.8

The Iterative Approach

XP is a significant departure from traditional software development methodologies and many organizations in different industries have developed successful software using it. One of the reasons for XP's success is because it stresses ongoing customer satisfaction. XP empowers developers to respond to changing customer and business requirements, even late in the systems development life cycle, and XP emphasizes teamwork. Managers, customers, and developers are all part of a team dedicated to delivering quality software. XP implements a simple, yet effective way to enable groupware-style development. The XP methodology promotes quickly being able to respond to changing requirements and technology.

Agile Methodology

The *agile methodology,* a form of XP, aims for customer satisfaction through early and continuous delivery of useful software components. Agile is similar to XP but with less focus on team coding and more on limiting project scope. An agile project sets a minimum number of requirements and turns them into a deliverable product. Agile means what it sounds like: fast and efficient; small and nimble; lower cost; fewer features; shorter projects.

The Agile Alliance is a group of software developers whose mission is to improve software development processes and whose manifesto includes the following tenets:

- Satisfy the customer through early and continuous delivery of valuable software.
- Welcome changing requirements, even late in development.
- Businesspeople and developers must work together daily throughout the project.
- Build projects around motivated individuals. Give them the environment and support they need, and trust them to get the job done.
- The best architectures, requirements, and designs emerge from self-organizing teams.
- At regular intervals, the team reflects on how to become more effective, then tunes and adjusts its behavior accordingly.[30]

DEVELOPING SUCCESSFUL SOFTWARE

The Gartner Group estimates that 65 percent of agile projects are successful. This success rate is extraordinary compared to the 10 percent success rate of waterfall projects. The following are the primary principles an organization should follow for successful agile software development.[31]

Slash the Budget

Small budgets force developers and users to focus on the essentials. Small budgets also make it easier to kill a failing project. For example, imagine that a project that has already cost $20 million is going down the tubes. With that much invested, it is tempting to invest another $5 million to rescue it rather than take a huge loss. All too often, the system fails and the company ends up with an even bigger loss.

Jim Johnson, chairman of The Standish Group, says he forced the CIO of one Fortune 500 company to set a $100,000 ceiling on all software development projects. There were no exceptions to this business rule without approval from the CIO and CEO. Johnson claims the company's project success rate went from 0 percent to 50 percent.[32]

If It Doesn't Work, Kill It

Bring all key stakeholders together at the beginning of a project and as it progresses bring them together again to evaluate the software. Is it doing what the business wants and, more important, requires? Eliminate any software that is not meeting business expectations. This is called triage, and it's "the perfect place to kill a software project," says Pat Morgan, senior program manager at Compaq's Enterprise Storage Group. He holds monthly triage sessions and says they can be brutal. "At one [meeting], engineering talked about a cool process they were working on to transfer information between GUIs. No one in the room needed it. We killed it right there. In our environment, you can burn a couple of million dollars in a month only to realize what you're doing isn't useful."[33]

Keep Requirements to a Minimum

Start each project with what the software must absolutely do. Do not start with a list of everything the software should do. Every software project traditionally starts with a requirements document that will often have hundreds or thousands of business requirements. The Standish Group estimates that only 7 percent of the business requirements are needed for any given application. Keeping requirements to a minimum also means that scope creep and feature creep must be closely monitored. **Scope creep** occurs when the scope of the project increases. **Feature creep** occurs when developers add extra features that were not part of the initial requirements. Both scope creep and feature creep are major reasons software development fails.[34]

Test and Deliver Frequently

As often as once a week, and not less than once a month, complete a part of the project or a piece of software. The part of the project must be working and it must be bug-free. Then have the customers test and approve it. This is the agile methodology's most radical departure from traditional development. In some traditional software projects, the customers did not see any working parts or pieces for years.

Assign Non-IT Executives to Software Projects

Non-IT executives should coordinate with the technical project manager, test iterations to make sure they are meeting user needs, and act as liaisons between executives and IT. Having the business side involved full-time will bring project ownership and a desire to succeed to all parties involved. SpreeRide, a Salt Lake City market research outfit, used the agile methodology to set up its company's Web site. The project required several business executives designated full-time. The company believes this is one of the primary reasons that the project was successfully deployed in less than three months.[35]

PROJECT MANAGING THE SYSTEMS DEVELOPMENT EFFORT

No one would think of building an office complex by turning loose 100 different construction teams to build 100 different rooms, with no single blueprint or agreed-upon vision of the completed structure. Yet this is precisely the situation in which many large organizations find themselves when managing systems development projects. Organizations routinely overschedule their resources (human and otherwise), develop redundant projects, and damage profitability by investing in nonstrategic efforts that do not contribute to the organization's bottom line. Project management offers a strategic framework for coordinating the numerous activities associated with organizational projects.

According to the Project Management Institute, ***project management*** is the application of knowledge, skills, tools, and techniques to project activities in order to meet or exceed stakeholder needs and expectations from a project. ***Project management software*** specifically supports the long-term and day-to-day management and execution of the steps in a project (such as building a new warehouse or designing and implementing a new IT system).

Project management is essential to the success of almost every aspect of IT. Without it, projects tend to be delayed, over budget, and often never reach completion. Horizon Blue Cross Blue Shield of New Jersey, a $6-billion-plus health insurance provider, allocated several hundred million dollars to IT over a five-year period to tackle tasks such as consolidating five enterprise software platforms, managing compliance with regulatory offices, and simplifying new product development. These IT initiatives involve hundreds of skilled people working on hundreds of concurrently developing projects. Horizon's executives needed to gain visibility into all projects, subsets of projects, and existing and planned projects collectively. The company considered a rigorous and formalized project management strategy fundamental to the project's success.

Horizon decided to implement IT project management software from Business Engine Inc. to manage its projects. The software collects information through standardized templates created for Microsoft Project, which are stored in an enterprise database, and then fed into Business Engine's analytical tool, called Ben. Each user can then view and manipulate spreadsheets and graphs, share documents, track revisions, and run what-if scenarios in their personalized digital dashboard view. With the help from Business Engine, Horizon is managing IT projects and assets as if they were investments, tracking their performance against business goals, assessing their individual return and value to the company, and helping sort out which projects require greater attention and resources and which require reduced attention and resources. Horizon currently finds itself in the position of being ahead of schedule on over 70 percent of its IT projects.[36]

Figure 5.9 displays the relationships between the three primary variables in any project—(1) time, (2) cost, and (3) scope. These three variables are interdependent. For example, decreasing a project's time frame means either increasing the cost of the project or decreasing the scope of the project to meet the new deadline. Increasing a project's scope means either increasing the project's time frame or increasing the project's cost—or both—to meet the

FIGURE 5.9

Project Management Interdependent Variables

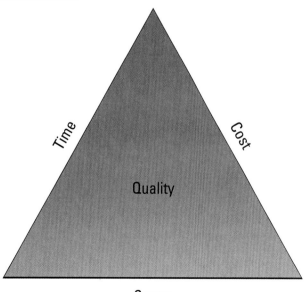

FIGURE 5.10

Why IT Projects Fall
Behind Schedule or Fail

Source: Information Week.

increased scope changes. Project management is the science of making intelligent trade-offs between time, cost, and scope. All three of the factors combined determine a project's quality.

Benjamin Franklin's timeless advice—by failing to prepare, you prepare to fail—especially applies to many of today's software development projects. A recent survey concluded that the failure rate of IT projects is much higher in organizations that do not exercise disciplined project management. Figure 5.10 displays the top six reasons why IT projects fail according to *Information Week*'s research survey of 150 IT managers.[37]

A successful project is typically on time, within budget, meets the business's requirements, and fulfills the customer's needs. The Hackett Group, an Atlanta-based consultancy, analyzed its client database (which includes 2,000 companies, including 81 Fortune 100 companies) and discovered:

- Three in 10 major IT projects fail.
- 21 percent of the companies state that they cannot adjust rapidly to market changes.
- One in four validate a business case for IT projects after completion.[38]

Nicolas Dubuc, collaborative project manager at Rhodia Inc., a $6 billion worldwide manufacturer of specialty chemicals, uses Microsoft's software to develop project management templates and methodologies for its 18 divisions. "We're designing a platform for rapid application development that will enhance opportunities for innovation," states Duboc.

Today, the leaders in the project management software market include Microsoft, Primavera, Oracle, PeopleSoft, and SAP. Microsoft Project is the core project-management tool for many organizations and dominates with more than 8 million users and over 80 percent of the market share. Figure 5.11 displays the expected growth for project management software over the next few years. If an organization wants to deliver successful, high-quality software on time and under budget, it must take advantage of project management software.

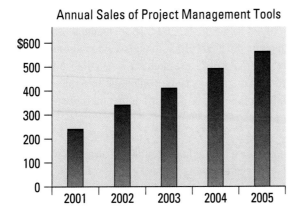

Annual Sales of Project Management Tools

FIGURE 5.11

Expected Growth for
Project Management
Software

Source: Gartner Dataquest
(in $millions).

1. List and describe the seven phases in the systems development life cycle and determine which phase is most important to Cisco when it is developing software.

2. Review the primary principles of successful software development and prioritize them in order of importance for Amazon.com's business strategy.

3. Explain why building agile software is important to all seven of the companies.

4. Assess the impact to IBM's business if it decided to use the waterfall methodology to build its customers' information systems.

Chapter Nineteen Case: Transforming the Entertainment Industry—Netflix

The online DVD rental pioneer Netflix is transforming the movie business with its unique business model and streamlined shipping strategy. Netflix is quickly becoming one of Hollywood's most promising new business partners and is experiencing staggering growth with over 1 million subscribers, accounting for 3 to 5 percent of all U.S. home video rentals.

Typically, traditional video rental stores focus on major films and ignore older movies and smaller titles with niche audiences. Netflix is turning that idea upside down by offering a serious market for every movie, not just blockbusters. How? Netflix attributes its success to its proprietary software, called the Netflix Recommendation System, which constantly suggests movies a customer might like, based on how the customer rates any of the 15,000 titles in the company's catalog. Beyond recommendations, Netflix has figured out how to get DVDs from one subscriber to the next with unbelievable efficiency.

Netflix operates by allowing its subscribers to rent unlimited videos for $20 a month, as long as they have no more than three DVDs rented at a time. Currently there are more than 3 million discs in the hands of its customers at any given time, with an average of 300,000 DVDs shipped out of the company's 20 leased distribution centers daily. To handle the rental logistics for its 5.5 million DVD library the company created a proprietary supply chain management system.

As with any change or market advance, when new competition invades, existing competitors will not stand still. Walmart.com recently launched its own version of the Netflix model, it has already built six distribution centers, and is charging $1.19 less per month for the same services offered by Netflix. Blockbuster purchased a similar service called FilmCaddy and is currently strategizing on how it will promote the service nationally. Other companies threatening to steal Netflix's market share are satellite and cable companies that now offer on-demand movies. To remain disruptive, Netflix will need to analyze its competition and strategize new ways to continue to increase subscriptions and revenues.[39]

Questions

1. Assess the business-related consequences of a failure in Netflix's proprietary supply chain management system.

2. List and describe the seven phases in the systems development life cycle and determine which phase you think is most important to Netflix when it is developing software.

3. Determine the primary differences between the waterfall development methodology and the agile development methodology. Which methodology would you recommend Netflix use and why?

4. Explain why prototyping would be a good idea for Netflix if it decides to build a CRM system.

<< PLUG-IN POINTERS

Review *Business Plug-In* **Systems Development** for in-depth coverage of the SDLC and its associated activities including performing feasibility studies, gathering business requirements, analyzing a buy vs. build decision, designing and building systems, writing and performing testing, supporting users, etc.

Review *Business Plug-In* **Project Management** for an overview of the fundamentals of project management including prioritizing projects and developing project plans, along with a detailed look at risk management and change management.

<< PLUG-IN POINTER

Review *Technology Plug-In* **Object-Oriented Technologies** for an overview of the fundamentals of object-oriented including information, procedures, classes, objects, messages, polymorphism, encapsulation, inheritance, and a detailed example of the benefits of building an object-oriented system.

Chapter Twenty: Developing a 21st Century Organization

20.1. List and describe the four 21st century trends that businesses are focusing on and rank them in order of business importance.

20.2. Explain how the integration of business and technology is shaping 21st century organizations.

O rganizations are facing changes more extensive and far reaching in their implications than anything since the modern industrial revolution took place in the early 1900s. Technology is one of the primary forces driving these changes. Organizations that want to survive in the 21st century must recognize the immense power of technology, carry out required organizational changes in the face of it, and learn to operate in an entirely different way. Figure 5.12 displays a few examples of the way technology is changing the business arena.

21ST CENTURY ORGANIZATION TRENDS

Twenty-first century organization trends on the business side are:

- Uncertainty in terms of future business scenarios and economic outlooks.
- Emphasis on strategic analysis for cost reduction and productivity enhancements.
- Focus on improved business resiliency via the application of enhanced security.

On the technology side, there has been a focus on improved business management of IT in order to extract the most value from existing resources and create alignment between business and IT priorities. Today's organizations focus on defending and safeguarding their existing market positions in addition to targeting new market growth. The four primary information technology areas where organizations are focusing include:

1. IT Infrastructures
2. Security
3. E-business
4. Integration

Increased Focus on IT Infrastructure

A significant trend for the 21st century is to increase the focus on *IT infrastructure*—the hardware, software, and telecommunications equipment that, when combined, provide the underlying foundation to support the organization's goals. Organizations in the past underestimated the importance that IT infrastructures have on the many functional areas of an organization.

FIGURE 5.12

Examples of How
Technology Is Changing
Business

Industry	Business Changes Due to Technology
Travel	Travel site Expedia.com is now the biggest leisure-travel agency, with higher profit margins than even American Express. Thirteen percent of traditional travel agencies closed in 2002 because of their inability to compete with online travel.[40]
Entertainment	The music industry has kept Napster and others from operating, but $35 billion annual online downloads are wrecking the traditional music business. U.S. music unit sales are down 20 percent since 2000. The next big entertainment industry to feel the effects of e-business will be the $67 billion movie business.[41]
Electronics	Using the Internet to link suppliers and customers, Dell dictates industry profits. Its operating margins have risen from 7.3 percent in 2002 to 8 percent in 2003, even as it takes prices to levels where rivals cannot make money.[42]
Financial services	Nearly every public e-finance company left makes money, with online mortgage service LendingTree growing 70 percent a year. Processing online mortgage applications is now 40 percent cheaper for customers.[43]
Retail	Less than 5 percent of retail sales occur online. eBay is on track this year to become one of the nation's top 15 retailers, and Amazon.com will join the top 40. Wal-Mart's e-business strategy is forcing rivals to make heavy investments in technology.[44]
Automobiles	The cost of producing vehicles is down because of SCM and Web-based purchasing. eBay has become the leading U.S. used-car dealer, and most major car sites are profitable.[45]
Education and training	Cisco saved $133 million last year by moving training sessions to the Internet, and the University of Phoenix online college classes please investors.[46]

In the early days of the Internet, the basic Internet infrastructure in terms of protocols and standards was unsophisticated (and still is), but software companies managed to enhance the Internet and offer compelling applications for functional business areas. The original design for the Internet and the Web was for simple e-mail, document exchange, and the display of static content, not for sophisticated and dynamic business applications that require access to back-end systems and databases.

Organizations today are looking to Internet-based cross-functional systems such as CRM, SCM, and ERP to help drive their business success. The days of implementing independent functional systems are gone. Creating an effective organization requires a 360-degree view of all operations. For this reason, the ownership of the IT infrastructure now becomes the responsibility of the entire organization and not just the individual users or functional department. This is primarily because the IT infrastructure has a dramatic influence on the strategic capabilities of an organization (see Figure 5.13).

Increased Focus on Security

With war and terrorist attacks at the top of many people's minds, security is a hot topic. For businesses, too, security concerns are widespread. Increasingly opening up their networks and applications to customers, partners, and suppliers using an ever more diverse set of computing devices and networks, businesses can benefit from deploying the latest advances in security technologies. These benefits include fewer disruptions to organizational systems, increased productivity of employees,

FIGURE 5.13

The Position of the
Infrastructure within
the Organization

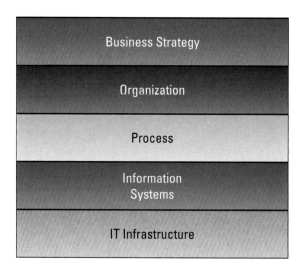

and greater advances in administration, authorization, and authentication techniques. For businesses it is important to have the appropriate levels of authentication, access control, and encryption in place, which help to ensure (1) that only authorized individuals can gain access to the network, (2) that they have access to only those applications for which they are entitled, and (3) that they cannot understand or alter information while in transit. Figure 5.14 displays a recent survey concerning both the level of physical security integration and the current security practices used by most organizations.

Business disrupted by security breaches not only is an inconvenience for business users and their customers and partners, but can also cost millions of dollars in lost revenues or lost market capitalization. Nor does business cost of inadequate security stop at simply inconvenience and loss of revenues or market valuation. It can even force a business out of existence. One example was the case in early 2002 of British Internet service provider CloudNine Communications, which was the victim of a distributed denial-of-service (DDoS) attack that forced the company to close operations and to eventually transfer over 2,500 customers to a rival organization. While "disruptive technologies" can help a company to gain competitive advantage and market share (and avoid real business disruptions), lack of security can have the opposite effect, causing profitable companies to lose market share or even their entire business within hours or days of an attack.[47]

It is now more important than ever for an organization to have well-rehearsed and frequently updated processes and procedures to insure against a variety of adverse scenarios—Internet e-mail and denial-of-service attacks from worms and viruses, loss of communications, loss of documents, password and information theft, fire, flood, physical attacks on property, and even terrorist attacks.

FIGURE 5.14

Physical Security
Integration and Best
Security Practices

Source: CSOonline.com.

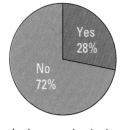

Is the organization's
physical security integrated
with IT security?

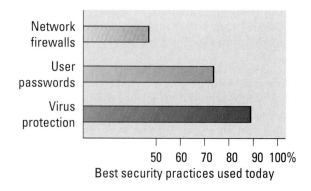

Best security practices used today

Increased Focus on E-Business

Mobility and wireless are the new focus in e-business, and some upcoming trends are mobile commerce, telematics, electronic tagging, and RFID.

- **Mobile commerce**—the ability to purchase goods and services through a wireless Internet-enabled device.
- **Telematics**—blending computers and wireless telecommunications technologies with the goal of efficiently conveying information over vast networks to improve business operations. The most notable example of telematics may be the Internet itself, since it depends on a number of computer networks connected globally through telecommunication devices.[48]
- **Electronic tagging**—a technique for identifying and tracking assets and individuals via technologies such as radio frequency identification and smart cards.
- **Radio frequency identification (RFID)**—technologies use active or passive tags in the form of chips or smart labels that can store unique identifiers and relay this information to electronic readers. Within the supply chain, RFID can enable greater efficiencies in business processes such as inventory, logistics, distribution, and asset management. On the mobile commerce side, RFID can enable new forms of e-business through mobile phones and smart cards. This can increase loyalty by streamlining purchases for the consumer. For example, RFID readers are being embedded in store shelving to help retailers, including Marks & Spencer and The Gap, to better manage their assets and inventories and understand customer behavior.[49]

These are all interesting subcategories within mobile business that open up new opportunities for mobility beyond simple employee applications. Electronic tagging and RFID are especially interesting because they extend wireless and mobile technologies not just to humans, but also to a wide range of objects such as consumer and industrial products. These products will gain intelligence via electronic product codes, which are a (potential) replacement for universal product code (UPC) barcodes, and via RFID tags with two-way communication capabilities.

Mobile employees will soon have the ability to leverage technology just as if they were in the office. Improvements in devices, applications, networks, and standards over the past few years have made this far more practical than it was when first introduced. The drivers for adoption are finally starting to outweigh the barriers. For example, major vendors such as IBM, Microsoft, Oracle, and Sybase are all playing a larger role and taking a greater interest in mobile business than they had previously. These vendors all have mature, proven offerings for enterprise mobility.

Mobile technology will help extend an organization out to its edges in areas such as sales force automation and enterprise operations. Benefits can include improved information accuracy, reduced costs, increased productivity, increased revenues, and improved customer service. Beyond being an additional channel for communications, mobile business will enable an organization to think about the powerful combination of business processes, e-business, and wireless communications.

Increased Focus on Integration

Information technology has penetrated the heart of organizations and will stay there in the future. The IT industry is one of the most dynamic in the global economy. As a sector, it not only creates millions of high-level jobs, but also helps organizations to be more efficient and effective, which in turn stimulates innovation. The integration of business and technology has allowed organizations to increase their share of the global economy, transform the way they conduct business, and become more efficient and effective (see Figure 5.15).

FIGURE 5.15

The Integration of
Business and
Technology

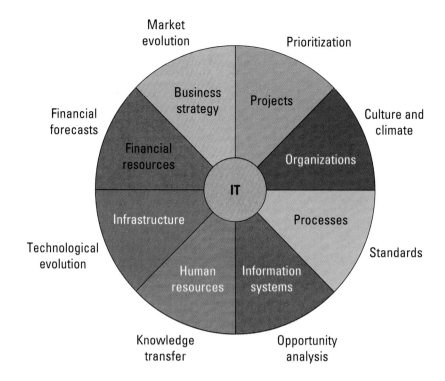

The past few years have produced a confluence of events that have reshaped the global economy. Around the world, free-market competition has flourished and a new globally interdependent financial system has emerged. Reflecting these changes, core business relationships and models are dramatically changing, including shifts from:

- Product-centricity to customer-centricity
- Mass production to mass customization
- The value in material things to the value of knowledge and intelligence

In concert with these trends, a new series of business success factors and challenges have emerged that are helping to determine marketplace winners and losers:

- Organization agility, often supported by a "plug and play" IT infrastructure (with a flexible and adaptable applications architecture)
- A focus on core competencies and processes
- A redefinition of the value chain
- Instantaneous business response
- The ability to scale resources and infrastructure across geographic boundaries

These developments add up to an environment that is vastly more complex than even five years ago. This in turn has resulted in organizations increasingly embracing new business models. The new environment requires organizations to focus externally on their business processes and integration architectures. The virtually integrated business model will cause a sharp increase in the number of business partners and the closeness of integration between them.

Never before have IT investments played such a critical role in business success. As business strategies continue to evolve, the distinction between "the business" and IT will virtually disappear.

1. Determine which of the seven companies would find it most important to focus on its IT infrastructure when determining its 21st-century strategy.

2. Determine which of the seven companies would find it most important to focus on security when determining its 21st-century strategy.

3. Determine which of the seven companies would find it most important to focus on e-business when determining its 21st-century strategy.

4. Determine which of the seven companies would find it most important to focus on integrations when determining its 21st-century strategy.

Chapter Twenty Case: Creating a Clearer Picture for Public Broadcasting Service (PBS)

One of the leaders in the transformation of the broadcasting industry is André Mendes, chief technology integration officer, or CTIO, at Public Broadcasting Service (PBS). Mendes oversees the company's technology organization, a 50-person group created last year by melding PBS's IT and broadcast-engineering departments. The new CTIO position replaces the formerly separate jobs of CIO and CTO at the nonprofit television network.

Mendes encountered a few roadblocks during his first few months as CTIO including resistance from the broadcast engineering staff, his limited knowledge of broadcast engineering, and breaking down barriers between the two departments. Mendes managed through the change with finesse and now refers to the experiences as a "bidirectional learning experience" for him and his staff. "Once you're in a new environment, you start asking a lot of questions," he says. "Every question requires the responder to think about the answer. That helped the process of evaluating why procedures and practices are done a certain way—and identifying possible improvements."

Michael Hunt, PBS's VP of Enterprise Applications, states that Mendes broke down many barriers and offered his employees a way to address and respond to change. The united team is currently working on large, sophisticated projects that are improving the efficiency of PBS and its member stations. "Projects are getting bigger and bigger, with more and more collaboration, with a more global picture," says Marilyn Pierce, director of PBS digital assets, who came from the broadcast-engineering side of the company.

"The broadcast environment is becoming an IT environment," states Mendes in reference to the fact that as the worlds of broadcast and traditional information technologies converge, this uncovers new ways to improve quality of service and increase opportunities for innovation through new digitized formats, which replace traditional analog video. The primary drivers of this convergence are advances in digital technologies and the Internet. Though those changes are unique to the television industry, it is not the first—or last—time that welding together different technology organizations has been responsible for advances in technology. For instance, companies pursuing voice-over-IP (VOIP) initiatives are combining their IT and telecommunications groups, and other industries face similar integration challenges as everything from automobiles to appliances becomes increasingly technology dependent.

The integration of broadcast and information technologies is raising the visibility of technology as an organizational infrastructure enabler and a strategic partner for new business models. PBS is launching several projects that are revamping the way the company does business. One project allows producers to send program content digitally rather than on videotapes. In the past, PBS rejected and returned 60 percent of the video content because it did not contain key technical information such as the number of frames in a program to allow for seamless merging of programs. "From a supply-chain standpoint, that was highly inefficient," Mendes says.

Another project is saving PBS tens of millions of dollars a year by transporting its programs to TV stations as e-mail files via TCP/IP over satellite. This delivery vehicle greatly improves quality by avoiding weather-related interference that can arise in transmitting programs by streaming signals over satellite. "The change in broadcast is similar to the transformation in the telecom industry as companies moved from switch circuitry to packet circuits," Mendes says. For PBS the business lines are blurring as the industry responds to technology changes, which is making the overall picture much clearer.[50]

Questions

1. Assess the impact to PBS's business if it failed to focus on IT infrastructures when determining its 21st-century business strategy.
2. Assess the impact to PBS's business if it failed to focus on security when determining its 21st-century business strategy.
3. Assess the impact to PBS's business if it failed to focus on e-business when determining its 21st-century business strategy.
4. Assess the impact to PBS's business if it failed to focus on integrations when determining its 21st-century business strategy.

PLUG-IN POINTER >>

Review *Technology Plug-In* **Valuing Technology** for an overview of Return on Investment (ROI), Net Present Value (NPV), Internal Rate of Return (IRR), Payback Period, and Total Cost of Ownership (TCO).

An organization must remain competitive in this quick-paced, constantly changing, global business environment. It must implement technology that is adaptive, disruptive, and transformable to meet new and unexpected customer needs. Focusing on the unexpected and understanding disruptive technologies can give an organization a competitive advantage.

Wireless technologies are quickly becoming one of the fastest growing disruptive technologies available today. Such things as RFID and WiMax are becoming trends in the e-business environment. Many of these wireless technologies are not quite ripe for mainstream adoption, but they pack enough punch to spark sudden changes in business and IT strategies. In fact, wireless networks, particularly those used in homes and small offices, are a disruptive technology that will have the same impact on the networking industry that wireless phones had on the telecommunications industry.

Organizations need software that users can transform quickly to meet the requirements of the rapidly changing business environment. Software that effectively meets employee needs will help an organization become more productive and make better decisions. Software that does not meet employee needs may have a damaging effect on productivity. Employee involvement along with using the right implementation methodology in developing software is critical to the success of an organization.

Four areas of focus for organizations heading into the 21st century are: (1) IT infrastructure, (2) security, (3) e-business (mobility), (4) integration. Information technology has rapidly expanded from a back-room resource providing competitive advantage (e.g., cost, time, quality) to a front-office resource (e.g., marketing, sales) that is a competitive necessity. The dynamic business and technical environment of the 21st century is driving the need for technology infrastructures and applications architecture that are increasingly flexible, integrated, and maintainable (while always providing functionality, cost effectiveness, timeliness, and security).

KEY TERMS

Agile methodology, 200
Analysis phase, 197
Business requirement, 197
Design phase, 197
Development phase, 197
Disruptive technology, 185
Electronic tagging, 209
Extreme programming (XP)
    methodology, 199
Feature creep, 201
Implementation phase, 197

IT infrastructure, 206
Maintenance phase, 197
Mobile commerce, 209
Planning phase, 196
Project management, 202
Project management
    software, 202
Prototype, 199
Radio frequency identification
    (RFID), 209

Rapid application development
    (RAD) (also called rapid
    prototyping) methodology, 199
Scope creep, 201
Sustaining technology, 185
Systems development life cycle
    (SDLC), 196
Telematics, 209
Testing phase, 197
Waterfall methodology, 198

CLOSING CASE ONE

Watching Where You Step—Prada

Prada estimates its sales per year at $22 million. The luxury retailer recently spent millions on IT for its futuristic "epicenter" store—but the flashy technology turned into a high-priced hassle. The company will need to generate annual sales of $75 million by 2007 to turn a profit on its new high-tech investment.

When Prada opened its $40 million Manhattan flagship, hotshot architect Rem Koolhaas promised a radically new shopping experience. And he kept the promise—though not quite according to plan. Customers were soon enduring hordes of tourists, neglected technology, and the occasional thrill of getting stuck in experimental dressing rooms. A few of the problems associated with the store:

1. **Fickle fitting rooms**—Doors that turn from clear to opaque confuse shoppers and frequently fail to open on cue.
2. **Failed RFID**—Touchscreens meant to spring to life when items are placed in the RFID "closets" are often just blank.
3. **Pointless PDAs**—Salesclerks let the hand-held devices gather dust and instead check the stockroom for inventory.
4. **Neglected network**—A lag between sales and inventory systems makes the wireless network nearly irrelevant.

This was not exactly the vision for the high-end boutique when it debuted in December 2001. Instead, the 22,000-square-foot SoHo shop was to be the first of four "epicenter" stores around the world that would combine cutting-edge architecture and 21st-century technology to revolutionize the luxury shopping experience. Prada poured roughly 25 percent of the store's budget into IT, including a wireless network to link every item to an Oracle inventory database in real-time using radio frequency identification (RFID) tags on the clothes. The staff would roam the floor armed with PDAs to check whether items were in stock, and customers could do the same through touchscreens in the dressing rooms.

But most of the flashy technology today sits idle, abandoned by employees who never quite embraced computing chic and are now too overwhelmed by large crowds to assist shoppers with hand-helds. On top of that, many gadgets, such as automated dressing-room doors and touchscreens, are either malfunctioning or ignored. Packed with experimental technology, the clear-glass dressing-rooms were designed to open and close automatically at the tap of a foot pedal, then turn opaque when a second pedal sent an electric current through the glass. Inside, an RFID-aware rack would recognize a customer's selections and display them on a touchscreen linked to the inventory system.

In practice, the process was hardly that smooth. Many shoppers never quite understood the pedals and disrobed in full view, thinking the door had turned opaque. That is no longer a problem, since the staff usually leaves the glass opaque, but often the doors get stuck. Some of the chambers are open only to VIP customers during peak traffic times.

With the smart closets and hand-helds out of commission, the wireless network in the store is nearly irrelevant, despite its considerable expense. As Prada's debt reportedly climbed to around $1 billion in late 2001, the company shelved plans for the fourth epicenter store, in San Francisco. A second store opened in Tokyo last year to great acclaim, albeit with different architects in a different market. Though that store incorporates similar cutting-edge concepts, architect Jacques Herzog emphasized that avant-garde retail plays well only in Japan. "This building is clearly a building for Tokyo," he told *The New York Times* in June. "It couldn't be somewhere else."

The multimillion-dollar technology spend is starting to look more like technology for technology's sake than an enhancement of the shopping experience, and already the store's failings have prompted Prada to reevaluate its epicenter strategy. The opening of the third epicenter store in Beverly Hills in July 2004 will demonstrate whether Prada has learned from its mistakes—or if similarly neglected technology will just leave Prada with more high-tech glitter that doesn't work well.

Questions

1. Would you consider Prada's use of technology disruptive? Why or why not?

2. Prada's attempt to use RFID to check inventory in real-time failed because of the staff's refusal to use the system. What could Prada have done to make the implementation of RFID successful?

3. How could prototyping have helped Prada work out the issues with its high-tech dressing rooms?

4. How could Prada have used agile development to increase the success of its high-tech systems?

5. What should Prada do differently when designing its fourth store to ensure its success?

6. Why should Prada focus on IT infrastructure, security, e-business, and integrations when it begins developing future stores?

CLOSING CASE TWO

Fear the Penguin

Linux has proved itself the most revolutionary software of the past decade. Estimates are that spending on Linux will reach $280 million by 2006. Linus Torvalds wrote the kernel (the core) of the Linux operating system at age 21. Torvalds posted the operating system on the Internet and invited other programmers to improve his code and users to download his operating system for free. Since then, tens of thousands of people have, making Linux perhaps the single largest collaborative project in the planet's history.

Today, Linux is everywhere. You can find Linux inside a boggling array of computers, machines, and devices. Linux is robust enough to run the world's most powerful supercomputers, yet sleek and versatile enough to run inside consumer toys like TiVo, television set-top boxes, cell phones, and hand-held portable devices. Even more impressive than Linux's increasing prevalence in living rooms and pockets is its growth in the market for corporate computers. According to a recent poll by CIO.com, 39 percent of IT managers agree that Linux will dominate corporate systems by 2007.

There is a reason why Linux is popping up everywhere. Since its introduction in 1991, no other operating system in history has spread as quickly across such a broad range of systems as Linux, and it has finally achieved critical mass. According to studies by market research firm IDC, Linux is currently the fastest-growing server operating system, with shipments expected to grow by over 34 percent per year over the next four years. With its innovative open source approach, strong security, reliability, and scalability, Linux can help companies achieve the agility they need to respond to changing consumer needs and stay ahead of the game.

Thanks to its unique open source development process, Linux is reliable and secure. A "meritocracy," a team specifically selected for their competence by the technical developer community, governs the entire development process. Each line of code that makes up the Linux kernel is extensively tested and maintained for a variety of different platforms and application scenarios.

This open collaborative approach means the Linux code base continually hardens and improves itself. If vulnerabilities appear, they get the immediate attention of experts from around the world, who quickly resolve the problems. According to Security Portal, which tracks vendor response times, it takes an average of 12 days to patch a Linux bug compared to an average of three months for some proprietary platforms. With the core resilience and reliability of Linux, businesses can minimize downtime, which directly increases their bottom line.

The Spread of Open Systems

Businesses and governments are opting for open-source operating systems like Linux instead of Windows.

- One of the attendees at the Linux Desktop Consortium in 2003 was Dr. Martin Echt, an avuncular cardiologist from Albany, New York. Dr. Echt, chief operating officer of Capital Cardiology Associates, an eight-office practice, discussed his decision to shift his business from Microsoft's Windows to Linux. Dr. Echt is not your typical computer geek or Linux supporter, and he is not the only one switching to Linux.
- The State Council in China has mandated that all ministries install the local flavor of Linux, dubbed Red Flag, on their PCs. In Spain, the government has installed a Linux operating system that incorporates the regional dialect. The city of Munich, despite a personal visit from Microsoft CEO Steve Ballmer, is converting its 14,000 PCs from Windows to Linux as early as 2004.
- "It's open season for open source," declared Walter Raizner, general manager of IBM Germany. One of the biggest corporate backers of Linux, IBM has more than 75 government customers worldwide, including agencies in France, Spain, Britain, Australia, Mexico, United States, and Japan.

The move toward Linux varies for each country or company. For Dr. Echt, it was a question of lower price and long-term flexibility. In China, the government claimed national security as a reason to move to open-source code because it permitted engineers to make sure there were no security leaks and no spyware installed on its computers. In Munich, the move was largely political. Regardless of the reason, the market is shifting toward Linux.

Microsoft vs. Linux

Bill Gates has openly stated that Linux is not a threat to Microsoft. According to IDC analysts, Microsoft's operating systems ship with 93.8 percent of all desktops worldwide. Ted Schadler, IDC research principal analyst, states that despite the push of lower-cost Linux players into the market, Microsoft will maintain its desktop market share for the following three reasons:

1. Linux is continuing to add features to its applications that most computer users have already come to expect.
2. Linux applications might not be compatible with Microsoft applications such as Microsoft Word or Microsoft Excel.
3. Microsoft continues to innovate and the latest version of Office is beginning to integrate word processing and spreadsheet software to corporate databases and other applications.

The Future of Linux

IDC analyst Al Gillen predicts that an open-source operating system will not enjoy explosive growth on the desktop for at least six or eight years. Still, even Gillen cannot deny that Linux's penetration continues to rise, with an estimated 18 million users. Linux's market share has nearly doubled from 1.5 percent at the end of 2000 to 2.8 percent at the beginning of 2003. According to IDC, by the end of 2004 it will have surpassed Apple's Mac OS, which has 2.9 percent of the market, as the second most popular operating system. Gartner Dataquest estimates Linux's server market share will grow seven times faster than Windows'.[51,52,53]

Questions

1. Would you consider Linux a disruptive technology? Why or why not?
2. Should Microsoft consider Linux a threat? Why or why not?

3. How is open-source software such as Linux a potential trend shaping 21st-century organizations?

4. How can you use Linux as an emerging technology to gain a competitive advantage?

5. Describe how open-source Linux differs from traditional software development.

6. Identify which development methodology you would recommend to someone developing a Linux application.

7. Research the Internet and discover potential ways that Linux might revolutionize business in the 21st century.

MAKING BUSINESS DECISIONS

1. Searching for Disruption

Scheduler.com is a large corporation that develops software that automates scheduling and record keeping for medical and dental practices. Scheduler.com currently holds 48 percent of its market share, has over 8,700 employees, and operates in six different countries. You are the VP of Product Development at Scheduler.com. You have just finished reading *The Innovator's Dilemma* by Clayton Christensen and you are interested in determining what types of disruptive technologies you can take advantage of, or should watch out for, in your industry. Use the Internet to develop a presentation highlighting the types of disruptive technologies you have found that have the potential to give the company a competitive advantage or could cause the company to fail.

2. Selecting a Systems Development Methodology

Exus Incorporated is an international billing outsourcing company. Exus currently has revenues of $5 billion, over 3,500 employees, and operations on every continent. You have recently been hired as the CIO. Your first task is to increase the software development project success rate, which is currently at 20 percent. In order to ensure that future software development projects are successful you want to standardize the systems development methodology across the entire enterprise. Currently, each project determines which methodology it uses to develop software.

Create a report detailing three additional system development methodologies that were not covered in this text. Compare each of these methodologies to the traditional waterfall approach. Finally, recommend which methodology you want to implement as your organizational standard. Be sure to highlight any potential roadblocks you might encounter when implementing the new standard methodology.

3. Applying Project Management Skills

You are a project management contractor attempting to contract work at a large telecommunications company, Hex Incorporated. Your interview with Debbie Fernandez, the senior VP of IT, went smoothly. The last thing Debbie wants to see from you before she makes her final hiring decision is a prioritized list of the projects below. You are sure to land the job if Debbie is satisfied with your prioritization. Create a report for Debbie prioritizing the projects and be sure to include the justifications for your prioritization.

- Upgrade accounting system
- Develop employee vacation tracking system
- Enhance employee intranet
- Cleanse and scrub data warehouse information

- Performance test all hardware to ensure 20 percent growth scalability
- Implement changes to employee benefits system
- Develop backup and recovery strategy
- Implement supply chain management system
- Upgrade customer relationship management system
- Build executive information system for CEO

4. **Transforming an Organization**

   Your college has asked you to help develop the curriculum for a new course titled "Building a 21st-Century Organization." Use the materials in this text, the Internet, and any other resources to outline the curriculum that you would suggest the course cover. Be sure to include your reasons why the material should be covered and the order in which it should be covered.

MAKING COLLABORATIVE DECISIONS

1. **Finding Innovation**

   Along with disruptive technologies there are also disruptive strategies. The following are a few examples of companies that use disruptive strategies to gain competitive advantages:

   - **Circuit City, Best Buy**—Disrupted the consumer electronics departments of full-service and discount department stores, which has sent them up-market into higher-margin goods.
   - **Ford**—Henry Ford's Model T was so inexpensive that he enabled a much larger population of people, who historically could not afford cars, to own one.
   - **JetBlue**—Whereas Southwest Airlines initially followed a strategy of new-market disruption, JetBlue's approach is low-end disruption. Its long-range viability depends on the major airlines' motivation to run away from the attack, as integrated steel mills and full-service department stores did.
   - **McDonald's**—The fast food industry has been a hybrid disruptor, making it so inexpensive and convenient to eat out that they created a massive wave of growth in the "eating out" industry. Their earliest victims were mom-and-pop diners.
   - **Plastic manufacturers**—Plastics as a category have disrupted wood and steel, in that the "quality" of plastic parts often was inferior to those of wood and steel. However, plastics' low cost and ease of shaping have replaced wood and steel in many areas. For example, look at how little plastics were used in automobiles 30 years ago versus extensive use today.[54]

   There are numerous other examples of corporations that have used disruptive strategies to create competitive advantages. In a team, prepare a presentation highlighting three additional companies that used disruptive strategies to gain a competitive advantage.

2. **Approving a Project**

   You are working in the IT development team for Gear International, a privately held sports and recreational equipment manufacturer. To date, you have spent the majority of your career developing applications for your corporate intranet. Your team has an idea to add an application that allows employees to learn about corporate athletic teams, register online, determine team schedules, post team statistics, etc. Your supervisor likes your idea and would like your team to prepare a short presentation with 5 to 10 slides that she can use to convince senior management to approve the project. Be sure to list benefits of the project along with your suggested methodology to help guarantee the project's development success.

3. Remote Patrol

Today's gadgets offer all-weather, all-knowing, anytime, anyplace. Whether you are trying to keep tabs on your children, your new home theater, or your streaming audio, here are a few wireless tools you can use around your house.

- **Wi-Fi camera**—A 5-inch-high Wireless Observer lets you take pictures at regular intervals or in response to motion and you can access it anytime through a Web browser.—www.veo.com
- **Security sensor**—This detector system alerts you to break-ins and errant pop flies. Its dual sensors record vibration and acoustic disturbances—signs of a shattered window—to help avoid false alarms.—www.getintellisense.com
- **GPS tracking device**—Total Parental Information Awareness is here. Lock this GPS locator to your kids' wrist and whenever you want to check on them just query Wherify's Web page. It pinpoints their location on a street map and displays an aerial photo.—www.wherify.com
- **Wireless speakers**—Sony's versatile 900-MHz speakers connect the RF receiver to your stereo, TV, or PC, and get crystal-clear audio anywhere within 150 feet.—www.sonystyle.com[55]

In a group, create a document discussing how these new wireless technologies could potentially change the business arena and list at least one company for each technology that should view these new products as potential threats.

4. Saving Failing Systems

Signatures Inc. specializes in producing personalized products for companies, such as coffee mugs and pens with company logos. The company generates over $40 million in annual revenues and has over 300 employees. The company is in the middle of a large multimillion-dollar SCM implementation and they have just hired your Project Management Outsourcing firm to take over the project management efforts. On your first day, your team is told that the project is failing for the following reasons:

- The project is using the traditional waterfall methodology.
- The SDLC was not followed and the developers decided to skip the testing phase.
- A project plan was developed during the analysis phase, but the old project manager never updated or followed the plan.

In a group determine what your first steps would be to get this project back on track.

Information Security

1. Describe the relationship between information security policies and an information security plan.
2. Summarize the five steps to creating an information security plan.
3. Provide an example of each of the three primary security areas: (1) authentication and authorization, (2) prevention and resistance, and (3) detection and response.
4. Describe the relationships and differences between hackers and viruses.

Introduction

The core units introduced *information security*, which is a broad term encompassing the protection of information from accidental or intentional misuse by persons inside or outside an organization. With current advances in technologies and business strategies such as CRM, organizations are able to determine valuable information such as who are the top 20 percent of the customers that produce 80 percent of all revenues. Most organizations view this type of information as valuable intellectual capital and they are implementing security measures to prevent the information from walking out the door or falling into the wrong hands. This plug-in discusses how an organization can implement information security lines of defense through people first and through technology second.

The First Line of Defense—People

Adding to the complexity of information security is the fact that organizations must enable employees, customers, and partners to access information electronically to be successful in this electronic world. Doing business electronically thus automatically creates tremendous information security risks for organizations. Surprisingly, the biggest issue surrounding information security is not a technical issue, but a people issue.

The 2003 CSI/FBI Computer Crime and Security Survey reported that 33 percent of respondents indicated security incidents originated within the enterprise. *Insiders* are legitimate users who purposely or accidentally misuse their access to the environment and cause some kind of business-affecting incident. Most information security breaches result from people misusing an organization's information either advertently or inadvertently. For example, many individuals freely give up their passwords or write them on sticky notes next to their computers, leaving the door wide open to intruders.[1]

Information security policies identify the rules required to maintain information security. An *information security plan* details how an organization will implement the information security policies. Figure B1.1 is an example of the University of Denver's Information Security Plan.

FIGURE B1.1

Sample Information Security Plan *(continued on the next page)*

INTERIM INFORMATION SECURITY PLAN

This Information Security Plan ("Plan") describes the University of Denver's safeguards to protect information and data in compliance ("Protected Information") with the Financial Services Modernization Act of 1999, also known as the Gramm Leach Bliley Act, 15 U.S.C. Section 6801. These safeguards are provided to:

■ Ensure the security and confidentiality of Protected Information;

■ Protect against anticipated threats or hazards to the security or integrity of such information; and

■ Protect against unauthorized access to or use of Protected Information that could result in substantial harm or inconvenience to any customer.

This Information Security Plan also provides for mechanisms to:

■ Identify and assess the risks that may threaten Protected Information maintained by the University of Denver;

■ Develop written policies and procedures to manage and control these risks;

■ Implement and review the plan; and

■ Adjust the plan to reflect changes in technology, the sensitivity of covered data and information and internal or external threats to information security.

Identification and Assessment of Risks to Customer Information

The University of Denver recognizes that it has both internal and external risks. These risks include, but are not limited to:

■ Unauthorized access of Protected Information by someone other than the owner of the covered data and information

■ Compromised system security as a result of system access by an unauthorized person

■ Interception of data during transmission

■ Loss of data integrity

■ Physical loss of data in a disaster

■ Errors introduced into the system

■ Corruption of data or systems

■ Unauthorized access of covered data and information by employees

■ Unauthorized requests for covered data and information

■ Unauthorized access through hardcopy files or reports

■ Unauthorized transfer of covered data and information through third parties

The University of Denver recognizes that this may not be a complete list of the risks associated with the protection of Protected Information. Since technology growth is not static, new risks are created regularly. Accordingly, the Information Technology Department and the Office of Student Affairs will actively participate with and seek advice from an advisory committee made up of university representatives for identification of new risks. The University of Denver believes current safeguards used by the Information Technology Department are reasonable and, in light of current risk assessments are sufficient to provide security and confidentiality to Protected Information maintained by the University.

Information Security Plan Coordinators

The University CIO and the Vice President for Student Affairs, in consultation with an advisory committee, have been appointed as the coordinators of this Plan. They are responsible for assessing the risks associated with unauthorized transfers of covered data and information and implementing procedures to minimize those risks to the University of Denver.

Design and Implementation of Safeguards Program

Employee Management and Training

During employee orientation, each new employee in departments that handle Protected Information will receive proper training on the importance of confidentiality of Protected Information.

INTERIM INFORMATION SECURITY PLAN *(continued)*

Physical Security

The University of Denver has addressed the physical security of Protected Information by limiting access to only those employees who have a business reason to know such information.

Information Systems

The University of Denver has policies governing the use of electronic resources and firewall and wireless policies. The University of Denver will take reasonable and appropriate steps consistent with current technological developments to make sure that all Protected Information is secure and to safeguard the integrity of records in storage and transmission. The University of Denver will develop a plan to ensure that all electronic Protected Information is encrypted in transit.

Selection of Appropriate Service Providers

Due to the specialized expertise needed to design, implement, and service new technologies, vendors may be needed to provide resources that the University of Denver determines not to provide on its own. In the process of choosing a service provider that will maintain or regularly access Protected Information, the evaluation process shall include the ability of the service provider to safeguard Protected Information. Contracts with service providers may include the following provisions:

- A stipulation that the Protected Information will be held in strict confidence and accessed only for the explicit business purpose of the contract;
- An assurance from the contract partner that the partner will protect the Protected Information it receives.

Continuing Evaluation and Adjustment

This Information Security Plan will be subject to periodic review and adjustment, especially when due to the constantly changing technology and evolving risks. The Coordinators, in consultation with the Office of General Counsel, will review the standards set forth in this policy and recommend updates and revisions as necessary. It may be necessary to adjust the plan to reflect changes in technology, the sensitivity of student/customer data and internal or external threats to information security.

FIGURE B1.1

Sample Information Security Plan *(concluded)*

The first line of defense an organization should follow is to create an information security plan detailing the various information security policies. A detailed information security plan can alleviate people-based information security issues. The following are the five steps for creating an information security plan:

1. **Develop the information security policies**—Identify who is responsible and accountable for designing and implementing the organization's information security policies. Simple, yet highly effective types of information security policies include requiring users to log off of their systems before leaving for lunches or meetings, never sharing passwords with anyone, and changing personal passwords every 60 days. The chief security officer (CSO) will typically be responsible for designing these information security policies.
2. **Communicate the information security policies**—Train all employees on the policies and establish clear expectations for following the policies. For example, let all employees know that they will receive a formal reprimand for leaving a computer unsecured.
3. **Identify critical information assets and risks**—Require the use of user IDs, passwords, and antivirus software on all systems. Ensure any systems that contain links to external networks have the appropriate technical protections such as firewalls or intrusion detection software. A ***firewall*** is hardware and/or software that guards a private network by analyzing the information leaving and entering the network. ***Intrusion detection software (IDS)*** searches out patterns in information and network traffic to indicate attacks and quickly respond to prevent any harm.
4. **Test and reevaluate risks**—Continually perform security reviews, audits, background checks, and security assessments.
5. **Obtain stakeholder support**—Gain the approval and support of the information security polices by the Board of Directors and all stakeholders.

The director of information security at a large health care company discovered how easy it was to create an information security breach when she hired outside auditors to test her company's security awareness. In one instance, auditors found

Top 10 Questions Managers Should Ask Regarding Information Security
1. Does our Board of Directors recognize information security is a board level issue that cannot be left to the IT department alone?
2. Is there clear accountability for information security in our organization?
3. Do our Board members articulate an agreed-upon set of threats and critical assets? How often do we review and update these?
4. How much is spent on information security and what is it being spent on?
5. What is the impact on the organization of a serious security incident?
6. Does our organization view information security as an enabler? (For example, by implementing effective security, could we enable our organization to increase business over the Internet?)
7. What is the risk to our business of getting a reputation for low information security?
8. What steps have we taken to ensure that third parties will not compromise the security of our organization?
9. How do we obtain independent assurance that information security is managed effectively in our organization?
10. How do we measure the effectiveness of our information security activities?

that staff members testing a new system had accidentally exposed the network to outside hackers. In another instance, auditors were able to obtain the passwords of 16 employees when the auditors posed as support staff; hackers frequently use such "social engineering" to obtain passwords. **Social engineering** is using one's social skills to trick people into revealing access credentials or other information valuable to the attacker. Dumpster diving, or looking through people's trash, is another way social engineering hackers obtain information.

Figure B1.2 provides the top 10 questions from Ernst & Young that managers should ask to ensure their information is secure.[2]

The Second Line of Defense—Technology

Arkansas State University (ASU) recently completed a major network upgrade that brought gigabit-speed network capacity to every dorm room and office on its campus. The university was concerned that the new network would be a tempting playground for hackers. To reduce its fear the university decided to install intrusion detection software (IDS) from Cisco Systems to stay on top of security and potential network abuses. Whenever the IDS spots a potential security threat, such as a virus or a hacker, it alerts the central management system. The system automatically pages the IT staff, who deal with the attack by shutting off access to the system, identifying the hacker's location, and calling campus security.[3]

Once an organization has protected its intellectual capital by arming its people with a detailed information security plan, it can begin to focus its efforts on deploying the right types of information security technologies such as the IDS installed at ASU.

International Data Corp. estimates that worldwide spending on IT security software, hardware, and services will top $35 billion in 2004. There are numerous technologies available that organizations can deploy to prevent information security breaches. When determining which types of technologies to invest in, it helps to understand the three primary information security areas:

1. Authentication and authorization
2. Prevention and resistance
3. Detection and response[4]

AUTHENTICATION AND AUTHORIZATION

Authentication is a method for confirming users' identities. Authentication techniques are broken down into three categories, and the most secure type of authentication involves a combination of all three:

1. Something the user knows such as a user ID and password
2. Something the user has such as a smart card or token
3. Something that is part of the user such as a fingerprint or voice signature

Something the User Knows such as a User ID and Password

The first type of authentication, using something the user knows, is the most common way to identify individual users and typically consists of a unique user ID and password. But this is actually one of the most *ineffective* ways for determining authentication because passwords are not secure. All it typically takes to crack a password is enough time. Over 50 percent of help-desk calls are password related, which can cost an organization significant money, and passwords are vulnerable to being coaxed out of somebody by a "social engineer." Figure B1.3 displays the amount of money lost to identity thefts based on stolen passwords, among other things. The worldwide total for identity theft is expected to hit between $2 and $5 trillion by 2005.[5]

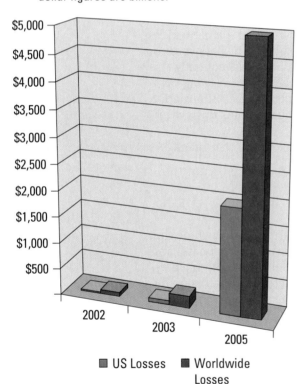

Identity thefts are expected to increase anywhere from 900% to 2,250% over the next two years; dollar figures are billions.

Something the User Has such as a Smart Card or Token

The second type of authentication, using something that the user has, offers a much more effective way to identify individuals than a user ID and password. Tokens and smart cards are two of the primary forms of this type of authentication. **Tokens** are small electronic devices that change user passwords automatically. The user enters his/her user ID and token displayed password to gain access to the network. A **smart card** is a device that is around the same size as a credit card, containing embedded technologies that can store information and small amounts of software to perform some limited processing. Smart cards can act as identification instruments, a form of digital cash, or a data storage device with the ability to store an entire medical record.

Something That Is Part of the User such as a Fingerprint or Voice Signature

The third kind of authentication, using something that is part of the user, is by far the best and most effective way to manage authentication. **Biometrics** (narrowly defined) is the identification of a user based on a physical characteristic, such as a fingerprint, iris, face, voice, or handwriting. Unfortunately, biometric authentication can be costly and intrusive. For example, iris scans are expensive and considered intrusive by most people. Fingerprint authentication is less intrusive and inexpensive but is also not 100 percent accurate.

PREVENTION AND RESISTANCE

Prevention and resistance technologies stop intruders from accessing intellectual capital. A division of Sony Inc., Sony Pictures Entertainment (SPE), defends itself from attacks by using an intrusion detection system to detect new attacks as they occur. SPE develops and distributes a wide variety of products including movies, television, videos, and DVDs. A compromise to SPE security could result in costing the company valuable intellectual capital as well as millions of dollars and months of time. The company needed an advanced threat management solution that would take fewer resources to maintain and require limited resources to track and respond to suspicious network activity. The company installed an advanced intrusion detection system allowing it to monitor all of its network activity including any potential security breaches.[6]

The cost of downtime or network operation failures can be devastating to any business. For example, eBay experienced a 22-hour outage in June 2000 that caused the company's market cap to plunge an incredible $5.7 billion. Downtime costs for businesses can vary from $100 to $1 million per hour. An organization must prepare for and anticipate these types of outages resulting most commonly from hackers and viruses. Technologies available to help prevent and build resistance to attacks include:

1. Content filtering
2. Encryption
3. Firewalls[7]

Content Filtering

Content filtering occurs when organizations use software that filters content to prevent the transmission of unauthorized information. Organizations can use content filtering technologies to filter e-mail and prevent e-mails containing sensitive information from transmitting, whether the transmission was malicious or accidental. It can also filter e-mails and prevent any suspicious files from transmitting such as potential virus-infected files. E-mail content filtering can also filter for *spam,* a form of unsolicited e-mail. Organizational losses from spam are estimated to be $190 billion in 2004.[8]

Encryption

Encryption scrambles information into an alternative form that requires a key or password to decrypt the information. If there is an information security breach and the information was encrypted, the person stealing the information will be unable to read it. Encryption can switch the order of characters, replace characters with other characters, insert or remove characters, or use a mathematical formula to convert the information into some sort of code. Companies that transmit sensitive customer information over the Internet, such as credit card numbers, frequently use encryption.

Firewalls

One of the most common defenses for preventing a security breach is a firewall. A *firewall* is hardware and/or software that guards a private network by analyzing the information leaving and entering the network. Firewalls examine each message that wants entrance to the network. Unless the message has the correct markings, the firewall prevents it from entering the network. Firewalls can even detect computers communicating with the Internet without approval. As Figure B1.4 illustrates, organizations typically place a firewall between a server and the Internet.

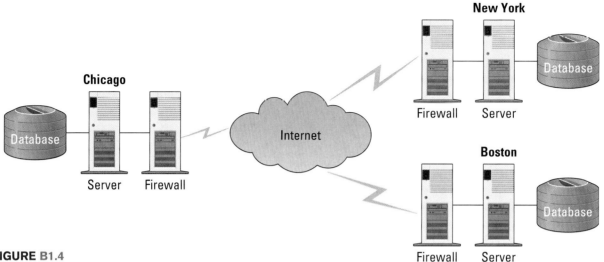

FIGURE B1.4

Sample Firewall
Architecture
Connecting Systems
Located in Chicago,
New York, and Boston

DETECTION AND RESPONSE

The final area where organizations can allocate resources is in detection and response technologies. If prevention and resistance strategies fail and there is a security breach, an organization can use detection and response technologies to mitigate the damage. The most common type of defense within detection and response technologies is antivirus software.

A single worm can cause massive damage. In August 2003, the "Blaster worm" infected computers worldwide and was one of the worst outbreaks of the year. Jeffrey Lee Parson, 18, was arrested by U.S. cyber investigators for unleashing the damaging worm on the Internet. The worm replicated itself repeatedly, eating up computer capacity, but did not damage information or programs. The worm generated so much traffic that it brought entire networks down.

The FBI used the latest technologies and code analysis to find the source of the worm. Prosecutors of the case said that Microsoft suffered financial losses that "significantly" exceeded $5,000, the statutory threshold in most hacker cases. Parson, charged with intentionally causing or attempting to cause damage to a computer, faces up to 10 years in prison and a $250,000 fine. "With this arrest, we want to deliver a message to cyber-hackers here and around the world," said U.S. Attorney John McKay in Seattle. "Let there be no mistake about it, cyber-hacking is a crime. We will investigate, arrest, and prosecute cyber-hackers."[9]

Typically, people equate viruses (the malicious software) with hackers (the people). While not all types of hackers create viruses, many do. Figure B1.5 provides an overview of the most common types of hackers and viruses.

Some of the most damaging forms of security threats to e-business sites include malicious code, hoaxes, spoofing, and sniffers. *Malicious code* includes a variety of threats such as viruses, worms, and Trojan horses. *Hoaxes* attack computer systems by transmitting a virus hoax, with a real virus attached. By masking the attack in a seemingly legitimate message, unsuspecting users more readily distribute the message and send the attack on to their co-workers and friends, infecting many users along the way. *Spoofing* is the forging of the return address on an e-mail so that the e-mail message appears to come from someone other than the actual sender. This is not a virus but rather a way by which virus authors conceal their identities as they send out viruses. A *sniffer* is a program or device that can monitor data traveling over a network. Sniffers can show all the data being transmitted over a network, including passwords and sensitive information. Sniffers tend to be a favorite weapon in the hacker's arsenal.

Hackers—people very knowledgeable about computers who use their knowledge to invade other people's computers.

- *White-hat hackers*—work at the request of the system owners to find system vulnerabilities and plug the holes.
- *Black-hat hackers*—break into other people's computer systems and may just look around or may steal and destroy information.
- *Hactivists*—have philosophical and political reasons for breaking into systems and will often deface the Web site as a protest.
- *Script kiddies* or *script bunnies*—find hacking code on the Internet and click-and-point their way into systems to cause damage or spread viruses.
- *Cracker*—a hacker with criminal intent.
- *Cyberterrorists*—seek to cause harm to people or to destroy critical systems or information and use the Internet as a weapon of mass destruction.

Viruses—software written with malicious intent to cause annoyance or damage.

- *Worm*—a type of virus that spreads itself, not only from file to file, but also from computer to computer. The primary difference between a virus and a worm is that a virus must attach to something, such as an executable file, in order to spread. Worms do not need to attach to anything to spread and can tunnel themselves into computers.
- *Denial-of-service attack (DoS)*—floods a Web site with so many requests for service that it slows down or crashes the site.
- *Distributed denial-of-service attack (DDoS)*—attacks from multiple computers that flood a Web site with so many requests for service that it slows down or crashes. A common type is the Ping of Death, in which thousands of computers try to access a Web site at the same time, overloading it and shutting it down.
- *Trojan-horse virus*—hides inside other software, usually as an attachment or a downloadable file.
- *Backdoor programs*—viruses that open a way into the network for future attacks.
- *Polymorphic viruses and worms*—change their form as they propagate.

Implementing information security lines of defense through people first and through technology second is the best way for an organization to protect its vital intellectual capital. The first line of defense is securing intellectual capital by creating an information security plan detailing the various information security policies. The second line of defense is investing in technology to help secure information through authentication and authorization, prevention and resistance, and detection and response.

Authentication, 224
Backdoor program, 227
Biometrics, 224
Black-hat hacker, 227
Content filtering, 225
Cracker, 227
Cyberterrorist, 227
Denial-of-service attack (DoS), 227
Distributed denial-of-service attack (DDoS), 227
Encryption, 225
Firewall, 222, 225

Hacker, 227
Hactivist, 227
Hoaxes, 226
Information security, 220
Information security plan, 221
Information security policy, 221
Insider, 220
Intrusion detection software (IDS), 222
Malicious code, 226
Polymorphic virus and worm, 227

Script kiddies or script bunnies, 227
Smart card, 224
Sniffer, 226
Social engineering, 223
Spam, 225
Spoofing, 226
Token, 224
Trojan-horse virus, 227
Virus, 227
White-hat hacker, 227
Worm, 227

Thinking Like the Enemy

David and Barry Kaufman, the founders of the six-year-old Intense School, recently added several security courses, including the five-day "Professional Hacking Boot Camp" and "Social Engineering in Two Days."

Information Technology departments must know how to protect organizational information. Therefore, organizations must teach their IT personnel how to protect their systems, especially in light of the many new government regulations, such as HIPPA, that demand secure systems. The concept of sending IT professionals to a hacking school seems counterintuitive; it is somewhat similar to sending accountants to an Embezzling 101 course. The Intense School does not strive to breed the next generation of hackers, however, but to teach its students how to be "ethical" hackers: to use their skills to build better locks, and to understand the minds of those who would attempt to crack them.

The main philosophy of the security courses at the Intense School is simply "To know thy enemy." In fact, one of the teachers at the Intense School is none other than Kevin Mitnick, the famous hacker who was imprisoned from 1995 to 2000. Teaching security from the hacker's perspective, as Mitnick does, is more difficult than teaching hacking itself: A hacker just needs to know one way into a system, David Kaufman notes, but a security professional needs to know *all* of the system's vulnerabilities. The two courses analyze those vulnerabilities from different perspectives.

The hacking course, which costs $3,500, teaches ways to protect against the mischief typically associated with hackers: worming through computer systems through vulnerabilities that are susceptible to technical, or computer-based, attacks. Mitnick's $1,950 social engineering course, by contrast, teaches the more frightening art of worming through the vulnerabilities of the people using and maintaining systems—getting passwords and access through duplicity, not technology. People that take this class, or read Mitnick's book, *The Art of Deception,* never again think of passwords or the trash bin the same way.

So how does the Intense School teach hacking? With sessions on dumpster diving (the unsavory practice of looking for passwords and other bits of information on discarded papers), with field trips to case target systems, and with practice runs at the company's in-house "target range," a network of computers set up to thwart and educate students.

One feature of the Intense School that raises a few questions is that the school does not check on morals at the door: Anyone paying the tuition can attend the school. Given the potential danger that an unchecked graduate of a hacking school could represent, it is surprising that the FBI does not collect the names of the graduates. But perhaps it gets them anyhow—several governmental agencies have sent students to the school.[10]

Questions

1. Describe how an organization can benefit from attending one of the courses offered at the Intense School.
2. Explain the two primary lines of security defense and how organizational employees can use the information taught by the Intense School when drafting an information security plan.
3. Determine the differences between the two primary courses offered at the Intense School, "Professional Hacking Boot Camp" and "Social Engineering in Two Days." Explain which course is more important for organizational employees to attend.

Homeland Security

"Our first priority must always be the security of our nation. . . . America is no longer protected by vast oceans. We are protected from attack only by vigorous action abroad, and increased vigilance at home."—President George W. Bush, State of the Union Address, January 29, 2002

Homeland Security Facts

- There are more than 1 million firefighters in the United States, of which approximately 750,000 are volunteers.
- Local police departments have an estimated 556,000 full-time employees including about 436,000 sworn law enforcement personnel. Sheriff's offices reported about 291,000 full-time employees, including about 186,000 sworn officers.
- There are more than 155,000 registered emergency medical technicians.
- The United States has a 7,500-mile land and air border shared with Canada and Mexico and an exclusive economic zone encompassing 3.4 million square miles.
- Each year, more than 500 million people are admitted into the United States, of which 330 million are noncitizens.
- On land, 11.2 million trucks and 2.2 million rail cars cross into the United States while 7,500 foreign-flag ships make 51,000 calls in U.S. ports annually.

The issue of homeland security is more paramount today than ever before, for all nations and around the world. Businesses and government agencies are experiencing new challenges in protecting their nation's interests, and they are continually searching for new and better ways to support security efforts.

One such effort includes exploring new ways to manage, mine, and share huge volumes of vital information. One terabyte of information is equal to one trillion bytes of information and can contain more than 300 feature length films. To implement strong homeland security, businesses and governments must share thousands of terabytes of information. Government agencies and corporations today are making tremendous strides in working together to deploy systems to help build strong homeland security. Here are a few examples of the new homeland security efforts taking place across the United States:

Oregon's Firehouse Responds Three Times Faster with New Emergency Response System

Gresham, Oregon, is the largest suburb of Portland and the fourth largest city in the state. Balancing rapid growth with a tight economy is difficult and the city is using technology to stretch its resources while providing the best possible services. One obstacle the city had to overcome was replacing its old systems, which could not even handle multiple users or provide simple information analysis. Gresham decided to implement a new system that helps fire, police, and emergency personnel better prepare for and respond to emergencies.

Firehouse, the Fire & Emergency Services System, allows fire personnel to enter information upon returning from an incident involving emergency medical care, fires, rescues, and/or hazardous material problems. The system records information on the location of the incident, the time of the emergency call, the time the crew arrived on the scene, the nature of the incident, treatments given, and so on. Firehouse then analyzes the information to ensure the fire personnel are providing the most effective and efficient means of delivering its services.

One example of how Gresham has used Firehouse's analysis capability was crunching through recent traffic accident information determining that most accidents occurred around 10:30 P.M. in a certain part of the city. Gresham officials then deployed extra emergency medical units in that location at that particular time. Being able to analyze information quickly and from many different angles supports planning accuracy based on hard information rather than guesswork. It helps Gresham allocate resources more intelligently and spend taxpayers' money more wisely.

California's Emergency Response Operations Center

Orange County, California, Emergency Operations Center (EOC) serves as a nerve center for countywide disaster-response operations for a population of nearly 3 million. The EOC must be up and running in 30 minutes in the event of a catastrophe and house many public safety officials and county department heads, allowing them to deliver a unified response to major emergencies. The center has a cart plugged in and ready to go with 20 preprogrammed wireless laptops loaded with all the software needed to handle information flows for emergency management. The technology allows the officials to network within the building as well as with state and local agencies and other EOCs to obtain the most current disaster information.

California's Enabled Motorcycle Officers

Laptop computers provide law enforcement personnel with access to vital database information including the department's records management system, warrants, restraining orders, driving records, and criminal histories. Laptops are relatively common in police patrol cars and for the first time ever the Newport Beach Police Department is going to deploy laptop computers to its motorcycle officers. The police department is mounting notebook computers on the back of its motorcycle officers' bikes. The system provides access to vital information and even provides court-calendar information, computer-aided dispatch information, and links to Newport Beach's vehicle location system. Dispatchers now have the ability to track officers' locations and quickly route them to emergency calls. The Newport Beach Police Department realizes that motorcycle officers have the same responsibilities, vulnerabilities, and need for information as the patrol officers. The new technology is enabling the police department to get as much information as possible into the field—to the people who really need it.

Texas Health Network

The public health officials in Texas use the Health Alert Network (HAN) to respond to health care crises and terrorist attacks. HAN is an advanced Web-based solution that integrates health departments across the state. HAN equips state and local health care agencies with the technology to react more effectively to disease outbreaks and terrorist attacks. It will also arm them to counter bioterrorism attacks, an important consideration in an era of heightened security. In the event of a bioterrorism attack, the system can share information among hospitals, clinics, and local health departments simultaneously, allowing the facilities to quickly realize that they have a health emergency and begin working on a solution.

The system currently supports 64 local health departments 24 hours a day, seven days a week. The system will need to eventually support several thousand health officials throughout the Texas public health care system.

Homeland security is crucial to our nation's future and by using technology in new and innovative ways, we will be able to ensure its integrity and vitality.[11]

Questions

1. Determine a few of the information security policies that might be implemented along with Gresham's new Firehouse system.

2. Identify how an information security plan can help the Newport Beach Police Department's vehicle location system be more successful.

3. How can the Texas Health Network use prevention and resistance technologies to assist in preventing a crisis?

4. Explain how Orange County California's Emergency Operations Center (EOC) might use authentication and authorization technologies to ensure the center's information security.

5. Research and identify an area of homeland security, not discussed in this case, that uses detection and response technologies to assist in protecting intellectual capital.

MAKING BUSINESS DECISIONS

1. Firewall Decisions

You are the CEO of Inverness Investments, a medium-sized venture capital firm that specializes in investing in high-tech companies. The company receives over 30,000 e-mail messages per year. On average, there are two viruses and three successful hackings against the company each year, which result in losses to the company of about $250,000. Currently, the company has antivirus software installed but does not have any firewalls installed.

Your CIO is suggesting implementing 10 firewalls for a total cost of $80,000. The estimated life of each firewall is about 3 years. The chances of hackers breaking into the system with the firewalls installed are about 3 percent. Annual maintenance costs on the firewalls is estimated around $15,000. Create an argument for or against supporting your CIO's recommendation to purchase the firewalls.

2. Drafting an Information Security Plan

Making The Grade is a nonprofit organization that helps students learn how to achieve better grades in school. The organization has 40 offices in 25 states and over 2,000 employees. The company is currently building a Web site to offer its services online. You have recently been hired by the CIO as the Director of Information Security. Your first assignment is to develop a document discussing the importance of creating information security polices and an information security plan. Be sure to include the following:

- The importance of educating employees on information security.
- A few samples of employee information security policies.
- Other major areas the information security plan should address.
- Signs the company should look for to determine if the new site is being hacked.
- The major types of attacks the company should expect to experience.

3. Preventing Identity Theft

The FBI states that identity theft is one of the fastest-growing crimes. If you are a victim of identity theft, your financial reputation can be ruined, making it impossible for you to cash a check or receive a bank loan. Learning how to avoid identity theft can be a valuable activity. Research the following Web sites and draft a document stating the best ways to prevent identity theft.

- The Federal Trade Commission Consumer Information on ID theft at www.consumer.gov/idtheft
- The Office of the Comptroller of the Currency at www.occ.treas.gov/chcktfd.idassume.htm
- The Office of the Inspector General at www.ssa.gov/oig/when.htm
- U.S. Department of Justice at www.usdoj.gov/criminal/fraud/idtheft.html

4. Discussing the Three Areas of Security

Great Granola Inc. is a small business operating out of northern California. The company specializes in selling unique homemade granola and its primary sales vehicle is through its Web site. The company is growing exponentially and expects its revenues to triple this year to $12 million. The company also expects to hire 60 additional employees to support its growing number of customers. Joan Martin, the CEO, is aware that if her competitors discover the recipe for her granola, or who her primary customers are, it could easily ruin her business. Joan has hired you to draft a document discussing the different areas of information security, along with your recommendations for providing a secure e-business environment.

Ethics

1. Summarize the guidelines for creating an information privacy policy.
2. Identify the differences between an ethical computer use policy and an acceptable use policy.
3. Describe the relationship between an e-mail privacy policy and an Internet use policy.
4. Explain the effects of spam on an organization.
5. Summarize the different monitoring technologies and explain the importance of an employee monitoring policy.

Introduction

The core units introduced *ethics,* which are the principles and standards that guide our behavior toward other people. Technology has created many new ethical dilemmas in our electronic society. The following are a few important concepts and terms related to ethical issues stemming from advances in technology:

- *Intellectual property*—intangible creative work that is embodied in physical form.
- *Copyright*—the legal protection afforded an expression of an idea, such as a song, video game, and some types of proprietary documents.
- *Fair use doctrine*—in certain situations, it is legal to use copyrighted material.
- *Pirated software*—the unauthorized use, duplication, distribution, or sale of copyrighted software.
- *Counterfeit software*—software that is manufactured to look like the real thing and sold as such.

The core units also introduced *privacy,* which is the right to be left alone when you want to be, to have control over your own personal possessions, and not to be observed without your consent. Privacy is related to *confidentiality,* which is the assurance that messages and data are available only to those who are authorized to view them. This plug-in takes a detailed look at *ePolicies*—policies and procedures that address the ethical use of computers and Internet usage in the business environment. ePolicies typically address information privacy and confidentiality issues and include the following:

- Ethical Computer Use Policy
- Information Privacy Policy
- Acceptable Use Policy
- E-Mail Privacy Policy
- Internet Use Policy
- Anti-Spam Policy

Ethics

Individuals form the only ethical component of an IT system. They determine how they use IT, and how they are affected by IT. How individuals behave toward each other, how they handle information and technology, are largely influenced by their ethics. Ethical dilemmas usually arise not in simple, clearcut situations but out of a clash between competing goals, responsibilities, and loyalties. Ethical decisions are complex judgments that balance rewards against responsibilities. Inevitably, the decision process is influenced by uncertainty about the magnitude of the outcome, by the estimate of the importance of the situation, by the perception of conflicting "right reactions," when there is more than one socially acceptable "correct" decision. Figure B2.1 contains examples of ethically questionable or unacceptable uses of information technology.

People make arguments for or against—justify or condemn—the behaviors in Figure B2.1. Unfortunately, there are few hard and fast rules for always determining what is and is not ethical. Knowing the law will not always help because what is legal might not always be ethical, and what might be ethical is not always legal. For example, in 2003, Joe Reidenberg received an offer for cell phone service from AT&T Wireless. The offer revealed that AT&T Wireless had used Equifax, a credit reporting agency, to identify Joe Reidenberg as a potential customer. Overall, this strategy seemed like good business. Equifax could generate additional revenue by selling information it already owned and AT&T Wireless could identify target markets, thereby increasing response rates to its marketing campaigns. Unfortunately, by law, credit information cannot be used to sell anything. The Fair Credit Reporting Act (FCRA) forbids repurposing credit information except when the information is used for "a firm offer of credit or insurance." In other words, the only product that can be sold based on credit information is credit. A spokesman for Equifax stated that "as long as AT&T Wireless (or any company for that matter) is offering the cell phone service on a credit basis, such as allowing the use of the service before the consumer has to pay, it is in compliance with the FCRA."[1] But is it ethical?

This is a good example of the ethical dilemmas facing many organizations today; because technology is so new and pervasive in unexpected ways, the ethics

Examples of Questionable Information Technology Use
Individuals copy, use, and distribute software.
Employees search organizational databases for sensitive corporate and personal information.
Organizations collect, buy, and use information without checking the validity or accuracy of the information.
Individuals create and spread viruses that cause trouble for those using and maintaining IT systems.
Individuals hack into computer systems to steal proprietary information.
Employees destroy or steal proprietary organization information such as schematics, sketches, customer lists, and reports.

FIGURE B2.1

Ethically Questionable or Unacceptable Information Technology Use

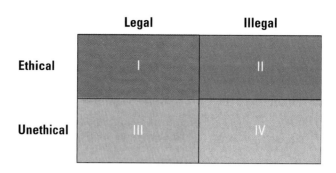

FIGURE B2.2

Acting Ethically and
Legally Are Not Always
the Same

surrounding information have not been all worked out. Figure B2.2 displays the four quadrants of ethical and legal behavior. The ideal goal for organizations is to make decisions within quadrant I that are both legal and ethical.

INFORMATION HAS NO ETHICS

Jerry Rode, CIO of Saab Cars USA, realized that he had a public relations fiasco on his hands when he received an e-mail from an irate customer. Saab had hired four Internet marketing companies to distribute electronic information about Saab's new models to its customers. Saab specified that the marketing campaign be *opt-in,* implying that it would contact only the people who had agreed to receive promotions and marketing material via e-mail. Unfortunately, one of the marketing companies apparently had a different definition of opt-in and was e-mailing all customers regardless of their opt-in decision.

Rode fired the errant marketing company and immediately developed a formal policy for the use of customer information. "The customer doesn't see ad agencies and contracted marketing firms. They see Saab USA spamming them," states Rode. "Finger-pointing after the fact won't make your customers feel better."[2]

Information has no ethics. Information does not care how it is used. It will not stop itself from spamming customers, sharing itself if it is sensitive or personal, or revealing details to third parties. Information cannot delete or preserve itself. Therefore, it falls on the shoulders of those who lord over the information to develop ethical guidelines on how to manage it. Figure B2.3 provides an overview of some of the important laws that individuals must follow when they are attempting to manage and protect information.

FIGURE B2.3

Established
Information-Related
Laws
(continued on next page)

Established Information-Related Laws	
Privacy Act—1974	Restricts what information the federal government can collect; allows people to access and correct information on themselves; requires procedures to protect the security of personal information; and forbids the disclosure of name-linked information without permission.
Family Education Rights and Privacy Act—1974	Regulates access to personal education records by government agencies and other third parties and ensures the right of students to see their own records.
Cable Communications Act— 1984	Requires written or electronic consent from viewers before cable TV providers can release viewing choices or other personally identifiable information.
Electronic Communications Privacy Act—1986	Allows the reading of communications by a firm and says that employees have no right to privacy when using their companies' computers.

Established Information-Related Laws *(continued)*	
Computer Fraud and Abuse Act—1986	Prohibits unauthorized access to computers used for financial institutions, the U.S. government, or interstate and international trade.
The Bork Bill (officially known as the Video Privacy Protection Act, 1988)	Prohibits the use of video rental information on customers for any purpose other than that of marketing goods and services directly to the customer.
Communications Assistance for Law Enforcement Act—1994	Requires that telecommunications equipment be designed so that authorized government agents are able to intercept all wired and wireless communications being sent or received by any subscriber. The Act also requires that subscriber call-identifying information be transmitted to a government when and if required.
Freedom of Information Act—1967, 1975, 1994, and 1998	Allows any person to examine government records unless it would cause an invasion of privacy. It was amended in 1974 to apply to the FBI, and again in 1994 to allow citizens to monitor government activities and information gathering, and once again in 1998 to access government information on the Internet.
Health Insurance Portability and Accountability Act (HIPPA)—1996	Requires that the health care industry formulate and implement regulations to keep patient information confidential.
Identity Theft and Assumption Deterrence Act—1998	Strengthened the criminal laws governing identity theft making it a federal crime to use or transfer identification belonging to another. It also established a central federal service for victims.
USA Patriot Act—2001 and 2003	Allows law enforcement to get access to almost any information, including library records, video rentals, bookstore purchases, and business records when investigating any act of terrorist or clandestine intelligence activities. In 2003, Patriot II broadened the original law.
Homeland Security Act—2002	Provided new authority to government agencies to mine data on individuals and groups including e-mails and Web site visits; put limits on the information available under the Freedom of Information Act; and gave new powers to government agencies to declare national heath emergencies.
Sarbanes-Oxley Act—2002	Sought to protect investors by improving the accuracy and reliability of corporate disclosures and requires companies to (1) implement extensive and detailed policies to prevent illegal activity within the company, and (2) to respond in a timely manner to investigate illegal activity.
Fair and Accurate Credit Transactions Act—2003	Included provisions for the prevention of identity theft including consumers' right to get a credit report free each year, requiring merchants to leave all but the last five digits of a credit card number off a receipt, and requiring lenders and credit agencies to take action even before a victim knows a crime has occurred when they notice any circumstances that might indicate identity theft.
CAN-Spam Act—2003	Sought to regulate interstate commerce by imposing limitations and penalties on businesses sending unsolicited e-mail to consumers. The law forbids deceptive subject lines, headers, return addresses, etc., as well as the harvesting of e-mail addresses from Web sites. It requires businesses that send spam to maintain a do-not-spam list and to include a postal mailing address in the message.

FIGURE B2.3

Established Information-Related Laws *(concluded)*

Developing Information Management Policies

Treating sensitive corporate information as a valuable resource is good management. Building a corporate culture based on ethical principles that employees can understand and implement is great management. In an effort to provide guidelines for ethical information management, *CIO* magazine (along with over 100 CIOs) developed the six principles for ethical information management displayed in Figure B2.4.

In order to follow the *CIO* six principles for ethical information management, a corporation should develop written policies establishing employee guidelines, personnel procedures, and organizational rules. These policies set employee expectations about the organization's practices and standards and protect the organization from misuse of computer systems and IT resources. If an organization's employees use computers at work, the organization should, at a minimum, implement ePolicies. *ePolicies* are policies and procedures that address the ethical use of computers and Internet usage in the business environment. ePolicies typically embody the following:

- Ethical Computer Use Policy
- Information Privacy Policy
- Acceptable Use Policy
- E-Mail Privacy Policy
- Internet Use Policy
- Anti-Spam Policy

ETHICAL COMPUTER USE POLICY

One of the essential steps in creating an ethical corporate culture is establishing an ethical computer use policy. An *ethical computer use policy* contains general principles to guide computer user behavior. For example, the ethical computer use policy might explicitly state that users should refrain from playing computer games during working hours. This policy ensures that the users know how to behave at work and that the organization has a published standard through which to deal with user infractions—for example, after appropriate warnings, terminating an employee who spends significant amounts of time playing computer games at work.

There are variations in how organizations expect their employees to use computers, but in any approach the overriding principle when seeking appropriate computer use should be informed consent. The users should be *informed* of the rules and, by agreeing to use the system on that basis, *consent* to abide by the rules.

FIGURE B2.4

CIO Magazine's Six Principles for Ethical Information Management

Six Principles for Ethical Information Management
1. Information is a valuable corporate asset and should be managed as such, like cash, facilities, or any other corporate asset.
2. The CIO is steward of corporate information and is responsible for managing it over its life cycle—from its generation to its appropriate destruction.
3. The CIO is responsible for controlling access to and use of information, as determined by governmental regulation and corporate policy.
4. The CIO is responsible for preventing the inappropriate destruction of information.
5. The CIO is responsible for bringing technological knowledge to the development of information management practices and policies.
6. The CIO should partner with executive peers to develop and execute the organization's information management policies.

An organization should make a conscientious effort to ensure that all users are aware of the policy through formal training and other means. If an organization were to have only one policy, it would want it to be an ethical computer use policy since it is the starting point and the umbrella for any other policies that the organization might establish.

INFORMATION PRIVACY POLICY

Scott Thompson is the executive vice president of Inovant, the company Visa set up to handle its technology. Thompson errs on the side of caution in regard to Visa's information: He bans the use of Visa's customer information for anything outside its intended purpose—billing.

Visa's customer information details such things as what people are spending their money on, in which stores, on which days, and even at what time of day. Sales and marketing departments around the country no doubt are salivating at any prospect of gaining access to Thompson's databases. "They would love to refine the information into loyalty programs, target markets, or even partnerships with Visa. There are lots of creative people coming up with these ideas," Thompson says. "This whole area of information sharing is enormous and growing. For the marketers, the sky's the limit." Thompson along with privacy specialists developed a strict credit card information policy, which the company follows. The question now is can Thompson guarantee that some unethical use of his information will not occur? Many experts do not believe that he can.

In fact, in a large majority of cases, the unethical use of information happens not through the malicious scheming of a rogue marketer, but rather unintentionally. For example, information is collected and stored for some purpose, such as record keeping or billing. Then, a sales or marketing professional figures out another way to use it internally, share it with partners, or sell it to a trusted third party. The information is "unintentionally" used for new purposes. The classic example of this type of unintentional information reuse is the Social Security number, which started simply as a way to identify government retirement benefits and is now used as a sort of universal personal ID, found on everything from driver's licenses to savings accounts.

An organization that wants to protect its information should develop an information privacy policy. An *information privacy policy* contains general principles regarding information privacy. The following are a few guidelines an organization can follow when creating an information privacy policy:

1. **Adoption and implementation of a privacy policy**—An organization engaged in online activities or e-business has a responsibility to adopt and implement a policy for protecting the privacy of personal information. Organizations should also take steps that foster the adoption and implementation of effective online privacy policies by the organizations with which they interact, for instance, by sharing best practices with business partners.

2. **Notice and disclosure**—An organization's privacy policy must be easy to find, read, and understand. The policy must clearly state:
   - What information is being collected
   - The use of information being collected
   - Possible third party distribution of that information
   - The choices available to an individual regarding collection, use, and distribution of the collected information
   - A statement of the organization's commitment to information security
   - What steps the organization takes to ensure information quality and access

3. **Choice and consent**—Individuals must be given the opportunity to exercise choice regarding how personal information collected from them online may be used when such use is unrelated to the purpose for which the information was collected. At a minimum, individuals should be given the opportunity to *opt out* of such use.

4. **Information security**—Organizations creating, maintaining, using, or disseminating personal information should take appropriate measures to assure its reliability and should take reasonable precautions to protect it from loss, misuse, or alteration.

5. **Information quality and access**—Organizations should establish appropriate processes or mechanisms so that inaccuracies in material personal information, such as account or contact information, may be corrected. Other procedures to assure information quality may include use of reliable sources, collection methods, appropriate consumer access, and protections against accidental or unauthorized alteration.

ACCEPTABLE USE POLICY

An *acceptable use policy (AUP)* is a policy that a user must agree to follow in order to be provided access to a network or to the Internet. *Nonrepudiation* is a contractual stipulation to ensure that e-business participants do not deny (repudiate) their online actions. A nonrepudiation clause is typically contained in an AUP.

It is common practice for many businesses and educational facilities to require that employees or students sign an acceptable use policy before being granted a network ID. When signing up with an Internet service provider (ISP), each customer is typically presented with an AUP, which states that they agree to adhere to certain stipulations (see Figure B2.5).

E-MAIL PRIVACY POLICY

E-mail is so pervasive in organizations that it requires its own specific policy. In a recent survey, 80 percent of professional workers identified e-mail as their preferred means of corporate communications. Trends also show a dramatic increase in the adoption rate of instant messaging (IM) in the workplace. While e-mail and IM are terrific business communication tools, there are risks associated with using them. Companies can mitigate many of the risks of using electronic messaging systems by implementing and adhering to an e-mail privacy policy.

One of the major problems with e-mail is the user's expectations of privacy. To a large extent, this exception is based on the false assumption that there exists e-mail privacy protection somehow analogous to that of U.S. first-class mail. This is simply not true. Generally, the organization that owns the e-mail system can operate the system as openly or as privately as it wishes. That means that if the organization

FIGURE B2.5

Acceptable Use Policy Stipulations

Acceptable Use Policy Stipulations
1. Not using the service as part of violating any law.
2. Not attempting to break the security of any computer network or user.
3. Not posting commercial messages to groups without prior permission.
4. Not performing any nonrepudiation.
5. Not attempting to send junk e-mail or spam to anyone who does not want to receive it.
6. Not attempting to mail bomb a site. A *mail bomb* is sending a massive amount of e-mail to a specific person or system resulting in filling up the recipient's disk space, which, in some cases, may be too much for the server to handle and may cause the server to stop functioning.

E-mail Privacy Policy Stipulations

1. The policy should be complementary to the ethical computer use policy.

2. It defines who legitimate e-mail users are.

3. It explains the backup procedure so users will know that at some point, even if a message is deleted from their computer, it will still be on the backup tapes.

4. It describes the legitimate grounds for reading someone's e-mail and the process required before such action can be taken.

5. It informs that the organization has no control of e-mail once it is transmitted outside the organization.

6. It explains what will happen if the user severs his or her connection with the organization.

7. It asks employees to be careful when making organizational files and documents available to others.

wants to read everyone's e-mail, it can do so. If it chooses not to read any, that is allowable too. Hence, it is up to the organization to decide how much, if any, e-mail it is going to read. Then, when it decides, it must inform the users, so that they can consent to this level of intrusion. In other words, an ***e-mail privacy policy*** details the extent to which e-mail messages may be read by others.

Organizations are urged to have some kind of e-mail privacy policy and to publish it no matter what the degree of intrusion. Figure B2.6 displays a few of the key stipulations generally contained in an e-mail privacy policy.

INTERNET USE POLICY

Similar to e-mail, the Internet has some unique aspects that make it a good candidate for its own policy. These include the large amounts of computing resources that Internet users can expend, thus making it essential that such use be legitimate. In addition, the Internet contains numerous materials that some might feel are offensive and, hence, some regulation might be required in this area. An ***Internet use policy*** contains general principles to guide the proper use of the Internet. Figure B2.7 displays a few important stipulations that might be included in an Internet use policy.

Internet Use Policy Stipulations

1. The policy should describe available Internet services because not all Internet sites allow users to access all services.

2. The policy should define the organization's position on the purpose of Internet access and what restrictions, if any, are placed on that access.

3. The policy should complement the ethical computer use policy.

4. The policy should describe user responsibility for citing sources, properly handling offensive material, and protecting the organization's good name.

5. The policy should clearly state the ramifications if the policy is violated.

ANTI-SPAM POLICY

Chief technology officer (CTO) of the law firm Fenwick and West, Matt Kesner reduced incoming spam by 99 percent and found himself a corporate hero. Prior to the spam reduction the law firm's partners (whose time is worth $350 to $600 an hour) found themselves spending hours each day sifting through 300 to 500 spam messages. The spam blocking engineered by Kesner traps between 5,000 and 7,000 messages a day.[3]

Spam is unsolicited e-mail. An *anti-spam policy* simply states that e-mail users will not send unsolicited e-mails (or spam). Spam plagues all levels of employees within an organization from receptionists to CEOs. Estimates indicate that spam accounts for 40 percent to 60 percent of most organizations' e-mail traffic. Ferris Research says spam cost U.S. businesses over $10 billion in 2003, and Nucleus Research stated that companies forfeit $874 per employee annually in lost productivity from spam alone. Spam clogs e-mail systems and siphons IT resources away from legitimate business projects.[4]

It is difficult to write anti-spam policies, laws, or software because there is no such thing as a universal litmus test for spam. One person's spam is another person's newsletter. End users have to be involved in deciding what spam is because what is unwanted can vary widely not just from one company to the next, but from one person to the next. What looks like spam to the rest of the world could be essential business communications for certain employees.

John Zarb, CIO of Libbey, a manufacturer of glassware, china, and flatware, tested Guenivere (a virus and subject-line filter) and SpamAssassin (an open-source spam filter). He had to shut them off after 10 days because they were rejecting important legitimate e-mails. As Zarb quickly discovered, once an organization starts filtering e-mail, it runs the risk of blocking legitimate e-mails because they look like spam. Avoiding an unacceptable level of "false positives" requires a delicate balancing act. The IT team tweaked the spam filters and today, the filters block about 70 percent of Libbey's spam, and Zarb says the "false positive" rate is far lower but not zero. Here are a few methods an organization can follow to prevent spam:

- **Disguise e-mail addresses posted in a public electronic place**—When posting an e-mail address in a public place be sure to disguise the address through simple means such as replacing "jsmith@domain.com" with "jsmith at domain dot com." This prevents spam from recognizing the e-mail address.

- **Opt-out of member directories that may place an e-mail address online**—Choose not to participate in any activities that place e-mail addresses online. If an e-mail address is placed online be sure it is disguised in some way.

- **Use a filter**—Many ISPs and free e-mail services now provide spam filtering. While filters are not perfect, they can cut down tremendously on the amount of spam a user receives.[5]

Ethics in the Workplace

There is a growing concern among employees that infractions of corporate policies—even accidental ones—will be a cause for disciplinary action. The Whitehouse.gov Internet site displays the U.S. president's official Web site and updates on bill signings and new policies. Whitehouse.com, however, leads to a trashy site that capitalizes on its famous name. A simple mistype from .gov to .com could potentially cost someone her or his job if the company has a termination policy for viewing illicit Web sites. Monitoring employees is one of the largest issues facing CIOs when they are developing information management policies.

The question of whether to monitor what employees do on company time with corporate resources has been largely decided by legal precedents that are already holding businesses financially responsible for their employees' actions. Increasingly, employee monitoring is not a choice; it is a risk-management obligation.

A 2003 survey of workplace monitoring and surveillance practices by the American Management Association (AMA) and the ePolicy Institute showed the degree to which companies are turning to monitoring:

- 82 percent of the study's 1,627 respondents acknowledged conducting some form of electronic monitoring or physical surveillance.
- 63 percent of the companies stated that they monitor Internet connections.
- 47 percent acknowledged storing and reviewing employee e-mail messages.[6]

MONITORING TECHNOLOGIES

Monitoring is tracking people's activities by such measures as number of keystrokes, error rate, and number of transactions processed. Figure B2.8 displays different types of monitoring technologies currently available.

If an organization is planning to engage in employee monitoring, the best path for it to take is open communication on the issue. A recent survey discovered that communication about monitoring issues is weak for most organizations. One in five companies did not even have an acceptable use policy and one in four companies did not have an Internet use policy. Companies that did have policies usually tucked them into the rarely probed recesses of the employee handbook, and even then the policies tended to be of the vague and legal jargon variety: "XYZ company reserves the right to monitor or review any information stored or transmitted on its equipment." Reserving the right to monitor is materially different from clearly stating up front that the company *does* monitor, listing what is tracked, describing what is looked for, and detailing the consequences for violations.

Common Monitoring Technologies	
Key logger, or key trapper, software	A program that, when installed on a computer, records every keystroke and mouse click.
Hardware key logger	A hardware device that captures keystrokes on their journey from the keyboard to the motherboard.
Cookie	A small file deposited on a hard drive by a Web site containing information about customers and their Web activities. Cookies allow Web sites to record the comings and goings of customers, usually without their knowledge or consent.
Adware	Software generates ads that install themselves on a computer when a person downloads some other program from the Internet.
Spyware (sneakware or stealthware)	Software that comes hidden in free downloadable software and tracks online movements, mines the information stored on a computer, or uses a computer's CPU and storage for some task the user knows nothing about.
Web log	Consists of one line of information for every visitor to a Web site and is usually stored on a Web server.
Clickstream	Records information about a customer during a Web surfing session such as what Web sites were visited, how long the visit was, what ads were viewed, and what was purchased.

FIGURE B2.8

Monitoring Technologies

EMPLOYEE MONITORING POLICIES

An organization must formulate the right monitoring policies and put them into practice. *Employee monitoring policies* explicitly state how, when, and where the company monitors its employees. CSOs that are explicit about what the company does in the way of monitoring and the reasons for it, along with actively educating their employees about what unacceptable behavior looks like, will find that employees not only acclimate quite quickly to a policy, but also reduce the CSO's burden by policing themselves. Figure B2.9 displays several common stipulations an organization can follow when creating an employee monitoring policy.

FIGURE B2.9

Employee Monitoring
Policy Stipulations

Employee Monitoring Policy Stipulations
1. Be as specific as possible.
2. Always enforce the policy.
3. Enforce the policy in the same way for everyone.
4. Expressly communicate that the company reserves the right to monitor all employees.
5. Specifically state when monitoring will be performed.
6. Specifically state what will be monitored (e-mail, IM, Internet, network activity, etc.).
7. Describe the types of information that will be collected.
8. State the consequences for violating the policy.
9. State all provisions that allow for updates to the policy.
10. Specify the scope and manner of monitoring for any information system.
11. When appropriate, obtain a written receipt acknowledging that each party has received, read, and understood the monitoring policies.

Advances in technology have made ethics a concern for many organizations. Consider how easy it is for an employee to e-mail large amounts of confidential information, change electronic communications, or destroy massive amounts of important company information all within seconds. Electronic information about customers, partners, and employees has become one of corporate America's most valuable assets. However, the line between the proper and improper use of this asset is at best blurry. Should an employer be able to search employee files without employee consent? Should a company be able to sell customer information without informing the customer of its intent? What is a responsible approach to document deletion?

The law provides guidelines in many of these areas, but how a company chooses to act within the confines of the law is up to the judgment of its officers. Since CIOs are responsible for the technology that collects, maintains, and destroys corporate information, they sit smack in the middle of this potential ethical quagmire.

One way an organization can begin dealing with ethical issues is to create a corporate culture that encourages ethical considerations and discourages dubious information dealings. Not only is an ethical culture an excellent idea overall, but it also acts as a precaution, helping prevent customer problems from escalating into front-page news stories. The establishment of and adherence to well-defined rules and policies will help organizations create an ethical corporate culture. These policies include:

- ePolicies
- Ethical Computer Use Policy
- Information Privacy Policy
- Acceptable Use Policy
- E-Mail Privacy Policy
- Internet Use Policy
- Anti-Spam Policy
- Employee Monitoring Policy

Acceptable use policy (AUP), 240
Adware, 243
Anti-spam policy, 242
Clickstream, 243
Confidentiality, 234
Cookie, 243
Copyright, 234
Counterfeit software, 234
E-mail privacy policy, 241
Employee monitoring policy, 244

ePolicies, 234, 238
Ethical computer use policy, 238
Ethics, 234
Fair use doctrine, 234
Hardware key logger, 243
Information privacy policy, 239
Intellectual property, 234
Internet use policy, 241
Key logger, or key trapper, software, 243
Mail bomb, 240

Monitoring, 243
Nonrepudiation, 240
Opt-in, 236
Pirated software, 234
Privacy, 234
Spam, 242
Spyware (sneakware or stealthware), 243
Web log, 243

Sarbanes-Oxley: Where Information Technology, Finance, and Ethics Meet

The Sarbanes-Oxley Act (SOX) of 2002 is legislation enacted in response to the high-profile Enron and WorldCom financial scandals to protect shareholders and the general public from accounting errors and fraudulent practices by organizations. One of the primary components of the Sarbanes-Oxley Act is the definition of which records are to be stored and for how long. For this reason, the legislation not only affects financial departments, but also IT departments whose job it is to store electronic records. The Sarbanes-Oxley Act states that all business records, including electronic records and electronic messages, must be saved for "not less than five years." The consequences for noncompliance are fines, imprisonment, or both. The following are the three rules of Sarbanes-Oxley that affect the management of electronic records.

1. The first rule deals with destruction, alteration, or falsification of records and states that persons who knowingly alter, destroy, mutilate, conceal, or falsify documents shall be fined or imprisoned for not more than 20 years, or both.

2. The second rule defines the retention period for records storage. Best practices indicate that corporations securely store all business records using the same guidelines set for public accountants which state that organizations shall maintain all audit or review workpapers for a period of five years from the end of the fiscal period in which the audit or review was concluded.

3. The third rule specifies all business records and communications that need to be stored, including electronic communications. IT departments are facing the challenge of creating and maintaining a corporate records archive in a cost-effective fashion that satisfies the requirements put forth by the legislation.

Essentially, any public organization that uses IT as part of its financial business processes will find that it must put in place IT controls in order to be compliant with the Sarbanes-Oxley Act. The following are a few practices you can follow to begin to ensure organizational compliance with the Sarbanes-Oxley Act.

- Overhaul or upgrade your financial systems in order to meet regulatory requirements for more accurate, detailed, and speedy filings.

- Examine the control processes within your IT department and apply best practices to comply with the act's goals. For example, segregation of duties within the systems development staff is a widely recognized best practice that helps prevent errors and outright fraud. The people who code program changes should be different from the people who test them, and a separate team should be responsible for changes in production environments.

- Homegrown financial systems are fraught with potential information-integrity issues. Although leading ERP systems offer audit-trail functionality, customizations of these systems often bypass those controls. You must work with internal and external auditors to ensure that customizations are not overriding controls.

- Work with your CIO, CEO, CFO, and corporate attorneys to create a document-retention-and-destruction policy that addresses what types of electronic documents should be saved, and for how long.

Ultimately, Sarbanes-Oxley compliance will require a great deal of work among all of your departments. Compliance starts with running IT as a business and strengthening IT internal controls.[7]

Questions

1. Define the relationship between ethics and the Sarbanes-Oxley Act.
2. Discuss why records management is an area of concern for the entire organization.
3. What are two policies an organization can implement to achieve Sarbanes-Oxley compliance?
4. Identify the biggest roadblock for organizations that are attempting to achieve Sarbanes-Oxley compliance.

CLOSING CASE TWO

Spying on Employees

Many employees use their company's high-speed Internet access to shop, browse, and just surf the Web. In fact, research firm ComScore Networks indicates that excluding auctions, 59 percent of all 2003 Web purchases in the United States were made from the workplace. A study by Vault.com determined that 47 percent of employees spend at least half an hour a day surfing the Web.

The research indicates that managers should monitor what their employees are doing with their Web access. Most managers do not want their employees conducting personal business during working hours. For these reasons many organization have increasingly been taking the Big Brother approach to Web monitoring with software that tracks Internet usage and even allows the boss to read employees' e-mail. Unfortunately, current research indicates that the effects of such employee monitoring are even worse than the lost productivity from employee Web surfing.

First, employee absenteeism is on the rise, almost doubling in 2003 to 21 percent. The lesson here might be that more employees are missing work to take care of personal business. Perhaps losing a few minutes here or there—or even a couple of hours—is cheaper than losing entire days.

Second, studies indicate that electronic monitoring results in lower job satisfaction, in part because people begin to believe the quantity of their work is more important than the quality.

Third, electronic monitoring also induces what psychologists call "psychological reactance": the tendency to rebel against constraints. If you tell your employees that they cannot shop, that they cannot use corporate networks for personal business, and that they cannot make personal phone calls, then their desire to do all these things will likely increase.

This is the thinking at SAS Institute, a private software company that is consistently ranked in the top 10 on many "Best Places to Work" surveys. SAS does not monitor its employees' Web usage. The company asks its employees to use company resources responsibly, but does not mind if they occasionally check sports scores or use the Web for shopping.

Many management gurus clearly state that organizations whose corporate cultures are based on trust are more successful than those whose corporate cultures are based on distrust. Before an organization implements monitoring technology it should ask itself, "What does this say about how the organization feels about its employees?" If the organization really does not trust its employees, then perhaps it should find new ones. If an organization does trust its employees, then it might want to treat them accordingly. An organization that follows its employees' every keystroke is unwittingly undermining its relationships with its employees.[8]

Questions

1. Explain the ethical issues involved in employee monitoring.
2. Summarize the adverse effects employee monitoring can have on employees. Summarize the potential issues an organization can face if it does not monitor its employees. If you were the CEO of an organization, would you choose to monitor your employees? Why or why not?
3. Identify the relationship between information privacy and e-mail monitoring.
4. Summarize the different monitoring technologies and rank them in order of least invasive to most invasive for employees.

✴ MAKING BUSINESS DECISIONS

1. Information Privacy

A new study by the Annenberg Public Policy Center at the University of Pennsylvania shows that 95 percent of people who use the Internet at home think they should have a legal right to know everything about the information that Web sites collect from them. Research also shows that 57 percent of home Internet users incorrectly believe that when a Web site has an information privacy policy it will not share personal information with other Web sites or companies. In fact, the research found that after showing the users how companies track, extract, and share Web site information to make money, 85 percent found the methods unacceptable, even for a highly valued site. Write a short paper arguing for or against an organization's right to use and distribute personal information gathered from its Web site.

2. Acting Ethically

Describe how you would react to the following scenarios:

- A senior marketing manager informs you that one of her employees is looking for another job and she wants you to give her access to look through her e-mail.
- A VP of sales informs you that he has made a deal to provide customer information to a strategic partner and he wants you to burn all of the customer information onto a CD.
- You start monitoring one of your employee's e-mail and discover that he is having an affair with one of the other employees in the office.
- You install a video surveillance system in your office and discover that employees are taking office supplies home with them.

3. Spying on E-Mail

Technology advances now allow individuals to monitor computers that they do not even have physical access too. New types of software can capture an individual's incoming and outgoing e-mail and then immediately forward that e-mail to another person. For example, if you are at work and your child is home from school and she receives an e-mail from John at 3:00 PM, at 3:01 PM you will receive a copy of that e-mail sent to your e-mail address. A few minutes later, if she replies to John's e-mail, within seconds you will again receive a copy of what she sent to John. Describe two scenarios (other than the above) for the use of this type of software: (1) where the use would be ethical, (2) where the use would be unethical.

4. Dealing with Difficult Decisions

Describe how you would react to the following scenarios:

■ You are assigned a parking space next to the CEO's in the company lot. You recently found a sizable dent on your car, along with flakes of your vehicle's paint on the CEO's bumper. The CEO has said nothing to you. What would you do?

■ You have recently persuaded a co-worker to quietly check himself into a substance-abuse program. Now the co-worker is back in the office, and while he is doing a great job, he is continually e-mailing everyone about his therapy meetings, progress, and new outlook on life. Other employees are complaining that he is making everyone in the office uncomfortable. What would you do?

■ You have recently spotted a memo from the CEO on your boss's desk which details who will be the targets of the next round of layoffs. What would you do?

5. Stealing Software

The issue of pirated software is one that the software industry fights on a daily basis. The major centers of software piracy are in places like Russia and China where salaries and disposable income are comparatively low. People in developing and economically depressed countries will fall behind the industrialized world technologically if they cannot afford access to new generations of software. Considering this, is it reasonable to blame someone for using pirated software when it could potentially cost him or her two months' salary to purchase a legal copy? Create an argument for or against the following statement: "Individuals who are economically less fortunate should be allowed access to software free of charge in order to ensure that they are provided with an equal technological advantage."

Supply Chain Management

Introduction

The core units introduced the supply chain and supply chain management. A **supply chain** consists of all parties involved, directly or indirectly, in the procurement of a product or raw material. **Supply chain management (SCM)** involves the management of information flows between and among stages in a supply chain to maximize total supply chain effectiveness and profitability.

This plug-in takes a detailed look at how an organization can create a supply chain strategy focusing on *efficiency* and *effectiveness*. **Efficiency IT metrics** measure the performance of the IT system including throughput, speed, availability, etc. **Effectiveness IT metrics** measure the impact IT has on business processes and activities including customer satisfaction, conversion rates, sell-through increases, etc. Once an organization determines its supply chain strategy it can begin to estimate the impact that its supply chain will have on its business and ultimately the performance of the organization. The payoff for a successful supply chain strategy can be tremendous. A study by Peter J. Metz, executive directory of the MIT Center for e-business, found that companies have achieved impressive bottom-line results from managing their supply chains—on average a 50 percent reduction in inventory and a 40 percent increase in timely deliveries.[1]

Supply Chain Strategies

General Motors, Ford, and DaimlerChrysler made history when the three automotive giants began working together to create a unified supply chain management system that all three companies and their suppliers could leverage. The Goldman

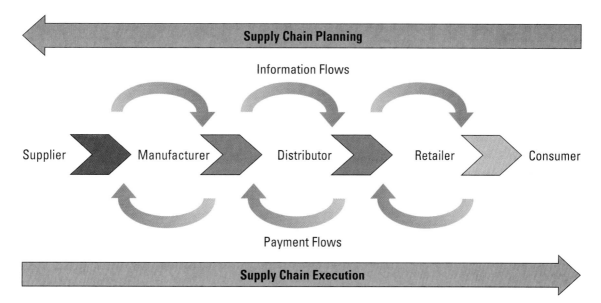

FIGURE B3.1

Supply Chain Planning and Supply Chain Execution Software's Correlation to the Supply Chain

Sachs Group's Senior Analyst, Gary Lapidus, estimates that Newco, the name of the joint venture, will have a potential market capitalization of between $30 billion and $40 billion once it goes public, with annual revenues of around $3 billion.

The combined automotive giants' purchasing power is tremendous with GM spending $85 billion per year, Ford spending $80 billion per year, and Daimler-Chrysler spending $73 billion per year. The ultimate goal of Newco is to Web-enable the entire automotive production process, from ordering production materials and forecasting future demand to making cars directly to consumer specifications. The automotive giants understand the impact strategic supply chain management can have on their business.[2]

Supply chain management software can be broken down into (1) supply chain planning software and (2) supply chain execution software. *Supply chain planning (SCP)* software uses advanced mathematical algorithms to improve the flow and efficiency of the supply chain while reducing inventory. SCP depends entirely on information for its accuracy. An organization cannot expect the SCP output to be accurate unless correct and up-to-date information regarding customer orders, sales information, manufacturing capacity, and delivery capability is entered into the system.

An organization's supply chain encompasses the facilities where raw materials, intermediate products, and finished goods are acquired, transformed, stored, and sold. These facilities are connected by transportation links, where materials and products flow. Ideally, the supply chain consists of multiple organizations that function as efficiently and effectively as a single organization, with full information visibility. *Supply chain execution (SCE)* software automates the different steps and stages of the supply chain. This could be as simple as electronically routing orders from a manufacturer to a supplier. Figure B3.1 details how SCP and SCE software correlate to the supply chain.

SUPPLY CHAIN DRIVERS

An organization's goals and strategic objectives should determine its overall supply chain management strategy. The SCM strategy in turn determines how the supply chain will perform with respect to efficiency and effectiveness. The four primary drivers of supply chain management are:

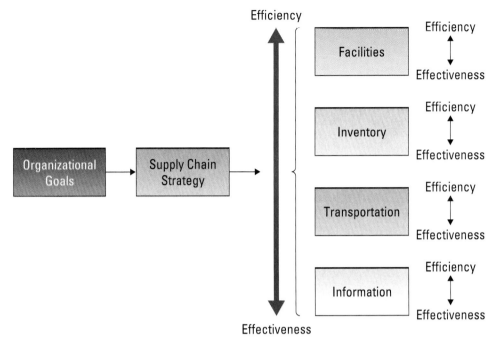

The combination of efficiency and effectiveness for all four supply chain drivers determines total supply chain efficiency or effectiveness.

1. Facilities
2. Inventory
3. Transportation
4. Information

An organization can use these four drivers in varying measure to push it toward either a supply chain strategy focusing on efficiency or a supply chain strategy focusing on effectiveness. The organization must decide on the trade-off it desires between efficiency and effectiveness for each driver. The selected combined impact of the various drivers then determines the efficiency and effectiveness of the entire supply chain. Figure B3.2 provides an overview of the four supply chain drivers in terms of their effect on overall efficiency and effectiveness.

FACILITIES DRIVER

A facility processes or transforms inventory into another product, or it stores the inventory before shipping it to the next facility. Toyota is an example of a company that stresses *effectiveness* in its facilities. Toyota's goal is to open a facility in every major market where it does business. These local facilities protect the company from currency fluctuations and trade barriers and thus are more effective for Toyota's customers. There are three primary components an organization should consider when determining its facilities strategy:

1. Location
2. Capacity
3. Operational design

Location

An organization must determine where it will locate its facilities, an important decision that constitutes a large part of its supply chain strategy. There are two primary options when determining facilities location: (1) centralize the location to gain economies of scale, which increases efficiency or (2) decentralize the locations to be closer to the customers, which increases effectiveness.

A company can gain economies of scale when it centralizes its facilities. However, this cost reduction decreases the company's effectiveness, since many of its customers may be located far away from the facility. The opposite is also true; having a number of different facilities located closer to customers reduces efficiency because of the increased costs associated with the additional facilities. Many other factors will influence location decisions including facility costs, employee expense, exchange rates, tax effects, etc.

Capacity

An organization must determine the performance capacity level for each of its facilities. If it decides a facility will have a large amount of excess capacity, which provides the flexibility to respond to wide swings in demand, then it is choosing an effectiveness strategy. Excess capacity, however, costs money and can therefore decrease efficiency.

Operational Design

An organization must determine if it wants a product focus or a functional focus for its facilities operational design. If it chooses a product focus design, it is anticipating that the facility will produce only a certain type of product. All operations, including fabrication and assembly, will focus on developing a single type of product. This strategy allows the facility to become highly efficient in producing a single product.

If it chooses a functional design, the facility will perform a specific function (e.g., fabrication only or assembly only) on many different products. This strategy allows the facility to become more effective since it can use a single process on many different types of products (see Figure B3.3).

FIGURE B3.3

The Facilities Driver's Effect on Efficiency and Effectiveness

Facilities Driver

Increases Efficiency
- Low number of facilities
- Centralized facilities
- Minimal amounts of excess capacity
- Single product focus

Increases Effectiveness
- High number of facilities
- Decentralized facilities
- Large amounts of excess capacity
- Multiple product focus

Efficiency

Effectiveness

INVENTORY DRIVER

Dillard's department store's competitive strategy is to appeal to higher-end customers who are willing to pay a premium to obtain products immediately. Dillard's carries large amounts of inventory to ensure products are always available for its customers. In return, its customers are willing to pay extra for their products.[3]

Companies require inventory to offset any discrepancies between supply and demand, but inventory is a major cost in any supply chain. Inventory's impact on a company's effectiveness versus efficiency can be enormous. Effectiveness results from more inventory, and efficiency results from less inventory. If a company's strategy requires a high level of customer effectiveness, then the company will locate large amounts of inventory in many facilities close to its customers, such as Dillard's strategy demands. If a company's strategy requires a high level of efficiency, the strategy of a low cost producer, for instance, then the company will maintain low levels of inventory in a single strategic location.

There are two facets of inventory an organization should consider when determining its inventory strategy:

1. Cycle inventory
2. Safety inventory

Cycle Inventory

Cycle inventory is the average amount of inventory held to satisfy customer demands between inventory deliveries. A company can follow either of two approaches regarding cycle inventory. The first approach is to hold a large amount of cycle inventory and receive inventory deliveries only once a month. The second

Inventory Driver

Increases Efficiency
- Maintains low levels of inventory
- Single inventory storage location

Efficiency

Increases Effectiveness
- Maintains large levels of inventory
- Multiple inventory storage locations close to customers

Effectiveness

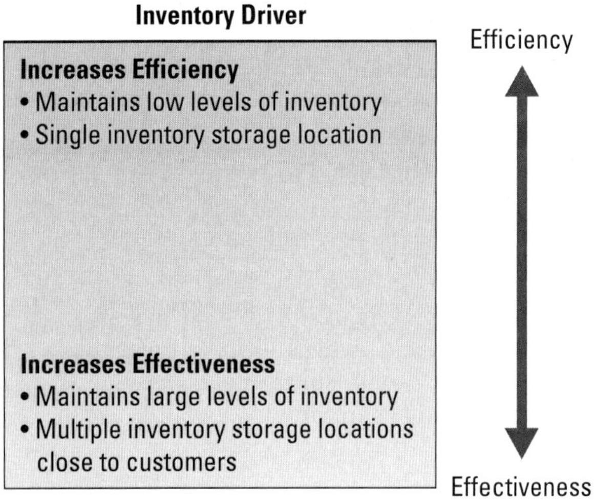

FIGURE B3.4

The Inventory Driver's Effect on Efficiency and Effectiveness

approach is to hold a small amount of inventory and receive orders weekly or even daily. The trade-off is the cost comparison between holding larger lots of inventory for an effective supply chain and ordering products frequently for an efficient supply chain.

Safety Inventory

Safety inventory is extra inventory held in the event demand exceeds supply. For example, a toy store might hold safety inventory for the Christmas season. The risk a company faces when making a decision in favor of safety inventory is that in addition to the cost of holding it, if it holds too much, some of its products may go unsold and it may have to discount them—after the Christmas season, in the toy store example. However, if it holds too little inventory it may lose sales and risks losing customers. The company must decide if it wants to risk the expense of carrying too much inventory or to risk losing sales and customers (see Figure B3.4).

TRANSPORTATION DRIVER

FedEx's entire business strategy focuses on its customers' need for highly effective transportation methods. Any company that uses FedEx to transport a package is focusing primarily on a safe and timely delivery and not on the cost of delivery. Many businesses even locate their facilities near FedEx hubs so that they can quickly transport inventory overnight to their customers.

An organization can use many different methods of transportation to move its inventories between the different stages in the supply chain. Like the other supply chain drivers, transportation cost has a large impact either way on effectiveness and efficiency. If an organization focuses on a highly effective supply chain, then it can use transportation to increase the price of its products by using faster, more costly transportation methods. If the focus is a highly efficient supply chain, the organization can use transportation to decrease the price of its products by using slower, less costly transportation methods. There are two primary facets of transportation an organization should consider when determining its strategy:

1. Method of transportation
2. Transportation route

Method of Transportation

An organization must decide how it wants to move its inventory through the supply chain. There are six basic methods of transportation it can choose from: truck, rail, ship, air, pipeline, and electronic. The primary differences between these methods are the speed of delivery and price of delivery. An organization might choose an expensive method of transportation to ensure speedy delivery if it is focusing on a highly effective supply chain. On the other hand, it might choose an inexpensive method of transportation if it is focusing on a highly efficient supply chain.

Transportation Route

An organization will also need to choose the transportation route for its products. Transportation route directly affects the speed and cost of delivery. For example, an organization might decide to use an effectiveness route and ship its products directly to its customers, or it might decide to use an efficiency route and ship its products to a distributor that ships the products to customers (see Figure B3.5).

INFORMATION DRIVER

Information is a driver whose importance has grown as companies use it to become both more efficient and more effective. An organization must decide what information is most valuable in efficiently reducing costs or in improving effectiveness. This decision will vary depending on a company's strategy and the design and organization of the supply chain. Two things to consider about information in the supply chain include:

1. Information sharing
2. Push vs. pull information strategy

Transportation Driver

Increases Efficiency
• Reduced speed of delivery
• Reduced cost of delivery
• Ship products to a distributor

Increases Effectiveness
• Increased speed of delivery
• Increased cost of delivery
• Ship products directly to customers

Efficiency

Effectiveness

Information Sharing

An organization must determine what information it wants to share with its partners throughout the stages of the supply chain. Information sharing is a difficult decision since most organizations do not want their partners to gain insight into strategic or competitive information. However, they do need to share information so they can coordinate supply chain activities such as providing suppliers with inventory order levels to meet production forecasts. Building trusting relationships is one way to begin to understand how much information supply chain partners require.

If an organization chooses an efficiency focus for information sharing then it will freely share lots of information to increase the speed and decrease the costs of supply chain processing. If an organization chooses an effectiveness focus for information sharing, then it will share only selected information with certain individuals, which will decrease the speed and increase the costs of supply chain processing.

Push vs. Pull Information Strategy

In a *push technology* environment, organizations send information. In a *pull technology* environment, organizations receive or request information. An organization must decide how it is going to share information with its partners. It might decide that it wants to push information out to partners by taking on the responsibility of sending information to them. On the other hand, it might decide that it wants its partners to take on the responsibility of getting information by having them directly access the information from the systems and pull the information they require.

Again, an organization must determine how much it trusts its partners when deciding on a push versus pull information sharing strategy. Using a push information sharing strategy is more effective because the organization has control over exactly what information is shared and when the information is shared. However, a push strategy is less efficient because there are costs associated with sending information such as computer equipment, applications, time, resources, and so forth.

Using a pull information sharing strategy is more efficient since the organization does not have to undertake the costs associated with sending information. However, the pull strategy is less effective since the organization has no control over when the information is pulled. For example, if the company needs inventory there is no guarantee that the suppliers will pick up the information. Hence, an organization could find itself in trouble if its partners forget to obtain the information and fail to deliver the required products (see Figure B3.6).

FIGURE B3.5

The Transportation Driver's Effect on Efficiency and Effectiveness

FIGURE B3.6

The Information Driver's Effect on Efficiency and Effectiveness

Information Driver

Increases Efficiency
• Openly shares information with all individuals
• Pull information strategy

Increases Effectiveness
• Selectively shares certain information with certain individuals
• Push information strategy

Efficiency

Effectiveness

APPLYING A SUPPLY CHAIN DESIGN

Figure B3.7 displays Wal-Mart's supply chain management design and how it correlates to its competitive strategy to be a reliable, low-cost retailer for a wide variety of mass consumption goods. Wal-Mart's supply chain emphasizes efficiency, but also maintains an adequate level of effectiveness.

■ **Facilities Focus—Efficiency:** Wal-Mart maintains few warehouses and will build a new warehouse only when demand is high enough to justify one.

■ **Inventory Focus—Efficiency:** Wal-Mart ships directly to its stores from the manufacturer. This significantly lowers inventory levels because stores maintain inventory, not stores and warehouses.

■ **Transportation Focus—Effectiveness:** Wal-Mart maintains its own fleet of trucks. The benefits in terms of overall supply chain efficiency justify the expense of maintaining its own trucks because effective transportation allows Wal-Mart to keep low levels of inventory.

■ **Information Focus—Efficiency:** Wal-Mart invests heavily in technology and the flow of information throughout its entire supply chain. Wal-Mart pushes inventory information all the way back up the supply chain to its suppliers who then manufacture only enough inventories to meet demand. The cost to build the information flows between its supply chain partners has been tremendous. However, the result of this investment is a highly successful and efficient supply chain.[4]

FIGURE B3.7

Wal-Mart's Supply
Chain Management
Drivers

Wal-Mart uses its four primary supply chain drivers to drive supply chain efficiency.

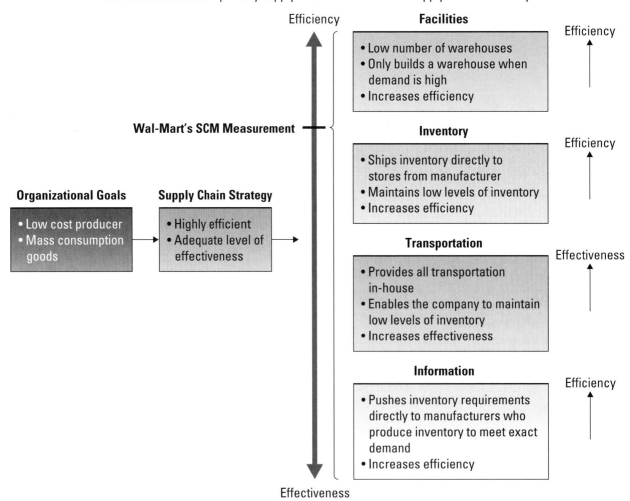

Future Trends

The functionality in supply chain management systems is becoming more and more sophisticated as supply chain management matures. Now and in the future, the next stages of SCM will incorporate more functions such as marketing, customer service, and product development. This will be achieved through more advanced communication, adoption of more user friendly decision support systems, and availability of shared information to all participants in the supply chain. SCM is an ongoing development as technology makes it possible to acquire information ever more accurately and frequently from all over the world, and introduces new tools to aid in the analytical processes that deal with the supply chain's growing complexity.

According to Forrester Research, Inc., U.S. firms will spend a total of $35 billion over the next five years to improve business processes that monitor, manage, and optimize their extended supply chains. The following are the fastest growing SCM components because they have the greatest potential impact on an organization's bottom line:[5]

- ***Supply chain event management (SCEM)*** enables an organization to react more quickly to resolve supply chain issues. SCEM software increases real-time information sharing among supply chain partners and decreases their response time to unplanned events. SCEM demand will skyrocket as more and more organizations begin to discover the benefits of real-time supply chain monitoring.

- ***Selling chain management*** applies technology to the activities in the order life cycle from inquiry to sale.

- ***Collaborative engineering*** allows an organization to reduce the cost and time required during the design process of a product.

- ***Collaborative demand planning*** helps organizations reduce their investment in inventory, while improving customer satisfaction through product availability.

New technologies are also going to improve the supply chain. Radio frequency identification (RFID) technologies use active or passive tags in the form of chips or smart labels that can store unique identifiers and relay this information to electronic readers. RFID will become an effective tool for tracking and monitoring inventory movement in a real-time SCM environment. The real-time information will provide managers with an instant and accurate view of inventories within the supply chain. Using current SCM systems, the RFID will check the inventory status and then trigger the replenishment process. Organizations using RFIDs will be able to quickly and accurately provide current inventory levels (in real-time) at any point in the supply chain as long as there are readers to detect their location. As inventory levels are reduced to their reorder points, replenishment orders can then be electronically generated. With quick and accurate information about inventories, the use of safety stock levels guarding against uncertainty can also be reduced. Hence, the potential benefits of RFIDs include a reduction of human intervention (or required labor) and holding fewer inventories, which nets a reduction in operating costs.

SCM applications have always been expensive, costing between $1 and $10 million. As the industry matures and competition increases, vendors will continue adapting their pricing models to attract mid-size and smaller companies.[6]

T he fundamental decisions an organization needs to make regarding its supply chain strategy concern:

- **Facilities**—An organization must decide between the cost of the number, location, and type of facilities (efficiency) and the level of effectiveness that these facilities provide.
- **Inventory**—An organization can increase inventory levels to make its supply chain more effective for its customers. This choice, however, comes at a cost as added inventory significantly decreases efficiency.
- **Transportation**—An organization can choose between the cost of transporting inventory (efficiency) and the speed of transporting inventory (effectiveness). Transportation choices also influence other drivers such as inventory levels and facility locations.
- **Information**—A focus on information can help improve both supply chain effectiveness and efficiency. The information driver also improves the performance of other drivers.

KEY TERMS

Collaborative demand
   planning, 257
Collaborative engineering, 257
Cycle inventory, 253
Effectiveness IT metric, 250
Efficiency IT metric, 250
Pull technology, 255

Push technology, 255
Safety inventory, 254
Selling chain management, 257
Supply chain, 250
Supply chain event
   management (SCEM), 257

Supply chain execution
   (SCE), 251
Supply chain management
   (SCM), 250
Supply chain planning
   (SCP), 251

CLOSING CASE ONE

Listerine's Journey

When you use Listerine antiseptic mouthwash, you are experiencing the last step in a complex supply chain spanning several continents and requiring months of coordination by countless businesses and individuals. The resources involved in getting a single bottle of Listerine to a consumer are unbelievable. As raw material is transformed to finished product, what will be Listerine travels around the globe and through multiple supply chains and information systems.

The Journey Begins

A farmer in Australia is harvesting a crop of eucalyptus for eucalyptol, the oil found in its leathery leaves. The farmer sells the crop to an Australian processing company, which spends about four weeks extracting the eucalyptol from the eucalyptus.

Meanwhile, in New Jersey, Warner-Lambert (WL) partners with a distributor to buy the oil from the Australian company and transport it to WL's Listerine manufacturing and distribution facility in Lititz, Pennsylvania. The load will arrive at Lititz about three months after the harvest.

At the same time, in Saudi Arabia, a government-owned operation is drilling deep under the desert for the natural gas that will yield the synthetic alcohol that gives Listerine its 43-proof punch. Union Carbide Corp. ships the gas via tanker to a refinery in Texas, which purifies it and converts it into ethanol. The ethanol is loaded onto another tanker, then transported from

Texas through the Gulf of Mexico to New Jersey, where it is transferred to storage tanks and transported via truck or rail to WL's plant. A single shipment of ethanol takes about six to eight weeks to get from Saudi Arabia to Lititz.

SPI Polyols Inc., a manufacturer of ingredients for the confectionery, pharmaceutical, and oral-care industries, buys corn syrup from farmers in the Midwest. SPI converts the corn syrup into sorbitol solution, which sweetens and adds bulk to the Cool Mint Listerine. The syrup is shipped to SPI's New Castle, Delaware, facility for processing and then delivered on a tank wagon to Lititz. The whole process, from the time the corn is harvested to when it is converted into sorbitol, takes about a month.

By now the ethanol, eucalyptol, and sorbitol have all arrived at WL's plant in Lititz, where employees test them, along with the menthol, citric acid, and other ingredients that make up Listerine, for quality assurance before authorizing storage in tanks. To mix the ingredients, flow meters turn on valves at each tank and measure out the right proportions, according to the Cool Mint formula developed by WL R&D in 1990. (The original amber mouthwash was developed in 1879.)

Next, the Listerine flows through a pipe to fillers along the packaging line. The fillers dispense the product into bottles delivered continuously from a nearby plastics company for just-in-time manufacturing. The bottles are capped, labeled, and fitted with tamper-resistant safety bands, then placed in shipping boxes that each hold one dozen 500-milliliter bottles. During this process, machines automatically check for skewed labels, missing safety bands, and other problems. The entire production cycle, from the delivery via pipe of the Listerine liquid to the point where bottles are boxed and ready to go, takes a matter of minutes. The line can produce about 300 bottles per minute—a far cry from the 80 to 100 bottles that the line produced per minute prior to 1994.

Each box travels on a conveyor belt to the palletizer, which organizes and shrink-wraps the boxes into 100-case pallets. Stickers with identifying bar codes are affixed to the pallets. Drivers forklift the pallets to the distribution center, located in the same Lititz facility, from which the boxes are shipped around the world.

Finally, the journey is completed when a customer purchases a bottle of Listerine at a local drug store or grocery store. In a few days, the store will place an order for a replacement bottle of Listerine. And so begins the cycle again.[7]

Questions

1. Summarize SCM and describe Warner-Lambert's supply chain strategy.
2. Detail Warner-Lambert's facilities strategy.
3. Detail Warner-Lambert's inventory strategy.
4. Detail Warner-Lambert's transportation strategy.
5. Detail Warner-Lambert's information strategy.
6. Describe what would happen to Warner-Lambert's business if a natural disaster in Saudi Arabia depletes its natural gas resources.

Crafting an SCM Strategy for Michaels

Michaels Stores, Inc., the largest retailer of arts and crafts materials in the United States, owns and operates 775 Michaels stores in 48 states and Canada; 155 Aaron Brothers stores, located primarily on the West Coast; and one wholesale operation in Dallas. Headquartered in Irving, Texas, Michaels' total annual sales exceed $2.8 billion.

A retailer's transportation system must do more than get the right product to the right place at the right time. It also needs to use the most efficient routes, optimize loads, and employ economical and reliable carriers. Although Michaels Stores, Inc., was achieving record growth, the company questioned whether its third-party logistics provider (3PL) was enabling it to make the best business decisions. "Our 3PL used inefficient communication methods rather than electronic communication," said Hal Feuchtwanger, Michaels Stores' director of Domestic Transportation. "Also, the quality and completeness of the data from an operational and financial perspective was falling short. There was always a question as to whether we were employing solid routing logic, utilizing the most cost-effective carriers, and generally making sound operational decisions."

Michaels decided to bring its transportation operations in-house and sought a solution that would support the processes from planning to payment. Adding further complexity to the already daunting task of reinventing its transportation management system, the company was on a tight timeline. Michaels wanted to have a new solution in place before its contract with its 3PL expired. Some of the challenges the SCM system had to overcome were:

- Optimize routing through efficient shipment consolidation.
- Enable efficient and effective carrier payment processes.
- Implement a new transportation solution before the 3PL contract expired.

The company chose to implement a solution from i2, which enabled Michaels to increase planning and processing efficiencies in order to gain visibility into transportation planning. Hal Feuchtwanger stated, "With the support of i2 consultants, and using in-house resources both from Michaels' transportation and IS organizations, we were successfully processing 100 percent of our inbound and outbound truckload and LTL shipments in just nine months." Other benefits from the i2 solution were:

- Ability to use "what-if" scenarios to validate new distribution network strategies.
- Automated audit and payment processes.
- Reduced man-hours associated with load planning and processing by nearly 50 percent.
- Gained visibility to project transportation management goals up to several years into the future.[8]

Questions

1. Describe Michaels' transportation strategy in terms of methods and routes.
2. Define the correlation between the information and transportation drivers. How can Michaels use the information driver to affect its transportation driver in terms of efficiency and effectiveness?
3. Explain how the new systems' ability to use "what-if" scenarios to validate new distribution network strategies will benefit Michaels.

MAKING BUSINESS DECISIONS

1. Focusing on Facilities

Focus is a large distributor of films and is owned and operated by Lauren O'Connell. The company has been in business for over 50 years and distributes motion pictures to theaters all over the United States and Canada. Focus is in the middle of a supply chain overhaul and is currently deciding its supply chain strategy. Lauren has asked you to create a report discussing the company's options for its facilities including location, capacity, and operational design. The report should include two primary focuses: one on efficiency and one on effectiveness.

2. Investing in Inventory

Poppa's Toy Store Inc. has over 150 stores in 38 states. The chain has been owned and operated for the last 30 years by CEO Taylor Coombe. Taylor has been reading reports on supply chain management and is particularly interested in updating the company's current supply chain. It is the beginning of April and Taylor wants a new SCM system up and running before the Christmas season starts in November. Taylor is particularly interested in demand planning and forecasting for the entire company's inventory during its busiest season—Christmas. Taylor has asked you to create a report discussing the company's options for its inventory management strategy including cycle and safety inventory. The report should include two primary focuses: one on efficiency and one on effectiveness.

3. Targeting Transportation

Extra Express Co. is an overnight freight and parcel delivery business that operates on a global level and has annual revenues in excess of $400 million. You have just been hired as the company's Director of Transportation. The CEO, Jeff Brewer, has asked you to put together a report detailing how the company can gain efficiencies by streamlining its transportation methods and routes.

4. Increasing Information

Galina's is a high-end auction house located in New York City. Galina's specializes in selling jewelry, art, and antique furniture primarily from estate sales. The owner, Galina Bucrya, would like to begin offering certain items for auction over the Internet. Galina is unfamiliar with the Internet and not quite sure how to pursue her new business strategy. You are working for Information Inc., a small business consulting company that specializes in e-business strategies. Galina has hired you to help her create her supply chain e-business strategy. Compile a report describing supply chain management, the potential benefits her company can receive from an SCM strategy, your recommendation for an efficient or effective SCM strategy, and your views on the future of SCM.

5. Increasing Revenues with SCM

Cold Cream is one of the premier beauty supply stores in the metro New York area. People come from all over to sample the store's unique creams, lotions, makeup, and perfumes. The company receives its products from manufacturers around the globe. The company would like to implement an SCM system to help it better understand its customers and their purchasing habits. Create a report summarizing SCM systems and explain how an SCM system can directly influence Cold Cream's revenues.

PLUG-IN

B4

Customer Relationship Management

LEARNING OUTCOMES

1. Describe the three CRM technologies used by marketing departments.
2. Describe and differentiate the CRM technologies used by sales departments and customer service departments.
3. Compare customer relationship management, supplier relationship management, partner relationship management, and employee relationship management.
4. Summarize the future of customer relationship management.

Introduction

The core units introduced *customer relationship management (CRM),* which involves managing all aspects of a customer's relationship with an organization to increase customer loyalty and retention and an organization's profitability. The two primary components of a CRM strategy are operational CRM and analytical CRM. *Operational CRM* supports traditional transactional processing for day-to-day front-office operations or systems that deal directly with the customers. *Analytical CRM* supports back-office operations and strategic analysis and includes all systems that do not deal directly with the customers. The primary difference between operational CRM and analytical CRM is the degree of direct interaction between the organization and its customers. See Figure B4.1 for an overview of operational CRM and analytical CRM.

An organization can find its most valuable customers by using a formula that industry insiders call "RFM"—**R**ecency, **F**requency, and **M**onetary Value. In other words, an organization must track:

- How recently a customer purchased items (Recency)
- How frequently a customer purchases items (Frequency)
- How much a customer spends on each purchase (Monetary Value)

Once a company has gathered this initial CRM information, it can compile it to identify patterns and create marketing campaigns, sales promotions, and services to increase business. For example, if Ms. Smith buys only at the height of the season, then the company should send her a special offer during the "off-season." If

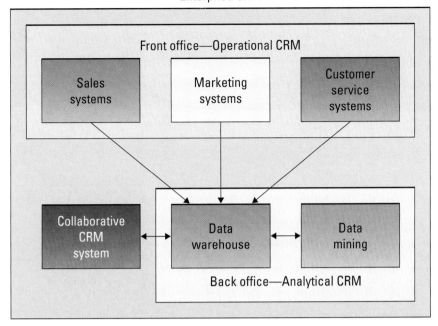

Enterprise CRM

Front office—Operational CRM

Sales systems

Marketing systems

Customer service systems

Collaborative CRM system

Data warehouse

Data mining

Back office—Analytical CRM

Mr. Jones always buys software but never computers, then the company should offer him free software with the purchase of a new computer.

The CRM technologies discussed in this plug-in can help organizations find answers to "RFM" and other tough questions such as who are their best customers and which of their products are the most profitable. The plug-in details the different operational and analytical CRM technologies an organization can use to strengthen its customer relationships and increase revenues.

The Evolution of CRM

Knowing the customer, especially knowing the profitability of individual customers, is highly lucrative in the financial services industry. Its high transactional nature has always afforded the financial services industry more access to customer information than other industries have, but it has embraced CRM technologies only recently.

Barclays Bank is a leading financial services company operating in more than 70 countries around the world. In the United Kingdom, Barclays has over 10 million personal customers and about 9.3 million credit cards in circulation, and serves 500,000 small business customers. Barclays decided to invest in CRM technologies to help it gain valuable insights into its business and customers.

With the new CRM system Barclays' managers are better able to predict the financial behavior of individual customers and assess whether a customer is likely to pay back a loan in full and within the agreed upon time period. This helps Barclays manage its profitability with greater precision because it can charge its customers a more appropriate rate of interest based on the results of the customer's risk assessment. Barclays also uses a sophisticated customer segmentation system to identify groups of profitable customers, both on a corporate and personal level, which it can then target for new financial products. One of the most valuable pieces of information Barclays discovered was that about 50 percent of its customers are nonprofitable and that less than 30 percent of its customers provide 90 percent of its profits.[1]

There are three phases in the evolution of CRM: (1) reporting, (2) analyzing, and (3) predicting. Reporting technologies help organizations identify their customers

FIGURE B4.2
Evolution of CRM

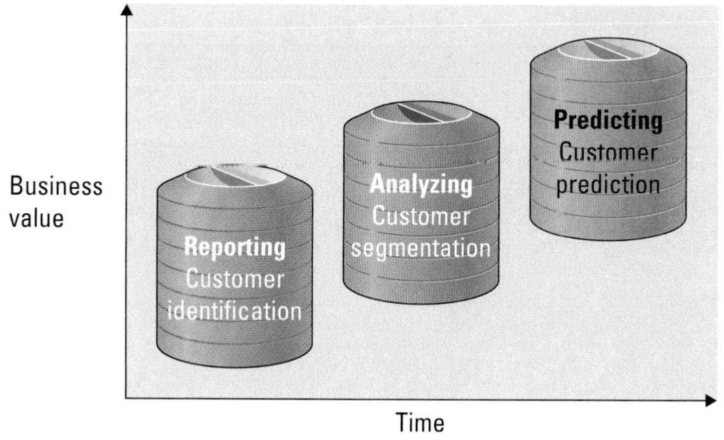

FIGURE B4.3
Reporting, Analyzing, and Predicting Examples

REPORTING "Asking What Happened"	ANALYZING "Asking Why It Happened"	PREDICTING "Asking What Will Happen"
What is the total revenue by customer?	Why did sales not meet forecasts?	What customers are at risk of leaving?
How many units did we manufacture?	Why was production so low?	What products will the customer buy?
Where did we sell the most products?	Why did we not sell as many units as last year?	Who are the best candidates for a mailing?
What were total sales by product?	Who are our customers?	What is the best way to reach the customer?
How many customers did we serve?	Why was customer revenue so high?	What is the lifetime profitability of a customer?
What are our inventory levels?	Why are inventory levels so low?	What transactions might be fradulent?

across other applications. Analysis technologies help organizations segment their customers into categories such as best and worst customers. Predicting technologies help organizations make predictions regarding customer behavior such as which customers are at risk of leaving (see Figure B4.2).

Both operational and analytical CRM technologies can assist in customer reporting (identification), customer analysis (segmentation), and customer prediction. Figure B4.3 highlights a few of the important questions an organization can answer using CRM technologies.

Operational CRM

Figure B4.4 displays the different technologies marketing, sales, and customer service departments can use to perform operational CRM.

FIGURE B4.4
Operational CRM Technologies for Sales, Marketing, and Customer Service Departments

Operational CRM Technologies		
Marketing	**Sales**	**Customer Service**
1. List Generator	1. Sales Management	1. Contact Center
2. Campaign Management	2. Contact Management	2. Web-Based Self-Service
3. Cross-Selling and Up-Selling	3. Opportunity Management	3. Call Scripting

MARKETING AND OPERATIONAL CRM

Companies are no longer trying to sell one product to as many customers as possible; instead, they are trying to sell one customer as many products as possible. Marketing departments are able to transform to this new way of doing business by using CRM technologies that allow them to gather and analyze customer information to deploy successful marketing campaigns. In fact, a marketing campaign's success is directly proportional to the organization's ability to gather and analyze the right information.

The three primary operational CRM technologies a marketing department can implement to increase customer satisfaction are:

1. List generator
2. Campaign management
3. Cross-selling and up-selling

List Generator

List generators compile customer information from a variety of sources and segment the information for different marketing campaigns. Information sources include Web site visits, Web site questionnaires, online and offline surveys, fliers, toll-free numbers, current customer lists, etc. After compiling the customer list, an organization can use criteria to filter and sort the list for potential customers. Filter and sort criteria can include such things as household income, education level, and age. List generators provide marketing departments with a solid understanding of the type of customer it needs to target for marketing campaigns.

Campaign Management

Campaign management systems guide users through marketing campaigns performing such tasks as campaign definition, planning, scheduling, segmentation, and success analysis. These advanced systems can even calculate quantifiable results for return on investment (ROI) for each campaign and track the results in order to analyze and understand how the company can fine-tune future campaigns.

Cross-Selling and Up-Selling

Two key sales strategies a marketing campaign can deploy are cross-selling and up-selling. *Cross-selling* is selling *additional* products or services to a customer. *Up-selling* is *increasing* the value of the sale. For example, McDonald's performs cross-selling by asking their customers if they would like an apple pie with their meal. McDonald's performs up-selling by asking their customers if they would like to super-size their meals. CRM systems offer marketing departments all kinds of information about their customers and their products, which can help them identify cross-selling and up-selling marketing campaigns.

California State Automobile Association (CSAA) had to take advantage of its ability to promote and cross-sell CSAA automotive, insurance, and travel services to beat its competition. Accomplishing this task was easy once the company implemented E.piphany's CRM system. The system integrated information from all of CSAA's separate databases, making it immediately available to all employees through a Web-based browser. Employees could quickly glance at a customer's profile and determine which services the customer currently had and which services the customer might want to purchase based on her or his needs projected by the software.[2]

SALES AND OPERATIONAL CRM

The sales department was the first to begin developing CRM systems. There were two primary reasons that sales departments needed to track customer sales information electronically. First, sales representatives were struggling with the overwhelming amount of customer account information they were required to maintain and track. Second, companies were struggling with the issue that much of their vital customer and sales information remained in the heads of their sales representatives. One of the first CRM components built to help address these issues was the sales force automation component. *Sales force automation (SFA)* is a system that automatically tracks all of the steps in the sales process. SFA products focus on increasing customer satisfaction, building customer relationships, and improving product sales by tracking all sales information.

Serving several million guests each year, Vail Resorts Inc. maintains dozens of systems across all seven of its properties. These systems perform numerous tasks including recording lift ticket, lodging, restaurant, conference, retail, and ski rental sales. Since a significant percentage of the company's revenue results from repeat guests, building stronger, more profitable relationships with its loyal customers is Vail Resorts first priority.

To improve customer service and marketing campaign success the company deployed the Ascential CRM system, which integrated the customer information from its many disparate systems. The CRM system is providing Vail Resorts with a detailed level of customer insight, which helps the company personalize its guest offerings and promotions. By using a CRM system that integrates information from across all of its resorts and business lines, the company can determine what, where, and how its guests behave across all of its properties. For example, the company can now offer discounts on lift ticket and ski rentals for customers staying in its resorts.[3]

The three primary operational CRM technologies a sales department can implement to increase customer satisfaction are:

1. Sales management
2. Contact management
3. Opportunity management

Sales Management

Figure B4.5 depicts the typical sales process, which begins with an opportunity and ends with billing the customer for the sale. *Sales management systems* automate each phase of the sales process, helping individual sales representatives coordinate and organize all of their accounts. Features include calendars to help plan customer meetings, alarm reminders signaling important tasks, customizable multi-

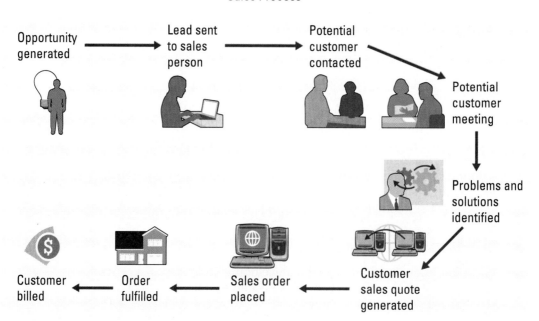

Sales Process

media presentations, and document generation. These systems even have the ability to provide an analysis of the sales cycle and calculate how each individual sales representative is performing during the sales process.

Contact Management

A *contact management system* maintains customer contact information and identifies prospective customers for future sales. Contact management systems include such features as maintaining organizational charts, detailed customer notes, and supplemental sale information. For example, a contact management system can take an incoming telephone number and display the caller's name along with notes detailing previous conversations. This allows the sales representative to answer the telephone and say, "Hi Sue, how is your new laptop working? How was your vacation to Florida?" without receiving any reminders of such details first from the customer. The customer feels valued since the sales associate knows her name and even remembers details of their last conversation!

3M, a $16 billion technology company, is a leader in the health care, safety, electronics, telecommunications, office, and consumer markets. The company began to focus on streamlining and unifying its sales processes with the primary goals of better customer segmentation and more reliable lead generation and qualification. To achieve these goals the company implemented a CRM system and soon found itself receiving the following benefits:

- Cutting the time it takes to familiarize sales professionals with new territories by 33 percent.
- Increasing management's visibility of the sales process.
- Decreasing the time it takes to qualify leads and assign sales opportunities by 40 percent.

One of the more successful campaigns driven by the CRM system allowed 3M to quickly deliver direct mail to targeted government agencies and emergency services in response to the anthrax attacks in 2002. All inquires to the mail campaign were automatically assigned to a sales representative who followed up with a quote. In little more than a week, the company had received orders for 35,000 respirator masks generating over $100,000 in revenues.[4]

Opportunity Management

Opportunity management systems target sales opportunities by finding new customers or companies for future sales. Opportunity management systems determine potential customers and competitors and define selling efforts including budgets and schedules. Advanced opportunity management systems can even calculate the probability of a sale, which can save sales representatives significant time and money when attempting to find new customers. The primary difference between contact management and opportunity management is that contact management deals with existing customers and opportunity management deals with new customers.

Figure B4.6 displays six CRM pointers a sales representative can use to increase prospective customers.

CUSTOMER SERVICE AND OPERATIONAL CRM

Sales and marketing are the primary departments that interact directly with customers prior to a sale. Most companies recognize the importance of building strong relationships during the marketing and sales efforts; however, many fail to realize the importance of continuing to build these relationships after the sale is complete. It is actually more important to build postsale relationships if the company wants to ensure customer loyalty and satisfaction. The best way to implement postsale CRM strategies is through the customer service department.

CRM Pointers for Gaining Prospective Customers	
1. **Get their attention**	If you have a good prospect, chances are that he or she receives dozens of offers from similar companies. Be sure your first contact is professional and gets your customer's attention.
2. **Value their time**	When you ask for a meeting, you are asking for the most valuable thing a busy person has—time. Many companies have had great success by offering high-value gifts in exchange for a meeting with a representative. Just be careful because some organizations frown on expensive gifts. Instead, offer these prospective customers a report that can help them perform their jobs more effectively.
3. **Overdeliver**	If your letter offered a free DVD in exchange for a meeting, bring a box of microwave popcorn along with the movie. Little gestures like these tell customers that you not only keep your word, but also can be counted on to overdeliver.
4. **Contact frequently**	Find new and creative ways to contact your prospective customers frequently. Starting a newsletter and sending out a series of industry updates are excellent ways to keep in contact and provide value.
5. **Generate a trustworthy mailing list**	If you are buying a mailing list from a third party be sure that the contacts are genuine prospects, especially if you are offering an expensive gift. Be sure that the people you are meeting have the power to authorize a sale.
6. **Follow up**	One of the most powerful prospecting tools is a simple thank-you note. Letting people know that their time was appreciated may even lead to additional referrals.

One of the primary reasons a company loses customers is bad customer service experiences. Providing outstanding customer service is a difficult task and there are many CRM technologies available to assist organizations with this important activity. For example, by rolling out Lotus Instant Messaging to its customers, Avnet Computer Marketing has established an efficient, direct route to push valuable information and updates out to its customers. The company uses Lotus Instant Messaging to provide real-time answers to customer questions by listing its support specialists' status by different colors on its Web site: green if they are available, red if they are not, or blue if they are out of the office. The customer simply clicks on a name to begin instant messaging or a chat session to get quick answers to questions.

Before Lotus Instant Messaging, customers would have to wait in "1-800" call queues or for e-mail responses for answers. The new system has increased customer satisfaction along with tremendous savings from fewer long-distance phone charges. Avnet also estimates that Lotus Instant Messaging saves each of its 650 employees 5 to 10 minutes a day.[5]

The three primary operational CRM technologies a customer service department can implement to increase customer satisfaction are:

1. Contact center
2. Web-based self-service
3. Call scripting

Contact Center

A ***contact center*** (or call center) is where customer service representatives (CSRs) answer customer inquiries and respond to problems through a number of different customer touchpoints. A contact center is one of the best assets a customer-driven organization can have because maintaining a high level of customer support is critical to obtaining and retaining customers. There are numerous systems available to help an organization automate its contact centers. A few of the features available in these systems are:

- *Automatic call distribution*—a phone switch routes inbound calls to available agents.
- *Interactive voice response (IVR)*—directs customers to use touch-tone phones or keywords to navigate or provide information.
- *Predictive dialing*—automatically dials outbound calls and when someone answers, the call is forwarded to an available agent.

Contact centers also track customer call history along with problem resolutions—information critical for providing a comprehensive customer view to the CSR. CSRs who can quickly comprehend and understand all of a customer's products and issues provide tremendous value to the customer and the organization. Nothing makes frustrated customers happier than not having to explain their problems to yet another CSR.

Web-Based Self-Service

Web-based self-service systems allow customers to use the Web to find answers to their questions or solutions to their problems. FedEx uses Web-based self-service systems to allow customers to track their own packages without having to talk to a CSR. Any FedEx customer can simply log onto FedEx's Web site and enter their tracking number. The Web site quickly displays the exact location of the package and the estimated delivery time.

Another great feature of Web-based self-service is click-to-talk buttons. *Click-to-talk* buttons allow customers to click on a button and talk with a CSR via the Internet. Powerful customer driven features like these add tremendous value to any organization by providing customers with real-time information without having to contact company representatives.[6]

Call Scripting

Being a CSR is not an easy task, especially when the CSR is dealing with detailed technical products or services. *Call scripting systems* access organizational databases that track similar issues or questions and automatically generate the details to the CSR who can then relay them to the customer. The system can even provide a list of questions that the CSR can ask the customer to determine the potential problem and resolution. This feature helps CSRs answer difficult questions quickly while also presenting a uniform image so two different customers do not receive two different answers.

Documedics is a health care consulting company that provides reimbursement information about pharmaceutical products to patients and health care professionals. The company currently supports inquiries for 12 pharmaceutical companies and receives over 30,000 customer calls per month. Originally, the company had a data file for each patient and for each pharmaceutical company. This inefficient process resulted in the potential for a single patient to have up to 12 different information files if the patient was a client of all 12 pharmaceutical companies. To answer customer questions a CSR had to download each customer file causing tremendous inefficiencies and confusion.

The company implemented a CRM system with a call scripting feature to alleviate the problem and provide its CSRs with a comprehensive view of every customer, regardless of the pharmaceutical company. The company anticipates 20 percent growth over the next year primarily because of the successful implementation of its new system.[7]

Analytical CRM Information Examples	
1. **Give customers more of what they want**	Analytical CRM can help an organization go beyond the typical "Dear Mr. Smith" salutation. An organization can use its analytical CRM information to make its communications more personable. For example, if it knows a customer's shoe size and preferred brand it can notify the customer that there is a pair of size 12 shoes set aside for them to try on the next time they visit the store.
2. **Find new customers similar to the best customers**	Analytical CRM might determine that an organization does a lot of business with women 35–45 years old who drive SUVs and live within 30 miles of a certain location. The company can then find a mailing list that highlights this type of customer for potential new sales.
3. **Find out what the organization does best**	Analytical CRM can determine what an organization does better than its competitors. For example, if a restaurant caters more breakfasts to mid-sized companies than its competition does, it can purchase a specialized mailing list of mid-sized companies in the area and send them a mailing that features the breakfast catering specials.
4. **Beat competitors to the punch**	Analytical CRM can determine sales trends allowing an organization to offer the best customers deals before the competition has a chance to. For example, a clothing store might determine its best customers for outdoor apparel and send them an offer to attend a private sale right before the competition runs their outdoor apparel sale.
5. **Reactivate inactive customers**	Analytical CRM can highlight customers who have not done any business with the organization in a while. The organization can then send them a personalized letter along with a discount coupon. It will remind them of the company and may help spark a renewed relationship.
6. **Let customers know they matter**	Analytical CRM can determine what customers want and need, so an organization can contact them with this information. Anything from a private sale to a reminder that the car is due for a tune-up is excellent customer service.

Analytical CRM

Analytical CRM relies heavily on data warehousing technologies and business intelligence to glean insights into customer behavior. These systems quickly aggregate, analyze, and disseminate customer information throughout an organization. Figure B4.7 displays a few examples of the kind of information insights analytical CRM can help an organization gain.

Data warehouses are providing businesses with information about their customers and products that was previously impossible to locate, and the resulting payback can be tremendous. Organizations are now relying on business intelligence to provide them with hard facts that can determine everything from which type of marketing and sales campaign to launch, to which customers to target, at what time. Using CRM along with business intelligence allows organizations to make better, more informed decisions and to reap amazing unforeseen rewards.

Sears, Roebuck and Company is the United States' third-largest retailer. Over the past two decades there has been a well-publicized encroachment by discount mass merchandisers. Even though Sears does not know exactly "who" its customers are (by name and address) since many customers use cash or non-Sears credit cards, it can still benefit from analytical CRM technologies. Sears uses these technologies to determine what its generic customers prefer to buy and when they buy it, which enables the company to predict what they will buy. Using analytical CRM, Sears can view each day's sales by region, district, store, product line, and individual item. Sears can now monitor the precise impact of advertising, weather, and other factors on sales of specific items. For the first time, Sears can even group together, or "cluster," widely divergent types of items. For example, merchandisers can track sales of a store display marked "Gifts under $25" that might include sweatshirts, screwdrivers, and other unrelated items. The advertising department can then follow the sales of "Gifts under $25" to determine which products to place in its newspaper advertisements.

Current Trends: SRM, PRM, and ERM

Organizations are discovering a wave of other key business areas where it is beneficial to take advantage of building strong relationships. These oncoming areas include supplier relationship management (SRM), partner relationship management (PRM), and employee relationship management (ERM).

SUPPLIER RELATIONSHIP MANAGEMENT

Supplier relationship management (SRM) focuses on keeping suppliers satisfied by evaluating and categorizing suppliers for different projects, which optimizes supplier selection. SRM applications help companies analyze vendors based on a number of key variables including strategy, business goals, prices, and markets. The company can then determine the best supplier to collaborate with and can work on developing strong supplier relationships with that supplier. The partners can then work together to streamline processes, outsource services, and provide products that they could not provide individually.

With the merger of the Bank of Halifax and Bank of Scotland, the new company, HBOS, implemented an SRM system to supply consistent information to its suppliers. The system integrates procurement information from the separate Bank of Halifax and Bank of Scotland operational systems, generating a single repository of management information for consistent reporting and analysis. Other benefits HBOS derived from the SRM solution include:

- A single consolidated view of all suppliers.
- Consistent, detailed management information allowing multiple views for every executive.
- Elimination of duplicate suppliers.[8]

PARTNER RELATIONSHIP MANAGEMENT

Organizations have begun to realize the importance of building relationships with partners, dealers, and resellers. *Partner relationship management (PRM)* focuses on keeping vendors satisfied by managing alliance partner and reseller relationships that provide customers with the optimal sales channel. PRM's business strategy is to select and manage partners to optimize their long-term value to an organization. In effect, it means picking the right partners, working with them to help them be successful in dealing with mutual customers, and ensuring that partners and the ultimate end customers are satisfied and successful. Many of the features of a PRM application include real-time product information on availability, marketing materials, contracts, order details, and pricing, inventory, and shipping information.

PRM is one of the smaller segments of CRM that has superb potential. PRM has grown from a $500 million business in 2001 to a $1 billion business in 2003. This is a direct reflection of the growing interdependency of organizations in the new economy. The primary benefits of PRM include:

- Expanding market coverage.
- Offerings of specialized products and services.
- Broadened range of offerings and a more complete solution.

EMPLOYEE RELATIONSHIP MANAGEMENT

Employee relationship management (ERM) provides employees with a subset of CRM applications available through a Web browser. Many of the ERM applications assist the employee in dealing with customers by providing detailed information on company products, services, and customer orders. Applications offer expense tracing, project management tracking, performance appraisals, training, benefits, and company news.

Grupo Gas Natural is a Spanish energy services organization that focuses on supply, commercialization, and distribution of natural gas in Spain and Latin America. The company implemented ERM and PRM systems to strengthen its market dominance. The PRM system extends access to third-party business partners such as energy-equipment installers allowing the scheduling of local independent installation technicians for Gas Natural customer visits. The company also implemented an ERM system to enhance communication throughout the organization by providing employees with a browser-based approach to managing activities and sharing strategic company information. The new systems are enabling the company to reach its goal of becoming a multiproduct, customer-centric organization.[9]

Future Trends

In the future, CRM applications will continue to change from employee-only tools to tools used by suppliers, partners, and even customers. Providing a consistent view of customers and delivering timely and accurate customer information to all departments across an organization will continue to be the major goal of CRM initiatives.

As technology advances (intranet, Internet, extranet, wireless), CRM will continue to be a major strategic focus for companies, particularly in industries whose product is difficult to differentiate. Some companies approach this problem by moving to a low-cost producer strategy. CRM will be an alternative way to pursue a differentiation strategy with a nondifferentiatable product.

CRM applications will continue to adapt wireless capabilities supporting mobile sales and mobile customers. Sales professionals will be able to access e-mail, order details, corporate information, inventory status, and opportunity information all from a PDA in their car or on a plane. Real-time interaction with human CSRs over the Internet will continue to increase.

CRM suites will also incorporate PRM and SRM modules as enterprises seek to take advantage of these initiatives. Automating interactions with distributors, resellers, and suppliers will enhance the corporation's ability to deliver a quality experience to its customers.

As organizations begin to migrate from the traditional product-focused organization toward customer-driven organizations, they are recognizing their customers as experts, not just revenue generators. Organizations are quickly realizing that without customers they simply would not exist and it is critical they do everything they can to ensure their customers' satisfaction. In an age when product differentiation is difficult, CRM is one of the most valuable assets a company can acquire.

Sales, marketing, and customer service departments can implement many different types of CRM technologies that can assist in the difficult tasks of customer identification, segmentation, and prediction (see Figure B4.8).

Analytical CRM relies on data warehousing and business intelligence to find insights into customer information in order to build stronger relationships. Organizations are also discovering a wave of other key business areas where it is beneficial to take advantage of building strong relationships including supplier relationship management (SRM), partner relationship management (PRM), and employee relationship management (ERM). The sooner a company embraces CRM the better off it will be and the harder it will be for competitors to steal loyal and devoted customers.

Operational CRM Technologies		
Marketing	**Sales**	**Customer Service**
1. List Generator	1. Sales Management	1. Contact Center
2. Campaign Management	2. Contact Management	2. Web-Based Self-Service
3. Cross-Selling and Up-Selling	3. Opportunity Management	3. Call Scripting

FIGURE B4.8

Operational CRM Technologies for Sales, Marketing, and Customer Service Departments

Analytical CRM, 262
Automatic call distribution, 269
Call scripting system, 269
Campaign management
    system, 265
Click-to-talk, 269
Contact center, 268
Contact management
    system, 267
Cross-selling, 265
Customer relationship
    management (CRM), 262

Employee relationship
    management (ERM), 272
Interactive voice response
    (IVR), 269
List generator, 265
Operational CRM, 262
Opportunity management
    system, 267
Partner relationship
    management (PRM), 271
Predictive dialing, 269

Sales force automation
    (SFA), 266
Sales management system, 266
Supplier relationship
    management (SRM), 271
Up-selling, 265
Web-based self-service
    system, 269

Fighting Cancer with Information

"The mission of the American Cancer Society (ACS) is to cure cancer and relieve the pain and suffering caused by this insidious disease," states Zachary Patterson, chief information officer, ACS.

The ACS is a nationwide voluntary health organization dedicated to eliminating cancer as a major health problem by supporting research, education, advocacy, and volunteer service. Headquartered in Atlanta, Georgia, with 17 divisions and more than 3,400 local offices throughout the United States, the ACS represents the largest source of private nonprofit cancer research funds in the United States.

To support its mission, the ACS must perform exceptionally well in three key areas. First, it must be able to provide its constituents—more than 2 million volunteers, patients, and donors—with the best information available regarding the prevention, detection, and treatment of cancer. Second, ACS must be able to demonstrate that it acts responsibly with the funds entrusted to it by the public. "Among other things, that means being able to provide exceptional service when someone calls our call center with a question about mammography screening or our latest antismoking campaign," says Terry Music, national vice president for Information Delivery at the ACS. Third, ACS must be able to continually secure donations of time and money from its constituent base. Its success in this area is directly related to providing excellent information and service, as well as having an integrated view of its relationship with constituents. "To succeed, we need to understand the full extent of each constituent's relationship with us so we can determine where there might be opportunities to expand that relationship," says Music.

The ACS was experiencing many challenges with its current information. "Our call center agents did not know, for example, if a caller was both a donor and a volunteer, or if a caller was volunteering for the Society in multiple ways," he says. "This splintered view made it challenging for American Cancer Society representatives to deliver personalized service and make informed recommendations regarding other opportunities within the Society that might interest a caller."

The ACS chose to implement a customer relationship management solution to solve its information issues. Critical to the CRM system's success was consolidating information from various databases across the organization to provide a single view of constituents and all information required to serve them. After an evaluation process that included participation from individuals across the organization, the ACS chose Siebel Systems as its CRM solution provider. The Society wanted to work with a company that could address both its immediate needs with a best-in-class e-business solution and its future requirements.

The Siebel Call Center is specifically designed for the next generation of contact centers, enabling organizations to provide world-class customer service, generate increased revenue, and create a closed-loop information flow seamlessly over multichannel sales, marketing, and customer service operations. Siebel Call Center empowers agents at every level by providing up-to-the-minute information and in-depth customer and product knowledge. This approach enables quick and accurate problem resolution and generates greater relationship opportunities. The ACS has received numerous benefits from the system including:

1. Increased constituent satisfaction and loyalty by supporting personalized interactions between constituents and cancer information specialists.
2. Improved productivity of cancer information specialists by consolidating all information required to serve constituents into a single view.
3. Increased donations of time and money by helping call center agents identify callers who are likely to be interested in expanding their relationship with the ACS.[10]

Questions

1. Explain how the ACS's marketing department could use operational CRM to strengthen its relationships with its customers.
2. Explain how the ACS's customer service department could use operational CRM to strengthen its relationships with its customers.

3. Review all of the operational CRM technologies and determine which one would add the greatest value to ACS's business.

4. Describe the benefits ACS could gain from using analytical CRM.

5. Summarize SRM and describe how ACS could use it to increase efficiency in its business.

CLOSING CASE TWO

Calling All Canadians

With multiple communication channels available and so many CRM failures, many companies are concluding that the best method for providing customer service is good old-fashioned customer service provided by a real live person. At the same time while companies consider outsourcing their customer service departments to other countries in order to save money, many worry about foreign accents as well as time-zone issues related to offshore outsourcing.

Canada has become one of the primary targets for outsourcing customer service centers by U.S. companies. Not only are accent and time-zone issues nonexistent, but companies also receive a favorable exchange rate. The Bank of Canada estimates that over the past five years, the currency exchange rate between the United States and Canada favors Americans by 44 percent. For every dollar an American business spends in Canada, it receives over a dollar and a half in goods and services.

Additional factors that make Canada even more attractive include a high Canadian unemployment rate estimated at 7.5 percent in 2003, while the U.S. unemployment rate was 5.9 percent. Canadians also have high education rates with 63 percent of Canadians over the age of 15 being high school graduates. The country's predominantly rural population and strong work ethic along with a declining industrial base have made call center outsourcing an attractive solution for Canada, too.

Canada has been a leader in the call center industry for over a decade. Since the early 1990s, "the Canadian call center industry has grown at an annual rate of 20 percent," according to Steve Demmings, president of Site Selection Canada of Winnipeg, Manitoba. Site Selection Canada promotes and assists site selection for American and Canadian firms. Demmings estimates there are 14,000 call centers in Canada with six or more agents employing 500,000 people, contributing about $36 billion (Canadian) in annual salaries.

In 1994, two Canadian provinces—Manitoba and New Brunswick—made a concerted effort to develop a local call center industry, recognizing the area's high unemployment with little native industry, says Demmings. The other provinces soon followed. Then the call center industry "made a big move" to bring educational institutions on board. "Many colleges have set up call center training programs," Demmings reports. The result has been an established industry with an excellent skilled labor pool. "American companies come up here to go shopping and we need to have the tableware on the table," states Demmings.

What is important to outsourcing buyers is that many Canadian call center customer service representatives have made it their career. Consequently, there is a much lower turnover rate for call centers than in the United States. Demmings reports the CSR turnover rate in the Province of Ontario was 18.3 percent last year. Compare that to the United States, where call center staffing can be a problem. Christopher Fletcher, vice president and research director of CRM for the Aberdeen Group, states, "It is tough to find people to staff a call center. Turnover ranges from 25 percent to 50 percent annually or above. The skill sets of the people you have available are often equivalent to McDonald's."[11]

Questions

1. What are the two different types of CRM and how can they be used to help an organization gain a competitive advantage?

2. Explain how a contact center (or call center) can help an organization achieve its CRM goals.

3. Describe three ways an organization can perform CRM functions over the Internet.

4. How will outsourcing contact centers (call centers) to Canada change as future CRM technologies replace current CRM technologies?

MAKING BUSINESS DECISION

1. Driving Up Profits with Successful Campaigns

Classic Cars Inc. operates high-end automotive dealerships that offer luxury cars along with luxury service. The company is proud of its extensive inventory, top-of-the-line mechanics, and especially its exceptional service, which even includes a cappuccino bar at each dealership.

The company currently has 40 sales representatives at four locations. Each location maintains its own computer systems and all sales representatives have their own contact management systems. This splintered approach to operations causes numerous problems including customer communication issues, pricing strategy issues, and inventory control issues. A few examples include:

- A customer shopping at one dealership can go to another dealership and receive a quote for a different price for the same car.
- Sales representatives are frequently stealing each other's customers and commissions.
- Sales representatives frequently send their customers to other dealerships to see specific cars and when the customer arrives, the car is not on the lot.
- Marketing campaigns are not designed to target specific customers; they are typically generic, such as 10 percent off a new car.
- If a sales representative quits, all of his/her customer information is lost.

You are working for Customer One, a small consulting company that specializes in CRM strategies. The owner of Classic Cars Inc., Tom Repicci, has hired you to help him formulate a strategy to put his company back on track. Develop a proposal for Tom detailing how a CRM system can alleviate the company's issues and create new opportunities.

2. Searching for Employee Loyalty

You are the CEO of Razz, a start-up Web-based search company, which is planning to compete directly with Google. The company had an exceptional first year and is currently receiving over 500,000 hits a day from customers all over the world. You have hired 250 people in the last four months, doubling the size of your organization. With so many new employees starting so quickly you are concerned about how your company's culture will evolve and whether your employees are receiving enough attention. You are already familiar with customer relationship management and how CRM systems can help an organization create strong customer relationships. However, you are unfamiliar with employee relationship management and you are wondering what ERM systems might be able to offer your employees and your company. Research the Web, create a report detailing features and functions of ERM systems, and determine what value will be added to your organization if you decide to implement an ERM solution.

3. **Creating Customer Support**

   You are the vice president of Customer Service at Health Star, one of the largest online health food distributors in the country. The company is currently receiving a tremendous number of calls regarding products, orders, and shipping information. Draft a proposal for a strategy to implement a contact center that can address the company's issues.

4. **Increasing Revenues with CRM**

   Cold Cream is one of the premier beauty supply stores in the metro New York area. People come from all over to sample the store's unique creams, lotions, makeup, and perfumes. The store is four stories high with each department located on a separate floor. The company would like to implement a CRM system to help it better understand its customers and their purchasing habits. Create a report summarizing CRM systems and detail how such a system can directly influence Cold Cream's revenues.

PLUG-IN

B5

Enterprise Resource Planning

Introduction

The core units discussed *enterprise resource planning (ERP),* which integrates all departments and functions throughout an organization into a single IT system (or integrated set of IT systems) so that employees can make enterprisewide decisions by viewing enterprisewide information on all business operations. This plug-in focuses on the two basic groups of ERP systems—core and extended.

Core and Extended ERP Components

Turner Industries grew from $300 million in sales to $800 million in sales in less than 10 years thanks to the implementation of an ERP system. Ranked number 369 on the Forbes 500 list of privately held companies, Turner Industries is a leading industrial services firm. Turner Industries develops and deploys advanced software applications designed to maximize the productivity of its 25,000 employees and construction equipment valued at more than $100 million.

The company considers the biggest challenges in the industrial services industry to be completing projects on time, within budget, while fulfilling customers' expectations. To meet these challenges the company invested in an ERP system and named the project Interplan. Interplan won Constructech's 2000 Vision award for software innovation in the heavy construction industry. Interplan runs all of Turner's construction, turnaround, shutdown, and maintenance projects and is so

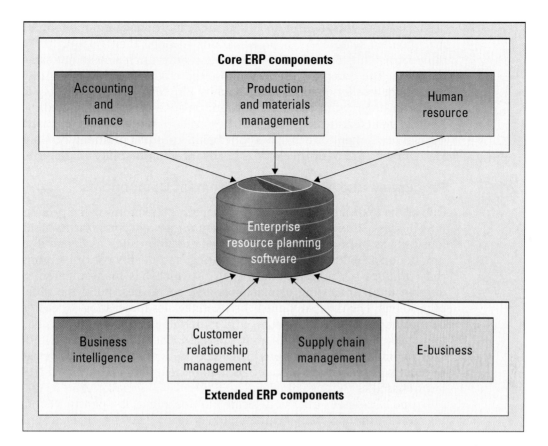

FIGURE B5.1

Core ERP Components
and Extended ERP
Components

adept at estimating and planning jobs that Turner Industries typically achieves higher profit margins on projects that use Interplan. As the ERP solution makes the company more profitable, the company can pass on the cost savings to its customers, giving the company an incredible competitive advantage.[1]

Figure B5.1 provides an example of an ERP system with its core and extended components. **Core ERP components** are the traditional components included in most ERP systems and they primarily focus on internal operations. **Extended ERP components** are the extra components that meet the organizational needs not covered by the core components and primarily focus on external operations.

CORE ERP COMPONENTS

The three most common *core* ERP components focusing on internal operations are:

1. Accounting and finance.
2. Production and materials management.
3. Human resource.

Accounting and Finance Components

Deeley Harley-Davidson Canada (DHDC), the exclusive Canadian distributor of Harley-Davidson motorcycles, has improved inventory, turnaround time, margins, and customer satisfaction—all with the implementation of a financial ERP system. The system has opened up the power of information to the company and is helping it make strategic decisions when it still has the time to impact and change things. The ERP system provides the company with ways to manage inventory, turnaround time, and utilize warehouse space more effectively.[2]

Accounting and finance components manage accounting data and financial processes within the enterprise with functions such as general ledger, accounts payable, accounts receivable, budgeting, and asset management. One of the most useful features included in an ERP accounting/finance component is its credit-management feature. Most organizations manage their relationships with customers by setting credit limits, or a limit on how much a customer can owe at any one time. The company then monitors the credit limit whenever the customer places a new order or sends in a payment. ERP financial systems help to correlate customer orders with customer account balances determining credit availability. Another great feature is the ability to perform product profitability analysis. ERP financial components are the backbone behind product profitability analysis and allow companies to perform all types of advanced profitability modeling techniques.

Production and Materials Management Components

One of the main functions of an ERP system is streamlining the production planning process. ***Production and materials management components*** handle the various aspects of production planning and execution such as demand forecasting, production scheduling, job cost accounting, and quality control. Companies typically produce multiple products, each of which has many different parts. Production lines, consisting of machines and employees, build the different types of products. The company must then define sales forecasting for each product to determine production schedules and materials purchasing. Figure B5.2 displays the typical ERP production planning process. The process begins with forecasting sales in order to plan operations. A detailed production schedule is developed if the product is produced and a materials requirement plan is completed if the product is purchased.

Grupo Farmanova Intermed, located in Costa Rica, is a pharmaceutical marketing and distribution company that markets nearly 2,500 products to approximately 500 customers in Central and South America. The company identified a need for software that could unify product logistics management in a single country. It decided to deploy PeopleSoft financial and distribution ERP components allowing the company to improve customer data management, increase confidence among internal and external users, and coordinate the logistics of inventory. With the new PeopleSoft software the company enhanced its capabilities for handling, distributing, and marketing its pharmaceuticals.[3]

FIGURE B5.2

The Production
Planning Process

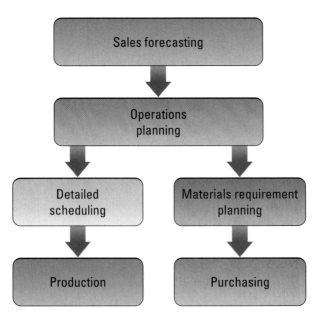

Human Resource Components

Human resource components track employee information including payroll, benefits, compensation, performance assessment, and assume compliance with the legal requirements of multiple jurisdictions and tax authorities. Human resource components even offer features that allow the organization to perform detailed analysis on its employees to determine such things as the identification of individuals who are likely to leave the company unless additional compensation or benefits are provided. These components can also identify which employees are using which resources, such as online training and long distance telephone services. They can also help determine whether the most talented people are working for those business units with the highest priority—or where they would have the greatest impact on profit.

EXTENDED ERP COMPONENTS

Extended ERP components are the extra components that meet the organizational needs not covered by the core components and primarily focus on external operations. There are numerous extended ERP components and many of these are Internet enabled and require interaction with customers, suppliers, and business partners outside the organization. The four most common extended ERP components are:

1. Business intelligence.
2. Customer relationship management.
3. Supply chain management.
4. E-business.

Business Intelligence Components

ERP systems offer powerful tools that measure and control organizational operations. Many organizations have found that these valuable tools can be enhanced to provide even greater value through the addition of powerful business intelligence systems. *Business intelligence* describes information that people use to support their decision-making efforts. The business intelligence components of ERP systems typically collect information used throughout the organization (including data used in many other ERP components), organize it, and apply analytical tools to assist managers with decisions. Data warehouses are one of the most popular extensions to ERP systems, with over two-thirds of U.S. manufacturers adopting or planning such systems.[4]

Customer Relationship Management Components

ERP vendors are expanding their functionality to provide services formerly supplied by customer relationship management (CRM) vendors such as PeopleSoft and Siebel. *Customer relationship management (CRM)* involves managing all aspects of a customer's relationship with an organization to increase customer loyalty and retention and an organization's profitability. CRM components provide an integrated view of customer data and interactions allowing organizations to work more effectively with customers and be more responsive to their needs. CRM components typically include contact centers, sales force automation, and marketing functions. These improve the customer experience while identifying a company's most (and least) valuable customers for better allocation of resources.

Supply Chain Management Components

ERP vendors are expanding their functionality to provide services formerly supplied by supply chain management vendors such as i2 Technologies and Manugistics. *Supply chain management (SCM)* involves the management of information flows between and among stages in a supply chain to maximize total supply chain effectiveness and profitability. SCM components help an organization to plan, schedule, control, and optimize the supply chain from its acquisition of raw materials to the receipt of finished goods by customers.

E-Business Components

The original focus of ERP systems was the internal organization. In other words, ERP systems are not fundamentally ready for the external world of e-business. The newest and most exciting extended ERP components are the e-business components. *E-business* means conducting business on the Internet, not only buying and selling, but also serving customers and collaborating with business partners. Two of the primary features of e-business components are e-logistics and e-procurement. *E-logistics* manages the transportation and storage of goods. *E-procurement* is the business-to-business (B2B) purchase and sale of supplies and services over the Internet.

E-business and ERP complement each other by allowing companies to establish a Web presence and fulfill orders expeditiously. A common mistake made by many businesses is deploying a Web presence before the integration of back-office systems or an ERP system. For example, one large toy manufacturer announced less than a week before Christmas that it would be unable to fulfill any of its Web orders. The company had all the toys in the warehouse, but unfortunately it could not organize the basic order processing function to get the toys delivered to the consumers on time.

Customers and suppliers are now demanding access to ERP information including order status, inventory levels, and invoice reconciliation. To make matters even worse the customers and partners want all this information in a simplified format available through a Web site. This is a difficult task to accomplish because most ERP systems are full of technical jargon, which is why employee training is one of the hidden costs associated with ERP implementations. Removing the jargon to accommodate untrained customers and partners is one of the more difficult tasks when Web-enabling an ERP system. To accommodate the growing needs of the e-business world, ERP vendors need to build two new channels of access into the ERP system information—one channel for customers (B2C) and one channel for businesses, suppliers, and partners (B2B).[5]

ERP Benefits and Risks (Cost)

There is no guarantee of success for an ERP system. ERPs focus on how a corporation operates internally and optimizing these operations takes significant time and energy. An organization should expect that it will take time, even years, to see tangible results from an ERP solution. According to Meta Group, it takes the average company a total of 8 to 18 months to see any benefits from an ERP system. The good news is that the average savings from new ERP systems are $1.6 million per year. Figure B5.3 displays a list of the five most common benefits an organization can expect to achieve from a successful ERP implementation.[6]

Along with understanding the benefits an organization can gain from an ERP system, it is just as important to understand the primary risk associated with an ERP implementation—cost. ERP systems do not come cheap. Meta Group recently published a study looking at the total cost of ownership (TCO) for an ERP system. The study included hardware, software, professional services, and internal staff costs. Sixty-three companies were surveyed ranging in size from small to large over a variety of industries. The average TCO was $15 million (highest $300 million and lowest $400,000). The price tag for an ERP system can easily start in the multiple millions of dollars and implementation can take an average of 23 months. Figure B5.4 displays a few of the costs associated with an ERP system.

Common ERP Benefits

1. **Integrate financial information:** In order to understand organizations' overall performance they must have a single financial view.

2. **Integrate customer order information:** With all customer order information in a single system it is easier to coordinate manufacturing, inventory, and shipping in order to send a common message to customers regarding order status.

3. **Standardize and speed up manufacturing processes:** ERP systems provide standard methods for manufacturing companies to use when automating steps in the manufacturing process. Standardizing manufacturing processes across an organization saves time, increases production, and reduces head count.

4. **Reduce inventory:** With the improved visibility into the order fulfillment process, an organization can reduce inventories and streamline deliveries to its customers.

5. **Standardize human resource information:** ERPs provide a unified method for tracking employees' time, as well as communicating HR benefits and services.

FIGURE B5.3

Common Benefits Received from ERP Systems

Associated ERP Costs

Software cost: Purchasing the software.

Consulting fees: Hiring external experts to help implement the system correctly.

Process rework: Redefining processes in order to ensure the company is using the most efficient and effective processes.

Customization: If the software package does not meet all of the companies needs, it may be required to customize the software.

Integration and testing: Ensuring all software products, including disparate systems not part of the ERP system, are working together or are integrated. Testing the ERP system includes testing all integrations.

Training: Training all new users.

Data warehouse integration and data conversion: Moving data from an old system into the new ERP system.

FIGURE B5.4

Associated ERP Costs

The Future of ERP

ERP places new demands not only on support and delivery information technology, but also on the way business processes have to be designed, implemented, monitored, and maintained. For example, several persons in different locations and with different hardware and software resources may simultaneously initiate a purchase process for the same product but with different selection criteria. Reliability, efficiency, and scalability are among the features that have to be embedded in e-business processes in ERP systems. Despite the rapid growth in the number of ERP installations, conducting ERP operations is still challenging.

Understanding the many different types of core and extended ERP components can help an organization determine which components will add the most value. The three biggest vendors in the ERP market are PeopleSoft, Oracle, and SAP. Figure B5.5 is an overview of a few of the components currently offered by each ERP vendor.

In the future, the line between ERP, SCM, and CRM will continue to blur as ERP vendors broaden the functionality of their product suites and redefine the packaging of their products. ERP vendors with comprehensive but modular components

PeopleSoft	
Component	**Description**
Application Integration	Integrate PeopleSoft and non-PeopleSoft applications at all levels with Portal Solutions, AppConnect, and Data Warehousing and Analytic Solutions.
Customer Relationship Management	Get immediate, seamless integration among customer, financial, supply chain, and employee management systems.
Enterprise Performance Management	Enable customers, suppliers, and employees to connect to set goals, develop plans, and measure progress with our integrated, scalable applications.
Financial Management	Get the power to compete in the business world with a comprehensive suite of pure Internet financial applications.
Human Capital Management (including Human Resources Management Solutions)	Manage and mobilize a unified, global workforce, and align workforce contribution with business objectives.
Service Automation	Optimize project investments, reduce project delivery costs, and maximize resources to increase utilization and value to your organization.
Supplier Relationship Management	Manage all aspects of supplier relationships including indirect and direct goods, as well as services procurement.
Supply Chain Management	Take advantage of solutions that promote business-to-business interaction throughout the supply chain, from customer to supplier.

Oracle	
Component	**Description**
Oracle Financials	Financial applications manage the flow of cash and assets into, out of, and within your enterprise: tracking thousands of transactions, setting fiscal goals for various departments, and allowing you to project future financial health as you record today's profits.
Oracle Human Resources Management	Oracle Human Resources Management System (HRMS) empowers businesses with the tools to find, extract, and analyze data related to human capital. This intelligence readies a company to rapidly deploy the best resources for maximum employee productivity, satisfaction, and retention.
Oracle Intelligence	Oracle Daily Business Intelligence accesses and shares unified information and analysis across the enterprise with a single definition of customers, suppliers, employees, and products.
Oracle Learning Management	Oracle Learning Management (Oracle iLearning, Oracle Training Management, and Oracle Human Resources Management System) provides a complete infrastructure that lets organizations manage, deliver, and track training, in both online and classroom environments.
Oracle Supply Chain Management	Oracle Supply Chain Management lets organizations gain global visibility, automate internal processes, and readily collaborate with suppliers, customers, and partners.
Oracle Manufacturing	Oracle Manufacturing optimizes production capacity beginning with raw materials through final products.
Oracle Order Management	Oracle's support of the complete fulfillment process from order to cash.
Oracle Marketing	Oracle Marketing drives profit by intelligently marketing to the most profitable customers. By leveraging a single repository of customer information, marketing professionals can better target and personalize their campaigns, and refine them in real time with powerful analytical tools.
Oracle Projects	To consistently deliver on time and on budget, an organization must fine-tune execution, align global organization with projects, and assign the right resources to the most important initiatives at the right time.
Oracle Sales	Oracle Sales allows an organization to learn more about its entire business to identify and target profitable opportunities.

FIGURE B5.5

Enterprise Resource Planning Vendor Components *(continued on next page)*

will dominate the next high-growth phase of the enterprise applications market. Since core functionality is virtually the same for all vendors, a vendor's success will primarily depend upon how quickly it incorporates other kinds of functionality such as the Internet, interface, and wireless technology.

SAP	
Component	**Description**
mySAP™ Customer Relationship Management	The fully integrated CRM solution that facilitates world-class service across all customer touchpoints.
mySAP™ Financials	The leading solution for operational, analytical, and collaborative financial management.
mySAP™ Human Resources (mySAP HR)	The HR resource that helps more than 7,800 organizations worldwide maximize their return on human capital.
mySAP™ Marketplace	An online marketplace solution that allows your company to buy, sell, and conduct business around the clock and around the world.
mySAP™ Product Lifecycle Management	The collaborative solution that helps designers, engineers, and suppliers achieve new levels of innovation.
mySAP™ Supplier Relationship Management	Covers the full supply cycle—from strategic sourcing for lower costs to faster process cycles.
mySAP™ Supply Chain Management	Gives an organization the power to dramatically improve its planning, responsiveness, and execution.

FIGURE B5.5

Enterprise Resource Planning Vendor Components *(concluded)*

INTERNET

The adoption of the Internet is one of the single most important forces reshaping the architecture and functionality of ERP systems and is responsible for the most important new developments in ERP. The Internet serves as a basis for extending ERP's traditional vision of integrating data and processes across an organization's functional departments to include sharing data and processes among multiple enterprises.

INTERFACE

Most ERP suites offer a customizable browser that allows each employee to configure his/her own view of the system. A manager can also customize each employee's views of the system. This feature allows managers to control access to highly sensitive information such as payroll and performance appraisals. The same customizable browser will be used in the future to allow customers and partners to see only select ERP information via the Internet.

WIRELESS TECHNOLOGY

Wireless technologies provide a means for users with hand-held devices, such as PDAs and Web-enabled telephones, to connect to and interact with ERP systems. Most large ERP vendors will acquire smaller companies that specialize in wireless access. If they fail to do so, they will need to develop their own expertise in this area to build wireless access packages.

Wireless technologies will enable users to carry out the same transactions from their mobile devices as they used to do from any fixed device. Being able to buy and sell goods and services over mobile devices is an important step toward achieving the anywhere-anytime paradigm. In the future, location and time will no longer constrain organizations from completing their operations.

C ore ERP components are the traditional components included in most ERP systems and they primarily focus on internal operations:

- Accounting and finance components.
- Production and materials management components.
- Human resource components.

Extended ERP components are the extra components that meet the organizational needs not covered by the core components and primarily focus on external operations:

- Business intelligence.
- Customer relationship management.
- Supply chain management.
- E-business.

ERP vendors with comprehensive but modular components will dominate the next high-growth phase of the enterprise applications market. Since core functionality is virtually the same for all vendors, a vendor's success will primarily depend upon how quickly it incorporates other kinds of functionality such as the Internet, interfaces, and wireless technologies.

★ KEY TERMS

Accounting and finance
  component, 279
Business intelligence, 281
Core ERP component, 279
Customer relationship
  management (CRM), 281
E-business, 282

E-logistics, 282
Enterprise resource planning
  (ERP), 278
E-procurement, 282
Extended ERP component, 279
Human resource
  component, 281

Production and materials
  management
  component, 280
Supply chain management
  (SCM), 281

★ CLOSING CASE ONE

PepsiAmericas' Enterprises

Headquartered in Rolling Meadows, Illinois, PepsiAmericas generates $2.97 billion in revenues yearly. The company has over 15,000 employees and 365,000 customers. The challenge facing PepsiAmericas was the integration of its enterprise systems. The company chose to implement a PeopleSoft ERP solution to enable it to deliver top-line growth and superior customer service through improved selling and delivery methods using standard processes along with proven technology.

With the introduction of numerous products, distribution gaps, and lost promotion opportunities, PepsiAmericas realized it needed a new strategy for managing its enterprise. It needed real-time access to enterprise information and seamless integration between its systems. The company especially required real-time customer information for its telemarketing agents to be able to effectively do their jobs. "It's important for a tel-sell (telemarketing) agent to understand if the customer has any issues or needs based on what's going on with the account. An error in credit status, a balance history, issues they've logged with the company—all of this will have an impact on how they interact with the customer," says John Kreul, director of Enterprise Applications for PepsiAmericas.

One of the biggest benefits of the PeopleSoft ERP solution was that it provided complete integration between PepsiAmericas' front-office and back-office systems. This integration allowed tel-sell agents to gain a clear picture of customers and their relationship with the company. "We can more readily see additional sales opportunities. For example, if the customer ordered certain products in the past and there's a promotion going on for a similar product, the agents can offer that to the customer," states Kreul.

PepsiAmericas also implemented PeopleSoft's supply chain management component to automate its inventory accounting. Prior to implementing PeopleSoft SCM, portions of the company's monthly inventory accounting were done manually and took two weeks to conduct. "Now product inventory accounting is done at period end automatically. It provides us much greater control of the data and has shaven one to two days off our close," says Dave Van Volkenburg, manager of IT Applications. Transferring products from one division to another was also a problem with the old system. Differences in product quantities shipped and received would create bottlenecks and result in days spent going back and forth between divisions to determine the accurate amount of products transferred. The SCM component changed all that. "Now our divisions have to send and receive product transfers within the system—so there's much tighter control on the activity, and the data is more accurate," Van Volkenburg says.

The following are the overall benefits PepsiAmericas received from its PeopleSoft ERP solution:

- Convert disparate sales systems to a single, integrated Internet application solution.
- Integrate computer telephony for Tel-Sell/Pre-Sell methodology.
- Deliver a 360-degree view of entire customer base.
- Improve customer distribution and profit potential.
- Simplify the issue resolution process.
- Provide more accurate and timely deliveries of products.
- Reduce product inventory close time by one to two days.[7]

Questions

1. How have core ERP components helped PepsiAmericas improve its business?
2. How have extended ERP components helped PepsiAmericas improve its business?
3. Explain how future ERP systems will help PepsiAmericas increase revenues.
4. Assess the impact on PepsiAmericas' business if it failed to implement the CRM component of PeopleSoft's ERP system.
5. Review the different PeopleSoft components in Figure B5.5. Which component would you recommend PepsiAmericas implement if it decided to purchase an additional PeopleSoft component?

CLOSING CASE TWO

Demanding Chocolate

Ghirardelli, incorporated in 1852, produces some of the world's finest chocolate confections, baking chocolate, and beverages, as well as industrial products for the confectionery, bakery, dairy, and food service industries. The company is the longest continuously operating chocolate manufacturer in the United States and is one of the few companies in the world that controls the entire chocolate manufacturing process, from the cocoa bean to the finished product. The company prides itself on being a marketing-driven business and its goals are to enhance inventory control and provide timely information that support strategic decision making.

Ghirardelli improved inventory management and profitability through the implementation of an ERP system. The company operates nine production lines in a 24 × 7 × 365 facility, making on-time and real-time information critical for handling raw materials and developing production schedules. From a manufacturing point of view, the company had to have at least enough raw materials to run two weeks' worth of production. Prior to implementing the ERP system, the company's 700 employees had to make manual inventory picks and bring back pieces of paper for data entry to confirm the picks. With the Warehouse Management and Wireless Warehouse ERP components, this process is now a one-step execution. Other results Ghirardelli gained from its ERP system include:

- Real-time inventory management.
- One-step execution of inventory distribution.
- Improved customer service performance.

For the future, Ghirardelli is evaluating additional ERP components including Advanced Planning. "Now that we've streamlined a lot of our manufacturing processes with the help of our ERP system, we're seeing even more clearly how Ghirardelli could benefit from even better forecasting capabilities, so we're considering Demand Consensus," says Jerry Baughman, director of IT. In the next year, Ghirardelli also has plans to expand its implementation of Warehouse Management. "Right now, our use of Warehouse Management is focused largely in shipping and receiving. We're planning on integrating it even more closely with our manufacturing systems so that we will be able to do production reporting by using wireless scanners right off the production line," says Baughman.[8]

Questions

1. Which additional core ERP components would you recommend Ghirardelli implement?
2. Which additional extended ERP components would you recommend Ghirardelli implement?
3. How can implementing an Advanced Planning ERP component help Ghirardelli's business?

1. CRM, SCM, and ERP Vendors

Health Caring Inc. recently purchased 12 hospitals in the Denver, Colorado, area. Three of the 12 hospitals currently use SAP products for their CRM and SCM systems. The other 9 hospitals use systems from a variety of vendors including PeopleSoft, Oracle, IBM, and Microsoft. With so many separate systems it is currently impossible to track patients, nurses, doctors, inventory, food services, etc. Health Caring Inc. wants to be able to leverage economies of scale by using its buying clout to drive down prices of such things as inventory and food service, along with creating an environment for flexible staffing in the hospitals for its nurses and doctors. The company's mission is to become known as the "Hospital That Cares." Treating its patients with understanding, care, and high quality service is vitally important to the company's success.

You are the newly appointed CIO and the Board of Directors is expecting you to develop a plan for moving Health Caring Inc. into the future. The plan should include details of the issues the company is likely to experience with so many disparate systems, along with your recommendation and reasons for implementing an ERP solution.

2. Building an ERP Solution—Cirris Minerals

You are working for Cirris Minerals, a multibillion-dollar mining company, which operates over 3,000 mines in 25 countries. The company is currently looking at implementing an ERP system to help streamline its operations and manage its 150,000 employees. You are leading the team that has to make the decision as to whether the company should buy or build an ERP solution. For the most part, your company's system requirements are similar to other companies' in your industry. Compile a list of questions you would require answers to in order to make your buy vs. build decision.

3. **Building an ERP Solution—Cirris Minerals (continued)**

You (in the decision above) have recommended that Cirris Minerals implement a People-Soft ERP solution. The CEO is on board with your recommendation. However, she wants you to use a phased approach to implementation. This means you must implement the new system in phases until it is evident that the new system performs correctly. The company will implement the remaining phases as soon as the first phase is completed successfully. You must now recommend which components the company should implement first. From the table below, choose the first two components that Cirris Minerals should implement. Be sure to include the justifications for the implementation of these components.

4. **Most Popular ERP Component**

Mackenzie Coombe is currently thinking about implementing an ERP solution in her online music company, The Burford Beat. The company is generating over $12 million in revenues and is growing by 150 percent a year. Create a one-page document explaining the advantages and disadvantages of ERP systems, why ERP systems include CRM and SCM components, and why the most popular ERP component in today's marketplace is the accounting and finance core component.

5. **Increasing Revenues with ERP**

Cold Cream is one of the premier beauty supply stores in the metro New York area. People come from all over to sample the store's unique creams, lotions, makeup, and perfumes. The company receives its products from manufacturers around the globe. The company would like to implement an ERP system to help it better understand its customers and their purchasing habits. Create a report summarizing ERP systems and explain how an ERP system can directly influence Cold Cream's revenues.

PeopleSoft	
Component	**Description**
Application Integration	Integrate PeopleSoft and non-PeopleSoft applications at all levels with Portal Solutions, AppConnect, and Data Warehousing and Analytic Solutions.
Customer Relationship Management	Get immediate, seamless integration among customer, financial, supply chain, and employee management systems.
Enterprise Performance Management	Enable customers, suppliers, and employees to connect to set goals, develop plans, and measure progress with our integrated, scalable applications.
Financial Management	Get the power to compete in the business world with a comprehensive suite of pure Internet financial applications.
Human Capital Management (including Human Resources Management Solutions)	Manage and mobilize a unified, global workforce, and align workforce contribution with business objectives.
Service Automation	Optimize project investments, reduce project delivery costs, and maximize resources to increase utilization and value to your organization.
Supplier Relationship Management	Manage all aspects of supplier relationships including indirect and direct goods, as well as services procurement.
Supply Chain Management	Take advantage of solutions that promote business-to-business interaction throughout the supply chain, from customer to supplier.

Strategic Outsourcing

LEARNING OUTCOMES

1. Explain the business benefits of outsourcing.
2. Identify the three primary outsourcing options.
3. Describe the benefits and challenges of outsourcing.
4. Compare offshore outsourcing and nearshore outsourcing.
5. Summarize a list of leading offshore outsourcing countries.
6. Summarize a list of up-and-coming offshore outsourcing countries.
7. Summarize a list of rookie offshore outsourcing countries.
8. Describe the future trend of multisourcing and how it can support a business need for outsourcing.

Introduction

The core units introduced the concept of *outsourcing,* an arrangement by which one organization provides a service or services for another organization that chooses not to perform them in-house. Typically, the outsourced process or function is a noncore business activity; what is outsourced can range from high volume, repetitive processes such as electronic transaction processing to more customized services such as a help desk.

This plug-in describes outsourcing as a strategic mechanism that aligns technology initiatives and business goals, manages technology operations in a difficult business environment, and reduces operating costs. Often, companies begin the process by outsourcing nonessential business operations, which may include applications, assets, people, and other resources. As organizations realize the benefits of outsourcing, they extend this approach to other business functions or processes.

Yet outsourcing carries risks: loss of control, inflexibility, and geopolitical uncertainty. Not all functions and processes can, or should be, outsourced, at least not without careful analysis of the advantages and disadvantages.

The Outsourcing Phenomenon

The outsourcing market has experienced strong growth over the last several years because of businesses' need to focus on core competencies, Web implementation initiatives, consolidation across industries, and a tight labor pool. The outsourcing of noncore, transaction-based processes has gained significant momentum over the last few years as organizations have become more comfortable with the concept of outsourcing and its advantages.

Organizations elect to outsource for a variety of reasons. Some of these reasons are tactical, while others are strategic. In the past, outsourcing was often used tactically, as a quick-fix, short-term solution to a particular need or problem which did not form part of an overall business strategy. In recent years, many companies have begun to use strategic outsourcing where an organization works with suppliers in order to make a significant improvement in business performance.

No one would seriously expect an oil company to outsource its exploration and refining functions; pharmaceutical companies probably would not outsource their research and development; and few, if any, major automakers would consider outsourcing their production planning or marketing campaigns. These activities are core to their businesses and often the means for differentiation in the marketplace and a source of competitive advantage. Businesses outsource their noncore functions, such as payroll and IT. By outsourcing IT, most organizations can cut costs, improve service, and focus on their core business. According to research firm IDC, the worldwide IT outsourcing market will reach $164 billion by 2005.[1]

Best Buy Co. Inc. is the number one United States specialty retailer for consumer electronics, personal computers, entertainment software, and appliances. Best Buy needed to find a strategic IT partner that could help the company leverage its IT functions in order to meet its business objectives. Best Buy further wanted to integrate its disparate enterprise systems and minimize its operating expenses. Best Buy outsourced these functions to Accenture, a global management consulting, technology services, and outsourcing company. The comprehensive outsourcing relationship that drove Best Buy's transformation produced spectacular results that were measurable in every key area of its business, such as a 20 percent increase in key category revenue that translated into a $25 million profit improvement.[2]

According to PricewaterhouseCoopers' survey of CEOs from 452 of the fastest growing U.S. companies, "Businesses that outsource are growing faster, larger, and more profitably than those that do not. In addition, most of those involved in outsourcing say they are saving money and are highly satisfied with their outsourcing service providers." Figure B6.1 lists common areas for outsourcing opportunities across industries.[3]

Industry	Outsourcing Opportunities
Banking and Finance	Check and electronic payment processing, credit report issuance, delinquency management, securities, and trades processing
Insurance	Claims reporting and investigation, policy administration, check processing, risk assessment
Telecommunications	Invoice and bill production, transaction processing
Healthcare	Electronic data interchange, database management, accounting
Transportation	Ticket and order processing
Government	Loan processing, Medicaid processing
Retail	Electronic payment processing

FIGURE B6.1

Outsourcing Opportunities

The drivers behind the rapid growth of the outsourcing industry include the following:

- **Globalization:** As markets open worldwide, competition heats up. Companies may engage outsourcing service providers to deliver international services.
- **The Internet:** Barriers to entry, such as lack of capital, are dramatically reduced in the world of e-business. New competitors enter the market daily.
- **Growing economy and low unemployment rate:** Building a competitive workforce is much harder and more expensive.
- **Technology:** Technology is advancing at such an accelerated rate that companies often lack the resources, workforce, or expertise to keep up.
- **Deregulation:** As private industries such as telecommunications and energy deregulate, markets open and competition increases.

OUTSOURCING BENEFITS

The many benefits associated with outsourcing include:

- Increased quality and efficiency of a process, service, or function.
- Reduced operating expenses.
- Outsourcing noncore processes or nonrevenue producing areas allows businesses to focus resources on their core profit-generating competencies.
- Reduced exposure to risks involved with large capital investments.
- Access to outsourcing service provider's economies of scale.
- Access to outsourcing services provider's expertise and best-in-class practices.
- Access to advanced technologies.
- Increased flexibility with the ability to respond quickly to changing market demands.
- Avoid costly outlay of capital funds.
- Reduced headcount and associated overhead expense.
- Reduced frustration and expense related to hiring and retaining employees in an exceptionally tight job market.
- Reduced time to market for products or services.

FIGURE B6.2

Outsourcing Models and Cost Savings

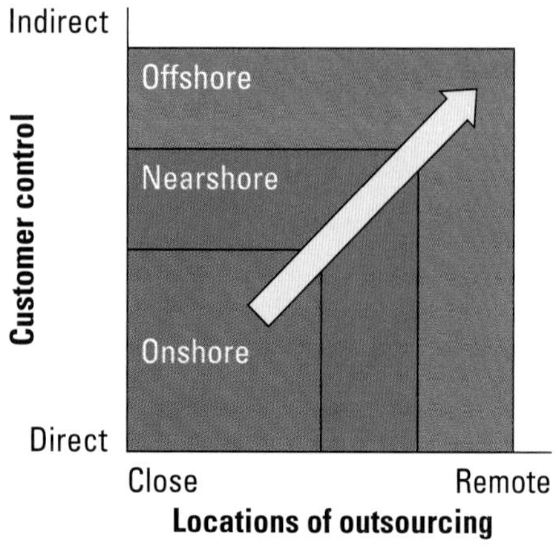

Locations of outsourcing

Outsourcing Options

In the early 1990s, British Petroleum (BP) began looking at IT outsourcing as a way to radically reduce costs and gain more flexible and higher quality IT resources that directly improve the overall business. Over the past decade, all companies within the global BP Group have incorporated outsourcing initiatives in their business plans. BP's information technology costs were reduced by 40 percent globally over the first three years of the outsourcing engagement and have continued at a 10 percent reduction year after year, leading to hundreds of millions of dollars in savings to BP.

Information technology outsourcing enables organizations to keep up with market and technology advances—with less strain on human and financial resources and more assurance that the IT infrastructure will keep pace with evolving business priorities (see Figure B6.2). Planning, deploying, and managing IT environments is both a tactical and a strategic challenge that must take into account a company's organizational, industrial, and technological concerns. There are three different forms of outsourcing options:

Category	Country
Leaders	India, Canada, China, Czech Republic, Hungary, Ireland, Israel, Mexico, Northern Ireland, Philippines, Poland, Russia, South Africa
Up-and-comers	Argentina, Belarus, Brazil, Caribbean, Egypt, Estonia, Latvia, Lithuania, New Zealand, Singapore, Ukraine, Venezuela
Rookies	Bangladesh, Cuba, Ghana, Korea, Malaysia, Mauritius, Nepal, Senegal, Sri Lanka, Taiwan, Thailand, Vietnam

1. **Onshore outsourcing** is the process of engaging another company within the same country for services.

2. **Nearshore outsourcing** refers to contracting an outsourcing arrangement with a company in a nearby country. Often this country will share a border with the native country.

3. **Offshore outsourcing** is using organizations from developing countries to write code and develop systems. In offshore outsourcing the country is geographically far away. Figure B6.3 illustrates the "Who's Who" in offshore outsourcing, such as India, the Ukraine, and the Philippines.

For many companies, certain IT services, such as application development, maintenance, and help desk support, fall within the category of functions that are ideal for outsourcing, including offshore outsourcing.

OFFSHORE OUTSOURCING

Since the mid-1990s, major U.S. companies have been sending significant portions of their software development work offshore—primarily to vendors in India, but also to vendors in China, Eastern Europe (including Russia), Ireland, Israel, and the Philippines. The big selling point for offshore outsourcing to these countries is "inexpensive good work." A programmer who earns as much as $63,000 per year in the United States is paid as little as $5,000 per year overseas (see Figure B6.4). Companies can easily realize cost savings of 30 percent to 50 percent through offshore outsourcing and still get the same, if not better, quality of service.[4]

Developed and developing countries throughout Europe and Asia offer some IT outsourcing services, but most are hampered to some degree by language, telecommunications infrastructure, or regulatory barriers. The first and largest offshore marketplace is India, whose English-speaking and technologically advanced population have built its IT services business into a $4 billion industry. Infosys, NIIT, Satyam, TCS, and Wipro are among the biggest Indian outsourcing service providers, each with a significant presence in the United States. There are currently three categories of outsourcing countries (see Figure B6.5):

1. The Leaders—countries that are leading the outsourcing industry

2. The Up-and-Comers—countries that are beginning to emerge as solid outsourcing options

3. The Rookies—countries that are just entering the outsourcing industry[5]

Country	Salary Range Per Year
China	$ 5,000–$ 9,000
India	6,000– 10,000
Philippines	6,500– 11,000
Russia	7,000– 13,000
Ireland	21,000– 28,000
Canada	25,000– 50,000
United States	60,000– 90,000

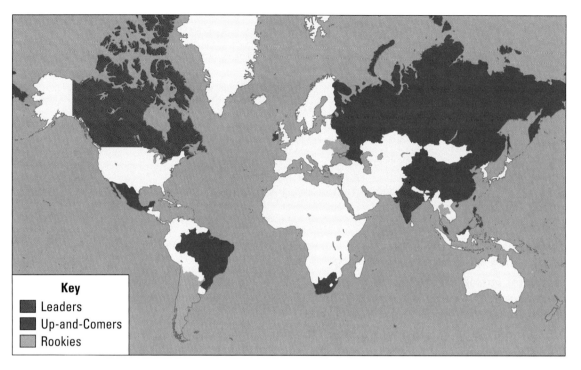

Key
- Leaders
- Up-and-Comers
- Rookies

FIGURE B6.5

Categories of
Outsourcing Countries

The Leaders

The following countries are leaders in the outsourcing industry:

- Canada
- India
- Ireland
- Israel
- Philippines

CANADA

Expertise	■ Software development/maintenance, contact centers, technical support.
Major Customers	■ Allmerica, Agilent.
Advantages	■ Though labor costs are high, geographic proximity and cultural affinity with the United States make it highly desirable. ■ Contact center turnover is low.
Disadvantage	■ High cost of labor pool, but still less expensive than outsourcing in the United States.

INDIA

Expertise	■ Software development/maintenance, contact centers, financial processing.
Major Customers	■ Citigroup, GE Capital, American Express.
Advantages	■ India is the leader in business process and IT services outsourcing. ■ Two million English-proficient speakers graduate every year from more than 1,000 colleges that offer information technology education. ■ Strong history of software development. ■ Highly skilled labor pool. ■ Favorable cost structure.
Disadvantages	■ Political instability. ■ Labor costs are rising as demand for IT workers begins to exceed supply. ■ High turnover, particularly in contact centers, is becoming an issue.

Expertise	■ European shared-services centers, software development, contact centers.
Major Customers	■ Intel, Dell, Microsoft.
Advantages	■ Reputation for producing highly skilled IT professionals. ■ Strong cultural affinity with the United States. ■ Low political or financial risk. ■ Solid telecommunications infrastructure. ■ Strong educational system.
Disadvantage	■ High cost of IT salaries, however, labor costs are still lower than in the United States.

Expertise	■ Software development/maintenance, packaged software implementation, application integration, security, e-business.
Major Customers	■ Merrill Lynch, Shaw Industries.
Advantages	■ Highly skilled workforce including scientists and engineers from Eastern Europe and Russia. ■ Excellent educational system. ■ Hotbed for IT innovation.
Disadvantages	■ Political instability. ■ Employee safety is a cause for concern. ■ High cost of IT salaries.

Expertise	■ Accounting, finance, contact centers, human resources.
Major Customers	■ Procter & Gamble, American International Group, Citigroup.
Advantages	■ The population boasts a high percentage of English speakers with American accents. ■ Culture dictates aim-to-please attitude. ■ Estimated 15,000 technology students graduate from universities annually.
Disadvantages	■ Filipinos are not nearly as strong in software development and maintenance as other outsourcing countries. ■ Political instability.

The Up-and-Comers

The following countries are up-and-coming in the outsourcing industry:

- Brazil
- China
- Malaysia
- Mexico
- Russia
- South Africa

BRAZIL

Expertise	■ Software development/maintenance.
Major Customers	■ General Electric, Goodyear, Xerox.
Advantages	■ Big cost savings from a large supply of IT labor. ■ Brazil is Latin America's largest economy with a strong industrial base. ■ Brazil's national focus is on growing small and midsize businesses, including IT services. ■ Affinity with U.S. culture including minimal time zone differences.
Disadvantage	■ Remains on priority watch list of International Intellectual Property Alliance for copyright infractions.

CHINA

Expertise	■ Transaction processing, low-end software development/maintenance.
Major Customers	■ HSBC Bank, Microsoft.
Advantages	■ Large pool of educated IT workers with broad skill sets. ■ Government provides strong support for IT outsourcing industry. ■ Telecommunications infrastructure is improving. ■ Entry into World Trade Organization winning confidence of foreign investors. ■ Government has established 15 national software industrial parks.
Disadvantages	■ English proficiency low. ■ Workers lack knowledge of Western business culture. ■ Workers lack project management skills. ■ Intellectual property protections weak. ■ Piracy. ■ Red tape and corruption from a highly bureaucratic government.

MALAYSIA

Expertise	■ Wireless applications.
Major Customers	■ IBM, Shell, DHL, Motorola, Electronic Data Systems Corporation.
Advantages	■ Good business environment with strong government support for IT and communications industries. ■ Workforce has strong global exposure. ■ World-class telecommunications infrastructure. ■ Over half of the 250,000 students in higher education major in scientific or technical disciplines.
Disadvantages	■ Labor costs higher than India. ■ Few suppliers, which limits business choices. ■ Shortage of skilled IT talent.

MEXICO

Expertise	■ Software development, contact centers.
Major Customers	■ AOL Time Warner, General Motors, IBM.
Advantages	■ Solid telecommunications infrastructure. ■ Shares cultural affinity and time zones with the United States. ■ Second-largest U.S. trading partner. ■ Programmers highly proficient on latest technologies, including Sun's J2EE and Microsoft's .NET.
Disadvantages	■ English proficiency low. ■ Government corruption.

RUSSIA

Expertise	■ Web design, complex software development, aerospace engineering.
Major Customer	■ Boeing.
Advantages	■ Large number of highly skilled workers with degrees in science, engineering, and math. ■ Strong venue for research and development. ■ Programmers have skills for both cutting-edge projects and working with legacy applications. ■ European-based companies benefit from historic cultural affinity and geographic proximity.
Disadvantages	■ English proficiency not as widespread as in India or the Philippines, making contact centers impractical. ■ Government corruption and red tape. ■ Copyright piracy. ■ Outsourcing industry is fragmented and many firms have 20 programmers or less, making them unattractive to companies with large IT projects. ■ Telecommunications infrastructure needs work.

SOUTH AFRICA

Expertise	■ Contact centers, e-business, software development, IT security.
Major Customers	■ AIG, Old Mutual, Sage Life, Swissair.
Advantages	■ Time zone compatibility with Europe. ■ English is a native language. ■ Solid telecommunications infrastructure.
Disadvantages	■ Small pool of IT skilled workers. ■ IT talent tends to emigrate. ■ Crime.

The Rookies

The following countries are just beginning to offer outsourcing and are considered rookies in the industry:

- ■ Argentina
- ■ Chile
- ■ Costa Rica
- ■ New Zealand
- ■ Thailand
- ■ Ukraine

ARGENTINA

Expertise	■ Software development/maintenance, contact centers.
Major Customers	■ BankOne, Citibank, Principal Financial Group.
Advantages	■ Low costs resulting from an economic collapse in 2001. ■ Economy began to rebound in 2003, growing more than 8 percent, but unemployment remains high. ■ Large labor pool, including solid base of engineering talent.
Disadvantages	■ Country has yet to reach agreement with creditors on restructuring debt. ■ Foreign investors are cautious.

CHILE

Expertise	■ Software development/maintenance.
Major Customers	■ Compaq.
Advantages	■ Large highly skilled pool of IT talent. ■ State-of-the-art telecommunications infrastructure. ■ Good satellite connectivity and digital network. ■ Government actively supports business process and software development sectors. ■ Government plans to begin offering English classes to technical workers.
Disadvantages	■ English proficiency lacking. ■ Slightly higher costs than neighboring countries.

COSTA RICA

Expertise	■ Contact centers, e-business.
Major Customers	■ Unisys.
Advantages	■ Business-friendly environment. ■ Highly skilled pool of engineering talent. ■ Well-educated workforce. ■ Favorable cost structure. ■ English and Spanish widely spoken.
Disadvantage	■ Relatively small labor supply.

NEW ZEALAND

Expertise	■ Contact centers, e-business, Web hosting, Web design.
Major Customers	■ IBM, Microsoft, Cisco.
Advantages	■ Stable political and economic environment. ■ Well-established telecommunications infrastructure. ■ Thriving contact center industry. ■ Limited supply of domestic labor. To meet demand, the government has eased visa restrictions allowing entry of workers from countries such as Bangladesh.
Disadvantage	■ New Zealand cannot compete on costs with India and the Philippines.

THAILAND

Expertise	■ Software development/maintenance.
Major Customers	■ Dell, Glovia, Sungard.
Advantages	■ Reasonable telecommunications infrastructure. ■ Cost structure is slightly lower than Malaysia.
Disadvantages	■ Demand for skilled IT labor exceeds supply. ■ Population is not as educated as in neighboring countries. ■ English is not widely spoken.

UKRAINE

Expertise	■ Software development, Web site development.
Major Customers	■ Sears, Roebuck and Company, Target Corporation.
Advantages	■ History of training highly educated scientists and engineers. (The Soviet Union based the majority of its space and aviation technology work here.) ■ Information technology outsourcing growth predicted to double over the next couple of years.
Disadvantages	■ Unstable political climate. ■ Fears that the country is drifting away from democracy and pro-Western stance.

In summary, there are many countries racing to participate in the outsourcing phenomenon. When an organization outsources, it needs to analyze all of its options and weigh all of the advantages and disadvantages. When faced with an outsourcing decision, be sure to evaluate the outsourcing countries on such things as geopolitical risk, English proficiency, and salary cost (see Figure B6.6).

THE CHALLENGES OF OUTSOURCING

There are several challenges in outsourcing. These arguments are valid and should be taken into consideration when a company is thinking about outsourcing. Many challenges can be avoided with proper research on the outsourcing service provider. Some challenges of outsourcing include:

- **Contract length**—Most of the outsourced IT contracts are for a relatively long time period (several years). This is because of the high cost of transferring assets and employees as well as maintaining technological investment. The long time period of the contract causes three particular problems:
  1. Difficulties in getting out of a contract if the outsourcing service provider turns out to be unsuitable.
  2. Problems in foreseeing what the business will need over the next 5 or 10 years (typical contract lengths), hence creating difficulties in establishing an appropriate contract.
  3. Problems in reforming an internal IT department after the contract period is finished.
- **Competitive edge**—Effective and innovative use of IT can give an organization a competitive edge over its rivals. A competitive business advantage provided by an internal IT department that understands the organization and is committed to its goals can be lost in an outsourced arrangement. In an outsourced arrangement, IT staff are striving to achieve the goals and objectives of the outsourcing service provider, which may conflict with those of the organization.

FIGURE B6.6

Outsourcing Options

THE LEADERS			
Country	Geopolitical Risk	English Proficiency	Average Programmer Salary
Canada	Low	Good	> $12K
India	Moderate	Good	$4K-$12K
Ireland	Low	Good	> $12K
Israel	Moderate	Good	> $12K
Philippines	Moderate	Good	$4K-$12K
THE UP-AND-COMERS			
Country	Geopolitical Risk	English Proficiency	Average Programmer Salary
Brazil	Moderate	Poor	$4K-$12K
China	Low	Poor	$4K-$12K
Malaysia	Low	Fair	$4K-$12K
Mexico	Moderate	Poor	> $12K
Russia	Moderate	Poor	$4K-$12K
South Africa	Moderate	Good	> $12K
THE ROOKIES			
Country	Geopolitical Risk	English Proficiency	Average Programmer Salary
Argentina	Moderate	Fair	$4K-$12K
Chile	Low	Poor	< $4K
Costa Rica	Moderate	Good	$4K-$12K
New Zealand	Low	Good	> $12K
Thailand	Low	Poor	$4K-$12K
Ukraine	Moderate	Poor	$4K-$12K

- **Confidentiality**—In some organizations, the information stored in the computer systems is central to the enterprise's success or survival. For example, information about pricing policies, product mixing formulas, or sales analysis. There are examples of companies deciding against outsourcing for fear of placing confidential information in the hands of the outsourcing service provider, particularly if the outsourcing service provider offer services to companies competing in the same marketplace. Although the organization usually dismisses this threat, claiming it is covered by confidentiality clauses in a contract, the organization must assess the potential risk and costs of a confidentiality breach in determining the net benefits of an outsourcing agreement.

- **Scope definition**—Most IT projects suffer from problems associated with defining the scope of the system. The same problem afflicts outsourcing arrangements. Many difficulties result from contractual misunderstandings between the organization and the outsourcing service provider. In such circumstances, the organization believes that the service they require is within the contract scope while the service provider is sure it is outside the scope and so is subject to extra fees.

Future Trends

Companies are getting smarter about outsourcing and about aligning efficiency with core business priorities. As businesses become increasingly networked (for instance, via the Internet)—global, commoditized, $24 \times 7 \times 365$, and collaborative—outsourcing is becoming less of a cost-saving strategy and more an overall context for business.

Outsourcing is rapidly approaching commodity status, and this will transform the outsourcing value equation from high margins and vendor control into a classic buyers' market with competition driving down margins, adding features and services, and increasing buyer choices. U.S. companies should consider Mexico and Canada for nearshore outsourcing since those countries often provide very competitive pricing. Vendors in these countries can be viable alternatives, such as IBM Global Services (Mexico and Canada), Softtek (Mexico), CGI (Canada), and Keane (Canada).[6]

Companies should look for value-based pricing rather than the lowest possible price. The emerging trend of companies using reverse auction bidding to select offshore vendors is a dangerous one—it could result in low prices, but also low value and low customer satisfaction.

MULTISOURCING

For many years, outsourcing has predominantly been a means to manage and optimize businesses' ever-growing IT infrastructures and ensure return on IT investments—or at a minimum, more cost-effective operations. As businesses move to Internet-based models, speed and skill have become more important than cost efficiencies giving way to a "utility" service provider model called "multisourcing." *Multisourcing* is a combination of professional services, mission-critical support, remote management, and hosting services that are offered to customers in any combination needed. Like the general contractor model, multisourcing brings together a wide set of specialized IT service providers, or "subcontractors," under one point of accountability. The goal of multisourcing is to integrate a collection of IT services into one stable and cost-effective system. Therefore, multisourcing helps companies achieve the advantages of a best-of-breed strategy.

A multisourcing service provider can offer a seamless, inexpensive migration path to whatever delivery model makes sense at that time. For instance, HR processes are outsourced to one best-of-breed outsourcing service provider. Logistics are outsourced to another. IT development and maintenance to another. Although multisourcing mitigates the risk of choosing a single outsourcing service provider, additional resources and time are required to manage multiple service providers.

Outsourcing IT services and business functions is becoming an increasingly common global practice among organizations looking for competitive advantage. The guiding principle is that noncore and critical activities of an enterprise can be handed over to companies with expertise in those activities, thereby freeing internal resources to focus on enhancing the added-value of the organization's core business.

Outsourcing is no longer a simple matter of cutting costs and improving service levels. As more companies consider the benefits of outsourcing their IT functions and their business processes, they will find new ways to create business value. Companies that succeed will find innovative solutions to help drive costs down, select only the problem areas to outsource, and more important, learn to use outsourcing as a strategic weapon.

Companies continue to outsource at an increasing rate, despite reports of organizations disappointed and disillusioned by the process. The ultimate goal is multisourcing, combining professional services, mission-critical support, remote management, and hosting services.

★ KEY TERMS

Multisourcing, 301   Onshore outsourcing, 293
Nearshore outsourcing, 293   Outsourcing, 290
Offshore outsourcing, 293

★ CLOSING CASE ONE

Mobil Travel Guide

For the past 45 years, the *Mobil Travel Guide* has been providing information on destinations, route planning, resorts, accommodations, restaurant reviews, and other travel-related subjects for people traveling in the United States and Canada. Print versions of the *Mobil Travel Guide* are created and updated annually at the company's Park Ridge, Illinois, headquarters, and are sold at most major booksellers and other publishing outlets.

Mobil Travel Guide, a well-known name in the travel industry, wanted to leverage its brand recognition by providing a highly responsive, real-time online service for leisure travelers that include customized travel planning, an around-the-clock customer service center, and a variety of privileges and rewards at a linked network of hotels and restaurants.

Mobil's existing online solution offered only a limited amount of static Web content that ran on just four servers, which were unable to process the site's considerable traffic, resulting in downtime for customers. Mobil needed a more robust solution that would provide real-time services such as route planning and fast access to the company's vast travel information database. The solution also had to be flexible and resilient enough to handle seasonal usage fluctuations, including anticipated spikes during the summertime and over major holidays. Mobil Travel Guide's internal goals also created a challenge for any solution. The site was expected to grow rapidly, but the company did not want to invest in an infrastructure capable of supporting its vision for the Web site.

Instead of using stand-alone Web, application, and database servers, Mobil Travel Guide decided to outsource all these functions to IBM. Because IBM delivers e-business infrastructure capacity as a utility, Mobil Travel Guide pays only for the processing, storage, and networking capacity it needs and can scale its virtual infrastructure up to meet demand spikes.

By avoiding up-front capital investment without sacrificing scalability, reliability, or flexibility, Mobil Travel Guide is positioned for success. The company can optimize its spending by scaling its infrastructure dynamically to meet demands and channeling resources toward generating new business and revenue. "Otherwise, we would have to buy enough infrastructure to handle the biggest day we could imagine, but typically it would sit unused. Now, we can take advantage of any market sweet spot we find, because we can scale with minimal lead time and capital dollars," explains Paul Mercurio, chief information officer for Mobil Travel Guide.

What is more, this capability moves portions of the Web-serving workload from Mobil Travel Guide's site onto servers located at strategic network points, so end users get faster responses even while Mobil Travel Guide lowers its per-transaction costs. "Because our service level ramps up or down dynamically in response to peaks and valleys in demand, we pay only for the capacity we need at any given moment in time," says Mercurio.

The on-demand delivery has already benefited Mobil Travel Guide in an unexpected way. After initially setting a committed capacity level that was too high, the company was able to leverage the flexibility of its IBM solution to "right-size" its capacity by reducing its contracted capacity level.

By outsourcing the solution to IBM, Mobil anticipates it will save about 35 percent in overall maintenance and software costs, while deploying an excellent e-business infrastructure solution that guarantees high availability, rapid scalability, and easy management of usage fluctuations.[7]

Questions

1. What are the main reasons Mobil Travel Guide used an outsourcing option?
2. What other areas would you recommend Mobil Travel Guide outsource?
3. What advantages and disadvantages would offshore outsourcing or nearshore outsourcing have for Mobil Travel Guide?
4. Make a list of the countries where Mobil could outsource its *Travel Guide.*

Outsourcing Brew

Coors Brewing Company, the third-largest brewer in the United States, manufactures and markets more than a dozen varieties of beer and malt beverages in 30 markets around the world. In a rapidly consolidating industry, Coors had a choice: keep growing or be acquired. To create the optimal conditions for growth, the company needed to improve access to information, consolidate systems, and reduce costs.

In less than a decade, Coors Brewing Company had more than doubled in size. Managing that growth became increasingly difficult for the company's internal IT staff. The company wanted to maintain responsibility for the technologies directly related to making and selling beer. Therefore, Coors was looking for a partner with deep industry expertise, mature application experience, and global reach to help revitalize its technology to support its business goals—including bringing new acquisitions online quickly.

The company decided to outsource its day-to-day management of its technical operations, conversion of legacy applications, and systems. Coors outsourced these functions to EDS in order to create a globally integrated enterprise solution, helping to optimize the supply chain from beginning to end. EDS is an experienced outsourcing services company with more than 130,000 employees and 2003 revenues of $21.5 billion, ranked 80th on the Fortune 500.

EDS offered Coors an infrastructure "on demand." Coors avoids a huge up-front investment in infrastructure, but is able to access increased capacity when business volumes increase. Now IT costs are predictable, and additional infrastructure is instantly available when the company needs it. Coors also controls costs by using EDS's Best ShoreSM Services, which enables Coors to reduce the cost of applications management by as much as 40 percent through a combination of offshore, nearshore, and local service centers and personnel.

EDS's solutions at Coors deliver much more than lower costs and increased reliability. As EDS assumed control of Coors's help desk, staff increased service levels while identifying patterns that let Coors focus training where it was most needed and kept the company aware of where potential problems lay. Standardizing the company's desktop environment has allowed Coors to get rid of many obsolete applications.

EDS is much more than an information technology outsourcing service provider, they are Coors's business partner. "They work with us on project management and root-cause analysis, which have helped us to add a lot of discipline in our organization," says CIO Virginia Guthrie. With a modernized and efficient information environment taking shape, EDS and Coors have ambitious plans for the future, from improving manufacturing processes to enhancing Coors's global presence. Guthrie goes on to say, "What we really want here is for this partnership to be a poster child for how outsourcing partnerships should work."

With the help of EDS, Coors was able to:

- Within just 60 days, reduce cost of application maintenance by 70 percent.
- Save more than $1.2 million on project resources related to SAP implementation.
- Reduce applications in use by 48 percent.
- Work to retire 70 percent of legacy systems.[8]

Questions

1. Describe an alternative approach that Coors could have used instead of outsourcing to EDS.
2. What would be the advantages of offshore outsourcing Coors' IT department?
3. What are some other reasons Coors outsourced its information technology functions that were not mentioned in the case?
4. Describe some of the factors causing Coors to be "forced" to outsource its information technology functions.

MAKING BUSINESS DECISIONS

1. Sports Sourcing

Sierra Sports Network launched its Web site SierraSports.com in 2001. With a huge influx of new visitors expected this football season, it is critical that SierraSports.com attracts, retains, and handles its Web traffic. What they need is an overhaul of its existing Web site. Since Sierra Sports Network does not have the in-house skills to support the needed changes, it needs to look at outsourcing its Web development. Some of the company's needs are working with an outsourcing service provider who is proficient in English, has a solid telecommunications infrastructure, and operates in a similar time zone. Make a list of the outsourcing countries that could assist Sierra Sports in their Web development needs, in addition to the advantages that each country could give to the company.

2. Ops.com

Contact center Ops.com provides information to those who are involved in real-time customer service. Contact centers have emerged as *the* critical link between a company and its customers. The growth in contact centers has resulted in a strong demand for Ops.com's services; so much that it now needs to outsource part of its operation. One main reason for the move to an outsourcing service provider is its need to develop a new service to collect information, such as account numbers, via an automated attendant and tie it back to a database. Ops.com can tap the database information to give callers automated access to more information, such as account balances, and create priority queuing for their most important customers. Describe the advantages that outsourcing would give Ops.com and list the outsourcing options along with a recommendation of prospective countries that have the resources available to be considered.

3. The Travel Store

In 2004, The Travel Store faced a dilemma. The retailer had tripled in size over a three-year period to $1 billion in sales, but it had done so in spite of operational deficiencies. The company's inability to evolve its business processes as it grew was causing problems. Within a year, sales and profits fell below expectations, and its stock price plummeted from approximately $10 a share to less than $2 a share. The Travel Store is determined to take quick and decisive action to restore profitability and improve its credibility in the marketplace. One of its top priorities is to overhaul its inventory management system in an effort at creating optimal levels of inventory to support sales demand. This would prevent higher volume stores from running out of key sale items while also ensuring that lower sales stores would not be burdened with excess inventory that could only be moved at closeout prices. The company would like to outsource this function but is worried about the challenges of transferring the responsibility of this important business function, as well as the issues surrounding confidentiality, and scope definition. Make a list of the competitive advantages outsourcing could give to the The Travel Store, along with recommendations for addressing the company's outsourcing concerns.

4. Software Solutions

Founded in 2003, Gabster Software provides innovative search software, Web site demographics, and testing software. All serve as part of its desktop and enterprise resource planning solutions for government, corporate, educational, and consumer markets. Web site publishers, digital media publishers, content managers, document managers, business users, consumers, software companies, and consulting services companies use the Gabster's solutions. The company is currently thinking about offshore outsourcing its call center functions, e-business strategies, and its application development. Describe how Gabster could use multisourcing along with the potential advantages it might receive.

PLUG-IN

B7

E-Business Models

LEARNING OUTCOMES

1. Describe the business-to-business (B2B) and business-to-consumer (B2C) e-business models.
2. Describe the four main areas where companies conduct business online.
3. Differentiate between a vertical marketplace and a horizontal marketplace.
4. Summarize the current and future trends for e-business models.

Introduction

As organizations, governments, and academia embrace the Internet to conduct business, new approaches in the way they reach their target customers have resulted in numerous e-business models. Some of these models are further developments of traditional models while others, namely "pure plays," are the outcome of technological advancements. A *pure play* is an Internet retailer that has no physical store, such as Expedia.com and Amazon.com. New technologies, competition, and cost savings along with the global nature of the Internet have significantly transformed traditional businesses into e-businesses.

The core units introduced the concepts of e-business as well as a few of the e-business models. *E-business,* derived from the term e-commerce, is conducting business on the Internet, not only buying and selling but also serving customers and collaborating with business partners. An *e-business model* is an approach to conducting electronic business through which a company can become a profitable business on the Internet. This plug-in will build on the units' discussion, providing specific details on the functions of e-business models as well as current and future trends.

E-Business: Commerce on the Internet

In the past, a company's business model was the primary strength of its value; today a company is valued on its strategy, business model, and ability to market itself. With technology driving new competition, a Fortune 500 company that once seemed unstoppable is now challenged by a start-up company that efficiently uses

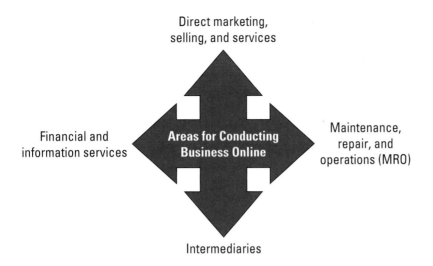

Direct marketing,
selling, and services

Financial and
information services

**Areas for Conducting
Business Online**

Maintenance,
repair, and
operations (MRO)

Intermediaries

Internet technologies, integrates its systems, and performs business processes more effectively. By capitalizing on a sustained business proposition and correctly applying technology, start-ups are able to reduce the barriers to entry while increasing their market reach. For e-businesses, the premise "first to market equals first to success" is often the case.[1]

Businesses communicate with customers and partners through channels. The Internet is one of the newest and, for many purposes, the best business communication channel. It is fast, reliable, inexpensive, and universally accessible. The four main areas in which companies conduct business online are:

1. Direct marketing, selling, and services.
2. Financial and information services.
3. Maintenance, repair, and operations (MRO).
4. Intermediaries (see Figure B7.1).

DIRECT MARKETING, SELLING, AND SERVICES

More Web sites focus on direct marketing, selling, and service than on any other type of e-business. Direct selling was the earliest type of e-business, and has proven to be a stepping stone to more complex commerce operations for many companies. Successes such as eBay, Barnes and Noble, Dell Computer, and the introduction of e-tickets by major airlines have sparked the growth of this segment, proving customer acceptance of e-business. Across consumer-targeted e-business sites, there are several keys to success:

- Marketing that creates site visibility and demand, targets customer segments with personalized offers, and generates qualified sales leads through analysis of customer behavior.

- Sales-enhancing site design that allows personalized content and adaptive selling processes that do more than just list catalog items.

- Integrated sales processing capabilities that provide secure credit card authorization, payment, automated tax calculation, order fulfillment, and tight integration with existing back-office systems.

- Automated customer service features that generate responsive feedback to consumer inquiries, track information about consumer requests, and automatically provide customized services based on personal needs and interests.

*Dell Computer
Direct Selling*

FINANCIAL AND INFORMATION SERVICES

Sites that offer a broad range of financial and information services performed over the Internet are enjoying rapid growth. These sites are popular because they help consumers, businesses, and financial institutions distribute important information over the Internet with greater convenience and richness than is available using other channels. Some of the financial and information services available are:

- **Online banking**—Consumers and small businesses can save time and money by performing their banking on the Internet. Paying bills, making transfers between accounts, trading stocks, bonds, and mutual funds can be performed electronically by using the Internet to connect customers with their financial institutions.

- **Online billing**—Companies can achieve significant cost savings and marketing benefits using Internet-based bill delivery and receiving systems.

- **Secure information distribution**—To many businesses, information is their most valuable asset. Although the Internet can enable businesses to reach new markets for that information, businesses must also safeguard that information to protect their assets.

MAINTENANCE, REPAIR, AND OPERATIONS (MRO)

The Internet offers tremendous time and cost savings for corporate purchasing of low-cost, high-volume goods for maintenance, repair, and operations (MRO) activities. Typical MRO goods include office supplies (such as pens and paper), office equipment, furniture, computers, and replacement parts. The Internet can transform corporate purchasing from a labor- and paperwork-intensive process into a self-service application. For example, company employees can order equipment on Web sites, company officials can automatically enforce purchase approval policies through automated business rules, and suppliers can keep their catalog information centralized and up-to-date. Purchase order applications can then use the Internet to transfer the order to suppliers. In response, suppliers can ship the requested goods and invoice the company over the Internet.

In addition to reducing administrative costs, Internet-based corporate purchasing can improve order-tracking accuracy, better enforce purchasing policies, provide improved customer service, reduce inventories, and give companies more power in negotiating exclusive or volume-discount contracts.

INTERMEDIARIES

Intermediaries are agents, software, or businesses that bring buyers and sellers together that provide a trading infrastructure to enhance e-business. With the introduction of e-commerce there was much discussion about disintermediation of middle people/organizations; however, recent developments in e-business have seen more reintermediation. *Reintermediation* refers to using the Internet to reassemble buyers, sellers, and other partners in a traditional supply chain in new ways. Examples include New York–based e-Steel Corp. and Philadelphia-based PetroChemNet Inc. bringing together producers, traders, distributors, and buyers of steel and chemicals, respectively, in Web-based marketplaces. Some of the more commonly applied intermediaries and their functions are (also see Figure B7.2):

- *Content provider*s are companies that use the Internet to distribute copyrighted content, including news, music, games, books, movies, and many other types of information. Retrieving and paying for content is the second largest revenue source for B2C e-business.

Type of Intermediary	Description	Example
Internet service provider	Companies that make money selling a service, not a product	Earthlink.com Comcast.com AOL.com
Portals	Central hubs for online content	Yahoo!.com MSN.com Google.com
Content providers	Companies that use the Internet to distribute copyrighted content	wsj.com cnn.com espn.com
Online brokers	Act as intermediaries between buyers and sellers of goods and services	charlesschwab.com fidelity.com datek.com
Market makers	Aggregate three services for market participants: a place, rules, and infrastructure	amazon.com ebay.com priceline.com
Online service providers	Extensive online array of services	xdrive.com lawinfo.com
Intelligent agents	Software applications that follow instructions and learn independently	Sidestep.com WebSeeker.com iSpyNOW.com
Application service providers	Sell access to Internet-based software applications to other companies	ariba.com commerceone.com ibm.com
Infomediary	Provides specialized information on behalf of producers of goods and services and their potential customers	autobytel.com BizRate.com

FIGURE B7.2

Types of Intermediaries

- ***Online brokers*** act as intermediaries between buyers and sellers of goods and services. Online brokers, who usually work for commission, provide many services. For example, travel agents are information brokers who pass information from product suppliers to customers. They also take and process orders, collect money, and provide travel assistance including obtaining visas.
- ***Market makers*** are intermediaries that aggregate three services for market participants: (1) a place to trade, (2) rules to govern trading, and (3) an infrastructure to support trading. For example, eBay's e-business model focuses on creating a digital electronic environment for buyers and sellers to meet, agree on a price, and conduct a transaction.

E-Business Models

The critical role of Internet technologies and integration requirements has demanded that organizations build a comprehensive planning framework or an e-business model. This structured planning approach enables the organization to assess, plan for, and implement the multiple aspects of an e-business.

One of the largest privately held companies in the nation, Cargill, a 136-year-old, $49 billion agricultural food and trade company headquartered in Wayzata, Minnesota, started searching for ways to revitalize its bottom line. The company's EVentures group is a two-year-old division whose mission is to search out, invest in, and nurture promising Internet and technology start-ups. Cargill hopes that EVentures will bring promising new ideas and technologies into the company's old-economy businesses of agriculture, food, metals, minerals, and transportation.

The EVentures group has invested in seven B2B e-marketplaces that roughly parallel Cargill's own lines of business, including GSX, a steel exchange, and LevelSeas, an e-marketplace for bulk shipping. It has also started investing in technology start-ups such as DemandTec, which offers a price optimization service, and EPropose, which builds transactional and exchange technology.[2]

Building an e-business that takes advantage of the Internet's communications capabilities is a complex undertaking. The intricate integration requires an e-business to perform at high levels of availability and scalability. The value chain has integration and performance demands that exceed the requirements seen in traditional businesses. In a successful e-business, all of these areas are tightly integrated to provide an organization the ability to quickly and efficiently sell, manufacture, and deliver products or services.

E-business models are typically categorized under four major classifications (refer to Figure B7.3):

- Business-to-business (B2B)
- Business-to-consumer (B2C)
- Consumer-to-business (C2B)
- Consumer-to-consumer (C2C)

FIGURE B7.3
Basic e-Business Models

	Business	**Consumer**
Business	B2B grainger.com	B2C carfax.com
Consumer	C2B ideas.com	C2C eBay.com

BUSINESS-TO-BUSINESS (B2B) MODELS

Business-to-business (B2B) applies to businesses buying from and selling to each other over the Internet. Online access to data including expected shipping date, delivery date, and shipping status provided either by the seller or a third-party provider is widely supported by B2B models. With these developments in B2B e-business, businesses are adopting Web-based e-procurement capabilities to achieve volume purchasing power, a wider choice of buyers and suppliers, lower costs, better quality, improved delivery, and reduced paperwork. *E-procurement* is the B2B purchase and sale of supplies and services over the Internet. Large enterprises have Web-enabled their buy-side activities and implemented Web-based e-procurement capabilities. Initially the focus on e-procurement was for the purchase of nonstrategic products and services, such as MRO materials.

To understand B2B models, it is useful to understand *how* businesses buy, and *what* they buy. Businesses buy a diverse set of products and services ranging from paper clips to computer systems, and steel to machinery. At the broadest level, business purchases can be classified into *manufacturing inputs* and *operating inputs.* Manufacturing inputs are raw materials and components that go directly into the manufactured product or manufacturing process. Manufacturing inputs tend to be *vertical* in nature, because the finished products that they go into are industry-specific. They are typically sourced from industry-specific suppliers and distributors, and they require specialized logistics and fulfillment mechanisms.

Operating inputs, on the other hand, are indirect materials and services that do not go into finished products. Operating inputs, sometimes called MRO inputs, include industrial supplies, capital equipment, services, and travel-related services. Unlike manufacturing inputs, operating inputs tend to be *horizontal* in nature (with the exception of capital equipment and some industrial supplies).

The other important distinction in business purchasing lies in *how* businesses buy products and services. Businesses can engage either in systematic sourcing or in spot sourcing. *Systematic sourcing* involves buying through prenegotiated contracts with qualified suppliers. These contracts are often long-term in nature; therefore, systematic sourcing tends to be relationship-oriented. A large proportion of manufactured inputs are purchased through this mechanism. On the other hand, businesses can also buy commodity-like products, such as oil, steel, and energy, from *spot sourcing,* which is transaction-oriented and rarely involves a long-term or ongoing relationship between buyers and sellers.

The two-way classification—*manufacturing inputs* versus *operating inputs* (the "what"); and *systematic sourcing* versus *spot sourcing* (the "how") allows B2B models to be classified into four categories (see Figure B7.4):

1. MRO hubs (operating supplies, systematic sourcing, horizontal focus)
2. Yield managers (operating supplies, spot sourcing, horizontal focus)
3. Catalog hubs (manufacturing inputs, systematic sourcing, vertical focus)
4. Exchanges (manufacturing inputs, spot sourcing, vertical focus)

B2B exchanges are new organizational forms in digital space that can take place in any of the following forms (also see Figure B7.5):

- Buyer model (few buyers, many sellers)
- Marketplace model (many buyers, many sellers)
- Longer term relationship model (few buyers, few sellers)
- Seller model (many buyers, few sellers)

Buyer Model (Few Buyers, Many Sellers)

In the buyer model, the buyer is faced with many sellers, which allows the buyer to benefit from multiple competing suppliers while facing no major opposition from other buyers. The buyer model is appropriate for commodity items, where the

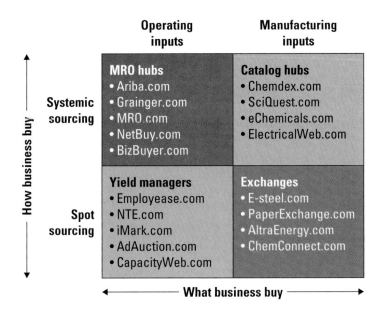

buyer is able to leverage its buying power through the use of reverse auction tools. In a reverse auction the winning bid is the lowest, rather than the highest, bid. (This is the opposite of the **English auction,** in which the highest bid wins.) Reverse auctions are common when buyers desire to pay the lowest price for a product. The supplier making the lowest bid wins. In this situation, buying power is with the buyer. This results in substantial value for the big buyers in terms of pricing, quality, and delivery terms.

Marketplace Model (Many Buyers, Many Sellers)

The **marketplace model** allows a virtually infinite number of businesses to transact electronically with minimal cost. Such exchanges allow buyers to choose among a large number of suppliers for a set of products and sellers to promote their products to many buyers. The presence of a large number of businesses in the marketplace prevents strong intercompany relationships that create value by matching many businesses through negotiated prices and by aggregating a large number of businesses. The marketplace model is appropriate when value can be created through third-party mediation of the matching process between buyers and sellers, or through aggregation of volume buying or selling.

Longer Term Relationship Model (Few Buyers, Few Sellers)

The **longer term relationship model** is for items requiring a high degree of planning between buyers and sellers either in the design stage or in fulfillment. The importance of planning can be due to technical complexity or demand characteristics

	Industry	Company
Owners facilitate trade	**Marketplace model** Many buyers, many sellers	**Seller model** Many buyers, few sellers
Owners are major traders	**Buyer model** Few buyers, many sellers	**Longer term relationship model** Few buyers, few sellers

driven by a time or phase requirement. Strategic relationships lead to few buyers and sellers, which results in improved service(s) and reduced risks from immature technical solutions. Close relationships between a small number of businesses promote collaboration, coordination, and expertise sharing.

Seller Model (Many Buyers, Few Sellers)

The *seller model* is appropriate when the supplier hosts value-added services on its Web site such as suppliers' product catalog and customers' order information. In this type of exchange, the seller can be a manufacturer or distributor selling to wholesalers, retailers, or businesses. While manufacturers must be real, intermediaries may be virtual. The value proposition for buyers is that the seller provides product information on the Web to which buyers have $24 \times 7 \times 365$ access. This is an effective opportunity for small and medium enterprises and individual buyers and sellers who would otherwise find it too expensive to join a marketplace.

BUSINESS-TO-CONSUMER (B2C) BUSINESS MODELS

Business-to-consumer (B2C) applies to any business that sells its products or services to consumers over the Internet. Carfax (carfax.com) is not your typical dotcom. It has been in the vehicle history report business for 18 years. "The Internet was just a new way for us to reach the consumer market," says Carfax President Dick Raines. That is what Carfax continues to do—use the Internet to expand its business beyond its original customer base of used car dealers in an effort to saturate the used car buying market. Carfax spent $20 million on print and TV ads to attract those customers to its Web site to purchase a Carfax report for $14.95 or six days of reports for $19.95. Carfax has now launched an affiliate program for small dealers' Web sites and a cash-back program offering customers 20 percent of revenues received for their referrals. "We continue to look for more and more ways to add value," Raines says.

The following "e" models are commonly applied to the B2C arena:[3]

- E-Shops
- E-Malls

E-Shop

E-shops, sometimes referred to as *e-stores* or *e-tailers,* are a version of a retail store where customers can shop at any hour of the day without leaving home or office. These are online stores that sell and support a variety of products and services. Some of these online businesses, or pure plays, are channeling their goods and services via the Internet only, such as Amazon.com. The others are an extension of traditional retail outlets that sell online as well as through a traditional physical store. They are generally known as "bricks and clicks," or "bricks and mortar," or "clicks and mortar" organizations, such as the Gap (www.gap.com) and Best Buy (www.bestbuy.com).

E-Mall

An *e-mall* consists of a number of e-shops; it serves as a gateway through which a visitor can access other e-shops. An e-mall may be generalized or specialized depending on the products offered by the e-shops it hosts. Revenues for e-mall operators include membership fees from participating e-shops, advertising, and possibly a fee on each transaction if the e-mall operator also processes payments. E-shops on the other hand benefit from brand reinforcement and increased traffic as visiting one shop on the e-mall often leads to browsing "neighboring" shops. An example of an e-mall is the Arizona e-mall, www.1az1.com/shopping.

CONSUMER-TO-BUSINESS (C2B) BUSINESS MODELS

Consumer-to-business (C2B) applies to any consumer that sells a product or service to a business over the Internet. One example of this e-business model is price-line.com where bidders (or customers) set their prices for items such as airline tickets or hotel rooms, and a seller decides whether to supply them. The demand for C2B e-business models is expected to increase in the next few years due to customers consistently demanding greater convenience and lower prices. From the consumer's perspective, C2B e-business facilitates the following:

- **Social interaction.** Consumers can communicate with businesses through various electronic means, such as e-mail, teleconferencing, and news groups.
- **Personal finance management.** Consumers can use electronic applications, for example Quicken, to manage investments and personal finances using online banking tools.
- **Purchasing products and information.** Consumers can use various electronic applications to find online information about products and services as well as to make purchases.

CONSUMER-TO-CONSUMER (C2C) BUSINESS MODEL

Consumer-to-consumer (C2C) applies to sites primarily offering goods and services to assist consumers interacting with each other over the Internet.

eBay, the Internet's most successful C2C online auction Web site, links like-minded buyers and sellers for a small commission. C2C online communities, or virtual communities, interact via e-mail groups, Web-based discussion forums, or chat rooms. C2C business models are consumer-driven where most consumers' needs, ranging from finding a mortgage to job hunting, are arranged. They are global swap shops based on customer-centered communication. An example of C2C community, KazaA, allows users to download MP3 music files, enabling users to exchange files. Many C2C communities are thriving on the Internet, such as:

- **Communities of interest**—people interact with each other on specific topics, such as golfing and stamp collecting.
- **Communities of relations**—brings together people who share certain life experiences, such as cancer patients, senior citizens, and car enthusiasts.
- **Communities of fantasy**—imaginary environments, such as fantasy football teams and playing one-on-one with Michael Jordan.

E-BUSINESS CHALLENGES

Although it is simple to describe the benefits of e-business, it is not nearly as easy to develop and deploy e-business systems. Companies can face significant implementation issues:

- **Cost**—E-business requires significant investments in new technologies that can touch many of a company's core business processes. As with all major business systems, e-business systems require significant investments in hardware, software, staffing, and training. Businesses need comprehensive solutions with greater ease of use to help foster cost-effective deployment.
- **Value**—Businesses want to know that their investments in e-business systems will produce a return. Business objectives such as lead generation, business-process automation, and cost reduction must be met. Systems used to reach these goals need to be flexible enough to change when the business changes.

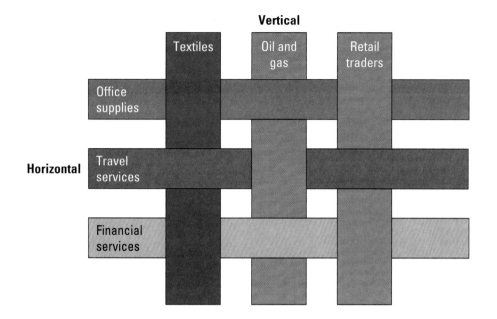

- **Security**—The Internet provides universal access, but companies must protect their assets against accidental or malicious misuse. System security, however, must not create prohibitive complexity or reduce flexibility. Customer information also needs to be protected from internal and external misuse. Privacy systems should safeguard the personal information critical to building sites that satisfy customer and business needs.

- **Leverage existing systems**—Most companies already use information technology to conduct business in non-Internet environments, such as marketing, order management, billing, inventory, distribution, and customer service. The Internet represents an alternative and complementary way to do business, but it is imperative that e-business systems integrate existing systems in a manner that avoids duplicating functionality and maintains usability, performance, and reliability.

- **Interoperability**—When systems from two or more businesses are able to exchange documents without manual intervention, businesses achieve cost reduction, improved performance, and more dynamic value chains.

Current Trends: E-Marketplaces

E-marketplaces and e-markets are sometimes referred to as "Net marketplaces" and "Net exchanges." Although e-marketplaces and e-markets are terms used interchangeably in the e-business literature, in this text *e-marketplaces* are interactive business communities providing a central market space where multiple buyers and sellers can engage in e-business activities.

Electronic marketplaces can be said to represent a new wave in the e-business propagation and extending the Business and Consumer combinations (B2B, B2C, C2B, and C2C) aiming primarily at the B2B area. E-marketplaces present structures for commercial exchange, consolidating supply chains, and creating sales channels. Their primary goal is to increase market efficiency by tightening and automating the relationship between supplier and buyer. Existing e-marketplaces allow participants to access various mechanisms to buy and sell almost anything, from services to direct materials.

Two broad types of e-marketplaces, as shown in Figure B7.6, have taken a strong hold on the e-business market:

1. *Horizontal marketplaces* connect buyers and sellers across many industries, primarily by simplifying the purchasing process. Horizontal MRO marketplaces for office supplies, travel, shipping, and financial services are now quite conventional. To participate in these e-marketplaces, an organization will need systems capable of interacting with the e-marketplace, such as inventory management and billing systems.

2. *Vertical marketplaces* provide products that are specific to trading partners in a given industry (textile, oil and gas, and retail, for instance). They can also serve as hubs for integrating business processes between companies. To be successful, they must provide much more than the simple aggregation of goods and services into an electronic catalog. They must add value chain services and collaborations well beyond the basic catalog transaction typical of horizontal MRO e-marketplaces.

At Dell Computer customers can specify the exact configuration of a computer system from available processors, memory modules, disk drives, monitors, audio and video enhancements, on its Web site. Once the order is received, the customer can continue to check on its status as it goes through the manufacturing process. Meanwhile, using dedicated Web pages, Dell keeps track of the capacities, capabilities, inventories, and actual cost structures of its top 20 suppliers who provide 90 percent of the components used in Dell products. Eventually, any feedback from the customer concerning quality and reliability of any component can be shared directly with the suppliers through this network. By treating both customers and suppliers as partners and collaborators sharing timely and critical information, companies like Dell become "virtually integrated" with the help of the Web.

Before e-marketplaces buyers were tied to a single supplier or a handful of suppliers over tightly controlled networks. Now, with e-marketplaces, they can perform one-stop comparison shopping across thousands of suppliers and go to the best source in real-time or near real-time.

The Big Three automakers have placed increased pressure on their 150,000 suppliers to reduce costs. Detroit-based General Motors Corporation plans to reduce the average cost of processing a purchase order from $100 to $10 by using Covisint, a B2B e-marketplace created by Ford Motor Company, General Motors Corporation, and DaimlerChrysler AG. The world's largest automaker spends more than $80 billion in procurements each year, so even a minor improvement in how these activities are handled could save the company billions.[4]

E-MARKETPLACE BENEFITS AND REVENUE MODELS

In the long list of potential benefits that can be derived from the participation in an e-marketplace, some are of financial nature while others are not. Typical ones include costs savings, revenue growth, and timesavings.

While the revenue model of an e-marketplace can be based solely on a single fee type, it is most often preferable that the revenue model rests on a combination of fees. Figure B7.7 presents the advantages and limitations of various types of revenue models. The revenue model should continuously be adjusted to reflect the dynamic set-up, the stage of the lifecycle and the specific competitive situation of the e-marketplace.

THE "CONTENT" PERSPECTIVE OF E-MARKETPLACES

A key element of e-marketplaces is their ability to provide not only transaction capabilities but dynamic, relevant content to trading partners. The original e-business Web sites provided shopping cart capabilities built around "product catalogs." As a result of the complex e-marketplace emergence that must support existing business processes and systems, content is becoming even more critical for e-marketplaces. Buyers need good content description to make informed purchases and

Revenue Models	Advantages	Limitation
Transaction fees	■ Can be directly tied to savings (both process and price savings) ■ Important revenue source when high level of liquidity (transaction volume) is reached	■ If process savings are not completely visible, use of the system is discouraged (incentive to move transactions offline) ■ Transaction fees likely to decrease with time
License fees	■ Creates incentives to do many transactions ■ Customization and back-end integration leads to lock-in of participants	■ Up front fee is a barrier to entry for participants ■ Price differentiation is complicated
Subscription fees	■ Creates incentives to do transactions ■ Price can be differentiated ■ Possibility to build additional revenue from new user groups	■ Fixed fee is a barrier to entry for participants
Fees for value-added services	■ Service offering can be differentiated ■ Price can be differentiated ■ Possibility to build additional revenue from established and new user groups (third parties)	■ Cumbersome process for customers to continually evaluate new services
Advertising fees	■ Well-targeted advertisements can be perceived as value-added content by trading participants ■ Easy to implement	■ Limited revenue potential ■ Overdone or poorly targeted advertisements can be disturbing elements on the Web site

FIGURE B7.7

The Advantages and Limitations of Various E-Marketplace Revenue Models

sellers use content to properly market and differentiate themselves from the competition. Content and product description establish the common understanding between both parties to the transaction. As a result, the accessibility, usability, accuracy, and richness of that content directly affects the transaction.

Future Trends: E-Channels, E-Portals, and E-Government

Traditional market channels are giving way to new channels, production-centric processes are yielding to customer-centric processes, old business models are morphing to new models, information is replacing inventory, and physical goods are being replaced by digital products. Consider the emerging structural patterns that characterize the new economy, such as e-channels, e-portals, and e-government.

E-channels are Web-based business channels. The first step is developing a stand-alone channel, or spin-off.com, independent of the parent company (for example, Procter and Gamble spin-off venture Reflect.com). The second step is a stand-alone channel with some connection to the parent company (Wal-Mart.com). The new phase, channel synchronization, is a tightly integrated click-and-brick strategy, like CVS.com, that serves customers seamlessly no matter what the entry point is.

An *e-portal* is a single gateway through which to gain access to all the information, systems, and processes used by stakeholders of an organization. E-portals have evolved in three phases in the last few years. The first was developing appropriate traffic (e.g., Yahoo!). The second was fighting for transactions (e.g., Amazon.com). Now in the third phase, companies are beginning to battle for margins with click-and-brick partnerships such as Amazon.com and Target. This is a developing environment; expect to see more partnerships like this. E-portals have been shown to provide these benefits:

	Business	Consumer	Government
Business	B2B conisint.com	B2C dell.com	B2G lockheedmartin.com
Consumer	C2B priceline.com	C2C ebay.com	C2G eGov.com
Government	G2B export.gov	G2C medicare.gov	G2G disasterhelp.gov

- Improved levels of customer interaction with an increase in customer service.
- Improved customer and business partner loyalty.
- Improved understanding of Web visitor information.
- Improved employee communications and productivity with enhanced business processes.

Some organizations believe they may also gain competitive advantage by enhancing their relationships with key suppliers or by increasing their customer base through customer service improvement. E-portals can be used to trace behavior of customers and suppliers in order to allow for constant service enhancements.

Personalization features of e-portals enable the user to select the information sources in which he or she is most interested, and often the colors and format in which the information is displayed. This sometimes means that users are more likely to return—presumably making the e-portal more effective at achieving its aims.

Ultimately, the purpose for business is always increased return on investment. In e-business systems, employing e-portals can lead to reduced EDI costs, postage costs, and travel costs to meetings, as well as reduced administration/paper costs. Increased return can also come from reduced error rates (because decisions are made based on more up-to-date information) and reduced staffing costs (because customers can take advantage of self-service features and so on).

The challenge of the e-portal is to reduce information overload by presenting only the information the user requires, preferably at the time when the user requires it.

The more recent business models that have arisen to enable organizations to take advantage of the Internet and create value are within e-government. *E-government* involves the use of strategies and technologies to transform government(s) by improving the delivery of services and enhancing the quality of interaction between the citizen-consumer within all branches of government(s) (refer to Figure B7.8).

One example of an e-government portal, FirstGov.gov, the official United States gateway to all government information, is the catalyst for a growing electronic government. Its powerful search engine and ever-growing collection of topical and customer-focused links connect users to millions of Web pages, from the federal government, to local and tribal governments, to foreign nations around the world.

Specific e-business models as they relate to e-government include:

- **Consumer-to-government (C2G)**—C2G will mainly constitute the areas where a consumer (or citizen) interacts with the government. It will include areas like elections when citizens vote for government officials; census where the consumer provides demographic information to the government; taxation where the consumer is paying taxes to the government.

- **Government-to-business (G2B)**—This model includes all government interaction with business enterprises whether it is procurement of goods and services from suppliers or information regarding legal and business issues that is transmitted electronically.

- **Government-to-consumer (G2C)**—Governments around the world are now dealing with consumers (or citizens) electronically, providing them with updated information. Governments are also processing applications for visas, renewal of passports and driver's licenses, advertising of tender notices, and other services online.

- **Government-to-government (G2G)**—Governments around the world are now dealing with other governments electronically. Still at an inception stage, this e-business model will enhance international trade and information retrieval, for example, on criminal records of new migrants. At the state level, information exchange and processing of transactions online will enable enhanced efficiencies.

With the advent of the Internet and e-commerce, new e-business models have been emerging. To capitalize on e-business and create new channels that cut expenses, speed delivery time, and open new markets, new strategic business models are needed. To establish an environment conducive to e-business, companies are required to change their strategies, realign their organizations with emerging opportunities, and articulate the new strategies to partners.

Merely deciding to adopt a new e-business model does not guarantee success. Implementing a new e-business model in an established organization involves considerable disruption. Technical adjustments, such as integration, debugging, software integration, and effective Web sites are necessary. Effectively managing the changes associated with the implementation of new e-business models will lead to success.

✳ KEY TERMS

Business-to-business (B2B), 311
Business-to-consumer (B2C), 313
Consumer-to-business (C2B), 314
Consumer-to-consumer
   (C2C), 314
Content provider, 309
E-business, 306
E-business model, 306
E-channel, 317
E-government, 318

E mall, 313
E-marketplace, 315
English auction, 312
E-portal, 317
E-procurement, 311
E-shop (e-store or e-tailer), 313
Horizontal marketplace, 316
Intermediary, 309
Longer term relationship
   model, 312

Market makers, 310
Marketplace model, 312
Online broker, 310
Pure play, 306
Reintermediation, 309
Seller model, 313
Spot sourcing, 311
Systematic sourcing, 311
Vertical marketplace, 316

✳ CLOSING CASE ONE

E-Business@eBay

eBay.com is the largest e-marketplace. Founded in 1995, eBay.com created a powerful platform for the sale of goods and services by a community of individuals and businesses. On any given day, there are millions of items across thousands of categories for sale on eBay.com, as well as on Half.com, eBay.com's site dedicated to fixed price trading. eBay.com enables trade on a local, national, and international basis with customized sites in markets around the world.

From its humble origins as a trading post for Beanie Babies, eBay.com is indeed morphing into something entirely new and a lot bigger than most people realize. Margaret C. Whitman took over as CEO of eBay in early 1998, after founder Pierre Omidyar already had it growing 70 percent a month. Whitman initially was not sure what to make of what looked like a funky online garage sale. But under her stewardship, eBay has grown into the world's largest e-marketplace, offering everything from its trademark Pez dispensers and Beanie Babies to automobiles and homes.

In 2003, at least 30 million people bought and sold well over $20 billion in merchandise on eBay, more than the gross domestic product of all but 70 of the world's countries. More than 150,000 entrepreneurs earned a full-time living selling everything from diet pills and Kate Spade handbags to BMWs.

eBay's powerful whirlwind is pulling ever larger players into its economy. The company's sellers are stretching far beyond its specialty of used and remaindered goods; they are now pushing into the heart of traditional retailing, a $2 trillion market. Among eBay's 12 million daily listings are new Crest toothbrushes and the latest DVD players. Retail giants such as Sears, Roebuck and Co. and Walt Disney Co. are selling brand new items there as well. More than a quarter of the offerings are listed at fixed prices familiar to mass-market consumers.

Nimble management at eBay is apparent in its financials. In 2003, profits rocketed 176 percent, to $250 million. Net sales, from transaction fees on $15 billion in gross revenues, hit $1.2 billion. In the second quarter, revenues shot up 91 percent from a year ago, to $509 million. It now looks as if eBay's forecast two years ago that it would grow to $3 billion in net revenues by 2005, which could have been considered a stretch at the time, will be met easily, barring an unexpected slowdown.

For now, the big brands, which still account for fewer than 5 percent of eBay's gross sales, seem to be bringing in more customers than they steal. Motorola Inc., for example, helped kick off a new wholesale business for eBay in 2003, selling excess and returned cell phones in large lots. "We bring a community of buyers to eBay," says Chip Yager, a director of channel development at Motorola PCS. Thanks to the initiative of established companies such as Motorola, eBay's wholesale business jumped nine-fold, to $23 million, in the first quarter.

As businesses on eBay grow larger, they spur the creation of even more businesses. A new army of merchants, for instance, are making a business out of selling for other people. From almost zero a couple of years ago, these so-called "Trading Assistants" now number nearly 23,000. One of them, a start-up called AuctionDrop Inc., plans to open a nationwide chain of storefronts where people can drag in stuff for AuctionDrop to sell on eBay.com.[5]

Questions

1. eBay is one of the only major Internet "pure plays" to consistently make a profit from its inception. What is eBay's e-business model and why has it been so successful?

2. Other major Web sites, like Amazon.com and Yahoo!, have entered the auction e-marketplace with far less success than eBay. How has eBay been able to maintain its dominant position?

3. eBay has long been an e-marketplace for used goods and collectibles. Today, it is increasingly a place where major businesses come to auction their wares. Why would a brand name vendor set up shop on eBay?

CLOSING CASE TWO

Mail with PostalOne

Despite billions of dollars invested in automation and information technology since the early 1970s, the 226-year-old United States Postal Service's (USPS) productivity grew by only 11 percent over the past three decades. The 800,000 employees at USPS faced a fiscal deficit of $2.4 billion in 2001. Factors in the shortfall included the slow economy, rising fuel costs, and electronic alternatives to paper mail.

Agency leaders maintain that technology is one of the keys to making the USPS more competitive, as they have started a heavy campaign to combat declining revenues using a series of Web technology projects. One of the most significant projects for the USPS is a Web front-end for PostalOne, a system that seeks to eliminate the administrative paperwork for bulk mail, which accounts for 70 percent of total mail volume and 50 percent of the agency's $65 billion in revenue. More than 770,000 businesses use the USPS to send bulk mail.

PostalOne is one of the main customer-facing portions of the USPS's plan to build the Information Platform, which comprises the core IT systems that receive, process, transport, and deliver the mail. There is a tremendous amount of paperwork associated with verifying a mailing to receive a discounted postage rate and creating related documentation. Business customers will install a USPS application that will reside on their server and manage the online paperwork, validate and encrypt files, and handle communications with PostalOne servers.

As part of the Information Platform, there is a Web interface to the agency's Processing Operations Information System (POIS), which collects, tracks, and ultimately delivers performance data on the agency's more than 350 processing and distribution facilities. These efforts follow several e-business projects:

- **NetPost Mailing Online** is a service that lets small businesses transmit documents, correspondence, newsletters and other first-class, standard, and nonprofit mail over the Web to the USPS. Electronic files are transmitted to printing contractors, which print the documents, insert them into addressed envelopes, sort the mail pieces, and then add postage. The finished pieces are taken to a local post office for processing and delivery. Customers get the automated first-class rate, which is a few cents less per piece than the first-class rate.

- **Post Electronic Courier Service,** or PosteCS, a secure messaging product, lets mailers send documents by e-mail or over the Web to recipients via a secure communication session. PosteCS has an electronic postmark, an electronic time and date stamp developed by USPS, embedded for proof of delivery. PosteCS is used mainly to transfer large files, such as financial statements. Cost is based on security option chosen and file size.

- **NetPost.Certified,** a secure messaging product, was developed to help federal agencies comply with the Government Paperwork Elimination Act. NetPost.Certified is used, for example, by the Social Security Administration to receive notification by prisons when inmates are no longer eligible for benefits. NetPost.Certified includes an electronic postmark and a public key infrastructure. The service costs 50 cents per transaction.

- **EBillPay** lets customers receive, view, and pay their bills via the agency's Web site. The Postal Service partners with CheckFree, which offers its service on the USPS site and performs back-end processing. There are some enhancements that are currently being developed to this service including an embedded electronic postmark, person-to-person payments, and the ability to receive and pay bills via e-mail. The ability to offer businesses and consumers online bill payment options is vital for the Postal Service, which estimates that $17 billion in annual revenue is at risk from first-class mail going through electronic alternatives for bill payment and presentment.

Despite its problems, the USPS has been resilient over the years, in large part because of its enormous resources. It is the nation's second largest employer behind Wal-Mart and its revenue would rank it eighth in the Fortune 500.[6]

Questions

1. Do you think the USPS's steps are far-reaching enough to ensure its relevance in e-business?
2. What other strategic alliances, akin to its partnership with CheckFree, can the USPS develop to stay competitive?
3. Why would the USPS compete in a market that private companies already serve well?

1. **Implementing an E-Business Model**

   The Genius is a revolutionary mountain bike with full-suspension and shock-adjustable forks that is being marketed via the Internet. The Genius needs an e-business solution that will easily enable internal staff to deliver fresh and relevant product information throughout its Web site. To support its large audience, they also need the ability to present information in multiple languages and serve over 1 million page-views per month to visitors in North America and Europe. Explain what e-business model you would use to market The Genius on the Internet.

2. **P2P File Sharing**

   GigaMedia.com is a new Internet based company that provides subscription-based digitally downloadable games via its Web site. It also provides online Web-based games and allows users of multiplayer online games to view one another's actions. At the moment GigaMedia.com has 200,000 subscribers in 10 countries and charges a subscription rate of $10 per month. Online gaming has been a powerful driver in the P2P e-marketspace. How can GigaMedia.com protect themselves against public sharing of games such as the music industry has seen?

3. **Online Auction Sites**

   You are working for a new Internet start-up company, eMart.com, an online marketplace for the sale of goods and services. It offers a wide variety of features and services that enable online members to buy and sell their goods and services quickly and conveniently. eMart.com's mission is to provide a global trading platform where anyone can trade practically anything. Suggest some ways that eMart.com can extend their market reach beyond that of its competitor, eBay.com.

4. **Brewing Marketplace**

   Founded in 2003, the Foothills Brewing Company, foothillsbrew.com, is a pure play Internet brewing master. In its first year, the brewery sold 1,500 barrels of beer online. Its lagers and ales are brewed in small batches, hand-crafted by a team of dedicated workers with only the highest ideals of quality. This pride, along with its brewing process, is what creates the great brews. Identify the reasons why foothillsbrew.com should continue to be a pure play–only company in the midst of a highly competitive marketplace.

B8

Emerging Trends and Technologies

1. Identify the trends that will have the greatest impact on future business.
2. Identify the technologies that will have the greatest impact on future business.
3. Explain why understanding trends and new technologies can help an organization prepare for the future.

Introduction

The core units brought out how important it is for organizations to anticipate and prepare for the future by studying emerging trends and new technologies. Having a broad view of emerging trends and new technologies as they relate to business can provide an organization with a valuable strategic advantage. Those organizations that can most effectively grasp the deep currents of technological evolution can use their knowledge to protect themselves against sudden and fatal technological obsolescence.

This plug-in identifies several emerging trends and new technologies that can help an organization prepare for future opportunities and challenges.

Reasons to Watch Trends

Organizations anticipate, forecast, and assess future events using a variety of rational, scientific methods including:

- ■ **Trend analysis:** The examination of a trend to identify its nature, causes, speed of development, and potential impacts.
- ■ **Trend monitoring:** Trends viewed as particularly important in a specific community, industry, or sector are carefully monitored, watched, and reported to key decision makers.
- ■ **Trend projection:** When numerical data is available, a trend can be plotted on graph paper to display changes through time and into the future.
- ■ **Computer simulation:** Complex systems, such as the U.S. economy, can be modeled by means of mathematical equations and different scenarios can be run against the model to determine "what if" analysis.

Top Reasons to Study Trends	
1. Generate ideas and identify opportunities	Find new ideas and innovations by studying trends and analyzing publications.
2. Identify early warning signals	Scan the environment for potential threats and risks.
3. Gain confidence	A solid foundation of awareness about trends can provide an organization with the confidence to take risks.
4. Beat the competition	Seeing what is coming before others can gives an organization the lead time it requires to establish a foothold in the new market.
5. Understand a trend	Analyzing the details within a trend can help separate truly significant developments from rapidly appearing and disappearing fads.
6. Balance strategic goals	Thinking about the future is an antidote to a "profit now, worry later" mentality that can lead to trouble in the long term.
7. Understand the future of specific industries	Organizations must understand everything inside and outside their industry.
8. Prepare for the future	Any organization that wants to compete in this hyperchanging world needs to make every effort to forecast the future.

FIGURE B8.1

Top Reasons to Study Trends

- *Historical analysis:* The study of historical events in order to anticipate the outcome of current developments.

Foresight is one of the secret ingredients of business success. Foresight, however, is increasingly in short supply because almost everything in our world is changing at a faster pace than ever before. Many organizations have little idea what type of future they should prepare for in this world of hyperchange. Figure B8.1 displays the top reasons organizations should look to the future and study trends.[1]

Trends Shaping Our Future

According to the World Future Society, the following trends have the potential to change our world, our future, and our lives.[2]

- The world's population will double in the next 40 years
- Population in developed countries is living longer
- The growth in information industries is creating a knowledge-dependent global society
- The global economy is becoming more integrated
- The economy and society are dominated by technology
- Pace of technological innovation is increasing
- Time is becoming one of the world's most precious commodities

THE WORLD'S POPULATION WILL DOUBLE IN THE NEXT 40 YEARS

The countries that are expected to have the largest increases in population between 2000 and 2050 are:

- Palestinian Territory—217 percent increase
- Niger—205 percent increase
- Yemen—168 percent increase

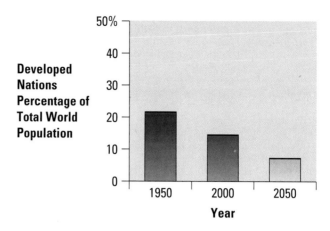

- Angola—162 percent increase
- Democratic Republic of the Congo—161 percent increase
- Uganda—133 percent increase

In contrast, developed and industrialized countries are expected to see fertility rates decrease below population replacement levels, leading to significant declines in population (see Figure B8.2).

Potential Business Impact

- Global agriculture will be required to supply as much food as has been produced during all of human history to meet human nutritional needs over the next 40 years.
- Developed nations will find that retirees will have to remain on the job to remain competitive and continue economic growth.
- Developed nations will begin to increase immigration limits.

POPULATION IN DEVELOPED COUNTRIES IS LIVING LONGER

New pharmaceuticals and medical technologies are making it possible to prevent and cure diseases that would have been fatal to past generations. This is one of the reasons that each generation lives longer and remains healthier than the last. On average, each generation in the United States lives three years longer than the previous. An 80-year-old in 1950 could expect to live 6.5 years longer today. Many developed countries are now experiencing life expectancy over 75 years for males and over 80 years for females (see Figure B8.3).

FIGURE B8.3

Rising Life Expectancy
in Developed Countries

Rising Life Expectancy in Developed Countries		
Country	Life Expectancy (Born 1950–1955)	Life Expectancy (Born 1995–2000)
United States	68.9	76.5
United Kingdom	69.2	77.2
Germany	67.5	77.3
France	66.5	78.1
Italy	66.0	78.2
Canada	69.1	78.5
Japan	63.9	80.5

Potential Business Impact

- Global demand for elderly products and services will grow quickly in the coming decades.
- The cost of health care is destined to skyrocket.
- Pharmaceutical companies will be pushed for advances in geriatric medicine.

THE GROWTH IN INFORMATION INDUSTRIES IS CREATING A KNOWLEDGE-DEPENDENT GLOBAL SOCIETY

Estimates indicate that 83 percent of American management personnel will be knowledge workers by 2005. Estimates for knowledge workers in Europe and Japan are not far behind. A typical large organization in 2010 will have fewer than half the management levels of its counterpart in 1990, and about one-third the number of managers. Soon, large organizations will be composed of specialists who rely on information from co-workers, customers, and suppliers to guide their actions. Employees will gain new power as they are provided with the authority to make decisions based on the information they acquire.

Potential Business Impact

- Top managers must be computer-literate to retain their jobs and achieve success.
- Knowledge workers are generally higher paid and their proliferation is increasing overall prosperity.
- Entry-level and unskilled positions are requiring a growing level of education.
- Information now flows from front-office workers to higher management for analysis. Thus, in the future, fewer mid-level managers will be required, flattening the corporate pyramid.
- Downsizing, restructuring, reorganization, outsourcing, and layoffs will continue as typical large organizations struggle to reinvent and restructure themselves for greater flexibility.

THE GLOBAL ECONOMY IS BECOMING MORE INTEGRATED

International outsourcing is on the rise as organizations refuse to pay high salaries for activities that do not contribute directly to the bottom line. The European Union has relaxed its borders and capital controls making it easier for companies to outsource support functions throughout the continent.

The Internet is one of the primary tools enabling our global economy. Internet users numbered about 500 million worldwide in 2003. One of the primary reasons for the increase in Internet use is the increase in connectivity technology. China's Internet users are growing by 6 percent each month, to 33 million users in 2003. India's Internet users are close to 25 million in 2003 (see Figure B8.4 for India's statistics). The increase in Internet use is increasing revenues for e-businesses. Total online consumer sales, excluding auctions, reached $6 billion in 2002.

Potential Business Impact

- Demand for personnel in distant countries will increase the need for foreign-language training, employee incentives suited to other cultures, and many other aspects of performing business globally.
- The growth of e-business and the use of the Internet to shop globally for raw materials and supplies will reduce the cost of doing business.
- The Internet will continue to enable small companies to compete with worldwide giants with relatively little investment.

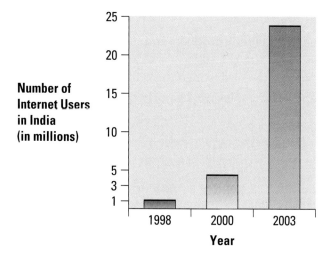

- Internet-based operations require sophisticated knowledge workers and thus people with the right technical skills will be heavily recruited over the next 15 years.

- Estimated world savings in business expenses on the Internet totaled $2.3 trillion in 2003.

THE ECONOMY AND SOCIETY ARE DOMINATED BY TECHNOLOGY

Computers are becoming a part of our environment. Mundane commercial and service jobs, environmentally dangerous jobs, standard assembly jobs, and even the repair of inaccessible equipment such as space stations will be increasingly performed by robots. Personal robots will appear in the home by 2010. By 2007, artificial intelligence and expert systems will help most companies and government agencies assimilate data and solve problems beyond the range of today's computers including energy prospecting, automotive diagnostics, insurance underwriting, and law enforcement.

Superconductors operating at economically viable temperatures are expected to be in commercial use by 2015. Products eventually will include supercomputers the size of a three-pound coffee can, electronic motors 75 percent smaller and lighter than those in use today, and power plants.

Potential Business Impact

- New technologies provide dozens of new opportunities to create businesses and jobs.

- Automation will continue to decrease the cost of products and services, making it possible to reduce prices while improving profits.

- The Internet is expected to push prices of most products to the commodity level.

- The demand for scientists, engineers, and technicians will continue to grow.

PACE OF TECHNOLOGICAL INNOVATION IS INCREASING

Technology is advancing at a phenomenal pace. Medical knowledge is doubling every eight years. Half of what students learn in their freshman year of college about innovative technology is obsolete, revised, or taken for granted by their senior year. In fact, all of today's technical knowledge will represent only 1 percent of the knowledge that will be available in 2050.

Potential Business Impact

- The time to get products and services to market is being shortened by technology. Products must capture their market quickly before the competition can copy them. During the 1940s the average time to get a product to market was 40 weeks. Today, a product's entire life cycle seldom lasts 40 weeks.
- Industries will face tighter competition based on new technologies. Those who adopt state-of-the-art technology first will prosper, while those who ignore it eventually will fail.

TIME IS BECOMING ONE OF THE WORLD'S MOST PRECIOUS COMMODITIES

In the United States, workers today spend around 10 percent more time on the job than they did a decade ago. European executives and nonunionized workers face the same trend. This high-pressured environment is increasing the need for any product or service that saves time or simplifies life.

Potential Business Impact

- Companies must take an active role in helping their employees balance their time at work with their family lives and need for leisure.
- Stress-related problems affecting employee morale and wellness will continue to grow.
- As time for shopping continues to evaporate, Internet and mail-order marketers will have a growing advantage over traditional stores.

Technologies Shaping Our Future

The following technologies have the potential to change our world, our future, and our lives.[3]

- Digital ink
- Digital paper
- Radio frequency identification (RFID)
- Teleliving
- Alternative energy sources
- Autonomic computing

DIGITAL INK

Digital ink (or *electronic ink*) refers to technology that digitally represents handwriting in its natural form (see Figure B8.5). E Ink Corporation, headquartered in

FIGURE B8.5

Digital Ink

Cambridge, Massachusetts, has developed a proprietary technology called electronic ink, which provides significant advantages over other display technologies. E Ink was founded in 1997 to advance electronic ink, develop applications, and create markets for displays based on this unique technology.

Potential Business Impact

- Digital ink has broad usage in many applications, from point-of-sale signs in retail stores, to next generation displays in mobile devices and PDAs, to thin, portable electronic books and newspapers. E Ink has collaborated with various companies like Lucent Technologies to produce reusable paper with digital ink.

- The ultimate dream of E Ink is *RadioPaper,* a dynamic high-resolution electronic display that combines a paperlike reading experience with the ability to access information anytime, anywhere. RadioPaper will be thin and flexible and could be used to create an electronic book or newspaper with real pages.

DIGITAL PAPER

Digital paper (or *electronic paper*) is any paper that is optimized for any type of digital printing. In some ways, digital paper is produced much like a sheet of paper. It comes from a pulp and the finished product has the flexibility to be rolled into scrolls of "paper." However, the major difference between paper produced from a tree and paper produced in a laboratory is that information on a digital paper sheet can be altered thousands of times and not degrade over time (see Figure B8.6). Digital paper offers excellent resolution and high contrast under a wide range of viewing angles, requires no external power to retain its image, is extremely lightweight, costs less, and is remarkably flexible, unlike computer displays.

FIGURE B8.6

Digital Paper

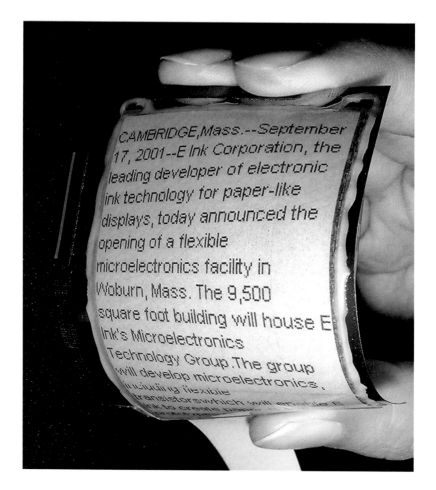

Date	Technology
April 1996	MIT's Media Lab starts work on electronic paper prototype
April 1997	E Ink is founded to commercialize MIT's electronic paper displays
May 1999	E Ink debuts Immedia electronic paper display products
November 2000	E Ink and Lucent Technologies demonstrate first flexible electronic products
December 2000	Gyricon Media is spun off from Xerox PARC
February 2001	E Ink teams with Philips Components to develop a high-resolution display for smart hand-helds
March 2001	Gyricon introduces digital paper technology
June 2001	Macy's is scheduled to test digital paper for in-store signage use
Late 2001	Delivery of E Ink/Philips hand-held prototype
2004/2005	E Ink electronic paper hand-held devices expected to become available to users
Mid-2000s	Possible debut of E Ink's RadioPaper wireless electronic publishing technology

Macy's department store was the first company to experiment by placing digital paper signs in the children's section at a New Jersey store. As the company is currently spending more than $250,000 a week on changing its in-store signs, such renewable signage could prove highly desirable. A networked programmable sign will run for two years on three AA batteries (see Figure B8.7).[4]

As a laboratory prototype, digital ink and digital paper have been around for some time with demonstration of the technologies often leading to wild predictions about e-books and e-newspapers (see Figure B8.8).

Potential Business Impact

- Digital paper is driving a new wave of innovation in the content distribution field. Paperlike displays will replace newspapers, magazines, and books since they will be almost as manageable as paper and allow display resolution close to print.

- The concept of a reusable paper product is an environmentally sound idea considering that a major portion of the world's paper goes to printing newspapers, magazines, pamphlets, etc.

RADIO FREQUENCY IDENTIFICATION (RFID)

Radio frequency identification (RFID) technologies use active or passive tags in the form of chips or smart labels that can store unique identifiers and relay this information to electronic readers. Even though radio frequency identification (RFID) technology has been around for some time, it has only recently become a significant enabling technology to enhance efficiencies across the supply chain. RFID already is demonstrating measurable results that have the potential to transform how business is conducted for both retailers and their suppliers.

RFID technology is attracting considerable attention as a complement or even replacement for bar codes (or UPC) because of the significant range, speed, and unattended reading advantages it provides (refer to Figure B8.9). Unlike bar code–based tracking systems, an RFID system can read the information on a tag without requiring line of sight and without the need for a particular orientation. That means RFID systems can be largely automated, reducing the need for manual scanning. In addition, RFID tags hold much more data than UPC labels. The tag can be programmed to hold information such as an item's serial number, color, size, manufacture date, and current price, as well as a list of all distribution points the item touched before arriving at a store.[5]

Potential Business Impact

- Incorporating RFID technology into existing supply chain operations can reduce the labor required to monitor goods movement and inventory flow. Benefits include reduced labor costs, simplified business processes, improved inventory control, and increased sales.

FIGURE B8.9

Comparison of Bar Code Labeling to RFID Technology

Bar Code Labeling and Scanning Technology	RFID Technology
Bar codes are currently cheaper per item than RFID.	Current RFID tags are expensive compared to bar code labels, but new polymer-based tags are being developed in the less than $0.01 range.
Bar codes are limited by space, and typically only store identifiers like lot #, SKU #.	Some RFID tags can hold a substantial amount of data, reducing the need for a back-end database to track each material transaction.
Once applied, bar code labels cannot be modified, only reprinted and reapplied.	Once affixed to the material, some RFID tags may be overwritten and updated with new information very easily, without removal.
Requires line-of-sight between reader and label.	Does not require line-of-sight between reader and label.
Bar codes can include human-readable information.	RFID tags cannot be read without a special reading device; however, hybrid labels are available.
Bar codes are completely passive.	Intelligent RFID tags (smart labels) are being built that can track variables like temperature as they travel with the material.

- Bar code–based tracking systems are an effective tool for basic inventory tracking. Used in conjunction with a bar code system or as a stand-alone inventory tracking application, RFID allows manufacturers and retailers to complement existing systems while gathering more information throughout a supply chain.
- Systems with the power to update the information that moves with an individual product provide complete supply chain visibility without the prohibitive labor costs and error rates a similar manual system would entail.
- RFID can act like a security guard at a gateway. As goods are moved from shipping dock to truck to store, RFID can conduct automatic inventories and compare the goods with the manifest.

TELELIVING

Lifestyle changes will emerge as computers develop capabilities that are more sophisticated. *Teleliving* refers to using information devices and the Internet to conduct all aspects of life seamlessly. This can include such things as shopping, working, learning, playing, healing, and praying. Even today, homes, autos, and work environments are wired into intelligent networks that interact with one another. Each year, four billion chips are embedded in everything from coffee makers to Cadillacs.

Potential Business Impact

- In the future, people will move through a constant stream of information summoned at the touch of a finger. They will interact with life-sized images, data, and text in homes and offices. The days of hunching over a computer will be gone.
- The *virtual assistant (VA)* will be a small program stored on a PC or portable device that monitors e-mails, faxes, messages, and phone calls. Virtual assistants will help individuals solve problems in the same way a real assistant would. In time, the VA will take over routine tasks such as writing a letter, retrieving a file, and making a phone call.
- Robotic sales people will take on human appearances and have the ability to perform all tasks associated with a sales job.

ALTERNATIVE ENERGY SOURCES

By the end of the decade wind, geothermal, hydroelectric, solar, and other alternative energy sources will increase from their present level of 10 percent of all energy use to about 30 percent. Worldwide wind-power generating capacity grew by 6,500 megawatts in 2003, the fastest rate of growth yet recorded and 50 percent more than the previous year (see Figure B8.10). Nuclear plants will supply 16 percent of the energy in Russia and eastern Europe by 2010. New sources of carbon fuels are frequently being discovered and more-powerful extraction methods are being developed, thereby keeping supply up and costs down.

Potential Business Impact

- China, Asia, India, South America, and Russia are modernizing their economies, which increasingly use large amounts of energy.
- The cost of alternative energy sources is dropping with technical advances. This growing competition from other energy sources will help limit the price of oil.
- The imminent deregulation of the energy industry is expected to create a huge spurt of innovative entrepreneurship, fostering a wide variety of new energy sources.

■ Oil will remain the world's most important energy resource. However, in two
or three decades a declining reliance on oil will help reduce air and water pol-
lution. By 2060, a costly but pollution-free hydrogen economy may become
possible.

AUTONOMIC COMPUTING

Autonomic computing is a self-managing computing model named after, and patterned on, the human body's autonomic nervous system. Autonomic computing
is one of the building blocks of widespread computing, an anticipated future computing model in which small—even invisible—computers will be all around us,
communicating through increasingly interconnected networks. Many industry
leaders, including IBM, HP, Sun, and Microsoft, are researching various components of autonomic computing. However, autonomic computing is not an overnight revolution in which systemwide, self-managing environments suddenly appear. As described in Figure B8.11, autonomic computing is a gradual evolution
that delivers new technologies that are adopted and implemented at various stages
and levels.[6]

Potential Business Impact

■ The complex IT infrastructures of the future will require more computer automation than ever before. Autonomic computing will be used in a variety of
areas that include security, storage, network management, and new redundancy and failover capabilities.

■ Autonomic computers will continuously seek out ways to optimize computing. In the autonomic environment, computers will monitor components and
fine-tuning workflows to achieve system performance goals.

Level	Technologies Implemented
Level 1: Basic	The starting point where most systems are today, this level represents manual computing in which all system elements are managed independently by an extensive, highly skilled IT staff. The staff sets up, monitors, and eventually replaces system elements.
Level 2: Managed	Systems management technologies can be used to collect and consolidate information from disparate systems onto fewer consoles, reducing administrative time. There is greater system awareness and improved productivity.
Level 3: Predictive	The system monitors and correlates data to recognize patterns and recommends actions that are approved and initiated by the IT staff. This reduces the dependency on deep skills and enables faster and better decision making.
Level 4: Adaptive	In addition to monitoring and correlating data, the system takes action based on the information, thereby enhancing IT agility and resiliency with minimal human interaction.
Level 5: Autonomic	Fully integrated systems and components are dynamically managed by business rules and policies, enabling IT staff to focus on meeting business needs with true business agility and resiliency.

- Autonomic computers will be able to "self-heal." In the event of a component failure, an autonomic computer will be able to diagnose the failure and develop a workaround that allows the computer to continue with its functions.
- Autonomic computers will be able to "self-protect." Protection for computing resources primarily takes the form of fighting off invasive viruses and security intrusion attempts.

Organizations that can think ahead will be prepared to take advantage of all the new opportunities that rapid social and technological progress is creating. Trends shaping our future include:

- The world's population will double in the next 40 years
- Population in developed countries is living longer
- The growth in information industries is creating a knowledge-dependent global society
- The global economy is becoming more integrated
- The economy and society are dominated by technology
- Pace of technological innovation is increasing
- Time is becoming one of the world's most precious commodities

Technologies shaping our future include:

- Digital ink
- Digital paper
- Radio frequency identification (RFID)
- Teleliving
- Alternative energy sources
- Autonomic computing

★ KEY TERMS

Autonomic computing, 334
Computer simulation, 324
Digital ink (or electronic ink), 329
Digital paper (or electronic paper), 330

Historical analysis, 325
Radio frequency identification (RFID), 332
RadioPaper, 330
Teleliving, 333

Trend analysis, 324
Trend monitoring, 324
Trend projection, 324
Virtual assistant (VA), 333

★ CLOSING CASE ONE

Autonomic Railways

Canadian Pacific Railway (CPR), based in Calgary, Alberta, Canada, is one of the largest railway systems in North America. With more than 14,400 miles of rail line in Canada and the United States, this $2.6 billion (US) transportation company serves virtually every major industry, from the resource-based industries of the West, to the manufacturing bases and consumer markets in central Canada and the northern United States.

Shippers expect fast, reliable services and on-time delivery of goods. As a result, CPR designed many programs—from improving asset management, to strengthening service reliability, to accounting for fluctuating costs—to help it respond to market forces with agility and ease. Val King, manager of IT security for CPR, explains that security management is an essential element in the delivery of these on demand services. King states, "We must protect our operations from technology attacks, while providing our customers easy, reliable access to information and services online."

The goal of the company's IT security team is simple: minimize risk while optimizing user satisfaction. Yet the team's greatest challenges are lack of resources and tight budgets. "We had to look to technology to help us accomplish our goals," explains King. CPR collaborated with IBM to deliver solutions that are both automated (they can control a defined process without human intervention) and autonomic (they can sense and respond to conditions in accordance with business policies). As a result, IT employees can deliver consistent, reliable service levels at reduced costs since they collaborated with IBM using autonomic computing resources such as Tivoli Risk Manager, Tivoli Access Manager, Tivoli Identity Manager, and Tivoli Decision Support. "The automation of processes through the intelligent self-managing features of Tivoli software can help companies respond to threats more quickly," says King. "The benefit is that organizations can strengthen the resiliency of their environments even as the number of security events increases."

CPR is realizing measurable results from its implementation of Tivoli Security Management solutions and King sees the already-realized benefits as only the "tip of the iceberg." Some of the notable ROI from CPR's investment in Tivoli Security Management solutions include:

1. **Improved productivity**—The IT Security team spends less time managing security incidents with Tivoli Risk Manager. The IT staff also expects to spend less time on reporting because data from the various security monitors will be integrated.
2. **Reduced costs**—The application development team estimates that a centralized security model helps accelerate development time. The help desk organization reports a reduction in user calls, due to the password-reset capabilities of Tivoli Identity Manager.
3. **Increased business resiliency**—Using Tivoli Risk Manager, Tivoli Enterprise Console, Tivoli Decision Support and Tripwire, a data integrity assurance solution from Tripwire, Inc., CPR tests show that if an attack shuts down a service, administrators can get systems back online much faster.
4. **Improved audit compliance**—Before the implementation of Tivoli Access Manager for e-business, security staff would need to look at each system or application to see if it properly applied security policy. Now, security policies are consistent enterprisewide.[7]

Questions

1. Which of the trends shaping our future discussed in this plug-in will have the greatest impact on CPR's business?
2. Which of the trends will have the least impact on CPR's business?
3. How are the functions of autonomic computing providing CPR with a competitive advantage?
4. How can CPR take advantage of other technological advances to improve security?

CLOSING CASE TWO

Wireless Progression

Progressive Corporation is the fourth-largest automobile insurer in the United States with more than 8 million policyholders and net premiums of $6.1 billion. Progressive offers wireless Web access to holders of its auto insurance policies, a move that analysts have said fits the company's reputation as a technology leader in the insurance industry and its emphasis on customer service.

Customers can use their Web-enabled phones to get price quotes, report claims, locate nearby independent agents by ZIP code, and access real-time account information through the company's Web site. Progressive also has the ability to push time-sensitive data to policyholders via wireless connections, instantly delivering information about an auto-recall notice to a customer's cell phone.

As a cost-saving measure, and in keeping with a corporate tradition of internal development, Ohio-based Progressive decided to build its own wireless applications. Policyholders simply have to type Progressive's Web address into their phones or connect to the site through search engines that specialize in wireless e-business.

Stephen Williams, president of the Insurance Institute of Indiana, a nonprofit trade association that represents insurers in that state, said it's "not uncommon for Progressive to be on the cutting edge with its use of technology." If Progressive is starting to take advantage of the wireless Web, other companies could follow its lead, he added. Jeffrey Kagan, an Atlanta-based wireless technology analyst, called Progressive "the Nordstrom's of insurance because of its emphasis on customer service." The addition of wireless access to its Web site "is a simple but smart way to use technology" to further improve the company's service, Kagan said. Progressive.com leads the insurance industry in consumer-friendly innovations. It was the first auto insurance Web site (1995), the first to offer online quoting and comparison rates (1996), first to offer instantaneous online purchase of an auto policy (1997), and first to offer after-the-sale service (1998).

The progressive.com Web site leads the insurance industry in consumer-friendly innovations and functionality. Progressive.com was recognized as one of the "top 10 Web sites that work" by *InfoWeek Magazine* and was named to the Smart Business 50 by *Smart Business Magazine* for successful use of the Internet to enhance and expand its business.[8]

Questions

1. Which of the trends shaping our future discussed in this plug-in will have the greatest impact on Progressive's business?
2. Which of the trends will have the least impact on Progressive's business?
3. What other forms of advanced technology would you expect Progressive to deploy in the near future?

MAKING BUSINESS DECISIONS

1. Identifying and Following Trends

What's Hot.com is a new business that specializes in helping companies identify and follow significant trends in their industries. You have recently been hired as a new business analyst and your first task is to highlight current trends in the e-business industry. Using the Internet and any other resources you have available highlight five significant trends not discussed in this text. Prepare a PowerPoint presentation that lists the trends and discusses the potential business impacts for each trend.

2. Reading the Ink on the Wall

iPublish.com is an e-book-only imprint publisher. While large publishers find that e-books are not selling as expected, iPublish.com continues to report positive growth. However, iPublish.com feels threatened by digital ink and digital paper inventions that seem to be revolutionizing the publishing environment and endangering the global paper industry. You have been hired by iPublish.com to develop a strategy in order to embrace this new technology. Create a detailed report listing the reasons iPublish.com needs to support these two new technologies.

3. Pen Pal

StyleUs is a digital pen that writes on ordinary paper printed with a unique dot pattern almost invisible to the naked eye. A tiny camera in the pen registers the pen's movement across a printed grid and stores it as a series of map coordinates. These coordinates correspond to the exact location of the page that is being written on. The dot pattern makes up a huge map of tiny distinctive squares, so small portions of it can also be given specific functions, such as "send," "store," or "synchronize." When a mark is made in the send box with the digital pen, it is instructed to send the stored sequence of map coordinates, which are translated into an image. The result is an exact copy of the handwriting displayed on the computer, mobile phone, or received as a fax anywhere in the world.

Analyze this new technology and identify how it might affect the digital ink or digital paper market. Be sure to include a Porter's Five Forces analysis of the market.

4. Less Is More

Your organization is teetering on the edge of systems chaos. Your systems administrator is stressed beyond tolerance by too many systems, too many applications, too few resources, and too little time. The scope, frequency, and diversity of demand are causing greater risk than anyone dares to admit. Automating (and reducing complexity) the operating environment is critical for your business to survive. Research autonomic computing and write a report discussing how this technology can help an organization gain control over its systems.

B9

Systems Development

1. Summarize the activities associated with the planning phase in the SDLC.
2. Summarize the activities associated with the analysis phase in the SDLC.
3. Summarize the activities associated with the design phase in the SDLC.
4. Summarize the activities associated with the development phase in the SDLC.
5. Summarize the activities associated with the testing phase in the SDLC.
6. Summarize the activities associated with the implementation phase in the SDLC.
7. Summarize the activities associated with the maintenance phase in the SDLC.

Introduction

Today, systems are so large and complex that teams of architects, analysts, developers, testers, and users must work together to create the millions of lines of custom-written code that drive enterprises. For this reason, developers have created a number of different system development methodologies including waterfall, prototyping, rapid application development (RAD), extreme programming, agile, and others. All these methodologies are based on the *systems development life cycle (SDLC),* which is the overall process for developing information systems from planning and analysis through implementation and maintenance (see Figure B9.1).

The systems development life cycle is the foundation for all systems development methodologies and there are literally hundreds of different activities associated with each phase in the SDLC. Typical activities include determining budgets, gathering system requirements, and writing detailed user documentation. The activities performed during each systems development project will vary. This plug-in takes a detailed look at a few of the more common activities performed during the systems development life cycle, along with common issues facing software development projects (see Figure B9.2).

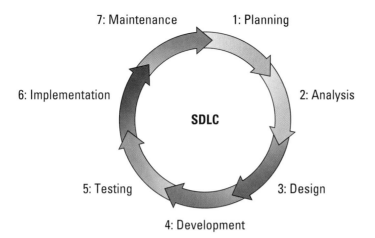

SDLC Phase	Activities
1. Planning	■ Identify and select the system for development ■ Assess project feasibility ■ Develop the project plan
2. Analysis	■ Gather business requirements ■ Create process diagrams ■ Perform a buy vs. build analysis
3. Design	■ Design the IT infrastructure ■ Design system models
4. Development	■ Develop the IT infrastructure ■ Develop the database and programs
5. Testing	■ Write the test conditions ■ Perform the system testing
6. Implementation	■ Determine implementation method ■ Provide training for the system users ■ Write detailed user documentation
7. Maintenance	■ Build a help desk to support the system users ■ Perform system maintenance ■ Provide an environment to support system changes

Systems Development Life Cycle

PHASE 1: PLANNING

The *planning phase* involves establishing a high-level plan of the intended project and determining project goals. The three primary activities involved in the planning phase are:

1. Identify and select the system for development.
2. Assess project feasibility.
3. Develop the project plan.

Identify and Select the System for Development

Systems are only successful when they solve the right problem or take advantage of the right opportunity. Systems development focuses on either solving a problem or taking advantage of an opportunity. Determining which systems are required to

Evaluation Criteria	Description
Value chain analysis	The value chain determines the extent to which the new system will add value to the organization. Systems with greater value are given priority over systems with less value.
Strategic alignment	Projects that are in line with the organization's strategic goals and objectives are given priority over projects not in line with the organization's strategic goals and objectives.
Cost/benefit analysis	A cost/benefit analysis determines which projects offer the organization the greatest benefits with the least amount of cost.
Resource availability	Determine the amount and type of resources required to complete the project and determine if the organization has these resources available.
Project size, duration, and difficulty	Determine the number of individuals, amount of time, and technical difficulty of the project.

support the strategic goals of an organization is one of the primary activities performed during the planning phase. Typically, employees generate proposals to build new information systems when they are having a difficult time performing their jobs. Unfortunately, most organizations have limited resources and cannot afford to develop all proposed information systems. Therefore, they look to critical success factors to help determine which systems to build.

A *critical success factor (CSF)* is a factor that is critical to an organization's success. In order to determine which system to develop an organization tracks all the proposed systems and prioritizes them by business impact or critical success factors. This allows the business to prioritize which problems require immediate attention and which problems can wait. Figure B9.3 displays possible evaluation criteria for determining which projects to develop.

Assess Project Feasibility

A *feasibility study* determines if the proposed solution is feasible and achievable from a financial, technical, and organizational standpoint. Typically, an organization will define several alternative solutions that it can pursue to solve a given problem. A feasibility study is used to determine if the proposed solution is achievable, given the organization's resources and constraints in regard to technology, economics, organizational factors, and legal and ethical considerations. There are many different types of feasibility studies an organization can perform including:

- **Economic feasibility study** (often called a **cost-benefit analysis**) identifies the financial benefits and costs associated with the systems development project.
- **Operational feasibility study** examines the likelihood that the project will attain its desired objectives.
- **Technical feasibility study** determines the organization's ability to build and integrate the proposed system.
- **Schedule feasibility study** assesses the likelihood that all potential time frames and completion dates will be met.
- **Legal and contractual feasibility study** examines all potential legal and contractual ramifications of the proposed system.

Develop the Project Plan

Developing a project plan is one of the final activities performed during the planning phase and it is one of the hardest and most important activities. The project plan is the guiding force behind on-time delivery of a complete and successful system. It logs and tracks every single activity performed during the project. If an activity is missed, or takes longer than expected to complete, the project plan must be updated to reflect these changes. Continuous updating of the project plan is an activity that must be performed in every subsequent phase during the systems development effort.

PHASE 2: ANALYSIS

The **analysis phase** involves analyzing end-user business requirements and refining project goals into defined functions and operations of the intended system. The three primary activities involved in the analysis phase are:

1. Gather business requirements.
2. Create process diagrams.
3. Perform a buy vs. build analysis.

Gather Business Requirements

Business requirements are the detailed set of business requests that the system must meet in order to be successful. At this point, there is little or no concern with any implementation or reference to technical details. For example, the types of technology used to build the system, such as an Oracle database or the Java programming language, are not yet defined. The only focus is on gathering the true business requirements for the system. A sample business requirement might state, "The system must track all customer sales by product, region, and sales representative." This requirement states what the system must do from the business perspective, giving no details or information on how the system is going to meet this requirement.

Gathering business requirements is basically conducting an investigation in which users identify all the organization's business needs and take measurements of these needs. There are a number of ways to gather business requirements including:

- Performing a **joint application development (JAD)** session where employees meet, sometimes for several days, to define or review the business requirements for the system.
- Conducting interviews with different individuals to determine current operations and current issues.
- Compiling questionnaires to survey employees to discover issues.
- Making observations to determine how current operations are performed.
- Reviewing business documents to discover reports, policies, and how information is used throughout the organization.

The **requirements definition document** contains the final set of business requirements, prioritized in order of business importance. The system users review the requirements definition document and determine if they will sign-off on the business requirements. **Sign-off** is the system users' actual signatures indicating they approve all of the business requirements. One of the first major milestones on the project plan is usually the users' sign-off on business requirements.

A large data storage company implemented a project called Python whose purpose was to control all the company's information systems. Seven years later, tens of millions of dollars later, and 35 programmers later, Python was cancelled. At the end of the project, Python had over 1,800 business requirements of which 900 came from engineering and were written in order to make the other 900 customer requirements work. By the time the project was cancelled, it was unclear what the primary goals, objectives, and needs of the project were. Management should have realized Python's issues when the project's requirements phase dragged on, bulged, and took years to complete. The sheer number of requirements should have raised a red flag.[1]

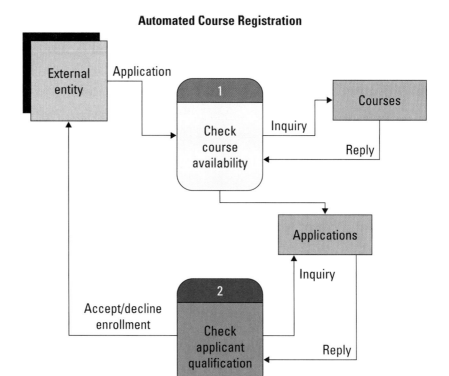

Automated Course Registration

External
entity

Application

1

Check
course
availability

Inquiry

Courses

Reply

Applications

Inquiry

2

Check
applicant
qualification

Reply

Accept/decline
enrollment

Create Process Diagrams

Once a business analyst takes a detailed look at how an organization performs its work and its processes, the analyst can recommend ways to improve these processes to make them more efficient and effective. *Process modeling* involves graphically representing the processes that capture, manipulate, store, and distribute information between a system and its environment. One of the most common diagrams used in process modeling is the data flow diagram. A *data flow diagram (DFD)* illustrates the movement of information between external entities and the processes and data stores within the system (see Figure B9.4). Process models and data flow diagrams establish the specifications of the system. *Computer-aided software engineering (CASE)* tools are software suites that automate systems analysis, design, and development. Process models and data flow diagrams can provide the basis for the automatic generation of the system if they are developed using a CASE tool.

Perform a Buy vs. Build Analysis

An organization faces two primary choices when deciding to develop an information system: (1) it can *buy* the information system from a vendor or (2) it can *build* the system itself. *Commercial off-the shelf (COTS)* software is a software package or solution that is purchased to support one or more business functions and information systems. Most customer relationship management, supply chain management, and enterprise resource planning solutions are COTS. Typically, a cost/benefit analysis forms the basis of the buy vs. build decision. Organizations must consider the following during the buy vs. build decision:

- Are there any currently available products that fit the organizations needs?
- Are there features that are not available and important enough to warrant the expense of in-house development?
- Can the organization customize or modify an existing COTS to fit its needs?
- Is there a justification to purchase or develop based on the cost of acquisition?

Three key factors an organization should also consider when contemplating the buy vs. build decision are: (1) time to market, (2) corporate resources, and (3) core competencies. Weighing the complex relationship between each of these three variables will help an organization make the right choice.

1. **Time to market**—If time to market is a priority then purchasing a good base technology and potentially building on to it will likely yield results faster than starting from scratch.

2. **Availability of corporate resources**—The buy vs. build decision is a bit more complex to make when considering the availability of corporate resource. Typically, the costs to an organization to buy systems such as SCM, CRM, and ERP are extremely high. These costs can be so high, in the multiple millions of dollars, that acquiring these technologies might make the entire concept economically unfeasible. Building these systems, however, can also be extremely expensive, take indefinite amounts of time, and constrain resources.

3. **Corporate core competencies**—When considering the buy vs. build decision with respect to core competencies, the more an organization wants to build a technical core competency the less likely it will want to buy it.

When making the all-important buy vs. build decision consider when the product must be available, how many resources are available, and how the organization's core competencies affect the product. If these questions can be definitely answered either yes or no, then the answer to the buy vs. build question is easy. However, most organizations cannot answer these questions with a solid yes or no. Most organizations need to make a trade-off between the lower cost of buying a system and the need for a system that meets all of their requirements. Finding a system to buy that meets all an organization's unique business requirements is next to impossible.

PHASE 3: DESIGN

The *design phase* involves describing the desired features and operations of the system including screen layouts, business rules, process diagrams, pseudo code, and other documentation. The two primary activities involved in the design phase are:

1. Design the IT infrastructure.
2. Design system models.

Design the IT Infrastructure

The system must be supported by a solid IT infrastructure or chances are the system will crash, malfunction, or not perform as expected. The IT infrastructure must meet the organization's needs in terms of time, cost, technical feasibility, and flexibility. Most systems run on a computer network with each employee having a client and the application running on a server. During this phase, the IT specialists recommend what types of clients and servers to buy including memory and storage requirements, along with software recommendations. An organization typically explores several different IT infrastructures that must meet current as well as future system needs. For example, databases must be large enough to hold the current volume of customers plus all new customers that the organization expects to gain over the next several years (see Figure B9.5).

Design System Models

Modeling is the activity of drawing a graphical representation of a design. An organization should model everything it builds including reports, programs, and databases. There are many different types of modeling activities performed during the design phase including:

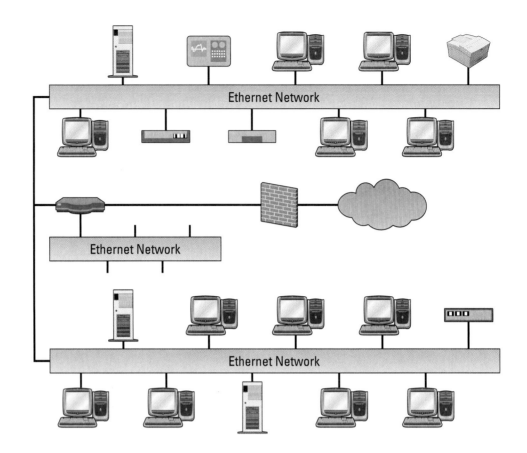

- The *graphical user interface (GUI)* is the interface to an information system. *GUI screen design* is the ability to model the information system screens for an entire system using icons, buttons, menus, and submenus.

- *Data models* represent a formal way to express data relationships to a database management system (DBMS).

- *Entity relationship diagram (ERD)* is a technique for documenting the relationships between entities in a database environment (see Figure B9.6).

PHASE 4: DEVELOPMENT

The *development phase* involves taking all of the detailed design documents from the design phase and transforming them into the actual system. The two primary activities involved in the development phase are:

1. Develop the IT infrastructure.
2. Develop the database and programs.

Develop the IT Infrastructure

The platform upon which the system will operate must be built prior to building the actual system. In the design phase, an organization creates a blueprint of the proposed IT infrastructure displaying the design of the software, hardware, and telecommunication equipment. In the development phase, the organization purchases and implements the required equipment to support the IT infrastructure.

Most new systems require new hardware and software. It may be as simple as adding memory to a client or as complex as setting up a wide area network across several states.

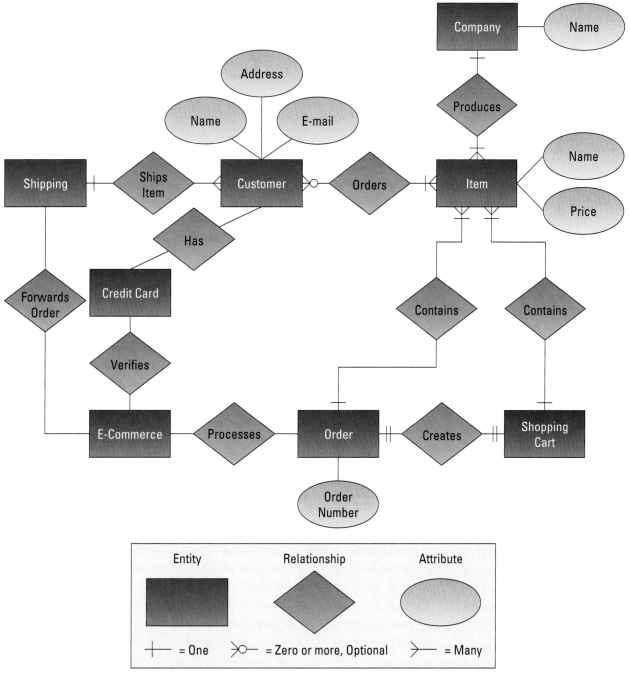

FIGURE B9.6

Sample Entity Relationship Diagram

Develop the Database and Programs

Once the IT infrastructure is built, the organization can begin to create the database and write the programs required for the system. IT specialists perform these functions and it may take months or even years to design and create all the needed elements to complete the system.

PHASE 5: TESTING

According to a report issued in June 2003 by the National Institute of Standards and Technology (NIST), defective software costs the U.S. economy an estimated $59.5 billion each year. Of that total, software users incurred 64 percent of the costs and software developers 36 percent. NIST suggests that improvements in testing could reduce this cost by about a third, or $22.5 billion, but that unfortunately testing improvements would not eliminate all software errors.[2]

The *testing phase* involves bringing all the project pieces together into a special testing environment to test for errors, bugs, and interoperability, in order to verify that the system meets all the business requirements defined in the analysis phase. The two primary activities involved in the testing phase are:

1. Write the test conditions.
2. Perform the system testing.

Write the Test Conditions

Testing is critical. An organization must have excellent test conditions in order to perform an exhaustive test. *Test conditions* are the detailed steps the system must perform along with the expected results of each step. Figure B9.7 displays several test conditions for testing user logon functionality in a system. The tester will execute each test condition and compare the expected results with the actual results in order to verify that the system functions correctly. Notice in Figure B9.7 how each test condition is extremely detailed and states the expected results that should occur when executing each test condition. Each time the actual result is different from the expected result a "bug" is generated and the system goes back to development for a bug fix.

Test condition 6 in Figure B9.7 displays a different actual result than the expected result because the system failed to allow the user to logon. After this test condition fails, it is obvious that the system is not functioning correctly and it must be sent back to development for a bug fix.

FIGURE B9.7

Sample Test Conditions

Test Condition Number	Date Tested	Tester	Test Condition	Expected Result	Actual Result	Pass/ Fail
1	1/1/05	Emily Hickman	Click on System Start Button	Main Menu appears	Same as expected result	Pass
2	1/1/05	Emily Hickman	Click on Logon Button in Main Menu	Logon Screen appears asking for Username and Password	Same as expected result	Pass
3	1/1/05	Emily Hickman	Type Emily Hickman in the User Name Field	Emily Hickman appears in the User Name Field	Same as expected result	Pass
4	1/1/05	Emily Hickman	Type Zahara123 in the password field	XXXXXXXXX appears in the password field	Same as expected result	Pass
5	1/1/05	Emily Hickman	Click on O.K. button	User logon request is sent to database and user name and password are verified	Same as expected result	Pass
6	1/1/05	Emily Hickman	Click on Start	User name and password are accepted and the system main menu appears	Screen appeared stating logon failed and username and password were incorrect	Fail

A typical system development effort has hundreds or thousands of test conditions. Every single test condition must be executed to verify that the system performs as expected. Writing all the test conditions and performing the actual testing of the software takes a tremendous amount of time and energy. Testing is critical to the successful development of any system.

Perform the System Testing

System developers must perform many different types of testing to ensure that the system works as expected. The following are a few of the more common types of test performed during testing:

- **Unit testing**—tests each unit of code as soon as the unit is complete to expose faults in the unit regardless of its interaction with other units.
- **Application (or system) testing**—verifies that all units of code work together and the total system satisfies all of its functional and operational requirements.
- **Integration testing**—exposes faults in the integration of software components or software units.
- **Regression testing**—is performed after making a functional improvement or repair to the system to determine if the change has affected (or impacted) the other functional aspects of the software.
- **Backup and recovery testing**—tests the ability of an application to be restarted after failure.
- **Documentation testing**—verifies that the instruction guides are helpful and accurate.
- **User acceptance testing (UAT)**—formal tests conducted to determine whether or not a system satisfies its acceptance criteria and to enable the customer to determine whether or not to accept a system.

PHASE 6: IMPLEMENTATION

The *implementation phase* involves placing the system into production so users can begin to perform actual business operations with the system. The three primary activities involved in the implementation phase are:

1. Write detailed user documentation.
2. Determine implementation method.
3. Provide training for the system users.

Write Detailed User Documentation

Systems users require *user documentation* that highlights how to use the system. This is the type of documentation that is typically provided along with the new system. Systems users find it extremely frustrating to have a new system without documentation.

Determine Implementation Method

An organization must choose the right implementation method to ensure a successful system implementation. There are four primary implementation methods an organization can choose from:

1. **Parallel implementation**—using both the old and new systems until it is evident that the new system performs correctly.
2. **Plunge implementation**—discarding the old system completely and immediately starting to use the new system.

3. **Pilot implementation**—having only a small group of people use the new system until it is evident that the new system performs correctly and then adding the remaining people to the new system.

4. **Phased implementation**—implementing the new system in phases (e.g., accounts receivables then accounts payable) until it is evident that the new system performs correctly and then implementing the remaining phases of the new system.

Provide Training for the System Users

An organization must provide training for the system users. The two most popular types of training are online training and workshop training. *Online training* runs over the Internet or off a CD-ROM. System users perform the training at any time, on their own computers, at their own pace. This type of training is convenient for system users because they can set their own schedule for the training. *Workshop training* is set in a classroom-type environment and led by an instructor. Workshop training is recommended for difficult systems where the system users require one-on-one time with an individual instructor.

PHASE 7: MAINTENANCE

The *maintenance phase* involves performing changes, corrections, additions, and upgrades to ensure the system continues to meet the business goals. Once a system is in place, it must change as the organization changes. The three primary activities involved in the maintenance phase are:

1. Build a help desk to support the system users.
2. Perform system maintenance.
3. Provide an environment to support system changes.

Build a Help Desk to Support the System Users

A *help desk* is a group of people who respond to internal system user questions. Typically, internal system users have a phone number for the help desk they call whenever they have issues or questions about the system. Providing a help desk that answers internal user questions is an excellent way to provide comprehensive support for new systems.

Perform System Maintenance

Maintenance is fixing or enhancing an information system. There are many different types of maintenance that must be performed on the system to ensure it continues to operate as expected. These include:

- **Adaptive maintenance**—making changes to increase system functionality to meet new business requirements.
- **Corrective maintenance**—making changes to repair system defects.
- **Perfective maintenance**—making changes to enhance the system which improves such things as processing performance and usability.
- **Preventive maintenance**—making changes to reduce the chance of future system failures.

Provide an Environment to Support System Changes

As changes arise in the business environment, an organization must react to those changes by assessing the impact on the system. It might well be that the system needs to adjust to meet the ever-changing needs of the business environment. If so, an organization must modify its systems in order to support the business environment.

A *change management system* includes a collection of procedures to document a change request and define the steps necessary to consider the change based on the expected impact of the change. Most change management systems require that a change request form be initiated by one or more project stakeholders (users, customers, analysts, developers). Ideally, these change requests are reviewed by a *change control board (CCB)* responsible for approving or rejecting all change requests. The CCB's composition typically includes a representative for each business area that has a stake in the project. The CCB's decision to accept or reject each change is based on an impact analysis of the change. For example, if one department wants to implement a change to the software that will increase both deployment time and cost then the other business owners need to agree that the change is valid and that it warrants the extended timeframe and increased budget.

Software Problems Are Business Problems

Only 28 percent of projects are developed within budget and delivered on time and as promised, says the Standish Group, a Massachusetts-based consultancy, in its most recent report. The primary reasons for project failure are:

- Unclear or missing business requirements.
- Skipping SDLC phases.
- Failure to manage project scope.
- Failure to manage project plan.
- Changing technology.[3]

UNCLEAR OR MISSING BUSINESS REQUIREMENTS

The most common reason systems fail is because the business requirements are either missing or incorrectly gathered during the analysis phase. The business requirements drive the entire system. If they are not accurate or complete, the system will not be successful.

It is important to discuss the relationship between the SDLC and the cost for the organization to fix errors. An error found during the analysis and design phase is relatively inexpensive to fix. All that is typically required is a change to a Word document. However, exactly the same error found during the testing or implementation phase is going to cost the organization an enormous amount to fix because it has to change the actual system. Figure B9.8 displays how the cost to fix an error grows exponentially the later the error is found in the SDLC.

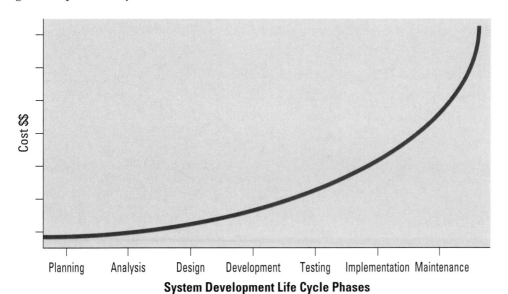

FIGURE B9.8

The Cost of Finding Errors

SKIPPING SDLC PHASES

The first thing individuals tend to do when a project falls behind schedule is to start skipping phases in the SDLC. For example, if a project is three weeks behind in the development phase the project manager might decide to cut testing down from six weeks to three weeks. Obviously, it is impossible to perform all the testing in half the time. Failing to test the system will lead to unfound errors, and chances are high that the system will fail. It is critical that an organization perform all phases in the SDLC during every project. Skipping any of the phases is sure to lead to system failure.

FAILURE TO MANAGE PROJECT SCOPE

As the project progresses, the project manager must track the status of each activity and adjust the project plan if an activity is added or taking longer than expected. *Scope creep* occurs when the scope of the project increases. *Feature creep* occurs when developers add extra features that were not part of the initial requirements. Scope creep and feature creep are difficult to manage and can easily cause a project to fall behind schedule.

FAILURE TO MANAGE PROJECT PLAN

Managing the project plan is one of the biggest challenges during systems development. The project plan is the road map the organization follows during the development of the system. Developing the initial project plan is the easiest part of the project manager's job. Managing and revising the project plan is the hard part. The project plan is a living document since it changes almost daily on any project. Failing to monitor, revise, and update the project plan can lead to project failure.

CHANGING TECHNOLOGY

Many real-world projects have hundreds of business requirements, take years to complete, and cost millions of dollars. Gordon Moore, co-founder of Intel Corporation, observed in 1965 that chip density doubles every 18 months. This observation, known as Moore's law, simply means that memory sizes, processor power, etc., all follow the same pattern and roughly double in capacity every 18 months. As Moore's law states, technology changes at an incredibly fast pace; therefore it is possible to have to revise an entire project plan in the middle of a project as a result of a change in technology. Technology changes so fast that it is almost impossible to deliver an information system without feeling the pain of changing technology.

T he systems development life cycle (SDLC) is the foundation for all systems development methodologies. Understanding the phases and activities involved in the systems development life cycle is critical when developing information systems regardless of which methodology is being used. The SDLC contains the following phases:

1. The *planning phase* involves establishing a high-level plan of the intended project and determining project goals.
2. The *analysis phase* involves analyzing end-user business requirements and refining project goals into defined functions and operations of the intended system.
3. The *design phase* involves describing the desired features and operations of the system including screen layouts, business rules, process diagrams, pseudo code, and other documentation.
4. The *development phase* involves taking all the detailed design documents from the design phase and transforming them into the actual system.
5. The *testing phase* involves bringing all the project pieces together into a special testing environment to test for errors, bugs, and interoperability, in order to verify that the system meets all the business requirements defined in the analysis phase.
6. The *implementation phase* involves placing the system into production so users can begin to perform actual business operations with the system.
7. The *maintenance phase* involves performing changes, corrections, additions, and upgrades to ensure the system continues to meet the business goals.

Analysis phase, 343
Business requirement, 343
Change control board
    (CCB), 351
Change management
    system, 351
Commercial off-the shelf
    (COTS), 344
Computer-aided software
    engineering (CASE), 344
Critical success factor
    (CSF), 342
Data flow diagram (DFD), 344
Data model, 346
Design phase, 345

Development phase, 346
Entity relationship diagram
    (ERD), 346
Feasibility study, 342
Feature creep, 352
Graphical user interface
    (GUI), 346
GUI screen design, 346
Help desk, 350
Implementation phase, 349
Joint application development
    (JAD), 343
Maintenance, 350
Maintenance phase, 350
Modeling, 345

Online training, 350
Planning phase, 341
Process modeling, 344
Requirements definition
    document, 343
Scope creep, 352
Sign-off, 343
Systems development life cycle
    (SDLC), 340
Test condition, 348
Testing phase, 348
User documentation, 349
Workshop training, 350

Disaster at Denver International Airport

One of the best ways to learn how to develop successful systems is to review past failures. One of the most infamous system failures is Denver International Airport's (DIA) baggage system. When the automated baggage system design for DIA was introduced, it was hailed as the savior of modern airport design. The design relied on a network of 300 computers to route bags and 4,000 telecars to carry luggage across 21 miles of track. Laser scanners were to read barcoded luggage tags, while advanced scanners tracked the movement of toboggan-like baggage carts.

When DIA finally opened its doors for reporters to witness its revolutionary baggage handling system the scene was rather unpleasant. Bags were chewed up, lost, and misrouted in what has since became a legendary systems nightmare.

One of the biggest mistakes made in the baggage handling system fiasco was that not enough time was allowed to properly develop the system. In the beginning of the project, DIA assumed it was the responsibility of individual airlines to find their own way of moving the baggage from the plane to the baggage claim area. The automated baggage system was not involved in the initial planning of the DIA project. By the time the developers of DIA decided to create an integrated baggage system, the time frame for designing and implementing such a complex and huge system was not possible.

Another common mistake that occurred during the project was that the airlines kept changing their business requirements. This caused numerous issues including the implementation of power supplies that were not properly updated for the revised system design, which caused overloaded motors and mechanical failures. Besides the power supplies design problem, the optical sensors did not read the barcodes correctly, causing issues with baggage routing.

Finally, BAE, the company that designed and implemented the automated baggage system for DIA, had never created a baggage system of this size before. BAE had created a similar system in an airport in Munich, Germany, where the scope was much smaller. Essentially, the baggage system had an inadequate IT infrastructure since it was designed for a much smaller system.

DIA simply could not open without a functional baggage system and the city had no choice but to delay the opening date for over 16 months, costing taxpayers roughly $1 million per day, which totaled around $500 million.[4,5]

Questions

1. One of the problems with DIA's baggage system was inadequate testing. Describe the different types of tests DIA could have used to help ensure its baggage system's success.
2. Evaluate the different implementation approaches and choose the one that would have most significantly increased the chances of the project's success.
3. Explain the cost of finding errors and how more time spent in the analysis and design phase could have saved Colorado taxpayers hundreds of millions of dollars.
4. Explain why BAE could not take an existing IT infrastructure and simply increase its scale and expect it to work.

Reducing Ambiguity in Business Requirements

The number one reason projects fail is bad business requirements. Business requirements are considered "bad" because of ambiguity or insufficient involvement of end users during analysis and design.

A requirement is unambiguous if it has the same interpretation for all parties. Different interpretations by different participants will usually result in unmet expectations. Here is an example of an ambiguous requirement and an example of an unambiguous requirement:

- **Ambiguous requirement:** The financial report must show profits in local and U.S. currencies.
- **Unambiguous requirement:** The financial report must show profits in local and U.S. currencies using the exchange rate printed in *The Wall Street Journal* for the last business day of the period being reported.

Ambiguity is impossible to prevent completely because it is introduced into requirements in natural ways. For example:

- Requirements can contain technical implications that are obvious to the IT developers but not to the customers.
- Requirements can contain business implications that are obvious to the customer but not to the IT developers.
- Requirements may contain everyday words whose meanings are "obvious" to everyone, yet different for everyone.
- Requirements are reflections of detailed explanations that may have included multiple events, multiple perspectives, verbal rephrasing, emotion, iterative refinement, selective emphasis, and body language—none of which are captured in the written statements.

Tips for Reviewing Business Requirements

When reviewing business requirements always look for the following words to help dramatically reduce ambiguity:

- **"And and Or"** have well defined meanings and ought to be completely unambiguous, yet they are often understood only informally and interpreted inconsistently. For example, consider the statement "The alarm must ring if button T is pressed and if button F is pressed." This statement may be intended to mean that to ring the alarm, both buttons must be pressed or it may be intended to mean that either one can be pressed. A statement like this should never appear in a requirement because the potential for misinterpretation is too great. A preferable approach is to be very explicit, for example, "The alarm must ring if both buttons T and F are pressed simultaneously. The alarm should not ring in any other circumstance."
- **"Always"** might really mean "most of the time," in which case it should be made more explicit. For example, the statement "We always run reports A and B together" could be challenged with "In other words, there is never any circumstance where you would run A without B and B without A?" If you build a system with an "always" requirement, then you are actually building the system to never run report A without report B. If a user suddenly wants report B without report A, you will need to make significant system changes.
- **"Never"** might mean "rarely," in which case it should be made more explicit. For example, the statement "We never run reports A and B in the same month" could be challenged

with, "So that means that if I see that A has been run, I can be absolutely certain that no one will want to run B." Again, if you build a system that supports a "never" requirement then the system users can never perform that requirement. For example, the system would never allow a user to run reports A and B in the same month, no matter what the circumstances.

■ **Boundary conditions** are statements about the line between true and false and do and do not. These statements may or may not be meant to include end points. For example, "We want to use method X when there are up to 10 pages, but method Y otherwise." If you were building this system, would you include page 10 in method X or in method Y? The answer to this question will vary causing an ambiguous business requirement.[6]

Questions

1. Why are ambiguous business requirements the leading cause of system development failures?

2. Explain why the words "and" and "or" tend to lead to ambiguous requirements.

3. Research the Web and determine other reasons for "bad" business requirements.

4. What is wrong with the following business requirement: "The system must support employee birthdays since every employee always has a birthday every year."

MAKING BUSINESS DECISIONS

1. Understanding Project Failure

You are the Director of Project Management for Stello, a global manufacturer of high-end writing instruments. The company sells to primarily high-end customers and the average price for one of its fine writing instruments is about $350. You are currently implementing a new customer relationship management system and you want to do everything you can to ensure a successful systems development effort. Create a document summarizing the five primary reasons why this project could fail, along with your strategy to eliminate the possibility of system development failure on your project.

2. Missing Phases in the Systems Development Life Cycle

Hello Inc. is a large concierge service for executives operating in Chicago, San Francisco, and New York. The company performs all kinds of services from dog walking to airport transportation. Your manager, Dan Martello, wants to skip the testing phase during the company's financial ERP implementation. Dan feels that since the system came from a vendor it should work correctly. In order to meet the project's looming deadline he wants to skip the testing phase. Draft a memo explaining to Dan the importance of following the SDLC and the ramifications to the business if the financial system is not tested.

3. Saving Failing Systems

Crik Candle Company manufactures low-end candles for restaurants. The company generates over $40 million in annual revenues and has over 300 employees. You are in the middle of a large multimillion dollar supply chain management implementation. Your project manager has just come to you with the information that the project might fail for the following reasons:

- Several business requirements were incorrect and the scope has to be doubled.
- Three developers recently quit.
- The deadline has been moved up a month.

Develop a list of options that your company can follow in order to ensure the project remains on schedule and within budget.

4. **Refusing to Sign-Off**

You are the primary client on a large extranet development project. After carefully reviewing the requirements definition document you are positive that there are missing, ambiguous, inaccurate, and unclear requirements. The project manager is pressuring you for your sign-off since he has already received sign-off from five of your co-workers. If you fail to sign-off on the requirements, you are going to put the entire project at risk since the time frame is nonnegotiable. What would you do?

5. **Feasibility Studies**

John Lancert is the new managing operations director for a large construction company, LMC. John is currently looking for an associate who can help him prioritize the 60 proposed company projects. You are interested in working with John and have decided to apply for the job. John has asked you to compile a report detailing why project prioritization is critical for LMC, along with the different types of feasibility studies you would recommend that LMC use when determining which projects to pursue.

PLUG-IN

B10

Project Management

1. Describe the three primary activities performed by a project manager.
2. Explain change management and how an organization can prepare for change.
3. Explain risk management and how an organization can mitigate risk.
4. Summarize the different strategies a project manager can use to ensure a successful project.

Introduction

The core units introduced project management. A ***project*** is a temporary endeavor undertaken to create a unique product or service. According to the Project Management Institute, ***project management*** is the application of knowledge, skills, tools, and techniques to project activities in order to meet or exceed stakeholder needs and expectations from a project. This plug-in takes a detailed look at the fundamentals of project management, along with change management and risk management.

Project Management Fundamentals

Project deliverables are any measurable, tangible, verifiable outcome, result, or item that is produced to complete a project or part of a project. Examples of project deliverables include design documents, testing scripts, and requirements documents. ***Project milestones*** represent key dates when a certain group of activities must be performed. For example, completing the planning phase might be a project milestone. If a project milestone is missed, then chances are the project is experiencing problems. A ***project manager*** is an individual who is an expert in project planning and management, defines and develops the project plan, and tracks the plan to ensure all key project milestones are completed on time. The art and science of project management must coordinate numerous activities as displayed in Figure B10.1. Project managers perform numerous activities, and three of these primary activities are:

1. Choosing strategic projects.
2. Setting the project scope.
3. Managing resources and maintaining the project plan.

CHOOSING STRATEGIC PROJECTS

Calpine Corp., a large energy producer, uses project management software to look at its IT investments from a business perspective. The company classifies projects in one of three ways: (1) run the business, (2) grow the business, and (3) transform the business. Calpine splits its $100 million in assets accordingly: 60 percent for running the business, 20 percent for growing the business, and 20 percent for transforming the business. Calpine evaluates each of its 30 to 35 active projects for perceived business value against project costs. For the company to pursue a project it must pass a return on investment (ROI) hurdle. A business project must minimally provide two times ROI, and a transformation project must provide five times ROI.[1]

One of the most difficult decisions organizations make is determining the projects in which to invest their time, energy, and resources. An organization must identify what it wants to do and how it is going to do it. The "what" part of this question focuses on issues such as justification for the project, definition of the project, and expected results of the project. The "how" part of the question deals with issues such as project approach, project schedule, and analysis of project risks. Determining which projects to focus corporate efforts on is as necessary to projects as each project is to an organization. The three common techniques an organization can use to select projects include:

1. Focus on organizational goals
2. Categorize projects
3. Perform a financial analysis (see Figure B10.2)

Techniques for Choosing Strategic Projects

1. **Focus on organizational goals**—Managers are finding tremendous value in choosing projects that align with the organization's goals. Projects that address organizational goals tend to have a higher success rate since they are important to the entire organization.

2. **Categorize projects**—There are various categories that an organization can group projects into to determine a project's priority. One type of categorization includes problem, opportunity, and directives. Problems are undesirable situations that prevent an organization from achieving its goals. Opportunities are chances to improve the organization. Directives are new requirements imposed by management, government, or some other external influence. It is often easier to obtain approval for projects that address problems or directives because the organization must respond to these categories to avoid financial losses.

3. **Perform a financial analysis**—A number of different financial analysis techniques can be performed to help determine a project's priority. A few of these include net present value, return on investment, and payback analysis. These financial analysis techniques help determine the organization's financial expectations for the project.

Prior to its merger with Hewlett-Packard, Compaq decided to analyze and prioritize its system development projects. Knowing that the CIO wanted to be able to view every project, project management leaders quickly identified and removed nonstrategic projects. At the end of the review process, the company cancelled 39 projects, saving the organization $15 million. Most Fortune 100 companies are receiving bottom-line benefits similar to Compaq's from implementing a project management solution.[2]

Organizations also need to choose and prioritize projects in such a way that they can make responsible decisions as to which projects to eliminate. Jim Johnson, chairman of the Standish Group, has identified project management as the process that can make the difference in project success. According to Johnson, "Companies need a process for taking a regular look at their projects and deciding, again and again, if the investment is going to pay off. As it stands now, for most companies, projects can take on a life of their own."[3]

It is important to note that an organization must build in continuous self-assessment, which allows earlier termination decisions on failing projects, with the associated cost savings. This frees up capital and personnel for dedication to projects that are worth pursuing. The elimination of a project should be viewed as successful resource management, not as an admission of failure.

SETTING THE PROJECT SCOPE

Once an organization defines the projects it wants to pursue, it must set the project scope. *Project scope* defines the work that must be completed to deliver a product with the specified features and functions. The project scope statement is important because it specifies clear project boundaries. The project scope typically includes the following:

- *Project product*—a description of the characteristics the product or service has undertaken.
- *Project objectives*—quantifiable criteria that must be met for the project to be considered a success.
- *Project deliverables*—any measurable, tangible, verifiable outcome, result, or item that is produced to complete a project or part of a project.
- *Project exclusions*—products, services, or processes that are not specifically a part of the project.

The project objectives are one of the most important areas to define because they are essentially the major elements of the project. When an organization achieves the project objectives, it has accomplished the major goals of the project and the project scope is satisfied. Project objectives must include metrics so that the project's success can be measured. The metrics can include cost, schedule, and quality metrics along with a number of other metrics. Figure B10.3 displays the SMART criteria—useful reminders on how to ensure that the project has created understandable and measurable objectives.

- **S**pecific
- **M**easurable
- **A**greed upon
- **R**ealistic
- **T**ime framed

MANAGING RESOURCES AND MAINTAINING THE PROJECT PLAN

Managing people is one of the hardest and most critical efforts a project manager undertakes. How to resolve conflicts within the team and how to balance the needs of the project with the personal/professional needs of the team are a few of the challenges facing project managers. More and more project managers are the main (and sometimes sole) interface with the client during the project. As such, communication, negotiation, marketing, and salesmanship are just as important to the project manager as financial and analytical acumen. There are many times when the people management side of project management made the difference in pulling off a successful project.

A **project plan** is a formal, approved document that manages and controls project execution. A well-defined project plan is characterized by the following:

- Easy to understand.
- Easy to read.
- Communicated to all key participants (key stakeholders).
- Appropriate to the project's size, complexity, and criticality.
- Prepared by the team, rather than by the individual project manager.

The most important part of the plan is communication. The project manager must communicate the plan to every member of the project team and to any key stakeholders and executives. The project plan must also include any project assumptions and be detailed enough to guide the execution of the project. A key to achieving project success is earning consensus and buy-in from all key stakeholders. By including key stakeholders in project plan development, the project manager allows them to have ownership of the plan. This often translates to greater commitment, which in turn results in enhanced motivation and productivity.

The two primary diagrams most frequently used in project planning are PERT and Gantt charts. A **PERT (Program Evaluation and Review Technique) chart** is a graphical network model that depicts a project's tasks and the relationships between those tasks. A **dependency** is a logical relationship that exists between the project tasks, or between a project task and a milestone. PERT charts define dependency between project tasks before those tasks are scheduled (see Figure B10.4). The boxes in Figure B10.4 represent project tasks and the project manager can adjust the contents of the boxes to display various project attributes such as schedule and actual start and finish times. The arrows indicate that one task is dependent on the start or completion of another task. The **critical path** is a path from the start to the finish that passes through all the tasks that are critical to completing the project in the shortest amount of time. PERT charts frequently display a project's critical path.

A **Gantt chart** is a simple bar chart that depicts project tasks against a calendar. In a Gantt chart, tasks are listed vertically and the project's timeframe is listed horizontally. A Gantt chart works well for representing the project schedule. It also shows actual progress of tasks against the planned duration. Figure B10.5 displays a software development project using a Gantt chart.

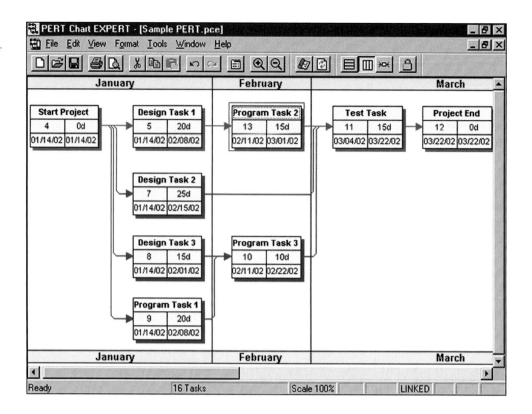

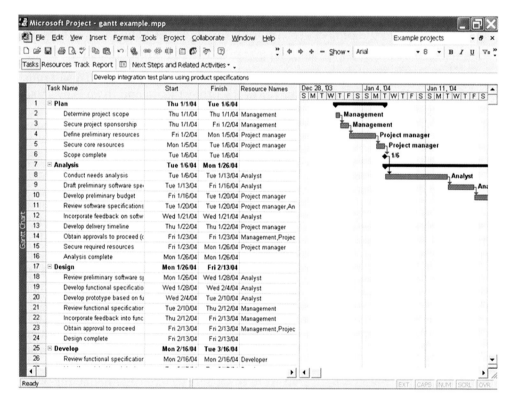

Change Management and Risk Management

Business leaders face a rapidly moving and unforgiving global marketplace that will force them to use every possible tool to sustain competitiveness. A good project manager understands not only the fundamentals of project management, but also how to effectively deal with change management and risk management.

Common Reasons Why Change Occurs
1. An omission in defining initial scope
2. A misunderstanding of the initial scope
3. An external event such as government regulations that create new requirements
4. Organizational changes, such as mergers, acquisitions, and partnerships, that create new business problems and opportunities
5. Availability of better technology
6. Shifts in planned technology that force unexpected and significant changes to the business organization, culture, and/or processes
7. The users or management simply wanting the system to do more than they originally requested or agreed to
8. Management reducing the funding for the project or imposing an earlier deadline[5]

FIGURE B10.6

Common Reasons Change Occurs

CHANGE MANAGEMENT

What works at Snap-on, a maker of tools and equipment for specialists such as car mechanics, is the organization's ability to manage change. The company recently increased profits by 12 percent while sales were down 6.7 percent. Dennis Leitner, VP of IT, runs the IT group on a day-to-day basis and leads the implementation of all major software development initiatives. Each software development initiative is managed by both the business and IT. In fact, business resources are on the IT group's payroll and they spend as much as 80 percent of their time learning what a business unit is doing and how IT can help make it happen. Leitner's role focuses primarily on strategic planning, change management, and setting up metrics to track performance.[4]

Dynamic organizational change is inevitable and an organization must effectively manage change as it evolves. With the numerous challenges and complexities that organizations face in today's rapidly changing environment, effective change management thus becomes a critical core competency. *Change management* is a set of techniques that aid in evolution, composition, and policy management of the design and implementation of a system. Figure B10.6 displays a few of the more common reasons change occurs.

A *change management system* includes a collection of procedures to document a change request and define the steps necessary to consider the change based on the expected impact of the change. Most change management systems require that a change request form be initiated by one or more project stakeholders (systems owners, users, customers, analysts, developers). Ideally, these change requests are considered by a *change control board (CCB)* that is responsible for approving or rejecting all change requests. The CCB's composition typically includes a representative from each business area that has a stake in the project. The CCB's decision to accept or reject each change is based on an impact analysis of the change. For example, if one department wants to implement a change to the software that will increase both deployment time and cost, then the other business owners need to be in agreement that the change is valid and that it warrants the extended timeframe and increased budget.

Preparing for Change

Change is an opportunity, not a threat. Realizing that change is the norm rather than the exception will help an organization stay ahead. Becoming a change leader and accepting the inevitability of change can help ensure that an organization can survive and even thrive in times of change. Change leaders make change effective both inside and outside their organization by following three important guidelines:

Three Important Guidelines for Effectively Dealing with Change Management
1. **Institute change management polices**—Create clearly defined policies and procedures that must be followed each time a request for change is received.
2. **Anticipate change**—View change as an opportunity and embrace it.
3. **Seek change**—Every 6 to 12 months look for changes that may be windows of opportunity. Review successes and failures to determine if there are any opportunities for innovation.

1. Institute change management policies
2. Anticipate change
3. Seek change (see Figure B10.7)

General Electric has successfully tackled change management through an innovative program trademarked "Work Out." Work Out is shorthand for the idea of taking excess work out of the system. The purpose is to eliminate bureaucracy and free up people's time for more productive activities. The positive time-saving and productivity-enhancing results of the Work Out change management program include:

- **Reports:** Teams calculated the time it took to prepare routine reports and compared it with the value generated from the reports. It quickly became apparent that much more effort went into preparing the reports than their comparative value to the recipients warranted. Valuable time was freed when those reports were eliminated or scaled back.

- **Approvals:** The approval process was questioned and adjusted accordingly. One instance discovered that a simple purchase order request required 12 approval signatures.

- **Meetings:** Teams evaluated the need for meetings and changed the way they were conducted to take advantage of technologies like teleconferencing.[6]

Change, whether it comes in the form of a crisis, a market shift, or a technological development, is challenging for all organizations. Successful organizations and successful people learn to anticipate and react appropriately to change.

RISK MANAGEMENT

Altria Group, Inc., the tobacco and food-products conglomerate, has a well-defined process for choosing projects based on project risk. The company gathers project information such as cash flow, return on investment, interfaces, and regulatory-compliance issues and creates a risk-based score of each project. The company then plots them on a grid with risk on the horizontal axis and value on the vertical axis. Managers then choose projects based on an optimal balance of risk and return.[7]

Project risk is an uncertain event or condition that, if it occurs, has a positive or negative effect on a project objective(s). ***Risk management*** is the process of proactive and ongoing identification, analysis, and response to risk factors. The best place to address project risk is during the project plan creation. Elements of risk management are outlined in Figure B10.8.

Risks vary throughout a project and in general are more significant at the later phases of a project. Risk factors that may not be immediately obvious and are often the root causes of IT project success or failure are displayed in Figure B10.9.

Elements of Risk Management
Risk identification—determining which risks might affect the project and documenting their characteristics
Qualitative risk analysis—performing a qualitative analysis of risks and conditions to prioritize their effects on project objectives
Quantitative risk analysis—measuring the probability and consequences of risks as well as estimating their implications for the project objectives
Risk response planning—developing procedures and techniques to enhance opportunities and reduce threats to the project's objectives

FIGURE B10.8

Elements of Risk Management

Common Project Risk Factors
Changing business circumstances that undermine expected benefits
Reluctance to report negative information or to "blow the whistle" on a project
Significant change management issues including resistance to change
The rush to get a project done quickly, often compromising the end result and desired outcome
Executives who are strongly wedded to a project and unwilling to admit that it may have been a mistake
A common tendency in IT projects to overengineer technology solutions, stemming from a belief in the superiority of technical solutions over simpler, people-based solutions
Building the project plan in conjunction with the budget or to validate some basic assumptions about the project's fiscal requirements and business base payback calculations

FIGURE B10.9

Common Project Risk Factors

Mitigating Risk

An organization must devise strategies to reduce or mitigate risk. A wide range of strategies can be applied, with each risk category necessitating different mitigation strategies. When considering risk mitigation the importance of choice, opportunities, and inexactitude should be kept clearly in mind. Organizations should take several actions at the enterprise level to improve risk management capabilities—these are displayed in Figure B10.10.

Actions to Improve Risk Management Capabilities
Promote project leadership skills—Hire individuals with strong project management and project leadership skills as well as business management skills. These individuals can be extremely helpful in advisory and steering committee roles as well as coaching roles.
Learn from previous experience—Over many years of collective experiences, organizations have encountered hundreds of large IT projects. Document and revisit development methodologies, software tools, and software development best practices in order to share this vital information across the organization.
Share knowledge—Working in team or group environments tends to yield the most successful projects since individuals can share their unique learning experiences.
Create a project management culture—Orient people from day one on the importance of project management, change management, and risk management. Be sure to measure and reward project management skills and promote individuals based on successful projects.

FIGURE B10.10

Actions to Improve Risk Management Capabilities

Audit and tax firm KPMG LLP and software maker SeeCommerce unveiled a service, called SeeRisk, to help companies assess supply chain management risk. SeeRisk helps a company establish common metrics and measure performance against them by identifying operational problems and risks. The SeeRisk system is integrated with operational and transactional systems along with external vendor systems. The goal of the system is to improve revenue as well as reduce costs by increasing visibility of inventory, and by knowing what is on the shelf and what is downstream in production. SeeRisk can calculate the implications that defective components would have on revenue, operating costs, what it would cost to start production over, and ultimately the effect on corporate profitability.[8]

Successful Project Management Strategies

Recreational Equipment, Inc. (REI), needs to consistently develop high-quality products and decrease the time to deliver them to market. To do that, REI needs to efficiently manage product development processes, projects, and information. The REI Gear and Apparel division takes an integrated project management approach to designing, managing, and tracking its product development projects, while collaborating and managing its workflow. REI's strategy entails combining Microsoft .NET technology, the Microsoft Office Enterprise Project Management (EPM) Solution, and software based on Microsoft Office Visio 2003 to create an integrated business solution it can use to model as-is business processes, experiment with what-if scenarios, and then convert the optimized processes into detailed project plans.

Project managers can further develop these plans, assign resources division-wide, manage projects online, and collaborate globally. REI predicts this integrated solution will help it improve its efficiency, consistency, and scalability so it can deliver its products to market more quickly.[9] Figure B10.11 displays the top five successful project management strategies outlined in CIO magazine.

FIGURE B10.11

Top Five Successful Project Management Strategies

Top Five Successful Project Management Strategies

1. **Define project success criteria**—At the beginning of the project, make sure the stakeholders share a common understanding of how they will determine whether the project is successful. Too often, meeting a predetermined schedule is the only apparent success factor, but there are certainly others. Some examples are increasing market share, reaching a specified sales volume or revenue, achieving specific customer satisfaction measures, retiring a high-maintenance legacy system, and achieving a particular transaction processing volume and correctness.

2. **Develop a solid project plan**—The hard part of developing a plan is the thinking, negotiating, balancing, and communication project managers will have to do to develop a solid and realistic plan. The time they spend analyzing what it will take to solve the business problem will reduce the number of changes later in the project.

3. **Divide and conquer**—Break all large tasks into multiple small tasks to provide more accurate estimates, reveal hidden work activities, and allow for more accurate, fine-grained status tracking.

4. **Plan for change**—Things never go precisely as planned on a project; therefore, the budget and schedule should include some contingency buffers at the end of major phases to accommodate change.

5. **Manage project risk**—Failure to identify and control risks will allow the risks to control the project. Be sure to spend significant time during project planning to brainstorm possible risk factors, evaluate their potential threat, and determine the best way to mitigate or prevent them.[10]

L arge IT projects require significant investment of time and resources. Successful software development projects have proven challenging and often elusive, wasting many resources and jeopardizing the goodwill of stakeholders, including customers and employees. Bringing strong, effective project, change, and risk management disciplines to large IT projects is essential to successful organizations. The days when a project manager could just concentrate on bringing a project in on time, on budget, and with agreed-upon deliverables are fading.

Change control board
    (CCB), 363
Change management, 363
Change management
    system, 363
Critical path, 361
Dependency, 361
Gantt chart, 361

PERT (Program Evaluation and
    Review Technique) chart, 361
Project, 358
Project deliverable, 358
Project exclusion, 360
Project management, 358
Project manager, 358
Project milestone, 358

Project objective, 360
Project plan, 361
Project product, 360
Project risk, 364
Project scope, 360
Risk management, 364

Staying on Track—Toronto Transit

Schedules are at the heart of Toronto Transit Commission's (TTC) celebrated transit system, which services over 1 million customers daily. There are over 50 large engineering and construction projects currently under way to expand, upgrade, and maintain Toronto's transit systems and structures. One such project is the Sheppard project, which consists of constructing the new six-kilometer line north of the city. Sheppard is estimated to take more than five years to complete, with a total cost of $875 million.

TTC's challenge is to keep its 50 individual projects, most of which fall within the $2 million to $100 million price range and span an average of five years, on schedule and under budget. Staying on top of so many multifaceted, multiyear, and often interdependent projects adds additional complexity for the company. TTC uses Primavera Project Planner (P3) to create a single Master Schedule for all of its engineering and construction projects.

TTC's 50 individual projects average 100–150 activities each, with some projects encompassing as many as 500–600 activities. "Seeing the big picture is important, not only for the 300 people who work in the Engineering and Construction branch of the TTC, but for the entire 9,000 person organization," says Vince Carroll, head scheduler for the Engineering and Construction branch. "Engineering managers need to see how other projects may impact their own. Materials and procurement managers need to track project progress. Senior managers need to be able to communicate with city government to secure funding. Marketing and public relations people need the latest information to set public expectations. And most important of all," says Carroll, "the operations group needs to stay informed of what is happening so that they can adjust the schedules that run the trains."

Carroll and his team of 25 people create, update, and publish a single Master Schedule that summarizes the individual status of each project, shows the logical links between projects, and provides an integrated overview of all projects. The Master Schedule helps the team effectively and regularly communicate the status of all projects currently under way throughout the Toronto Transit system.

The Master Schedule organizes projects according to their location in the capital budget. For example, projects can be organized according to those that have been allotted funding for expansion, state of good repair, legislative reasons, or environmental reasons. Each project is organized by its logical flow—from planning, analysis, design, through the maintenance phase. The final report shows positive and negative balances for each project and a single overview of the status of all the engineering and construction projects. Carroll and his team use PERT charts to create time-scaled logic diagrams and then convert this information to bar charts for presentation purposes in the Master Schedule. TTC is currently in the process of linking its Master Schedule directly to its payroll system, enabling it to track the number of hours actually worked versus hours planned.[11]

Questions

1. Describe Gantt charts and explain how TTC could use one to communicate project status.
2. Describe PERT charts and explain how TTC could use one to communicate project status.
3. Determine how TTC could use its Master Schedule to gain efficiencies in its supply chain.
4. Discuss how TTC could use its Master Schedule to identify change management and risk management issues.

CLOSING CASE TWO

Automating Autodesk

Autodesk, one of the world's leading digital design and content companies, provides popular graphics applications and Internet portal services to more than 4 million customers in over 150 countries. Autodesk is the developer of the popular Computer Aided Design (CAD) and Computer Aided Manufacturing (CAM) software products. The company offers a broad range of integrated, interoperable solutions that combine industry-leading software with innovative Internet, mobile, and wireless technologies. Autodesk helps companies "turn designs into reality."

Autodesk needed to capitalize on its existing IT budget for maximum project completion, overall budget control, and improved management of IT resources across multiple geographies such as Japan, Switzerland, California, and New Hampshire. The company was experiencing several issues including managing processes and projects via a myriad of spreadsheets and Word documents, which did not adequately address the needs of its global IT department. Through the implementation of Evolve's integrated project management suite, Autodesk's Global IT department has achieved the following:

- Improved planning and prioritizing of its mission-critical projects.
- Created a flexible global workforce.
- Improved its ability to track project costs against budget.
- Streamlined its use of contractors.
- Better strategic alignment of people and projects.

With the Evolve Time-and-Expense Manager, Autodesk can control costs and bill customers more effectively, while the multicurrency function supports and streamlines its international operations. Autodesk's Evolve implementation connects professionals across North America, Canada, and Europe using the Opportunity, Resource, and Time & Expense Manager applications.[12]

Questions

1. Explain why project management, change management, and risk management are critical to a global company such as Autodesk.

2. Assess the impact on Autodesk's business if it failed to implement Evolve's project management solution and continued to manage its projects using a myriad of spreadsheets and Word documents.

3. Explain why Opportunity, Resource, and Time & Expense Manager applications would be of value to a company like Autodesk.

★ MAKING BUSINESS DECISIONS

1. Explaining Project Management

Prime Time Inc. is a large consulting company that specializes in outsourcing people with project management capabilities and skills. You are in the middle of an interview for a job with Prime Time. The manager performing the interview asks you to explain why managing a project plan is critical to a project's success. The manager also wants you to explain scope creep and feature creep and your tactics for managing them on a project. Finally, the manager wants you to elaborate on your strategies for delivering successful projects and reducing risks.

2. Applying Project Management Techniques

You have been hired by a medium-sized airline company, Sun Best. Sun Best currently flies over 300 routes in the eastern region. The company is experiencing tremendous issues coordinating its 3,500 pilots, 7,000 flight attendants, and 2,000 daily flights. Determine how Sun Best could use a Gantt chart to help it coordinate its pilots, flight attendants, and daily flights. Using Excel, create a sample Gantt chart highlighting the different types of activities and resources Sun Best could track with the tool.

3. Prioritizing Projects

Nick Zele is the new managing operations director for a large construction company, CMA. Nick is currently looking for a project manager who can help him manage the 60 ongoing company projects. You are interested in working with Nick and have decided to apply for the job. Nick has asked you to compile a report detailing why project prioritization is critical for CMA, along with the different types of prioritization techniques you would recommend CMA use when determining which projects to pursue.

4. Managing Expectations

Trader is the name for a large human resource project that is currently being deployed at your organization. Your boss, Pam Myers, has asked you to compile an expectations management matrix for the project. The first thing you need to determine are management's expectations. Compile a list of questions you would ask to help determine management's expectations for the Trader project.

5. Mitigating Risk

Alicia Fernandez owns and operates a chain of nine seafood restaurants in the Boston area. Alicia is currently considering purchasing one of her competitors which would give her an additional six restaurants. Alicia's primary concerns with the purchase are the constantly changing seafood prices and high staff turnover rate in the restaurant industry. Explain to Alicia what risk management is and how she can use it to mitigate the risks for the potential purchase of her competitor.

PLUG-IN

T1

Hardware and Software

Introduction

Information technology (IT) is any computer-based tool that people use to work with information and support the information and information-processing needs of an organization. Therefore, information technology is composed of the Internet, a personal computer, a cell phone that can access the Web, a personal digital assistant, presentation software, just to name a few. All of these technologies help to perform specific information processing tasks, which are detailed in this plug-in.

The Basics of Hardware and Software

There are two basic categories of technology: hardware and software. **Hardware** is the physical aspect of computers, telecommunications, and other information technology devices. **Software** is a general term for the various kinds of programs used to operate computers and related devices. Software, such as Microsoft Excel, and various hardware devices such as a keyboard and a monitor interact to create a graph, for instance. A keyboard is used to enter data, Excel provides specific rules to create the graph, and a monitor enables the user to see the graph.

All hardware falls into one of six categories:

1. An *input device* is equipment used to capture information and commands (e.g., keyboard, scanner).

2. An *output device* is equipment used to see, hear, or otherwise accept the results of information processing requests (e.g., monitor, printer).

3. A *storage device* is equipment used to store information (e.g., diskette, hard drive, CD).

4. The *central processing unit (CPU)* is the actual hardware that interprets and executes the program (software) instructions and coordinates how all the other hardware devices work together.

5. A *telecommunications device* is equipment used to send information and receive it from one location to another (e.g., modem).

6. **Connecting devices** are equipment such as parallel ports that connect a printer to a computer and connector cords (e.g., printer cable, USB cable).

There are two main types of software: application and system. *Application software* is software used to solve specific problems or perform specific tasks. Microsoft PowerPoint, for example, can help create slides for a presentation and Microsoft FrontPage assists with creating and publishing a Web page or Web site. From an organizational perspective, payroll software, collaborative software such as videoconferencing (within groupware), and inventory management software are all examples of application software.

System software handles tasks specific to technology management and coordinates the interaction of all technology devices. System software includes both operating system software and utility software. *Operating system software* and its functions support the application software and manages how the hardware devices work together. Popular personal operating system software includes Microsoft Windows XP, Mac OS X (for Apple computers), and Linux (an open source operating system). There are also operating systems for networks (Microsoft Windows NT is an example), operating systems for personal digital assistants (Windows CE is an example), and operating systems for just about every other type of technology configuration.

Utility software provides additional functionality to the operating system. Utility software includes antivirus software, screen savers, disk optimization software, and anti-spam software.

COMPUTER CATEGORIES

Computers come in different shapes, sizes, and colors. Some are small enough to carry around, while others are the size of a telephone booth. Size does not always correlate to power, speed, and price.

Personal Digital Assistants (PDAs)

A *personal digital assistant (PDA)* is a small hand-held computer that performs simple tasks such as taking notes, scheduling appointments, and maintaining an address book and a calendar. The PDA screen is touch-sensitive, allowing a user to write directly on the screen, capturing what is written.

Notebook Computers

A *notebook computer* is a fully functional computer designed to be carried around and run on battery power. Notebooks come equipped with all of the technology that a personal desktop computer has, yet weigh as little as 4 pounds.

Personal Data Assistant (PDA)

Tablet Computers

A *tablet computer* is a pen-based computer that provides the screen capabilities of a PDA with the functional capabilities of a notebook or desktop computer. Similar to PDAs, tablet PCs use a writing pen or stylus to write notes on the screen and touch the screen to perform functions such as clicking on a link while visiting a Web site. Tablet PCs come in two designs—convertibles and slates. Convertible tablet PCs look like notebook computers, including a screen that lifts up and sets in position with a full keyboard and touch pad underneath. Using a convertible PC, a swivel screen allows a user to lay it flat on the keyboard, converting it into a notebook computer with no top.

Slate tablet PCs come with no integrated physical keyboard, making the tablet the entire computer. Docking stations are available for a slate tablet PC, giving the ability to connect a keyboard and mouse.

Tablet Computer

Desktop Computers

A *desktop computer* is still one of the most popular choices for personal computing needs. Desktop computers are available with a horizontal system box (the box is where the CPU, RAM, and storage devices are held) with a monitor on top, or there are desktop computers with a vertical system box (called a tower) that are usually placed on the floor within a work area.

What category of computer is needed, PDA, notebook, tablet PC, or desktop computer, is a function of unique individual needs. PDAs offer great portability allowing a user to keep a calendar, send and receive e-mail, take short notes, and even access the Web. However, they are limited in capacity; for example, a user would typically not write a term paper, build a Web site, or create a complex graph with statistical software on a PDA. For any of those tasks, either a notebook or a desktop computer would be the best choice.

The capabilities of PDAs will continue to improve dramatically, allowing users to perform "complex" tasks such as creating an elaborate spreadsheet or graph and even integrating speech recognition.

Minicomputers, Mainframe Computers, and Supercomputers

PDAs, notebooks, and desktop computers are designed to meet personal information processing needs. In business, however, many people often need to access and use the same computer simultaneously. In this case, businesses need computing technologies that multiple people can access and use at the same time. Computers of this type include minicomputers, mainframe computers, and supercomputers.

A *minicomputer* (sometimes called a *mid-range computer*) is designed to meet the computing needs of several people simultaneously in a small to medium-size business environment. Minicomputers are more powerful than desktop computers but also cost more, ranging in price from $5,000 to several hundred thousand dollars. Businesses often use minicomputers as servers, either for creating a Web presence or as an internal computer on which shared information and software are placed. For this reason, minicomputers are well suited for business environments in which people need to share common information, processing power, and/or certain peripheral devices such as high quality, fast laser printers.

Supercomputer

A *mainframe computer* (sometimes just called a mainframe) is designed to meet the computing needs of hundreds of people in a large business environment. Mainframe computers are a step up in size, power, capability, and cost from minicomputers. Mainframes can cost in excess of $1 million. With processing speeds greater than 1 trillion instructions per second (compared to a typical desktop that can process about 2.5 billion instructions per second), mainframes can easily handle the processing requests of hundreds of people simultaneously. **Supercomputers** are the fastest, most powerful, and most expensive type of computer. Organizations such as NASA that are heavily involved in research and "number crunching" employ supercomputers because of the speed with which they can process information. Other large, customer-oriented businesses such as General Motors and AT&T employ supercomputers just to handle customer information and transaction processing.

Software

Software contains the instructions that the hardware executes to perform an information processing task. Without the aid of software, the computer (e.g., hardware) is useless. As previously stated, there are two categories of software: application and system.

APPLICATION SOFTWARE

Application software is used for specific information processing needs, including payroll, customer relationship management, project management, training, and many others.

Personal Productivity Software

Personal productivity software is used to perform personal tasks such as writing a memo, creating a graph, or creating a slide presentation. Some of the more popular personal productivity software tools include Microsoft Word and Excel, Internet Explorer, and Quicken (personal finance software).

Vertical and Horizontal Market Software

Vertical market software is application software that is unique to a particular industry. For example, the health care industry has a variety of application software that is unique to it, including radiology software, patient scheduling software, nursing allocation software, and pharmaceutical software.

   Horizontal market software is general enough to be suitable for use in a variety of industries. Inventory management, payroll, accounts receivable, and billing applications are examples of horizontal market software. Many of these functions are very similar, if not identical, in many different industries.

   There are some key differences between personal productivity software and horizontal and vertical market software. One difference is price. A full suite of personal productivity software sells for less than $400. In contrast, some individual horizontal and vertical market software packages may cost as much as $500,000 or more. Second is the issue of customizability. When purchasing personal productivity software, the way in which the software works cannot be changed. However, horizontal and vertical market software is often able to be modified to fit specific business needs.

SYSTEM SOFTWARE

System software controls how the various technology tools work together along with the application software. System software includes two basic categories: operating system and utility.

Operating System Software

Operating system software controls the application software and manages how the hardware devices work together. For example, when using Excel to create and print a graph, the operating system software controls the process, ensures that a printer

MacIntosh OS X

is attached and has paper, and sends the graph to the printer along with instructions on how to print it.

The operating system software also supports a variety of useful features, one of which is multitasking. **Multitasking** allows more than one piece of software to be used at a time. As an example, multitasking is used when creating a graph in Excel and inserting it into a word processing document. With multitasking, both pieces of application software can be open at the same time; both may be visible on the screen. Therefore, when completing the creation of a graph, it is an easy task to copy and paste the graph into a word processing document without having to go through a series of steps to exit the spreadsheet software and then start the word processing software.

There are different types of operating system software for personal environments and for organizational environments that support many users simultaneously. Popular personal operating systems include:

- **Microsoft Windows XP**—Microsoft's latest operating system for personal computers.
- **Mac OS X**—the latest operating system for Apple computers.
- **Linux**—an open source ("open source" refers to any program whose source code is made available for use or modification as users or other developers see fit) operating system that provides a rich environment for high-end workstations and network servers.

Utility Software

Utility software is software that adds additional functionality to an operating system. As an example, screen saver software (which is probably also a part of the operating system) is considered utility software. Most important, utility software includes antivirus software that scans for and often eliminates viruses from computers. There are other types of utility software including:

- **Crash-proof software** helps save information if a computer crashes.
- **Uninstaller software** can remove software from a computer that is no longer needed.
- **Disk optimization software** organizes information on a hard disk in the most efficient way.
- **Spyware software** removes any software that employs a user's Internet connection in the background without their knowledge or explicit permission.

Hardware

To understand the significant role of hardware, it helps to know something about how the computer works. Computers work in terms of bits and bytes using electrical pulses that have two states: on and off.

A **binary digit (bit)** is the smallest unit of information that a computer can process. A bit can be either a 1 (on) or a 0 (off). The challenge from a technological point of view is to be able to represent all the characters, special symbols, and numbers in binary form. Using ASCII is one way to do this. **ASCII (American Standard Code for Information Interchange)** is the coding system that most personal computers use to represent, process, and store information. In ASCII, a group of eight bits represents one natural language character and is called a **byte**.

COMMON INPUT DEVICES

An input device is equipment used to capture information and commands. For example, a keyboard is used to type in information and a mouse is used to point and click on buttons and icons. There are numerous input devices available in many different environments, some of which have applications that are more suitable in a business setting than in a personal setting. Some common input devices include:

- **Keyboard**—the most popular input technology.
- **Point-of-sale (POS)**—used for capturing information at the point of a transaction, typically in a retail environment.
- **Microphone**—used for capturing sounds such as a voice (for automatic speech recognition).
- **Mouse**—the most popular "pointing" input device.
- **Pointing stick**—a small rubberlike pointing device that causes the pointer to move on the screen applying directional pressure (popular on notebooks).
- **Touch pad**—another form of a stationary mouse on which the movement of a finger causes the pointer on the screen to move (popular also on notebooks).

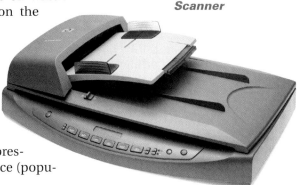

Scanner

- **Touch screen**—a special screen that allows the use of a finger to point at and touch a particular function to perform.
- **Bar code reader**—captures information that exists in the form of vertical bars whose width and distance apart determine a number.
- **Optical mark recognition (OMR)**—detects the presence or absence of a mark in a predetermined place (popular for multiple-choice exams).
- **Scanner**—captures images, photos, and artwork that already exist on paper.

COMMON OUTPUT DEVICES

An output device is equipment used to see, hear, or otherwise accept the results of information processing requests. Among output devices, printers and monitors are the most common; however, speakers and plotters (special printers that draw output on a page) are becoming widely used. In addition, output devices are responsible for converting computer-stored information into a form that can be understood.

Monitors

Monitors come in two varieties: cathode-ray tube (CRT) or flat-panel displays. *Cathode-ray tubes (CRTs)* are monitors that look like traditional television sets, while *flat-panel displays* are thin, lightweight monitors that take up much less space than CRTs. Flat-panel displays are either liquid crystal display or gas plasma. *Liquid crystal display (LCD) monitors* make the image by sending electricity through crystallized liquid trapped between two layers of glass or plastic. *Gas plasma displays* send electricity through gas trapped between two layers of glass or plastic to create an image. A gas plasma display usually provides a better image, but is more expensive than a comparably sized LCD monitor.

Monitor size reflects how large the entire monitor is, measured diagonally from corner to corner. Monitor size, especially for CRTs,

Gas Plasma Display

gives an indication of the amount of space the monitor will require. However, the size that really is of interest is viewable screen size, often expressed as VIS or viewable inch screen. Viewable screen size describes the size of the screen, which is measured diagonally from corner to corner and is always smaller than monitor size. Viewable screen size refers to the size of the screen that actually displays the application or utility software.

The number of picture elements or pixels determine screen resolution. *Pixels* are the dots that make up an image on the computer screen. For example, a monitor with a resolution given as $1,024 \times 768$ has 1,024 pixels horizontally and 768 pixels vertically. The number of dots varies with the type of monitor, but larger numbers (of pixels) provide clearer and crisper screen images than smaller ones. Monitor types range from basic VGA (with a resolution of 640×480) to QXGA (with a resolution of $2,048 \times 1,536$).

Dot pitch is the distance between the centers of a pair of like-colored pixels. Therefore, a monitor with .24 mm dot pitch (.24 millimeter between pair of like-colored pixels) is better than one with .28 mm dot pitch because the dots are smaller and closer together, giving a better quality image.

Printers

Printers are another common type of output device, creating output on paper. A printer's sharpness and clarity depends on its resolution. The resolution of a printer is the number of dots per inch (dpi) it produces, which is the same principle as the resolution in monitors. So, the more dots per inch, the better the image, and usually, the more costly the printer.

Most high-end personal printers have a resolution of $1,200 \times 1,200$ dpi or better. Multiplying these numbers together gives 1,440,000 dots per square inch. In addition, printers which have the same number of dots per inch both vertically and horizontally provide a better quality image. The common types of printers include:

Multifunction Printer

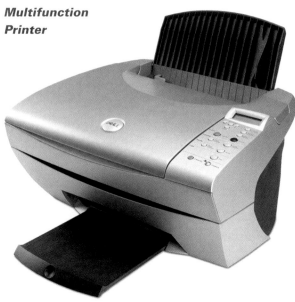

- **Inkjet printers** make images by forcing ink droplets through nozzles. Standard inkjet printers use four colors: black, cyan (blue), magenta (purplish pink), and yellow. Some inkjet printers produce high-quality images and are often advertised as photo printers. These have six colors (offering a second shade of magenta and cyan).

- **Laser printers** form images using an electrostatic process, the same way a photocopier works. Laser printers are more expensive than inkjet printers, but provide higher quality images. Most common personal laser printers print only in black and white.

- **Multifunction printers** scan, copy, and fax, as well as print. These are becoming quite popular in the personal technology arena, mainly because they cost less than if they are bought as separate tools (printer, scanner, copier, and fax machine). Multifunction printers can be either inkjet or laser, with the laser being more expensive and providing better quality.

Characteristics of CPUs and RAM

Together, the CPU and RAM make up the real brains of a computer. The CPU will largely determine the price of a computer system. The *central processing unit (CPU)* is the actual hardware that interprets and executes the program (software) instructions and coordinates how all the other hardware devices work together. *Random access memory (RAM)* is temporary storage that holds the current information, the application software currently being used, and the operating system software.

The CPU is often referred to as a microprocessor or a CPU chip. The dominant manufacturers of CPUs today include Intel (with its Celeron and Pentium lines for personal computers) and AMD (with its Athlon series). The most helpful information when comparing CPUs is their relative speeds. CPU speed is usually quoted in megahertz and gigahertz. *Megahertz (MHz)* is the number of millions of CPU cycles per second. *Gigahertz (GHz)* is the number of billions of CPU cycles per second. The number of CPU cycles per second determines how fast a CPU carries out the software instructions; more cycles per second means faster processing and faster CPUs cost more than their slower counterparts.

A CPU contains two primary parts: control unit and arithmetic/logic unit. The ***control unit*** interprets software instructions and literally tells the other hardware devices what to do, based on the software instructions. The ***arithmetic/logic unit (ALU)*** performs all arithmetic operations (for example, addition, and subtraction) and all logic operations (such as sorting and comparing numbers).

The control unit and A/L unit perform different functions. The control unit actually gets another instruction from RAM, which contains the software. It then interprets the instruction, decides what each other device must do, and finally tells each device what to do. The A/L unit, on the other hand, responds to the control unit and does whatever it dictates, performing either arithmetic or logic operations.

Random access memory (RAM) is "temporary" memory. When the computer is turned off, everything in RAM is literally wiped clean. RAM capacity is expressed in bytes, with megabytes being the most common. A megabyte (MB or M or Meg) is roughly 1 million bytes. Therefore, a computer with 256MB of RAM translates into the RAM being able to hold roughly 256 million characters of information and software instructions.

COMMON STORAGE DEVICES

Storage devices do not lose their contents when the computer is turned off. When considering storage devices, there are two questions to consider: (1) Is updating or modifying the information an option? and (2) How much information needs to be stored?

Abbreviation	Binary Term	Size
KB	Kilobyte	1,024 Bytes
MB	Megabyte	1,048,576 Bytes
GB	Gigabyte	1,073,741,824 Bytes | One billion Bytes
TB	Terrabyte	1024 GB
PB	Pettabyte	1024 TB
EB	Exabyte	1024 PB
ZB	Zettabyte	1024 EB
YB	Yottabyte	1024 ZB

Some storage devices, such as a hard disk, offer easy update capabilities and a large storage capacity. Others, such as floppy disks, offer easy update capabilities but limited storage capacities. Still others, such as CD-ROM, offer limited update capabilities but do possess large storage capacities. Storage device capacities are measured in terms of bytes including megabytes, gigabytes, and terabytes. A *gigabyte (GB)* is roughly 1 billion characters. A *terabyte (TB)* is roughly 1 trillion bytes (refer to Figure T1.1). Most standard desktops have a hard disk with storage capacity in excess of 40GB. Hard disks (sometimes referred to as hard disk packs) for large organizational computer systems can hold in excess of 100TB of information. For example, a typical double-spaced page of pure text is roughly 2,000 characters. Therefore, a 20GB (20 gigabyte or 20 billion characters) hard disk can hold approximately 10 million pages of text. Common storage devices include:

- *High-capacity floppy disk*—great for portability and ease of updating and holds between 100MB and 250MB of information, such as superdisks and Zip disks.

- *Hard disk*—rests within the system box and offers both ease of updating and great storage capacity.

- *CD-ROM (compact disk-read-only memory)*—optical or laser disc that offers no updating capability with about 800MB of storage capacity. Most software today is distributed on a CD-ROM.

- *CD-R (compact disc-recordable)*—optical or laser disc that offers one-time writing capability with about 800MB of storage capacity.

- *CD-RW (compact disc-rewritable)*—offers unlimited writing and updating capabilities on the CD.

- *DVD-ROM*—optical or laser disc that offers no updating capability with upward of 17GB of storage capacity. The trend is now for movie rentals to be on DVD.

- *DVD-R*—optical or laser disc that offers one-time writing capability with upward of 17GB of storage capacity.

- *DVD-RW,* or *DVD+RW* (different names by different manufacturers)—optical or laser disc that offers unlimited writing and updating capabilities on the DVD.

- *Flash memory device*—a storage device that is small enough to fit on a key ring and plugs directly into the USB port on a computer.

- *Memory card*—flash memory cards have high-capacity storage laminated inside a small piece of plastic.

TELECOMMUNICATIONS DEVICES

Telecommunications is the most dynamic, changing, exciting, and technically complicated aspect of IT. Telecommunications implies the ability to be connected, to almost anyone, anywhere, and at anytime. Telecommunications enables the concept of a network. A computer network (which is simply referred to as a net-

Carrier Technology	Description	Speed	Comments
Dial-up Access	On demand access using a modem and regular telephone line (POT).	2400 bps to 56 Kbps	■ Cheap but slow.
Cable	Special cable modem and cable line required.	512 Kbps to 20 Mbps	■ Must have existing cable access in area. ■ Bandwidth is shared.
DSL Digital Subscriber Line	This technology uses the unused digital portion of a regular copper telephone line to transmit and receive information. A special modem and adapter card are required.	128 Kbps to 8 Mbps	■ Doesn't interfere with normal telephone use. ■ Bandwidth is dedicated. ■ Must be within 5 km (3.1 miles) of telephone company switch.
Wireless (LMCS)	Access is gained by connection to a high-speed cellular like local multipoint communications system (LMCS) network via wireless transmitter/receiver.	30 Mbps or more	■ Can be used for high-speed data, broadcast TV, and wireless telephone service.
Satellite	Newer versions have two-way satellite access, removing need for phone line.	6 Mbps or more	■ Bandwidth is not shared. ■ Some connections require an existing Internet service account. ■ Setup fees can range from $500–$1000.

FIGURE T1.2

Modem Speeds Comparison

work) connects two or more computers so that they can communicate with each other and share information, software, peripheral devices, and/or processing power. A simple example of a network is two computers connected to the same printer. The most well-known (and complicated) example of a network is the millions of computers connected all over the world that make up the Internet.

The simplest form of communication device is a modem. There are many types of modems, including (refer to Figure T1.2):

■ Telephone modems (dial-up)

■ Cable modems

■ Digital Subscriber Line (DSL) modems

■ Wireless modems

■ Satellite modems

A telephone modem is a device that connects a computer to a phone line in order to access another computer or network. A telephone modem is necessary when using the standard telephone line for connecting to a network, because it acts as a converter of sorts. The computer works in terms of digital signals, while a standard telephone line works in terms of analog signals. Digital signals are discrete with each signal representing a bit (either 0 or 1). The modem must convert the digital signals of a computer into analog signals so they can be sent across the telephone line. At the other end, another modem translates the analog signals into digital signals, which can then be used by the other computer or network. The actual connection between devices cannot exist without the use of communications software, specifically:

■ **Connectivity software** enables a computer to "dial up" or connect to another computer.

■ **Web browser software** allows a computer (i.e., user) to surf the Web.

■ **E-mail software** enables electronic communication with other people by sending and receiving e-mail.

CONNECTING DEVICES

Connecting devices enable all the hardware components to communicate with each other. For example, a parallel connector is used to plug a printer into a system box. The parallel connector interfaces with a parallel port that is connected to an expansion card. That card is connected to the expansion bus (via an expansion slot), which moves information between various devices and RAM. The expansion bus is a part of the larger system bus, which moves information between the RAM and CPU and to and from various other devices.

Buses, Expansion Slots, and Expansion Cards

The system bus consists of the electronic pathways that move information between basic components on the motherboard, between the CPU and RAM. A part of the system bus is called the *expansion bus,* which moves information from the CPU and RAM to all of the other hardware devices such as a microphone and printer.

Along the expansion bus are expansion slots. An *expansion slot* is a long skinny socket on the motherboard into which an expansion card is inserted. An *expansion card* is a circuit board that is inserted into an expansion slot. Expansion cards include such things as video cards (for a monitor), sound cards (for speakers and microphone), and modem cards. Each expansion card contains one or more ports into which a connector is linked to some other hardware device such as a printer.

When buying a complete computer system, it will come already equipped with the expansion cards inserted into the expansion slots. The task after purchasing the new systems is to plug the appropriate connectors into the right ports.

Ports and Connectors

Different hardware devices require different kinds of ports and connectors. *Ports* are simply the plug-ins found on the outside of the system box (usually in the back) into which a connector is plugged. Popular connectors include:

- *Universal serial bus (USB)* is the most popular means of connecting devices to a computer. Most standard desktops and laptops have at least two USB ports.
- *Serial connector* usually has nine holes but may have 25, which fit into the corresponding number of pins in the port. Serial connectors are often most used for monitors and certain types of modems.
- *Parallel connector* has 25 pins, which fit into the corresponding holes in the port. Most printers use parallel connectors.

A special type of port called an infrared data association or IrDA has no physical corresponding connector. IrDA ports are for wireless devices that work in essentially the same way as the remote control on a TV. To use IrDA, both the computer and the wireless device (such as a mouse) must have an IrDA port.

Wireless Connections

Wireless devices transfer and receive information in the form of waves, either infrared or radio waves. Different types of waves have different frequencies (refer to Figure T1.3). The three types most frequently used in personal and business computer environments are (1) infrared, (2) Bluetooth, and (3) WiFi.

1. *Infrared*—also called *IR* or *IrDA (infrared data association)*—uses red light to send and receive information. Infrared light has a frequency below what the eye can see. It is used for TV remotes and other devices that operate over short distances that are free of obstacles.
2. *Bluetooth*—a standard for transmitting information in the form of short-range radio waves over distances of up to 30 feet and is used for purposes such as wirelessly connecting a cell phone or a PDA to a computer.

Type	Connection Speed	Range	Information
Wireless G (802.11g)	54Mbps	150 feet	Wi-Fi. The fastest most advanced. Compatible with 802.11b.
Wireless B (802.11b)	11Mbps	150 feet	Lowest cost solution.
Wireless A (802.11a)	54Mbps	255 feet	Cordless phones, used in densely populated areas.
Bluetooth	22Kbps	30 feet	Intended to replace peripheral cables.
Infrared (IR)	75Kbps	10 feet	Home-entertainment remote-control boxes, wireless local area networks, links between notebook computers and desktop computers.

3. **WiFi (wireless fidelity)**—a standard for transmitting information in the form of radio waves over distances up to about 300 feet. WiFi has several forms; for example, WiFi is called IEEE 802.11a, b, or g, each of which is a unique type. WiFi is usually the type of wireless communication used in a network environment.

I nformation technology (IT) is any computer-based tool that people use to work with information and support the information and information-processing needs of an organization. IT includes cell phones, PDAs, software such as spreadsheet software, and a printer. Categories of computers by size include personal digital assistants, notebook computers, desktop computers, minicomputers, mainframe computers, and supercomputers.

Personal productivity software helps perform personal tasks—such as writing a memo, creating a graph, and creating a slide presentation. System software handles tasks specific to technology management and coordinates the interaction of all technology devices.

* KEY TERMS

Application software, 371
Arithmetic/logic unit (ALU), 377
ASCII (American Standard Code for Information Interchange), 374
Binary digit (bit), 374
Bluetooth, 380
Byte, 374
CD-R, 378
CD-ROM, 378
CD-RW, 378
Central processing unit (CPU), 371
Control unit, 377
Crash-proof software, 374
Desktop computer, 372
Disk optimization software, 374
DVD-R, 378
DVD-ROM, 378
DVD–RW or DVD+RW, 378
Expansion bus, 380
Expansion card (board), 380
Expansion slot, 380

Flash memory device, 378
Gigabyte (GB or Gig), 378
Gigahertz (GHz), 377
Hard disk, 378
Hardware, 370
High capacity floppy disk, 378
Horizontal market software, 373
Infrared, IR, or IrDA (infrared data association), 380
Input device, 371
Linux, 374
Mainframe computer (mainframe), 372
Megahertz (MHz), 377
Memory card, 378
Minicomputer (mid-range computer), 372
Multitasking, 374
Notebook computer, 371
Operating system software, 371
Output device, 371
Parallel connector, 380
Personal digital assistant, 371

Personal productivity software, 373
Pixels, 376
Port, 380
Random access memory (RAM), 376
Serial connector, 380
Software, 370
Spyware software, 374
Storage device, 371
Supercomputer, 373
System software, 371
Tablet computer, 372
Telecommunications device, 371
Terabyte (TB), 378
Uninstaller software, 374
Universal serial bus (USB), 380
Utility software, 371
Vertical market software, 373
WiFi (wireless fidelity), 381

* MAKING BUSINESS DECISIONS

1. Customizing a Computer Purchase

One of the great things about the Web is the number of e-tailers now offering you a variety of products and services online. One such e-tailer is Dell, which allows you to customize and buy a computer. Connect to Dell's Web site at www.dell.com. Go to the portion of Dell's site that allows you to customize either a notebook or a desktop computer. First, choose an already prepared system and note its price and capability in terms of CPU speed, RAM size, monitor quality, and storage capacity. Now, customize that system to increase CPU speed, add more RAM, increase monitor size and quality, and add more storage capacity. What's the difference in price between the two? Which system is more in your price range? Which system has the speed and capacity you need?

2. **Web-Enabled Cell Phones and Web Computers**
   When categorizing computers by size for personal needs, we focused on PDAs, notebook computers, and desktop computers. There are several other variations including Web-enabled cell phones that include instant text messaging and Web computers. For this project, you will need a group of four people, which you will then split into two groups of two. Have the first group research Web-enabled cell phones, their capabilities, and their costs. Have that group make a purchase recommendation based on price and capability. Have the second group do the same for Web computers. What is your vision of the future? Will we ever get rid of clunky notebooks and desktops in favor of more portable and cheaper devices such as Web-enabled cell phones and Web computers? Why or why not?

3. **Operating System Software for PDAs**
   The personal digital assistant (PDA) market is ferocious, dynamic, and uncertain. One of the uncertainties is which operating system for PDAs will become dominant. Today, Microsoft operating systems dominate the notebook and desktop market. Research the more popular PDAs available today. What are the different operating systems? What different functionality do they offer? Are they compatible with each other? Determine which one will dominate in the future.

4. **Types of Monitors and Their Quality**
   The monitor you buy will greatly affect your productivity. If you buy a high-resolution, large-screen monitor, you will see the screen content better than if you buy a low-resolution, small-screen monitor. One factor in this is the monitor type. There are seven major monitor types available today: HDTV, QXGA, SVGA, SXGA, UXGA, VGA, and XGA. Research these monitor types, rank them from best to worst in terms of resolution. Also, rank the monitors in terms of price.

PLUG-IN T2

Networks and Telecommunications

1. Summarize the individual components of a computer network.
2. Describe the three main network topologies.
3. Explain the difference between the three main forms of network access methods.
4. Summarize the difference between guided media and unguided media.
5. Explain how a network operating system works.
6. List the transmitting and receiving devices used in a computer network.
7. Describe the function of TCP/IP.
8. Summarize the use of a virtual private network (VPN).

Introduction

A *computer network* (or just *network*) is a group of two or more computer systems linked together using wires or radio waves over a geographical area. Computer networks that do not use physical wires are called *wireless*—one of the fastest growing areas in IT and business.

In the business world, a computer network is more than a collection of interconnected devices. For many businesses, the computer network is the resource that enables them to gather, analyze, organize, and disseminate information that is essential to their profitability. The rise of intranets and extranets—business networks based on Internet technology—is an indication of the critical importance of computer networking to businesses.

Networks now take a whole variety of forms—they can exist within an entire building, a city, a country, or the world. There are networks that access each other at will or at the whim of individual users who can connect to them any time over telephone lines or a wireless satellite link.

This plug-in takes a detailed look at the key concepts that are integrating computer networks and data communications into the business world.

The Need for Networking

On the most fundamental level, a computer network interconnects a collection of devices that enables the storage, retrieval, and sharing of information. Commonly connected devices include personal computers, printers, pagers, and various data-storage devices. Recently, other types of devices have become network connectable, including interactive televisions, videophones, hand-held devices, and navigational environmental control systems.

A network provides two principle benefits: the ability to communicate and the ability to share. A network supports communication among users in ways that other media cannot. E-mail, the most popular form of network communication, provides low-cost, printable correspondence with the capability for forwarding, acknowledgment, storage, retrieval, and attachment. Sharing involves not only information (database records, e-mail, graphics, etc.), but also resources (applications, printers, modems, disk space, scanners, etc.).

Through its ability to share, a network promotes collaboration. This is the main attraction of software called groupware that is designed to allow multiple users to hold electronic meetings and work concurrently on projects. **Groupware** is software that supports team interaction and dynamics including calendaring, scheduling, and videoconferencing.

THE BENEFITS OF COMPUTER NETWORKING

The most obvious benefit of computer networking is that it can store virtually any kind of information at, and retrieve it from, a central location on the network as well as access it from any connected computer. Anyone can store, retrieve, and modify textual information such as letters and contracts, audio information such as voice messages, and visual images such as facsimiles, photographs, medical X rays, and even video segments.

A network also combines the power and capabilities of diverse equipment providing a collaborative medium to combine the skills of different people, regardless of physical location. Networking enables people to share information and ideas easily, so they can work more efficiently and productively. Networks also improve commercial activities such as purchasing, selling, and customer service (B2B and B2C activities). Networks are making traditional business processes more efficient, more manageable, and less expensive.

NETWORKING BASICS

Information travels over the cables (unless the network is wireless), allowing network users to exchange documents and data with each other, print to the same printers, and generally share hardware or software that is connected to the network. Each computer, printer, or other peripheral device that is connected to the network is called a *node.* Networks can have tens, thousands, or even millions of nodes.

Networks are assembled according to certain rules. Cabling, for example, has to be a certain length; each cabling strand can support only a certain amount of network traffic. **Topology** refers to the actual physical organization of the computers (and other network devices) including connections. **Bandwidth** indicates how much information can be carried in a given time period (usually a second) over a wired or wireless communications link. Speed is expressed as megabits per second (or mbps), where one "bit" (short for binary digit) is the smallest unit of data in a computer. A bit has a single binary value, either 0 or 1.

For historical reasons, the network industry refers to nearly every type of network as an "area network." The most commonly discussed categories of computer networks include the following:

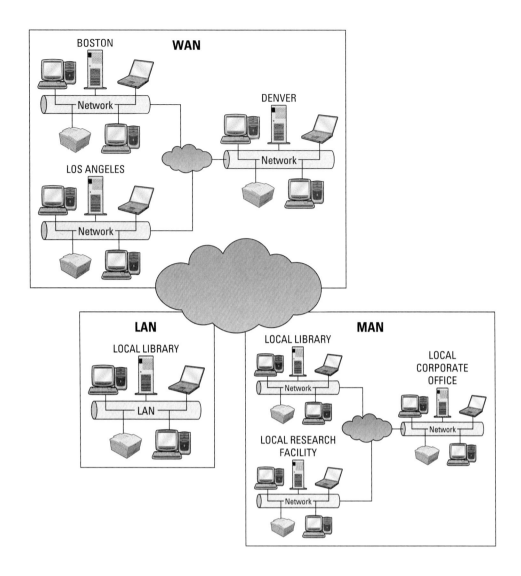

- Local Area Network (LAN)
- Wide Area Network (WAN)
- Metropolitan Area Network (MAN)

A *local area network (LAN)* connects network devices over a relatively short distance, such as a building or a campus, whereas a *wide area network (WAN)* is a geographically dispersed telecommunications network, such as the Internet. LANS and WANS (see Figure T2.1) are the most often referred to of the network designs. The concept of "area" makes good sense because a key distinction between a LAN and a WAN involves the physical distance that the network spans. A third category, equally popular, is the *metropolitan area network (MAN)* that interconnects users with computer resources in a geographic area or region larger than that covered by even a large local area network, but smaller than the area covered by a wide area network. In terms of geographic breadth, MANs are larger than LANs, but smaller than WANs.

Local Area Network (LAN) Basics

A LAN connects network devices over a relatively short distance. A networked office building, school, or home usually contains a single LAN, although sometimes one building will contain a few small LANs, and occasionally a LAN will span a group of nearby buildings.

Wide Area Network (WAN) Basics

As the term implies, a wide area network spans a large physical distance. The Internet is a WAN that spans most of the world. A wide area network is a geographically dispersed telecommunications network. The term distinguishes a broader telecommunications structure from a local area network. A wide area network may be privately owned or rented, but the term usually implies the inclusion of public (shared user) networks.

Metropolitan Area Network (MAN) Basics

A MAN interconnects users in a geographical area larger than a LAN, but smaller than a WAN, such as a city, with dedicated or high-performance hardware. For instance, a university or college may have a MAN that joins together many of its local area networks situated around its campus. Then from its MAN it could have several wide area network links to other universities or the Internet.

Networks—The Big Picture

There are a number of networks in the computing world, ranging from tiny two-computer local area networks to the biggest network of all, the Internet. Networks vary a great deal, but they all share one simple idea—they allow people to extend the reach of their computers beyond the devices and shared information that are sitting on their desktop. Networks give computer users the power to use the resources—such as hard disks, printers, and CD-ROM drives—of other computers without forcing anyone to physically move to those other computers to use them. Before the development of network technology, individual computers were isolated from each other and limited in their range of applications. By linking these individual computers over networks, the computers' usefulness and productivity have been increased enormously.

A network is made up of many physical elements in addition to the computers, printers, and other devices that are the main components of the network. Using network hardware, the computers and other devices in a specific area are literally hooked up to each other. After the connections are made, special networking software is enabled on the networked computers so the computers can communicate with each other. The manner in which all these items are connected is often referred to as the network topology. Because of the specific nature of computer network technology, networks must be arranged in a particular way in order to work properly. These arrangements are based on the network hardware's capabilities and the characteristics of the various modes of data transfer. Network topologies are further subdivided into two categories:

- Physical topologies
- Logical topologies

PHYSICAL TOPOLOGIES

The *physical topology* refers to the actual physical organization of the computers on the network and its connections. Physical topologies vary depending on cost and functionality. There are five principal topologies used in LANs:

1. *Bus topology*—all devices are connected to a central cable, called the bus or backbone. Bus networks are relatively inexpensive and easy to install for small networks (see Figure T2.2).
2. *Star topology*—all devices are connected to a central device, called a hub. Star networks are relatively easy to install and manage, but bottlenecks can occur because all data must pass through the hub (see Figure T2.2).

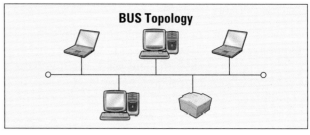

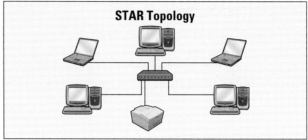

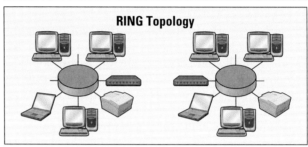

3. **Ring topology**—all devices are connected to one another in the shape of a closed loop, so that each device is connected directly to two other devices, one on either side of it. Ring topologies are relatively expensive and difficult to install, but they offer high bandwidth and can span large distances (see Figure T2.2).

4. **Tree topology**—combines the characteristics of the bus and star topologies. It consists of groups of star-configured workstations connected to a linear bus backbone cable (see Figure T2.3).

5. **Wireless topology**—devices are connected by a receiver/transmitter to a special network interface card that transmits signals between a computer and a server, all within an acceptable transmission range (see Figure T2.3).

NETWORK ACCESS METHODS (PROTOCOLS)

A **protocol** is the predefined way that someone (who wants to use a service) talks with or utilizes that service. The "someone" could be a person, but more often it is a computer program like a Web browser. Simply put, for one computer (or computer program) to talk to another computer (or computer program) they must both be talking the same language, and this language is called a protocol.

A protocol is based on an agreed-upon and established standard, and this way all manufacturers of hardware and software that are utilizing the protocol do so in a similar fashion to allow for interoperability. The Institute of Electrical and Electronics Engineers (IEEE) is the governing body that determines the standards. Through extensive testing, collaboration, and industry feedback, standards are solidified into working blueprints for communicating. The most popular network protocols used are:

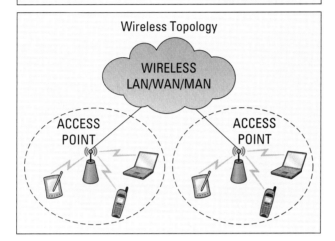

- Token Ring
- Ethernet
- Fiber Distributed Data Interface (FDDI)

Token Ring

A *token ring* network is a LAN in which all computers are connected in a ring or star topology (as suggested by Figure T2.4), and a token-passing scheme is used in order to prevent the collision of data between two computers that want to send messages at the same time. The token ring protocol is the second most widely used protocol on local area networks after Ethernet. IBM originally developed the token ring network in the 1970s that is still IBM's primary local area network (LAN) technology. The token ring technology provides for data transfer rates of either 4 or 16 megabits per second, comparatively slower than the Ethernet technology.

Ethernet

Ethernet is a physical and data layer technology for LAN networking. Ethernet is the most widely installed LAN access method originally developed by Xerox and then developed further by Xerox, Digital Equipment Corporation, and Intel. When it first began to be widely deployed in the 1980s, Ethernet supported a maximum theoretical data transfer rate of 10 megabits per second (Mbps). More recently, Fast Ethernet has extended traditional Ethernet technology to 100 Mbps peak, and Gigabit Ethernet technology extends performance up to 1000 Mbps.

Ethernet has survived as the major LAN technology (it is currently used for approximately 85 percent of the world's LAN-connected PCs and workstations) because its protocol has the following characteristics:

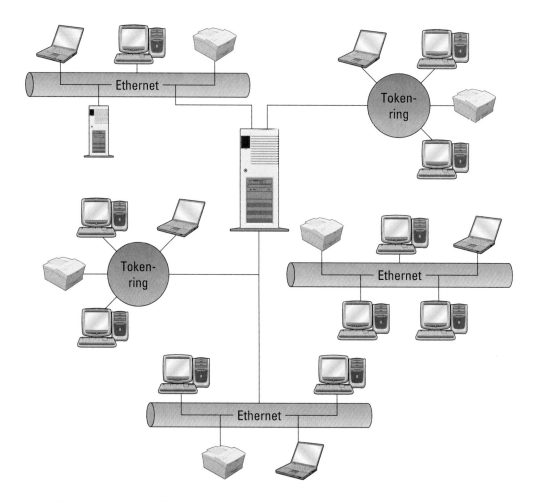

- Easy to understand, implement, manage, and maintain.
- Allows low-cost network implementations.
- Provides extensive flexibility for network installation.
- Guarantees successful interconnection and operation of standards-compliant products, regardless of manufacturer.

Fiber Distributed Data Interface (FDDI)

Fiber Distributed Data Interface (FDDI) is a set of protocols for sending digital data over fiber optic cable. FDDI networks are token-passing networks that support data rates of up to 100 megabits per second. FDDI networks are typically used as backbones for wide area networks (see Figure T2.5).

FIGURE T2.5

Fiber Distributed Data
Interface (FDDI)

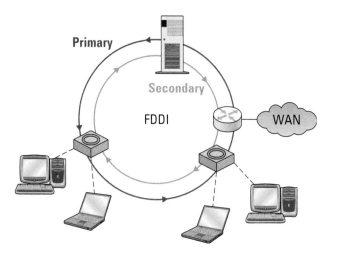

Networking Hardware

The hardware used to transport the data from one computer to another can generally be divided into network transmission media and transmitting and receiving devices. *Network transmission media* refers to the various types of media used to carry the signal between computers. Transmitting and receiving devices are the devices placed at either end of the network transmission media to either send or receive the information.

When information is sent across the network, it is converted into electrical signals. These signals are generated as electromagnetic waves (analog signaling) or as a sequence of voltage pulses (digital signaling). To be sent from one location to another, a signal must travel along a physical path. The physical path that is used to carry a signal between a signal transmitter and a signal receiver is called the transmission media. There are two types of transmission media:

- Guided
- Unguided

GUIDED MEDIA

Guided media are transmission material manufactured so that signals will be confined to a narrow path and will behave predictably. The three most commonly used types of guided media are (see Figure T2.6):

- Twisted-pair wiring
- Coaxial cable
- Fiber optic cable

Twisted-Pair Wiring

Twisted-pair wiring refers to a type of cable composed of four (or more) copper wires twisted around each other within a plastic sheath. The wires are twisted to reduce outside electrical interference. There are "shielded" and "unshielded" varieties of twisted-pair cables. Shielded cables have a metal shield encasing the wires that acts as a ground for electromagnetic interference. Unshielded twisted-pair (UTP) is the most popular and is generally the best option for LAN networks. The quality of UTP may vary from telephone-grade wire to high-speed cable. The cable has four pairs of wires inside the jacket. Each pair is twisted with a different number of twists per inch to help eliminate interference from adjacent pairs and other electrical devices. The RJ-45 connectors on twisted-pair cables resemble large telephone connectors.

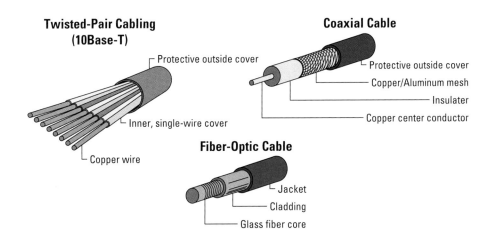

Twisted-Pair Cabling (10Base-T)
- Protective outside cover
- Inner, single-wire cover
- Copper wire

Coaxial Cable
- Protective outside cover
- Copper/Aluminum mesh
- Insulater
- Copper center conductor

Fiber-Optic Cable
- Jacket
- Cladding
- Glass fiber core

FIGURE T2.6

Twisted-Pair, Coaxial Cable, and Fiber Optic Cable

Coaxial Cable

Coaxial cable is cable that can carry a wide range of frequencies with low signal loss. It consists of a metallic shield with a single wire placed along the center of a shield and isolated from the shield by an insulator. This type of cable is referred to as "coaxial" because it contains one copper wire (or physical data channel) that carries the signal and is surrounded by another concentric physical channel consisting of a wire mesh. The outer channel serves as a ground for electrical interference. Because of this grounding feature, several coaxial cables can be placed within a single conduit or sheath without significant loss of data integrity. Coaxial cable is divided into two different types: (1) thinnet and (2) thicknet.

1. *Thinnet coaxial cable* is similar to the cable used by cable television companies. Thinnet is not as flexible as twisted-pair, but it is still used in LAN environments. The connectors on coaxial cable are called BNC twist-on connectors and resemble those found on television cables.

2. *Thicknet coaxial cable* is similar to thinnet except that it is larger in diameter. The increase in size translates into an increase in maximum effective distance. The drawback to the increase in size, however, is a loss of flexibility. Since thicknet is much more rigid than thinnet, the deployment possibilities are much more limited and the connectors are much more complex. Thicknet is used primarily as a network backbone with thinnet "branches" to the individual network components.

Fiber Optic Cable

Fiber optic (or *optical fiber*) refers to the technology associated with the transmission of information as light impulses along a glass wire or fiber. 10Base-FL and 100Base-FX optical fiber cable are the same types of cable used by most telephone companies for long distance service. Optical fiber cable can transmit data over long distances with little loss in data integrity. In addition, because data is transferred as a pulse of light, optical fiber is not subject to interference. The light pulses travel through a glass wire or fiber encased in an insulating sheath.

As with thicknet, optical fiber's increased maximum effective distance comes at a price. Optical fiber is more fragile than wire, difficult to split, and labor intensive to install. For these reasons, optical fiber is used primarily to transmit data over extended distances where the hardware required to relay the data signal on less expensive media would exceed the cost of optical fiber installation. It is also used where large amounts of data need to be transmitted on a regular basis.

Figure T2.7 summarizes the cable specifications, cable types, and maximum lengths. Figure T2.8 summarizes the common relationships between the physical topology, cabling, and protocol.

FIGURE T2.7

Cable Summary

Specification	Cable Type	Maximum Length
10BaseT	Unshielded Twisted-Pair	100 meters
10Base2	Thin Coaxial	185 meters
10Base5	Thick Coaxial	500 meters
10BaseF	Faber Optic	2000 meters
100BaseT	Unshielded Twisted-Pair	100 meters
100BaseTX	Unshielded Twisted-Pair	220 meters

Physical Topology	Common Cable	Common Protocol
Bus	Twisted-Pair Coaxial Fiber	Ethernet LocalTalk
Star	Twisted-Pair Fiber	Ethernet LocalTalk
Ring	Twisted-Pair	Token Ring
Tree	Twisted-Pair Coaxial Fiber	Ethernet

FIGURE T2.8

Physical Topology, Cable, and Protocol Relationship

UNGUIDED MEDIA

Unguided media are natural parts of the Earth's environment that can be used as physical paths to carry electrical signals. The atmosphere and outer space are examples of unguided media that are commonly used to carry signals. These media can carry such electromagnetic signals as microwave, infrared light waves, and radio waves.

Network signals are transmitted through all media as a type of waveform. When transmitted through wire and cable, the signal is an electrical waveform. When transmitted through fiber optic cable, the signal is a light wave: either visible or infrared light. When transmitted through the Earth's atmosphere, the signal can take the form of waves in the radio spectrum, including microwaves, infrared, or visible light.

Recent advances in radio hardware technology have produced significant advancements in wireless networking devices: the cellular telephone, wireless modems, and wireless LANs. These devices use technology that in some cases has been around for decades but until recently was too impractical or expensive for widespread use.

TRANSMITTING AND RECEIVING DEVICES

Once a transmission media has been selected, devices that can propagate signals across the media and devices that can receive the signals when they reach the other end of the media are needed. Such devices are designed to propagate a specific type of signal across a particular type of transmission medium. Transmitting and receiving devices used in computer networks include the following:

- Network adapters
- Modems
- Repeaters
- Concentrators, hubs, and switches
- Bridges, routers, and gateways
- Microwave transmitters
- Infrared and laser transmitters
- Cellular transmitters
- Wireless LAN transmitters

Network Adapters

A *network adapter* is the hardware installed in computers that enables them to communicate on a network. Network adapters are manufactured in a variety of forms. The most common form is designed to be installed directly into a standard expansion slot inside a PC. Many manufacturers of desktop workstation motherboards include network adapters as part of the motherboard. Other network adapters are designed for mobile computing: they are small and lightweight and can be connected to portable computers so that the computer and network adapter can be easily transported from network to network.

Network adapters are manufactured for connection to virtually any type of guided medium, including twisted-pair wire, coaxial cable, and fiber optic cable. They are also manufactured for connection to devices that transmit and receive visible light, infrared light, and radio microwaves.

Modems

Modems provide the means to transmit computer data (digital) over analog transmission media, such as ordinary telephone lines. The transmitting modem converts the encoded data signal to an audible signal and transmits it. A modem connected at the other end of the line receives the audible signal and converts it back into a digital signal for the receiving computer. Modems are commonly used for inexpensive, intermittent communications between a network and geographically isolated computers.

While dial-up Internet connections such as the 56K modem are still the most pervasive in the United States, cable modems are quickly catching up in popularity to the traditional form of connectivity. With each passing day, the number of cable TV systems that provide this high-speed connection service is increasing.

Repeaters

Repeaters are used to increase the distance over which a network signal can be propagated. As a signal travels through a transmission medium, it encounters resistance and gradually becomes weak and distorted. The technical term for this signal weakening is "attenuation." All signals attenuate, and at some point, they become too weak and distorted to be received reliably. Repeaters are used to overcome this problem. A simple, dedicated repeater is a device that receives the network signal and retransmits it at the original transmission strength. Repeaters are placed between transmitting and receiving devices on the transmission medium at a point at which the signal is still strong enough to be retransmitted. Dedicated repeaters are seldom used within current networks since they are considered "dumb" devices, meaning that they do not have the capability to analyze what they are repeating. They therefore will repeat all signals, including those that should not be repeated, which increases network traffic. Repeating capabilities are now built into other, more complex networking devices that can analyze and filter signals. For example, virtually all modern network adapters, hubs, and switches incorporate repeating capabilities.

Concentrators, Hubs, and Switches

Concentrators, hubs, and switches provide a common physical connection point for computing devices. Most hubs and all wiring concentrators and switches have built-in signal repeating capability to perform signal repair and retransmission (these devices also perform other functions). In most cases, hubs, wiring concentrators, and switches are proprietary, standalone hardware. Occasionally, hub technology consists of hub cards and software that work together in a standard computer.

Bridges, Routers, and Gateways

The devices used to interconnect network segments are divided into three classifications: bridges, routers, and gateways. *Bridges* and *routers* are generally used to connect networks that use similar protocols (e.g., TCP/IP), while *gateways* are used to connect networks that use dissimilar protocols (TCP/IP and IPX). Bridges and routers are usually separate hardware components that are connected directly to the transmission media at the intersection point of the two separate networks. There are also bridges and routers that are software-based and function as part of a server's network operating system (discussed in detail later on in this plug-in) or run in conjunction with the network operating system. Software-based bridges and routers can also be installed on standard computers to create dedicated, standalone devices.

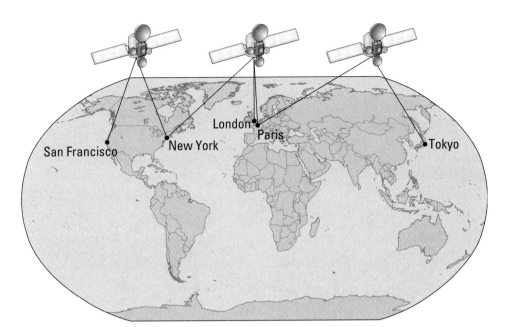

Gateways, on the other hand, are usually a combination of both hardware and software, and they perform much more advanced functions than either bridges or routers.

Microwave Transmitters

Microwave transmitters and receivers, especially satellite systems, are commonly used to transmit network signals over great distances. A microwave transmitter uses the atmosphere (or outer space) as the transmission medium to send the signal to a microwave receiver. The microwave receiver then either relays the signal to another microwave transmitter or translates the signal to some other form, such as digital impulses, and relays it on another suitable medium to its destination as illustrated in Figure T2.9. Originally, this technology was used almost exclusively for satellite and long-range communication. Recently, however, there have been developments in cellular technology that allow complete wireless access to networks, intranets, and the Internet via microwave transmission.

Infrared and Laser Transmitters

Infrared and *laser transmitters* are similar to microwave systems: they use the atmosphere and outer space as transmission media. However, because they transmit light waves rather than radio waves, they require a line-of-sight transmission path. Infrared and laser transmissions are useful for signaling across short distances where it is impractical to lay cable. However, infrared and laser signals are in the light spectrum—rain, fog, and other environmental factors can cause transmission problems.

Cellular Transmitters

Cellular transmitters are radio transmissions that have the advantage of being able to penetrate solid objects. The cellular base station at the center of each cell consists of low-power transmitters, receivers, antennas, and computer control equipment. The cell tower usually has a triangular array of antennas on top. Unlike conventional radio and television transmitters, whose primary purpose is to cover the largest area possible, cellular transmitters emit signals that do not carry much farther than a few cells. Cellular devices are configured to operate at low power to avoid interfering with other cellular devices in the area.

Type of Wireless Media	Use	Transfer Rate	Range	Advantage	Disadvantage
Cellular	Telephone	19.2kbps	Each cell has .5–50 mile radius, nationwide coverage	Widespread, inexpensive	Noise
Infrared	Short distance data transfer	16Mbps	1.5 miles	Fast, inexpensive	Short distances, line of sight required
Microwave	Long haul, building to building	100Mbps	20–30 miles	Reliable, high speed, high volume	Expensive, potential interference
Wireless LAN	Local area networks	2Mbps–54Mbps	<100 meters	Ease of use, inexpensive	Too many standards

FIGURE T2.10

Overview of Wireless Media

Wireless LAN Transmitters

Wireless LAN transmitters or access points function like hubs and switches in a wired environment, only they propagate signals through radio waves or infrared light instead of wires. An access point consists of a transceiver, usually positioned in a high place such as a tower or near a ceiling in a building that physically connects to the hard wiring of the LAN. An access point that is connected to the LAN via radio waves is called an extension point. Wireless networking operates under the same principal as cellular phones: each access point or extension point covers a cell and then users are handed off from one cell to the next. Therefore, a user with a hand-held device can connect to the network in one room, walk to another part of the building or campus, and still maintain connectivity.

Other kinds of wireless transmitters reside in wireless devices and interface directly with similar devices, creating an ad hoc, peer-to-peer network when they are near one another. These transmitters also operate at low power to avoid unwanted interference. Figure T2.10 summarizes the wireless media discussed in this plug-in.

The Network Operating System

In order for a network to communicate successfully, all the separate functions of the individual components discussed in this plug-in must be coordinated. This task is performed by the *network operating system (NOS),* an operating system that includes special functions for connecting computers and devices into a local area network. The NOS is the "brain" of the entire network, acting as the command center and enabling the network hardware and software to function as one cohesive system. Network operating systems are divided into two categories: client-server and peer-to-peer. Networks based on client-server NOSs are composed of client workstations that access network resources made available through the server. On the other hand, networks based on peer-to-peer NOSs involve computers that are equal, all with the same networking abilities.

CLIENT-SERVER NETWORKS

A *client-server network* is a versatile, message-based, and modular infrastructure that is intended to improve usability, flexibility, interoperability, and scalability as compared to centralized, mainframe computing. A client is defined as a requester of services and a server is defined as the provider of services. A single machine can be both a client and a server depending on the software configuration. The client-server model has become one of the central ideas of network computing. Most business applications being written today use the client-server model.

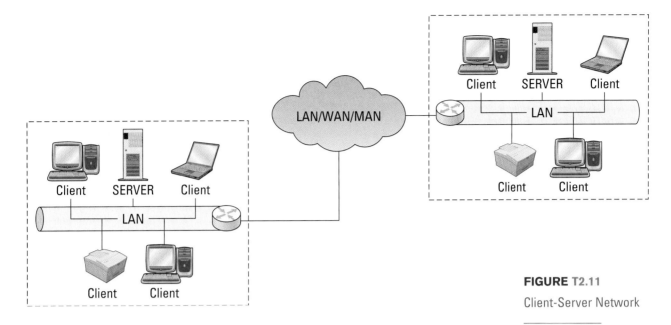

In the usual client-server network model, a server is activated and awaits client requests. Typically, multiple client programs share the services of a common server program. A Web browser is a client program that requests services (the sending of Web pages or files) from a Web server on the Internet.

In a client-server network, the NOS runs on a computer called the network server. A client-server NOS is responsible for coordinating the use of all resources and services available from the server on which it is running. The client part of a client-server network is any other network device or process that makes requests to use server resources and services, as illustrated in Figure T2.11. For example, network computer users request the use of services and resources though client software, which runs on the computer and communicates with the NOS on the server by means of a common protocol, such as TCP/IC.

The NOS provides many services or tasks performed by a server, such as coordinating file access and file sharing, managing data security, scheduling tasks for processing, coordinating printer access, and managing Internet communications. Among the most important functions performed by a client-server NOS are ensuring the reliability of data stored on the server and managing server security.

THIN CLIENT-SERVER NETWORKS

A variation on the client-server network is the server-based network or thin client-server network. This kind of network also consists of servers and clients, but the relationship between client and server is different. *Thin clients* are similar to terminals connected to mainframes; the server performs the bulk of the processing, and the client presents the interface. Unlike mainframe terminals, however, thin clients are connected to a network, not directly to the server.

The term "thin client" usually refers to a specialized PC that possesses little computing power and is optimized for network connections. Thin clients are usually devoid of floppy drives, expansion slots, and hard disks; consequently, the "box" or central processing unit is much smaller than that of a conventional PC.

The "thin" in thin client refers both to the client's reduced processing capabilities and to the amount of traffic generated between client and server. In a typical thin-client environment, only the keystrokes, mouse movements, and screen updates travel across the connection. The term "thin" is also used generically to describe any computing process or component that uses minimal resources.

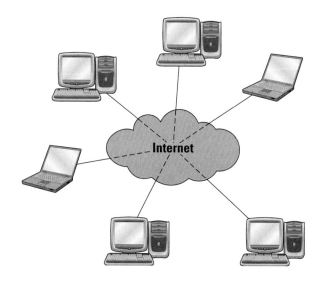

PEER-TO-PEER NETWORKS

Peer-to-peer networks enable networked computers to function as both servers and workstations. In a wired peer-to-peer network the NOS is installed on every networked computer so that any networked computer can provide resources and services to all other networked computers, as illustrated in Figure T2.12. For example, each networked computer can allow other computers to access its files and use connected printers while it is in use as a workstation without the aid of a server. In a wireless peer-to-peer network, each networked device contains a short-range transceiver that interfaces with the transceivers of nearby devices or with access points. Like their wired counterparts, wireless peer-to-peer networks offer file and resource sharing.

Peer-to-peer networks provide fewer services than client-server networks. In addition, the services they provide are less robust than those provided by client-server networks. Moreover, the performance of peer-to-peer networks decreases significantly both with heavy use and as the network grows. Maintenance is also often more difficult. Since there is no method of centralized management, there can be many servers (or peer computers) to manage (rather than one centralized server or peer), and many people may have the rights to change the configuration of different computers. In the case of wireless peer-to-peer networks, however, an access point may be one node in the network, allowing users both to share files directly from their hard drives and to access resources from the servers on the LAN.

Internet Technology

The Internet's history can be traced to 1957, when the Department of Defense (DoD) formed the Advanced Research Projects Agency (ARPA) in response to Russia's launch of Sputnik, the first artificial earth satellite. ARPA (later renamed DARPA) sponsored a number of studies to research how to make a few university supercomputers available to many research scientists across the country. In 1969, the first computer network was created. Called ARPANET, it interconnected UCLA, Stanford Research Institute, and UC Santa Barbara in California with the University of Utah. As time passed, more and more organizations joined this growing computer network.

Now the Internet is the world's largest computer network, linking thousands of networks and millions of individual computers around the world. The interlinked networks and individual computers belong to a myriad of private individuals, government agencies, universities, hospitals, private businesses of all kinds, and other organizations in almost every country in the world.

On a daily basis, millions of users send and receive e-mail, download and upload files, perform research, and conduct business on the Internet. E-business alone is expected to account for billions of dollars in sales over the next few years.

Given that the Internet is so popular and widely used, many of its technologies have spilled over into the private computer networking market. Two of the most influential technologies are the Transmission Control Protocol/Internet Protocol (TCP/IP) suite and the World Wide Web (WWW). These technologies, and the addressing scheme that supports them, have become integral to computer networking that is shaping the future of the network industry.

TRANSMISSION CONTROL PROTOCOL/INTERNET PROTOCOL (TCP/IP)

Transmission Control Protocol/Internet Protocol (TCP/IP) was originally developed by the Department of Defense to connect a system of computer networks that became known as the Internet. *Transmission Control Protocol/Internet Protocol (TCP/IP)* is a group, or suite, of networking protocols used to connect computers on the Internet. TCP and IP are the two main protocols in the suite. TCP provides transport functions, ensuring, among other things, that the amount of data received is the same as the amount transmitted. The IP part of TCP/IP provides the addressing and routing mechanism, that acts as a postmaster.

TCP/IP uses a special transmission method that maximizes data transfer and automatically adjusts to slower devices and other delays encountered on a network. The TCP/IP suite of applications include (see Figure T2.13):

1. *File Transfer Protocol (FTP)* allows files containing text, programs, graphics, numerical data, and so on to be downloaded off or uploaded onto a network.
2. *Simple Mail Transfer Protocol (SMTP)* is TCP/IP's own messaging system for e-mail.
3. *Telnet* protocol provides terminal emulation that allows a personal computer or workstation to act as a terminal, or access device, for a server.
4. *Hypertext Transfer Protocol (HTTP)* allows Web browsers and servers to send and receive Web pages.
5. *Simple Network Management Protocol (SNMP)* allows the management of networked nodes to be managed from a single point.

WORLD WIDE WEB (WWW)

The World Wide Web has become the dominant Internet service, taking only a few short years to catch on after it was introduced to Internet users in 1991 by Tim Berners-Lee and CERN (a European consortium for nuclear research).

The World Wide Web is a client-server environment where information is managed through Web sites on computers called Web servers. Accessing Web sites is done through the use of client software (i.e., a browser) and the Internet's HTTP.

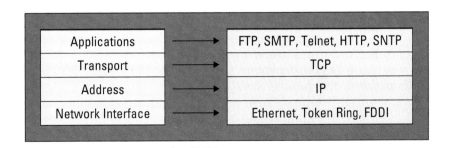

FIGURE T2.13

The TCP/IP Protocol Suite

The computers and Web sites on the Internet are linked through documents called Web pages. The basic format of a Web page is a text document written in HTML, which is made up of codes that tell how the page will be displayed on the browser. The HTML document also includes the text that will be displayed as well as the addresses, or Uniform Resource Locators (URLs), of other Web pages that have links in the document. These links appear as underlined or highlighted text that includes hidden cross-references, or hyperlinks, to additional information. Clicking on this highlighted text allows users to jump to the Web page referenced by the link. Web pages may also display icons and images as links to other pages.

In order for these links to work, however, the addressing scheme must be specific and the links must reference an appropriate URL. The URL is then used to determine the location of the site referenced by the link.

Intranet

An *intranet* is an internalized portion of the Internet, protected from outside access, that allows an organization to provide access to information and application software to only its employees. The term *intranet* appeared when companies discovered that they could use Internet technologies to make internal information available to all employees, no matter where the employees were located or what kind of hardware they were using. They could still secure the information from unwanted access by outsiders and make the information available at the lowest possible cost.

The main reason for a company to implement an intranet is that it enables the collection, management, and dissemination of information more quickly and easily. Intranet publishing is the ultimate in electronic publishing because it is based on the Internet technologies that were developed specifically for allowing information sharing among dissimilar computing systems.

Extranet

An *extranet* is a private network that uses the Internet protocol and the public telecommunications system to securely share part of a business's information or operations with suppliers, vendors, partners, customers, or other businesses. On an extranet, each connected company usually makes some selected part of its intranet accessible to the employees of one or more other companies. For example, several companies might create an extranet to consolidate data gathering and to share data, to jointly develop and share training programs, or to coordinate project management for a common work project. On an extranet, each company uses the security inherent in its own intranet to keep employees of other companies from accessing information they do not need to see.

Virtual Private Network (VPN)

A *virtual private network (VPN)* is a way to use the public telecommunications infrastructure (e.g., Internet) to provide secure access to an organization's network. By contrast, traditional WAN connections are made by means of dedicated communications equipment and dedicated leased lines. Although VPNs may not provide the same data-transfer performance as a dedicated-line WAN, there are some advantages that a VPN has over a dedicated-line WAN that have made VPNs increasingly popular. The most obvious advantage is the cost of implementation. Since VPNs use the Internet as the backbone, there is no need to lay cable or lease dedicated lines between the remote sites needing to connect. This eliminates an incredible amount of overhead. With a conventional dedicated-line network, an additional Internet connection would be required. Using a VPN, businesses can network remote offices into one large WAN and provide access to the Internet.

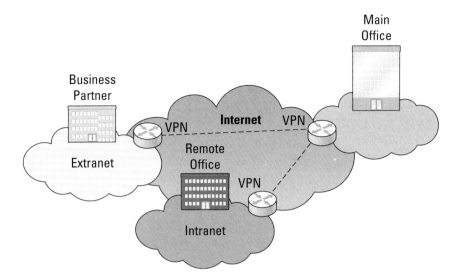

FIGURE T2.14

Intranet, Extranet, and
VPN Technologies

The TCP/IP suite and the World Wide Web have drastically changed the future of computer networking. Businesses and individuals who have become familiar with the Internet and its workings have recognized the advantages of this technology and applied it to their business networks in the form of intranets, extranets, and virtual private networks (VPNs) (refer to Figure T2.14).

Networks come in all sizes from two computers connected to share a printer, to the Internet, which is the largest network of all, joining millions of computers of all types all over the world. In between are business networks, which vary in size from a dozen or fewer computers to many thousands.

Each computer on a network must have a network card that provides the communication doorway for information traffic to and from other computers. A network usually has at least one connecting device (like a hub or a router) that ties the computers on the network together and acts as a switchboard for passing information. There must be communications media such as cables or radio waves connecting network hardware devices. The communications media transport information around the network between computers and the connecting device(s). Each computer must have software that supports the movement of information in and out of the computer. This could be modem software and/or a network operating system.

★ KEY TERMS

Bandwidth, 385
Bridge, 394
Bus topology, 387
Cellular transmitter, 395
Client-server network, 396
Coaxial cable, 392
Computer network (network), 384
Concentrator, hub, and
    switch, 394
Ethernet, 389
Extranet, 400
Fiber distributed data interface
    (FDDI), 390
Fiber optic (optical fiber), 392
File transfer protocol (FTP), 399
Gateway, 394
Groupware, 385
Guided media, 391
Hypertext transfer protocol
    (HTTP), 399
Infrared transmitter, 395
Intranet, 400

Laser transmitter, 395
Local area network (LAN), 386
Metropolitan area network
    (MAN), 386
Microwave transmitter, 395
Modem, 394
Network adapter, 393
Network operating system
    (NOS), 396
Network transmission
    media, 391
Peer-to-peer network, 398
Physical topology, 387
Protocol, 388
Repeater, 394
Ring topology, 388
Router, 394
Simple mail transfer protocol
    (SMTP), 399
Simple network management
    protocol (SNMP), 399

Star topology, 387
Telnet, 399
Thicknet coaxial cable, 392
Thin client, 397
Thinnet coaxial cable, 392
Token ring, 389
Topology, 385
Transmission Central
    Protocol/Internet Protocol
    (TCP/IP), 399
Tree topology, 388
Twisted-pair, 391
Unguided media, 393
Virtual private network
    (VPN), 400
Wide area network (WAN), 386
Wireless, 384
Wireless LAN transmitter, 396
Wireless topology, 388

★ MAKING BUSINESS DECISIONS

1. Secure Access

Organizations that have traditionally maintained private, closed systems have begun to look at the potential of the Internet as a ready-made network resource. The Internet is inexpensive and globally pervasive: every phone jack on earth is a potential connection. However, what the Internet has lacked as a network is security. What obstacles must organizations overcome to allow secure connections? What type of network infrastructure must they develop?

2. LAN Growth

The introduction of Ethernet technology as well as the availability of powerful, affordable personal computers has driven the growth of local area networks. As a result, applications that once were possible only on mainframe computers are now running on LANs. Network speed and availability are critical requirements for these applications. Existing applications and a new generation of multimedia, groupware, imaging, and database products can easily overwhelm a network running at Ethernet's traditional speed of 10 megabits per second (Mbps). With more applications requiring faster LAN speeds for acceptable performance, network managers face several choices for implementing high-speed LAN technology. Make a detailed list of the alternatives to using traditional Ethernet, listing advantages and disadvantages for each.

3. Why Is the Network Slow?

When network managers hear a user complain, "Why is the network slow?" they typically do not have an immediate answer because they do not have a complete picture of what the network is doing. Having a completely instrumented network would show them the flows of data through their network at different times of the day and provide an immediate picture of who is transmitting and receiving information through interfaces on the network. Explain why it is almost impossible for network managers to have a complete picture of their networks.

4. Rolling Out with Networks

As organizations begin to realize the benefits of adding a wireless component to their network, they must understand how to leverage this emerging technology. Wireless solutions have come to the forefront of many organizations with the rollout of more standard, cost-effective, and secure wireless protocols. With wireless networks, increased business agility may be realized by continuous data access and synchronization. However, with the increased flexibility come many challenges. Develop a list outlining the challenges that a wireless network presents along with recommendations for any solutions.

Decision-Analysis Tools in Excel

1. Describe the use of a PivotTable.
2. Summarize the tools used when building a PivotTable.
3. Compare the functions of Goal Seek and Solver.
4. List the advantages of using the Scenario Manager.

Introduction

There are many decision-analysis tools on the market. However, most of them focus on one specific analytical technique, like simulation or decision trees. Most of them are tailored to a specific industry need, such as insurance claims modeling. Furthermore, the cost of these tools can run into the tens of thousands, even millions, of dollars—such as SAS and Cognos. One integrated set of tools that combines the best analytical methods, can be applied to different problems, and is reasonably priced is Microsoft Excel. It is a standard application within the Microsoft Office Suite.

The measure of any business intelligence solution is its ability to derive knowledge from data, as discussed in the core units of this book. This plug-in will examine a few of the advanced business analysis tools that have the capability to identify patterns, trends, and rules and create "what-if" analyses. There are four areas in this plug-in:

1. The PivotTable function is an analysis tool that displays fields and records.
2. The Goal Seek function is used to find an unknown value that produces a desired result.
3. The Solver function is used to calculate an optimum solution based on several variables and constraints.
4. The Scenario Manager function is used to create and evaluate a collection of "what-if" scenarios containing multiple input values.

PivotTables

A powerful built-in data-analysis feature in Excel is the PivotTable. A **PivotTable** analyzes, summarizes, and manipulates data in large lists, databases, worksheets, or other collections. It is called a *PivotTable* because fields can be moved within the table to create different types of summary lists providing a "pivot." PivotTables offer flexible and intuitive analysis of data.

Although the data that appears in PivotTables looks like any other worksheet data, the data in the data area of the PivotTable cannot be directly entered or changed. The PivotTable is linked to the source data; the output in the cells of the table are read-only data. The formatting (number, alignment, font, etc.) can be changed as well as a variety of computational options such as SUM, AVERAGE, MIN, and MAX.

PIVOTTABLE TERMINOLOGY

There are a few PivotTable terms worth noting:

- **Row field**—Row fields have a row orientation in a PivotTable report and are displayed as row labels. These appear in the ROW area of a PivotTable report layout.
- **Column field**—Column fields have a column orientation in a PivotTable report and are displayed as column labels. These appear in the COLUMN area of a PivotTable report layout.
- **Data field**—Data fields from a list or table contain summary data in a Pivot-Table, such as numeric data (e.g., statistics, sales amounts). These are summarized in the DATA area of a PivotTable report layout.
- **Page field**—Page fields filter out the data for other items and display one page at a time in a PivotTable report.

BUILDING A PIVOTTABLE

Build a PivotTable with the Data, PivotTable, and PivotChart Report option, which displays a series of PivotTable Wizard dialog boxes. The wizard steps through the process of creating a PivotTable, allowing a visual breakdown of the data in the Excel list or database. When the wizard steps are complete, a diagram, such as Figure T3.1, with the labels PAGE, COLUMN, ROW, and DATA appears. The next step is to drag the field buttons onto the PivotTable grid. This step tells Excel about the data needed to be analyzed with a PivotTable.

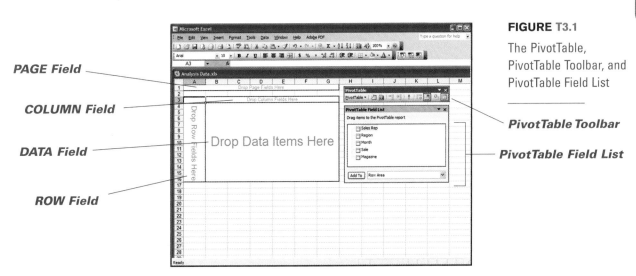

FIGURE T3.1

The PivotTable, PivotTable Toolbar, and PivotTable Field List

PAGE Field

COLUMN Field

DATA Field

ROW Field

PivotTable Toolbar

PivotTable Field List

Using the PivotTable Feature

1. Select the **PivotTable Data** worksheet from the **Analysis Data.xls** workbook that accompanies this textbook. Click any cell in the list. Now the active cell is within the list, and Excel knows to use the data in the Excel list to create a PivotTable.

2. Choose **Data, PivotTable and PivotChart Report.** The PivotTable and Pivot-Chart Wizard—Step 1 of 3 dialog box opens, as shown in Figure T3.2.

3. In the **Where Is the Data That You Want to Analyze?** area, choose **Microsoft Excel List** or **Database** if it is not already selected.

4. In the **What Kind of Report Do You Want to Create?** area, choose **PivotTable.**

5. Click the **Next** button. The PivotTable and PivotChart Wizard—Step 2 of 3 dialog box opens. In the Range box, the range should be $A$1:$E$49, which defines the data range to use for the PivotTable. The range must include the column headings in row 1, which will be the names of the fields to drag into the PivotTable.

6. Click the **Next** button. The PivotTable and PivotChart Wizard—Step 3 of 3 dialog box opens. This dialog box is used to tell Excel whether to place the PivotTable on an existing or new worksheet. Select **New Worksheet.**

7. The next step is to design the layout of the PivotTable. Click the **Layout button.** Excel opens the PivotTable and PivotChart Wizard–Layout dialog box, as shown in Figure T3.3.

8. The fields appear on buttons to the right in the dialog box. These currently are the column fields. The four areas you can define to create your PivotTable are ROW, COLUMN, DATA, and PAGE.

FIGURE T3.2

The PivotTable and PivotChart Wizard— Step 1 of 3 Dialog Box

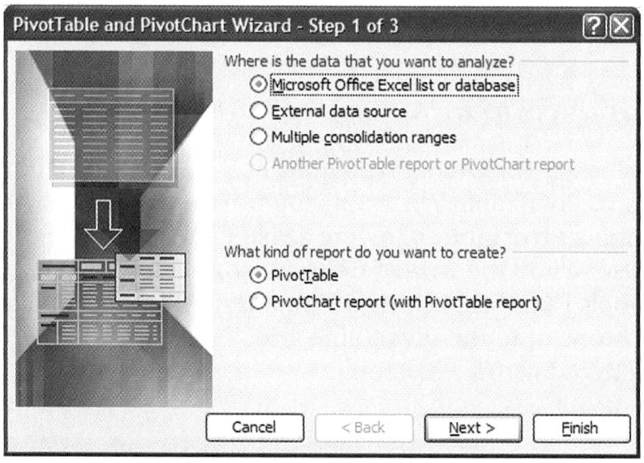

FIGURE T3.3

The PivotTable and PivotChart Wizard–Layout Dialog Box

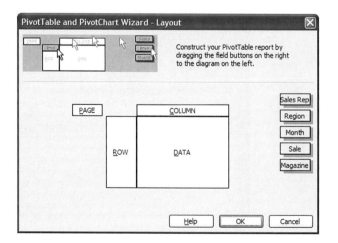

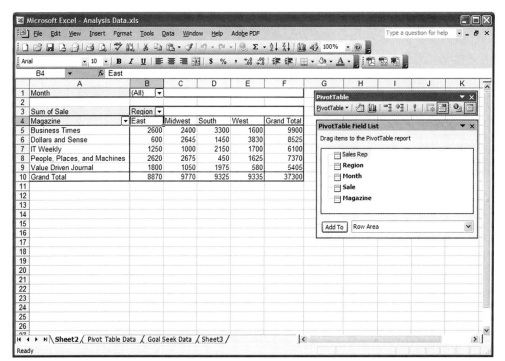

9. Drag the field buttons to the areas to define the layout of the PivotTable. For example, to summarize the values in a field in the body of the table, place the field button in the DATA area. To arrange items in a field in columns with the labels across the top, place the field button in the COLUMN area. To arrange items in a field of rows with labels along the side, place the field button in the ROW area. To show data for one item at a time, one item per page, place the field button in the PAGE area.

10. Drag the **Month** button to the **PAGE** area. The page field operates like the row and column fields but provides a third dimension to the data. It allows another variable to be added to the Pivot Table without necessarily viewing all its values at the same time.

11. Drag the **Sale** button to the **DATA** area. The data field is the variable that the Pivot Table summarizes.

12. Drag the **Region** button to the **COLUMN** area. The column field is another variable used for comparison.

13. Drag the **Magazine** button to the **ROW** area. A row field in a PivotTable is a variable that takes on different values.

14. Click **OK** to return to the PivotTable and PivotChart Wizard—Step 3 of 3 dialog box.

15. Click the **Finish** button. The PivotTable Wizard places the table in the new worksheet called Sheet2, as illustrated in Figure T3.4. In addition, the Pivot-Table toolbar and the PivotTable Field List should appear.

MODIFYING A PIVOTTABLE VIEW

After a PivotTable is built, modifications can be done at any time. For example, examining the sales for a particular month would mean that the Month field would need to be changed. Use the drop-down list to the right of the field name. Select a month and click OK. Click on the red ! button on the PivotTable toolbar to refresh the data with the new criteria. The grand total dollar amounts by region are at the bottom of each item, which have been recalculated according to the selected month.

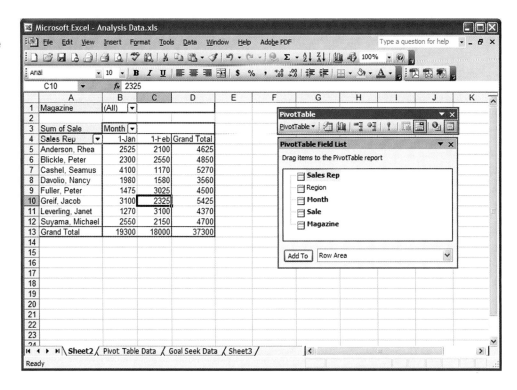

This report can be used in various ways to analyze the data. For instance, click the PivotTable down arrow button on the PivotTable toolbar, choose PivotTable Wizard, and click the Layout button. Drag the buttons off the diagram and arrange the fields like this:

- **Magazine** in the **PAGE** area
- **Month** in the **COLUMN** area
- **Sale** in the **DATA** area
- **Sales Rep** in the **ROW** area.

The completed PivotTable dialog box should look like the one in Figure T3.5. The PivotTable now illustrates the sales by month for each salesperson, along with the total amount for the sales for each sales representative.

PIVOTTABLE TOOLS

- **PivotTable**—A menu that contains commands for working with a PivotTable.
- **Format Report**—Enables the user to format the PivotTable report.
- **Chart Wizard**—Enables the user to create a chart using the data in the Pivot-Table.
- **Hide Detail**—Hides the detail information in a PivotTable and shows only the totals.
- **Show Detail**—Shows the detail information in a PivotTable.
- **Refresh External Data**—Allows the user to refresh the data in the PivotTable after changes to data are made in the data source.
- **Include Hidden Items in Totals**—Lets the user show the hidden items in the totals.
- **Always Display Items**—Always shows the field item buttons with drop-down arrows in the PivotTable.
- **Field Settings**—Displays the PivotTable Field dialog box so that the user can change computations and their number format.
- **Hide Field List**—Hides and shows the PivotTable Field List window.

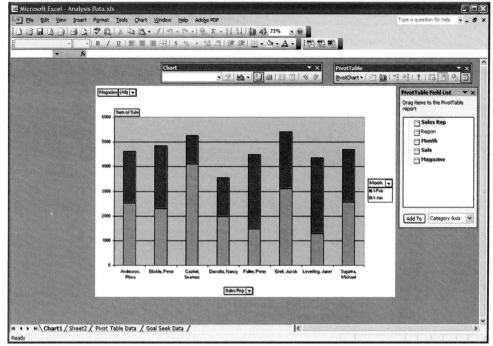

BUILDING A PIVOTCHART

A *PivotChart* is a column chart (by default) that is based on the data in a PivotTable. The chart type can be changed if desired. Use the Excel list created on Sheet2 earlier. To build a PivotChart:

1. Click the **Chart Wizard** on the PivotTable toolbar. Excel will automatically create a new worksheet, labeled Chart 1, and display the current PivotTable information in chart form like Figure T3.6.

2. Modifications to the PivotChart can be done by selecting the drop-down lists to the right of the field names.

3. **Note:** Whatever changes are selected on the PivotChart are also made to the PivotTable, as the two features are linked dynamically.

Goal Seek

Goal Seek is an analytical function, which allows a value in a formula to be adjusted in order to reach a desired result or answer. Goal Seek can eliminate unnecessary calculations that can be used to determine a single variable value in a formula. For example, a salesperson might participate in a bonus program that pays 3 percent of all sales dollars. The salesperson wants to receive a bonus of at least $2,500 and needs to know the target sales dollar amount needed. Create a worksheet with the following information (see Figure T3.7 for a layout sample):

Label	Cell Address	Value
Sales Dollars	B1	(unknown—leave blank)
Bonus Percentage	B2	3%
Bonus Amount	B3	=B1*B2

When the Goal Seek command starts to run, it repeatedly tries new values in the variable cell to find a solution to the problem. This process is called *iteration,* and it continues until Excel has run the problem 100 times or has found an answer

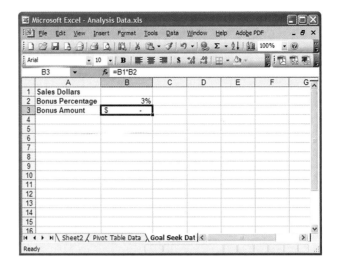

within .001 of the target value specified. The iteration settings can be adjusted by choosing Tools, Options, and adjusting the Iteration options in the Calculations tab. It calculates so fast, the Goal Seek command can save significant time and effort over the brute force method of trying one number after another in a formula.

Using the Goal Seek Command

The Goal Seek feature is used to fill in the target value of the cell containing the *Sales Dollar* amount. The Goal Seek values read "Set cell = B3, To value = 2500, By changing cell = $B$1." To use the Goal Seek command:

1. Choose **Tools, Goal Seek.**
2. Specify the cell that contains the desired value in the Set cell text box. Type in or select **B3.**
3. Enter the desired value or answer in the **To value** text box. Type in **2500.**
4. Enter the cell whose value will be changed in the **By changing cell** text box. Type in or select **$B$1.**
5. The Goal Seek dialog box should look like Figure T3.8.
6. Choose **OK.**
   a. If a solution is found, the Goal Seek Status dialog box appears.
   b. The results are shown in Figure T3.9.
7. Select **OK.**

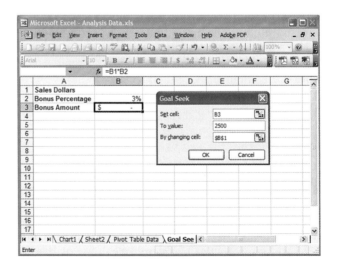

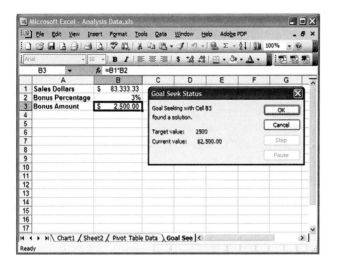

Goal Seek is used to adjust a single variable in a formula. Use the Solver feature to adjust multiple variables in a formula, as described in the next section.

Solver

Solver is part of a suite of functions sometimes called *what-if analysis tools* used when forecasting for problems that contain more than one variable. The Solver add-in utility is needed to analyze the scenarios in decision-making situations that involve consideration of values and constraints for several variables simultaneously. This powerful function uses multiple changing variables and constraints to find the optimal solution to solve a problem.

As an example, there is a coffee shop that currently sells three beverages: (1) regular fresh-brewed coffee, (2) premium caffe latte, and (3) premium caffe mocha. The current price for regular coffee is set at $1.25, caffe latte at $2.00, and caffe mocha at $2.25, but the revenue potential is uncertain. What special emphasis (or marketing) should be given to each of the beverages to maximize revenue? Although the premium coffees bring in more money, their ingredients are more expensive and they take more time to make than regular coffee. Making some basic calculations by hand is easy, but there needs to be some structure to the sales data in a worksheet so that periodic changes can be made and analyzed. To set up the Solver scenario, follow these steps:

INSTALLING SOLVER

Both Goal Seek and Solver tools come with the standard Excel package, but Solver has to be installed. If it has not already been installed, do the following:

1. Open Excel and go to **Tools, Add-Ins.**
2. After clicking **Add-Ins,** scroll down to **Solver Add-in** and click the box.

SETTING UP THE PROBLEM

The first step in using the Solver command is to build a "Solver-friendly" worksheet. This involves creating a target cell to be the goal of your problem—for example, a formula that calculates total revenue—and assigning one or more variable cells that the Solver can change to reach the goal.

1. Set up a worksheet similar to Figure T3.10.
2. The three variable cells in the worksheet are cells D5, D9, and D13. These are the cells whose values the Solver needs to determine to maximize the weekly revenue.

FIGURE T3.10

Coffee Sales Data
Sheet for Solver

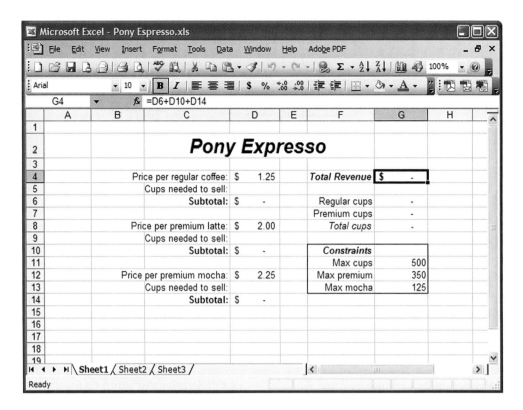

3. In the bottom-right corner of the table is a list of constraints to use for forecasting.

4. The worksheet must contain cells (G6 through G8) that include the formulas used as constraints. The limiting values for the constraints are listed in cells G11 through G13.

- No more than 500 total cups of coffee (both regular and premium)
- No more than 350 cups of premium coffee (both caffe latte and caffe mocha)
- No more than 125 caffe mochas

5. The subtotals for cells D6, D10, D14 need to be calculated, as well as the Total Revenue (sum of D6, D10, and D14) in G4.

6. The value for cell G6 should equal the value that will be calculated for D5 and the value for cell G7 will be the sum of the values from D9 and D13. The calculation of G8 = SUM of D5, D9, and D13.

7. Click the target cell **G4**—the one containing the formula that is based on the variable cells you want the Solver to determine.

8. Choose **Tools, Solver.** The Solver Parameters dialog box opens, as shown in Figure T3.11. Select the **Set Target Cell** text box (unless it already contains the

FIGURE T3.11

Solver Parameters
Dialog Box

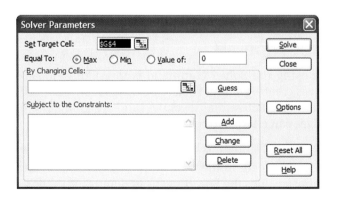

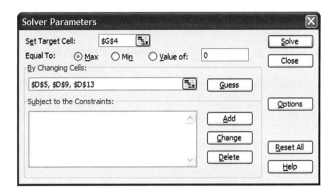

correct reference), and then click cell **G4** to insert **$G$4** as the target cell. The Equal To option button (Max) is already selected. Do not change this since the problem requests the maximum value for the target cell.

9. Select the **By Changing Cells** text box. Click the button in the text box to collapse the dialog box. Select each of the variable cells by holding down the **Ctrl key** and clicking **D5, D9,** and **D13.** This places commas between the three cell entries in the text box: $D$5, $D$9, $D$13 (refer to Figure T3.12).

10. This problem has three constraints. Click **Add** to add the first constraint in the Add Constraint dialog box.

    a. The first constraint is Pony Espresso can sell only 500 cups of coffee in one week. To enter this constraint, click cell **G8,** click <= in the operator drop-down list, and with the insertion point in the Constraint text box, type or click cell **G11.**

    b. Click **Add** to enter the first constraint and begin the second constraint—Pony Espresso can sell only 350 premium coffees in one week. With the insertion point in the Cell Reference text box, click cell **G7,** click <= in the operator drop-down list, and in the Constraint text box, type or click cell **G12.**

    c. Click **Add** to enter the second constraint and begin the third—Pony Espresso can sell only 125 caffe mochas in one week. Click cell **D13,** click <= in the operator drop-down list, and in the Constraint text box, type, or click cell **G13.**

    d. Click **OK** to add all three constraints to the Solver Parameters dialog box as shown in Figure T3.13.

11. Click **Solve** to calculate the result.

12. Solver displays a dialog box describing the results of the analysis. If the Solver runs into a problem, an error message will be displayed. If the Solver finds a solution, a Solver Results dialog box like Figure T3.14 will appear.

13. To display the new solution in the worksheet, click the **Keep Solver Solution** option button, and then click **OK.** The Solver places an optimum value in the target cell and fills the variable cells with the solutions that satisfy the constraints specified and provide the optimal result, as shown in Figure T3.15.

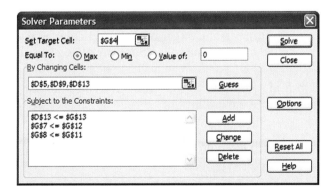

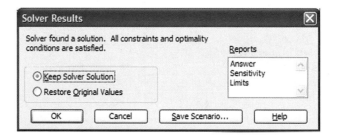

Solver Results

Solver found a solution. All constraints and optimality
conditions are satisfied.

Reports

Answer
Sensitivity
Limits

⊙ Keep Solver Solution
○ Restore Original Values

| OK | Cancel | Save Scenario... | Help |

Microsoft Excel - Pony Espresso.xls

File   Edit   View   Insert   Format   Tools   Data   Window   Help   Adobe PDF

Arial   10   B   I $ %

H20

Pony Expresso

Price per regular coffee:	$	1.25	**Total Revenue**	$	918.75
Cups needed to sell:		150		
Subtotal:	$	187.50	Regular cups	150
			Premium cups	350
Price per premium latte:	$	2.00	Total cups	500
Cups needed to sell:		225		
Subtotal:	$	450.00	*Constraints*	
			Max cups	500
Price per premium mocha:	$	2.25	Max premium	350
Cups needed to sell:		125	Max mocha	125
Subtotal:	$	281.25		

Sheet1 / Sheet2 / Sheet3 /

Ready

EDITING A SOLVER FORECAST

The Solver tool is very useful in modifying the constraints to evaluate new goals and possibilities. For example, if Pony Espresso wants to earn exactly $800 per week from coffee drinks, use the Solver to "solve" for the optimum combination of drinks. Setting a target value in the Solver is a little like using the Goal Seek command to determine a value for an unknown variable, although Solver can use more than one variable. To edit the Solver forecast to find the variables to reach a specific goal, follow these steps:

1. Choose **Tools, Solver.** The Solver Parameters dialog box appears, still displaying the variables and constraints of the last Solver problem. These will be adjusted to compute a new forecasting goal.

2. Click the **Value Of** option button and type **800** in the text box to the right. The Value Of option button sets the target cell to a particular goal to determine the variable mix needed to reach the milestone. The dialog box should look similar to Figure T3.16.

3. Click **Solve** to find a solution to the problem. When the Solver has finished, click **OK** to display the new solution.

4. Figure T3.17 shows the new solution that Solver generates.

Note: The results presented in Figure T3.17 is one possible solution that Solver may return.

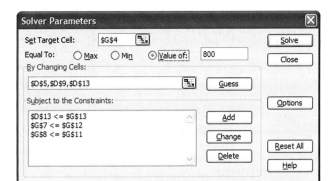

FIGURE T3.16

Editing Solver Forecast

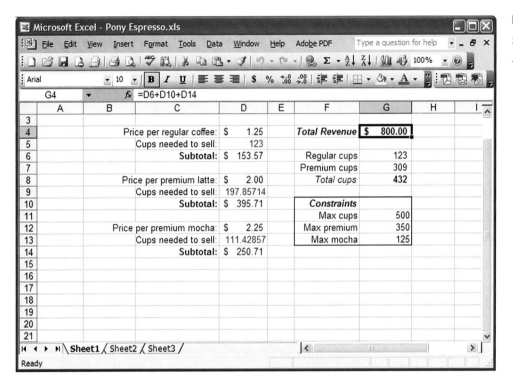

FIGURE T3.17

Solver Solution

Scenario Manager

A *scenario* is a set of input values and corresponding results from calculations that Excel can save and report as needed. A worksheet can be used to conduct a "what-if" analysis on a particular set of data. Several input values in a worksheet might change depending on different situations or circumstances. Values that produce different results can be stored as scenarios.

Excel's *Scenario Manager* allows 32 different scenarios or groups of values to be defined. The Scenario Manager can then be used to selectively display the desired values or scenario in the worksheet. The Scenario Manager eliminates the need to have multiple copies of the same worksheet representing different situations. For each group of input values a scenario must be named and stored before it can be used.

SETTING UP SCENARIOS

Each group of input values or scenarios must be named and stored before it can be used. Scenarios are stored with the worksheet. To set up a scenario:

1. Open the file **Scenario Data.xls** (see Figure T3.18).
2. Select the cells containing the first set of values to store in a scenario.

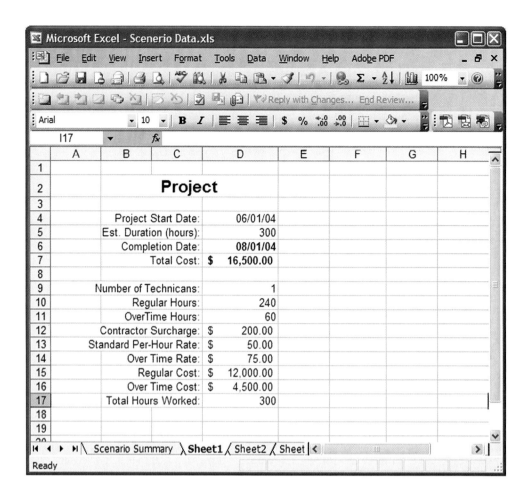

3. On the toolbar, select **Tools, Scenarios.**
4. Click **Add** to display the Add Scenario dialog box.
5. Enter **Original** for the Scenario name.
6. In the Changing Cells text box, type **D9:D11** or use the Collapse Dialog button at the right side of the text box to manually select the cells that hold the Number of Technicians, Regular Hours, and Over Time Hours values.
7. Choose **OK.** The Scenario Values dialog box appears.
8. The Scenario Values dialog box will display the values for cells D9, D10, and D11 as 1, 300, and 0, respectively, as shown in Figure T3.19. Click **OK.**
9. Once the Original has been saved, the what-if scenarios need to be created.
10. Click **Add.** In the Add Scenario dialog box, type **Single Contractor Overtime.**
11. Click **OK.** In the Scenario Values dialog box for cell D10, type **300** and for cell D11 enter **40.** The value in D9 remains at **1.**

FIGURE T3.19

Scenario Values Dialog
Box Values

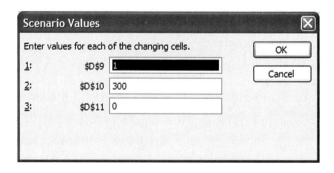

FIGURE T3.20

Single Contractor
Overtime Scenario

```
Microsoft Excel - Scenerio Data.xls
File  Edit  View  Insert  Format  Tools  Data  Window  Help          Type a question for help
Arial          10    B  I  U
D12          fx  200
```

	A	B	C	D	E	F	G	H	I	J	K
1											
2			**Project**								
3											
4		Project Start Date:		06/01/04							
5		Est. Duration (hours):		300							
6		Completion Date:		08/01/04							
7		Total Cost:	$	18,000.00							
8											
9		Number of Technicans:		1							
10		Regular Hours:		300							
11		OverTime Hours:		40							
12		Contractor Surcharge:	$	200.00							
13		Standard Per-Hour Rate:	$	50.00							
14		Over Time Rate:	$	75.00							
15		Regular Cost:	$	15,000.00							
16		Over Time Cost:	$	3,000.00							
17		Total Hours Worked:		340							

Scenario Manager dialog:

Scenarios: Single Contractor Overtime / Original

Buttons: Show, Close, Add..., Delete, Edit..., Merge..., Summary...

Changing cells: $D$9:$D$11

Comment: Created by amyphill on 3/26/2004

Sheet tabs: Scenario Summary \ Sheet1 / Sheet2 / Sheet3

Ready

12. Click **OK.** Ensure that the Single Contractor Overtime scenario is selected, and click **Show.** Excel reports that this project will need an additional $3,000, as shown in Figure T3.20.

13. Create one more scenario. In the Scenario Manager dialog box, click **Add** again.

14. The Add Scenario dialog box appears. In the Scenario Name text box, type **Two Contractors No Overtime.**

15. The Changing Cells (D9:D11) should already appear in the proper text box; if not, enter that range. Click **OK** to invoke the Scenario Values dialog box.

16. Two outside contractors are brought in (by charging $200 for each additional technician). Enter **2** in the text box for cell D9 and **0** in the text box for cell D11. This time in cell D10's text box, type **=300/2** since there will be two technicians to split the time. Click **OK.** A message box shown in Figure T3.21 says that Excel converted the formula into a value.

17. Click **OK** to dismiss the message, and Excel returns you to the Scenario Manager dialog box.

18. Select **Two Contractors** and click **Show.** Excel displays 150 in cell D10 even though the total hours are 300. This scenario gives a completion cost of $15,200.

FIGURE T3.21

Message Dialog Box

```
Microsoft Excel
 ⚠  Names and results of formulas were converted into values.
                    OK
```

Compare the Scenarios

Compare each scenario to determine the best solution, such as:

Scenario	Cost
Original	$15,000
Single Contractor Overtime	$18,000
Two Contractors No Overtime	$15,200

MODIFYING A SCENARIO

Once scenarios have been defined, the data values in the scenarios can be modified, as needed. To modify a scenario:

1. Choose **Tools, Scenarios.**
2. Select the desired scenario name.
3. Choose **Edit.**
4. Modify the scenario information as desired.
5. Close the Scenario Manager dialog box.

CREATING A SCENARIO SUMMARY REPORT

Included in the Scenario Manager is a feature called the Summary Report that creates a report that summarizes the result cells that are affected by a scenario. The Summary Report appears in the form of a summary table that is placed on a new worksheet, which can be printed.

To create a Scenario Summary Report:

1. Choose **Tools, Scenarios.**
2. Choose **Summary.**
3. Choose **Scenario summary** in the Report type group box.
4. In the Result cells text box, type in **D7, D12, D15, D16, D17.** Result cells are the cells affected by the specified scenario.
5. Choose **OK.**
6. Excel produces a Scenario Summary Report like Figure T3.22.

FIGURE T3.22

Scenario Summary Report

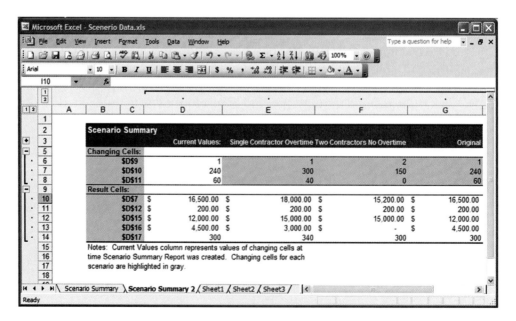

T echnology can and does play a vitally important role in both supporting decision making and, in some instances, actually making decisions or recommendations. Microsoft Excel is spreadsheet software that has an integrated set of tools that combine the analytical methods that can be applied to different problems. PivotTables, PivotCharts, Goal Seek, Solver, and Scenario Manager are analysis tools that have the capability to identify patterns, trends, and rules and create *"what-if"* analyses.

KEY TERMS

Goal Seek, 409	PivotTable, 405	Scenario Manager, 415
PivotChart, 409	Scenario, 415	Solver, 411

MAKING BUSINESS DECISIONS

1. Production Errors

Established in 2002, t-shirts.com has rapidly become the place to find, order, and save on T-shirts. One huge selling factor is that they manufacture their own T-shirts. However, the quality manager for the production plant, Kasey Harnish, has noticed an unacceptable number of defective T-shirts being produced. You have been hired to assist Kasey in understanding where the problems are concentrated. He suggests using a PivotTable to perform an analysis and has provided you with a data file, tshirt-production.xls. The following is a brief definition of the information within the data file:

A. **Batch**—A unique number that identifies each batch or group of products produced.

B. **Product**—A unique number that identifies each product.

C. **Machine**—A unique number that identifies each machine on which products are produced.

D. **Employee**—A unique number that identifies each employee producing products.

E. **Batch Size**—The number of products produced in a given batch.

F. **Num Defect**—The number of defective products produced in a given batch.

2. Scheduling Solver

AirPlains Airline is a new airline company that maintains a schedule of two daily flights each way between Salt Lake City, Denver, and Chicago. AirPlains Airline must strategically position itself as a low-cost provider in a volatile industry. Therefore, they must work toward finding a minimum cost for assigning flight crews to a given flight schedule while satisfying restrictions dictated by the Federal Aviation Administration.

Using Excel Solver, determine all the possible crew rotations. You will want to find an approximate expected cost of each combination and then solve the original crew scheduling problem by using these costs. Secondly, you will want to calculate the crew constraints in order to determine the decision variables, constraints, and objective.

The AirPlains Airline flight schedule is as follows:

From	To	Departure	Arrival
Salt Lake City	Denver	9:00AM	12:00PM
Salt Lake City	Denver	2:00PM	5:00PM
Salt Lake City	Chicago	10:00AM	2:00PM
Salt Lake City	Chicago	3:00PM	7:00PM
Denver	Salt Lake City	8:00AM	11:00AM
Denver	Salt Lake City	2:00PM	5:00PM
Denver	Chicago	9:00AM	11:00AM
Denver	Chicago	3:00PM	5:00PM
Chicago	Salt Lake City	8:00AM	12:00PM
Chicago	Salt Lake City	2:00PM	6:00PM
Chicago	Denver	10:00AM	12:00PM
Chicago	Denver	4:00PM	6:00PM

Apply the following business rules (constraints) to your model:

1. A crew that leaves a city in the morning has to return to the same city at night.
2. The crew can return on another airplane. There are six airplanes in use.
3. When a crew is flying, the cost is $200 per hour.
4. When a crew is waiting or returning, the cost is $75 per hour.

3. **Coffee Trends**

College chums Hannah Baltzan and Tyler Phillips are working on opening a third espresso drive-thru stand in Highlands Ranch, Colorado, called Brewed Awakening. Their original drive-thru stand, Jitters, and their second espresso stand, Bean Scene, have done well in their current locations in Englewood, Colorado, five miles away. Since Hannah and Tyler want to start with low overhead, they need assistance analyzing the data from the past year on the different types of coffee and amounts that they sold from both drive-thru stands. What Hannah and Tyler would like is a recommendation of the four top sellers to start offering when Brewed Awakening opens. They have provided you with the data file, JittersCoffee.xls for you to perform the analysis that will support your recommendation.

4. **DVD Sales**

Hans Hultgren, the sales manager for DVD Sales, wants to maximize his profit on the sale of portable DVD players. He already has two portable models he plans to sell:

Products	Retail Price	Wholesale Cost
Panasonic DVD–LS50	$349.95	$192.47
Mintek MDP–1720	$225.95	$124.27

Hans would like you to use the Web to locate the retail price of two other portable DVD players. The wholesale price of each unit is 55 percent of the retail price for both units you find. The only constraint is that Hans has $200,000 to purchase new DVD players. The total wholesale cost of the four types of DVD units must be less than $200,000. You want to maximize total profit for Hans with the cost constraint, limiting the number of units to positive integers.

5. Maximizing Profit

HotSprings Spas manufactures and sells two spa models: the Steamboat and the Classic. HotSprings Spas receives spa bodies from another manufacturer and then adds a pump and tubing to circulate the water. The Steamboat model demands 15.5 hours to labor and 14.5 feet of tubing. The Classic model requires 10.5 hours of labor and uses 20 feet of rubing. Based on selling patterns, the owner, Deborah Liebson, has determined that the Steamboat model generates a profit of $400 per unit, and the Classic model generates $345 profit. While Deborah would like a large labor capacity and sufficient tubing and motors to build any number of spas, her resources are limited. For the next production period, Deborah has 2,650 labor hours, 3,450 feet of tubing, and 231 pumps available. Deborah needs assistance in figuring out how many Steamboat and Classic models to build in order to maximize her profit. Given the constraints above, assist Deborah in her what-if analysis.

6. Budget Constraints

Joanne Krull wants to purchase a newer model automobile to replace her rusty 1989 car. The bank where Joanne has a checking account, US Bank, is advertising an annual interest rate of 6.75 percent for a three-year loan on used cars. By selling her old car and using some cash she has accumulated, Joanne has $3,000 available as a down payment. Under her current budget, Joanne figures that the maximum monthly loan payment she can afford is $300. She wants to find out the maximum car price she can afford and keep the monthly payment no higher than $300. She cannot alter the interest rate, or the three-year term. Use the Excel Goal Seek command to figure out the highest purchase price Joanne can afford.

PLUG-IN

T4

Designing Database Applications

LEARNING OUTCOMES

1. Describe the purpose of the relational database model in a database management system.
2. List the relational database model's basic components.
3. Describe why entities and attributes are organized into tables.
4. Describe how data redundancy is handled in the relational database model.
5. Explain the need for an entity-relationship diagram in a database management system.
6. Describe the Chen model symbols used in entity-relationship modeling.
7. Explain the purpose of normalization.
8. List the three normal forms typically used in normalization.

Introduction

Businesses rely on their database systems for accurate, up-to-date information. Without those databases of mission critical information, most businesses would be unable to perform their normal daily transactions, much less create summary reports that help management make strategic decisions. To be useful, the information must be accurate, complete, and organized in such a way that it can be retrieved when needed and in the format required.

The core units introduced the *database,* which maintains information about various types of objects (inventory), events (transactions), people (employees), and places (warehouses). A *database management system (DBMS)* is software through which users and application programs interact with a database. The *relational database model* is a type of database that stores its information in the form of logically related two-dimensional tables. This plug-in will build on the core units by providing specific details about how to design relational database applications.

Entities and Data Relationships

There are numerous elements in a business environment that need to store information, and those elements are related to one another in a variety of ways. Thus a database must contain not only the information but also information about the relationships between the information.

The idea behind a database is that the user, either a person working interactively or an application program, has no need to worry about the way in which information is physically stored on disk. A database management system translates between the user's request for information and the physical storage.

A *data model* is a formal way to express data relationships to a database management system (DBMS). The underlying relationships in a database environment are independent of the data model and therefore independent of the DBMS that is being used. Before designing a database for any data model, data relationships need to be defined. An *entity-relationship diagram (ERD)* is a technique for documenting the relationships between entities in a database environment.

ENTITIES AND THEIR ATTRIBUTES

An *entity* is a person, place, thing, transaction, or event about which information is stored. A customer is an entity, as is a merchandise item. Entities are not necessarily tangible; for instance, an appointment to see the doctor is an entity. *Attributes,* also called fields or columns, are characteristics or properties of an entity class. For example, a *CUSTOMER* entity can be described by a *Customer Number, First Name, Last Name, Street, City, State, Zip Code, Phone Number, Credit Card No,* and *Credit Card Exp* (refer to Figure T4.1).

When entities in a database are represented, only the attributes are stored. Each group of attributes models a single entity type in the real world, and values assigned to these attributes represent instances of objects (entity occurrences) corresponding to the entity. For example, in Figure T4.2, there are four instances of a *CUSTOMER* entity stored in a database. If there are 1,000 customers in the database, then there will be 1,000 instances of *CUSTOMER* entities.

Entity Identifiers

An *entity identifier* ensures that each entity instance has a unique attribute value that distinguishes it from every other entity instance (an entity identifier is also referred to as a primary key, which will be discussed later in the plug-in). The primary purpose for entering the information that describes an entity in a database is to retrieve the information at some later date. This means there must be some way of distinguishing one entity from another in order to retrieve the correct entity. An

FIGURE T4.1

Entities and Attributes
Example

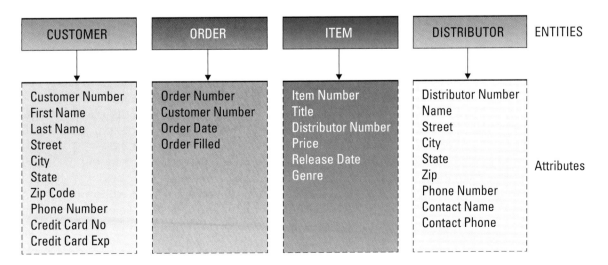

CUSTOMER #1111
Sam Smith
101 Main Street
Denver Colorado 80208
555-555-5555

CUSTOMER #0001
Bill Miller
101 North Main Street
Englewood Colorado 80211
777-777-7777

CUSTOMER #1212
John Doe
101 Main Street
Vail Colorado 88888
666-666-6666

CUSTOMER #0505
Jane Cook
101 South Main Street
Littleton Colorado 80126
444-444-4444

entity identifier ensures that each entity has a unique attribute value that distinguishes it from every other entity.

Assume, for example, that a local video store, Mega-Video, has two customers named John Smith. If an employee searches for the items John Smith has ordered, which John Smith will the DBMS retrieve? In this case, both of them. Since there is no way to distinguish between the two customers, the result of the query will be inaccurate. Mega-Video can solve the problem by creating an entity identifier.

Some entities, such as *ORDER*, come with natural identifiers, such as an *Order Number*. Typically, a unique, randomly generated number is assigned to entity identifiers.

A ***constraint*** is a rule to which some elements in a database must adhere. All entities must have a unique identifier that is a constraint. That is to say, when an instance of an entity in a database is stored, the DBMS needs to ensure that the new instance has a unique identifier. The enforcement of a variety of database constraints helps to maintain data consistency and accuracy.

SINGLE-VALUED VERSUS MULTI-VALUED ATTRIBUTES

When creating a relational database, the attributes in the data model must be single-valued. ***Single-valued*** means having only a single value of each attribute at any given time. For example, a *CUSTOMER* entity allows only one *Phone Number* for each *CUSTOMER*. If a *CUSTOMER* has more than one *Phone Number* and wants them all included in the database, then the *CUSTOMER* entity cannot handle them.

The existence of more than one *Phone Number* turns the *Phone Number* attribute into a multi-valued attribute. ***Multi-valued*** means having the potential to contain more than one value for an attribute at any given time. An entity in a relational database cannot have multi-valued attributes. Those attributes must be handled by creating another entity to hold them.

In the case of the multiple *Phone Number*(s), a *PHONE NUMBER* entity needs to be created. Each instance of the entity would include the *Customer Number* of the person to whom the *Phone Number* belonged along with the *Phone Number*. If a customer had two *Phone Number*(s), then there would be two instances of the *PHONE NUMBER* entity for the *CUSTOMER* (see Figure T4.3).

Multi-valued attributes can cause problems with the meaning of data in the database, significantly slow down searching, and place unnecessary restrictions on the amount of data that can be stored. Relational databases do not allow multi-valued attributes for this reason. For example, an *EMPLOYEE* entity with attributes for the *Name(s)* and *Birthdate(s)* of dependents would be considered multi-valued.

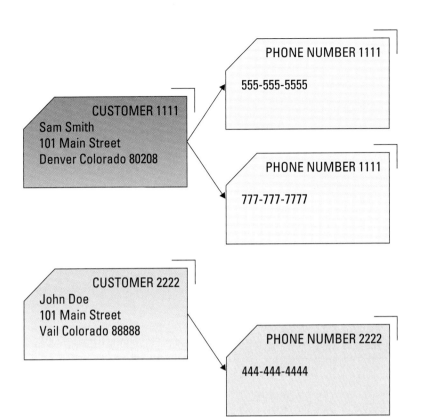

PHONE NUMBER 1111

555-555-5555

CUSTOMER 1111

Sam Smith
101 Main Street
Denver Colorado 80208

PHONE NUMBER 1111

777-777-7777

CUSTOMER 2222

John Doe
101 Main Street
Vail Colorado 88888

PHONE NUMBER 2222

444-444-4444

When searching a multi-valued attribute, a DBMS must search each value in the attribute, most likely scanning the contents of the attribute sequentially. A sequential search is the slowest type of search available.

Generally, a multi-valued attribute is a major hint that another entity is needed. The only way to handle multiple values of the same attribute is to create an entity for which multiple instances can be stored, one for each value of the attribute. In the case of the *EMPLOYEE* entity, a *DEPENDENT* entity that could be related to the *EMPLOYEE* entity needs to be created. There would be one occurrence of the *DEPENDENT* entity related to an occurrence of the *EMPLOYEE* entity for each of an employee's dependents. In this way, there is no limit to the number of an employee's dependents. In addition, each occurrence of the *DEPENDENT* entity would contain the *Name* and *Birthdate* of only one dependent, eliminating any confusion about which *Name* was associated with which *Birthdate,* as suggested in Figure T4.4. Searching would also be faster because the DBMS could use quicker search techniques on the individual *DEPENDENT* entity occurrences, without resorting to the slow sequential search.

Documenting Logical Data Relationships

The two most commonly used styles of ERD notation are Chen, named after the originator of entity-relationship modeling, Dr. Peter Chen, and Information Engineering, which grew out of work by James Martin and Clive Finkelstein. It does not matter which is used, as long as everyone who is using the diagram understands the notation.

The Chen model uses rectangles to represent entities. Each entity's name appears in the rectangle and is expressed in the singular, as in *CUSTOMER*. The original Chen model did not provide a method for showing attributes on the ERD itself. However, many people have extended the model to include the attributes in ovals as illustrated in Figure T4.5.

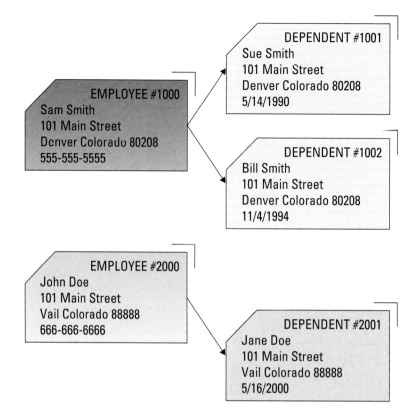

BASIC DATA RELATIONSHIPS

The relationships that are stored in a database are between instances of entities. For example, a Mega-Video customer is related to the *ITEM*(s) he or she *ORDER*(s). Each instance of the *CUSTOMER* entity is related to instances of the specific *ITEM* ordered (see Figure T4.6). This is a purely conceptual representation of what is in the database and is completely unrelated to the physical storage of the data.

When data relationships are documented, such as drawing an ERD, types of relationships among entities are shown, displaying the possible relationships that are allowable in the database. Unless a relationship is mandatory, there is no requirement that every instance of an entity be involved in the documented relationships. For example, Mega-Video could store information about a *CUSTOMER* without the customer having any current *ORDER*(s) to which it is related.

Once the basic entities and their attributes in a database environment have been defined, the next task is to identify the relationships among those entities. There are three basic types of relationships: (1) one-to-one, (2) one-to-many, and (3) many-to-many.

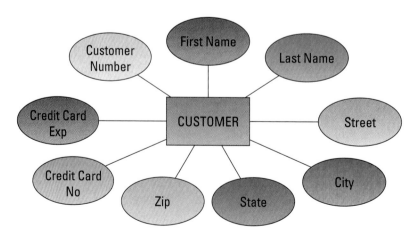

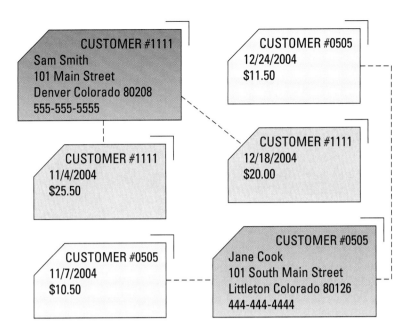

One-to-One Relationship

A ***one-to-one relationship (1:1)*** is between two entities in which an instance of entity A can be related to only one instance of entity B and entity B can be related to only one instance of entity A. Consider an airport in a small town and the town in which the airport is located, both of which are described in a database of small town airports (this would not be true for some major metropolitan cities, such as New York City with two major airports). Each of these might be represented as an instance of a different type of entity. As shown in Figure T4.7, the relationships between the two instances can then be expressed as "The airport is located in one and only one town and the town contains one and only one airport." The Chen method, as displayed in Figure T4.7, uses rectangles to document entities, a diamond to represent the relationship, and numbers to show the type of relationship in this example, 1:1).

This is a true one-to-one relationship because at no time can a single *AIRPORT* be related to more than one *TOWN* and no *TOWN* can be related to more than one *AIRPORT*. Although there are municipalities that have more than one *AIRPORT*, the *TOWN*(s) in this database are too small for that to happen.

True one-to-one relationships are rare in business. For example, assume that Mega-Video decides to start dealing with a new distributor of DVDs. At first, the company orders only one specialty title from the new distributor. The instance of the *DISTRIBUTOR* entity in the database is related to just the one merchandise *ITEM* instance. This would then appear to be a one-to-one relationship. Over time, Mega-Video may choose to order more titles from the new distributor, which would violate the rule that the distributor must be related to no more than one merchandise item. Therefore, this is not a true one-to-one relationship (this is an example of a one-to-many relationship, which is discussed below).

What if Mega-Video created a special *CREDIT CARD* entity to hold data about the credit cards that *CUSTOMER*(s) used to secure their rentals? Each *CUSTOMER* has only one credit card on file with the store. There would therefore seem to be a one-to-one relationship between the instance of a *CUSTOMER(s)* entity and the

FIGURE T4.7

A One-to-One Relationship

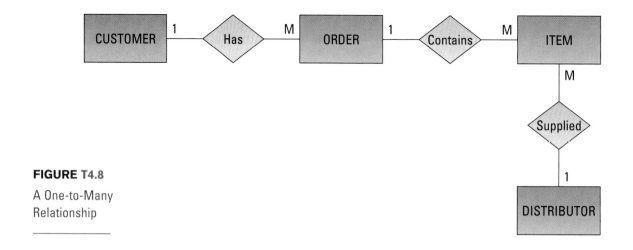

FIGURE T4.8

A One-to-Many
Relationship

instance of the *CREDIT CARD* entity. In this case, it is a single entity. The *Credit Card Number,* the *Type of Credit Card,* and the *Credit Card Expiration Date* can all become attributes of the *CUSTOMER(s)* entity. Given that only one credit card is stored for each customer, the attributes are not multi-valued; no separate entity is needed.

One-to-Many Relationship

A ***one-to-many relationship (1:M)*** is between two entities, in which an instance of entity A can be related to zero, one, or more instances of entity B and entity B can be related to only one instance of entity A. This is the most common type of relationship. In fact, most relational databases are constructed from the rare one-to-one relationship and numerous one-to-many relationships. Mega-Video typically *ORDER*(s) many *ITEM*(s) (in this scenario, an item is a DVD title) from each *DISTRIBUTOR* and a given *ITEM* comes from only one *DISTRIBUTOR* as Figure T4.8 demonstrates. Similarly, a *CUSTOMER* places many *ORDER*(s), but an *ORDER* comes from only one *CUSTOMER.*

When specifying data relationships, there needs to be an indication of the possible relationships, but an indication is not necessary that all instances of all entities participate in every documented relationship. There is no requirement that a *DISTRIBUTOR* be related to any merchandise *ITEM,* much less one or more merchandise *ITEM*(s). It might not make much sense to have a *DISTRIBUTOR* in the database from whom the company did not *ORDER,* but there is nothing to prevent data about that *DISTRIBUTOR* from being stored.

Many-to-Many Relationship

A ***many-to-many relationship (M:N)*** is between two entities in which an instance of entity A can be related to zero, one, or more instances of entity B and entity B can be related to zero, one, or more instances of entity A. There is a many-to-many relationship between a Mega-Video *CUSTOMER* and the merchandise *ITEMs* carried by the store (refer to Figure T4.9). A *CUSTOMER* can order many *ITEM*(s) and each *ITEM(s)* can be ordered from many *CUSTOMERs.*

Many-to-many relationships bring two major problems to a database's design. These issues and the way in which they are solved are discussed in the section "Dealing with Many-to-Many Relationships" below.

FIGURE T4.9

A Many-to-Many
Relationship

CUSTOMER 1 (1,1) — Places — M (0,N) ORDER

RELATIONSHIP CONNECTIVITY AND CARDINALITY

Cardinality expresses the specific number of entity occurrences associated with one occurrence of the related entity. In the Chen model, the cardinality is indicated by placing numbers beside the entities in the format of (x, y). The first number in the cardinality represents the minimum value and the second number stands for the maximum value.

The data relationships discussed thus far have defined those relationships by starting each with "zero," indicating that the cardinality in a given instance of an entity in a relationship is optional. Mega-Video can store data about a *CUSTOMER* in its database before the *CUSTOMER* places an *ORDER*. An instance of the *CUSTOMER* entity does not have to be related to any instances of the *ORDER* entity, meaning there is an *optional* cardinality.

However, the reverse is not true for the Mega-Video database. An *ORDER must* be related to a *CUSTOMER*. Without a *CUSTOMER*, an *ORDER* cannot exist. As a result, an *ORDER* is an example of a **weak entity,** one that cannot exist in the database unless a related instance of another entity is present and related to it. An instance of the *CUSTOMER* entity can be related to zero, one, or more orders. An instance of the *ORDER* entity must be related to one and only one *CUSTOMER*, having a cardinality of (1, 1). The "zero" option is not available to a weak entity. The relationship between an instance of the *ORDER* entity and the *CUSTOMER* is a mandatory relationship, as illustrated in Figure T4.10.

Identifying weak entities and their associated mandatory relationships is important for maintaining the consistency and integrity of the database. Consider the effect of storing an *ORDER* without knowing the *CUSTOMER* to which it belongs. There would be no way to ship the *ITEM* to the *CUSTOMER*, causing a company to lose business.

There is a need to define the relationship between an *ORDER* and the *ORDER LINES* (the specific items on the order) as one-to-many because an *ORDER LINE* cannot exist in the database without its being related to an *ORDER*. An *ORDER LINE* is meaningless without knowing the *ORDER* to which it belongs.

In contrast, a merchandise *ITEM* can exist in a database without indicating the *DISTRIBUTOR* from which it comes (assuming that there is only one source per item). Data about a new *ITEM* can be stored before a *DISTRIBUTOR* is selected. In this case, the relationship between a *DISTRIBUTOR* and an *ITEM* is actually zero-to-many.

Documenting Relationships—The Chen Method

As briefly described earlier, the Chen method uses diamonds for relationships and lines to show the type of relationship between entities. Figure T4.11 displays the relationship between a Mega-Video *CUSTOMER* and an *ORDER*. The number "1" next to the *CUSTOMER* entity indicates that an *ORDER* belongs to at most one *CUSTOMER*. The letter "M" next to the *ORDER* entity indicates that a *CUSTOMER* can place one or more *ORDER*(s). The word within the relationship diamond gives some indication of the meaning of the relationship.

There is one major limitation to the Chen method of drawing ERDs—there is no obvious way to indicate weak entities and mandatory relationships. An *ORDER*

CUSTOMER 1 — Has — M ORDER

should not exist in the database without a *CUSTOMER. ORDER* is a weak entity and its relationship with a *CUSTOMER* is mandatory.

Some database designers have added a new symbol to the Chen method for a weak entity, a double-bordered rectangle, as shown in Figure T4.12. Whenever a weak entity is introduced into an ERD, it indicates that the relationship between that entity and at least one of its parents is mandatory.

DEALING WITH MANY-TO-MANY RELATIONSHIPS

There are problems associated with many-to-many relationships. One problem is straightforward—the relational data model cannot handle many-to-many relationships directly; it is limited to one-to-one and one-to-many relationships. This means that the many-to-many relationships need to be replaced with a collection of one-to-many relationships in a relational DBMS.

A second problem is a bit more subtle. To understand it, consider the relationship between an *ORDER* Mega-Video places with a *DISTRIBUTOR* and the merchandise *ITEM* on the *ORDER*. There is a many-to-many relationship between the *ORDER* and the *ITEM* because each *ORDER* can be for many *ITEM*(s) and, over time, each *ITEM* can appear on many *ORDER*(s). Whenever Mega-Video places an *ORDER* for an *ITEM,* the number of copies of the *ITEM* varies, depending on the perceived demand for the *ITEM* at the time the *ORDER* is placed. Now the question: Where should we store the *Quantity* being ordered? It cannot be part of the *ORDER* entity because the *Quantity* depends on which item is being ordered. Similarly, the *Quantity* cannot be part of the *ITEM* entity because the *Quantity* depends on the specific *ORDER*.

Composite Entities

Entities that exist to represent the relationship between two other entities are known as ***composite entities.*** As an example of how composite entities work, consider the relationship between an *ORDER* placed by a *CUSTOMER* and the *ITEM*(s) in the *ORDER*. There is a many-to-many relationship between an *ITEM* and an *ORDER*: An *ORDER* can contain many *ITEM*(s) and over time, the same *ITEM* can appear on many *ORDER*(s).

What is needed is an entity that displays a specific title that appears on a specific order. Refer to Figure T4.13; there are three *ORDER* instances and three merchandise *ITEM* instances. The first *ORDER* for *Customer Number* 1111 (*Order Number* 1000) contains only one *ITEM* (*Item Number* 9244). The second *ORDER* for *Customer Number* 1111 (*Order Number* 1001) contains a second copy of *Item Number* 9244, but ordered on a different date. *Order Number* 1002, which belongs to *Customer Number* 1211, has two *ITEM*(s) in it (*Item Number* 9250 and *Item Number* 9255).

Therefore, a composite entity called a *LINE ITEM* (thinking of it as a line item on a packing slip) is created to represent the relationship between an *ORDER* and a *PRODUCT*. Figure T4.14 demonstrates the Chen notation for ERDs; the symbol for a composite entity is the combination of a rectangle and a diamond.

Each *ORDER* is related to one *LINE ITEM* instance for each *ORDER* on which it appears. Each *LINE ITEM* instance is related to one and only one *ORDER;* it is also related to one and only one *PRODUCT* item. As a result, the relationship between an *ORDER* and its *LINE ITEM* is one-to-many (one order has one or more line items) and the relationship between an *ITEM* and the *ORDER* on which it appears

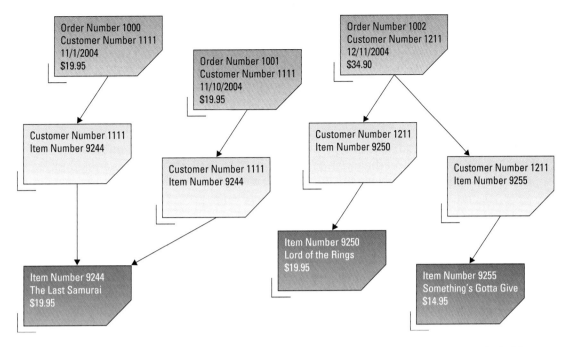

Composite Entity
Example

is one-to-many (one item appears in zero, one, or more line items). The presence of the composite entity has removed the original many-to-many relationship and turned it into two one-to-many relationships.

SCHEMAS

A *schema* is a completed entity-relationship diagram representing the overall, logical plan of a database. This is the way in which the people responsible for maintaining the database will view the design. Users (both interactive users and application programs) may work with only a portion of the logical schema. In addition, both the logical schema and the users' views of the data are at the same time distinct from the physical storage.

The underlying physical storage, which is managed by the DBMS, is known as the *physical schema.* It is for the most part determined by the DBMS (only very large DBMSs give any control over physical storage). The benefit of this arrangement is that both database designers and users do not need to be concerned about physical storage, greatly simplifying access to the database and making it much easier to make modifications.

FIGURE T4.14

ERD of Composite
Entity

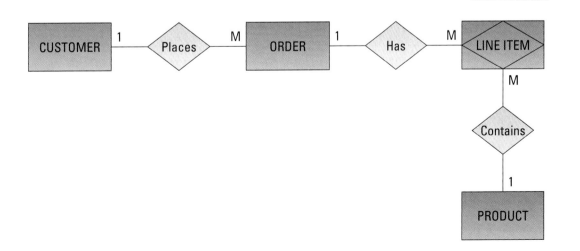

The Relational Data Model

Once the ERD is completed, it can be translated from a conceptual logical schema into the formal data model required by the DBMS. Most database installations are based on the relational data model.

The relational data model is the result of the work of one person, Edgar (E. F.) Codd. During the 1960s, Dr. Codd, trained as a mathematician, began working with existing data models. His experience led him to believe that these were clumsy and unnatural ways of representing data relationships. He therefore went back to mathematical set theory and focused on the construct known as a relation. Dr. Codd extended that concept to produce the relational database model, which he introduced in a historic seminal paper in 1970.

UNDERSTANDING RELATIONS

In mathematical set theory, a relation is the definition of a *table* with columns (e.g., attributes) and rows (e.g., records). The word "table" is used synonymously with "entity." The definition specifies what will be contained in each column of the table, but does not include information. When rows of information are included, an *instance* of a relation is created, such as the *CUSTOMER* relation in Figure T4.15.

At first glance, a relation looks much like a portion of a spreadsheet. Since it has its underpinnings in mathematical set theory, a relation has some very specific characteristics that distinguish it from other ways of looking at information. Each of these characteristics forms the basis of a constraint that will be enforced by the DBMS.

Columns and Column Characteristics

Two or more tables within the same relational schema may have columns with the same names; in fact, in some circumstances, this is highly desirable. But a single table must have unique column names. When the same column name appears in more than one table and tables that contain that column are used in the same operation (e.g., query), the name of the column must be qualified by preceding it with the name of the table and a period, as in:

CUSTOMER.Customer Number, First Name, Last Name, Phone Number

Note the proper notation is to capitalize the table name (e.g., *CUSTOMER*) and all columns are in title case (Customer Number).

Rows and Row Characteristics

A row in a relation has the following properties:

- Only one value at the intersection of a column and row—a relation does not allow multi-valued attributes.
- Uniqueness—there are no duplicate rows in a relation.
- A primary key—a **primary key** is a field (or group of fields) that uniquely identifies a given entity in a table.

FIGURE T4.15

A Sample Customer Relation

CUSTOMER			
Customer Number	**First Name**	**Last Name**	**Phone Number**
0001	Bill	Miller	777-777-7777"
0505	Jane	Cook	444-444-4444
1111	Sam	Smith	555-555-5555
1212	John	Doe	666-666-6666

Primary Key

A primary key makes it possible to uniquely identify every row in a table. The primary key is important to define to be able to retrieve every single piece of information put into a database.

As far as a relational database is concerned, there are only three pieces of information to retrieve for any specific bit of information: (1) the name of the table, (2) the name of the column, and (3) the primary key of the row. If primary keys are unique for every row, then the results will be exactly what was searched for. If they are not unique, then the data being retrieved will be a row with the primary key value, which may not be the row containing the data being searched.

The proper notation to use when documenting the name of the table, the column name, and primary key is as follows:

CUSTOMER(<u>Customer Number</u>, First Name, Last Name, Phone Number)

Notice that the table name is capitalized, the primary key is underlined, and it is the first attribute listed in the parenthetical statement containing the column names.

Along with being unique, a primary key must not contain the value *null*. Null is a special database value meaning "unknown." It is not the same as a zero or a blank. If one row has a null primary key, then the data structure is all right. The minute a second one is introduced, the property of uniqueness is lost. The presence of nulls in any primary key column is forbidden. This constraint, known as entity integrity, will be enforced by a DBMS whenever information is entered or modified. ***Entity integrity*** is a constraint on a relation that states that no part of a primary key can be null.

Selecting a primary key can be a challenge. Some entities have natural primary keys, such as purchase order numbers. Primary keys are often arbitrary, unique identifiers, such as a company attaches to the orders it sends to vendors. Two qualities of all primary keys are:

1. A primary key should contain some value that is unlikely ever to be null.

2. A primary key should never change.

REPRESENTING DATA RELATIONSHIPS

The use of identifiers in more than one relation was mentioned in the preceding section. This is the way in which relational databases represent relationships between entities (see Figure T4.16).

Each table (or entity) in Figure T4.16 is directly analogous to the entity by the same name in the Mega-Video ERD. The *ITEM* entity is identified by an *Item Number,* an arbitrary unique primary key. The *ORDER* entity is identified by an *Order Number,* another arbitrary unique primary key assigned by Mega-Video. The third entity, *ORDER LINE*, tells the company which *ITEM*(s) are part of which *ORDER*. This table requires a *concatenated primary key* because multiple *ITEM*(s) can appear on multiple *ORDER*(s). The selection of this primary key, however, has more significance than simply identifying each row; it also represents a relationship between the *ORDER LINE*(s), the *ORDER* on which they appear, and the *ITEM*(s) being ordered.

The *Item Number* column in the *ORDER LINE* relation is the same as the primary key of the *ITEM* table. This indicates a one-to-many relationship between the two tables. Similarly, there is also a one-to-many relationship between the *ORDER* and *ORDER LINE* tables because the *Order Number* column in the *ORDER LINE* table is the same as the primary key of the *ORDER* table.

When a table contains a column that is the same as the primary key of another table, the column is called a foreign key. A ***foreign key*** is a primary key of one table that appears as an attribute in another table and acts to provide a logical relationship between the two tables. The matching of foreign keys to primary keys represents data

ITEM

Item Number	Title	Distributor Number	Price
9244	The Last Samurai	002	19.95
9250	Lord of the Rings	002	19.95
9255	Something's Gotta Give	004	14.95

ORDER

Order Number	Customer Number	Order Date
1000	1111	11/1/2004
1001	1111	11/10/2004
1002	1211	12/11/2004

ORDER LINE

Order Number	Item Number	Quantity	Shipped?
1000	9244	1	Y
1001	9244	1	Y
1002	9250	1	Y
1002	9255	1	Y

relationships in a relational database. As far as the user of a relational database is concerned, there are no structures that show relationships other than the matching columns.

Foreign keys may be a part of a concatenated primary key or they may not be part of their table's primary key at all. Consider a pair of Mega-Video *CUSTOMER* and *ORDER* relations:

CUSTOMER(Customer Number, First Name, Last Name, Phone Number)

ORDER(Order Number, Customer Number, Order Date)

The *Customer Number* column in the *ORDER* table is a foreign key that matches the primary key of the *CUSTOMER* table. It represents the one-to-many relationship between *CUSTOMER*(s) and the *ORDER*(s) they place. However, the *Customer Number* is not part of the primary key of the *ORDER* table; it is a nonkey attribute that is nonetheless a foreign key, which is represented by using the double underline notation.

Technically, foreign keys need not have values unless they are part of a concatenated primary key; they can be null. However, in this particular database, Mega-Video would be in serious trouble if a *Customer Number* was null, since there would be no way to know which *CUSTOMER* placed an *ORDER*.

A relational DBMS uses the relationships indicated by matching data between primary and foreign keys. Assume that a Mega-Video employee wanted to see what *Titles* had been ordered with *Order Number* 1002. First, the DBMS identifies the rows in the *LINE ITEM* table that contain an *Order Number* of 1002. Then, it takes the *Item Number*(s) from the rows and matches them to the *Item Number*(s) in the *ITEM* table. In the rows where there are matches, the DBMS finally retrieves the associated *Title*.

Foreign Keys and Primary Keys in the Same Table

Foreign keys do not necessarily need to reference a primary key in a different table; they need only reference a primary key. As an example, consider the following employee relation:

EMPLOYEE(<u>Employee Number</u>, First Name, Last Name, Department, Manager Number)

A manager is also an employee. Therefore, the *Manager Number,* although named differently from the *Employee Number,* is actually a foreign key that references the primary key of its own table. The DBMS will therefore always ensure that whenever a user enters a *Manager Number,* that manager already exists in the table as an employee.

Referential Integrity

The procedure described in the preceding section works very well unless for some there is no *Order Number* in the *ORDER* table to match a row in the *ORDER LINE* table. This is undesirable since there is no way to ship the ordered *ITEM* because there is no way to find out which *CUSTOMER* placed the *ORDER.*

The relational data model enforces a constraint called **referential integrity,** which states that every non-null foreign key value must match an existing primary key value. Of all the constraints in a relational database, this is probably the most important because it ensures the consistency of the cross-references among tables.

Referential integrity constraints stored in the database are enforced automatically by the DBMS. As with all other constraints, each time a user enters or modifies data, the DBMS checks the constraints and verifies that they are met. If the constraints are violated, the data modification will not be allowed.

The Data Dictionary

The **data dictionary** is a file that stores definitions of information types, identifies the primary and foreign keys, and maintains the relationships among the tables. The structure of a relational database is stored in the database's data dictionary, or catalog. The data dictionary is made up of a set of relations, identical in properties to the relations used to hold information. No user can modify the data dictionary tables directly. Data manipulation language commands (e.g., Structured Query Language) that create and remove database structural elements work by modifying rows in data dictionary tables.

The following types of information are typically found in a data dictionary:

- Definitions of the columns that make up each table.
- Integrity constraints placed on relations.
- Security information (which user has the right to perform which operation of which table).

When a user attempts to access information in any way, a relational DBMS first goes to the data dictionary to determine whether the database elements the user has requested are actually part of the schema. In addition, the DBMS verifies that the user has the access rights to whatever he or she is requesting.

When a user attempts to modify information, the DBMS goes to the data dictionary to look for integrity constraints that may have been placed on the relation (see Figure T4.17). If the information has met the constraints, the modification is permitted. Otherwise, the DBMS returns an error message and does not allow the change.

All access to a relational database is through the data dictionary. Relational DBMSs are said to be *data dictionary driven.*

RELATIONSHIPS AND BUSINESS RULES

In many ways, database design is as much an art as a science. The "correct" design for a specific business depends on the business rules; what is correct for one organization may not be correct for another.

FIGURE T4.17

Data Dictionary Example

Table Name	Attribute Name	Contents	Type	Length	Format	Range	Req'd	Key	Referenced Table
CUSTOMER	Customer Number	Customer Number	VCHAR	10	X(10)		Y	PK	
	First Name	First Name	VCHAR2	12	X(12)		Y		
	Last Name	Last Name	VCHAR2	15	X(15)		Y		
	Street	Street Address	VCHAR2	20	X(20)		Y		
	City	City	VCHAR2	20	X(20)		Y		
	State	State	VCHAR2	2	X(2)		Y		
	Zip	Zip Code	NUMBER	5	99999		Y		
	Credit Card No	Credit Card Number	NUMBER	15	X(15)		Y		
	Credit Card Exp	Credit Card Expiration Date	DATE	8	MM/DD/YYYY				
ORDER	Order Number	Order Number	NUMBER	5	99999	1-99999	Y	PK	
	Customer Number	Customer Number	NUMBER	5	99999	1-99999	Y	FK	CUSTOMER
	Order Date	Order Date	DATE	8	MM/DD/YYYY		Y		
	Order Filled	Ordered Filled	DATE	8	MM/DD/YYYY		Y		
ORDER LINE	Order Number	Order Number	NUMBER	5	99999	1-99999	Y	FK	ORDER
	Item Number	Item Number	NUMBER	5	99999	1-99999	Y	FK	ITEM
	Quantity	Quantity	NUMBER	3	999	1-999	Y		
	Price	Selling Price	NUMBER	5	$999.99		Y		
	Shipped	Shipped	VCHAR2	1	X	Y/N	Y		

436 ★ **Plug-In T4** Designing Database Applications

Assume there is more than one store when creating a database for a retail establishment. One of the elements being modeled in the database is an employee's schedule. Before that can be done, the question of the relationship between an employee and a store needs to be answered: Is it one-to-many or many-to-many? Does an employee always work at only one store, in which case the relationship is one-to-many, or can an employee split his or her time between more than one store, producing a many-to-many relationship? This is not a matter of right or wrong database design, but an issue of how the business operates.

Normalization

Normalization is the process of placing attributes into tables that avoid the problems associated with poor database design. Given any group of entities and attributes, there is a large number of ways to group them into relations.

There are at least two ways to approach normalization. The first is to work from an ERD. If the diagram is drawn correctly, then there are some simple rules to use to translate it into relations that will avoid most relational design problems. The drawback to this approach is that it can be difficult to determine whether the design is correct. The second approach is to use the theoretical concepts behind good design to create relations. This is a bit more difficult than working from an ERD, but often results in a better design.

NORMAL FORMS

Normal forms are the theoretical rules that the design of a relation must meet. Each normal form represents an increasingly stringent set of rules. Theoretically, the higher the normal form, the better the design of the relation.

As illustrated in Figure T4.18, there are six nested normal forms, indicating that if a relation is in one of the higher, inner normal forms, it is also in all of the normal forms surrounding it. In most cases, if relations are in third normal form (3NF), then most of the problems common to bad relational designs are avoided. Boyce-

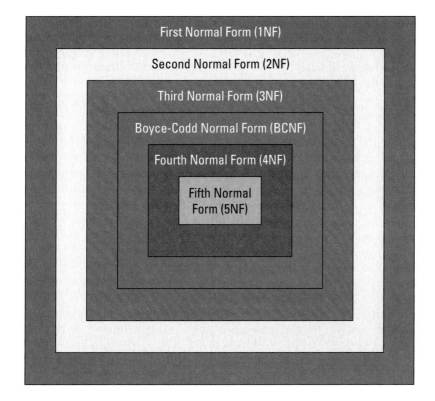

First Normal Form (1NF)

Second Normal Form (2NF)

Third Normal Form (3NF)

Boyce-Codd Normal Form (BCNF)

Fourth Normal Form (4NF)

Fifth Normal Form (5NF)

FIGURE T4.18

Normal Forms

Codd (BCNF) and fourth normal form (4NF) handle special situations that arise only occasionally. Fifth normal form (5NF) is a complex set of criteria that are extremely difficult to work with. It is very difficult to verify that a relation is in 5NF. Most practitioners do not bother with 5NF, knowing that if their relations are in 3NF (or 4NF if the situation warrants), then their designs are generally problem free. BCNF, 4NF, and 5NF are beyond the scope of this plug-in; therefore they will not be discussed beyond what is mentioned in this section.

First Normal Form (1NF)

First normal form (1NF) is where each field in a table contains different information. For example, in the column labeled "Customer," only customer names or numbers are permitted. A table is in first normal form (1NF) if the data are stored in a two-dimensional table with no repeating groups.

Although first normal form relations have no repeating groups, they are full of other problems. Expressed in the notation for relations that have been used in this plug-in, the relation notation would look like the following:

ORDER(Customer Number, First Name, Last Name, Street, City, State, Zip, Phone, Order Number, Order Date, Item Number, Title, Price, Has Shipped)

The first thing is to determine the primary key for this table. The *Customer Number* alone will not be sufficient because the customer number repeats for every item ordered by the customer. The *Item Number* will also not suffice, because it is repeated for every order on which it appears. The *Order Number* cannot be used because it is repeated for every item on the order. The only solution is a concatenated key, in this example the combination of the *Order Number* and the *Item Number*.

Given that the primary key is made up of the *Order Number* and the *Item Number*, there are two important things that cannot be done with this relation:

- Data about a customer cannot be added until the customer places at least one order because without an order and an item on that order, there is no complete primary key.
- Data about a merchandise item cannot be added without that item being ordered. There must be an *Order Number* to complete the primary key.

First normal form relations can also present problems when deleting data. Consider, for example, what happens if a customer cancels the order of a single item:

- In cases where the deleted item was the only item on the order, all data about the order is lost.
- In cases where the order was the only order on which the item appeared, data about the item is lost.
- In cases where the deleted item was the only item ordered by a customer, all data about the customer is lost.

There is a final type of inconsistency in the *ORDER*(s) relation that is not related to the primary key: a modification, or update, anomaly. The *ORDER*(s) relation has a great deal of unnecessary duplicated data, in particular information about customers. When a customer moves, then the customer's data must be changed in every row, for every item on every order ever placed by the customer. If every row is not changed correctly, then data that should be the same are no longer the same.

Second Normal Form (2NF)

Second normal form (2NF) is when the relation is in first normal form and all non-key attributes are functionally dependent on the entire primary key. The solution to anomalies in a first normal form relation is to break the relation down so that there is one relation for each entity in the 1NF relation. The *ORDER(s)* relation, for example, will break down into four relations (*CUSTOMER, ITEM, ORDER,* and *LINE ITEM*). Such relations are in at least 2NF.

Although second normal form eliminates problems from many relations, relations that are in second normal form still exhibit anomalies. Assume that each DVD title that Mega-Video carries comes from one *DISTRIBUTOR* and that each *DISTRIBUTOR* has only one warehouse, which has only one *Warehouse Phone Number*. The following relation is therefore in 2NF:

ITEM(<u>Item Number</u>, Title, Distributor, Warehouse Phone Number)

From each *Item Number,* there is only one value for the item's *Title, Distributor,* and *Warehouse Phone Number.* There is one insertion anomaly—data cannot be inserted about a *DISTRIBUTOR* until an item from the *DISTRIBUTOR* is entered. There is a deletion anomaly as well: if the only item from the *DISTRIBUTOR* is deleted, the data about the *DISTRIBUTOR* is lost.

Third Normal Form (3NF)

Third normal form (3NF) is when the relation is in second normal form and there are no transitive dependencies. In terms of entities, the items relation does contain two entities: the merchandise *ITEM* and the *DISTRIBUTOR*. The relation needs to be broken down into two smaller relations, both of which are now in 3NF:

ITEM(<u>Item Number</u>, Distributor Number)

DISTRIBUTOR(<u>Distributor Number</u>, Warehouse Phone Number)

NORMALIZED RELATIONS AND DATABASE PERFORMANCE

Normalizing the relations in a database separates entities into their own relations and makes it possible to enter, modify, and delete data without disturbing entities other than the one directly being modified. When relations are split so that relationships are represented by matching primary and foreign keys, DBMS is forced to perform matching operations between relations whenever a query requires data from more than one table. In a normalized database, data is stored about an *ORDER* in one relation, data about a *CUSTOMER* in a second relation, and data about the *ORDER LINE*(s) in yet a third relation. The operation typically used to bring the data into a single table to prepare an output, such as an *INVOICE,* is known as a join. A ***join*** is an operation that combines two relations by matching rows based on values in columns in the two tables. The matching relationship is usually primary key to foreign key.

In theory, a join looks for rows with matching values between two tables and creates a new row in a result table every time it finds a match. In practice, however, performing a join involves manipulating more data than the simple combination of the two tables being joined would suggest. Joins of large tables (those of more than a few hundred rows) can significantly slow down the performance of a DBMS.

A database management system, or DBMS, is considered a basic component of data processing. The main advantage of using a DBMS is to enforce a logical and structured organization of the data. Additionally, using a DBMS provides a central store of data that can be accessed by multiple users, from multiple locations. Data can be shared among multiple applications, instead of new iterations of the same data being reproduced and stored in new files for every new application.

The principal type of database used is a relational DBMS. Designing a database requires both a logical and physical design. The organization's data model should reflect its key business processes and decision-making requirements. Entity relationship diagrams and normalization are processes used to design a relational database.

Attribute, 423
Cardinality, 429
Composite entity, 430
Constraint, 424
Database, 422
Database management
  system, 422
Data dictionary, 435
Data model, 423
Entity, 423
Entity identifier, 423
Entity integrity, 433

Entity-relationship diagram
  (ERD) , 423
First normal form (1NF) , 438
Foreign key, 433
Join, 439
Many-to-many relationship
  (M:N), 428
Multi-value, 424
Normal form, 437
Normalization, 437
One-to-many relationship
  (1:M), 428

One-to-one relationship
  (1:1), 427
Physical schema, 431
Primary key, 432
Referential integrity, 435
Relational database model, 422
Schema, 431
Second normal form (2NF), 438
Single-value, 424
Third normal form (3NF), 439
Weak entity, 429

1. Foothills Athletics

Foothills Athletics is an athletic facility offering services in the greater Highlands Ranch, Colorado, area. All property owners living in Highlands Ranch are members of the Recreation Function of the Highlands Ranch Community Association (HRCA). Foothills Athletics consists of a recreation facility where residents have the opportunity to participate in athletic activities, enroll their children in day camp or preschool, or participate in an HRCA program.

Personnel: Foothills Athletics has a number of employees, primarily fitness course instructors and administrative personnel (e.g., billing clerks, equipment managers, etc.). Records are kept on each employee, past and present, detailing employee name, address, phone number, date of hire, position, and status as either a current or former employee. Employees are assigned a unique four-digit Employee ID number when they are hired.

Members: When joining the Foothills Athletic center, individuals are assigned a unique four-digit Member ID number. This information along with their name, address, phone number, gender, birth date, and date of membership are recorded. At the time of enrollment, each member decides on one of three available membership types along with a fixed membership fee: Platinum ($400), Gold ($300), and Silver ($200). This is a one-time fee that establishes a lifetime membership.

Facilities and Equipment: Foothills Athletics has a variety of facilities and equipment choices. Each facility has a unique room number and a size limitation associated with it. Some of the rooms contain pieces of exercise equipment; all have a serial number (provided by its manufacturer) that is used for inventory purposes. In addition, for each piece of equipment, purchase date and the date of its last maintenance are recorded. Each piece of equipment belongs to a specific equipment type, such as stair master machine, and is assigned a unique three-digit identification number. The description, the manufacturer's model number, and the recommended maintenance interval for that model of equipment are also kept on file. Each equipment type is associated with a single manufacturer that is referenced by a unique two-digit manufacturer ID number. Additional information maintained on each manufacturer is the company name, address, and phone number.

The Task: You have been hired to assist Foothills Athletics with creating a database structure that will incorporate all the features and business rules mentioned above. You should start out developing an ERD and then proceed to create a normalization structure in 3NF.

2. **On-the-Vine Vineyard**

On-the-Vine Vineyard, Inc., is one of California's largest winemaking facilities in Sonoma Valley, striving to make both a visit to the vineyard and the wine tasting an unforgettable experience. On-the-Vine is a small, family-owned winery, specializing in limited production of premium quality Chardonnay, Sauvignon Blanc, Merlot, Syrah, Zinfandel, Sangiovese, Viognier, and Cabernet.

The Employees: On-the-Vine currently employs over 12 full-time employees, with positions ranging from administrative assistant to winemaker. Among the employees, supervisors have been appointed to manage the work of other employees. Each supervised employee reports to only one supervisor. Each employee, upon employment, is assigned a unique employee identification number. In addition to the employee's name, position, and identification number, the company also records each employee's social security number, address, phone number, and emergency contact.

The Vineyard: The grounds of On-the-Vine Vineyard include the Estate house with an award-winning rose garden, winery, and two vineyard plots of 40 acres each in separate locations. Each vineyard is managed by a single employee and is referred to by its own unique name, Sonoma Cellar and Sonoma Barrel. No employee manages more than one vineyard. Each vineyard is dedicated to the growing of a single grape variety per year.

As mentioned above, On-the-Vine Vineyard currently grows eight different grape varieties:

1. Chardonnay
2. Sauvignon Blanc
3. Merlot
4. Syrah
5. Zinfandel
6. Sangiovese
7. Viognier
8. Cabernet

The Winery: Each wine produced is given a unique identification number in addition to its name. Other information recorded for each wine is its vintage year, category (e.g., dry red, dessert, etc.), and percent alcohol, which is a legal requirement. Also recorded is the employee in charge of making that wine. Winemakers may be responsible for more than one wine at a time.

The composition of a wine may be entirely from a single grape variety or may be a blend of more than one variety. Several of the grape varieties are used in more than one blended wine.

The Customers: On-the-Vine customers are mainly restaurants and wine shops, but the winery also sells to individuals via the Internet. All customers are assigned a unique customer identification number and this number is recorded along with their address and phone number. Individual customers also have their first name, last name, and date of birth, in order to demonstrate legal age, recorded. Restaurants and wine shops have their company name and tax identification number recorded.

All customers obtain their products by placing orders directly with On-the-Vine. Each order is assigned a unique order number, and the date the order is received, the product or products ordered, and the quantity or quantities desired are all recorded at the same time. A shipment status of "pending" is assigned to an order until it is actually shipped, whereupon the status is then changed to "shipped."

The Task: You have been hired to assist On-the-Vine Vineyard with creating a database structure that will incorporate all the features and business rules mentioned above. You should start out developing an ERD and then proceed to create a normalization structure in 3NF.

PLUG-IN

T5

Touring Access

1. Describe the primary functions of Microsoft Access.
2. List and describe the steps for creating a table in Microsoft Access.
3. List and describe the steps for creating relationships in Microsoft Access.
4. List and describe the steps for creating a form in Microsoft Access.
5. List and describe the steps for creating a query in Microsoft Access.
6. List and describe the steps for creating a report in Microsoft Access.

Introduction

As presented in the core units, a ***database*** maintains information about various types of objects (inventory), events (transactions), people (employees), and places (warehouses). The ***relational database model*** is a type of database that stores its information in the form of logically related two-dimensional tables.

Most organizations maintain and manage large amounts of information (i.e., data). One of the most efficient and powerful information management computer-based applications is the relational database. The technology plug-in "Designing Database Applications" discussed in detail how to design a relational database.

Information can be stored, linked, and managed using a single relational data-base application and its associated tools. This plug-in details how to build a relational database using Microsoft Access 2003. Access provides a powerful set of tools that are sophisticated enough for professional developers, yet easy to learn for new users. This plug-in focuses on the four basic objects of Access that an end user would use: (1) Tables, (2) Forms, (3) Queries, and (4) Reports.

Creating an Access Database

Access is a relational database management system (DBMS). At the most basic level, a database management system is software through which users and application programs interact with a database. Although the term "database" typically refers to a collection of related data tables, an Access database includes more than just data. In addition to tables, an Access database contains several different types of database objects:

- Saved queries for retrieving and organizing data.
- Forms for entering and displaying data.
- Reports for printing data or the results of queries.

Before creating a database, it is very important to plan it carefully. Data the database will store and analyze, as well as how the data stored will be used, needs to be identified. There are four steps in producing and using a database:

1. Define the tables in which to store the data, the data integrity constraints (such as primary keys and validation rules), and the relationships between the tables (including enforcing referential integrity).
2. Add data to the database, either directly into the table or using a form.
3. Extract data from the database using a query.
4. Create a report to present the data in the database.

FIGURE T5.1

New File Task Pane

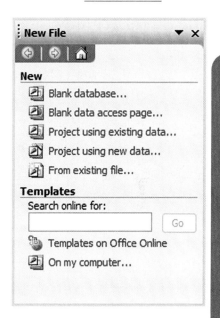

TRY IT—CREATING A NEW DATABASE

To build a database from scratch, create a blank database and then manually add tables and other database objects one at a time. To create a blank database, follow these steps:

1. If the New File task pane (illustrated in Figure T5.1) is not visible, click the **New** toolbar button, select **File, New,** or press **Ctrl + N.**
2. Click the **Blank Database** command in the New area of the New File task pane.
3. Select a location to save the file and enter **Slopeside Bikes** for the database file name in the File New Database dialog box.
4. Access will save the new, blank database in the specified database file (which will have the .mdb extension), and it will open the Database window within the main Access window.

SAVING A DATABASE IN ACCESS

The way an Access database is saved on disk is different from the way a typical Microsoft Word document is saved, such as:

- When data is added, changed, or deleted—Access automatically saves the changes in the database file.
- Due to the automatic data-saving feature of Access, when a new database is created, Access saves it to a file before starting work on the database.

USING THE DATABASE WINDOW AND OBJECT VIEWS

Whenever a database is open, Access displays the Database window (shown in Figure T5.2), which serves as the central location for working with the database objects (tables, forms, queries, reports, etc.) in the opened database.

The following are among the important ways to work with database objects using the Database window:

- To work with a particular type of database object, click the corresponding button in the left column of the Database window—Tables, Queries, Forms, Reports.
- To view a database object, select the object and then click the Open button in the Database window, or just double-click the object.
- To change the design of a database object, select the object and click the Design button in the Database window.

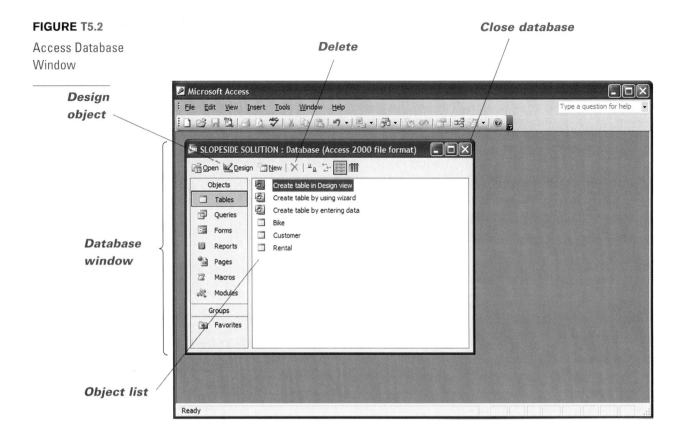

Access Database Window

- To create a new database object, click the New button to open the New Object dialog box (New Table, New Query, New Form, or New Report). The New Object dialog box will display a list of all the ways to create a new database object (the list varies according to the type of object that is being created).
- To make a copy of a database object, right-click the object and choose Copy from the shortcut menu. Then right-click a blank spot in the Database window and choose Paste from the shortcut menu.
- To rename a database object, select the object and press F2.
- To delete a database object, select the object and press the Delete key or click the Delete button in the Database window.
- To close the current database, together with the Database window, click the Close button in the upper-right corner of the window.

Access provides several different views for working with database objects. When a database object is selected in the Database window:

- Click the Open button (or the Preview button for a report) or double-click an object.
- Access will open the object in a view that is appropriate for examining and modifying the object's data, such as:
  - Datasheet view for a table or query
  - Form view for a form
  - Page view for a data access page
  - Print Preview view for a report
- When the Design button is clicked, Access will open the object in Design view, where the object's design can be modified (for instance, the fields, and their data types for a table).

Once a database object is opened in any view, switch to any other available view by choosing a different view from the View menu or by clicking the down arrow on the View toolbar button and choosing a different view from the drop-down menu. Again, the available views depend upon the type of the database object.

Designing a Database

To build a database, create a blank database and then manually add tables and other database objects one at a time. Use the Design view to define the design of a new blank table created using the Design view option.

Design view is used to:

- Add, remove, or rearrange fields
- To define the name, the data type, and other properties of each field
- To designate a primary key for the table

CREATE A TABLE

To create a new, blank table in Design view and to add fields and define their properties, select the Table object and click on the Design button. The Design view Window appears, as shown in Figure T5.3.

The top portion of the Design view window lists the fields in the table, one per row, and gives the name, data type, and an optional description for each field. The tabs at the bottom portion of the window show all the other properties for the current field. The current field is the one that is selected in the field list—it is marked with an arrow in the box at the left side of the row. Each property is displayed in a separate box within the grid.

Adding a Field

To add a new field to a table, click in the *Field Name* column of the first blank row in the top portion of the Design view window. There are up to 64 characters for the field name, including spaces. Make the name short and descriptive of the field's contents. The field can be labeled with a "friendlier" name, including spaces if desired (for example, Type of Bike rather than BikeID), assigned to the field's *Caption* property, located in the General tab.

Setting the Field Properties

Each of the fields in a table is described by a set of properties. The field's properties determine how the field's data is stored, handled, or displayed. The properties

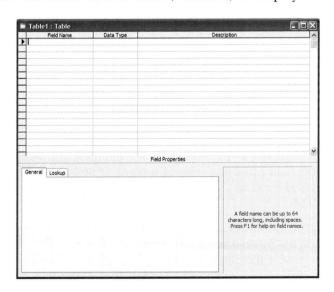

FIGURE T5.3

Design View Window

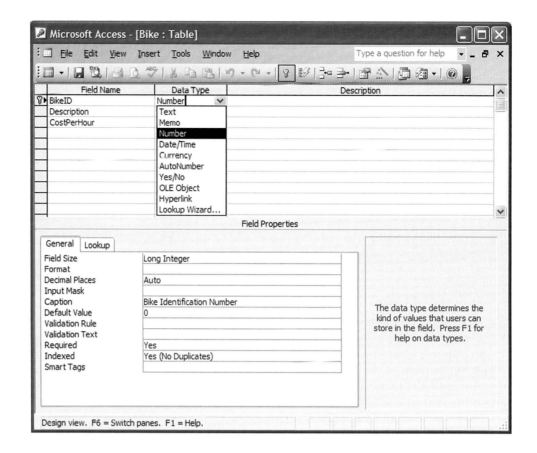

include the field name, the data type, the description, and other features such as the field size, format, validation rule, and caption (see Figure T5.4, for example). Note that when the insertion point is within a property box, Access displays information about that property in the lower-right corner of the window. Detailed information can be viewed by pressing F1.

When a new field is added, a name for it must be entered. Access will assign all of the field's other properties a default setting. For some fields the default setting is no value; that is, the property box will initially be blank.

Setting the Data Type

Every field is assigned a specific data type, which determines the type of data that can be entered into the field such as text, number, or date/time. The default data type of a new field is Text. To change a field's data type, click in the *Data Type* column for that field, and select a new data type from the drop-down list, as shown in Figure T5.4.

Field Size Property

The *Field Size* property controls the amount of space that is allocated for a particular field. It is available only for a field that has the Text or Number Data Type. For a Text field, the Field Size specifies the maximum number of characters that can be stored in the field (a value between 1 and 255, the default value is 50). For a Number field, select a value from the drop-down list that determines the size and type of number that the field can store, such as Integer, Long Integer, or Decimal.

Format Property

The *Format* property determines how the data is displayed on the screen or how it is printed. Choose the format needed from the drop-down list. For example, for a field that has the Date/Time data type, choose Long Date to display the date as Saturday, January 1, 2005, or select Short Date to display a date as 1/1/2005.

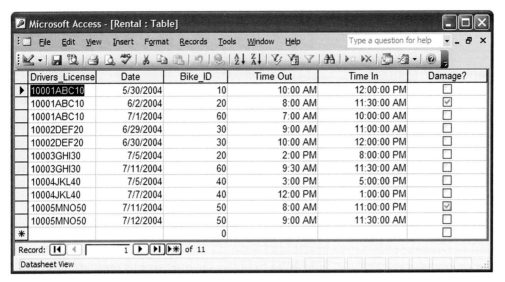

Decimal Places Property

The *Decimal Places* property sets the number of decimal places that Access displays for a field that has the Number or Currency data type. It affects only the way the number is displayed, not the precision of the value that is stored internally. Choose a specific number of decimal places from the drop-down list or choose Auto (the default value) to display the default number of decimal places for the field's Format property setting.

Input Mask Property

Most data types give the option to define an input mask (by default, there is no input mask). An *Input Mask* assists in entering valid data into a field. It demonstrates placeholder characters, displaying the number of characters that need to be entered; it includes separator characters such as the parentheses and hyphen in a telephone number so they do not have to be typed, and it prevents anyone from typing an inappropriate character. Figure T5.5 illustrates an Input Mask applied to a field with the Date/Time data type, as it is displayed in the Datasheet view. This input mask makes it easier to enter a valid date in the mm/dd/yyyy format.

The fastest way to define an input mask is to run the Input Mask Wizard by clicking the ellipsis (. . .) button that appears at the right of the Input Mask property box.

Caption Property

Access will use the *Caption* property to label the field in Datasheet view, at the top of the field's column. If the Caption box is left empty (the default value), Access labels the field using the field name. This property gives flexibility in the way the fields are labeled in Datasheet view, without having to change the actual field name.

Default Value Property

When creating a database in which a field usually contains the same value—for example, the City field in an address database in which most of the addresses are in the same city (e.g., Denver)—that value can be assigned to the *Default Value* property (by default, this property is blank).

Validation Rule

A *Validation Rule* is an expression that can precisely define the set of values that will be accepted in one or several fields in a record. A validation rule can be used on a field containing the date an employee was hired to prevent a date in the future from being entered. Or it can limit deliveries to only certain local areas, when a validation rule is used on the phone field or ZIP code field to refuse entries from other areas.

Validation rules can be typed in by hand, or can be created using the Expression Builder. If an entry does not satisfy the rule, Access rejects the entry and displays a message explaining why.

Validation Text

The *Validation Text* property sets the message displayed if the Validation Rule is rejected, such as "Area code must be 303 or 720."

Required Property

If the *Required* property box is set to "Yes," Access will require that a value be entered into the field when a record is created or modified. If the property box is set to "No" (the default value), the field can be left empty.

Indexed Property

The *Indexed* property controls whether a field is indexed—that is, whether Access builds an index for the field. Indexing a field significantly speeds up searching, sorting, or running queries on that field, but it requires more space for storing the information and can make adding, deleting, or updating records slower. The primary key for a table is automatically indexed.

Smart Tags

Smart tags provide a way to integrate an Access database with other applications. Since Access cannot recognize smart tags dynamically, a smart tag for a field or control needs to be defined. The smart tag will then be available regardless of the contents of the field or control. Smart tags are similar to hyperlinks, but they extend the hyperlink by providing for the automatic recognition of smart tags once they have been described.

DESIGNATING A PRIMARY KEY

The primary key consists of one or more fields that Access can use to uniquely identify the records contained within a table. A table must have a primary key if it is on the "one" side of a one-to-many relationship, as explained in the plug-in "Designing Database Applications."

When a single field is designated as the primary key, the field's Indexed property is automatically set to "Yes" (No Duplicates). This setting cannot be changed. When data in a record is entered or modified, Access will not allow a primary key field to be left blank.

To designate a field, or a group of fields, as the primary key, select the field in the field list and choose Edit, Primary Key or click the Primary Key toolbar button. To select several fields as a primary key, click the row selector for the first field, and then click the row selector for each additional field while holding down the Ctrl key. Access will mark the primary key field(s) with a key icon, as shown in Figure T5.6. To remove the primary key designation from a field, select it and choose the Primary Key command or click the Primary Key toolbar button again.

TRY IT—BUILD TABLES

1. In the left column of the Database window, make sure that the **Tables** object is selected.
2. Click **Design** on the Database dialog box.
3. Create fields and attributes for the following:
   a. Field Name = BikeID, Data Type = Number, Field Size = Long Integer, <u>Primary Key</u>
   b. Field Name = Description, Data Type = Text, Field Size = 25
   c. Field Name = CostPerHour, Data Type = Currency

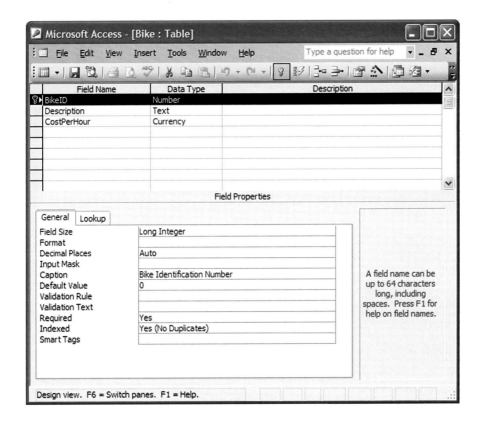

4. **Close** the Tables dialog box, and click **Yes** to Save the changes. Enter **Bike** as the Table name.

5. Create fields for each entry in Figure T5.7, using field sizes and descriptions as appropriate. Set the primary key and the **Required** property to **"Yes"** as applicable.

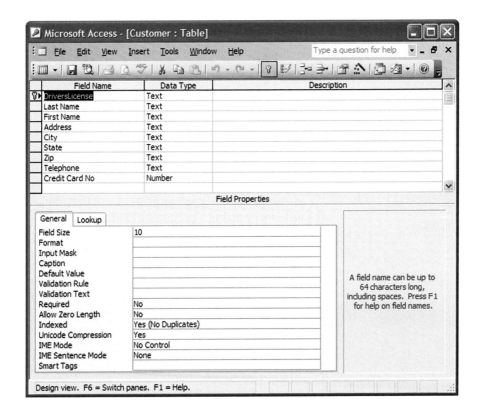

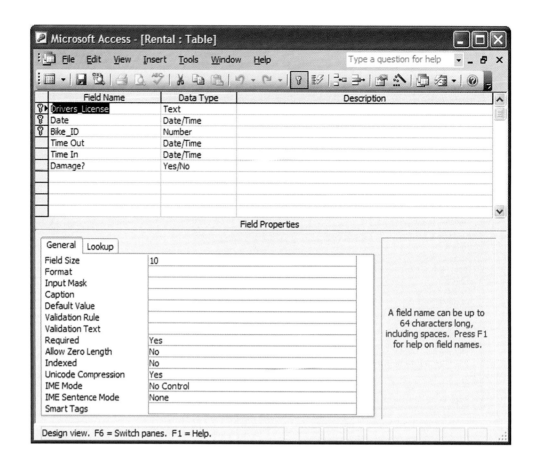

6. **Close** the Tables dialog box, and click **Yes** to Save the changes. Enter **Customer** as the Table name.

7. Create fields for each entry in Figure T5.8, using field sizes and descriptions as appropriate. Since there are three primary keys in this scenario (each acts as an associate key that creates one primary key), make sure all three are selected by holding down the **CTRL** key when clicking each field, then select the **Primary Key** button on the toolbar.

8. **Close** the Tables dialog box, and click **Yes** to Save the changes. Enter **Rental** for the Table name.

SETTING UP TABLE RELATIONSHIPS

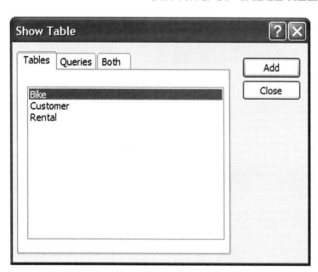

Before Access can work with relational data, the relationships between associated tables must be explicitly defined—for example, to create a query that displays data from two or more related tables. Explicitly defining a relationship also allows Access to maintain integrity of the related data.

To view existing relationships, define new ones, or change relationship properties, close any tables that are opened. Open the Relationships window by choosing *Tools, Relationships*. The Show Table dialog box appears as shown in Figure T5.9. Select each table listed and click the *Add* button. Clicking on the Primary key field from one table and dragging it onto the linking table will allow a line (or link) to be created between the primary key and the foreign key. The lines between the field lists in the

Relationships window indicate relationships between specific fields. A field in a single record in the primary table can match the same field for several records in the related table; the relationship between these fields is called a *one-to-many* relationship. The *one* side of a relationship line is marked with a "1" and the *many* side is marked with an infinity symbol (∞). However, the infinity symbol will only show up when *enforce referential integrity* has been selected, by double-clicking on the relationship link. **Referential integrity** states that every non-null foreign key value must match an existing primary key value. When one table has a foreign key to another table, the concept of referential integrity states that a record to the table that contains the foreign key cannot be added unless there is a corresponding record in the linked table.

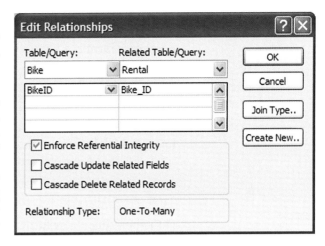

FIGURE T5.10

Edit Relationship Dialog Box

Try IT—Create Relationships

1. Open the Relationships window by choosing **Tools, Relationships** or, if the Database window is active, by clicking the Relationships toolbar button.

2. In the Show Table dialog box, select each table listed (i.e., **Bike, Customer,** and **Rental**) and click the **Add** button.

3. To define a new relationship, click and drag the **BikeID** from the **Bike** table and drop it on the **BikeID** in the **Rental** table. Click the **Create** button in the Edit Relationships dialog box (see Figure T5.10). Make sure that the Table names and field names are the correct ones being linked. Select the **Enforce Referential Integrity** box. Note that related fields do not need to have the same name, only the same data type (although it is best to give the same name to clarify the relationship).

   a. To change the features of a relationship, double-click the relationship's line (the line that connects the two tables) in the Relationships window.

   b. To delete a relationship, click the line to select it and then press the **Delete** key.

4. Complete the diagram with the Relationships shown in Figure T5.11.

5. **Close** the Relationships window, and **Save** the layout.

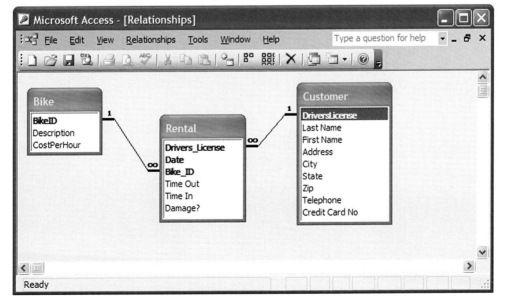

FIGURE T5.11

Completed Relationship Window

Creating Forms and Data Access Pages

An Access form is a window, similar to a dialog box, that contains a set of controls (such as labels, text boxes, and check boxes) to view, enter, or edit database information, typically one record at a time.

In a form, data is obtained directly from one or more tables or data that has been extracted using a query. Although it is possible to directly enter and edit the information in tables from the Datasheet view, a database usually includes a set of forms, which can make entering and editing data considerably easier and can limit the fields that can be viewed or modified.

TRY IT—CREATE A FORM USING THE FORM WIZARD

For generating a new form using the Form Wizard follow these steps:

1. In the left column of the Database window, make sure that the Forms object is selected.
2. Click **New** on the Database dialog box.
3. In the New Form dialog box, select the **Form Wizard** option and click the **OK** button. The Form Wizard will start running.
4. In the first Form Wizard dialog box, shown in Figure T5.12, select all the fields needed to display on the form.
5. Select the **Bike** table from the Tables/Query drop-down list. This table will become the record source for the table, and all the fields that belong to it will be displayed in the Available Fields list.
6. Move **BikeID, Description, CostPerHour** from the Available Fields list to the Selected Fields list, using the four buttons located between the lists.
7. Click the **Next** button to display the second Form Wizard dialog box.
8. In the second Form Wizard dialog box, select the **Columnar** radio button, shown in Figure T5.13. This is the basic arrangement of the controls on the form.
9. Click the **Next** button.
10. In the third Form Wizard dialog box, shown in Figure T5.14, select the **Standard** style. This style affects the background color or pattern, the fonts, the look of the controls, and other features of the form.
11. Click the **Next** button to open the final wizard dialog box.

FIGURE T5.12

Form Wizard Step One

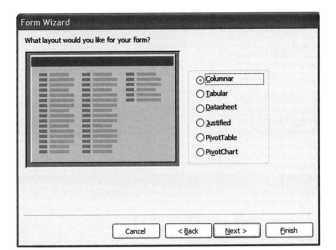

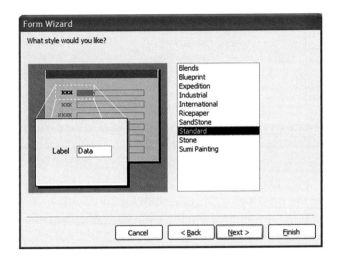

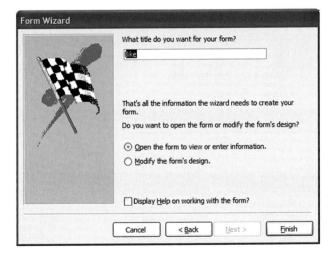

12. In the final Form Wizard dialog box, shown in Figure T5.15, the **Bike** table name is inserted into the title text box. This assigns a name to the form and chooses the way the form will initially be opened.

13. Click the **Finish** button to have Access create the form.

14. The completed form is shown in Figure T5.16.

15. Using the **Bike** form, enter the information displayed in Figure T5.17.

FIGURE T5.16

Completed Bike Form

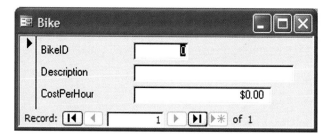

FIGURE T5.17

Bike Information

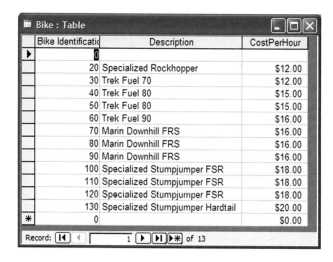

16. Using the steps above, create and populate a new form from the **Customer** table using the information displayed in Figure T5.18.

17. Create and populate a new form from the **Rental** table using the information displayed in Figure T5.19.

FIGURE T5.18

Customers Information

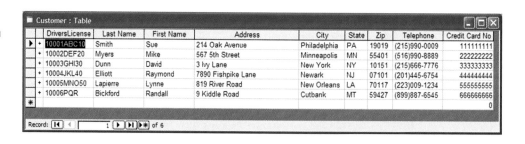

Customer : Table

	DriversLicense	Last Name	First Name	Address	City	State	Zip	Telephone	Credit Card No
+	10001ABC10	Smith	Sue	214 Oak Avenue	Philadelphia	PA	19019	(215)990-0009	111111111
+	10002DEF20	Myers	Mike	567 5th Street	Minneapolis	MN	55401	(516)990-8889	222222222
+	10003GHI30	Dunn	David	3 Ivy Lane	New York	NY	10151	(215)666-7776	333333333
+	10004JKL40	Elliott	Raymond	7890 Fishpike Lane	Newark	NJ	07101	(201)445-6754	444444444
+	10005MNO50	Lapierre	Lynne	819 River Road	New Orleans	LA	70117	(223)009-1234	555555555
+	10006PQR	Bickford	Randall	9 Kiddle Road	Cutbank	MT	59427	(899)887-6545	666666666
*									0

Record: of 6

FIGURE T5.19

Rentals Information

Rental : Table

Drivers_License	Date	Bike_ID	Time Out	Time In	Damage?
10001ABC10	5/30/2004	10	10:00 AM	12:00:00 PM	☐
10001ABC10	6/2/2004	20	8:00 AM	11:30:00 AM	☑
10001ABC10	7/1/2004	60	7:00 AM	10:00:00 AM	☐
10002DEF20	6/29/2004	30	9:00 AM	11:00:00 AM	☐
10002DEF20	6/30/2004	30	10:00 AM	12:00:00 PM	☐
10003GHI30	7/5/2004	20	2:00 PM	8:00:00 PM	☐
10003GHI30	7/11/2004	60	9:30 AM	11:30:00 AM	☐
10004JKL40	7/5/2004	40	3:00 PM	5:00:00 PM	☐
10004JKL40	7/7/2004	40	12:00 PM	1:00:00 PM	☐
10005MNO50	7/11/2004	50	8:00 AM	11:00:00 PM	☑
10005MNO50	7/12/2004	50	9:00 AM	11:30:00 AM	☐
*		0			☐

Record: of 11

Creating a Query

A query is a tool for extracting, combining, and displaying data from one or more tables, according to any criteria specified. For example, in the Slopeside Bikes database create a query to view a list of all bike rentals over the past month. In a query, information is sorted, summarized (e.g., totals, averages, counts), and displayed according to sort criteria and/or results of calculations on data. The results of a query can be viewed in a tabular format (that is, a Datasheet view, as shown in Figure T5.20) or can be viewed through a form or on a report.

CREATING A BASIC QUERY WITH THE SIMPLE QUERY WIZARD

The following is the procedure for creating a query using the Simple Query Wizard. The query draws information from the Bike, Rental, and Customer tables.

Try IT—Create a Query

1. In the left column of the Database window, make sure that the **Queries** object is selected.

2. Click **New** on the Database dialog box, then select the **Simple Query Wizard** option in the New Query dialog box and click the **OK** button.

3. In the first Simple Query Wizard dialog box, select the **LastName, First Name,** and **City** from the **Customer** table to include in the query. Move these fields from the Available Fields list to the Selected Fields list, using the four buttons located between the lists.

4. Repeat this operation to include the **BikeID** from the **Bike** table and the **Date** and **Damage?** fields from the Rental table (see Figure T5.21).

5. Click the **Next** button to open the second wizard dialog box.

6. When one or more numeric field has been selected in addition to the primary key (such as the BikeID in the example query), Access will display the second Simple Query Wizard dialog box shown in Figure T5.22. (If a numeric field in the first dialog box is not selected, the wizard will immediately display the final dialog box, discussed in the next step.) In the second dialog box in Figure T5.22, select the type of query, as follows:

   ■ To show the information on the query from every matching record, select **Detail.**

   ■ To display summary information from each *group* of matching records, rather than showing the information from all matching records, select **Summary.** The type of summary value to be calculated is sum, average, minimum, or maximum.

FIGURE T5.20

Query Datasheet View

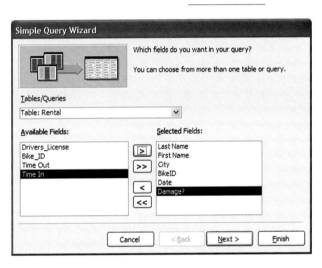

FIGURE T5.21

Simple Query Wizard Step One

FIGURE T5.22

Simple Query Wizard Step Two

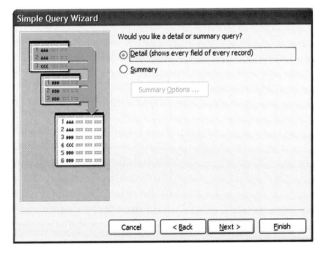

FIGURE T5.23

Simple Query Wizard
Step Three

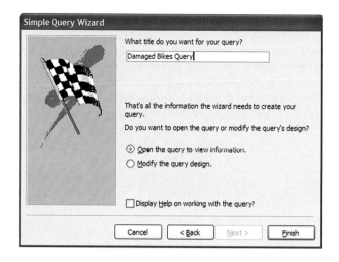

Simple Query Wizard

What title do you want for your query?

| Damaged Bikes Query |

That's all the information the wizard needs to create your query.

Do you want to open the query or modify the query's design?

⊙ _O_pen the query to view information.

○ _M_odify the query design.

☐ Display _H_elp on working with the query?

| Cancel | < _B_ack | _N_ext > | _F_inish |

FIGURE T5.24

Results of Using Simple
Query Wizard

Damaged Bikes Query : Select Query

Last Name	First Name	City	BikeID	Date	Damage?
Smith	Sue	Philadelphia	10	5/30/2004	☐
Smith	Sue	Philadelphia	20	6/2/2004	☑
Dunn	David	New York	20	7/5/2004	☐
Elliott	Raymond	Newark	40	7/5/2004	☐
Lapierre	Lynne	New Orleans	50	7/11/2004	☑
Smith	Sue	Philadelphia	60	7/1/2004	☐
Myers	Mike	Minneapolis	30	6/29/2004	☐
Myers	Mike	Minneapolis	30	6/30/2004	☐
Elliott	Raymond	Newark	40	7/7/2004	☐
Lapierre	Lynne	New Orleans	50	7/12/2004	☐
Dunn	David	New York	60	7/11/2004	☐
*					☐

Record: |◄| ◄ | 1 | ► | ►| | ►* | of 11

---

7. In this query example there is no need to use the Summary option. Click the **Next** button.

8. In the final Simple Query Wizard dialog box, enter **Damaged Bikes Query** for a query title in the text box (as shown in Figure T5.23).

9. Select the **Open the query to view information** option to open the query in the Datasheet view.

10. Click the **Finish** button to proceed.

Figure T5.24 shows the example query displayed in Datasheet view.

MODIFYING A QUERY

The Design view is used to define a new query, customize a new query, or modify an existing query of any type. Figure T5.25 shows an example of the query created in the previous section opened in Design view. The top portion of the Query Design view window displays field lists for the tables in the database and shows the relationships between these objects in the same way these relationships are shown in the Relationships window. The query is defined in the grid in the lower portion of the window. Each column in the Query Design grid defines a field that is displayed in the query, or is used to sort rows or select records.

In the Query Design view window, one or more of the following actions are used to define or modify the query:

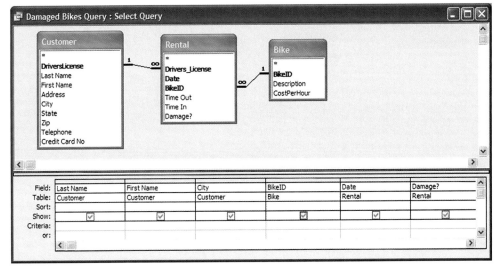

FIGURE T5.25

Query Design View

- If the table or query that contains a field to display or use in the query is not shown in the top portion of the Design window, choose Show Table from the Query menu and select one or more tables or queries in the Show Table dialog box. To remove a field list, click it, and then either choose Query, Remove Table, or press the Delete key.

- To add a field to a query, select it in the drop-down list in the Field row. Or, drag the field from the field list that displays it and drop it on the query design grid; this will insert a new column for that field to the left of the column where the field is dropped. To display *all* fields belonging to a particular table or other query, select or drag the asterisk (*) item.

- To sort the rows of the query by a particular field, select a sort type—Ascending or Descending—in the Sort row of the field's column.

- To display a particular field in the query, check the box in the Show row of the field's column. To use a field to sort rows or select records, but not appear in the query, clear the box.

- To restrict the rows displayed in the query, enter a value into the Criteria of a particular field. For instance, to display only those bikes that were damaged in the example query of Figure T5.25, type *"Yes"* in the Criteria row of the Damaged? column. Access will add quotation marks around the text when the query is saved. With a numeric or date field, enter a comparison using the standard operators (>, <, >=, <=, and <>). As an example, to display only bikes that were damaged after July 1, 2004, type *">7/1/2004"* into the Criteria row of the Date column.

- To combine several selection criteria using *And* logic, enter them all into the Criteria row. For example, to show bikes that were damaged *and* were damaged after July 1, 2004, enter both of the criteria described in the previous item into the Criteria row.

- To add a selection criterion using *Or* logic, enter it into the Or row. For instance, to display bikes that were damaged or bike rentals after July 1, 2004, enter *"Yes"* into the Criteria row of the Damaged? column and enter *">7/1/2004"* into the Or row of the Date column. The query would list all of the bikes that were damaged, plus all of the bikes rented after July 1, 2004. To add further Or criteria, use additional rows at the bottom of the query design grid.

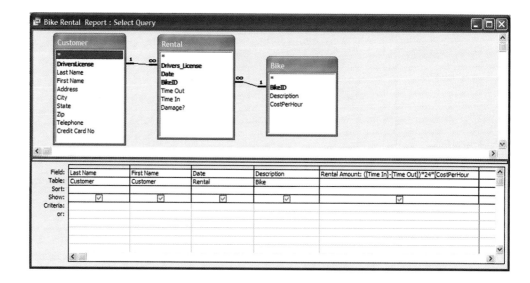

- To create a calculated field, click in the Field row in a blank column. Rather than typing the name of a field to be used in the calculation, a calculation can be used to determine the rental amount, such as Rental Amount: ([Time In]-[Time Out])*24*[CostPerHour] (refer to Figure T5.26). Formulas for calculating fields are similar to formulas entered into cells in Microsoft Excel spreadsheets—the main difference is that rather than referring to cell addresses, Access refers to field names.

- To delete all the entries in a particular row or column, click in that row or column and choose *Delete Rows* or *Delete Columns* from the Edit menu. To delete all entries in the query design grid, choose Edit, Clear Grid.

- To display the results of the query (that is, to run the query using the database's current contents), choose View, Datasheet View, choose Query, Run, or click the Run toolbar button.

Try IT—Modify a Query

1. Make a copy of the Damaged Bikes Query and rename it **Bike Rental Report.**
2. Open the **Bike Rental Report** in Design view.
3. Select the **City** column, right mouse click and click **Cut.**
4. Change the **BikeID** field and select **Description.**
5. Select the **Damaged?** field, right mouse click and click **Cut.**
6. Select an empty column, type in **Rental Amount: ([Time In]-[Time Out])*24* [CostPerHour]** in the field row (refer to Figure T5.26).
7. Run the modified Query, by clicking on the **Run** button (i.e., the red exclamation mark) on the tool bar.

Generating Reports

Reports are used primarily for printing selected database information. A report labels, groups, sorts, and summarizes the data it presents (see Figure T5.27). Like a form, a report can display data directly from one or more tables or it can display the results of a query.

Slopeside Bike Rental Report

Description	Date	Last Name	First Name	Rental Amount
Specialized Rockhopper				
	5/30/2004	Smith	Sue	$24.00
	6/2/2004	Smith	Sue	$42.00
	7/5/2004	Dunn	David	$72.00
Summary for Specialized Rockhopper (3 detail records)				$138.00
Trek Fuel 70				
	6/29/2004	Myers	Mike	$24.00
	6/30/2004	Myers	Mike	$24.00
Summary for Trek Fuel 70 (2 detail records)				$48.00
Trek Fuel 80				
	7/5/2004	Elliott	Raymond	$30.00
	7/7/2004	Elliott	Raymond	$15.00
	7/11/2004	Lapierre	Lynne	$225.00
	7/12/2004	Lapierre	Lynne	$37.50
Summary for Trek Fuel 80 (4 detail records)				$307.50
Trek Fuel 90				
	7/1/2004	Smith	Sue	$48.00
	7/11/2004	Dunn	David	$32.00
Summary for Trek Fuel 90 (2 detail records)				$80.00
Grand Total				$573.50

FIGURE T5.27

Access Report

TRY IT—USE THE REPORT WIZARD

To create a report using the Report Wizard, follow these steps:

1. In the left column of the Database window, make sure that the **Reports** object is selected.
2. Double-click **Create report by using wizard** in the Database window.
3. In the first Report Wizard dialog box, select the query that was created in the previous section, **Bike Rental Report,** to be included in the report. Move from the Available Fields to the Selected Fields, **Description, Date, Last Name, First Name,** and **Rental Amount.** Make sure to move them in the order that is shown in Figure T5.28.
4. Click the **Next** button to open the next Report Wizard dialog box.

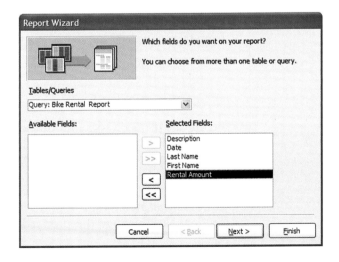

FIGURE T5.28

Report Wizard Step One

5. Selecting fields from more than one table or query in the previous step will enable the second Report Wizard dialog box to appear. Choose the **Description** field for grouping the information in the report.

6. Click the **Next** button.

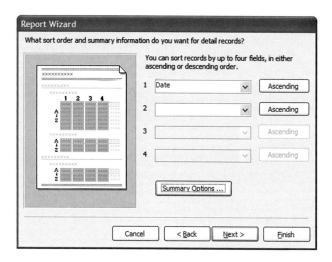

7. In the third Report Wizard dialog box, shown in Figure T5.29, choose **Date** for the sorting order for the Detail section in the report. Note that the report groups are automatically sorted on the fields used for grouping. In this dialog box, however, the date will be used for sorting the detail lines falling within each group.

8. One button in the third Report Wizard dialog box is crucial but easy to overlook: the Summary Options button. Click this button to open the **Summary Options** dialog box. This dialog box lists each of the numeric or currency fields included in the report's Detail section. Access can summarize the values in one or more of these fields for each group in the report. Check the **Sum** box for the Rental Amount shown in Figure T5.30.

9. Click **OK** to return to the third Report Wizard dialog box.

10. The fourth Report Wizard dialog box sets the report's layout and orientation. Select the **Stepped** option. The model at the left of the dialog box gives a view of how the report will look. Each layout option in this dialog box specifies how much of the database information is repeated at each level of the report.

11. Click the **Next** button to go to the fifth dialog box.

12. The fifth dialog box of the Report Wizard formats the style for the report. Select the **Bold** style. These styles automatically apply fonts, borders, and spacing to the report design.

13. Click the **Next** button to move to the sixth dialog box.

14. In the sixth and final Report Wizard dialog box name the report and choose whether to immediately preview the report's printed appearance or open it in Design view to modify its design. Type in **Slopeside Bike Rental Report** in the title text box and click the **Preview the report** button.

15. Click the **Finish** button to generate and open the report.

Figure T5.31 shows the example report, opened in Print Preview mode. As is typical of a report generated by the Report Wizard, the field sizes and positions need some adjustment so that text is not cut off and the column headings would benefit from friendlier names.

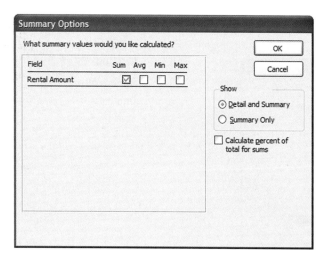

16. **Close** the Report Window.

MODIFYING A REPORT

Figure T5.31 needs some modifications to visually resemble Figure T5.27. This section will use the Design view to adjust the report that was created by using the Report Wizard in the previous section. Design view is used to add, remove, or modify the controls that make up a report, work with report sections, and change the properties of the report itself.

Slopeside Bike Rental Report

Description	Date	Last Name	First Name	Rental Amount
Specialized Rockhopper				
	5/30/2004	Smith	Sue	24
	6/2/2004	Smith	Sue	42
	7/5/2004	Dunn	David	72
Summary for 'Description' = Specialized Rockhopper (3 detail records)				
Sum				138
Trek Fuel 70				
	6/29/2004	Myers	Mike	24
	6/30/2004	Myers	Mike	24
Summary for 'Description' = Trek Fuel 70 (2 detail records)				
Sum				48
Trek Fuel 80				
	7/5/2004	Elliott	Raymond	30
	7/7/2004	Elliott	Raymond	15
	7/11/2004	Lapierre	Lynne	225
	7/12/2004	Lapierre	Lynne	37.5
Summary for 'Description' = Trek Fuel 80 (4 detail records)				
Sum				307.5
Trek Fuel 90				
	7/1/2004	Smith	Sue	48
	7/11/2004	Dunn	David	32
Summary for 'Description' = Trek Fuel 90 (2 detail records)				
Sum				80
Grand Total				573.5

Try IT—Modify a Report

1. In the left column of the Database window, make sure that the **Reports** object is selected.
2. Click **Design** on the Database dialog box.
3. Under the Detail section, right mouse click on the **Rental Amount** box, select **Properties,** click on the **Format tab,** select the **Format** text box, click on the drop-down arrow and select **Currency.**
4. **Close** the Text box.
5. Repeat the same functions from step three and four for the **=Sum** text box under the **Description Footer** and the **=Sum** text box under the **Report Footer.**
6. **Close** the Text Box.
7. Click **View** on the toolbar and then select **Print Preview.**
8. To return to the Design view, click **View** on the toolbar and then select **Design.**
9. Make any other needed modifications in order to match the report in Figure T5.27.

M ost organizations maintain and manage large amounts of information. One of the most efficient information management, computer-based applications is Microsoft Access 2003. Access provides a powerful set of tools for creating and maintaining a relational database. Specific modules that most users utilize when working with Access are building tables and relationships, creating forms for data entry, developing queries for data extraction, and generating reports.

* **KEY TERMS**

Database, 444	Referential integrity, 453	Relational database model, 444

* **MAKING BUSINESS DECISIONS**

1. Technology Conference

The Association of Information Technology Professionals is an association for scholars (academics), students, executives, and managers involved or interested in IT. You have been asked to assist the association in developing a database for its annual one-day conference being held by one of the member institutions.

In the past, each host institution has handled the paper submission and registration process differently, using a combination of paper and electronic formats. This approach has led to duplication of effort and disorganization within and across institutions over the years and has complicated conference planning and reporting.

Programs: The association will have a variety of programs for registrants to select from; however, the programs will only be offered once during the conference. Each program needs to be identified by a unique code. The program topics are:

- Customer relationship management, enterprise resource planning, and supply chain management
- E-business models and strategies
- Ethics and security
- Outsourcing
- Project management

Each program can have more than one presentation, which is referred to as a session. Each session has a unique code, a session title, and presenter(s).

Presenters: Information needs to be recorded for each presenter. Each program must have at least one presenter, but can have more than one (e.g., session). The following information needs to be recorded for each presenter:

- Last name, first name, title, name of institution or company, phone number, and e-mail
- Program topic and title of presentation (session)

Conference registration: For each registrant, the following information needs to be recorded:

- Last name, first name, address, phone number, and e-mail
- Date of registration
- Status (academic, student, executive, or manager)

Conference fees vary according to participant's status. The table to the right provides the registration fee information.

Payments can be made via check, money order, or credit card. For each conference participant, the payment amount, date received, and method are recorded.

Report requirements: To facilitate conference planning and evaluation, the association will need the following reports:

Registration Status	Fee
Academic (Professor, Dean, Provost)	$285
Student	$200
Executive (CIO, CEO)	$300
Manager	$225

- Breakdown of participants by status (academic, student, executive, manager)
- Number of registrations per program and the number of sessions in each program
- A summary revenue report (as shown to the right), displaying the number of registrations and revenue by registration status

Type of Registrant	Number	Revenue by Type
Academic	4	$1140
Student	3	600
Executive	5	1500
Manager	2	450
Total	**14**	**$3490**

The association has provided you with a data file, conference participants.xls, for the participants and presenters who have registered thus far. Use this information to populate the database after you create it.

2. Consulting

Capital Consulting, a Denver-based firm, has asked you to evaluate a spreadsheet that contains the following column structure:

Field Name	Data	Field Name	Data	Field Name	Data
Client Number	300	Contract Type 3		Consultant Name 2	Mary Blaine
Client Name	Damian Smith	Contract Type 4		Consultant Number 3	
Date	1/1/2005	Region	Southwest	Consultant Name 3	
Contract Number	5101	Consultant Number 1	210	Consultant Number 4	
Contract Type 1	ERP	Consultant Name 1	James Monroe	Consultant Name 4	
Contract Type 2	CRM	Consultant Number 2	342		

The spreadsheet was created to enable the manager to match clients with consultants within a given region and to make sure that the clients' need for specific consulting services is properly matched to the consultants' expertise. For example, if the client is in need of ERP services and is located in the Southeast, the objective is to make a match with a consultant who is located in the Southeast and whose expertise is ERP services.

Using Microsoft Access, create a database from the spreadsheet information using proper relational database structure, specifying the field names, data types, descriptions, validation rules (if any), default values (if any), and primary keys for each table.

Create forms to input data for the tables. The design of the forms should be aesthetically pleasing and appropriate to a consulting firm. In addition, the company has asked you to create the following reports:

- A breakdown of consultants by region and expertise
- A breakdown of clients by region and need
- A summary of consultants by region, expertise, and clients

Capital Consulting has provided you with a data file, Capital data.xls, listing its clients and consultants to use for populating the database.

Object-Oriented Technologies

Introduction

The explosion of object-oriented technologies is radically changing the way businesses view information and develop information systems. Object-oriented technologies are everywhere in the business world today. It is difficult to find a business or IT department that is not using object-oriented concepts and technologies. People everywhere are quickly learning how to write software in object-oriented programming languages, create databases using object-oriented database management systems, and design new systems using object-oriented analysis and design techniques.

This plug-in presents:

- The traditional technology approach.
- The object-oriented technology approach.
- The five primary concepts of object-oriented technologies: information, procedures, classes, objects, and messages.
- The three fundamental principles of object-oriented technologies: inheritance, encapsulation, and polymorphism.
- A detailed business case example.
- Types of object-oriented technologies.

Traditional Technology Approach

The **traditional technology approach** has two primary views of any system—information and procedures—and it keeps these two views separate and distinct at all times.

INFORMATION VIEW

The terms data, variables, and attributes all refer to the same thing and in this plug-in these are referred to as information. Information is a key characteristic stored within a system. For example, if a system stores customer information, key characteristics could include *Last Name* or *Phone Number.* The **information view** includes all of the information stored within a system. Figure T6.1 displays all of the different types of information required to build a student grading system, such as *Student Last Name, Student ID,* and *Final Exam Grade.* The information view simply focuses on the information required to develop the system. The problem with the information view is that it gives no thought to how the information is used by the system. For example, it does not define the weights associated with each assignment or exam to derive the *Final Course Grade.*

PROCEDURE VIEW

There are many terms that describe procedures including formulas, functions, and methods. All of these terms refer to the same thing and in this plug-in these are referred to as procedures. A **procedure** manipulates or changes information. For example, a student would need to change her address in the system if she moved. The way this is performed is by running an *Update Student Address* procedure that changes the *Student Address information.* The **procedure view** contains all of the procedures within a system.

There are four primary procedures, or ways, a system can manipulate information; create, read, update, and delete. These four procedures are commonly referred to as **CRUD** (**C**reate, **R**ead, **U**pdate, **D**elete). Other procedures can include such things as *Calculate, Run, Save, Cut, Copy, Spell Check, Select, Overwrite,* etc. The procedures in Figure T6.1 include the basic CRUD on most of the information and a *Calculate Final Course Grade* procedure that calculates the average, based on various weights, for all of a student's grades. These procedures define how the system uses the information. One issue with the procedure view is that it gives no thought as to what information is stored in the system. For example, there is a *CRUD Student Address* procedure, but there is nothing that ensures there is a *Student Address* information field.

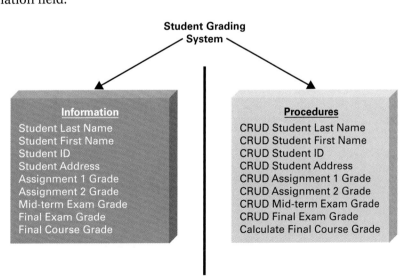

FIGURE T6.1

Student Grading System: Separate Information and Procedure Views

THE PROBLEM WITH THE TRADITIONAL TECHNOLOGY APPROACH

The primary problem with the traditional technology approach is that these separate views can lead to potential disconnects between the information and procedures. For example, it is possible to have the correct information but not be able to do anything with it because the corresponding procedures are missing. Likewise, the system might have the correct procedures but not be able to do anything with it because it does not have the corresponding information. In the first instance, it is rather like having a spreadsheet, but no spreadsheet software. In the second instance, it is like having the spreadsheet software but no information to work with.

Object-Oriented Technology Approach

The object-oriented approach bridges the gap between information and procedures by providing a holistic view of an information system. That is, an ***object-oriented approach*** combines information and procedures into a single view.

INFORMATION AND PROCEDURE VIEWS COMBINED

Figure T6.2 represents the same student grading system as in Figure T6.1, except this diagram uses an object-oriented approach. Notice the diagram represents a holistic view of the entire system with the information in the middle and the procedures surrounding the information.

When you build an object-oriented system you think of the procedures and information as a single unit. Think about how easy it would be for a person to look at this diagram and instantly understand what types of information are in the system and what kinds of procedures can be performed on the information. People who use the object-oriented approach, looking at both information and procedures combined, find it easier to perform the following three important tasks:

1. Understand the entire system.
2. Determine if any key information is missing that would be required in order to perform all of the procedures.
3. Determine if any key procedures, which are required to manipulate the information, are missing.

FIGURE T6.2

Student Grading System: Combined Information and Procedures

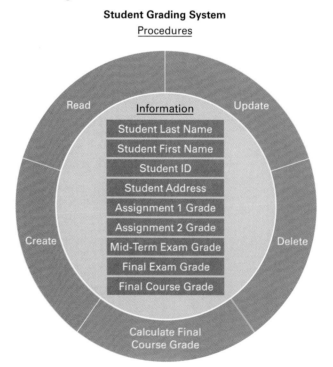

OBJECT-ORIENTED APPROACH AND THE REAL WORLD

The object-oriented approach improves overall systems development because the system more closely models the real world. In the real world, a given process is viewed as a combination of information and the procedures required to act on that information. For example, when you purchase a product that requires assembly such as a bicycle or a gas grill the instruction booklet is contained in the box with the product. The instructions include detailed steps concerning assembly along with a description of the various parts. Both the information and procedures are provided together, which is similar to an object-oriented approach. The set of instructions is not found separate from the description of the parts; they are combined because this makes logical sense.

If a person viewed only the procedures in the student grading system example, it would be difficult to understand the procedures without understanding the information. For example, it would be impossible to understand the *Calculate Final Course Grade* procedure without knowing what type of information was used in the calculation.

Consider a business process such as *Track Inventory*. It is easy to immediately identify several key characteristics required to perform this process, such as *Part Number, Part Name, Part Manufacturer, Quantity on Hand, Reorder Point,* and *Cost.* These are all examples of information. At the same time, it is easy to identify how the information needs to be manipulated to perform this process, such as *Calculate Quantity to Order, Add a New Part,* and *Change a Part Cost.* These are all examples of procedures. In short, both information and procedures are integrated parts of the track inventory process. Therefore, object-oriented concepts basically provide a real-world view in which information and procedures are combined together.

Five Primary Concepts of Object-Oriented Technologies

There are five basic object-oriented concepts: information, procedures, classes, objects, and messages.

INFORMATION

Information comprises key characteristics stored within a system. For example, if you were building an information system for tracking members at an athletic club you would want to track such things as *Member Name, Member ID, Address, Phone, Weight, Height,* and *Membership Type.* These are all examples of the different types of information the member tracking system might store.

PROCEDURES

A *procedure* manipulates or changes information. Examples of procedures that the athletic club member tracking system might contain include *CRUD Member Name* and *CRUD Member ID.* Procedures perform many functions and operations extending far beyond simple CRUD. Examples could include *Calculating Membership Costs* or *Reserving Equipment.*

CLASSES

A **class** contains information and procedures and acts as a template to create objects. Classes are simply the combination of information and procedures as displayed in Figure T6.3. It sometimes helps to think of classes as similar to definitions in a dictionary. If you look up the definition of the word *member* in a dictionary, it will give you an overview of what a member is and perhaps explain the role of a

Class: Member
Procedures

member. A class does exactly the same thing. If you look at the class Member in Figure T6.3, you can quickly understand all of the information required to describe a member and many of the procedures the Member class can perform including *Calculate Membership Costs* and *Reserve Equipment.*

Multiple Classes

Only a single class has been identified for the student grading system and the member tracking system. Classes become a little more complex when you take into consideration that a single system can have anywhere from 5 to 500 classes. The reason that a system has multiple classes is that you simply cannot put all the information for one system into one class. Imagine putting all the information for the member tracking system into a single class. This class would be enormous. If all the information is in a single class, the class quickly becomes unmanageable. Determining which types of information belong to which procedures would be impossible. Breaking down the information and procedures for ease of use and understandability, or practicing **information decomposition,** is the proper way to structure information systems. Practicing information decomposition makes IT specialists' and users' jobs easier because the information is in understandable pieces.

OBJECTS

An **object** is an instance of a class. An easier way to think of an object is the actual item represented by the class. Review the two objects (Alana and Samuel) of the class Member represented in Figure T6.4. It is easy to describe the primary difference between the Member class diagram in Figure T6.3 and the Member object diagrams in Figure T6.4. The Member object diagrams contain the information representing the actual members that the system is tracking. Using Figure T6.4, you can describe the first object, Alana. Alana Smith is a yearly member who lives at 112 Baker Street. You can also describe the second object, Samuel. Samuel Scola is a monthly member who lives at 3A 16th Street. Every member the system tracks is a separate object, and every member object is an instance of (or created from) the class Member. Alana and Samuel are both examples of objects of the class Member.

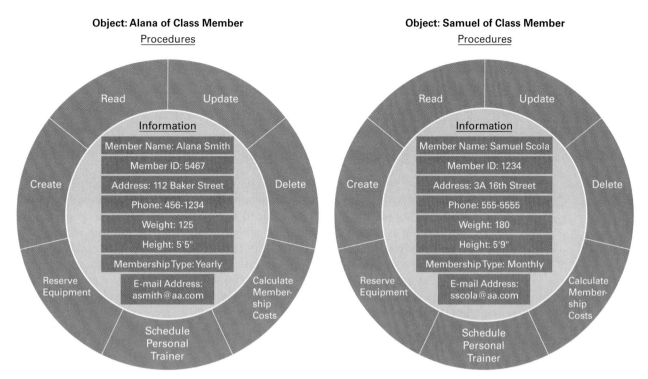

FIGURE T6.4

Alana and Samuel: Two Instances (Objects) of Class Member

MESSAGES: HOW CLASSES AND OBJECTS INTERACT

Essentially, a class is a blank template that defines all the different types of information the system can store about an object. Once you create an object from the class, you can fill in the template with the actual information. For example, the Member class can give you a high-level definition of a member object, such as *Member Name,* but it cannot tell you the actual name of the member. The class will tell you only that it can store information for the member's name. The object stores the actual information and can tell you that the member's name is Alana.

Messages are how objects communicate with each other. One object can send a message to another object asking it to perform a certain procedure. In general, systems are created by developing many different classes that work together to perform tasks. Refer back to our student grading system. If you build this system, you might have one class representing students, a second class representing courses, and a third class representing instructors. Objects from each of the classes communicate with each other in order to enter the student's course grades. The student object passes a request to enroll in courses to the course object. The instructor object passes a request to teach specific courses to the course object. The instructor object also passes the student's final course grades to the course object. Combining these three classes together gives you a fully functioning student grading system.

HOW THE FIVE PRIMARY CONCEPTS INTERACT

Information, procedures, classes, objects, and messages relate to each other in the following ways:

- Information and procedures create classes.
- Classes create objects.
- Objects communicate with other objects via messages.

Another way to understand object-oriented systems is to review the differences between system developers and system users. *System developers* are the individuals who build the systems and are responsible for building the classes which contain information and procedures. *System users* are the individuals who use the system and are responsible for inputting the actual information or creating the objects. If you think about the member tracking system, you can easily identify which individuals are responsible for the different tasks. The system developer would be responsible for building the Member class and the associated information and procedures. The athletic club employees, or system user, would be responsible for creating the objects or inputting the actual member information.

REAL-WORLD OBJECT-ORIENTED EXAMPLE

Reviewing how the five primary object-oriented concepts interact begins to mimic the real world. For example, a car's steering wheel, tires, and engine are different components that work together in order to accomplish the common goal of driving. A computer is another example of several different components working together and sending messages to each other in order to accomplish a common task. The keyboard, monitor, mouse, and operating system all work together to run applications. A home stereo system is a perfect analogy for an object-oriented system. If you created classes to represent each stereo component, they could include some or all of the following:

- Amplifier
- CD player
- Cassette deck
- Equalizer
- Speakers
- CDs
- Cassettes

Some of the information items stored within the CD class would include *Title, Artist, Date Recorded,* and *Number of Songs.* The number of objects created from the CD class would vary depending on the number of CDs. *Set Volume* might be one of the primary procedures for the amplifier object.

In order for the system to work, objects are created from each class, and each of the objects works with specific information and procedures. The information for the CD player, for example, could include the *Manufacturer Name, Model Number,* or *Play Speed.* The procedures for the CD player could include *Play, Fast Forward, Rewind, Skip,* or *Stop.* To hear music the CD player must play the CD, and then send a message to the amplifier object, which sends a message to the speaker object, to play the music. A home stereo system is a true example of a real-world object-oriented system. Each component must work together with the others in order for the system to function correctly. Thus, each component in a home stereo system really is an object. As an object, each component works with only certain information and performs certain procedures. If one component needs another procedure performed, it must send a message to another object (or component) that can perform that procedure.

Three Fundamental Principles of Object-Oriented Technologies

A business can gain huge advantages by using object-oriented technologies. The three fundamental principles of object-oriented technologies are:

1. Inheritance
2. Encapsulation
3. Polymorphism

INHERITANCE

One of the most powerful features of object-oriented technologies is inheritance. **Inheritance** is the ability to define superclass and subclass relationships among classes. Generalization (parent) and specialization (child) relationships are another way of thinking of superclass and subclass relationships. Review Figure T6.5 and determine which class is the superclass and which classes are the subclasses. The Car class is the superclass and the Bronco and Porsche classes are the subclasses. Another way to state this relationship is that the Bronco and Porsche subclasses inherit all the information and procedures from the Car superclass. For example, the *CRUD* procedures are not defined in the Bronco and Porsche subclasses because they are inherited from the Car superclass.

Defining inheritance is simply a matter of defining generic and specific information and procedures. Generic information and procedures apply to all classes. Specific information and procedures apply only to a particular subclass. For example, notice that the Car superclass in Figure T6.5 contains generic information and procedures that are shared by both the Bronco and Porsche subclasses. Both the Bronco and Porsche subclasses have a *Model, Year, Price,* and *Color* and both can *Honk Horn, Brake,* and *Drive.*

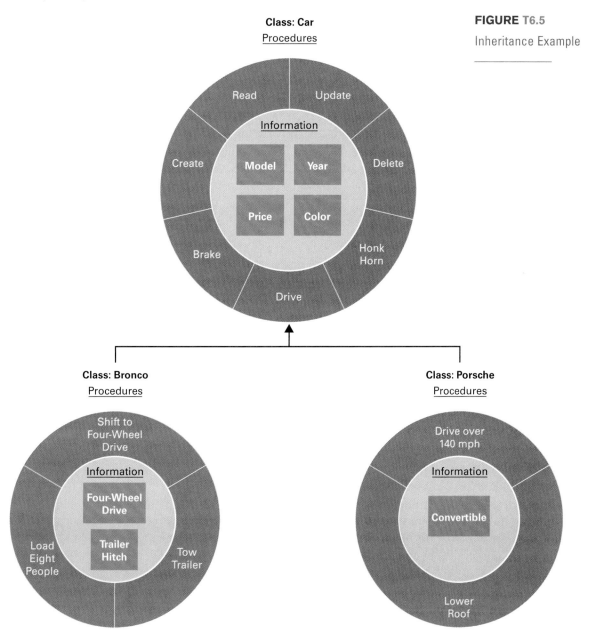

FIGURE T6.5

Inheritance Example

The subclasses contain specific information and procedures that are unique to each particular subclass. The Bronco subclass contains information for *4-Wheel Drive* and the Porsche subclass contains a procedure to *Drive over 140 mph*. These unique features are stored in the subclass because they are not generic enough to store in the Car superclass. If you store the procedure for *Drive over 140 mph* in the Car superclass, then every subclass of Car inherits this procedure. This is a rather serious mistake since there are many types of cars that cannot drive over 140 mph. Hence, you must store this unique feature at the subclass level.

Primary Business Benefit of Inheritance: Reuse

The true business benefit gained from using inheritance is the ability to easily expand and maintain a system. For example, if you decided to add a piece of information called *Mileage* to the Car class, it is only developed in one place, the Car class, and it is automatically inherited by every subclass. The *Mileage* information is reused by all of the subclasses.

If you were using the traditional approach to develop this system, the *Mileage* information would have to be developed in each of the Car, Bronco, and Porsche classes because the traditional approach does not support the concept of inheritance or reuse. Obviously, if you used the traditional approach it would take a great deal of time and energy to build *Mileage* information into all 50 subclasses. Using the object-oriented approach you build it only once and all 50 subclasses automatically inherit this valuable piece of information.

Another example of how inheritance makes it easy to expand a system would be if you decide to add a new class, Volkswagen Beetle, to the system. If you place this class as a subclass of Car, it automatically inherits all the information and procedures already developed in the Car class. All you need to develop is any unique information or procedures that the Volkswagen Beetle class requires. If you added a Volkswagen Beetle class using the traditional approach, you would have to build every single piece of information and every procedure including *Model, Year, Price, Color, CRUD, Honk Horn, Drive,* and *Brake.*

Inheritance is a valuable principle for businesses in terms of saving money, effort, and time when developing and maintaining information systems.

ENCAPSULATION

Encapsulation means information hiding. This concept has a simple definition and provides tremendous benefits when building an information system. Objects are sometimes referred to as black boxes, whereby the information inside an object is hidden and all that can be viewed is the object. Imagine you are in a park and you see a dog. You can instantly determine that the dog is an object of the class Dog. However, you do not know all the information about the dog. You cannot tell the dog's name, weight, height, or other characteristics just by looking at it. Hence, the actual information stored in the object is hidden, or encapsulated, but this does not prevent you from seeing the dog and being able to communicate with the dog.

For example, if you order AT&T digital cable, you receive a remote control that is used as the interface to the digital cable box. An ***interface*** is any device that calls procedures and can include such things as a keyboard, mouse, and touch screen. Recently, AT&T changed its entire digital cable system including the menu colors, item locations, and cable features. Suddenly, when a user turned on the television everything on the digital cable menu looked completely different. However, the remote control, or system interface, continued to work exactly the same as it did before the system changed. The same buttons on the remote control were used to turn the TV on and off, to adjust the volume up and down, and to select different menu items. Since the remote control did not change, the customers could use their system exactly the same way as they did before. The only change the users had to deal with was getting used to the new look and feel of the improved digital cable system.

Primary Business Benefit of Encapsulation: Quality

AT&T used encapsulation to hide the digital cable system changes from its users. The system changed significantly but, because the user's remote control, or interface, continued to work exactly the same as before, the users were unaffected. The users continued to receive the same high-quality service from AT&T. In other words, the system changes were hidden from the system users. The users operated the digital cable system exactly the same way as they did before the changes, through their remote control. This is a great example of the huge benefits a company can receive by using encapsulation. Just imagine the millions of dollars AT&T would be required to spend if it had to retrain all of its customers every time it wanted to make a system change.

POLYMORPHISM

Polymorphism simply means "to have many forms." An example of polymorphism is the word *bark*. The word *bark* can refer to a dog's bark or to tree bark. This is true polymorphism, the ability to use the same word to mean different things.

Figure T6.6 displays an example of polymorphism. Notice that the Rectangle, Square, and Circle classes all contain procedures called *CalculateArea*. However, the *CalculateArea* procedure is different for each class. The formula to calculate the area of a rectangle (*Length * Width*) is completely different from the formula to calculate the area of a square (*Side * Side*). This is an example of polymorphism because each class has an identically named procedure that performs different calculations.

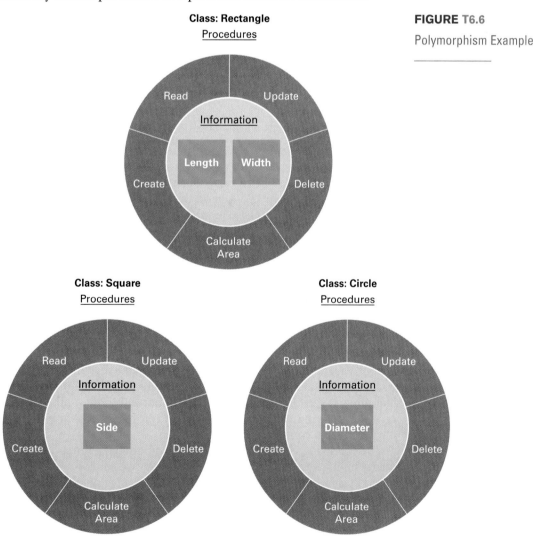

FIGURE T6.6

Polymorphism Example

Primary Business Benefit of Polymorphism: Productivity

If you build a procedure using a traditional technology, you must ensure that the procedure has a unique name. Imagine how difficult and time-consuming it would be if there were 50,000 procedures in the system. Using an object-oriented approach removes the problem of defining complex naming structures which increases productivity.

Ice Blue Snowboards

An Object-Oriented Business Example

Ice Blue Snowboards manufactures and sells snowboards, bindings, boots, and apparel. In order to prepare for the launch of the business, you researched similar businesses to discover any problems they have encountered so you could avoid making the same mistakes. The following is a list of common competitor problems:

- 18 months to get a new product to market.
- Inventory control.
- Scalability and expandability.

18 MONTHS TO GET A NEW PRODUCT TO MARKET

In order for your business to be competitive you must be able to get your new products into the market as soon as they are finished. Having a fast time-to-market is critical for the success of any new business. Eighteen months is simply too long for you to wait to get a new product on the market. Using an object-oriented approach will help you reduce this critical time-to-market factor. The typical high-level processes for developing new products include the following:

- Generating and accepting the idea.
- Manufacturing the product.
- Updating all current systems to support the new product.
- Implementing the new product.

Each time a new product is developed, it takes almost 18 months for your competitors to get it on the market. The reason this process takes so long is primarily because several applications must be changed every time a new product is introduced. A typical business will have a different system for every business function including inventory, sales, orders, marketing, billing, and so forth. Every system must be updated with the new product information before you can begin selling the product to your customers.

The following is an example of how you could define an object-oriented snowboard selling system. First, a class called Snowboard would be created. The Snowboard class would be responsible for tracking all snowboard information including *Pricing, Model, Features, Discounts,* and so on. The Snowboard class would also be responsible for establishing all the procedures associated with marketing and selling snowboards including advertising in magazines and competitor pricing analysis.

Second, an interface would be designed to perform all these procedures. This would encapsulate the information and procedures in the Snowboard superclass and allow you the flexibility to change things without affecting the system users.

Third, you would practice inheritance. A subclass would be created for each particular type of snowboard. Defining subclasses, or using inheritance, saves you a great deal of time and energy because each subclass inherits all the information and procedures from the superclass. The only work required to create a subclass is defining the unique information or procedures associated with the subclass. After creating each class once, you can reuse the classes across all your business applications.

Finally, you would create objects that communicate with all the other objects across every system in your business.

ONE HOUR TO LAUNCH A NEW PRODUCT

Defining a new snowboard product would now require no more than one hour. The following are the steps required to define a new product:

- Create a single subclass for the new product.
- Assign a superclass/subclass relationship between the new class and the Snowboard class.
- Define any unique pieces of information for the new product subclass.
- Define any unique procedures for the new product subclass.
- Reuse the new product subclass by copying it directly into every business application.
- Create objects from the new subclass.

By understanding and using object-oriented technologies, you have decreased your product introduction time from 18 months to 1 hour. The key to reducing the time-to-market for your products is having business systems that use the same generic interfaces for dealing with products. Every time you introduce a new product, as long as it conforms to the common generic interface, all the business applications are able to add it without any modification or interruption to the knowledge workers.

Figure T6.7 provides an example of a snowboard business case class diagram. This figure assumes your business offers an electronic catalog on the Internet listing all the snowboarding products you sell. By creating a catalog object whose primary procedure is to update the electronic catalog, you will not be required to change anything when adding a new product to the catalog. The catalog object already understands how products are added and listed in the catalog. The new product object simply sends a message to the catalog object to execute the update catalog procedure. The new product will be added to the catalog without any need for system modification.

INVENTORY CONTROL

Controlling inventory is one of the largest problems facing businesses today. Businesses need to be able to have sufficient inventory on hand to meet current production needs while minimizing the associated expenses including storing the inventory, transporting the inventory, and maintaining the inventory. This problem is a part of supply chain management and it hits all businesses small and large. Managing the supply chain is fundamental to the success of any business. If you neglect to manage your supply chain, then you will find your business experiencing high storage costs, the inability to manufacture products because of low inventories, and lost inventory.

You can use object-oriented technology to define Shipping, Distribution, and Vehicle classes. Creating shipping, distribution, and vehicles objects allows you to

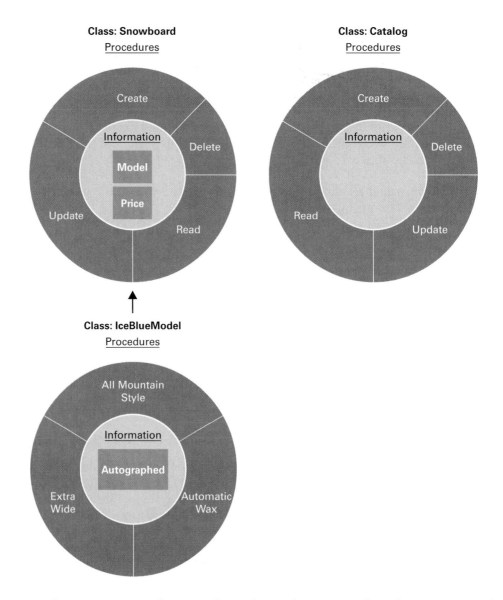

control your inventory. Shipping objects know their origin, their destinations, and their primary goal of arriving at the destination on time with the lowest expense. Distribution objects designate which modes of transportation will be used to ship the inventory. Vehicle objects move the inventory. Using these three objects will help your business track and maintain correct inventory levels.

SCALABILITY AND EXPANDABILITY

Scalability refers to how well a system can adapt to increased demands. Increased demands can include such things as additional users, information, and processing speeds. When a system grows, the size of the database that stores the information grows. As the database grows, the system tends to perform procedures slower. *Expandability* refers to how easy it is to add features and functions to a system. If you design a system without thinking about expandability, you will run into major problems when your business starts to grow.

Review Figure T6.8 and explain why the ExpertSnowModel class was unable to be placed in a superclass/subclass relationship with the Snowboard class. As we discussed, it is important to take advantage of inheritance as it saves time and effort when developing a system. The reason the ExpertSnowModel class cannot inherit the functionality from the Snowboard class is because of the procedure called *Deep Powder Specific. Deep Powder Specific* is a procedure that does not ap-

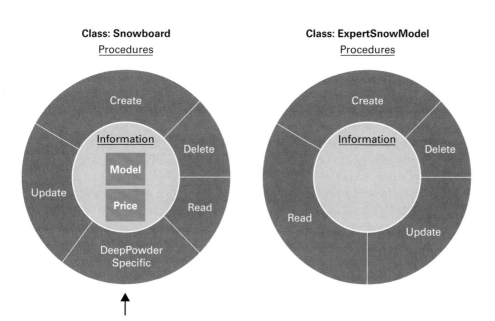

Class: Snowboard
Procedures

Create

Information

Model

Price

Delete

Update

Read

DeepPowder
Specific

Class: ExpertSnowModel
Procedures

Create

Information

Delete

Read

Update

Class: IceBlueModel
Procedures

All Mountain
Style

Information

Autographed

Extra
Wide

Automatic
Wax

ply to all types of snowboards. Snowboards are designed for powder, ice, and all mountain terrain. For this reason, the ExpertSnowModel class cannot be designated as a Snowboard subclass. If you did place the ExpertSnowModel class as a subclass of Snowboard, then an ExpertSnowModel is now able to perform the *Deep Powder Specific* procedure. This is a rather large system error. Defining superclasses that are too specific and not being able to take advantage of inheritance is a common problem with object-oriented systems.

Did you notice anything else wrong with the class diagram? The ExpertSnowModel class does not contain any information. This indicates a disconnect between the information and procedures. The ExpertSnowModel class contains the *Create, Read, Update,* and *Delete* procedures, but what are these procedures going to manipulate if there is not any information? This is a typical error if you are using the traditional technology approach because information and procedures are viewed separately. Using the object-oriented approach, you notice this disconnect right away.

Types of Object-Oriented Technologies

Many technologies in use today support object-oriented concepts and techniques. Many more of these technologies are being developed every day as the business world continues to rush toward the use of objects. It is important that you have some general knowledge of the different types of object-oriented technologies available and used throughout IT departments.

OBJECT-ORIENTED PROGRAMMING LANGUAGES

In general, programs are what make computers work. A ***program*** is a set of instructions that, when executed, cause a computer to behave in a specific manner. A program is almost like a recipe. It contains ingredients and directions, or information and procedures that tell the computer how to perform different tasks.

A ***programming language*** is the tool developers use to write a program. For example, English, French, and Italian are all different types of languages you can use to write a paper. Java and C# are two different types of languages you can use to write a program. An ***object-oriented programming language*** is a programming language used to develop object-oriented systems. Programming languages that are not object oriented cannot handle classes, objects, messages, inheritance, or encapsulation. Currently, there are close to 100 different object-oriented programming languages available. The three most popular languages today are Java, C++, and C#.

OBJECT-ORIENTED DATABASE SYSTEMS

Relational databases organize information into fields, records, and files (or relations). ***Object-oriented databases*** work with traditional database information and also complex data types such as diagrams, schematic drawings, video, and sound.

The relational database model, although it may allow you to store and view such data types, does not include good mechanisms for allowing you to manipulate and change information within those data types. For example, you can include a CAD drawing of a part as a field in a relational database, but it is literally impossible to work with any specific information in the drawing (such as cuts, specific components, and the ordering of assembly) without having that information also stored in other fields.

Another feature of object-oriented databases is that you are not restricted to two-dimensional tables. This gives you greater flexibility in storing and defining procedures that work with complex data types. In fact, most of today's multimedia applications rely on the use of objects and object-oriented databases.

Most other database models also restrict you to working with specific data types: alphabetic, numeric, decimal, currency, and date. In an object-oriented database environment, however, you can create and work with data types that may be unique to a specific business process. For example, if you had an object that included an address you could easily design this field to include a street address and a unit number. You could then define a procedure that required the entry of both pieces of information. This is an example of a unique data type that requires not only a street address but also a unit number.

OBJECT-ORIENTED TECHNOLOGIES
AND CLIENT/SERVER ENVIRONMENTS

Client/server is the emerging blueprint for organizational networks, and most organizations are choosing to develop client/server networks through object-oriented technologies. Spreading objects across a client/server network makes logical sense: client workstations contain objects with local procedures for working with local information, and servers contain objects with global procedures for working with global information.

In Figure T6.9, the server handles the entire data management function, the client handles the entire presentation function, and both share in processing the logic or business rules. So the server object contains procedures for retrieving and

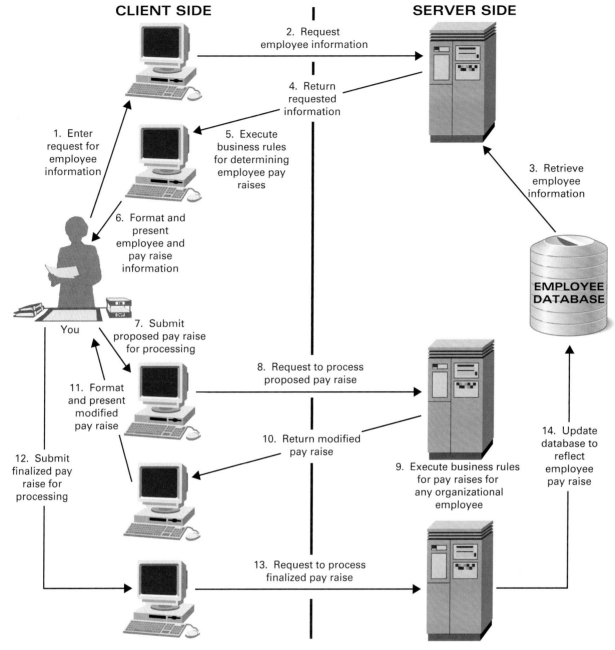

CLIENT SIDE | **SERVER SIDE**

2. Request employee information

4. Return requested information

1. Enter request for employee information

5. Execute business rules for determining employee pay raises

3. Retrieve employee information

6. Format and present employee and pay raise information

You

7. Submit proposed pay raise for processing

11. Format and present modified pay raise

8. Request to process proposed pay raise

EMPLOYEE DATABASE

10. Return modified pay raise

14. Update database to reflect employee pay raise

12. Submit finalized pay raise for processing

9. Execute business rules for pay raises for any organizational employee

13. Request to process finalized pay raise

FIGURE T6.9

Object-Oriented Technologies and Client/Server—The Perfect Match

storing information (data management) and for processing some of the logic or business rules. Likewise, the client object contains procedures for some of the logic or business rules and for presenting information (the presentation function). To demonstrate, assume you are the manager of the manufacturing division in an organization and need to give pay raises to each of your employees. For assigning pay raises, you also have to follow several rules—some for just your division and some for all organizational employees.

In an object-oriented environment, your client workstation contains an object for assigning pay raises to manufacturing division employees according to manufacturing division rules. The server contains an object for assigning pay raises according to organizational rules and for retrieving information from and saving information to the database.

Take a look at how this would actually work. First, your client object, or Manufacturing Employee object, asks you for an employee and sends a message to the server object, or Organizational Employee object, to retrieve that employee's information from the database. Your client object then executes the rules for determining a pay raise for a manufacturing employee, displays that information to you, and sends the proposed pay raise to the server object. The server object then executes the organizational rules for assigning a pay raise and returns the modified pay raises to your client object. Your client object then displays that information to you and allows you to submit the finalized pay raises for processing to the server object. Finally, the server object updates the Employee database to reflect the employee's pay raise.

It is possible that while you are assigning pay raises to employees of your manufacturing division, various managers of other departments could be assigning pay raises for their employees. In this instance, you and any other managers essentially share the server object—another excellent example of reuse.

T he object-oriented approach combines information and procedures into a single view. The five primary object-oriented concepts are *information, procedures, classes, objects,* and *messages.* The three fundamental principles of object-oriented technologies are *inheritance, encapsulation,* and *polymorphism.* The number of object-oriented development tools increases daily and thus so does the importance of understanding object-oriented concepts. In the future, object-oriented technologies will perform tasks and provide functionality that have not even been thought of yet.

* KEY TERMS

Class, 469
CRUD (Create, Read, Update, Delete), 467
Encapsulation, 474
Expandability, 478
Information decomposition, 470
Information view, 467
Inheritance, 473

Interface, 474
Messages, 471
Object, 470
Object-oriented approach, 468
Object-oriented database, 480
Object-oriented programming language, 480
Polymorphism, 475

Procedure, 467
Procedure view, 467
Program, 480
Programming language, 480
Scalability, 478
Traditional technology approach, 467

* MAKING BUSINESS DECISIONS

1. Schultz Landscape Inc.

You have been hired to build an inventory tracking system for the Schultz landscaping company. Schultz is excited about the use of inheritance in object-oriented systems and wants to see how you are going to use it in the system. Schultz has already defined the Tree, Grass, Flowers, Fence, Equipment, and Plant classes. Your job is to define all of the information and procedures for each class and the inheritance structure of the classes, or the superclass and subclass relationships. Please provide a class diagram that displays all of the classes for the Schultz inventory tracking system and be sure to include inheritance.

2. Object-Oriented Concepts and the Real World

List all of a computer's parts. Be sure to include the monitor, keyboard, mouse, hard drive, disk drive, memory, CD-ROM drive, software, and printer. Write a brief explanation answering each of the following:

- What types of information are associated with the computer?
- What types of procedures are associated with the computer?
- What parts of the computer, if any, represent the classes?
- What parts of the computer, if any, represent the objects?
- How many classes are there?
- How many objects are there?
- How are messages used?
- How do all the components work together to create a complete system?

3. Explaining Object-Oriented Technologies

Assume you are working for a large oil and gas company. Your current manager has little experience with object-oriented technologies and has asked you to create a document describing, in generic terms, each of the following object-oriented concepts. Be sure to include explanations as to how using these object-oriented concepts will contribute to building and implementing successful information systems.

- Encapsulation
- Polymorphism
- Inheritance

4. Creating a Video Store

Consider your local video rental store. What would be three important classes? How many different objects do you think there are for each class? On a separate sheet of paper, draw a class diagram displaying all the classes along with the different types of information and procedures they contain. Do you think video rental stores in general use object-oriented systems? Why or why not?

5. Finding Object-Oriented Errors

Review the following class diagram and determine any potential errors.

Class Diagram Example

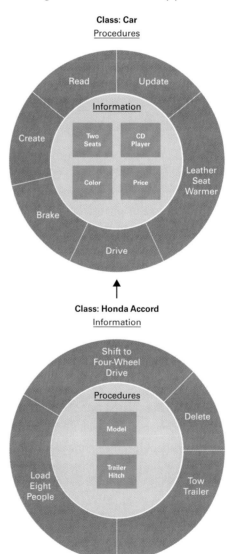

Valuing Technology

1. Summarize the three areas an organization can use to assess the financial health of an information technology project.

2. Describe the different financial metrics an organization can use to determine the value of an information technology project.

3. Explain customer metrics and their importance to an organization.

4. Describe the different types of comparative metrics an organization can use to determine the efficiency and effectiveness of its information technology resources.

Introduction

The core units introduced efficiency and effectiveness metrics, which are the two primary types of IT metrics. *Efficiency IT metrics* measure the performance of the IT system including throughput, speed, availability, etc. *Effectiveness IT metrics* measure the impact IT has on business processes and activities including customer satisfaction, conversion rates, sell-through increases, etc.

An organization's *strategic resources* include those assets available after an organization has cautiously spent what it must to keep its existing business operating at its current level. Strategic resources are typically used to fund more promising strategic ventures. Decisions regarding strategic resource allocation for IT projects are among the most difficult of all tactical resource decisions. Many organizations routinely analyze efficiency and effectiveness metrics to measure the performance of IT projects. This plug-in takes a step beyond simple efficiency and effectiveness metrics by covering a number of tools commonly used in IT investment decisions including financial, customer, and comparative metrics.

Metrics—Measuring IT Value

In today's highly automated business world, the strategies and directions of the IT department increasingly form the basis for the overall corporate strategy. Once regarded as merely a service department, decisions made regarding IT can influence a company's competitive position and often dictate its ability to exploit market

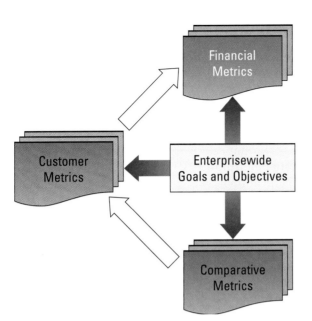

opportunities. For example, manufacturing firms depend on their supply chain infrastructure to respond quickly to shifting production demands, while retailers look to the intelligence built into their inventory management systems to withstand economic downturns.

Metrics provide vital feedback to the firm, quickly confirming success or immediately identifying corrective actions needed such as changes in processes, strategy, or product offerings. Furthermore, the act of specifying concrete goals with precise measurements can help senior managers clarify their strategic priorities and set clear directions, strategies, and goals throughout the organization.

BUSINESS METRICS IN IT

Information technology groups with a metrics-based culture constantly think in terms of how their efforts will be measured by the corporation. All initiatives are reflected against a clear set of objectives, with an eye toward determining whether these initiatives will draw them closer to achieving enterprisewide goals and objectives. Organizations must strive to identify and present a clear set of metrics. This enables the staff to stay abreast of what has transpired, which goals are being met, and what needs to be changed.

The financial metrics, customer metrics, and comparative metrics best capture a firm's performance. Taken together, they enable managers to understand information technology's value and performance (see Figure T7.1).

Financial Metrics

Financial metrics assess the financial performance of a company. Typical financial metrics include revenue growth, gross margins, operating income, earnings per share, and cash flow. The investment community weights financial metrics heavily and the organization's financial performance is of ultimate interest to its shareholders.

An IT investment should not be treated any differently from any other business investment; therefore, financial metrics are used to assess IT investments. Each IT investment needs to have a business case that justifies the reason for the investment. If an IT project measures up to the corporate criteria (or corporate goals), then the company should feel comfortable moving forward with the project.

CAPITAL BUDGETING

Capital budgeting is the process of planning for purchases of assets whose returns are expected to continue beyond one year. A *capital expenditure* is a cash outlay that is expected to generate a flow of future cash benefits lasting longer than one year. Many information technology initiatives fall under the categories of capital budgeting and capital expenditures. Capital expenditures are important to an organization because they require large cash outlays and have long-term impact on the organization's performance. An organization's capital expenditures affect its future profitability and determine its strategic direction.

Typically, an organization has several different IT projects that it wants to pursue and it must determine where to invest its strategic resources. *Capital rationing* is the process of limiting the number of capital expenditure projects because of insufficient funds to finance all projects that otherwise meet the organization's criteria for acceptability. An organization must perform capital rationing on its prospective IT projects, that is, choose which projects it is going to pursue.

PROJECT CLASSIFICATIONS

Organizations commonly undertake three types of IT projects:

1. *Independent projects*—projects whose acceptance or rejection does not directly eliminate other projects from consideration. For example, an organization might decide to install a wireless network in its office and replace its payroll system at approximately the same time. In the absence of a constraint on the availability of funds, both projects could be adopted if they meet minimum investment criteria.

2. *Mutually exclusive projects*—projects whose acceptance precludes the acceptance of one or more alternative proposals. Because two mutually exclusive projects have the capacity to perform the same function for an organization, only one should be chosen. For example, if an organization is looking at installing a new database, it might have to choose between Oracle and Sybase. The organization would have to choose one over the other. It could not install both.

3. *Contingent projects*—projects whose acceptance is dependent on the adoption of one or more other projects. For example, if an organization is considering installing a wireless network it must also upgrade all its hardware for wireless capabilities. When an organization is considering contingent projects, it must consider all projects that are dependent on one another and treat them as a single project for evaluation purposes.

The Five Common Financial Metrics

The following are financial metrics that an organization can use to measure the business value of its information technology investments:

1. Net present value (NPV)
2. Internal rate of return (IRR)
3. Return on investment (ROI)
4. Payback period (PB)
5. Total cost of ownership (TCO)

NET PRESENT VALUE (NPV)

Present value is the value of cash to be received in the future expressed in today's dollars. *Net present value (NPV)* of a capital expenditure project is the present value of the stream of net (operating) cash flows from the project minus the proj-

Year	Project A	Project B
Net Investment	$ 50,000	$50,000
1	12,500	5,000
2	12,500	10,000
3	12,500	15,000
4	12,500	15,000
5	12,500	25,000
6	12,500	30,000
NPV	$ – 1,387.50	$ 7,735

Year	Project X	Project Y	Project Z
Net Investment	$10,000	$10,000	$10,000
NPV	$13,000	$80,000	$30,500

ect's net investment. Essentially, NPV makes a comparison between the cost of an investment and the present value of uncertain future cash flows generated by the project. The net present value method is often referred to as the *discounted cash flow technique* because the cash flows are discounted at the firm's required rate of return.

Decision Rule—NPV

In theory, a project should be accepted if its NPV is greater than or equal to zero and rejected if its NPV is less than zero. Review Figure T7.2 for an example of using NPV to compare two different projects. In this example, Project A would be rejected because it has a negative NPV, and Project B would be accepted because it has a positive NPV ($7,735).

If two or more mutually exclusive projects have positive net present values, the project having the largest NPV is the one selected. In Figure T7.3 Project Y would be chosen because it offers the highest NPV ($80,000).

INTERNAL RATE OF RETURN (IRR)

PeopleSoft calculated an IRR in the fourth year of 203 percent on a new streaming media system. PeopleSoft employs thousands of employees in dozens of offices around the world, who require the same information, presentations, and professional development opportunities. The company implemented a system that distributes company information in audio and video formats using streaming media. Integrating steaming media increased the impact of information, improved the retention of complex concepts, and accelerated the distribution of new ideas and innovations. The system was so successful that the initial investment of $300,000 paid for itself in the first year in terms of reduced travel expenses and conference call charges.[1]

Internal rate of return (IRR) is the rate at which the NPV of an investment equals zero. This is often referred to as the *discounted cash flow (DCF) rate of return*. Essentially, the IRR is the interest rate, when applied to the cost and benefits of a project, which discounts the cash flows to zero.

Decision Rule—IRR

The IRR is often compared against the **hurdle rate,** the minimum ROI percentage a project must meet to be considered for management approval. A project with an IRR in excess of the hurdle rate is worth pursuing. Generally, the internal rate of return method indicates that a project whose internal rate of return is greater than or equal to the firm's cost of capital should be accepted, whereas a project whose internal rate of return is less than the firm's cost of capital should be rejected.

When two or more mutually exclusive projects are being considered, it is generally preferable to accept the project having the highest IRR. NPV and IRR are typically used in conjunction with return on investment (ROI) and provide a more thorough measure than ROI because they take into account the expected life of an investment.

RETURN ON INVESTMENT (ROI)

Return on investment (ROI) indicates the earning power of a project and is measured by dividing the benefits of a project by the investment. The tangible benefits typically include cost reductions and revenue increases. The investment equals the total cost of the project over the measurement period. In analyzing projects, the risk factor should be included in the evaluation. For example, a high ROI for "risky projects" may not be as good as a lower ROI for "safe projects." Typically, an IT investment should generate a high ROI. The ROI equation is as follows:

$$\text{ROI} = \frac{\text{Increased Revenues or Cost Saving}}{\text{Investment}}$$

For a simple example assume the organization has a 1-year project costing $40,000 with a return of $100,000. The ROI equals:

$$\frac{\$100,000}{\$40,000} = 2.5 \text{ times or } 250\% \text{ ROI}$$

If the analysis period exceeds one year then the interest rate factor needs to be applied which can include inflation expectations, interest rate assumptions, and even a risk profile. For example, using a 15 percent discount rate, a 3-year depreciation period, a project cost of $100,000, and a return of $50,000 per year, the ROI calculation is:

$$\frac{\dfrac{50,000}{1.15} + \dfrac{50,000}{1.15 * 1.15} + \dfrac{50,000}{1.15 * 1.15 * 1.15}}{100,000} = 114\% \text{ ROI}$$

Decision Rule—ROI

In general, when the expected ROI is greater than or equal to the required return, an organization will find the investment attractive. It is important to note that although ROI is easily measured in standard business functions such as purchasing and sales, measuring ROI on a technology project is a challenging task. For example, how does a company place an ROI on a piece of software that protects corporate information such as a firewall. Dividing the benefits of the firewall by the amount invested in the firewall is not going to derive the true ROI. The true ROI is the number of times the firewall prevents hackers from stealing corporate information, which could cause immeasurable lost revenues. Estimating an ROI on a firewall is similar to attempting to estimate the ROI of a fire extinguisher, it is impossible. Placing traditional business metrics on something as valuable as information security is challenging.

PAYBACK PERIOD (PB)

The reciprocal of ROI is the **_payback period (PB)_** of an investment or the period of time required for the cumulative cash inflows (net cash flows) from a project to equal the initial cash outlay (net investment). PB essentially determines the amount of time required for a project to pay for itself. Organizations typically require that projects pay back quickly, usually in less than 18 months. PB is used by most organizations as an initial screen for project prioritization, which means that the longer projects are usually not even considered. PB is taking a dominating role in industry as the initial yardstick for project approval.

Imagine that an organization is considering a project that requires a net investment of $100,000 and is expected to generate net cash inflows of $25,000 a year. Since the expected net cash inflows are equal in each year, the payback period is the ratio of the net investment to the annual net cash inflows:

$$\text{Payback Period (PB)} = \frac{\text{Net Investment}}{\text{Annual Net Cash Inflows}}$$

The payback period for the preceding example is:

$$PB = \frac{\$100,000}{\$25,000} = \text{Project payback is 4 years}$$

Decision Rule—PB

The payback period method does not take into account the time value of money and gives equal weight to all cash inflows. The payback period method also ignores all cash flows occurring after the payback period. For these reasons, it should not be used to determine acceptance or rejection of an investment project.

TOTAL COST OF OWNERSHIP (TCO)

The **_total cost of ownership (TCO)_** consists of the costs, direct and indirect, incurred throughout the life cycle of an asset, including acquisition, deployment, operation, support, and retirement. Essentially, TCO attempts to properly state the costs of an IT investment. TCO was originally developed in the late 1980s by the research firm Gartner to determine the cost of owning and deploying personal computers. Gartner's initial finding, through the use of TCO, was that a single PC cost an enterprise nearly $10,000 per year as a result of additional software, hardware, and maintenance expenses. This finding caused quite a stir as Gartner's methodology was carefully examined and, over the ensuing years, accepted as a standard way to evaluate total costs.[2]

TCO is calculated by compiling all the direct and indirect costs, computed on an annual basis, and then totaling them to provide the total cost of ownership. Direct costs include such things as hardware, software, operations, and administration. Indirect costs include such things as end user operations and downtime. TCO results provide some stunning realizations for an organization. For example, a printer costing $200 could easily have a TCO of over $1,000 when all the paper, toner, and maintenance costs are included.

Decision Rule—TCO

Organizations typically hire consultants and vendors to assist in the task of determining TCO for different IT areas. This calculation is important because an organization can drastically underestimate the cost of an IT investment if it fails to consider the total cost of ownership. Essentially, there are no hard rules for TCO calculations and they are typically analyzed on a project-by-project basis.

ASSESSING THE VALUE OF IT

The best measurement to use when assessing the value of information technology is the one that is correctly scaled to the size of the project.

- *Net present value (NPV)* and *internal rate of return (IRR)* are primarily used for large projects where the time value of money is a big factor, or where the corporation requires projects to exceed its forecasted expectations.

- *Return on investment (ROI)* is most valuable when used to decide between different projects or competing priorities.

- *Payback period (PB)* is typically applied to projects of short duration.

- *Total cost of ownership (TCO)* is used on projects of varying sizes because it provides a framework for good financial analysis of IT investments.

Customer Metrics

Stock market analysts tend to have a bias toward financial metrics. Clearly this emphasis is important—however, focusing only on financial measurements is limiting since financial metrics are only one factor that an organization can use to rate and rank competitive IT projects. **Customer metrics** assess the management of customer relationships by the organization. These metrics typically focus on a set of core measurements including market share, customer acquisition, customer satisfaction, and customer profitability.

Traffic on the Internet retail site for Wal-Mart has grown 66 percent in the last year. The site has over 500,000 visitors daily, 2 million Web pages downloaded daily, 6.5 million visitors per week, and over 60,000 users logged on simultaneously. Wal-Mart's primary concern is maintaining optimal performance for online transactions. A disruption to the Web site directly affects the company's bottom line and customer loyalty. The company monitors and tracks the hardware, software, and network running the company's Web site to ensure high quality of service, which saved the company $1.1 million dollars last year.[3]

Customers are primarily concerned with the quality of service they receive from an organization. Anyone using the Internet knows that it is far from perfect and often slow. One of the biggest problems facing Internet users is congestion caused by capacity too small to handle large amounts of traffic. Corporations are continually benchmarking and monitoring their systems in order to ensure high quality of service. The most common quality of service metrics that are benchmarked and monitored include throughput, speed, and availability.

- **Throughput** equals the amount of information that can travel through the system at any point in time.

- **Speed** establishes the amount of time allowed for the system to perform a transaction.

- **Availability** denotes the number of hours that the system must be available for use by customers and employees. In today's electronic world, many systems need to be available $24 \times 7 \times 365$ in order to meet global customer and employee needs.

A company must continually monitor these behaviors to determine if the system is operating above or below expectations. If the system begins to operate below expectations, system administrators must take immediate action to bring the system back to acceptable operating levels. For example, if a company suddenly began taking two minutes to deliver a Web page to a customer, the company would need to fix this problem as soon as possible to keep from losing customers and ultimately revenue.

WEB TRAFFIC ANALYSIS

Most companies measure the traffic on a Web site as the primary determinant of the Web site's success. However, a lot of Web site traffic does not necessarily indicate large sales. Many organizations with lots of Web site traffic have minimal sales. A company can go further and use Web traffic analysis to determine the revenue generated by Web traffic, the number of new customers acquired by Web traffic, any reductions in customer service calls resulting from Web traffic, and so on. The Yankee Group reports that 66 percent of companies determine Web site success solely by measuring the amount of traffic. New customer acquisition ranked second on the list at 34 percent, and revenue generation ranked third at 23 percent.[4]

Analyzing Web site traffic is one way organizations can understand the effectiveness of Web advertising. A *cookie* is a small file deposited on a hard drive by a Web site containing information about customers and their Web activities. Cookies allow Web sites to record the comings and goings of customers, usually without their knowledge or consent. A *click-through* is a count of the number of people who visit one site and click on an advertisement that takes them to the site of the advertiser. A *banner ad* is a small ad on one Web site that advertises the products and services of another business, usually another dot-com business. Advertisers can track how often customers click on banner ads resulting in a click-through to their Web site. Often the cost of the banner ad depends on the number of customers who click on the banner ad. Tracking the number of banner ad clicks is a great way to begin to understand the effectiveness of the ad on its target audience.

Tracking effectiveness based on click-throughs guarantees exposure to target ads; however, it does not guarantee that the visitor liked the ad, spent any substantial time viewing the ad, or was satisfied with the information contained in the ad. In order to help understand advertising effectiveness, interactivity measures are tracked and monitored. *Interactivity* measures the visitor interactions with the target ad. Such interaction measures include the duration of time the visitor spends viewing the ad, the number of pages viewed, and even the number of repeat visits to the target ad. Interactivity measures are a giant step forward for advertisers, since traditional methods of advertising through newspapers, magazines, outdoor such as billboards and buses, and radio and television provide no way to track effectiveness metrics. Interactivity metrics measure actual consumer activities, something that was impossible to do in the past and provides advertisers with very useful information.

The ultimate outcome of any advertisement is a purchase. Knowing how many visitors make purchases on a Web site and the dollar amount of the purchases creates critical business information. It is easy to communicate the business value of a Web site or Web application when an organization can tie revenue amounts and new customer creation numbers directly back to the Web site, banner ad, or Web application.

Behavioral Metrics

Firms can observe through click-stream data the exact pattern of a consumer's navigation through a site. *Click-stream data* is a virtual trail that a Web user leaves behind while using the Internet. Click-stream data can reveal a number of basic data points on how consumers interact with Web sites. Metrics based on click-stream data include:

- The number of page-views (i.e., the number of times a particular page has been presented to a visitor)
- The pattern of Web sites visited, including most frequent exit page and most frequent prior Web sites
- Length of stay on the Web site
- Dates and times of visits
- Number of registrations filled out per 100 visitors

- Number of abandoned registrations
- Demographics of registered visitors
- Number of customers with shopping carts
- Number of abandoned shopping carts

Figure T7.4 provides definitions of common metrics based on click-stream data. To interpret such data properly, managers try to benchmark against other companies. For instance, consumers seem to visit their preferred Web sites regularly, even checking back to the Web site multiple times during a given session. Consumers tend to become loyal to a small number of Web sites, and they typically revisit those Web sites a number of times during a particular session.

FIGURE T7.4

Web Site Metrics

Visitor	Visitor Metrics
Unidentified visitor	A visitor is an individual who visits a Web site. An "unidentified visitor" means that no information about that visitor is available.
Unique visitor	A unique visitor is one who can be recognized and counted only once within a given period of time. An accurate count of unique visitors is not possible without some form of identification, registration, or authentication.
Session visitor	A session ID is available (e.g., cookie) or inferred by incoming address plus browser type, which allows a visitor's responses to be tracked within a given visit to a Web site.
Tracked visitor	An ID (e.g., cookie) is available which allows a user to be tracked across multiple visits to a Web site. No information, other than a unique identifier, is available for a tracked visitor.
Identified visitor	An ID is available (e.g., cookie or voluntary registration), which allows a user to be tracked across multiple visits to a Web site. Other information (name, demographics, possibly supplied voluntarily by the visitor) can be linked to this ID.
Exposure	**Exposure Metrics**
Page exposures (page-views)	The number of times a particular Web page has been viewed by visitors in a given time period, without regard to duplication.
Site exposures	The number of visitor sessions at a Web site in a given time period, without regard to visitor duplication.
Visit	**Visit Metrics**
Stickiness (visit duration time)	The length of time a visitor spends on a Web site. Can be reported as an average in a given time period, without regard to visitor duplication.
Raw visit depth (total Web pages exposure per session)	The total number of pages a visitor is exposed to during a single visit to a Web site. Can be reported as an average or distribution in a given time period, without regard to visitor duplication.
Visit depth (total unique Web pages exposure per session)	The total number of unique pages a visitor is exposed to during a single visit to a Web site. Can be reported as an average or distribution in a given time period, without regard to visitor duplication.
Hit	**Hit Metrics**
Hits	When visitors reach a Web site, their computer sends a request to the site's computer server to begin displaying pages. Each element of a requested page (including graphics, text, interactive items) is recorded by the Web site's server log file as a "hit."
Qualified hits	Exclude less important information recorded in a log file (such as error messages, etc.).

Comparative Metrics

Comparative metrics assess how the organization is performing compared to other organizations, industries, and markets. One of the best ways to demonstrate business value is by tracking costs and contributions over time. An organization can develop cost breakdowns and compare them to industry standards to help determine if its information technology costs are in line with other industries.

IT SPENDING BY ACTIVITY AND RESOURCE

Reviewing organizational IT spending by activity and resource allows management to easily compare spending among departments and even compare other organizations' spending against its own. Understanding if an organization's IT spending is in line with other similar organizations can provide a great amount of comfort to skeptical business managers. Knowing IT spending by activity and resource metrics is particularly helpful when managers are preparing budgets for the following year. Figure T7.5 displays the average IT costs by activity and resource for several industries provided by the Gartner Group.[5]

IT SPENDING AS A PERCENTAGE OF REVENUE

Industries have various technology needs and therefore spend differing amounts of money on technology. The total level of IT spending, measured as a percentage of the revenue of the organization, is one indicator that the company is or is not spending the right amount on information technology. Figure T7.6 shows an example of IT

IT Spending by Activity (%)	1999	2000	2001	2002	2003
Development/major enhancements	9	15	16	19	18
Maintenance/minor enhancements	16	20	19	23	25
Production/operations	47	44	43	29	26
End user computing/help desk	10	11	11	18	21
Planning, administration, other	18	10	11	11	10
	100	100	1000	100	100

IT Spending by Resource (%)	1999	2000	2001	2002	2003
Hardware	29	26	26	22	18
Software	8	8	8	13	13
Personnel	40	36	37	35	37
Outside services	12	19	18	16	11
Datacom and other	11	11	11	14	20
	100	100	1000	100	100

FIGURE T7.5

IT Cost by Activity and by Resource

Industry Group	IT Spending as % of Revenue				
	1999	2000	2001	2002	2003
Communications (Telcos)	4.7	5.8	4.1	6.7	13.9
Electric/water/gas/sanitary services	1.6	1.6	1.8	2.8	3.4
Finance, insurance, banking	3.6	2.6	2.5	6.5	8.6
Hospitals and health care	2.3	2.5	2.3	3.9	5.3
Manufacturing	1.9	2.0	1.8	1.8	3.0
All industries	3.0	2.5	2.6	4.1	5.5

FIGURE T7.6

IT Spending as a Percentage of Revenue

spending-to-revenue data provided by the Gartner Group. The percentage of revenue spent on IT can help an organization's managers understand their company's spending in comparison to industry averages.

If a company is underspending on technology relative to its industry peers, it may be missing a competitive advantage that its competition is enjoying. For example, a business might be growing at a fast pace, but outgrowing its technology capability, which will leave the company exposed to its competition. If a company is overspending on technology relative to its industry peers, it may be hurting its cost structure only to realize a diminishing marginal benefit. For example, the company might benefit from spending the money on advertising or manufacturing instead of IT.

IT BUDGET ALLOCATED PER EMPLOYEE

Dividing the IT budget by the number of employees generates the IT budget allocated per employee. If the business is currently satisfied with the quality of service from the IT department then it can determine the amount per employee that the business is paying for this service. For example, if the annual IT budget is $300 million and the company has 25,000 employees, the IT budget per employee is $12,000. If a department hires additional human resources, the IT budget will need to increase accordingly in order to deliver the same quality of service. This allows managers to make educated decisions about the dollars they spend for the services they obtain.

THE VALUE OF THE HELP DESK

One of the easiest measurements of an IT organization's effectiveness is measuring the value of the help desk. Since most help desks track detailed trouble tickets, it is easy to apply metrics to determine the value provided by the help desk. Each trouble ticket typically tracks the department origin, time to complete, and IT employee assigned. Figure T7.7 displays the calculations of the percentage of tickets per department, times the total salary for all help-desk employees, which generates the value of the help desk in resolving problems.

FIGURE T7.7

Valuing the Help Desk

	Department			
	Accounting/ Finance	Sales/ Marketing	Operations/ Manufacturing	Human Resources
Percent of trouble tickets	15%	45%	30%	10%
Number of trouble tickets generated annually per department (5 million total)	750,000	2,250,000	1,500,000	500,000
Help desk costs allocated per department ($8 million total)	$1,200,000	$3,600,000	$2,400,000	$800,000
Annual cost per trouble ticket = $1.60				

E volving technologies are continually changing the speed and form of business in almost every industry. Organizations spend enormous sums of money on IT in order to remain competitive. Many organizations spend up to 50 percent of their total capital expenditure on IT. More than ever, there is a need to understand the payoff of these large IT investments, the impact on business performance, and the overall business value gained with the use of technology. The financial, customer, and comparative metrics discussed in this plug-in help organizations make wise decisions regarding IT investments that will maximize the value to the enterprise.

KEY TERMS

Banner ad, 493
Capital budgeting, 488
Capital expenditure, 488
Capital rationing, 488
Click-stream data, 493
Click-through, 493
Comparative metric, 495
Contingent project, 488
Cookie, 493

Customer metric, 492
Effectiveness IT metric, 486
Efficiency IT metric, 486
Financial metrics, 487
Hurdle rate, 490
Independent project, 488
Interactivity, 493
Internal rate of return (IRR), 489
Mutually exclusive project, 488

Net present value (NPV), 488
Payback period (PB), 491
Present value, 488
Return on investment (ROI), 490
Strategic resource, 486
Throughput, 492
Total cost of ownership
   (TCO), 491

MAKING BUSINESS DECISIONS

1. **Assessing the Business Value of Information Technology**

   Pizza Planet is a large pizza chain that operates 700 franchises in 15 states. The company is currently contemplating implementing a new ERP system from PeopleSoft, which is expected to cost $7 million and take 18 months to implement. Once the system is completed, it is expected to generate $12 million a year in decreased costs and increased revenues. You are working in the finance department for the company and your boss has asked you to compile a report detailing the different financial metrics you can use to assess the business value of the new ERP system. Once your report is completed, the company will make a decision about purchasing the ERP system.

2. **Comparing Financial Metrics**

   Nick Zele is the new managing operations director for a large publishing company, Covers Inc. Nick is your manager and he wants you to help him prioritize the six ongoing company projects. Nick has asked you to review the following and compile a report detailing prioritization for the projects.

Year	ROI	IRR	NPV
Project 1	22%	30%	$350,000
Project 2	45	23	100,000
Project 3	14	8	500,000
Project 4	38	40	400,000
Project 5	12	12	50,000
Project 6	20	10	500,000

3. Analyzing Web Sites

Stars Inc. is a large clothing corporation that specializes in reselling clothes worn by celebrities. The company's four different Web sites generate 75 percent of its sales. The remaining 25 percent of sales occur directly through the company's warehouse. You have recently been hired as the director of Sales. The only information you can find on the success of the four Web sites follows:

Web Site	Classic	Contemporary	New Age	Traditional
Traffic analysis	5,000 hits/day	200 hits/day	10,000 hits/day	1,000 hits/day
Stickiness (average)	20 min.	1 hr.	20 min.	50 min.
Number of abandoned shopping carts	400/day	0/day	5,000/day	200/day
Number of unique visitors	2,000/day	100/day	8,000/day	200/day
Number of identified visitors	3,000/day	100/day	2,000/day	800/day
Average revenue per sale	$1,000	$1,000	$50	$1,300

You decide that maintaining four separate Web sites is expensive and adds little business value. You want to propose consolidating to one Web site. Create a report detailing the business value gained by consolidating to a single Web site, along with your recommendation for consolidation. Be sure to include your Web site profitability analysis.

4. Comparing Organizations

Joan Martin works for the government helping small businesses operate and compete. Joan realizes that technology can be very expensive for organizations. Joan wants to produce a document discussing how a small business can decide how much to spend on technology, along with how to allocate the spending. Help Joan prepare a report that determines the different types of comparative metrics a small business can use to help it understand its information technology investments.

Project 1:
The Importance of Information Technology

Managers need to be involved in information technology—any computer-based tool that people use to work with information and support the information and information-processing needs of an organization—for the following (primary) reasons:

- The sheer magnitude of the dollars spent on IT must be managed to ensure business value.

- Research has consistently shown that when managers are involved in information technology, it enables a number of business initiatives, such as gaining a competitive advantage, streamlining business processes, and even transforming entire organizations.

- Research has consistently shown that when managers are not involved in IT, systems fail, revenue is lost, and even entire companies can fail all as a result of poorly managed IT.[1]

Project Focus:

One of the biggest challenges your organization will face is, "How do we get general business managers involved in IT?" Research has shown that involvement is highly correlated with personal experience with IT and IT education, including university classes and IT executive seminars. Once general business managers understand IT through experience and education, they are more likely to be involved in IT, and more likely to lead their organizations in achieving business success through IT.

1. Search the Internet to find examples of the types of technologies that are currently used in the field or industry that you plan to pursue. For example, if you are planning on a career in accounting or finance you should become familiar with financial systems such as Oracle Financials and PeopleSoft. If you are planning a career in logistics or distribution then you should research supply chain management systems or if you are planning a career in marketing then you should research customer relationship management systems.

2. Create a simple report of your findings; include a brief overview of the type of technologies you found.

3. IT is described as an enabler/facilitator of competitive advantage, organizational effectiveness, and organizational efficiency. As a competitive tool, IT can differentiate a company's products, services, and prices from its competitors by improving product quality, shortening product development or delivery time, creating new IT-based products and services, and improving customer service before, during, and after a transaction. Search the Internet and find several examples of companies in the industry where you plan to work that have achieved a competitive advantage through IT.

4. Create a simple report of your findings; include a brief description of the companies and how they are using IT to achieve a competitive advantage.

File: None

Project 2:
Strategic and Competitive Advantage

Pony Espresso is a small business that sells specialty coffee drinks at office buildings. Each morning and afternoon, trucks arrive at offices' front entrances, and the office employees purchase various beverages such as Java du Jour and Café de Colombia. The business is profitable. But Pony Espresso offices are located to the north of town, where lease rates are less expensive, and the principal sales area is south of town. This means that the trucks must drive cross-town four times each day.

The cost of transportation to and from the sales area, plus the power demands of the truck's coffee brewing equipment, is a significant portion of variable costs. Pony Espresso could reduce the amount of driving and, therefore, the variable costs, if it moved the offices closer to the sales area.

Pony Espresso presently has fixed costs of $10,000 per month. The lease of a new office, closer to the sales area, would cost an additional $2,200 per month. This would increase the fixed costs to $12,200 per month.

Although the lease of new offices would increase the fixed costs, a careful estimate of the potential savings in gasoline and vehicle maintenance indicates that Pony Espresso could reduce the variable costs from $0.60 per unit to $0.35 per unit. Total sales are unlikely to increase as a result of the move, but the savings in variable costs should increase the annual profit.

You have been hired by Pony Espresso to assist in the cost analysis and new lease options to determine a growth in profit margin. You will need to calculate a degree of operating leverage (DOL) to better understand the company's profitability. Degree of operating leverage will give the owner of Pony Espresso a great deal of information for setting operating targets and planning profitability.

Project Focus:

Consider the information provided to you from the owner, PonyEspresso.xls. Especially look at the change in the variability of the profit from month to month. From November through January, when it is much more difficult to lure office workers out into the cold to purchase coffee, Pony Espresso barely breaks even. In fact, in December of 2004, the business lost money.

1. Develop the cost analysis on the existing lease information using the monthly sales figures provided to you in the file PonyEspresso.xls.
2. Develop the cost analysis from the new lease information provided above.
3. Calculate the variability that is reflected in the month-to-month standard deviation of earnings for the current cost structure and the projected cost structure.
4. Do not consider any association with downsizing such as overhead—simply focus on the information provided to you.
5. You will need to calculate the EBIT—earnings before interest and taxes.
6. Would the DOL and business risk increase or decrease if Pony Espresso moved its office? **Note:** Variability in profit levels, whether measured as EBIT, operating income, or net income, does not necessarily increase the level of business risk as the DOL increases.

File: PonyEspresso.xls

Project 3:
Assessing the Value of Information

In 2004, a national study announced that Boulder, Colorado, was one of the healthiest places to live in the United States. Since then housing development projects have been springing up all around Boulder. Six housing development projects are currently dominating the Boulder market—Crested Butte, Pinon Pointe, Wildcat Canyon, Pawnee Springs, Summer Hawk, and Bolder Boulder. These six projects each started with 100 homes, have sold all of them, and are currently developing phase 2.

Column	Name	Description
A	LOT #	The number assigned to a specific home within each project.
B	PROJECT #	A unique number assigned to each of the six housing development projects (see Figure AYK.2).
C	ASK PRICE	The initial asking price for the home.
D	SELL PRICE	The actual price for which the home was sold.
E	LIST DATE	The date the home was listed for sale.
F	SALE DATE	The date on which the final contract closed and the home was sold.
G	SQ. FT.	The total square footage for the home.
H	# BATH	The number of bathrooms in the home.
I	# BDRMS	The number of bedrooms in the home.

As one of the three partners and real estate agents of H.O.M.E.S Real Estate, it is your responsibility to analyze the information concerning the past 600 home sales and choose which development project to focus on for selling homes in phase 2. You and your partners have decided that the firm should focus on selling homes in only one of the development projects.

From the Colorado Real Estate Association you have obtained a spreadsheet file, RealEstate.xls, which contains information concerning each of the sales for the first 600 homes. Figure AYK.1 displays the information description.

Figure AYK.2 exhibits the project numbers and project names that have been assigned to each of the housing development projects.

It is your responsibility to analyze the sales list and prepare a report that details which housing development project your real estate firm should focus on. Your analysis should be from as many angles as possible.

Project Focus:

1. You do not know how much each development project cost, but you do have data supporting the sale of each house. Therefore, you cannot consider the amount of profit in your decision.
2. Phase 2 for each housing development project will develop homes similar in style, price, and square footage to their respective first phases.
3. As you consider the information provided to you, think in terms of what information is important and what information is not important. Be prepared to justify how you went about your analysis.
4. Upon completing your analysis, please provide concise, yet detailed and thorough documentation (in narrative, numeric, and graphic forms) that justifies your decision.

File: RealEstate.xls

Project Number	Project Name
10	Crested Butte
20	Pinon Pointe
30	Wildcat Canyon
40	Pawnee Springs
50	Summer Hawk
60	Bolder Boulder

Project 4:
Network Security

Empty cans of Pringles could be helping malicious hackers spot wireless networks that are open to attack. Security companies have demonstrated that a directional antenna made with a Pringles container can significantly improve the chances of finding the wireless computer networks being used. An informal survey carried out by i-sec (an Internet security research company) using the homemade antenna has found that over two-thirds of the networks surveyed were doing nothing to protect themselves. Known as the "PringlesCantenna," these networks are rapidly becoming popular because they are cheap (under $10) and easy to set up.

Not surprisingly, wireless network security, particularly regarding wireless local area networks (WLANs), is the number one concern of network managers, and, as such, an entire industry has grown to serve the ever-changing demands of wireless network–based information integrity. As enterprises have gradually adopted wireless technology, it was assumed that special security precautions would be required to deal with the unique nature of wireless communications. After all, wireless purposely puts valuable enterprise information out on the airwaves, and anyone within range and equipped with an appropriate receiver (e.g., Pringles-Cantenna) would be able to grab this data and put it to all kinds of questionable use. Since this is the case, many wireless networks implement inherent authentication and encryption mechanisms to provide basic assurance to customers that their data will at least be difficult to decrypt and their networks at least challenging to crack.

Project Focus:

1. Create a report based on a thorough Internet search that discusses the tips, techniques, and best practices to protect against this type of amateur hacking. Include a summary of the types of detection and prevention technologies available, specifically the use of firewalls and intrusion detection software.

2. In your report, include the current statistics on identity theft, the number of times networks are hacked, and the total annual cost of online security breaches to corporations. You might also consider finding statistics on the percentage of companies that have yet to implement adequate security measures and the percentage of companies that spend 5 percent or less of their IT budget on network security.

File: None

Project 5:
Qualitative Analysis

One of the main products of the Fairway Woods Company is custom-made golf clubs. The clubs are manufactured at three plants (Denver, Colorado; Phoenix, Arizona; and Dallas, Texas) and are then shipped by truck to five distribution warehouses in Sacramento, California; Salt Lake City, Utah; Chicago, Illinois; Albuquerque, New Mexico; and New York City, New York. Since shipping costs are a major expense, management has begun an analysis to determine ways to reduce them. For the upcoming golf season, an estimate has been made of what the output will be from each manufacturing plant and how much each warehouse will require to satisfy its customers. The CIO from Fairway Woods Company has created a spreadsheet for you, Fairways.xls, of the shipping costs from each manufacturing plant to each warehouse as a baseline analysis.

Some business rules and requirements you should be aware of:

■ The problem presented involves the shipment of goods from three plants to five regional warehouses.

■ Goods can be shipped from any plant to any warehouse, but it costs more to ship goods over long distances than over short distances.

Project Focus:

1. Your goal is to minimize the costs of shipping goods from production plants to warehouses thereby meeting the demand from each metropolitan area while not exceeding the supply available from each plant. To complete this project it is recommended that you use the Solver function in Excel to assist with the analysis.

2. Specifically you want to focus on:

   a. Minimize the total shipping costs.

   b. Total shipped must be less than or equal to supply at a plant.

   c. Total shipped to warehouses must be greater than or equal to the warehouse demand.

   d. Number to ship must be greater than or equal to 0.

File: Fairways.xls

Project 6:
Small Business Analysis

Schweitzer Distribution specializes in distributing fresh produce to local restaurants in the Chicago area. The company currently sells 12 different products through the efforts of three sales representatives to 10 restaurants. The company, like all small businesses, is always interested in finding ways to increase revenues and decrease expenses.

The company's founder, Bob Schweitzer, has recently hired you as a new business analyst. You have just graduated from college with a degree in Marketing and a specialization in Customer Relationship Management. Bob is anxious to hear your thoughts and ideas on how to improve the business and help the company build strong lasting relationships with its customers.

Project Focus:

1. Bob has provided you with last year's sales information in the file RestaurantSales.xls. Perform a detailed analysis on the current operations to determine your suggestions for improvements.

2. Some example analysis questions might include:

   Who are your best customers?

   Who are your worst customers?

   Which sales representative was the most productive?

   Which sales representative was the most productive by customer?

   What are your best-selling products?

   Which products would you eliminate if you had to get rid of your two worst products?

   Which customers would you eliminate if you wanted to get rid of your two worst customers?

   If you had to fire one sales representative who would it be?

   What are the best-selling products for your best customer per month?

File: RestaurantSales.xls

Project 7:
Mining Information

Employee turnover rates are at an all-time high at Global Manufacturing Inc. The company is currently experiencing severe worker retention issues, which are leading to productivity and quality control problems. The majority of the company's workers perform a variety of tasks and are paid by the hour. The company currently tests each potential applicant to ensure they have the skills necessary for the intense mental concentration and dexterity required to fill the

Variable	Definition
Gender	0 = Female; 1 = Male
Education	Years of education
MSASTAT	Metropolitan statistical area
Wage	Wage per hour
Output	Output per hour (in units)
Dexterity Score	High score on dexterity equals greater dexterity
Quit Rate	Quit within first 6 months
	0 = no, 1 = yes
Hire Method	1 = unsolicited, 2 = Employee recommendation, 3 = Response to advertisement
Tenure	Tenure in days

positions. Since there are significant costs associated with employee turnover, Global Manufacturing wants to find a way to predict which applicants have the characteristics of being a short-term versus a long-term employee.

Project Focus:

1. Review the information that Global Manufacturing has collected from two of its different data sources. The first file, GlobalWageData.xls, contains information regarding employee wages. The second file, GlobalRetentionData.xls, contains information regarding employee retention. Figure AYK.3 outlines the definitions of the categories found in each file.

2. Using Excel analysis functions, determine the employee characteristics that you would recommend Global Manufacturing look for when hiring new personnel. It is highly recommended that you use PivotTables as part of your analysis.

3. Prepare a report based on your findings (which should include several forms of graphical representation) for your recommendations.

Files: GlobalWageData.xls, GlobalRetentionData.xls

Project 8:
Data Warehouse and CRM Challenge

Martin Resorts, Inc., owns and operates four Spa and Golf resorts in Colorado. The company has five traditional lines of business: (1) golf sales; (2) golf lessons; (3) restaurants; (4) retail and rentals; and (5) hotels. David Logan, director of Marketing Technology at Martin Resorts, Inc., and Donald Mayer, the lead strategic analyst for Martin Resorts are soliciting your input for their CRM strategic initiative.

Martin Resorts IT infrastructure is pieced together with various systems and applications. Currently, the company has a difficult time with CRM because its systems are not integrated. The company cannot determine vital information such as which customers are golfing and staying at the hotel or which customers are staying at the hotel and not golfing.

For example, the three details that the customer Diego Titus (1) stayed four nights at a Martin Resorts' managed hotel, (2) golfed three days, and (3) took an all-day spa treatment the first day, are discrete facts housed in separate systems. Martin Resorts hopes that by using data warehousing technology to integrate its data, the next time Diego reserves lodging for another trip, sales associates may ask him if he would like to book a spa treatment as well, and even if he would like the same masseuse that he had on his prior trip.

Martin Resorts is excited about the possibility of taking advantage of customer segmentation and CRM strategies to help increase its business.

Project Focus:

The company wants to use CRM and data warehouse technologies to improve service and personalization at each customer touchpoint. Using a data warehousing tool, important customer information can be accessed from all of its systems either daily, weekly, monthly, or once or twice per year. Analyze the sample data in Martin.xls for the following:

1. Currently, the quality of the data within the above disparate systems is low. Develop a report for David and Donald discussing the importance of high-quality information and how low-quality information can affect Martin Resorts' business.

2. Review the data that David and Donald are working with from the data warehouse in the file Martin.xls and Key.doc.

    a. Give examples from the data showing the kind of information Martin Resorts might be able to use to gain a better understanding of its customers. Include the types of data quality issues the company can anticipate and the strategies it can use to help avoid such issues.

    b. Determine who are Martin Resorts' best customers and provide examples of the types of marketing campaigns the company should offer these valuable customers.

    c. Prepare a report that summarizes the benefits Martin Resorts can receive from using business intelligence to mine the data warehouse. Include a financial analysis of the costs and benefits.

Files: Martin.xls, Key.doc

Project 9:
Analyzing a Supply Chain

Hoover Transportation, Inc., is a large distribution company located in Denver, Colorado. The company is currently looking to gain some operational efficiencies in its supply chain by reducing the number of transportation carriers that it is currently using to outsource. Operational efficiencies for Hoover Transportation, Inc., suggest that reducing the number of carriers from the Denver distribution center to warehouses in the selected states will lead to reduced costs. Brian Hoover, the CEO of Hoover Transportation, requests that the number of carriers transporting products from its Denver distribution center to wholesalers in the states of AZ, AR, IA, MO, MT, OK, OR, and WA be reduced from the current five carriers to one or two carriers.

Project Focus:

Carrier selection should be based on the assumptions that all environmental factors are equal and historical cost trends will continue. Review the historical raw data from the past several years to determine your recommendation for the top two carriers that Hoover Transportation should continue to use.

1. Analyze the last 24 months of Hoover's Transportation carrier transactions found in HooverTransportation.xls.

2. Create a report detailing your recommendation for the top two carriers with which Hoover Transportation should continue to do business. Be sure to use PivotTables and PivotCharts in your report. A few questions to get you started include:

    a. Calculate the average cost per carrier.

    b. Calculate the total shipping costs per state.

    c. Calculate the total shipping weights per state.

    d. Calculate the average shipping costs per lb.

    e. Calculate the average cost per carrier.

File: HooverTransportation.xls

Project 10:
Outsourcing Information Technology

Founded in 2000, Innovative Software provides advanced search software, Web site accessibility testing/repair software, and usability testing/repair software. All serve as part of its desktop and enterprise content management solutions for government, corporate, educational, and consumer markets. The company's solutions are used by Web site publishers, digital media publishers, content managers, document managers, business users, consumers, software companies, and consulting services companies. Innovative Software solutions help organizations develop long-term strategies to achieve Web content accessibility, enhance usability, and comply with U.S. and search standards.

In its five-year history, Innovative Software has continually focused on providing outstanding customer service. With the informal motto of "Grow big, but stay small," the company takes pride in achieving 100 percent customer care callback. Its personal service has been an integral part of its outstanding customer service. However, the success of its "grow big" philosophy has presented new challenges.

Innovative Software has experienced rapid growth to six times its original customer-base size and is forced to deal with difficult questions for the first time, such as, "Can we serve this many customers?" "How do we ensure our commitment to personal service is not compromised as we grow?" In addition, the number of phone calls from customers having problems with one of the newer applications is on the rise.

As customer service manager for Innovative Software, your goal is to maintain the company's reputation for excellent customer service. You have been considering the option of outsourcing as a means of keeping up with the expanding call volume and are currently reviewing e-Bank, a company that has had great success with outsourcing. e-BANK outsourced its customer service to handle its large number of customers who interact with the company through several customer interaction channels. e-BANK felt that its competencies were primarily in finance, rather than in customer service, and that it could greatly benefit from the expertise of a customer service–focused provider. e-BANK discovered that it was cost effective to outsource its customer service center. Additionally, the outsourcing approach was relatively hassle-free, since e-BANK did not have to set up its own customer contact center (i.e., call center).

Project Focus:

1. Create an analysis from the data provided in Forecast.xls, which includes:
   a. DATE—the actual date of the phone calls made to customer service about the search software
   b. SALES VOLUME—the number of search software units sold that day
   c. NUMBER OF CALLS—the number of calls received in customer service for the search software

2. Here are several business assumptions to assist in this analysis:
   - Innovative Software's customer service department is already near its call volume capacity. Any significant increase in calls would result in a decline in the company's 100 percent callback record.
   - You need to consider what approach would be more cost effective—adding customer service representatives or outsourcing—if your forecast predicts sudden growth in call volume. All else being equal, it would cost 30 percent less to increase call volume capacity by 50 percent if you outsourced.
   - The price of the products, the actual product type, and any warrantee information is irrelevant.

- Develop a growth, trend, and forecast analysis. You should use a three-day moving average: a shorter moving average might not display the trend well and a much longer moving average would shorten the trend too much. Hint: A three-day moving average is done by taking the Actual Calls and dividing that by the Forecast Calls over a three-day period. As an example, on the 4th day you would calculate the average for the Actual Calls for days 1, 2, and 3.

- You can create an effective forecast as long as you have a reasonable baseline to create a forecast. A baseline is a set of numeric observations made over time that is ordered from the earliest observation to the most recent. All the time periods in the baseline are of equal length.

- You will want to use the TREND worksheet function in Excel to create a regression forecast. The regression approach to forecasting will help you to make projections into the future. The TREND function creates forecasts based on a linear relationship between the times that the observation was made. However, you will have to create a GROWTH pattern to determine the nonlinear forecasts if the line has a dramatic upward or downward curve to it.

3. Upon completing your analysis, provide detailed and thorough documentation (in narrative, numeric, and graphic forms) that justifies your outsourcing recommendations.

File: Forecast.xls

PROJECT 11:
E-Business

e-Grocery.com, based in Longmont, Colorado, is using the Internet for food retailing services. Founded in 2004, e-Grocery.com is a member of an online grocery/drugstore shopping and delivery service that already has thousands of customers in the Phoenix, Seattle, and Denver areas.

Established on the idea that people will buy groceries over the Internet, e-Grocery.com has an online database of over 25,000 grocery and drugstore items, and allows comparison shopping based on price, nutritional content, fat, and calories. e-Grocery.com membership offers users additional benefits such as electronic coupons, retailer preferred customer discounts, recipes, and tips.

Eighty-five to 90 percent of e-Grocery.com's orders come in via computer; the rest are faxed or phoned. e-Grocery.com orders are taken centrally and then e-mailed to its local partners. The store receives the order, the delivery address, and driving instructions. Each order is filled by an e-Grocery.com employee who shops the aisles of the store. The employee pays for the groceries at special e-Grocery.com counters in the back of the store. The order is then taken to a holding area in the supermarket, where the appropriate items are kept cold or frozen until the deliverer picks up the orders for delivery. e-Grocery.com members are charged actual shelf prices, plus a per-order charge of $5.00 or 5 percent of the order amount, whichever is greater.

Project Focus:

1. e-Grocery.com is using interactive technology to change the shopping experience. The success of e-Grocery.com lies within many areas. Analyze the e-Grocery.com business model using the questions below. Feel free to think "outside the box" to develop your own analysis of online grocery shopping and e-business models.

- What is e-Grocery.com's e-business model?
- How does e-Grocery.com compete with traditional retailers?
- What value can e-Grocery.com offer as a true competitive advantage in this marketplace?
- What is the threat of new entrants in this market segment?

- How is e-Grocery.com using technology to change the shopping experience?
- What are the logistics for making e-Grocery.com profitable?
- How does e-Grocery.com profit from online customer interaction?

File: None

Project 12:
Emerging Trends and Technology

"Intelligent wireless hand-held devices are going to explode, absolutely explode over the next several years."

—Steve Ballmer, CEO, Microsoft

Wireless, mobility, pervasive computing, the anytime network—whatever name you choose—it is here. The price of easy-to-handle devices which provide access to a variety of applications and information is rapidly falling while the efficiencies of such devices are increasing. More and more, the business user is looking to use mobile devices to perform tasks that previously could only be handled by the desktop PC. End user adoption is skyrocketing. The next 18 months will demonstrate a true growing period for mobile computing as the world changes to one characterized by the mobile user.

As this market sector grows, software and information companies are beginning to evolve their products and services. Wireless mobility and associated functionality provide new market opportunities for both established companies and new entrants to increase efficiency and take advantage of new revenue possibilities. The services available to Internet-enabled wireless devices create a vast array of new business opportunities for companies as they develop products and services that utilize location, time, and immediate access to information in new and innovative ways.

Technologies that are currently being developed at this time include:

- Hard drives for wireless devices
- Global-roaming devices
- Mobile power supplies that run on next-generation fuel cells
- Biometrics

All four could bring about significant changes in wireless space.

Project Focus:

Using the list of wireless solution providers and manufacturers provided in the Wireless.htm file, develop a report that addresses the following issues:

1. Identify some of the key concerns organizations have when contemplating a wireless/mobile strategy. How does this differ from a traditional (LAN, WAN) network strategy?
2. How would an organization calculate its return on investment (ROI) or the total cost of ownership (TCO) for a wireless/mobile strategy?
3. What are some of the best practices an organization should use when implementing a wireless/mobile strategy.

File: Wireless.htm

PROJECT 13:
Open Source on a Large Scale

Initially, open source was used deep within IT departments. These expert groups have the technical prowess to manage and evaluate such technologies; they know where they should be widely deployed and where they should have limited use. Google is at one end of the open source use scale. To process more than 200 million Internet searches a day, Google claims to possess the world's largest open source Linux cluster, with over 10,000 servers. It stores more than 3 billion Web pages on its index and is currently the dominant Internet search provider. Because it executes only a single type of business function, it stripped all unneeded code out of Linux to maximize the performance and speed of its technology.

The use of open source is not limited to a few companies that want to be on the edge. Companies that are using open source, such as Linux, for commercial applications include Winnebago Industries, Merrill Lynch and Co., and L. L. Bean.

Project Focus:

1. The growing use and the continued expansion of open source technologies are changing the way traditional vendors provide value. Open source solutions have started to emerge on the desktop as well. Create an analysis of the following issues as they relate to open source technology. Provide detailed documentation (in narrative, numeric, and graphic forms) along with numerous business examples that are currently using open source technology. Specifically address:

   - Fundamental issues with open source software development
   - Legal risks
   - Licensing issues
   - Areas (departments, companies, industries, etc.) where open source makes most sense
   - An assessment of the competition (e.g., open source vs. Microsoft)
   - Security issues
   - The need for standards

File: None

Project 14:
Aligning IT with Business Goals

Most companies would like to be in the market-leading position of JetBlue, Harrah's, Dell, or Wal-Mart. The use of information technology has secured their respective spots in the marketplace. These companies have a relentless goal of keeping the cost of technology down by combining the best of IT and business leadership.

Nevertheless, it takes more than a simple handshake between groups to start on the journey toward financial gains   it requires operational discipline and a linkage between business and technology units. Only recently have companies not on the "path for profits" followed the lead of their more successful counterparts that require more operational discipline from their IT groups as well as more IT participation from their business units. Bridging this gap is one of the greatest breakthroughs a company can make.

Companies that master the art of finely tuned, cost-effective IT management will have a major advantage. Their success will force their competitors to also master the art or fail miserably. This phenomenon has already occurred in the retail and wholesale distribution markets, which have had to react to Wal-Mart's IT mastery, as one example. Other industries will follow. This trend will change not only the face of IT, but also the future of corporate America.

As world markets continue to grow, the potential gains are greater than ever. However, so are the potential losses. The future belongs to those who are perceptive enough to grasp the significance of IT and resourceful enough to synchronize business management and information technology.

Project Focus:

1. Use any resource to answer the question, "Why is business-IT alignment so difficult?" Use the following questions to begin your analysis:

   - How do companies prioritize the demands of various business units as they relate to IT?
   - What are some of the greatest IT challenges for the coming year?

- What drives IT decisions?
- Who or what is the moving force behind IT decisions?
- What types of efficiency metrics and effectiveness metrics might these companies use to measure the impact of IT?
- How are financial metrics used to monitor and measure IT investments? What are some of the issues with using financial metrics to evaluate IT.

File: None

Project 15:
Transforming Campaign Finance

When it comes to campaign finance, Americans want a system that minimizes the influence of "fat cats" and organized money, that keeps campaign spending at sensible levels, that fosters healthy electoral competition, that does not give advantage to wealthy candidates, and that does not require candidates to spend all of their waking hours raising money.

Indeed, the much maligned congressional campaign finance system we have now is itself a product of well-intended reform efforts, passed by Congress in 1974 to achieve these ideals. Moreover, dozens of new reform plans have emerged during the 1990s that also reach for these goals. Yet no reform scheme, however well intended, is likely to produce a perfect congressional campaign finance system.

The city of Highlands Ranch, Colorado, wishes to organize its campaign contributions records in a more organized and logical format. The city council is considering various executive information system packages that can show overall views of contribution information as well as give the ability to access more detailed information.

Figure AYK.4 displays a list of the information that will be the foundation for the reports in the proposed executive information system. To help you develop realistic reports, the city has provided you with a spreadsheet file, Contribute.xls, that contains specific contributions over the last six months.

Project Focus:

What the city council is most interested in is viewing several overall reports and then being able to request more detailed reports. As a consultant your goal is to develop different sets of reports that illustrate the concept of drilling down through information. For example, you should develop a report that shows overall campaign contributions by district (each of the eight different districts) and then develop more detailed reports that show contribution by political party and contribution by type.

1. The council would much rather see information graphically than numerically. As you develop your reports do so in terms of graphs that illustrate the desired relationships.

2. As you consider the information provided to you, think in terms of overall views first and then detailed views second. This will help you develop a logical series of reports.

FIGURE AYK.4

Contribute.xls Column Names and Descriptions

Column	Name	Description
A	DATE	The actual date that the contribution was made
B	CONTRIBUTOR	The name of the person or organization that made the contribution
C	DISTRICT	The district number that the councilperson belongs to
D	AMOUNT	The amount of the contribution
E	TYPE	The description type of where the contribution amount was given
F	COUNCILPERSON	The councilperson's name
G	PARTY	The councilperson's political party

3. If you wish, you can explore a variety of software tools to help you create the reports. Then prepare your presentation using a presentation graphics package, such as PowerPoint, that lets you create a dramatic presentation of your recommendations.

4. Your goal is not to create reports that point toward a particular problem or opportunity. Rather you are to design a series of logical reports that illustrate the concept of drilling down.

File: Contribute.xls

Project 16:
Relational Data Structure

Foothills Animal Hospital is a full-service small animal veterinary hospital located in Morrison, Colorado, specializing in routine medical care, vaccinations, laboratory testing, and surgery. The hospital has experienced tremendous growth over the past six months due to customer referrals. While Foothills Animal Hospital has typically kept its daily service records in a spreadsheet format, it feels the need to expand its reporting capabilities to develop a relational database as a more functional structure.

Foothills Animal Hospital needs help developing a database, specifically:

■ Create a customer table—name, address, phone, and date of entrance.

■ Create a pet table—pet name, type of animal, breed, gender, color, neutered/spayed, weight, and comments.

■ Create a medications table—medication code, name of medication, and cost of medication.

■ Create a visit table—details of treatments performed, medications dispensed, and the date of the visit.

■ Produce a daily invoice report.

Figure AYK.5 displays a sample daily invoice report that the Foothills Animal Hospital accountants have requested. Foothills Animal Hospital organizes its treatments using the codes displayed in Figure AYK.6.

The entity classes and primary keys for the database have been identified in Figure AYK.7. The following business rules have been identified:

1. A customer can have many pets but must have at least one.

2. A pet must be assigned to one and only one customer.

3. A pet can have one or more treatments per visit but must have at least one.

4. A pet can have one or more medications but need not have any.

Project Focus:

Your job is to complete the following tasks as they relate to this project:

1. Develop and describe the entity-relationship diagram.

2. Use normalization to assure the correctness of the tables (relations).

3. Create the database using a personal DBMS package (preferably Microsoft Access).

4. Use the data in Figure AYK.5 to populate your tables. Feel free to enter your own personal information.

5. Use the DBMS package to create the basic report in Figure AYK.5.

File: None

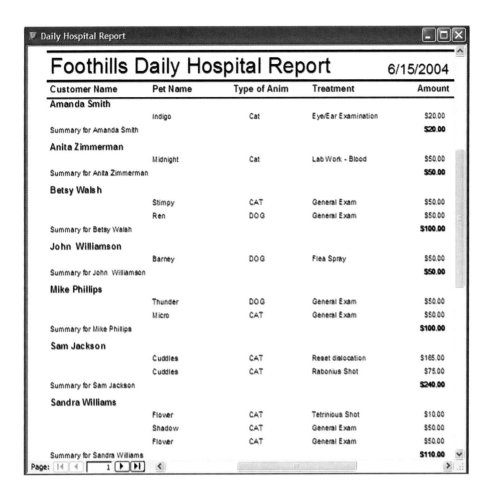

FIGURE AYK.5

Foothills Animal
Hospital Daily Invoice
Report Sample

Treatment Code	Treatment	Price
0100	Tetrinious Shot	$10.00
0201	Rabonius Shot	$20.00
0300	General Exam	$50.00
0303	Eye/Ear Examination	$20.00
0400	Spay/Neuter	$225.00
0405	Reset Dislocation	$165.00
0406	Amputation of Limb	$450.00
0407	Wrap Affected Area	$15.00
0408	Cast Affected Area	$120.00
1000	Lab Work—Blood	$50.00
1003	Lab Work—Misc	$35.00
2003	Flea Spray	$25.00
9999	Other Not Listed	$10.00

FIGURE AYK.6

Treatment Codes,
Treatments, and Price
Descriptions

Entity	Primary Key
CUSTOMER	Customer Number
PET	Pet Number
VISIT	Visit Number
VISIT DETAIL	Visit Number and Line Number (a composite key)
TREATMENT	Treatment Code
MEDICATION	Medication Code

FIGURE AYK.7

Entity Names and
Primary Keys for
Foothills Animal
Hospital

Project 17:
Building a Relational Database

On-The-Level Construction Company is a Denver-based construction company that specializes in subcontracting the development of single-family homes. In business since 1998, On-The-Level Construction has maintained a talented pool of certified staff and independent consultants providing the flexibility and combined experience required to meet the needs of its nearly 300 completed projects in the Denver metropolitan area. The field of operation methods that On-The-Level Construction is responsible for includes structural development, heating and cooling, plumbing, and electricity.

The company charges its clients by billing the hours spent on each contract. The hourly billing rate is dependent on the employee's position according to the field of operations (as noted above).

Figure AYK.8 shows a basic report that On-The-Level Construction foremen would like to see every week concerning what projects are being assigned, the overall assignment hours, and the charges for the assignment. On-The-Level Construction organizes its internal structure in four different operations—Structure (500), Plumbing (501), Electrical (502), and Heating and Ventilation (503). Each of these operational departments can and should have many subcontractors who specialize in that area.

Due to the boom in home sales over the last several years, On-The-Level Construction has decided to implement a relational database model to track project details according to project name, hours assigned, and charges per hour for each job description. Originally, On-The-Level Construction decided to let one of its employees handle the construction of the database. However, that employee has not had the time to completely implement the project. On-The-Level Construction has asked you to take over and complete the development of the database.

FIGURE AYK.8

On-The-Level Construction Project Detail Report

ON-THE-LEVEL CONSTRUCTION PROJECT DETAIL

PROJECT NAME	ASSIGN DATE	EMPLOYEE LAST NAME	FIRST NAME	JOB DESCRIPTION	ASSIGN HOUR	CHARGE/HOUR
Chatfield						
	6/10/2004	Olenkoski	Glenn	Structure	2.1	$35.75
	6/10/2004	Ramora	Anne	Plumbing	2.6	$98.75
	6/10/2004	Sullivan	David	Electrical	1.2	$105.00
	6/11/2004	Frommer	Matt	Plumbing	1.4	$98.75
Summary of Assignment Hours and Charges					7.30	$588.08
Evergreen						
	6/10/2004	Sullivan	David	Electrical	1.8	$105.00
	6/10/2004	Jones	Anne	Heating and Ventalation	3.4	$84.50
	6/11/2004	Frommer	Matt	Plumbing	4.1	$98.75
	6/16/2004	Bawangi	Terry	Plumbing	4.1	$98.75
	6/16/2004	Newman	John	Electrical	1.7	$105.00
Summary of Assignment Hours and Charges					15.10	$1,448.15
Roxborough						
	6/10/2004	Ramora	Anne	Plumbing	2.6	$98.75
	6/10/2004	Washberg	Jeff	Plumbing	3.9	$98.75
	6/11/2004	Smithfield	William	Structure	2.4	$35.75
	6/11/2004	Bawangi	Terry	Plumbing	2.7	$98.75
	6/16/2004	Joen	Denise	Plumbing	2.5	$98.75
	6/16/2004	Johnson	Peter	Electrical	5.2	$105.00
Summary of Assignment Hours and Charges					19.30	$1,763.78

The entity classes and primary keys for the database have been identified in Figure AYK.9.

The following business rules have been identified:

1. A job can have many employees assigned but must have at least one.
2. An employee must be assigned to one and only one job number.
3. An employee can be assigned to work on one or more projects.
4. A project can be assigned to only one employee but need not be assigned to any employee.

Entity	Primary Key
PROJECT	Project Number
EMPLOYEE	Employee Number
JOB	Job Number
ASSIGNMENT	Assignment Number

FIGURE AYK.9

Entity Classes and Primary Keys for On-The-Level Construction

Project Focus:

Your job is to complete the following tasks:

1. Develop and describe the entity-relationship diagram.
2. Use normalization to assure the correctness of the tables (relations).
3. Create the database using a personal DBMS package (preferably Microsoft Access).
4. Use the DBMS package to create the basic report in Figure AYK.8.
5. You may not be able to develop a report that looks exactly like the one in Figure AYK.8. However, your report should include the same information.
6. Complete personnel information is tracked by another database. For this application, include only the minimum: employee number, last name, and first name.
7. Information concerning all projects, employees, and jobs is not readily available. You should, however, create information for several fictitious projects, employees, and jobs to include in your database.

File: None

Project 18:
Buy or Lease

On-The-Vine-Grapes, a leading supplier of grapes to the wine-producing industry in California, wants to enlarge its delivery services and expand its reach to market by increasing its current fleet of delivery trucks. Some of the older vehicles were acquired through closed-end leases with required down payments, mileage restrictions, and hefty early termination penalties. Other vehicles were purchased using traditional purchase-to-own loans which often resulted in high depreciation costs and large maintenance fees. All vehicles were acquired one at a time through local dealers.

On-The-Vine-Grapes has asked you to assist in developing a lease/buy cost analysis worksheet to make the most cost-effective decision. The director of operations has identified a 2004 Ford F-550 4x2 SD Super Cab XLT as the truck of choice. This vehicle has a retail price of $34,997 or a lease price of $600/month through Ford Motor Credit Company. Figure AYK.10 displays some basic fees and costs that you need to consider.

Project Focus:

1. The director of operations has provided you with a template, BuyOrLease.xls, which you can use to enter the information above. There is also a worksheet included that has been developed to assist you with annual depreciation.
2. Create a detailed summary worksheet of the lease/buy option for On-The-Vine-Grapes, including a narrative description of your analysis.

File: BuyOrLease.xls

1. Lease Costs	
Refundable Security Deposit	$500
First Month's Payment at Inception	$500
Other Initial Costs	$125
Monthly Lease Payment for Remaining Term	$600
Last Month Payment in Advance	No
Allowable Annual Mileage	15,000
Estimated Annual Miles to Be Driven	20,000
Per Mile Charge for Excess Miles	$0.10
2. Purchase Costs	
Retail Price including Sales Taxes, Title	$34,997
Down Payment	$4,000
Loan Interest Rate	4.75%
Will Interest Be Deductible Business or Home Equity Interest	Yes
3. Common Costs and Assumptions	
Total Lease/Loan Term	36
Discount Percent	8.75%
Tax Bracket—Combined Federal and State	33%
Business Use Percentage	100%

Project 19:
Gathering Business Requirements

First Information Corporation is a large consulting company that specializes in systems analysis and design. The company has over 2,000 employees and first-quarter revenues reached $15 million. The company prides itself on maintaining an 85 percent success rate for all project implementations. The primary reason attributed to the unusually high project success rate is the company's ability to define accurate, complete, and high-quality business requirements.

The GEM Athletic Center located in Cleveland, Ohio, is interested in implementing a new payroll system. The current payroll process is manual and takes three employees, two days each month to complete. The GEM Athletic Center does not have an IT department and is outsourcing the entire procurement, customization, and installation of the new payroll system to First Information Corporation.

You have been working for First Information for a little over one month. Your team has just been assigned the GEM Athletic Center project and your first task is to define the initial business requirements for the development of the new payroll system.

Project Focus:

1. Review the testimony of three current GEM Athletic Center accounting employees who detail the current payroll process along with their wish list for the new system. Use the files MaggieCleaver.doc, AnneLogan.doc, JimPoulos.doc.

2. Review the *Characteristics of Good Business Requirements* document, BusinessRequirements.doc, that highlights several techniques you can use to develop solid business requirements.

3. After careful analysis create a report detailing the business requirements for the new system. Be sure to list any assumptions, issues, or questions in your document.

Files: MaggieCleaver.doc, AnneLogan.doc, JimPoulos.doc, BusinessRequirements.doc

Project 20:
Project Management

Time Keepers Inc. is a small firm that specializes in project management consulting. You are a Senior Project Manager and you have recently been assigned to the Tahiti Tanning Lotion account. The Tahiti Tanning Lotion company is currently experiencing a 10 percent success rate (90 percent failure rate) on all internal IT projects. Your first assignment is to analyze one of the current project plans being used to develop a new CRM system (see Figure AYK.11).

Project Focus:

1. Review the project plan in Figure AYK.11 and create a document listing the numerous errors in the plan. Be sure to also provide suggestions on how to fix the errors.

2. If you have access to Microsoft Project open the file BadProject.mpp. Fix the errors you found in question 1 directly to BadProject.mpp.

   (If you are new to using Microsoft Project review the document MSProjectGuidelines. doc for an overview of several tips for using Microsoft Project.)

File: BadProject.mpp, MSProjectGuidelines.doc

FIGURE AYK.11

Project Plan Sample

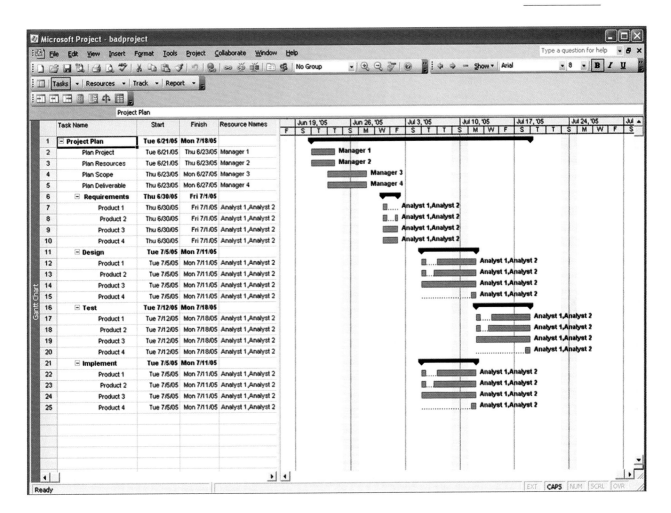

GLOSSARY

A

acceptable use policy (AUP)   A policy that a user must agree to follow in order to be provided access to a network or to the Internet.

accounting and finance component   Manages accounting data and financial processes within the enterprise with functions such as general ledger, accounts payable, accounts receivable, budgeting, and asset management.

adware   Software that generates ads that install themselves on a computer when a person downloads some other program from the Internet.

agile methodology   A form of XP, aims for customer satisfaction through early and continuous delivery of useful software components.

analysis phase   Analyzing end-user business requirements and refining project goals into defined functions and operations of the intended system.

analytical CRM   Supports back-office operations and strategic analysis and includes all systems that do not deal directly with the customers.

analytical information   Encompasses all organizational information and its primary purpose is to support the performing of managerial analysis tasks.

anti-spam policy   States that e-mail users will not send unsolicited e-mails (or spam).

application generation component   Includes tools for creating visually appealing and easy-to-use applications.

application service provider (ASP)   A company that offers an organization access over the Internet to systems and related services that would otherwise have to be located in personal or organizational computers.

application software   Software used to solve specific problems or perform specific tasks.

arithmetic/logic unit (ALU)   Performs all arithmetic operations (for example, addition and subtraction) and all logic operations (such as sorting and comparing numbers).

artificial intelligence (AI)   Simulates human intelligence such as the ability to reason and learn.

ASCII (American Standard Code for Information Interchange) The coding system that most personal computers use to represent, process, and store information.

association detection   Reveals the degree to which variables are related and the nature and frequency of these relationships in the information.

attribute   Characteristics or properties of an entity class.

authentication   A method for confirming users' identities.

automatic call distribution   A phone switch routes inbound calls to available agents.

B

autonomic computing   A self-managing computing model named after, and patterned on, the human body's autonomic nervous system.

backdoor program   Viruses that open a way into the network for future attacks.

backup   An exact copy of a system's information.

backward integration   Takes information entered into a given system and sends it automatically to all upstream systems and processes.

bandwidth   Indicates how much information can be carried in a given time period (usually a second) over a wired or wireless communications link.

banner ad   A small ad on one Web site that advertises the products and services of another business, usually another dot-com business.

benchmark   Baseline values the system seeks to attain.

benchmarking   The process of continuously measuring system results, comparing those results to optimal system performance (benchmark values), and identifying steps and procedures to improve system performance.

binary digit (bit)   The smallest unit of information that a computer can process.

biometric   The identification of a user based on a physical characteristic, such as a fingerprint, iris, face, voice, or handwriting.

black-hat hacker   Breaks into other people's computer systems and may just look around or steal and destroy information.

bluetooth   A standard for transmitting information in the form of short-range radio waves over distances of up to 30 feet and is used for purposes such as wirelessly connecting a cell phone or a PDA to a computer.

bridge   Used to connect networks that use similar protocols.

bus topology   Devices are connected to a central cable.

business intelligence   Information that people use to support their decision-making efforts.

business process   A standardized set of activities that accomplish a specific task, such as processing a customer's order.

business process outsourcing   The contracting of a specific business task, such as payroll, to a third-party service provider.

business requirement   The detailed set of business requests that the system must meet in order to be successful.

business-critical integrity constraint The rules that enforce business rules vital to an organization's success and often require more insight and knowledge than operational integrity constraints.

business-to-business (B2B) Applies to businesses buying from and selling to each other over the Internet.

business-to-business (B2B) marketplace An Internet-based service which brings together many buyers and sellers.

business-to-consumer (B2C) Applies to any business that sells its products or services to consumers over the Internet.

buyer power High when buyers have many choices of whom to buy from and low when their choices are few.

byte A group of eight bits represents one natural language character.

C

call scripting system Accesses organizational databases that track similar issues or questions and automatically generate the details to the CSR who can then relay them to the customer.

campaign management system Guides users through marketing campaigns performing such tasks as campaign definition, planning, scheduling, segmentation, and success analysis.

capital rationing The process of limiting the number of capital expenditure projects because of insufficient funds to finance all projects that otherwise meet the organization's criteria for accceptability.

capital budgeting The process of planning for purchases of assets whose returns are expected to continue beyond one year.

capital expenditure A cash outlay that is expected to generate a flow of future cash benefits lasting longer than one year.

cardinality Expresses the specific number of entity occurrences associated with one occurrence of the related entity.

CD-R (compact disc—recordable) Optical or laser disc that offers one-time writing capability with about 800MB of storage capacity.

CD-ROM (compact disc—read-only memory) Optical or laser disc that offers no updating capability with about 800MB of storage capacity.

CD-RW (compact disc—rewritable) Offers unlimited writing and updating capabilities on the CD.

cellular transmitter Radio transmissions that have the advantage of being able to penetrate solid objects.

central processing unit (CPU) The actual hardware that interprets and executes the program (software) instructions and coordinates how all the other hardware devices work together.

change control board (CCB) Responsible for approving or rejecting all change requests.

change management A set of techniques that aid in evolution, composition, and policy management of the design and implementation of a system.

change management system Includes a collection of procedures to document a change request and define the steps necessary to consider the change based on the expected impact of the change.

chief information officer (CIO) A senior executive who (1) oversees all uses of information technology and (2) ensures the strategic alignment of IT with business goals and objectives.

chief privacy officer (CPO) A senior executive responsible for ensuring the ethical and legal use of information within an organization.

chief security officer (CSO) A senior executive responsible specifically for ensuring the security of IT systems and developing strategies and IT safeguards against attacks from hackers and viruses.

chief technology officer (CTO) A senior executive responsible for ensuring the throughput, speed, accuracy, availability, and reliability of an organization's information technology.

class Contains information and procedures and acts as a template to create objects.

clickstream Records information about a customer during a Web surfing session such as what Web sites were visited, how long the visit was, what ads were viewed, and what was purchased.

click-stream data A virtual trail that a Web user leaves behind while using the Internet.

click-through A count of the number of people who visit one site and click on an advertisement that takes them to the site of the advertiser.

click-to-talk Buttons allow customers to click on a button and talk with a CSR via the Internet.

client-server network A versatile, message-based, and modular infrastructure that is intended to improve usability, flexibility, interoperability, and scalability as compared to centralized, mainframe computing.

cluster analysis A technique used to divide an information set into mutually exclusive groups such that the members of each group are as close together as possible to one another and the different groups are as far apart as possible.

coaxial cable Cable that can carry a wide range of frequencies with low signal loss.

cold site A separate facility that does not have any computer equipment, but is a place where employees can move after the disaster.

collaboration system An IT-based set of tools that supports the work of teams by facilitating the sharing and flow of information.

collaborative demand planning Helps organizations reduce their investment in inventory, while improving customer satisfaction through product availability.

collaborative engineering Allows an organization to reduce the cost and time required during the design process of a product.

commercial off-the shelf (COTS) A software package or solution that is purchased to support one or more business functions and information systems.

comparative metric Assess how the organization is performing compared to other organizations, industries, and markets.

competitive advantage A product or service that an organization's customers value more highly than similar offerings from a competitor.

composite entity   Entities that exist to represent the relationship between two other entities.

computer network (network)   A group of two or more computer systems linked together using wires or radio waves over a geographical area.

computer simulation   Complex systems, such as the U.S. economy, can be modeled by means of mathematical equations and different scenarios can be run against the model to determine "what if" analysis.

computer-aided software engineering (CASE)   Software suites that automate systems analysis, design, and development.

concentrators (hubs or switches)   Provide a common physical connection point for computing devices.

confidentiality   The assurance that messages and data are available only to those who are authorized to view them.

consolidation   Involves the aggregation of information and features simple roll-ups to complex groupings of interrelated information.

constraint   A rule to which some elements in a database must adhere.

consumer-to-business (C2B)   Applies to any consumer that sells a product or service to a business over the Internet.

consumer-to-consumer (C2C)   Applies to sites primarily offering goods and services to assist consumers interacting with each other over the Internet.

contact center (call center)   Customer service representatives (CSRs) answer customer inquiries and respond to problems through a number of different customer touchpoints.

contact management system   Maintains customer contact information and identifies prospective customers for future sales.

content filtering   Occurs when organizations use software that filters content to prevent the transmission of unauthorized information.

content management system   Provides tools to manage the creation, storage, editing, and publication of information in a collaborative environment.

content provider   Companies that use the Internet to distribute copyrighted content, including news, music, games, books, movies, and many other types of information.

contingent project   Project whose acceptance is dependent on the adoption of one or more other projects.

control unit   Interprets software instructions and literally tells the other hardware devices what to do, based on the software instructions.

cookie   A small file deposited on a hard drive by a Web site containing information about customers and their Web activities.

copyright   The legal protection afforded an expression of an idea, such as a song, video game, and some types of proprietary documents.

core competency   An organization's key strength or business function that it does better than any of its competitors.

core competency strategy   When an organization chooses to focus specifically on what it does best (its core competency) and forms partnerships and alliances with other specialist organizations to handle nonstrategic business processes.

core ERP component   Traditional components included in most ERP systems and they primarily focus on internal operations.

counterfeit software   Software that is manufactured to look like the real thing and sold as such.

cracker   A hacker with criminal intent.

crash-proof software   Saves information if a computer crashes.

critical path   A path from the start to the finish that passes through all the tasks that are critical to completing the project in the shortest amount of time.

critical success factor (CSF)   A factor that is critical to an organization's success.

cross-selling   Selling additional products or services to a customer.

CRUD   Four common procedures including Create, Read, Update, and Delete.

cube   The common term for the representation of multidimensional information.

customer metric   Assess the management of customer relationships by the organization.

customer relationship management (CRM)   Involves managing all aspects of a customer's relationship with an organization to increase customer loyalty and retention and an organization's profitability.

cyberterrorist   Seek to cause harm to people or to destroy critical systems or information and use the Internet as a weapon of mass destruction.

cycle inventory   The average amount of inventory held to satisfy customer demands between inventory deliveries.

D

data administration component   Provides tools for managing the overall database environment by providing facilities for backup, recovery, security, and performance.

database   Maintains information about various types of objects (inventory), events (transactions), people (employees), and places (warehouses).

database management system (DBMS)   Software through which users and application programs interact with a database.

data definition component   Helps create and maintain the data dictionary and the structure of the database.

data dictionary   A file that stores definitions of information types, identifies the primary and foreign keys, and maintains the relationships among the tables.

data flow diagram (DFD)   Illustrates the movement of information between external entities and the processes and data stores within the system.

data manipulation component   Allows users to create, read, update, and delete information in a database.

data mart   Contains a subset of data warehouse information.

data mining   The process of analyzing data to extract information not offered by the raw data alone.

data-mining tool   Use a variety of techniques to find patterns and relationships in large volumes of information and infer rules from them that predict future behavior and guide decision making.

data model   A formal way to express data relationships to a database management system (DBMS).

data warehouse   A logical collection of information—gathered from many different operational databases—that supports business analysis activities and decision-making tasks.

decision support system (DSS)   Models information to support managers and business professionals during the decision-making process

denial-of-service attack (DoS)   Floods a Web site with so many requests for service that it slows down or crashes the site.

dependency   A logical relationship that exists between the project tasks, or between a project task and a milestone.

design phase   Involves describing the desired features and operations of the system including screen layouts, business rules, process diagrams, pseudo code, and other documentation.

desktop computer   One of the most popular choices for personal computing needs.

development phase   Involves taking all of the detailed design documents from the design phase and transforming them into the actual system.

digital asset management system (DAM)   Though similar to document management, DAM generally works with binary rather than text files, such as multimedia file types.

digital Darwinism   Organizations which cannot adapt to the new demands placed on them for surviving in the information age are doomed to extinction.

digital dashboard   Integrates information from multiple components and present it in a unified display.

digital ink (or electronic ink)   Technology that digitally represents handwriting in its natural form.

digital paper (or electronic paper)   Any paper that is optimized for any type of digital printing.

disaster recovery cost curve   Charts (1) the cost to the organization of the unavailability of information and technology and (2) the cost to the organization of recovering from a disaster over time.

disaster recovery plan   A detailed process for recovering information or an IT system in the event of a catastrophic disaster such as a fire or flood.

disk optimization software   Organizes information on a hard disk in the most efficient way.

disruptive technology   A new way of doing things that initially does not meet the needs of existing customers.

distributed denial-of-service attack (DDoS)   Attacks from multiple computers that flood a Web site with so many requests for service that it slows down or crashes.

document management system (DMS)   Supports the electronic capturing, storage, distribution, archival, and accessing of documents.

drill-down   Enables users to get details, and details of details, of information.

DVD-R   Optical or laser disc that offers one-time writing capability with upward of 17GB of storage capacity.

DVD-ROM   Optical or laser disc that offers no updating capability with upward of 17GB of storage capacity.

DVD-RW or DVD+RW   Optical or laser disc that offers unlimited writing and updating capabilities on the DVD.

E

e-business   The conducting of business on the Internet, not only buying and selling, but also serving customers and collaborating with business partners.

e-business model   An approach to conducting electronic business through which a company can become a profitable business on the Internet.

e-channel   Web-based business channels.

e-commerce   The buying and selling of goods and services over the Internet.

effectiveness IT metric   Measure the impact IT has on business processes and activities including customer satisfaction, conversion rates, sell-through increases, etc.

efficiency IT metric   Measure the performance of the IT system itself including throughput, speed, availability, etc.

e-government   Involves the use of strategies and technologies to transform government(s) by improving the delivery of services and enhancing the quality of interaction between the citizen-consumer within all branches of government(s).

electronic data interchange (EDI)   A standard format for exchanging business data.

electronic marketplace, or e-marketplace   Interactive business communities providing a central market space where multiple buyers and suppliers can engage in e-business activities.

electronic tagging   A technique for identifying and tracking assets and individuals via technologies such as radio frequency identification and smart cards.

electronic trading network   Service providers that manage network services.

e-logistics   Manages the transportation and storage of goods.

e-mail privacy policy   Details the extent to which e-mail messages may be read by others.

e-mall   Consists of a number of e-shops, which serves as a gateway through which a visitor can access other e-shops.

employee monitoring policy   States how, when, and where the company monitors its employees.

employee relationship management (ERM)   Provides employees with a subset of CRM applications available through a Web browser.

encapsulation   Information hiding.

encryption   Scrambles information into an alternative form that requires a key or password to decrypt the information.

English auction   The highest bid wins.

enterprise application integration (EAI) middleware
Represents a new approach to middleware by packaging together commonly used functionality, such as providing prebuilt links to popular enterprise applications, which reduces the time necessary to develop solutions that integrate applications from multiple vendors.

enterprise information portal (EIP)   An Internet site owned and operated by an organization to support its operations.

enterprise resource planning (ERP) Integrates all departments and functions throughout an organization into a single IT system (or integrated set of IT systems) so that employees can make enterprisewide decisions by viewing enterprisewide information on all business operations.

entity In the relational database model is a person, place, thing, transaction, or event about which information is stored.

entity class In the relational database model is a collection of similar entities.

entity identifier Ensures that each entity instance has a unique attribute value that distinguishes it from every other entity instance.

entity integrity A constraint on a relation that states that no part of a primary key can be null.

entity-relationship diagram (ERD) A technique for documenting the relationships between entities in a database environment.

entry barrier A product or service feature that customers have come to expect from organizations in a particular industry and must be offered by an entering organization to compete and survive.

environmental scanning The acquisition and analysis of events and trends in the environment external to an organization.

ePolicies Policies and procedures that address the ethical use of computers and Internet usage in the business environment.

e-portal A single gateway through which to gain access to all the information, systems, and processes used by stakeholders of an organization.

e-procurement The B2B purchase and sale of supplics and services over the Internet.

e-shop (e-store or e-tailer) A version of a retail store where customers can shop at any hour of the day without leaving home or office.

ethernet A physical and data layer technology for LAN networking.

ethical computer use policy Contains general principles to guide computer user behavior.

ethics Principles and standards that guide our behavior toward other people.

executive information system (EIS) A specialized DSS that supports senior level executives within the organization.

expandability How easy it is to add features and functions to a system.

expansion bus Moves information from the CPU and RAM to all of the other hardware devices such as a microphone and printer.

expansion card A circuit board that is inserted into an expansion slot.

expansion slot A long skinny socket on the motherboard into which an expansion card is inserted.

expert system Computerized advisory programs that imitate the reasoning processes of experts in solving difficult problems.

explicit knowledge Consists of anything that can be documented, archived, and codified, often with the help of IT.

extended ERP component The extra components that meet the organizational needs not covered by the core components and primarily focus on external operations.

extraction, transformation, and loading (ETL) A process that extracts information from internal and external databases, transforms the information using a common set of enterprise definitions, and loads the information into a data warehouse.

extranet A private network that uses the Internet and the public telecommunication system to securely share part of a business's information or operations with suppliers, vendors, partners, customers, or other businesses.

extreme programming (XP) methodology Breaks a project into tiny phases, and developers cannot continue on to the next phase until the first phase is complete.

F

fair use doctrine In certain situations, it is legal to use copyrighted material.

feasibility study Determines if the proposed solution is feasible and achievable from a financial, technical, and organizational standpoint.

feature creep Occurs when developers add extra features that were not part of the initial requirements.

Fiber Distributed Data Interface (FDDI) A set of protocols for sending digital data over fiber optic cable.

fiber optic ("optical fiber") The technology associated with the transmission of information as light impulses along a glass wire or fiber.

File Transfer Protocol (FTP) Allows files containing text, programs, graphics, numerical data, and so on to be downloaded off or uploaded onto a network.

financial metric Assess the financial performance of a company.

firewall Hardware and/or software that guards a private network by analyzing the information leaving and entering the network.

first normal form (1NF) Each field in a table contains different information.

first-mover advantage An organization can significantly impact its market share by being first to market with a competitive advantage.

Five Forces model Helps determine the relative attractiveness of an industry.

flash memory device A storage device that is small enough to fit on a key ring and plugs directly into the USB port on a computer.

forecast Predictions made on the basis of time-series information.

foreign key A primary key of one table that appears as an attribute in another table and acts to provide a logical relationship between the two tables.

forward integration Takes information entered into a given system and sends it automatically to all downstream systems and processes.

G

Gantt chart   A simple bar chart that depicts project tasks against a calendar.

gateway   Used to connect networks that use dissimilar protocols.

gigabyte (GB)   Roughly 1 billion characters.

gigahertz (GHz)   The number of billions of CPU cycles per second.

goal seek   An analytical function which allows a value in a formula to be adjusted in order to reach a desired result or answer.

goal-seeking analysis   Finds the inputs necessary to achieve a goal such as a desired level of output.

graphical user interface (GUI)   The interface to an information system.

groupware   Software that supports team interaction and dynamics including calendaring, scheduling, and videoconferencing.

GUI screen design   The ability to model the information system screens for an entire system using icons, buttons, menus, and submenus.

guided media   Transmissions media manufactured so that signals will be confined to a narrow path and will behave predictably.

H

hacker   People very knowledgeable about computers who use their knowledge to invade other people's computers.

hactivist   Have philosophical and political reasons for breaking into systems and will often deface the Web site as a protest.

hard disk   Rests within the system box and offers both ease of updating and great storage capacity.

hardware   The physical aspect of computers, telecommunications, and other information technology devices.

hardware key logger   A hardware device that captures keystrokes on their journey from the keyboard to the motherboard.

help desk   A group of people who respond to internal system user questions.

hierarchial database   Stores related information in terms of predefined categorical relationships in a "tree-like" fashion.

high-capacity floppy disk   Great for portability and ease of updating and holds between 100MB and 250MB of information.

historical analysis   The study of historical events in order to anticipate the outcome of current developments.

hoaxes   Attack computer systems by transmitting a virus hoax, with a real virus attached.

horizontal market software   General enough to be suitable for use in a variety of industries.

horizontal marketplace   Connects buyers and sellers across many industries, primarily by simplifying the purchasing process.

hot site   A separate and fully equipped facility where the company can move immediately after the disaster and resume business.

human resource component   Tracks employee information including payroll, benefits, compensation, performance assessment, and assumes compliance with the legal requirements of multiple jurisdictions and tax authorities.

hurdle rate   The minimum ROI percentage a project must meet to be considered for management approval.

Hypertext Transfer Protocol (HTTP)   Allows Web browsers and servers to send and receive Web pages.

I

implementation phase   Involves placing the system into production so users can begin to perform actual business operations with the system.

independent project   Project whose acceptance or rejection does not directly eliminate other projects from consideration.

information cleansing or scrubbing   A process that weeds out and fixes or discards inconsistent, incorrect, or incomplete information.

information decomposition   Breaking down the information and procedures for ease of use and understandability.

information integrity   A measure of the quality of information.

information partnership   Occurs when two or more organizations cooperate by integrating their IT systems, thereby providing customers with the best of what each can offer.

information privacy policy   Contains general principles regarding information privacy.

information security   A broad term encompassing the protection of information from accidental or intentional misuse by persons inside or outside an organization.

information security plan   Details how an organization will implement the information security policies.

information security policy   Identifies the rules required to maintain information security.

information technology (IT)   Any computer-based tool that people use to work with information and support the information and information-processing needs of an organization.

information view   Includes all of the information stored within a system.

infrared (IR or IrDA Infrared data association)   Uses red light to send and receive information.

infrared transmitter (laser transmitter)   Transmitters that use the atmosphere and outer space as transmission media.

inheritance   The ability to define superclass and subclass relationships among classes.

input device   Equipment used to capture information and commands.

insider   Legitimate users who purposely or accidentally misuse their access to the environment and cause some kind of business-affecting incident.

insourcing   A common approach using the professional expertise within an organization to develop and maintain the organization's information technology systems.

integration   Allows separate systems to communicate directly with each other.

integrity constraint The rules that help ensure the quality of information.

intellectual property Intangible creative work that is embodied in physical form.

intelligent agent A special-purpose knowledge-based information system that accomplishes specific tasks on behalf of its users.

intelligent system Various commercial applications of artificial intelligence.

interactive voice response (IVR) Directs customers to use touch-tone phones or keywords to navigate or provide information.

interactivity Measures the visitors' interactions with the target ad.

interface Any device that calls procedures and can include such things as a keyboard, mouse, and touch screen.

intermediary Agents, software, or businesses that bring buyers and sellers together that provide a trading infrastructure to enhance e-business.

internal rate of return (IRR) The rate at which the NPV of an investment equals zero.

internet service provider (ISP) A company that provides individuals and other companies access to the Internet and other related services, such as Web site building.

internet use policy Contains general principles to guide the proper use of the Internet.

intranet An internalized portion of the Internet, protected from outside access, that allows an organization to provide access to information and application software to only its employees.

intrusion detection software (IDS) Searches out patterns in information and network traffic to indicate attacks and quickly respond to prevent any harm.

IT infrastructure Includes the hardware, software, and telecommunications equipment that, when combined, provide the underlying foundation to support the organization's goals.

J

join An operation that combines two relations by matching rows based on values in columns in the two tables.

joint application development (JAD) A session where employees meet, sometimes for several days, to define or review the business requirements for the system.

K

key logger, or key trapper, software A program that, when installed on a computer, records every keystroke and mouse click.

knowledge management Involves capturing, classifying, evaluating, retrieving, and sharing information assets in a way that provides context for effective decisions and actions.

knowledge management system (KMS) Supports the capturing and use of an organization's "know-how."

L

linkage The interconnection of different systems, information, and transactions to support a user action.

Linux An open source operating system that provides a rich environment for high-end workstations and network servers.

list generator Compiles customer information from a variety of sources and segment the information for different marketing campaigns.

local area network (LAN) Connects network devices over a relatively short distance.

logical view Focuses on how users logically access information to meet their particular business needs.

longer term relationship model For items requiring a high degree of planning between buyers and sellers either in the design stage or in fulfillment.

loyalty program Rewards customers based on the amount of business they do with a particular organization.

M

mail bomb Sends a massive amount of e-mail to a specific person or system resulting in filling up the recipient's disk space, which, in some cases, may be too much for the server to handle and may cause the server to stop functioning.

mainframe Designed to meet the computing needs of hundreds of people in a large business environment.

maintenance The fixing or enhancing of an information system.

maintenance phase Involves performing changes, corrections, additions, and upgrades to ensure the system continues to meet the business goals.

malicious code Includes a variety of threats such as viruses, worms, and Trojan horses.

management information system (MIS) The function that plans for, develops, implements, and maintains IT hardware, software, and the portfolio of applications that people use to support the goals of an organization.

many-to-many relationship (M:N) A relationship between two entities in which an instance of entity A can be related to zero, one, or more instances of entity B and entity B can be related to zero, one, or more instances of entity A.

market basket analysis Analyzes such items as Web sites and checkout scanner information to detect customers' buying behavior and predict future behavior by identifying affinities among customers' choices of products and services.

market makers Intermediaries that aggregate three services for market participants.

marketplace model Allows a virtually infinite number of businesses to transact electronically with minimal cost.

megahertz (MHz) The number of millions of CPU cycles per second.

memory card High-capacity storage laminated inside a small piece of plastic.

message How objects communicate with each other.

metropolitan area network (MAN)   Interconnects users with computer resources in a geographic area or region larger than that covered by even a large local area network, but smaller than the area covered by a wide area network.

microwave transmitter   Commonly used to transmit network signals over great distances.

middleware   Different types of software which sit in the middle of and provide connectivity between two or more software applications.

minicomputer (mid-range computer)   Designed to meet the computing needs of several people simultaneously in a small to medium-size business environment.

mobile commerce, or m-commerce   The ability to purchase goods and services through a wireless Internet-enabled device.

model   A simplified representation or abstraction of reality.

modeling   The activity of drawing a graphical representation of a design.

modem   Provides the means to transmit computer data (digital) over analog transmission media.

monitoring   Tracking people's activities by such measures as number of keystrokes, error rate, and number of transactions processed.

multisourcing   A combination of professional services, mission-critical support, remote management, and hosting services that are offered to customers in any combination needed.

multitasking   Allows more than one piece of software to be used at a time.

multi-valued   Having the potential to contain more than one value for an attribute at any given time.

mutually exclusive project   Project whose acceptance precludes the acceptance of one or more alternative proposals.

N

nearshore outsourcing   Contracting an outsourcing agreement with a company in a nearby country.

net present value (NPV)   The present value of the stream of net (operating) cash flows from the project minus the project's net investment.

network adaptor   The hardware installed in computers that enables them to communicate on a network.

network database   Used by a network installation tool to allocate and track network resources.

network operating system (NOS)   An operating system that includes special functions for connecting computers and devices into a local area network.

network transmission media   Various types of media used to carry the signal between computers.

neural network (an artificial neural network)   A category of AI that attempts to emulate the way the human brain works.

nonrepudiation   A contractual stipulation to ensure that e-business participants do not deny (repudiate) their online actions.

normal form   The theoretical rules that the design of a relation must meet.

normalization   The process of placing attributes into tables that avoid the problems associated with poor database design.

notebook computer   Fully functional computer designed to be carried around and run on battery power.

O

object   An instance of a class.

object-oriented approach   Combines information and procedures into a single view.

object-oriented database   Works with traditional database information and also complex data types such as diagrams, schematic drawings, video, and sound.

object-oriented programming language   A programming language used to develop object-oriented systems.

offshore outsourcing   Using organizations from developing countries to write code and develop systems.

one-to-many relationship (1:M)   A relationship between two entities, in which an instance of entity A can be related to zero, one, or more instances of entity B and entity B can be related to only one instance of entity A.

one-to-one relationship (1:1)   A relationship between two entities in which an instance of entity A can be related to only one instance of entity B and entity B can be related to only one instance of entity A.

online analytical processing (OLAP)   The manipulation of information to create business intelligence in support of strategic decision making.

online broker   Intermediaries between buyers and sellers of goods and services.

online service provider (OSP)   Offers an extensive online array of services of their own apart from the rest of the Internet and sometimes their own version of a Web browser.

online training   Runs over the Internet or off a CD-ROM.

online transaction processing (OLTP)   The capturing of transaction and event information, using technology to (1) process the information according to defined business rules, (2) store the information, and (3) update existing information to reflect the new information.

onshore outsourcing   The process of engaging another company within the same country for services.

open architecture (or **open system**)   A broad, general term that describes nonproprietary IT hardware and software made available by the standards and procedures by which their products work, making it easier to integrate them.

operating system software   Supports the application software and manages how the hardware devices work together.

operational CRM   Supports traditional transactional processing for day-to-day front-office operations or systems that deal directly with the customers.

operational integrity constraint   The rules that enforce basic and fundamental information-based constraints.

opportunity management system   Targets sales opportunities by finding new customers or companies for future sales.

opt-in   Implying that a company will contact only the people who have agreed to receive promotions and marketing material via e-mail.

output device   Equipment used to see, hear, or otherwise accept the results of information processing requests.

outsourcing   An arrangement by which one organization provides a service or services for another organization that chooses not to perform them in-house.

P

parallel connector   A computer connector that has 25 pins, which fit into the corresponding holes in the port.

partner relationship management (PRM)   Focuses on keeping vendors satisfied by managing alliance partner and reseller relationships that provide customers with the optimal sales channel.

payback period (PB)   The period of time required for the cumulative cash inflows (net cash flows) from a project to equal the initial cash outlay (net investment).

peer-to-peer (P2P)   Systems which allow collaboration in a shared information space to utilize, add to, or comment on any piece of information.

peer-to-peer network   Enables networked computers to function as both servers and workstations.

performance   Measures how quickly a system performs a certain process or transaction.

personal digital assistant (PDA)   Small hand-held computer that performs simple tasks such as taking notes, scheduling appointments, and maintaining an address book.

personalization   Occurs when a Web site can know enough about a person's likes and dislikes that it can fashion offers that are more likely to appeal to that person.

personal productivity software   Used to perform personal tasks such as writing a memo, creating a graph, or creating a slide presentation.

PERT (Program Evaluation and Review Technique) chart   A graphical network model that depicts a project's tasks and the relationships between those tasks.

physical schema   The underlying physical storage, which is managed by the DBMS.

physical topology   The actual physical organization of the computers on the network and its connections.

physical view   The physical storage of information on a storage device such as a hard disk.

pirated software   The unauthorized use, duplication, distribution, or sale of copyrighted software.

PivotChart   A column chart (by default) that is based on the data in a PivotTable.

PivotTable   Analyzes, summarizes, and manipulates data in large lists, databases, worksheets, or other collections.

pixel   Dots that make up an image on the computer screen.

planning phase   Involves establishing a high-level plan of the intended project and determining project goals.

polymorphic virus and worm   Change their form as they propagate.

polymorphism   Means "to have many forms."

portal   A Web site that offers a broad array of resources and services, such as e-mail, online discussion groups, search engines, and online shopping malls.

port   The plug-ins found on the outside of the system box (usually in the back) into which a connector is plugged.

predictive dialing   Automatically dials outbound calls and when someone answers, the call is forwarded to an available agent.

present value   The value of cash to be received in the future expressed in today's dollars.

primary key   A field (or group of fields) that uniquely identifies a given entity in a table.

privacy   The right to be left alone when you want to be, to have control over your own personal possessions, and not to be observed without your consent.

private exchange   A B2B marketplace in which a single buyer posts its need and then opens the bidding to any supplier who would care to bid.

procedure   Manipulates or changes information.

procedure view   Contains all of the procedures within a system.

process modeling   Involves graphically representing the processes that capture, manipulate, store, and distribute information between a system and its environment.

production and materials management component   Handles the various aspects of production planning and execution such as demand forecasting, production scheduling, job cost accounting, and quality control.

program   A set of instructions that, when executed, cause a computer to behave in a specific manner.

programming language   The tool developers use to write a program.

project   A temporary endeavor undertaken to create a unique product or service.

project deliverable   Any measurable, tangible, verifiable outcome, result, or item that is produced to complete a project or part of a project.

project exclusion   Products, services, or processes that are not specifically a part of the project.

project management   The application of knowledge, skills, tools, and techniques to project activities in order to meet or exceed stakeholder needs and expectations from a project.

project management software   Supports the long-term and day-to-day management and execution of the steps in a project.

project manager   An individual who is an expert in project planning and management, defines and develops the project plan, and tracks the plan to ensure all key project milestones are completed on time.

project milestone   Represents key dates when a certain group of activities must be performed.

project objective   Quantifiable criteria that must be met for the project to be considered a success.

project plan   A formal, approved document that manages and controls project execution.

project product   A description of the characteristics the product or service has undertaken.

project risk   An uncertain event or condition that, if it occurs, has a positive or negative effect on a project objective(s).

project scope   Defines the work that must be completed to deliver a product with the specified features and functions.

protocol   The predefined way that someone (who wants to use a service) talks with or utilizes that service.

prototype   A smaller-scale representation or working model of the user's requirements or a proposed design for an information system.

pull technology   Organizations receive or request information.

pure play   An Internet retailer that has no physical store, such as Expedia.com and Amazon.com.

push technology   Organizations send information.

Q

Query-by-example (QBE) tool   Allows users to graphically design the answers to specific questions.

R

radio frequency identification (RFID)   Technologies using active or passive tags in the form of chips or smart labels that can store unique identifiers and relay this information to electronic readers.

RadioPaper   A dynamic high-resolution electronic display that combines a paper-like reading experience with the ability to access information anytime, anywhere.

random access memory (RAM)   Temporary storage that holds the current information, the application software currently being used, and the operating system software.

rapid application development (RAD) (also called rapid prototyping)   Emphasizes extensive user involvement in the rapid and evolutionary construction of working prototypes of a system to accelerate the systems development process.

real-time information   Immediate, up-to-date information.

real-time system   Provides real-time information in response to query requests.

recovery   The ability to get a system up and running in the event of a system crash or failure and includes restoring the information backup.

redundancy   The duplication of information or storing the same information in multiple places.

referential integrity   States that every non-null foreign key value must match an existing primary key value.

reintermediation   Using the Internet to reassemble buyers, sellers, and other partners in a traditional supply chain in new ways.

relational database model   A type of database that stores its information in the form of logically related two-dimensional tables.

repeater   A device used to increase the distance over which a network signal can be propagated.

report generator   Allows users to define formats for reports along with what information they want to see in the report.

requirements definition document   Contains the final set of business requirements, prioritized in order of business importance.

response time   The time it takes to respond to user interactions such as a mouse click.

return on investment (ROI)   Indicates the earning power of a project and is measured by dividing the benefits of a project by the investment.

reverse auction   An auction format in which increasingly lower bids are solicited from organizations willing to supply the desired product or service at an increasingly lower price.

ring topology   All devices are connected to one another in the shape of a closed loop, so that each device is connected directly to two other devices, one on either side of it.

risk management   The process of proactive and ongoing identification, analysis, and response to risk factors.

rivalry among existing competitors   High when competition is fierce in a market and low when competition is more complacent.

router   Used to connect networks that use similar protocols (e.g., TCP/IP).

S

safety inventory   Includes extra inventory held in the event demand exceeds supply.

sales force automation (SFA)   A system that automatically tracks all of the steps in the sales process.

sales management system   Automates each phase of the sales process, helping individual sales representatives coordinate and organize all of their accounts.

scalability   Refers to how well a system can adapt to increased demands.

scenario   A set of input values and corresponding results from calculations that Excel can save and report as needed.

scenario manager   Allows 32 different scenarios or groups of values to be defined.

schema   A completed entity-relationship diagram representing the overall, logical plan of a database.

scope creep   Occurs when the scope of the project increases.

script kiddies or script bunnies   Finds hacking code on the Internet and click-and-point their way into systems to cause damage or spread viruses.

second normal form (2NF)   The relation is in first normal form and all nonkey attributes are functionally dependent on the entire primary key.

seller model   The supplier hosts value-added services on its Web site such as suppliers' product catalog and customers' order information.

selling chain management   Applies technology to the activities in the order life cycle from inquiry to sale.

sensitivity analysis   The study of the impact that changes in one (or more) parts of the model have on other parts of the model.

serial connector   A computer connector that usually has nine holes but may have 25, which fit into the corresponding number of pins in the port.

shopping bot   Software that will search several retailer Web sites and provide a comparison of each retailer's offerings including price and availability.

sign-off   The system users' actual signatures indicating they approve all of the business requirements.

Simple Mail Transfer Protocol (SMTP)   TCP/IP's own messaging system for e-mail.

Simple Network Management Protocol (SNMP)   Allows the management of networked nodes to be managed from a single point.

single-valued   Having only a single value of each attribute of an entity at any given time.

slice-and-dice   The ability to look at information from different perspectives.

smart card   A device that is around the same size as a credit card, containing embedded technologies that can store information and small amounts of software to perform some limited processing.

sniffer   A program or device that can monitor data traveling over a network.

social engineering   Using one's social skills to trick people into revealing access credentials or other information valuable to the attacker.

software   A general term for the various kinds of programs used to operate computers and related devices.

solver   Part of a suite of functions sometimes called what-if analysis tools.

spam   Unsolicited e-mail.

spoofing   The forging of the return address on an e-mail so that the e-mail message appears to come from someone other than the actual sender.

spot sourcing   Buying commodity-like products that are transaction-oriented and rarely involve a long-term or ongoing relationship between buyers and sellers.

spyware (sneakware or stealthware)   Software that comes hidden in free downloadable software and tracks online movements, mines the information stored on a computer, or uses a computer's CPU and storage for some task the user knows nothing about.

spyware software   Removes any software that employs a user's Internet connection in the background without their knowledge or explicit permission.

star topology   All devices are connected to a central device, called a hub.

storage device   Equipment used to store information.

strategic resource   Assets available after an organization has cautiously spent what it must to keep its existing business operating at its current level.

structured collaboration (or process collaboration)   Involves shared participation in business processes such as workflow in which knowledge is hard coded as rules.

structured query language (SQL)   A standardized fourth-generation query language found in most DBMSs.

supercomputer   The fastest, most powerful, and most expensive type of computer

supplier power   High when buyers have few choices of whom to buy from and low when their choices are many.

supplier relationship management (SRM)   Focuses on keeping suppliers satisfied by evaluating and categorizing suppliers for different projects, which optimizes supplier selection.

supply chain   Consists of all parties involved, directly or indirectly, in the procurement of a product or raw material.

supply chain event management (SCEM)   Enables an organization to react more quickly to resolve supply chain issues.

supply chain execution (SCE)   Software that automates the different steps and stages of the supply chain.

supply chain management (SCM)   Involves the management of information flows between and among stages in a supply chain to maximize total supply chain effectiveness and profitability.

supply chain planning (SCP)   Software that uses advanced mathematical algorithms to improve the flow and efficiency of the supply chain while reducing inventory.

sustaining technology   Produces an improved product customers are eager to buy, such as a faster car or larger hard drive.

switching cost   The costs that can make customers reluctant to switch to another product or service.

systematic sourcing   Buying through prenegotiated contracts with qualified suppliers.

systems development life cycle (SDLC)   The overall process for developing information systems from planning and analysis through implementation and maintenance.

system software   Handles tasks specific to technology management and coordinates the interaction of all technology devices.

T

tablet computer   A pen-based computer that provides the screen capabilities of a PDA with the functional capabilities of a notebook or desktop computer.

tacit knowledge   The knowledge contained in people's heads.

telecommunications device   Equipment used to send information and receive it from one location to another.

teleliving   Using information devices and the Internet to conduct all aspects of life seamlessly.

telematic   Blending computers and wireless telecommunications technologies with the goal of efficiently conveying information over vast networks to improve business operations.

telnet   Provides terminal emulation that allows a personal computer or workstation to act as a terminal, or access device, for a server.

terabyte (TB)   Roughly 1 trillion bytes.

test condition   The detailed steps the system must perform along with the expected results of each step.

testing phase   Involves bringing all the project pieces together into a special testing environment to test for errors, bugs, and interoperability, in order to verify that the system meets all of the business requirements defined in the analysis phase.

thicknet coaxial cable   Similar to thinnet except that it is larger in diameter.

thinnet coaxial cable   Similar to cable used by cable television companies.

thin client   Similar to terminals connected to mainframes; the server performs the bulk of the processing, and the client presents the interface.

third normal form (3NF)   The relation is in second normal form and there are no transitive dependencies.

threat of new entrants   High when it is easy for new competitors to enter a market and low when there are significant entry barriers to entering a market.

threat of substitute products or services   High when there are many alternatives to a product or service and low when there are few alternatives from which to choose.

throughput   The amount of information that can travel through a system at any point in time.

time-series information   Time-stamped information collected at a particular frequency.

token   Small electronic devices that change user passwords automatically.

token ring   A LAN in which all computers are connected in a ring or star topology and a token-passing scheme is used in order to prevent the collision of data between two computers that want to send messages at the same time.

topology   The actual physical organization of the computers including connections.

total cost of ownership (TCO)   Consists of the costs, direct and indirect, incurred throughout the life cycle of an asset, including acquisition, deployment, operation, support, and retirement.

traditional technology approach   Two primary views of any system—information and procedures—and it keeps these two views separate and distinct at all times.

transactional information   Encompasses all of the information contained within a single business process or unit of work and its primary purpose is to support the performing of daily operational tasks.

Transmission Control Protocol/Internet Protocol (TCP/IP)   A group, or suite, of networking protocols used to connect computers on the Internet.

tree topology   Combines the characteristics of the bus and star topologies.

trend analysis   The examination of a trend to identify its nature, causes, speed of development, and potential impacts.

trend monitoring   Trends viewed as particularly important in a specific community, industry, or sector are carefully monitored, watched, and reported to key decision makers.

trend projection   When numerical data is available, a trend can be plotted on graph paper to display changes through time and into the future.

Trojan-horse virus   Hides inside other software, usually as an attachment or a downloadable file.

twisted-pair   A type of cable composed of four (or more) copper wires twisted around each other within a plastic sheath.

U

unguided media   Natural parts of the Earth's environment that can be used as physical paths to carry electrical signals.

uninstaller software   Removes software from a computer that is no longer needed.

universal serial bus (USB)   The most popular means of connecting devices to a computer.

unstructured collaboration (information collaboration)   Includes document exchange, shared whiteboards, discussion forums, and e-mail.

up-selling   Increasing the value of a sale.

user documentation   Highlights how to use the system.

utility software   Provides additional functionality to the operating system.

V

value chain   Views an organization as a chain, or series, of processes, each of which adds value to the product or service for each customer.

value-added network (VAN)   A private network, provided by a third party, for exchanging information through a high capacity connection.

vertical marketplace   Provides products that are specific to trading partners in a given industry.

vertical market software   Application software that is unique to a particular industry.

view   Allows users to see the contents of a database, make any required changes, perform simple sorting, and query the database to find the location of specific information.

virtual assistant   A small program stored on a PC or portable devide that monitors e-mails, faxes, messages, and phone calls.

virtual private network (VPN)   A way to use the public telecommunication infrastructure (e.g., Internet) to provide secure access to an organization's network.

virus   Software written with malicious intent to cause annoyance or damage.

W

waterfall methodology   A sequential, activity-based process in which each phase in the SDLC is performed sequentially from planning through implementation and maintenance.

weak entity   An entity that cannot exist in the database unless a related instance of another entity is present and related to it.

Web-based self-service system   Allows customers to use the Web to find answers to their questions or solutions to their problems.

Web content management system (WCM)   Adds an additional layer to document and digital asset management that enables publishing content both to intranets and to public Web sites.

Web log   Consists of one line of information for every visitor to a Web site and is usually stored on a Web server.

Web traffic   Includes a host of benchmarks such as the number of page-views, the number of unique visitors, and the average time spent viewing a Web page.

what-if analysis   Checks the impact of a change in an assumption on the proposed solution.

white-hat hacker   Work at the request of the system owners to find system vulnerabilities and plug the holes.

wide area network (WAN)   A geographically dispersed telecommunication network.

WiFi (wireless fidelity)   A standard for transmitting information in the form of radio waves over distances up to about 300 feet.

wireless   Computer networks that do not use physical wires.

wireless Internet service provider (WISP)   An ISP that allows subscribers to connect to a server at designated "hot spots" or "access points" using a wireless connection.

wireless LAN transmitter   Propagate signals through radio waves or infrared light instead of wires.

wireless topology   Devices are connected by a receiver/transmitter to a special network interface card that transmits signals between a computer and a server all within an acceptable transmission range.

workflow management system   Controls the movement of work through a business process.

workshop training   Set in a classroom-type environment and led by an instructor.

worm   A type of virus that spreads itself, not only from file to file, but also from computer to computer.

NOTES

UNIT 1

1. Kim Girard, "How Levi's Got Its Jeans into Wal-Mart," *CIO Magazine,* July 15, 2003, www.cio.com/archive/071503/levis.html, accessed November 14, 2003.

2. www.synergyanywhere.com, accessed November 14, 2003.

3. "Amazon Finds Profits in Outsourcing," *CIO Magazine,* October 15, 2002, www.cio.com/archive/101502/tl_ec.html, accessed November 14, 2003.

4. www.wired.com, accessed November 15, 2003.

5. "The Net's Good Fortunes," *Wired,* March 2004, p. 57.

6. Gabriel Kahn and Cris Prystay, "'Charge It' Your Cellphone Tells Your Bank," *The Wall Street Journal,* August 13, 2003.

7. "Trek Standardizes Worldwide Operations on J. D. Edwards," www.jdedwards.com, accessed November 15, 2003.

8. Christopher Koch, "The ABC's of Supply Chain Management," www.cio.com, accessed October 12, 2003.

9. Sarah L. Roberts-Witt, "It's the Customer, Stupid!" *PC Magazine,* June 27, 2000, p. 26,

10. www.businessweek.com, accessed November 15, 2003.

11. "Integrated Solutions—The ABCs of CRM," www.integratedsolutionsmag.com, accessed November 12, 2003.

12. "Customer Success Stories," www.siebel.com, accessed November 12, 2003.

13. Dave Lindorff, "GE's Drive to Real-Time Measurement," *CIO Insight,* November 11, 2002.

14. Ken Blanchard, "Effectiveness vs. Efficiency," *Wachovia Small Business*

15. www.accenture.com, accessed November 10, 2003.

16. United Nations Division for Public Economics and Public Administration, www.un.com, accessed November 10, 2003.

17. *eBay Financial News,* Earnings and Dividend Release, January 15, 2002.

18. "Sun and eBay Celebrate Record Uptime," www.sun.com/service/about/features/ebay_and_sun.html, accessed January 14, 2004.

19. www.gartner.com, accessed January 13, 2004.

20. www.cio.com, accessed January 14, 2004.

21. John Heilemann, "What's Friendster Selling?" *Business 2.0,* March 2004, p. 46.

22. "What Concerns CIOs the Most?" www.cio.com, accessed November 22, 2003.

23. Michael Schrage, "Build the Business Case," *CIO Magazine,* March 15, 2003.

24. Scott Berianato, "Take the Pledge," *CIO Magazine,* www.cio.com, accessed November 17, 2003.

25. Ibid.

26. "Health Information Management," www.gartner.com, accessed November 16, 2003.

27. "Ticketmaster's Customer's Customer," www.business2.com, accessed November 16, 2003.

28. "Rewarding All-Stars," *Fast Company,* February 2004, www.fastcompany.com, accessed November 13, 2003.

29. "The Incredible Lateness of Delta," *CIO Magazine,* February 15, 2003, www.cio.com, accessed November 11, 2003.

30. "Can American Keep Flying?" *CIO Magazine,* November 1, 2002, www.cio.com, accessed November 10, 2003.

31. Max Hopper, "Rattling SABRE," *Harvard Business Review,* October 2002.

32. Ibid.

UNIT 2

1. Michael S. Malone, "IPO Fever," *Wired,* March 2004.

2. "Cyber Bomb—Search Tampering," *BusinessWeek,* March 1, 2004.

3. "Google Knows Where You Are," *BusinessWeek,* February 2, 2004.

4. www.google.com, accessed September 13, 2003.

5. "Google Reveals High-Profile Users of Data Search Machine," Reuters News Service, August 13, 2003, www.chron.com, accessed September 3, 2003.

6. Mitch Betts, "Unexpected Insights," *ComputerWorld,* April 14, 2003, www.computerworld.com, accessed September 4, 2003.

7. Ibid.

8. "Data Mining: What General Managers Need to Know," *Harvard Management Update,* October 1999.

9. Reimers, DePompa, Barbara, "Too Much of a Good Thing," *ComputerWorld,* www.computerworld.com, April 14, 2003.

10. Ibid.

11. "MSI Business Solutions Case Study: Westpac Financial Services," www.MSI.com, accessed August 4, 2003.

12. "Why Data Quality," www.trilliumsoft.com, accessed October 3, 2003.

13. Ibid.

14. Ibid.

15. "Alaska Fish and Game Yields a Bounty of High-Quality Information to Manage Natural Resources," www.oracle.com, accessed September 20, 2003.

16. www.oracle.com/successstories, accessed September 20, 2003.

17. Ibid., accessed September 22, 2003.

18. Ibid., accessed September 23, 2003.

19. Ibid.

20. Ibid., accessed September 22, 2003.

21. Ibid., accessed September 20, 2003.

22. Ibid.

23. Kathleen Melymuka, "Premier 100: Turning the Tables at Applebee's," *ComputerWorld,* www.computerworld.com, accessed February 24, 2003.

24. Alice LaPante, "Big Things Come in Smaller Packages," *Computerworld,* June 24, 1996, pp. DW/6–7.

25. Julia Kiling, "OLAP Gains Fans among Data-Hungry Firms," *ComputerWorld,* January 8, 2001, p. 54.

26. Nikhil Hutheesing, "Surfing with Sega," *Forbes,* November 4, 2002, p. 58.

27. Tommy Perterson, "Data Cleansing," *ComputerWorld,* www.computerworld.com, February 10, 2003.

28. "Dr Pepper/Seven Up, Inc.," www.cognos.com, accessed September 10, 2003.

29. Christine McGeever, "FBI Database Problem Halts Gun Checks," www.computerworld.com, accessed May 22, 2000.

30. "Distribution of Software Updates of Thousands of Franchise Locations Was Slow and Unpredictable," www.fountain.com, accessed October 10, 2003.

31. "What Every Executive Needs to Know," www.akamai.com, accessed September 10, 2003.

32. "Connect Austria," www.ncr.com, accessed October 10, 2003.

33. "Privacy, Security, Personal Health Records and the Enterprise," *CIO Magazine,* www.cio.com, accessed November 10, 2003.

34. Meridith Levinson, "Harrah's Knows What You Did Last Night," *Darwin Magazine,* May 2001.

35. "Harrah's Entertainment Wins TDWI's 2000 DW Award," www.hpcwire.com, October 10, 2003.

36. Gary Loveman, "Diamonds in the Data Mine," *Harvard Business Review* 81 (5) (May 2003), p. 109.

37. Levinson, "Harrah's Knows What You Did."

38. "NCR—Harrah's Entertainment, Inc.," www.ncr.com, October 12, 2003.

39. "Cognos and Harrah's Entertainment Win Prestigous Data Warehousing Award," 2002 News Release, www.cognos.com, October 14, 2003.

40. Kim Nash, "Casinos Hit Jackpot with Customer Data," www.cnn.com, October 14, 2003.

41. Rafe Needleman, "Success in the Army," *Business 2.0,* July 7, 2003, www.business20.com.

UNIT 3

1. www.investor.harley-davidson.com, accessed October 10, 2003.

2. Bruce Caldwell, "Harley-Davidson Revs up IT Horsepower," *Internetweek.com,* December 7, 2000.

3. "Computerworld 100 Best Places to Work in IT 2003," *Computerworld,* June 9, 2003, pp. 36–48.

4. Leroy Zimdars, "Supply Chain Innovation at Harley-Davidson: An Interview with Leroy Zimdars," *Ascet* 2 (April 15, 2000).

5. "Customer Trust: Reviving Loyalty in a Challenging Economy," *Pivotal Webcast,* September 19, 2002.

6. "Harley-Davidson Announces Go-Live: Continues to Expand Use of Manugistics Supplier Relationship Management Solutions," www.manugistics.com, May 7, 2002.

7. Roger Villareal, "Docent Enterprise Increases Technician and Dealer Knowledge and Skills to Maximize Sales Results and Customer Service," www.docent.com, August 13, 2002.

8. "1,000 Executives Best Skillset," *The Wall Street Journal,* July 15, 2003.

9. "The Visionary Elite," *Business 2.0,* December 2003, pp. S1–S5.

10. "Open Standards and The Taming of the Screw," www.ibm.com/services/thinking, accessed May 6, 2003.

11. Beth Bacheldor, "Steady Supply," *InformationWeek,* November 24, 2003, www.informationweek.com, accessed June 6, 2003.

12. Neil McManus, "Robots at Your Service," *Wired,* January 2003, p. O59.

13. "Put Better, Faster Decision-Making in Your Sights," www.teradata.com, accessed July 7, 2003.

14. McManus, "Robots at Your Service."

15. "Maytag—Washing Away Maintenance," www.sas.com, accessed October 3, 2003.

16. "How Creamy? How Crunchy?" www.sas.com, accessed October 3, 2003.

17. "Forecasting Chocolate," www.sas.com, accessed October 3, 2003.

18. "Finding the Best Buy," www.oracle.com, accessed April 4, 2003.

19. Ibid.

20. Bacheldor, "Steady Supply."

21. "The e-Biz Surprise," *BusinessWeek,* May 12, 2003, pp. 60–65.

22. "Creating a Value Network," *Wired,* September 2003, p. S13.

23. Fred Hapgood, "Smart Decisions," *CIO Magazine,* www.cio.com, August 15, 2001.

24. "Creating a Value Network."

25. Keving Kelleher, "BudNet: 66,207,896 Bottles of Beer on the Wall," *Business 2.0,* February 2004.

26. "1800 flowers.com," *Business 2.0,* February 2004.

27. "The 'New' New York Times," *Business 2.0,* January 2004.

28. "New York Knicks—Success," www.jdedwards.com, accessed January 15, 2004.

29. "Customer Success—Brother," www.sap.com, accessed January 12, 2004.

30. "Finding Value in the Real-Time Enterprise," *Business 2.0,* November 2003, pp. S1–S5.

31. "Customer Success—PNC Retail Bank," www.siebel.com, accessed May 5, 2003.

32. "Customer Success—Boise Office Solution," www.siebel.com, accessed May 5, 2003.

33. "Finding Value in the Real-Time Enterprise."

34. "Customer Success—REI," www.siebel.com, accessed May 5, 2003.

35. "Customer Success—UPS," www.sap.com, accessed April 5, 2003.

36. "Customer Success—Cisco," www.sap.com, accessed April 5, 2003.

37. "ERP Success," www.sap.com, accessed April 5, 2003.

38. "Hilton Hotels—Upgrading Its Infrastructure," *ComputerWorld,* February 2003, pp. 1–2.

39. "Customer Success—Lego," www.i2.com, accessed June 6, 2003.

40. "Customer Success—eBay," www.informatica.com, accessed June 6, 2003.

UNIT 4

1. "Case Study: Amazon.com," digitalenterprise.org/cases/amazon.html, accessed June 8, 2004.

2. S. Leschly, et al., "Amazon.com," *Harvard Business Online,* Case 9-803-098, February 13, 2003.

3. Joshua Ramo, "Jeffrey Bezos," www.time.com/time/poy2000/archive/1999.html, accessed June 8, 2004.

4. "Shop Amazon.com with your voice," www.amazon.com/exec/obidos/subst/misc/anywhere/anywhere.html/ref=gw_hp_ls_1_2/002-7628940-9665649, accessed June 8, 2004.

5. Juan Perez, "First-Mover Advantage," www.cio.com/archive/121503/tl_ecom.html, accessed June 8, 2004.

6. www.computerworld.com/managementtopics/outsourcing/story/0,10801,49190,00.html, accessed June 8, 2004.

7. Jennifer DiSabatino, "Circuit City Seeks E-mail Help for Training Program," www.cio.com/archive/050104/best.html, accessed June 8, 2004.

8. "How Many Online?" www.nua.ie/surveys/how_many_online/, accessed June 8, 2004.

9. Mary Hillebrand, "U.S. Steel Finds B2B E-Commerce Riveting," www.ecommercetimes.com/story/2590.html, accessed June 8, 2004.

10. "E-Commerce Taxation," www.icsc.org/srch/government/ECommerceFebruary2003.pdf, accessed June 8, 2004.

11. Phil Taylor, "Global Cellular Data Forecasts (2003–2008)," www.strategyanalytics.com/cgi-bin/list.cgi?type=reports&archive=yes&svc=15, accessed June 8, 2004.

12. Akira Ishikawa, "The Success of 7-Eleven Japan," October 2002, pp. 1–3.

13. Ibid.

14. "D-FW Defense Contractors Show Mixed Fortunes since September 11," www.bizjournals.com/dallas/stories/2002/09/09/focus2.htm, accessed June 8, 2004.

15. Steve Konicki, "Collaboration Is Cornerstone of $19B Defense Contract," www.business2.com/content/magazine/indepth/2000/07/11/17966, accessed June 8, 2004.

16. "Speeding Information to BMW Dealers," www.kmworld.com/resources/featurearticles/index.cfm?action=readfeature&Feature_ID=337, accessed June 8, 2004.

17. "What Is OAISIS?" www.comptroller.nyc.gov/bureaus/bis/oaisis_sec1.shtm, accessed June 8, 2004.

18. "Toyota's One-Stop Information Shop," www.istart.co.nz/index/HM20/PC0/PV21873/EX236/CS25653, accessed June 8, 2004.

19. "Driving Performance of e-Business," www.concord.com/aboutus/invest/pdfs/1999CCRD_AR.pdf, accessed June 8, 2004.

20. "Groove Workspace: Instant Messaging Grows Up," www.syllabus.com/article.asp?id=8291, accessed June 8, 2004.

21. "Once an Obscure Discipline, Knowledge Management Is Now a Business Necessity," www.chevrontexaco.com/news/archive/chevron_press/1999/99-01-11.asp, accessed June 8, 2004.

22. "Frito-Lay's Sales Force Sells More Chips through Information Collaboration," www.cio.com/archive/050101/crunch.html, accessed June 8, 2004.

23. "Merrill Lynch and Thomson Financial to Develop Wealth Management Workstation," www.advisorpage.com/modules.php?name=News&file=print&sid=666, accessed June 8, 2004.

24. Charles Pelton, "How to Solve the IT Labor Shortage Problem," www.informationweek.com/author/eyeonit15.htm, accessed June 8, 2004.

25. "Future Three Partners with Ideal Technology Solutions, U.S. for Total Automotive Network Exchange (ANX) Capability," www.itsusnow.com/news_future3.htm, accessed June 8, 2004.

26. "Sneaker Net," from www.cio.com/archive/webbusiness/080199_nike.html, accessed June 8, 2004.

27. Art Jahnke, "Kodak Stays in the Digital Picture," www.cnn.com/TECH/computing/9908/06/kodak.ent.idg/, accessed June 8, 2004.

28. Michael Kanellos, "IDC: PC market on the Comeback Trail," news.com.com/2100-1001-976295.html?part=dtx&tag=ntop, accessed June 8, 2004.

29. Stephanie Overby, "In or Out?" www.cio.com/archive/081503/sourcing.html, accessed June 8, 2004.

30. Jaikumar Vijayan, "Companies Expected to Boost Offshore Outsourcing," www.computerworld.com/managementtopics/outsourcing/story/0,10801,78583,00.html, accessed June 8, 2004.

31. "IBM Offshoring Presentation," www.allianceibm.org/articles/execoffshoremeet.htm, accessed June 8, 2004.

32. "CEOs Being Forced to Adapt to Internet Reality," www.morebusiness.com/running_your_business/management/d935705515.brc, accessed June 8, 2004.

33. "ChemConnect's Chalkboard Provides Vanguard Petroleum Real-time Access to NGL Market," www.communityb2b.com/library/, accessed June 8, 2004.

34. "Choosing an ISP," www.choosinganisp.com/, accessed June 8, 2004.

35. "Get More from Your Mobile Life," www.t-mobile.com/hotspot/services_about.htm, accessed June 8, 2004.

36. "Ask the Pilot," www.salon.com/tech/col/smith/2004/01/16/askthepilot70/index_np.html, accessed June 8, 2004.

37. "GM Pushes Web Services to the (Shop) Floor," www.cio.com/archive/091503/tl_web.html, accessed June 8, 2004.

38. Jonathan Fahey, "Can This Brand Be Saved?" http://www.forbes.com/forbes/2004/0329/062_print.html www.cio.com/archive/040197/outsourcing.html, accessed June 8, 2004.

39. "Business Reasons Driving Software/Application Development Outsourcing," www.ebstrategy.com/BPO/it_software/bus_reasons.htm, accessed June 8, 2004.

40. "DuPont: Launching eCommerce," www.accenture.com/xd/xd.asp?it=enweb&xd=industries%5Cresources%5Cchemical%5Ccase%5Cchem_dupontecomm.xml, accessed June 8, 2004.

UNIT 5

1. Kevin Kelleher, "The Wired 40," *Wired,* www.wired.com, accessed March 3, 2004.

2. "The Web Smart 50," *BusinessWeek,* www.businessweek.com, accessed March 3, 2004.

3. Adam Lashinsky, "Kodak's Developing Situation," *Fortune,* January 20, 2003, p. 176.

4. Adam Lashinsky, "The Disrupters," *Fortune,* August 11, 2003, pp. 62–65.

5. Ibid.

6. Clayton Christensen, *The Innovator's Dilemma* (Boston: Harvard Business School, 1997).

7. Ibid.

8. "The ITEC Outlook," *The BusinessWeek 50,* Spring 2003, pp. 153–58.

9. "Small Fry to the Rescue," *The BusinessWeek 50,* Spring 2003, pp. 43–45.

10. Christensen, *The Innovator's Dilemma.*

11. Ibid.

12. David Pescovitz, "Six Technologies That Will Change the World," *Business 2.0,* May 2003, pp. 116–20.

13. Stephen Wildstrom, "Keys That Remember and a Lot More," *BusinessWeek,* December 22, 2003, p. 30.

14. Pescovitz, "Six Technologies."

15. Wildstrom, "Keys That Remember."

16. "The Future of Wireless," www.cio.com, accessed December 4, 2003.

17. "Growing Technology," *Business 2.0,* October 2003, pp. s1–s7.

18. "The Real-Time Enterprise," www.cio.com, accessed December 12, 2003.

19. "The Brew Platform," www.cio.com, accessed December 12, 2003.

20. "More Work, Less Time," *BusinessWeek,* www.businessweek.com, accessed November 12, 2003.

21. Ibid.

22. "Customer Success Story—Weather.com," www.ibm.com, accessed January 1, 2004.

23. www.businessweek.com, accessed November 1, 2003.

24. Ibid.

25. "Software Costs," www.cio.com, accessed December 5, 2003.

26. Ibid.

27. "Defective Software Costs," National Institute of Standards and Technology (NIST), June 2002.

28. "Customer Success Story—PHH," www.informatica. com, accessed December 12, 2003.

29. "Building Events," www.microsoft.com, accessed November 15, 2003.

30. *Agile Alliance Manifesto,* www.agile.com, accessed November 1, 2003.

31. Ibid.

32. "Software Metrics," www.cio.com, accessed December 2, 2003.

33. "Building Software That Works," www.compaq.com, accessed November 14, 2003.

34. "Software Metrics," www.cio.com, accessed November 15, 2003.

35. www.agile.com, accessed November 10, 2003.

36. "Customer Success—Horizon," www.businessengine.com, accessed October 15, 2003.

37. "Top Reasons Why IT Projects Fail," *InformationWeek,* www.infoweek.com, accessed November 5, 2003.

38. Ibid.

39. Christopher Null, "How Netflix Is Fixing Hollywood," *Business 2.0,* July 2003, pp. 31–33.

40. www.expedia.com, accessed October 13, 2003.

41. www.apple.com, accessed October 13, 2003.

42. www.dell.com, accessed October 13, 2003.

43. www.lendingtree.com, accessed October 13, 2003.

44. www.amazon.com, accessed October 13, 2003.

45. www.ebay.com, accessed October 13, 2003.

46. www.cisco.com, accessed October 13, 2003.

47. Lashinsky, "The Disrupters."

48. www.wired.com, accessed October 15, 2003.

49. "A New View," *Business 2.0,* November 10, 2003, pp. S1–S5.

50. Tom Schultz, "PBS: A Clearer Picture," *Business 2.0,* January 2003.

51. Bruce Sterling, "Linux: The Next Generation," *Wired,* December 2003, pp. 108–11.

52. Erick Schonfeld, "Linux Takes Flight," *Business 2.0,* January 2003, pp. 103–5.

53. Otis Port, "Will the Feud Choke the Life Out of Linux?" *BusinessWeek,* July 7, 2003, p. 81.

PLUG-IN B1

1. "2002 CSI/FBI Computer Crime and Security Survey," www.gocsi.com, accessed November 23, 2003.

2. www.ey.com, accessed November 25, 2003.

3. "The Security Revolution," www.cio.com, accessed June 6, 2003.

4. Alice Dragoon, "Eight (Not So) Simple Steps to the HIPAA Finish Line," www.cio.com, accessed July 7, 2003.

5. "Losses from Identity Theft to Total $221 Billion Worldwide," www.cio.com, May 23, 2003.

6. "Sony Fights Intrusion with 'Crystal Ball,' " www.cio.com, accessed August 9, 2003.

7. Mark Leon, "Keys to the Kingdom," www.computerworld.com, April 14, 2003, accessed August 8, 2003.

8. "Spam Losses to Grow to $198 Billion," www.cio.com, accessed August 9, 2003.

9. "Teen Arrested in Internet 'Blaster' Attack," www.cnn.com, August 29, 2003.

10. Scott Berinato, and Sarah Scalet, "The ABCs of Information Security," www.cio.com, accessed July 7, 2003.

11. "Countermeasures to Protect the Enterprise," www.cio.com, accessed August 8, 2003.

PLUG-IN B2

1. Scott Berinato, "Take the Pledge—The CIO's Code of Ethical Data Management," *CIO Magazine,* July 1, 2002, www.cio.com, accessed March 7, 2004.

2. Ibid.

3. Alice Dragoon, "Be a Spam Slayer," *CIO Magazine,* November 1, 2003, www.cio.com, accessed March 9, 2004.

4. Paul Roberts, "Report: Spam Costs $874 per Employee per Year," www.computerworld.com, July 2, 2003, accessed March 9, 2004.

5. Ibid.

6. AMA Research, "Workplace Monitoring and Surveillance," www.amanet.org, April 2003, accessed March 1, 2004.

7. "Sarbanes-Oxley Act," www.workingvalues.com, accessed March 3, 2004.

8. AnchorDeskStaff, "How to Spy on Your Employees . . . and Why You May Not Want To," www.reviews-zdnet.com, August 21, 2003, accessed March 5, 2004.

PLUG-IN B3

1. Frank Quinn, "The Payoff Potential in Supply Chain Management," www.ascet.com, accessed June 15, 2003.

2. Walid Mougayar, "Old Dogs Learn New Tricks," *Business 2.0,* October 2000, www.Business2.com, accessed June 14, 2003.

3. Quinn, "The Payoff Potential."

4. William Copacino, "How to Become a Supply Chain Master," *Supply Chain Management Review,* September 1, 2001, www.manufacturing.net, accessed June 12, 2003.

5. Navi Radjou, "Manufacturing Sector IT Spending Profile for 2004," www.forrester.com, September 12, 2003, accessed March 15, 2004.

6. Ibid.

7. Jennifer Bresnahan, "The Incredible Journey," *CIO Enterprise Magazine,* August 15, 1998, www.cio.com, accessed March 12, 2004.

8. "Crafting Improved Transportation Processes at Micheals," www.i2.com, accessed June 14, 2003.

PLUG-IN B4

1. "Barclays, Giving Voice to Customer-Centricity," crm.insightexec.com, accessed July 15, 2003.

2. California State Automobile Association Case Study, www.epiphany.com/customers/detail_csaa.html, accessed July 4, 2003.

3. "Vail Resorts Implements FrontRange HEAT," *CRM Today,* October 16, 2003, www.crm2day.com/news/crm/EpyykllFyAqEUbqOhW.php, accessed December 2, 2003.

4. "3M Accelerates Revenue Growth Using Siebel eBusiness Applications," www.siebel.com, July 30, 2002, accessed July 10, 2003.

5. "Avnet Brings IM to Corporate America with Lotus Instant Messaging," websphereadvisor.com/doc/12196, accessed July 11, 2003.

6. www.FedEx.com, accessed July 13, 2003.

7. "Documedics," www.siebel.com, accessed July 10, 2003.

8. *Supply Chain Planet,* June 2003, http://newsweaver.co.uk/supplychainplanet/e_article000153342.cfm, accessed July 12, 2003.

9. "Grupo Gas Natural Exploding," www.siebel.com, accessed July 10, 2003.

10. "Partnering in the Fight against Cancer," www.siebel.com, accessed July 16, 2003.

11. "The Expanding Territory of Outsourcing," www.outsourcing.com, accessed August 15, 2003.

PLUG-IN B5

1. "Customer Success Story—Turner Industries," www.jdedwards.com, accessed October 15, 2003.

2. "Harley-Davidson on the Path to Success," www.peoplesoft.com/media/success, accessed October 12, 2003.

3. "Customer Success Story—Grupo Farmanova Intermed," www.jdedwards.com, accessed October 15, 2003.

4. www.jdedwards.com, accessed October 15, 2003.

5. Ibid.

6. Michael Doane, "A Blueprint for ERP Implementation Readiness," www.metagroup.com, accessed October 17, 2003.

7. "Customer Success Story—PepsiAmerica," www.peoplesoft.com, accessed October 22, 2003.

8. "Customer Success Story—Ghirardelli," www.peoplesoft.com, accessed October 22, 2003.

PLUG-IN B6

1. "IBM/Lotus Domino Server Hosting Service," www.macro.com.hk/solution_Outsourcing.htm, accessed June 8, 2004.

2. www.forrester.com/find?SortType=Date&No=350&N=32, accessed June 8, 2004.

3. Deni Connor, "IT Outlook Declines Due to Outsourcing, Offshoring," www.nwfusion.com/careers/2004/0531manside.html, accessed June 8, 2004.

4. "BP: WebLearn," www.accenture.com/xd/xd.asp?it=enweb&xd=industries%5Cresources%5Cenergy%5Ccase%5Cener_bpweblearn.xml, accessed June 8, 2004.

5. Datz, Todd, "Outsourcing World Tour," CIO Magazine, July 15, 2004, pp. 42–48.

6. "Call Center and CRM Statistics," www.cconvergence.com/shared/printableArticle.jhtml?articleID=7617915, accessed June 8, 2004.

7. Stan Gibson, "Global Services Plays Pivotal Role," www.eweek.com/article2/0,1759,808984,00.asp, accessed June 8, 2004.

8. "Coors Brewing Company," www.eds.com/case_studies/case_coors.shtml, accessed June 8, 2004.

PLUG-IN B7

1. "Cargill, Nourishing Potential," www.cargill.com/today/files/cb_english.pdf, accessed June 8, 2004.

2. Stephanie Overby, "Survivor III: Who's Left on the E-Commerce Island?" www.itworld.com/Tech/2401/CIO010501survivor/pfindex.html, accessed June 8, 2004.

3. Melissa Campanelli, "Consign of the Times," www.entrepreneur.com/article/0,4621,315172,00.html, accessed June 8, 2004.

4. Erich Luening, "Supplier Joins 'Big Three' Automakers' Online Marketplace," news.com.com/2100-1017-240837.html?legacy=cnet, accessed June 8, 2004.

5. www.ebay.com, accessed June 8, 2004.

6. "About NetPost Certified Mail," www.usps.com/netpost/certifiedmail/aboutcm.htm, accessed June 8, 2004.

PLUG-IN B8

1. "The Art of Foresight," *The Futurist,* May–June 2004, pp. 31–35.

2. Marvin Cetron and Owen Davies, "50 Trends Shaping the Future," *2003 World Future Society Special Report,* April 2004.

3. William Halal, "The Top 10 Emerging Technologies," *The Futurist Special Report,* July 2004.

4. Penelope Patsuris, "Marketing Messages Made to Order," *Forbes,* August 2003.

5. www.rfidnews.org, accessed June 18, 2004.

6. Stacy Crowley, "IBM, HP, MS Discuss Autonomic Computing Strategies," *Infoworld,* May 19, 2004.

7. Denise Dubie, "Tivoli Users Discuss Automation," *Network World,* April 14, 2003.

8. "Progressive Receives Applied Systems' 2003 Interface Best Practices Award," www.worksite.net/091203tech.htm, accessed June 18, 2004.

PLUG-IN B9

1. "Python Project Failure," www.systemsdev.com, accessed November 14, 2003.

2. Gary McGraw, "Making Essential Software Work," *Software Quality Management Magazine,* April 2003, www.sqmmagazine.com, accessed November 14, 2003.

3. www.standishgroup.com, accessed November 14, 2003.

4. "Overcoming Software Development Problems," www.samspublishing.com, October 7, 2002, accessed November 16, 2003.

5. "Baggage Handling System Errors," www.flavors.com, accessed November 16, 2003.

6. www.microsoft.com, accessed November 16, 2003.

PLUG-IN B10

1. www.calpine.com, accessed December 14, 2003.

2. "The Project Manager in the IT Industry," www.si2.com, accessed December 15, 2003.

3. www.standishgroup.com, accessed December 12, 2003.

4. www.snapon.com, accessed December 13, 2003.

5. "The Change Management Guide for Managers and Supervisors," www.change-management.org, accessed December 12, 2003.

6. www.change-management.org, accessed December 12, 2003.

7. www.altria.com, accessed December 15, 2003.

8. "Supply and Demand Chain," www.isourceonline.com, accessed December 14, 2003.

9. www.microsoft.com, accessed December 13, 2003.

10. "Successful Project Management Strategies," *CIO Magazine,* www.cio.com, accessed December 12, 2003.

11. "Staying on Track at the Toronto Transit Commission," www.primavera.com, accessed December 16, 2003.

12. www.autodesk.com, accessed December 16, 2003.

PLUG-IN T7

1. www.jdedwards.com, accessed January 13, 2004.

2. www.gartner.com, accessed January 13, 2004.

3. www.cio.com, accessed January 14, 2004.

4. www.yankeegroup.com, accessed January 14, 2004.

5. www.gartner.com, accessed January 13, 2004.

6. Ibid.

APPLY YOUR KNOWLEDGE PROJECT 1

1. "Why General Managers Need to Understand Information Technology," www.umsl.edu/~lacity/whymis.html, accessed June 15, 2004.

PHOTO CREDITS

Unit 1

Photo 1.1a, page 3, © Louise Gubb / The Image Works

Photo 1.1b, page 3, © Amy Etra / Photo Edit

Photo 1.1c, page 3, © James Leynse / Corbis

Photo 1.13a, page 18, Photo courtesy of Hyundai Motor America

Photo 1.13b, page 18, Photo Courtesy of Audi

Photo 1.13c, page 18, Copyright © 2004 Kia Motors America, Inc. All Rights Reserved

Photo 1.13d, page 18, Photo Courtesy of GM

Unit 2

Photo 2.1, page 51, Photo Courtesy of Cray Inc.

Photo 2.4, page 77, © Lester Lefkowitz / Corbis

Unit 3

Photo 3.1a, page 91, AP / Wide World Photos

Photo 3.1b, page 91, Scott Olson / Getty Images

Photo 3.1c, page 91, PRNewsFoto/Harley-Davidson / AP / Wide World Photos

Photo 3.2a, page 99, Alexander Heimann / AFP / Getty

Photo 3.2b, page 99, AP / Wide World Photos

Photo 3.2c, page 99, © Jeff Greenberg / Photo Edit

Photo 3.3, page 102, Photo courtesy of NCR Corporation

Unit 4

Photo 4.1a, page 133, © Macduff Everton/Corbis

Photo 4.1b, page 133, AP / Wide World Photos

Photo 4.1c, page 133, © Jack Kurtz / The Image Works

Unit 5

Photo 5.1a, page 181, Mario Tama / Getty Images

Photo 5.1b, page 181, Justin Sullivan/Getty Images

Photo 5.1c, page 181, Dan Krauss/Getty Images

Photo 5.2a, page 191, © Texas Instruments Inc. All Rights reserved.

Photo 5.2b, page 191, Photo Courtesy of Iomega Corporation

Photo 5.2c, page 191, Photo Courtesy of Advanced Micro Devices, Inc.

Plug-In B7

Photo B7.1, page 307, AP / Wide World Photos

Plug-In B8

Photo B8.5, page 329, © Copyright 2002 E Ink Corporation

Photo B8.6, page 330, AP / Wide World Photos

Photo B8.7, page 331, Gyricon, LLC

Photo B8.10, page 334, Getty Images

Plug-In T1

Photo T1.1, page 371, Courtesy of HP

Photo T1.2, page 372, Photo courtesy of Viewsonic

Photo T1.3, page 372, Photo Courtesy of Cray Inc.

Photo T1.4, page 374, Photo courtesy of Microsoft® Corp

Photo T1.5, page 374, Photo Courtesy of Apple

Photo T1.6, page 375, Courtesy of HP

Photo T1.7, page 375, Photo Courtesy of Panasonic

Photo T1.8, page 376, Courtesy of Dell Inc.

Photo T1.9, page 377, SimpleTech Inc.

Communicator, 199
Communities of fantasy, 314
Communities of interest, 314
Communities of relations, 314
Compact disc database (CDDB), 177
Compact disc—read-only memory (CD-ROM), 378, 519
Compact disc—recordable (CD-R), 378, 519
Compact disc—rewritable (CD-RW), 519
Compaq, 183, 201, 298, 360
Comparative metrics, 495–496, 519
    activity/resource spending on IT, 495
    allocations per employee, 496
    business decisions project, 498
    help desk value, 496
    revenue-percentage spending on IT, 495–496
Compensation programs, 44
Competition, 17–18, 99, 329
Competitive advantage, 15, 501, 519
Competitive advantages identification
    cell phone purchases (case study), 21
    Five Forces Model of, 15–18
    generic strategies for, 18–19
    value-chain strategy for, 19–20
Competitive advantages implementation, 22–28
    with customer relationship management, 24–25
    with enterprise resource planning, 26–27
    Saab (case study), 28
    with supply chain management, 22–24
Competitive analysis (project), 49
Competitive edge, 299
Competitive intelligence, 101
Competitive intelligence research (project), 49
Completeness of information, 57, 58
Composite entity, 430–431, 519
Comprehensiveness of enterprise resource planning, 121
Compton, Dean, 46
Computer Fraud and Abuse Act (1986), 237
Computer network (See Network)
Computer purchase (business decisions project), 382–383
Computer simulation, 324, 519
Computer-aided software engineering (CASE), 344, 520
Computerworld, 83, 91
ComScore Networks, 247
Concatenated primary key, 433
Concentrator, 394
Concur, 168
Confidentiality, 234, 300, 520
Congo, Democratic Republic of the, 326
Congruent goals, 119
Connecting devices, 371, 380–381
Connectivity, 327
Connectivity software, 379
Connectors, 380
Connor, Deni, 537
Consent, informed, 238
Consistency, 57, 58, 71
Consolidation, 98, 520
Constraint, 424, 435, 520
Constructech, 278
Consultant decision making (project), 129
Consulting (business decisions project), 465
Consumer protection, 141
Consumer-to-business (C2B), 314, 318, 520

Consumer-to-consumer (C2C), 314, 318, 520
Consumer-to-government (C2G), 318, 319
Contact center, 268, 281, 305, 520
Contact management system, 267, 520
Content filtering, 225, 520
Content management system (CMS), 147–148, 520
"Content" perspective (of e-marketplaces), 316, 317
Content provider, 309, 520
Contingent project, 488, 520
Contract length, 299
Control unit, 377, 520
Convenience, 191
Convenience goods, 138
Conversion rates, 31
Convertible tablet PCs, 372
Cookie, 33, 243, 493, 520
Cookin' with Google, 53
Coopetition, 139
Coors Brewing Company, 303–304
Copacino, William, 536
Copyright, 38, 234, 520
Cordless computer peripherals, 190
Core competency, 11, 159, 345, 520
Core competency strategy, 11, 520
Core ERP component, 279–281, 520
Corio, 168
Corporate core competency, 345
Corporate Email PLUS, 193
Corporate resources, 345
Corrective maintenance, 350
Cosmos Business Intelligence System (case study), 128–129
Cost
    of disaster recovery, 78
    of e-business, 314
    of enterprise resource planning, 283
    of low-quality information, 58
    and project time/scope, 202
    switching, 17
Cost leadership strategy, 18
Costa Rica, 297, 298
Cost/benefit analysis, 342
COTS (See Commercial off-the shelf)
Counterfeit software, 38, 234, 520
Covisint, 316
CPD (Chicago Police Department), 66
CPFR (collaborative planning, forecasting, and replenishment), 127
CPO (See Chief privacy officer)
CPU (See Central processing unit)
Cracker, 227, 520
Crash-proof software, 374
Create, Read, Update, and Delete (CRUD), 467, 520
Credit card fraud, 100
Credit cards, 21
Credit management, 280
Credit Union National Association, 100
Critical path, 361, 520
Critical success factor (CSF), 342, 520
CRM (See Customer relationship management)
CRM vendor comparison (project), 48–49
Cross-functional systems, 207
Cross-selling, 265, 520
Crowley, Stacy, 537
CRT (See Cathode Ray Tube)

CRUD (See Create, Read, Update, and Delete)
CSF (See Critical success factor)
CSI/FBI Computer Crime and Security Survey, 40, 220–221
CSO (See Chief security officer)
CSRs (See Customer service representatives)
CTO (See Chief technology officer)
Cube, 75, 76, 520
Culture
    at Harley-Davidson, 93
    project-management, 365
    trust-based, 247
    wireless, 192–193
Customer, 117
Customer metric, 32, 492–494, 520
Customer relationship management (CRM), 113–118, 262–277, 520
    American Cancer Society (case study), 273–275
    analytical, 270–271
    apply your knowledge project, 505–506
    auto dealership (business decisions project), 276
    Canada (case study), 275–276
    cluster analysis used for, 102
    and competitive advantages, 24–25
    decision making with analytical, 115–116
    defined, 24
    drivers of, 115
    employee loyalty (business decisions project), 276
    as ERP component, 281
    evolution of, 263–264
    growth of, 114–115
    increasing revenues (business decisions project), 277
    integrating SCM/ERP with, 121–122
    at 1–800–Flowers.com, 113
    operational, 264–269
    primary users/benefits of, 123
    and prospective customers, 268
    REI (case study), 118
    reporting/analyzing/predicting examples of, 264
    SCM/ERP comparison (business decisions project), 130
    by Siebel Automotive, 28
    spending on, 115
    strategies (collaborative decisions project), 130
    success factors for, 116–117
    support center (business decisions project), 277
    trends in, 271–272
Customer relationships, 92–93
Customer satisfaction, 31
Customer self-service, 15
Customer service, 267–269
Customer service representatives (CSRs), 268–269
Customer's customer relationship management (CCRM), 41–42
Customizability, 373
CVS.com, 317
Cybercenters, 167
Cyber-hacking, 226
Cybermediary, 139
Cyberterrorist, 227, 520
Cycle inventory, 253–254, 520

D

DaimlerChrysler, 250–251, 316
   ANX collaboration of, 158
   B2B cooperation of, 140
   and Internet, 174
DAM (*See* Digital asset management system)
DARPA, 398
Data administration component, 70, 520
Data definition component, 67, 520
Data dictionary, 67, 435, 436, 520
Data field (PivotTable), 405
Data flow diagram (DFD), 344, 520
Data manipulation component, 67–68, 520
Data mart, 75, 76, 520
Data mining, 520
   apply your knowledge project, 504–505
   association detection with, 102
   Best Buy data warehouse (case study), 105
   business decisions project, 86
   cluster analysis with, 102
   and decision making, 101–104
   defined, 76
   statistical analysis with, 103–104
Data model, 346, 423, 520
Data relationships
   basic, 426
   connectivity/cardinality of, 429–431
   logical, 425–431
   many-to-many, 428
   one-to-many, 428
   one-to-one, 427, 428
   schemas of, 431
Data type (Access), 448
Data warehouse, 10, 74–77, 81, 520
   and analytical CRM, 270
   apply your knowledge project, 505–506
   Best Buy data warehouse (case study), 105
   and business intelligence, 281
   Harrah's (case study), 83–84
The Data Warehousing Institute (TDWI), 76–77, 83
Database design, 422–442
   with Access (*See* Access)
   business decisions projects, 440–442
   entities/data relationships in, 423–425
   logical data relationships in, 425–431
   normalization of, 437–439
   relational model of, 432–437
Database management system (DBMS), 8, 66–71, 422, 520
   application generation/data administration components of, 68, 70
   components of, 67
   data definition component of, 67
   data manipulation component of, 67–70
   defined, 66
Databases, 61–73, 520
   Access (*See* Access)
   applications for, 9
   defined, 8, 61, 422–424, 444
   development of, 347
   multiple, 70–72
   object-oriented, 480
   relational, 61–63
Data-mining tool, 10, 76, 520

Davies, Owen, 537
DBMS (*See* Database management system)
DCF (discounted cash flow) (*See* Net present value)
DDoS (*See* Distributed denial-of-service attack)
DEC (*See* Digital Equipment Corporation)
Decimal places property (Access), 449
Decision making, 9–10, 94–105
   and artificial intelligence, 99–101
   Best Buy data warehouse (case study), 105
   business decisions projects for, 129–130
   collaborative decisions projects for, 130–131
   and data mining, 101–104
   decision support systems for, 96–97
   executive information systems for, 98–99
Decision support systems (DSS), 520
   defined, 96
   Dentix (business decisions project), 130
   examples of, 97
   reasons for growth of, 95
   research (collaborative decisions project), 131
   and SCM, 108–109
Decision-analysis tools, Excel (*See* Excel decision-analysis tools)
Dedicated server, 520
Deeley Harley-Davidson Canada (DHDC), 279
Default value property, 67, 449
Degree of operating leverage (DOL), 501
Delivery, project, 201
Dell Computer, 110, 295, 299, 316, 382
   as B2C e-business, 140
   as connected corporation, 121
   as e-business model, 307
   expected returns on investments/assets at, 186
   as innovative organization, 182–183
   as just-in-time model, 182–183
   as market leader, 510
   SCM analysis (project), 131
Delta Airlines, 45–47
Delta Technology, 46
DemandTec, 310
Demmings, Steve, 275
Democratic Republic of the Congo, 326
Denial-of-service attack (DoS), 227, 521
Dentix (business decisions project), 130
Denver International Airport (DIA), 354
Dependency, 361, 521
DePompa-Reimers, Barbara, 532
Deregulation, 292
Design phase (in systems development life cycle), 197, 345–347, 521
Desktop computer, 372
Detection and response technologies, 226–227
Development phase (in systems development life cycle), 197, 346, 347, 521
DFD (*See* Data flow diagram)
DHL, 296
DIA (Denver International Airport), 354
Diabetic patients, 24
Dial-up access, 379, 394
Differentiated strategy, 19
Digital asset management system (DAM), 147, 521

Digital Darwinism, 12, 521
Digital dashboard, 521
   collaborative decisions project, 49
   defined, 98
   examples of, 98–99
   Levi's and Wal-Mart (case study), 5
Digital Equipment Corporation (DEC), 158, 185, 186, 389
Digital Fountain, 78
Digital ink, 329, 521
Digital paper, 521
Digital signals, 379
Digital Subscriber Line (DSL), 379
Digital video recorder (DVR), 188
Dillard's, Inc., 253
Dimension, 75
Direct interaction, 66
Direct selling, 307
DiSabatino, Jennifer, 533
Disaster recovery cost curve, 78, 521
Disaster recovery plan, 78–79, 86–87, 521
Discounted cash flow (DCF) (*See* Net present value)
Discounted cash flow rate of return (*See* Internal rate of return)
Disk optimization software, 374
Disruptive strategies, 218
Disruptive technology, 185–189, 521
   building/implementing, 195
   business decisions project, 217
   Clayton Christensen on, 186
   companies using, 187
   defined, 185
   Internet as, 186–187
   laws of, 187–188
   TiVo (case study), 188–189
   wireless, 190–191
Distance groupware, 150
Distributed denial-of-service attack (DDoS), 208, 227, 521
DMS (*See* Document management system)
Doane, Michael, 537
Documedics, 269
Document management system (DMS), 11, 147, 521
Documentation testing, 349
Document-retention-and-destruction policy, 246
Documentum, 148
DoD (*See* U.S. Department of Defense)
DOL (degree of operating leverage), 501
DoS (*See* Denial-of-service attack)
Dot pitch, 376
Dots per inch (dpi), 376
Downtime, 80
Dpi (dots per inch), 376
Dr Pepper/Seven UP, Inc., 77
Dragoon, Alice, 536
Drill-down, 76, 98–99, 106, 521
Drilling up, 76
Drivers
   of outsourcing, 292
   supply-chain, 251–252
Drucker, Peter, 29
DSL (Digital Subscriber Line), 379
DSS (*See* Decision support systems)
Dubie, Denise, 537
Dubuc, Nicolas, 203

Ford Motor Company, 66, 218, 250–251, 316
    ANX collaboration of, 158
    B2B cooperation of, 140
    and Internet, 174
Forecast, 103–104, 522
Foreign key, 62, 67, 433–435, 522
Forester Research, 13
Form property, 67
Format property (Access), 448
Format report (PivotTable), 408
Forms, Access, 454–456
Forrester Research, Inc., 118, 160, 188, 257
Fortune, 91
Forward integration, 71, 522
4NF (fourth normal form), 438
Fourth normal form (4NF), 438
FoxMeyer, 196
France, 326
Franklin, Benjamin, 203
Freedom of Information Act, 237
Freenet, 38
Frequent-flyer programs, 16, 45
Friendster valuation (case study), 35
Frito-Lay, 15, 155–156
Frontier Airlines, 45
Fruit e-marketplace competitive advantage
    (project), 177
Fruit of the Loom, 139
FTP (*See* File Transfer Protocol)
Functional organization, 26
Future-orientation, 110

G

G2B (*See* Government-to-business)
G2C (*See* Government-to-consumer)
G2G (*See* Government-to-government)
G5 processor, 191
Gantt chart, 361, 362, 522
The Gap, 3, 137, 209, 313
Garden.com, 168
Gardner Group, 151
Gartner Dataquest, 117, 216
Gartner Group, 160, 191, 192, 201, 491, 495, 496
Gas plasma displays, 375
Gate and boarding applications, 46
Gates, Bill, 216
Gates (company), 6
Gateway, 394, 395, 522
GB (*See* Gigabyte)
GE Capital, 294
General Electric (GE), 29, 186, 296, 364
General Motors (GM) Corporation, 250–251,
    297, 316, 373
    ANX collaboration of, 158
    B2B cooperation of, 140
    expected returns on investments/assets at,
      186
    information as strategic asset at, 6
    online automobile sales with, 138
    Web services case study at, 174–176
General portals, 167, 168
Generic strategies (*See* Three generic
    strategies)
Germany, 326
Ghirardelli, 287–289
GHz (*See* Gigahertz)
Gibson, Stan, 537
Gigabit Ethernet technology, 389

Gigabyte (GB), 378, 522
Gigahertz (GHz), 377, 522
Gillen, Al, 216
Girard, Kim, 531
Global economy, 210, 327–328
Global Network, 166
Global outsourcing, 293–299
Global positioning system (GPS), 190
Global Product Information Network (GPIN),
    159
Global System for Mobile (GSM), 522
Globalization, 292
Glovia, 299
GMBuyPower.com, 175
Goal seek, 409–411, 421, 522
Goals, 110, 117, 119, 360, 361, 510–511
Goal-seeking analysis, 96, 97, 522
Goldman Sachs Group, 251
Goodyear, 296
Google, 35, 276, 509–510
    API for, 53
    case study of, 51–53
    as corporate information tool, 54
Google Alert, 53
Googlebot, 51
Government, 291
Government Paperwork Elimination Act, 322
Government-to-business (G2B), 318, 319
Government-to-consumer (G2C), 318, 319
Government-to-government (G2G), 318, 319
GPIN (Global Product Information Network),
    159
GPS (global positioning system), 190
GPS tracking device, 219
Gramm Leach Bliley Act, 221
Granola company (business decisions project),
    232
Granularity, 54, 55, 76
Graphical user interface (GUI), 346, 523
Green, Tonja, 22
Gresham, Oregon, 230
Grokster, 38
Groove Workspace, 152
Group 1 Software, 77
Groupware, 11, 150–151, 385, 523
Grupo Farmanova Intermed, 280
Grupo Gas Natural, 272
GSM (*See* Global System for Mobile)
GSX, 310
Guenivere filter, 242
GUI (*See* Graphical user interface)
GUI screen design, 346, 523
Guided media, 391–393, 523
    coaxial-cable, 391–393
    fiber-optic, 391–393
    twisted-pair, 391–393
Gurden, Dereck, 111
Guthrie, Virginia, 304
Guyaux, Joe, 115
Gyricon Media, 331

H

Hacker, 37, 53, 141, 226, 227, 228, 229, 231, 503,
    523
Hackett Group, 203
Hactivist, 227, 523
Halal, William, 537
Half.com, 320

Hammann, Greg, 4
HAN (Health Alert Network), 231
Hapgood, Fred, 533
Hard disk, 166, 378
Hard drives, 191
Hardware, 370–381, 523
    business decisions projects, 382–383
    categories of, 371–373
    connecting, 380–381
    CPUs/RAM, 376–377
    guided-media, 391–393
    input, 375
    mechanics of, 374
    networking, 391–396
    output, 375–376
    storage, 377–378
    telecommunications, 378–379
    transmitting/receiving, 393–396
    unguided-media, 393
Hardware key logger, 243, 523
Harley-Davidson, 91–93, 279
Harley-Davidson.com, 92
Harley's Owners Group (HOG), 93
Harrah, Bill, 83
Harrah's, 510
Harrah's Entertainment (case study), 82–85
Harris Interactive Report, 91, 93
HBOS, 271
Health Alert Network (HAN), 231
Health care industry, 24, 39, 274, 291
Health Information Management Society, 39
Health Insurance Portability and
    Accountability Act (HIPAA), 39, 237
Heilemann, John, 531
Heineken USA, collaborative system at, 145
Helfner AI Robot Cleaner, 99
Help desk, 350, 496, 523
Hershey Foods, 195
Herzog, Jacques, 214
Hewlett-Packard (HP), 167, 187, 334, 360
Hide detail (PivotTable), 408
Hide field list (PivotTable), 408
Hierarchical database, 61, 523
High-capacity floppy disk, 378
Highlands Ranch (Colorado), 511
High-quality information
    benefits of, 59
    characteristics of, 57
Hilton Hotels (case study), 124–125
HIPAA (*See* Health Insurance Portability and
    Accountability Act)
Historical analysis, 325, 523
Hit metrics, 34
Hits, 34, 494
Hoaxes, 226, 523
HOG (Harley's Owners Group), 93
Home Depot, 186
Home-entertainment-system control boxes,
    190
Homeland security, 229–231
Homeland Security Act (2002), 237
Homologation Timing System (HTS), 66
Honda, 187–188
Hopper, Max, 46, 531
Horizon Blue Cross Blue Shield of New Jersey,
    202
Horizontal inputs, 311
Horizontal market software, 373, 523
Horizontal marketplace, 315, 316, 523

Project objective, 360, 361, 526
Project plan, 361–362, 366, 526
Project product, 360, 526
Project risk, 364, 365, 526
Project scope, 360, 526
Project success criteria, 366
Promus Hotel Corporation, 125
Protecting organizational information (*See*
Viewing and protecting organizational
information)
Protocol, 388–390, 526
    ethernet, 389, 390
    FDDI, 390
    token-ring, 389, 390
Prototype, 199, 526
Prystay, Cris, 531
PSINet, 166
Psychological resistance, 247
P2P (*See* Peer-to-peer)
Public Broadcasting Service (PBS), 211–212
Public health, 231
Pull technology, 255, 526
Purchasing products and information, 314
Purdue Farms, 109
Pure play, 306, 526
Push technology, 255, 526
PVR (process variation reduction), 103

Q

QBT tool (*See* Query-by-example tool)
Quadstone, 81
Qualcomm, 142
Qualified hits, 34, 494
Qualitative analysis (apply your knowledge
project), 503–504
Quality of information, 77
    Alaska Department of Fish and Game (case
study), 59–60
    determining (business decisions project),
86
    improving (business decisions project), 86
    and information privacy policy, 240
    and integrity, 64
    valuing, 57–59
Quantum Corporation, 187
Queries, 68, 69, 457–460
Query processor, 52
Query-by-example (QBE) tool, 68, 69, 526
Quinn, Frank, 536
Qwest, 167
QXGA, 376

R

R. H. Forschner, 85
R/3 systems, 167
RAD (*See* Rapid application development)
Radio frequency identification (RFID), 190, 209,
214, 257, 332–333, 526
Radio paper, 330, 526
Raines, Dick, 313
Raizner, Walter, 216
RAM (*See* Random access memory)
Ramo, Joshua, 533
Ramsay, Mike, 188, 189
Random access memory (RAM), 376, 377, 526
Rapid application development (RAD), 199, 526

Rapid prototyping (*See* Rapid application
development)
RateMyProfessors.com, 53
Raw visit depth, 34, 494
Read-only access, 71
Real-time information, 23, 56–57, 257, 526
Real-time operations monitoring system, 29
Real-time system, 56, 526
Real-Time tool, 56
Receiving devices (*See* Transmitting and
receiving devices)
Recency, Frequency, and Monetary (RFM)
value, 261
Record keeping, 246
Recovery, 77–78, 87, 527
Recreational Equipment, Inc. (REI), 118, 137,
366
Red Flag, 216
Redundancy, 64, 527
Redundant information, 71
Redundant systems, 80
Referential integrity, 435, 453, 527
Reflect.com, 317
Refresh external data (PivotTable), 408
Registrations, Web, 493, 494
Regression testing, 349
REI (*See* Recreational Equipment, Inc.)
Reidenberg, Joe, 235
Reintermediation, 309, 527
Relational data
    apply your knowledge project, 512–513
Relational data model, 432–437
    and business rules, 435, 437
    columns in, 432
    data dictionary for, 435, 436
    foreign key in, 434–435
    performance and normalized, 439
    primary key in, 433–435
    referential integrity of, 435
    rows in, 432
Relational database model, 61, 422, 432–437,
444, 527
Relational databases, 61–66
    advantages of, 62, 64–66
    apply your knowledge project, 514–515
    entities/entity classes/attributes in, 62, 63
    Hotcourses educational database (case
study), 72–73
    keys/relationships in, 62
Reliability (in adaptable systems), 79
Remote patrol, 219
Repeater, 394, 527
Report generator, 67, 68, 460–463, 527
Reports, change-management, 364
Required property (Access), 450
Requirements definition document, 343, 527
Research in Motion BlackBerry, 193
Resistance technologies, 225
Resource availability, 342, 345
Response technologies, 226–227
Response time, 30, 527
Retail industry, 18, 207, 291
Return on investment (ROI), 98, 359, 490, 492,
527
Revenue generation, 32, 261, 277
Revenue models, 316, 317
Revenues, 196
Reverse auction, 17, 312, 527

Rewarding employees, 44–45
RFID (*See* Radio frequency identification)
RFM (Recency, Frequency, and Monetary)
value, 261
Rhodia Inc., 203
Riggio, Leonard, 135
RightNow, 167, 168
Ring topology, 388, 393, 527
Risk management, 364–366, 527
Rivalry among existing computers, 17–18, 527
RivalWatch, 99
RJ-45 connectors, 391
Robb, Curtis, 47
Roberts, Paul, 536
Roberts-Witt, Sarah L., 531
Robots, 99, 101, 183, 328, 333
Roche, Katrina, 195
Rode, Jerry, 236
ROI (*See* Return on investment)
Rosso, Wayne, 38
Router, 394, 527
Row field (PivotTable), 405
Rows, relational data model, 432
Royal Dutch/Shell Group, 140
Ruf Strategic Solutions, 76
Russia, 249, 293, 295, 297, 333

S

Saab
    consolidating touchpoints (case study), 28
    portal (collaborative decisions project),
179
Saab Cars USA, 28, 179, 236
SABRE, 45
Safety inventory, 254, 527
Sage Life, 297
Sales, 26, 265–267
Sales force automation (SFA), 266, 281, 527
Sales management system, 266, 527
Salesforce.com, 168
Salesnet, 168
Samsung Electronics, 54, 55
SAP, 283, 304
    ASP services of, 167
    and Brother International Corp., 114
    ERP solutions from, 27, 285
    as ERP vendor, 122
    and FoxMeyer, 196
    and Hershey Foods, 195
    as leading ERP vendor, 121
    as project management software vendor,
203
    and Universal Business Language, 170
    and UPS, 119
SAP software, 47
Sarbanes-Oxley Act (SOX), 237, 246–247
SAS, 77, 81
    datamining tools from, 104
    and 1–800–Flowers.com, 113
SAS Institute, 247
Satellite access, 379
Satellite systems, 395
Satellite television, 190
Satre, Phil, 83
Satyam, 293
Saving failing systems (collaborative decisions
project), 219